+3

THE HANDBOOK OF STRUCTURED FINANCE

ARNAUD DE SERVIGNY
NORBERT JOBST

McGraw-Hill

New York   Chicago   San Francisco   Lisbon   London
Madrid   Mexico City   Milan   New Delhi   San Juan
Seoul   Singapore   Sydney   Toronto

The **McGraw·Hill** Companies

1 2 3 4 5 6 7 8 9 0   DOC/DOC   0 9 8 7

ISBN-13 978-0-07-146864-0
ISBN-10   0-07-146864-1

This publication is designed to provide accurate and authoritative information in regard to the subject matter covered. It is sold with the understanding that neither the author nor the publisher is engaged in rendering legal, accounting, or other professional service. If legal advice or other expert assistance is required, the services of a competent professional person should be sought.

> —*From a Declaration of Principles jointly adopted by Committee of the American Bar Association and a Committee of Publishers.*

McGraw-Hill books are available at special quantity discounts to use as premiums and sales promotions, or for use in corporate training programs. For more information, please write to the Director of Special Sales, McGraw-Hill Professional, Two Penn Plaza, New York, NY 10121–2298. Or contact your local bookstore.

Library of Congress Cataloging-in-Publication Data

The handbook of structured finance / by
Arnaud de Servigny and Norbert Jobst, [et al.].
   p. cm.
   ISBN 0-07-146864-1 (hardcover : alk. paper)
  1. Asset-backed financing. 2. Asset-backed securities. 3. Mortgage-backed securities. 4. Credit–Management. 5. Risk management. I. Servigny, Arnaud de. II. Jobst, Norbert.

  HG4028.A84H366 2007
  332.63'2044–dc22   2006028075

CONTENTS

INTRODUCTION

The *Handbook of Structured Finance* presents many modern quantitative techniques used by investment banks, investors, and rating agencies active in the structured finance markets. In recent years, we have observed an exponential growth in market activity, knowledge, and quantitative techniques developed in industry and academia, such that the writing of a comprehensive book is becoming increasingly difficult. Rather than trying to cover all topics on our own, we have taken advantage from the expert wisdom of market participants and academic scholars and tried to provide a solid coverage of a wide range of structured finance topics, but choices had to be made.

The clear objective of this book is to blend three types of experiences in a single text. We always aim to consider the topics from an academic standpoint, as well as from a professional angle, while not forgetting the perspective of a rating agency.

The review in this book goes beyond a simple list of tools and methods. In particular, the various contributors try to provide a robust framework regarding the monitoring of structured finance risk and pricing. In order to do so, we analyze the most widely used methodologies in the structured finance community and point out their relative strengths and weaknesses whenever appropriate. The contributors also offer insight from their experience of practical implementation of these techniques within the relevant financial institutions.

Another feature of this book is that it surveys significant amounts of empirical research. Chapters dealing with correlation, for example, are illustrated with recent statistics that allow the reader to have a better grasp of the topic and to understand the practical implementation challenges.

Although the book focuses on collateral debt obligations (CDOs), it provides extensive insight related to other vehicles and techniques employed for residential mortgage-backed securities, Credit card securitization, Covered Bonds, and structured investment vehicles.

STRUCTURE OF THE BOOK

The book is divided into 16 chapters. We start with the building blocks that are necessary to price and measure risk on portfolio structures. This involves pricing techniques for single-name credit instruments (univariate pricing), and estimation/modeling techniques for default probabilities and loss given default (univariate risk) of such products. We then focus on dependence, and more specifically on correlation in general terms, applied to correlation among corporates as well as across structured tranches. Once this toolbox is available, we can move to the CDO space, the second part of this book. We investigate the techniques related to CDO pricing, CDO strategy, CDO hedging, the CDO risk assessment employed by Standard & Poor's, and we end up with an overview of recent developments in the CDO space. A third building block is based on a review of the methods used in the RMBS sector, for Covered Bonds, for Operating Companies, and finally we focus on Basel II both from a theoretical as well as from a case study perspective.

ACKNOWLEDGMENTS

As editors, we would like to thank all the contributors to this book: Alexander Batchvarov, Sven Sandow, Philippe Henrotte, Astrid Van Landschoot, Olivier Renault, Vivek Kapoor, Varqa Khadem, Francis Parisi, Cristina Polizu, Aymeric Chauve, and William Perraudin.

Our gratitude also goes to those who have helped us in carefully reading this book and providing valuable comments. We would like to thank in particular Jean-David Fermanian, Pieter Klaassen, Andre Lucas, Jean-Paul Laurent, Joao Garcia, Olivier Renault, Benoit Metayer, and Sriram Rajan.

ARNAUD DE SERVIGNY

NORBERT JOBST

CHAPTER 1

Overview of the Structured Credit Markets: Trends and New Developments

Alexander Batchvarov

OVERVIEW OF STRUCTURED FINANCE MARKETS AND TRENDS

The easiest way to highlight the development of the structured finance market is to quantify its new issuance volume. That volume has been steadily climbing all over the world, with U.S. leading, followed closely by Europe, and Japan and Australia a distant third and fourth. The rest of the world is now awakening to the opportunities offered by structured credit products to both issuers and investors and gearing up for a strong future growth. In that respect, it is worth mentioning Mexico, which is leading the way in Latin America; South Korea and Republic of China lead in continental Asia and Turkey in for the Middle East and Eastern Europe. It is only a matter of time before Central and Eastern Europe and China and India spring into action, and the Middle East launches its own version of securitization.

The data shown in Tables 1.1 to 1.4 are based on publicly available information about deals executed on each market. We believe such data to seriously understate the size of the respective markets due to several factors:

◆ the availability of private placement markets in many countries, data for which are not widely available;

◆ the execution of numerous transactions executed for a specific client, known as bespoke or custom-tailored deals, especially in the area of synthetic collateralized debt obligations (CDOs) and synthetic risk transfers;

♦ the exclusion from the count of many transactions based on synthetic indices, such as iTraxx and CDX, ABX, etc., whereby structured products are created using tranches from those indices.

That being said, the publicly visible size of the markets and their growth rates are sufficient to attract investors, issuers, and regulators. The structured finance market growth also stands out against the background of declining bond issuance volumes by corporates and the rising issuance volumes of covered bonds, which in turn are increasingly becoming more "structured" in nature.

The markets of United States, Australia, and Europe can be viewed as international markets, i.e., providing supply to both domestic and foreign investors on a regular basis and in significant amounts, whereas the other securitization markets remain predominantly domestic in their focus. The international or domestic nature of a given market is not only related to where the securities are sold and who the investors are, but also to the level of disclosure, availability of information and, subsequently, the level of quantification (as opposed to qualification) of the risks involved, in particular structured finance securities and underlying pools. If we were to rank the markets by the level of disclosure of information about the structured finance securities and their related asset pools, we should consider the U.S. market as the leader by far in terms of breadth, depth, and quality of the information provided—being the oldest structured finance market helps, but it is not the only reason: investor sophistication, type of instruments used (those subject to high convexity risk, for example), bigger share of lower credit quality securitization pools, higher trading intensity with related desire to find and explore pricing inefficiencies, etc. are all contributing factors.

Other structured finance markets, however, are making strides in that direction as well. Some of the reasons are associated with the type of instruments used: say, convexity-heavy-Japanese mortgages, refinancing-driven UK subprime, default- and correlation-dependent collateralized debt obligations (CDO) structures, etc. The existence of repeat issuers with large issuance programs and pools of information also helps. However, outside the United States, another major change is quietly driving toward more quantitative work: the need to quantify risks in structured finance bonds is moving from the esoteric (for many) area of back-office risk management to front-office investment decision making based on economic and regulatory

TABLE 1.1

U.S. Structured Product New Issuance Volume, 2000–2005

	Auto	CrCards	HEL	MH	Equip	StLoans	Other	Other ABS	CDO	CMBS
2000	64.72	50.45	55.73	9.13	9.56	12.42	16.90	38.89	68.45	48.9
2001	68.96	58.47	71.79	6.27	7.40	9.94	24.14	41.48	58.49	74.3
2002	93.08	70.04	148.14	4.30	6.54	20.18	12.41	39.14	59.23	67.3
2003	85.49	66.55	214.99	0.44	10.09	39.96	16.67	66.71	65.90	88
2004	77.02	50.36	320.11	0.50	5.92	44.99	6.73	57.64	106.06	103.221
2005	102.44	67.51	493.20	na	7.93	70.36	14.93	93.23	171.62	178.443

Abbreviations: na = not available; ABS = asset backed securitizations; CMBS = commercial mortgage backed securitizations; CDO = collateral debt obligations; Auto = automobile loan securitizations; CrCards = credit card securitizations; HEL = Home Equity Loans; MH = Manufactured Housing securitizations; Equip = Equipement / Utility recievables backed Securitizations; StLoans = Student Loans Securitizations.
Source: Merrill Lynch.

3

TABLE 1.2

U.S. CDO New Issuance by CDO Type, 2000–2005

	2000	2001	2002	2003	2004	2005
SF CBO	10.3	13.5	25.2	26.2	56.8	69.9
HY CLO	16.8	11.5	14.7	16.7	30.2	50.5
TruPS	0.3	2.2	4.3	6.5	7.5	9.0
HY CBO	17.5	15.2	1.5	0.8	0.6	0.0
IG CBO	13.1	5.2	4.4	0.0	0.0	0.0
Other	10.2	5.4	3.2	4.6	3.9	25.4
MV	0.2	0.0	0.0	0.0	0.9	—
Total	68.5	53.0	53.3	54.9	99.9	154.8
Synthetic	—	5.5	6.0	11.0	6.2	29.7
Total	68.5	58.5	59.2	65.9	106.1	184.5

Abbreviations: SF CBO = Structured Finance Collateralized Bond Obligation; HY CLO = High Yield Collateralized Loan Obligation; TruPS = Trust Preferred Securities; HY CBO = High Yield Collateralized Bond Obligation; IG CBO = Investment Grade Collateralized Bond Obligation; MV = Market Value Collateralized Debt Obligation.
Source: Merrill Lynch.

capital considerations, under the new regulatory guidelines of BIS2 (Basel 2 Banking Regulation) and Solvency2 (Regulation of Insurance Companies). Parallel with that, the increase in trading of structured finance securities beyond the United States, now in Europe, and in other markets over time, requires better pricing and, hence, more sophisticated pricing models.

Besides transparency and quantification, it is worth taking a look at some key recent developments in the U.S. and European structured finance

TABLE 1.3

European Funded Structured Product New Issuance Volume, 2000–2005

	2000	2001	2002	2003	2004	2005
ABS	16.195	28.325	30.652	36.929	47.821	53.517
CDO	14.900	26.528	20.966	20.892	32.690	57.657
CMBS	9.455	22.882	20.904	10.139	14.736	45.750
CORP	6.430	14.641	13.536	18.299	17.989	9.416
RMBS	42.186	54.001	69.463	110.653	125.933	159.748
Total	89.166	146.377	155.521	196.912	239.168	326.088

Abbreviations: ABS = asset backed securitizations; CDO = collateral debt obligations; CMBS = commercial mortgage backed securitizations; CORP = Corporate Securitization; RMBS = Residential Mortgage Backed Securitization.
Source: Merrill Lynch.

TABLE 1.4

European Funded CDO New Issuance Volume, 2000–2005

	2000	2001	2002	2003	2004	2005
ABS	0.66	0.20	1.83	3.15	5.80	3.62
CBO	3.85	8.19	3.39	2.10	0.40	1.86
CDS	0.97	0.67	1.59	1.22	1.60	0.90
CFO	0.00	0.00	0.85	0.24	0.56	0.56
CLO	6.56	10.18	6.19	4.37	7.94	15.49
MCDO	0.00	0.00	0.27	1.33	5.81	2.78
SME	2.86	7.29	6.84	8.48	10.58	32.46

Abbreviations: ABS = asset backed securitizations; CDS = credit default swap; CFO = Collateralized Fund Obligation; MCDO = Multiple-Credit-Dependent Obligations; SME = Small and Medium Enterprise Loan CDO.
Source: Merrill Lynch.

markets, being the major volume providers for international investors, over the last two years. We attempt to draw parallels as well as contrasts:

♦ Unlike the U.S. market in its ripening stage, the European market did not opt for commoditization of the securitization and structured products. Just the opposite, new structures and modifications of existing ones proliferated.

♦ Like the U.S. market, the European market saw compression of the marketing period. It was not uncommon to have deals oversubscribed even before the reds (sales reports) were printed.

♦ The shorter marketing period led to distortion in pipeline estimates, which in turn led to surprise over volume in December 2005, for example, catching many market participants totally unprepared to take advantage of it.

♦ Bespoke solutions proliferated, especially in the synthetic market, and were not restricted to deals backed by corporate portfolios.

♦ The avalanche of deals left little time for European investors to take in the bigger picture, the tiny details in the structure, the variations in the collateral, the variations in prepayments, etc., and whether they do matter. Unlike in the United States, structured finance investors in Europe are generally not specialized by sector of the structured finance market and, as a consequence, are less detail-oriented in their analysis.

♦ The collateral quality softened, sometimes visibly—in commercial real estate securitizations and in leveraged loans, for example; sometimes less so—in the residential mortgage deals, where reportedly prime mortgage pools contained products, which will not be viewed as prime in countries, where the differentiation is clearer, e.g., the UK. In contrast, in the United States, the subprime sector, usually associated with home equity loans of lower FICO (Fair Isaac & Co. Credit) score, experienced massive growth. The differentiation between prime and subprime pools, especially in the mortgage and consumer finance area, is clearly defined in the United States, and is further helped by the use of quantitative measurements of consumer credit quality, such as FICO scoring.

♦ European deal reporting and information disclosure is improving, although slowly. While the necessary information for residential mortgage pools is getting through in larger quantities, such information remains fairly sporadic for, say, commercial real estate transactions. The understanding of loan prepayment factors in either market remains largely in embryo.

While the above list of developments and trends is by no means exhaustive, it is consistent with the developments we expect in the coming years. Our positive views on the structured credit market are also supported by:

♦ The persistence of relatively weak supply of corporate paper and covered bonds. Structured products exceeded both corporate bond and covered bond supply for a second year in a row, which is expected to be the case in the future.

♦ Structured product spreads that remain attractive compared to similarly rated corporate and covered bonds. The predominantly triple-A supply (about 85 percent of new issuance on the structured product market) is offering a significant yield pick-up over sovereign, covered bond and bank paper. We do *not* attribute this pick-up in its entirety to a liquidity premium (except for bespoke structures, of course). The liquidity component *is* a more appropriate explanation for the yield differential between structured product, on the one hand, and the corporate bonds, on the other, at below-triple-A levels.

♦ The ability of structurers to offer bespoke deals addressing specific investor demands or concerns. That alone explains the large private volume in synthetic execution. The requirement for public rating for regulatory capital purposes may make some of this volume more visible in the future. We note the increasing flexibility and ingenuity applied by structurers in an effort to meet specific client's requirements and needs. Further customization of the market may lead to a less volatile and less tradable market at least for larger segments.

♦ The large range of structured product offerings dealing with repackaging of exposures. Many of these, which are otherwise unavailable to numerous investors, remain an attractive point for them; e.g., the investors can take direct exposure to consumer risk or real estate risk and leveraged or managed exposure to familiar and less familiar corporates.

♦ The "safe harbour" argument, which is as old as the structured credit market itself. There is a modification of this argument, though: investors in Europe are now becoming more concerned about mark-to-market of their bond holdings, and structured products, at least historically, have offered lower spread volatility, maybe due to their lower liquidity, given that their rating volatility was low. While the argument about lower event-risk sensitivity of structured products remains valid, many structured products have assumed more leverage, which by itself makes them more susceptible to volatility in the future. However, by their nature, structured products, in general, should remain more resilient to event-idiosyncratic risk, which is one of the main concerns of corporate bond investors. While individual events may have little impact on specific structured finance products, we note the delayed effect of accumulating credit risks in later years. We emphasize this point: credit deterioration has a cumulative negative effect in the predominantly static collateral pools backing the majority of structured bonds.

♦ The development of synthetic asset backed securitizations (ABS) exposures, be it on individual names [the European credit default swap (CDS) on ABS or U.S. PAYGO versions] or on a pool basis—through synthetic ABS pools or via the synthetic ABS index ABX in the United States—has dramatically changed the structured finance market. These innovations allow the ABS market to speed up execution, provide the exposures that the cash market cannot offer, and supply a mechanism to express a negative view on the

market, to hedge or speculate. The importance of these developments cannot be overestimated. In this regard, the United States is
leading Europe and the rest of the world, as has often been the
case in the structured finance market.

Having said all these nice things about the structured product market, let
us be more critical and highlight some of its shortcomings. Many of our
concerns have been voiced before, but they may take a new light now that
the market, by wide consensus, has reached the peak of the current cycle
and has nowhere to go but sideways and eventually descend. The starting point of that descent may be triggered by several weaknesses:

- Overall, deals are more leveraged: be it because of underlying
  consumer indebtedness, companies' financial ratios, or the deal
  structures. That should lead to bigger swings under unfavorable
  and/or unexpected market developments.

- Investors are stretched in their ability to absorb new deals, monitor old ones, and keep an eye on new developments. The
  growth of the market in complexity and volume has yet to be
  reflected in increasing investor specialization across asset sectors
  and products. Corporate analysts often know everything about
  a couple or so industries and the main companies within those
  industries; hence the need for several corporate analysts to manage a larger corporate bond portfolio. Structured credit analysts
  and portfolio managers, however, are expected to cope with
  numerous sectors, structures, and deals simply because they fall
  into the simplistic misnomer "structured."

- There is a serious need for more quantitative power dedicated to
  structured products. That power can be fully used only if there
  is more information about the structured product collateral.
  That power, though, is powerless in the face of unquantifiable
  quantities—say, the likelihood of prepayment of a given loan in
  a commercial real estate portfolio or the impact of a manager in
  a CDO under adverse market conditions. Under such circumstances, the good old reliance on "gut feeling" seems to be the
  one and only last resort for the investor.

- Lack of tiering to reflect differences in structure, pool composition, information availability, and servicer or manager capabilities. The deplored lack of tiering is an enduring feature of the
  European market and will properly change, we think, only under

market distress. We hope some signs of change are already in the air, say in commercial mortgage backed securitizations (CMBS) or CDO land, although with recent tight CMBS spreads pricing has looked haphazard, particularly for the more junior tranches.

♦ Regulatory uncertainty or uncertainty about the impact of regulations such as BIS2 and the respective national implementation guidelines, The accounting Standard IAS39, Solvency2, and the potential for a not-quite-level playing field they may be creating across countries and markets. One concern we have is that regulators' ambiguity about synthetics in some countries is hurting not only the market development, but also the regulated entities themselves, as they are precluded from using this market to their benefit.

THE NOT-SO-HOMOGENEOUS CDO SECTOR

One of the major market developments in recent years is the emergence of the CDO sector as a major market sector, with the capacity to influence developments in other seemingly independent market sectors. The CDO sector is not homogeneous and consists of many different subsectors and niches. Referring to the developments in any one CDO sector, and generalizing and applying the conclusions to all the others is wrong and grossly misleading. It can increase market volatility, deter investors from making reasonable investment decisions and, in the extreme, create a liquidity crisis in a specific market sector or on the entire market, if the panic spreads wide enough.

While this is fairly obvious, it is not fully appreciated by many market participants. Hence, there is a need to broadly differentiate among the several main categories of CDOs that are dominant on the market today, and highlight their interaction with the rest of the market.

Arbitrage Cash CDOs

The arbitrage cash CDO sector includes a number of CDO types, widely differentiated by the type of exposure used to rampup the CDO collateral pool. Among them are:

♦ cash CDOs comprising high grade and/or mezzanine ABS
♦ cash CLO of leveraged loans and/or middle market loans

♦ cash CDOs of insurance and bank trust preferred securities
♦ CDO of emerging markets exposures, both sovereign and corporate.

Each of these subsectors follows the credit and technical dynamics of its respective market. A CDO backed by a portfolio of such instruments is effectively a vehicle for creating tranched risk profile and leverage on that portfolio.

In the past, there were large subsectors of cash CDOs backed by high yield (HY) and high grade (HG) bonds, and their fortunes rose and sank with the movements in the HY or HG bonds backing them and, not least, with the strategy, behavior, and luck of the CDO managers running those portfolios.

We note that in a cash CDO, the asset and liability sides of the CDO are established at launch and may change little during the life of the transaction:

♦ The liability side (i.e., the capital structure of the CDO) is determined at deal's launch and changes only with the amortization of the senior tranches or the write-down of the equity and junior tranches in case of default and losses in the pools.

♦ The asset side (i.e., the pool of investments) is also determined at launch and may experience little change during the life of the deal. In the currently dominant types of cash CDOs (listed earlier), trading occurs to a very limited degree, if at all. In most deals, trading by the manager is restricted to credit impairment trade (due to expected or real deterioration of a given name) and credit improvement trade (upon certain spread tightening, but under condition that traded credit must be replaced by similar or better credit quality name).

♦ The asset–liability gap (i.e., the funding gap) determines the level of return that a CDO equity investor can expect (depending on the level of defaults in the investment pool) and is a key consideration in the placement of equity and overall economic viability of a cash CDO.

Hence, a cash arbitrage CDO is a structure mostly set at the beginning of the transaction and is meant to be maintained as stable as possible throughout its life, with the ultimate purpose of repaying debt investors and providing adequate return to equity investors over its scheduled life.

The initial and on-going pricing of the cash CDO tranches is market-based (rather than model-based). It takes into account where other similar transactions price on the primary and secondary market and, in case of significant defaults or downgrades in the pool, considers the value of the pool and how it relates to the outstanding CDO debt obligations that the pool is backing.

From this it follows that a cash CDO once launched has little on-going impact on the market, with its asset and liability side meant to be relatively stable. Looking at it the other way around: ongoing market changes may have little impact on the cash CDO, except for defaults and the mark-to-market of the CDO debt and equity tranches.

Hence, *defaults are the issue of main consideration for arbitrage cash CDOs*, as their occurrence or not, the degree thereof, and the subsequent crystallized loss will determine the yield on the debt tranches and return on the equity tranches of these transactions.

Synthetic CDOs

Synthetic CDOs are diverse in nature and include a number of instruments, which are not directly comparable in terms of investment characteristics and market impact. These include:

- Synthetic structured finance (or ABS) CDOs—an emerging sector, in which CDS on ABS in Europe and PAYGO SFCDS in the United States are used to build an ABS portfolio quickly and efficiently. Such a portfolio would be more difficult to execute in 100 percent cash due to allocation and sector and vintage limitations on the cash-structured finance market today. Such synthetic deals may be fully/partially funded or may be single tranche deals. The latter require hedging for the unfunded senior and junior (to the funded portion) tranches; hedging usually takes place through a combination of cash purchase and selling protection on the respective cash bonds and is usually adjusted downwards as the referenced exposures amortize or experience losses.

- Balance sheet synthetic CDOs/CLOs—associated with credit risk transfer of a bank bond or loan portfolio—their share of today's market is miniscule and their behavior is more akin to cash CDOs discussed earlier (relatively constant structure and primarily default-driven investment performance).

♦ Other synthetic CDO products, such as those based on constant maturity CDS, principle protected tranches of CDOs, etc., whose behavior is further modified by their specific structural features and will differ from that of other synthetic CDO subtypes.

♦ Bespoke synthetic CDOs—single tranche CDOs on corporate names, referenced through CDS.

♦ Standardized tranches of CDS indices—iTraxx in Europe and CDX in the United States.

The last two sectors tend to be also lumped together under the "correlation trades" moniker. The latter, because correlation is a derived variable from a pricing/trading model and a function of spread movements. The former, because to be priced, the implied correlation input is referenced from the standardized tranche market. These two sectors can be viewed as model-driven from the perspective of pricing and trading (exploring trading opportunities), but there are differences:

♦ The structure of a bespoke single-tranche CDO is set at its launch, but there is a need for the intermediary to hedge exposures senior and junior to the investor's tranche, creating an ongoing interaction with and impact on the market. The need to rebalance the delta hedges creates the need to trade certain CDS and thus influences the supply and demand for these credits in the market. The larger the size of the single-tranche market, the larger the impact such secondary delta-rebalancing trades may have on it: large and more single-tranche deals suggest larger and more referenced portfolios, whose senior and junior tranches must be hedged and the hedges rebalanced. However, the single-tranche investor may be relatively sheltered in his investment from such movements, as long as defaults do not cross certain threshold or he is in some way protected against trading/hedging losses.

♦ The standardized index tranches are used by investors to express a view (take a position) on spread direction and correlation, and as their view changes or the market developments do not justify such view (positioning), a need to trade arises. It may take place in order to adjust the position or to reverse it (to close a position altogether). That creates secondary market activity and, almost inevitably, market volatility. The standardized tranches market is also used to hedge positions or execute certain strategies. A desire to unwind the hedges or the positions when not needed or the market moves against them may further exacerbate market volatility.

From this it follows that correlation trades can have a strong on-going impact on the market either through the need to rebalance the hedges or to take a position and subsequently unwind it. The opposite is also true: ongoing market changes, such as spread movements, and the perception in correlation changes can have an impact on standardized index tranche pricing and associated positions. Hence, ongoing spread movements, actual downgrades/defaults, and the related perception of correlation are the main factors to consider in synthetic standardized tranche trades and in hedging single-tranche CDOs. From the perspective of the single-tranche CDO investor, though, the main concern is the level of default in the reference pool.

Different Investors "Own" Different CDO Sectors

The review of the CDO market so far indicates some fairly fundamental differences among the broadly defined cash arbitrage and synthetic CDO sectors. Such differences can be further illustrated by looking at the motivation and identity of the investors in the different sectors:

+ "Real" money accounts tend to focus on cash CDOs and tend to be buy-and-hold investors when buying synthetic and bespoke synthetic CDOs. In that space, different parts of the capital structure of a CDO attract a different type of investor—that spreads the slices of risk to the broadest possible range of market participants.

+ "Leveraged" money accounts (hedge funds) drive most of the activities on the standardized tranche market, although some real money accounts have become more active in recent months. The activities in that space are associated with taking a view on correlation and how spread changes in the market could trigger repricing of the different tranches of the synthetic indices. To some degree, this sector can be viewed as "speculative," although using it for the purposes of hedging is not uncommon.

Although this division is general and there are some investors who cross the line in both directions, it is certainly not imprecise.

The mark-to-market aspect affects the different investor types in a different way and is common to all fixed income instruments. We note that cash CDO "held to maturity" are not subject to mark-to-market, whereas all synthetic CDOs regardless of their classification are subject to mark-to-market. MTM issues are of a particular concern to European fixed income investors this year, as a result of the introduction of IAS39.

While the fall-out from the recent hedge fund standardized tranches investment strategy gone wrong could be wider spreads and high mark-to-market losses, there is no evidence in the market to suggest that the different cash and synthetic tranche CDOs have widened more than similarly rated other fixed income investments.

Liquidity and the "Unexpected" MTM Problem

A key market consideration is the liquidity of structured finance instruments and the associated mark-to-market volatility. The latter is a relatively recent concern associated with the introduction of mark-to-market accounting.

Table 1.5 demonstrates the spread movements for a variety of European structured products. Given the limited time frame of this analysis, as well as the limited time frame of a relatively mature European market, we suggest that readers do not focus on the nominal values, but rather on the relative magnitude across asset classes and sectors. If we assume that the period given in Table 1.5 embraces the tightest spreads seen on the market in recent years, it is natural to ask the question as to how much the spreads can widen. While we expect spread widening to be cyclical (trend-line), we foresee the actual spread movements to be shaped by technical and fundamental factors along the way (zigzagging along the trend line). From that perspective, it is important for investors to understand the expected behavior of the different sectors and subsectors of the European structured finance market, their reaction to technical and fundamental factors, and their interaction with each other.

When considering their portfolio strategies, investors can conceptualize the market and their portfolios in different ways. On that basis, they can re-examine their tolerance to mark-to-market and credit risk in a market

TABLE 1.5

Monthly Average Launch Spreads by Asset Class and Rating, 1998–2004

Asset Class	Sub type	Rating	1998 Ave	1998 Max	1998 Min	1999 Ave	1999 Max	1999 Min	2000 Ave	2000 Max	2000 Min	2001 Ave	2001 Max	2001 Min	2002 Ave	2002 Max	2002 Min	2003 Ave	2003 Max	2003 Min	March 2004 Ave	March 2004 Max	March 2004 Min
MBS	NCF	AAA	27	58	14	41	65	31	35	55	28	35	55	19	27	50	22	35	54	26	19	19	19
MBS	PRM	AAA	18	24	11	23	28	18	25	28	14	24	30	22	24	28	18	24	40	20	17	22	12
CMBS		AAA	47	47	47	44	55	27	34	51	25	37	44	24	43	63	28	45	50	40	38	38	38
CDO		AAA	15	39	7	15	30	11	37	43	26	45	57	35	55	68	25	71	81	61	57	64	48
ABS	CAR	AAA	45	45	45	32	50	19	31	35	26	24	28	14	24	38	13	30	42	11	15	15	15
ABS	CCD	AAA	22	30	14	18	20	15	20	30	16	25	28	23	20	22	16	20	27	5	13	22	15
ABS	UCC	AAA	23	36	17	24	36	16	28	33	25	32	35	28	31	36	28	25	31	20			3
MBS	NCF	A	70	83	40	125	160	85	124	150	85	139	203	100	109	125	98	164	188	135	95	95	95
MBS	PRM	A	57	80	35	63	77	50	69	86	48	68	77	63	64	83	45	71	85	65	52	62	39
CMBS		A				112	138	73	89	115	65	99	108	83	97	110	83	109	118	93	103	103	103
CDO		A	66	120	36	59	93	45	100	120	48	118	146	97	182	223	125	216	279	174	202	203	200
ABS	CAR	A	75	75	75	65	90	51	76	85	65	65	68	47	58	80	43	74	100	35	40	40	40
ABS	CCD	A				45	48	40	54	75	37	74	77	70	57	62	50	59	78	30	37	55	19
ABS	UCC	A	55	72	47	62	75	40	69	79	50	82	120	47	75	88	43	72	75	69			
MBS	NCF	BBB	139	175	92	244	275	200	256	300	200	256	300	218	240	270	207	326	350	300	212	212	212
MBS	PRM	BBB	88	93	82	153	160	150	145	188	130	144	165	135	141	179	120	140	163	127	103	121	81
CMBS		BBB	140	140	140	248	375	165	199	275	140	194	220	183	201	280	138	214	232	200			
CDO		BBB	131	183	77	124	188	59	159	200	85	238	311	168	322	467	215	348	490	285	375	500	300
ABS	CAR	BBB	175	175	175	75	75	75	178	180	175	225	225	225	150	150	150	160	170	155			
ABS	CCD	BBB				90	90	90	112	150	88	151	165	138	149	168	120	159	187	110			
ABS	UCC	BBB	130	130	130	160	160	160	175	175	175	217	275	188	150	170	125	153	170	140	83	120	45

Abbreviations: Ave = average; Max = maximum; Min = minimum.
Asset Class: MBS = mortgage backed securitizations; CMBS = commercial mortgage backed securitizations; CDO = collateral debt obligations; ABS = asset backed securitizations.
Subtypes: NCF = nonconforming; PRM = prime; CMBS = commercial mortgage backed securitizations; CDO = collateral debt obligations; CAR = automobiles; CCD = credit cards; UCC = unsecured consumer loans.
Source: Merrill Lynch.

downturn. Then, they can model how their current (at the peak of the market) portfolio will react to different levels of market downturn and determine what is the acceptable credit and marked-to-market loss they can bear.

Furthermore, investors can anticipate the evolution of their portfolio between today and some future point [factoring WAL (Weighted Average Loss) scheduled and unscheduled amortization, expected losses, etc.], when they expect the market downturn and see how such a portfolio will react to such downturn. Finally, investors must consider what steps to take now and in the near future to bring their current portfolio to that which is sensitive to credit and MTM losses and is consistent with their own (institutional or personal) tolerance.

CRITERIA FOR STRUCTURED FINANCE DEALS AND PORTFOLIOS

Review and Risk Tolerance

The analysis of structured finance products and portfolios is a complex undertaking. We highlight a number of criteria in no particular order:

Granularity

Granular deals with strong credit quality are less susceptible to event risk of single-name exposures than nongranular deals. Historical evidence suggests that more granular, high quality ABS have experienced little spread volatility compared with low quality granular deals and nongranular deals. These observations are true across ABS capital structures. They also hold for high grade mortgage backed securitizations (MBS) and CMBS as an example of highly granular and less granular deals, as well as for prime RMBS and subprime RMBS as an example of deals with similar granularity but different credit quality. While correct, this outcome may be influenced by the fact that granular deals in general are associated with consumer exposures and nongranular deals—with corporate exposures.

Types of Credit Exposure

Consumer ABS in Europe tends to demonstrate less spread volatility than corporate exposure ABS (in the form of CDOs and CMBS). That may be also associated with the granularity of the portfolios as mentioned earlier. In general, though, consumer pools' tranches tend to reflect tranching of the systemic risk, associated with a large securitization pool and reflect the state of the economy of the respective country.

In addition, consumer portfolios are exposed more to systemic risk, say widespread economic deterioration, than to event risk (collapse of a single company or an industrial sector). We caution, however, that today, in most countries, the consumer is over-indebted, i.e., the consumer sector is stretched or even over-stretched, which was not the case during the last corporate credit cyclical downturn. (The two countries, which in the past downturns have had relatively high consumer indebtedness—United States and UK, are even more indebted today, with the consumer debt stretching beyond residential mortgage debt.) Consumer lending and spending softened the blow during the last downturn—this buffer may not be as readily available in a future downturn. Hence, the economy as a whole and the consumer pools, in particular, may suffer more than previous downturns in history.

Senior versus Junior Tranches

It is a fact that senior tranches have more cushion against credit deterioration than junior tranches. The former seems to hold true for different asset classes, even ones of similar granularity. An interesting way to look at the credit cushion is to compare the level of credit enhancement for each tranche to the level of five-year cumulative losses of a given asset class. The challenge arises, when such cumulative loss numbers are not robust, statistically speaking.

As mentioned earlier, senior tranches tend to experience less spread volatility than junior tranches of the same asset class. Their bid-offer spread is much lower than the one for junior tranches. Almost always senior tranches are more liquid than junior tranches of the same deal. It is not uncommon for market participants to often use secondary trade-based pricing for marking-to-market their senior tranche positions and estimated pricing (on the basis of primary market or dealer talk) for mezzanine positions. In the case of the latter, there is the risk that one-off trade may lead to serious repricing and mark-to-market volatility.

Sensitivity to Third Parties (Originator, Servicer, Counterparty)

While structured finance bonds are set up in such a way as to minimize or eliminate the role of the asset originator and its potential bankruptcy, some linkages (in terms of credit or portfolio performance) remain—they may be with the originator or servicer, a third-party servicer and/or hedge counterparty. These linkages may have both direct and indirect effect on the bond pricing on the secondary market, and understanding the potential for problems from that corner is crucial in defending against mark-to-market losses, defaults or downgrades.

In addition, idiosyncratic aspects of underwriting and servicing should be taken into account in determining future pool performance—this is particularly true for subprime and commercial real estate sectors. Nonbank, nonrated servicers are of particular concern when anticipating the performance of the securitized pools and the headline risk of the respective bonds.

High versus Low Leverage Positions

In a low spread, low default market environment, leverage is a necessary way of achieving yield. In the course of the last couple years, investors had to take leverage to achieve their yield targets. The discussion about what leverage is in structured finance, how to estimate it, etc. is a never ending one, and we do not intend to reproduce it here. What is clear, though, is that leverage can enhance returns in good times and magnify losses in bad times. Hence, there is a need to review the amount of leverage, how it is achieved, and the extent to which it can be detrimental to the portfolio performance in a market downturn. Investors need to differentiate between de-levering structures (say, an MBS) and those that are meant to remain fully levered for life (say, a CDO Squared).

Pool versus Single-Name Exposures

While this may seem as a repetition of the granularity argument, it is not necessarily so. Single-name exposure may have many different connotations: it could be in the repetition of a given corporate name in numerous portfolios, or in the presence of the same servicer in multiple deals, or, alternatively, in the high dependence of a given transaction on the cash flows generated by a given entity. The need to estimate the accumulation of multiple exposures to a single name under different transactions is obvious, but the estimate is not that simple to make in practice. We suggest going beyond the issue of overlap, as know from CDO land, and considering all forms of exposure or potential exposure to a given name present in the structured finance portfolio.

Anticipated Impact of BIS2

We believe that BIS2 considerations should be an inextricable part of the European investment strategy over the next several years. BIS2 risk weights favor all senior securitization exposures and do not favor all subinvestment grade securitization exposures. Investors should factor the lower and higher capital requirements post January 1, 2007, when determining the adequate price for a securitization bonds, scheduled to mature after 2006. We also note the granularity adjustment differentiation for senior tranches of securitization exposures.

Other Country-Specific Considerations

Such considerations, e.g., may include:

♦ The changes in pension regulations and eventual new Real Estate Investment Trust (REITS) legislation in the UK should have a positive impact on commercial real estate pricing. That may make CMBS rarer, on one hand, and improve the property values for existing deals, on the other. In the short-term, this is offset by the growth in real estate conduits.

♦ The introduction of covered bonds in more countries should reduce the supply of MBS and make them more attractive.

♦ The reduction of budget support for SMEs in Spain should reduce their supply, change their geographic diversity, or convert them into stand-alone structures with higher subordination levels (more supply of non-triple-A paper).

We certainly do not intend an exhaustive list here, but suggest that investors consider these changes and how they could affect future supply and pricing in specific structured finance sectors.

Modeling

Structured finance securities are complex credit structures, which can perform differently under similar economic and market scenarios. All the more, when addressing the need to fully understand the variations in their performance, modeling comes handy. In that regard, availability of models and people able to use them properly becomes a key factor in better understanding the future performance of structured finance deals and related portfolios. The preceding discussion indicates that the simply rerunning historical scenarios are not enough for investors to fully understand the risk (credit, MTM, duration) of their holdings. One needs not only modellers, but also credit-savvy ones at that.

Increase Asset-Based Liquidity of the Portfolio

In a market downturn scenario the need for liquidity in a portfolio is most acutely felt, especially one with margin calls or with a potential for money withdrawals at a short notice. In that regard, we suggest that investors use the rating agencies guidelines for liquidity eligibility and haircuts for different asset classes of structured finance securities, in determining the asset-based liquidity of structured investment vehicles. Regulatory guidelines for repo eligibility and haircuts can also be useful, although the list of such securities is limited to primarily senior tranches of ABS backed by granular pools.

Distinguishing Between Cyclical Sectors

Distinguish between cyclical (CLOs, office CMBS, subprime consumer, etc.) and cycle-neutral sectors (retail CMBS, high quality consumer pools, etc.). Corporate ABS seems to be more affected by the event risk of down cycles than prime consumer ABS. Alternatively, high quality consumer-related ABS seems to be more cycle-neutral than low-credit-quality consumer-pool ABS. We refer here to the cyclical nature of the exposures comprising the pool of the respective structured financing. A CDO, e.g., being a derivative of the underlying corporate high-yield or high-grade sector will perform according to the cycles of that sector—the deal performance, however, will be modified by the actions of the CDO managers. Similarly, the performance of a subprime mortgage pool will be dependent on the performance of the economy and the housing market (hence, its cyclical nature), but modified by the actions of the respective servicer.

Senior Mezzanine-Equity Positions

That the credit risk and mark-to-market risk of the different tranches of structured financings are different is a given. What is more important is that such differences persist across the tranches of different asset classes, so the equity position of a CDO of senior ABS will have different susceptibility to the earlier risks than, say, the equity position of a CDO of high-yield loans, not to mention the mezzanine of prime mortgage master trust MBS compared to the mezzanine of a residential real estate mezzanine CDO, or the senior tranche of stand-alone amortizing Dutch prime MBS in comparison with senior tranche of a mixed lease Italian ABS.

BIS2 AND OTHER REGULATIONS—
LONGER-TERM IMPACT ON THE
STRUCTURED FINANCE MARKETS

As we noted on several occasions so far, BIS2 is expected to have a major effect on the structured finance market in all its aspects: supply, demand, spreads, and mark-to-market volatility. We explored some of the mark-to-market aspects earlier, and we turn our attention now to some of the more fundamental changes we anticipate BIS2 implementation will prompt. Here, we take into account only the consequences from the new capital treatment, as if securitization's only function were to achieve capital relief for the securitizing bank and as if banks invested only on the basis of regulatory capital considerations. We note that the number of banks expected to adopt the IRB (Internal Rating Based) approach is high in Europe, making this approach dominant in determining risk capital and the BIS2 impact in securitization.

From the Perspective of the Originating Bank

Again, if the only reason for securitization were capital relief, then the expected changes in capital requirements for different types of exposures on the banks' balance sheet should give a good understanding of which assets could conducive to securitization and which not. The chart above is based on QIS3 data and broadly indicates that banks will have reduced incentive to securitize consumer assets, and increased incentive to securitize special lending exposures, sovereign and to some degree other banks. That is because BIS2 leads to significant reduction in risk weights for retail exposures, particularly mortgages, and an increase in risk weights for specialized lending and sovereigns, particularly high volatility real estate. In more specific terms:

♦ There will be a seriously reduced capital relief benefit from securitizing mortgage portfolios and somewhat reduced benefit for retail and retail SME portfolios.

♦ The incentive should shift toward the securitization of higher-risk weighted assets such as lower investment and subinvestment grade corporate exposures, commercial real estate, specialized lending, etc.

♦ Securitization of mortgage and retail portfolios should be driven more by nonregulated companies, as well as by the funding considerations of banks.

These conclusions, however, should be further detailed on the basis of the credit quality of the underlying exposures, subject to securitization. The chart below compares the capital requirements for different types of retail exposures under both standardized and the IRB approaches.

In all cases, the bank should consider the capital requirement before securitization and after securitization (in the form of capital for retained portion of securitization exposure). To simplify, it will depend on whether the capital before securitization is higher, equal, or less than the equity piece of the securitization transactions, which is usually the piece retained by the bank originator. In that regard, the supervisor's and bank's own estimates for loss given default, EAD (Exposure at Default), and M (Maturity) play a key role in determining the benefits of securitization for a Foundation IRB bank.

In that respect, we note the wide range of corporate exposures listed under the IRB approach and the potential difficulty for banks to get supervisory approval to use their own inputs for capital calculation. That may lead the banks to use the prescribed risk weightings for specialized lending, as indicated in the discussion of IRB, and thus have regulatory capital incentives to securitize such exposures.

Banks who continue to dominate the issuance volume of structured products may modify their issuance patterns, as a result of incorporating regulatory capital treatment of the underlying exposures in the economics equation of securitization. Securitization of mortgages may be primarily done for funding purposes, given limited regulatory capital benefit for it, whereas securitization of commercial real estate, unsecured consumer loans, and project finance may be driven by regulatory capital relief considerations in the first place. Alternatively, banks using the standardized approach may still have a regulatory capital benefit from securitization, while that benefit will be largely unavailable for banks applying the IRB approach. All this could lead to a change in supply levels, types of products securitized, and servicer considerations.

To achieve better realignment of regulatory and economic capital, banks may be tempted to issue also double-Bs and single-Bs, and even sell first loss positions. That raises questions about the rating agencies' methodologies for rating below investment grade pieces and how reliable they are as well as about the breadth of investor base for such exposures.

From the Perspective of the Investing Bank

An investing bank naturally takes into account the cost of regulatory capital among other things when determining its investment interest in a securitization position. Again from the perspective of regulatory capital considerations alone, a bank investor should:

- Buy riskier sovereign, bank and corporate exposures (say, rated single B and below) rather than less risky securitization exposures (say, rated double-B).
- Avoid subinvestment grade securitization tranches regardless of their actual risk, unless of course the pricing of such tranches is sufficient to compensate the bank for both the risk of the tranche and the increased cost of capital. The placement of subordinated tranches may become more dependent on the appetite of nonregulated investors. In fact, the question of placement of noninvestment grade tranches of securitizations will become a key factor in determining the viability of many future securitization transactions.
- Standardized approach requires more capital for investment grade tranches (except for BBB–) and less capital for lower-rated tranches, which should lead to different investment incentives for standardized and IRB bank investors and lead them to modify their investment allocations.
- IRB banks are even less likely than standardized banks to invest in subordinated noninvestment grade securitization tranches, and even more likely than standardized banks to seek most senior investment grade tranches.
- The gap between senior secured corporate and securitization exposure risk weightings for noninvestment grade exposure widens even further. This creates even bigger disincentives for IRB banks to invest in subordinated securitization exposures and make them choose instead high-yield corporate exposures.
- The risk weightings for covered bonds and RMBS are converging, thus reducing or eliminating the regulatory capital advantage of covered bonds, characterizing the current investment decisions.

Given the reduced risk weights for senior tranches under BIS2, banks are expected to realize certain savings from holding such securitization positions. Given that banks are the dominant investors in securitization in Europe, it is highly likely that such savings are passed on to the market in the form of spread tightening. Those savings, which can be viewed as a potential range of spread tightening for securitization exposures. We note

the "dis-saving" BB exposures or increase in regulatory capital requirement for bank investors, which we already stated, should lead them to
shun away from such exposures.

To clarify further, a standardized bank investing in AAA RMBS
securitization tranche will use risk weight of 50 percent under BIS1 (Basel
1 regulation) and 20 percent under BIS2. That will translate into 40 bps
savings on average cost of capital. Those savings can be passed on to the
market in the form of spread tightening, although that will not be a one-
for-one transfer. The same bank needs to increase the risk weight for a BB
securitization exposure from 100 percent under BIS1 to 350 percent under
BIS2. The increase in its regulatory capital is 125 bps, which in turn should
see respective widening of the BB spreads of such exposure, to compensate the bank for the increased regulatory capital. Similar analysis can
be performed for the RBA approach to securitization to be applied by the
IRB banks under BIS2. The respective capital savings or "gains" are
slightly larger in comparison to the standardized approach.

Demand–Supply Dynamics

From the perspective of the demand–supply dynamics of the securitization market, our conclusions can be further expanded:

- Nonregulated companies may increase their share in consumer
  asset securitization, while banks could increase their share in the
  securitization of commercial real estate and other corporate
  assets. In addition, there will be differentiation of the incentives
  to securitize by asset class or at all across banks depending on
  the approach to regulatory capital they adopt.
- Spreads on subinvestment grade securitization tranches should
  widen, and on senior tranches should tighten, compared to present levels, although it is difficult to anticipate the changes in the
  overall cost of securitization, as the earlier movements may or
  may not be netted out.
- The spread movements of securitization tranches in comparison
  to similarly rated corporate exposures is somewhat less certain,
  although we would expect noninvestment grade securitization
  tranches to widen more than similarly rated corporate exposures.
- We expect ratings to continue to play a major role in the securitization market, probably more so than in the corporate market.

In that respect, further improvement in rating approaches and models for securitization tranching will likely become a matter of urgency, given the significant differentiation of risk weights by tranche's credit rating.

♦ The new BIS2 guidelines will probably slow down the securitization market, as we know it today, but simultaneously create new distortions that new structuring techniques will aim to address. Hence, while this may be the end of securitization, as we know it, it may be the beginning of a new stage of securitization and structured market development.

♦ Given that banks and related conduits account for two-thirds roughly of securitization paper placed on the market, it is conceivable that lower-risk weights should translate into lower-target spreads for such holdings. The potential for significantly lower-risk weights for senior tranches may be fuelling demand for them in expectation for spread tightening, as those weights are introduced (or less spread widening if their introduction coincides with a softening market):

  ○ Entities, which benefit from such spread tightening as it occurs, but do not have the permanent benefit of regulatory capital reduction, may be induced to sell once the tightening is over, i.e., once the risk weight effect is fully priced in.
  ○ Entities, which benefit from the permanent reduction of regulatory capital will be exposed to different regulatory capital and, subsequently, potentially higher spread volatility as their securitization holdings are upgraded or, God forbid, are downgraded.
  ○ In both cases, the aforementioned result may be more trading and more volatility.
  ○ Downgrades may lead to higher than before spread movements, especially on the border points, where one tranche moves from one type of investors to another; particularly given the fact that at least, at present, the breadth and depth of the investor base rapidly declines from senior to junior tranches.

♦ Banks may be more sensitive to downgrades in the future, as they will have to tolerate both MTM losses and regulatory capital increase. As a result, they may be more likely to sell upon a downgrade.

♦ More pronounced differentiation of investor base by tranche
will eventually subject the pricing and dynamics of each tranche
to the developments in its respective specialized investor base,
which in turn may suggest more opportunities to arbitrage the
capital structure of structured products (akin to correlation arbitrage of the different layers of standardized tranches of iTraxx).

♦ Given the lack of clarity about regulatory capital treatment of
many structured products (say, combo notes, CPPI, securitization of a single commercial real estate loan, etc.), the consequences of a treatment away from market expectation or
practices may be dramatic: no demand and oversell are two that
come to mind.

REGULATORY CHANGES PARALLEL TO BIS2

Two other regulatory changes are already putting their stamp on the
structured finance market. One is the change in accounting practices, the
other is the introduction of regulatory capital requirements for insurance
companies and pension funds, loosely tailored after BIS1 (rather than
BIS2). The accounting changes strike at the heart of securitization practices, affecting off-balance sheet treatment of securitization, accounting
for securitization exposures, etc. Given the uncertainty about the final res-
olution of numerous points here below we highlight only one of them—
the accounting for synthetic securitizations. Solvency2, on the other hand,
is an exercise similar to the introduction of BIS1 years ago and could
change the way insurance companies and pension funds go about doing
their business in the future.

IAS/Accountancy

While IAS may seem more straightforward, its consequences remain
under scrutiny. The main issue of ambiguity there is related to synthetic
securitizations, in general, and synthetic CDOs, in particular. The question has taken on a magnitude worthy almost of Hamlet: to invest or not
to invest? The requirement for bifurcation of synthetic CDOs has introduced unnecessary complexity.

In some cases, auditors have taken the Draconian approach of
stopping certain institutions from investing in the product altogether.
Not to mention that different auditors have adopted different views and

interpretations of the issue. This suggests replacement of economic sense with auditor's inclination. The American FASB has left some hope that bifurcation issue may find a quiet end for the benefit of all parties concerned. If that is to be the solution, the interest in single tranche synthetics and their secondary and tertiary derivatives will likely be rejuvenated.

Solvency2

As for Solvency2 (the insurance companies and pension funds equivalent to BIS2), it may be too early to discuss yet—it is not coming into force before 2009, but it suffices to point to two potential developments: more demand from insurance companies and pension funds for structured products and more insurance companies becoming originators of securitization in their own right.

CHAPTER 2

Univariate Risk Assessment*

Arnaud de Servigny and Sven Sandow

INTRODUCTION

In this chapter, we discuss the credit risk that is associated with a single debt instrument and various methods to assess this risk. The credit risk associated with a defaultable debt instrument can be decomposed into two components: default risk and recovery risk. The former captures the uncertainty related to a possible default while the latter reflects the uncertainty related to recovery in the case of default. We shall discuss both types of risk in this chapter while keeping the focus on single credits; the risk associated with portfolios of defaultable instruments is discussed in Chapters 4 to 10.

Default risk can be analyzed from various perspectives. One of these perspectives is provided by the rating approach, in which default risk is quantified by means of a credit rating. These credit ratings are assigned by rating agencies, such as Standard & Poor's (S&P), Moody's, and Fitch, and the ratings assigned by these agencies are widely used as default risk indicators by market participants. We shall review the rating approach in the next section.

Another widely used approach to quantifying credit risk is the application of statistical techniques. In this approach, one uses historical data and analyzes them by means of methods from classical statistics or

---

*This chapter contains material from de Servigny and Renault (2004).

machine learning. The result of such an analysis can be a credit score or a probability of default (PD) for an obligor. The thus estimated PDs can refer to a fixed period of time, typically one year, or they can provide a complete term structure for the possible default event. These statistical approaches are the topic of Section 2.

From a fundamental perspective, one can view default as the exercise of an option by the shareholders of a firm. Therefore, one can, at least in principle, derive PDs based on the Black–Scholes option pricing framework. This leads to the so-called structural or Merton models, which are analyzed in the section "The Merton Approach."

Yet another perspective on default risk is provided by spreads of traded bonds and credit default swaps. These spreads contain information about the market's view on default risk. Although these spreads depend on other factors as well, they can be used for the extraction of default risk information. We shall discuss these in the section "Spreads."

Recovery risk is not as well understood as default risk. However, recovery risk has received a lot of attention in recent years; this is in part driven by the Basel II requirements. A number of models have been developed, which will be reviewed in the section "Recovery Risk." In the final section, we will discuss the combined effect of recovery and default risk. In particular, we shall focus on the effect of common factors underlying the two types of risk.

Some of the models and results reviewed in this chapter are discussed more rigorously and in more detail in various textbooks on credit risk such as the ones by Bielicki and Rutkowski (2002), Duffie and Singleton (2003), Schönbucher (2003), de Servigny and Renault (2004), and Lando (2004). A more detailed review of models for recovery risk is provided by Altman et al. (2005). Other results are not included in these books; we shall give references for those below.

Many of the modeling approaches that we discuss in this chapter, as well as many other approaches that practitioners use for quantifying credit risk, rely on standard statistical methods as well as on methods from the field of machine learning. For a more detailed discussion of statistical methods, we refer the reader to statistics textbooks, e.g., to the ones by Davidson and MacKinnon (1993), Gelman et al. (1995), or Greene (2000). Good overviews of machine learning approaches are provided by Hastie et al. (2003), Jebara (2004), Mitchell (1997), and Witten and Frank (2005). We would also like to refer the reader to the textbooks by Andersen et al. (1993), Hougaard (2000), and Klein and Moeschberger (2003) on survival analysis, which underlies most of the commonly used default term-structure models.

THE RATING APPROACH

What is a Rating?

A credit rating represents the agency's opinion about the creditworthiness of an obligor, with respect to a particular debt security or other financial obligation (*issue-specific credit ratings*). It also applies to an issuer's general creditworthiness (*issuer credit ratings*). There are generally two types of assessment corresponding to different financial instruments: long-term and short-term ones. One should stress that ratings from various agencies do not convey the same information. S&P perceives its ratings primarily as an opinion on the likelihood of default of an issuer,[*] while Moody's ratings tend to reflect the agency's opinion on the expected loss (probability of default times loss severity) on a facility.

Long-term issue-specific credit ratings and issuer ratings are divided into several categories, e.g., from "AAA" to "D" for S&P. Short-term issue-specific ratings can use a different scale (e.g., from "A-1" to "D"). Figure 2.1 reports Moody's and S&P rating scales. Although these grades are not directly comparable as recalled earlier, it is common to put them in parallel. The rated universe is broken down into two very broad categories: investment grade (IG) and noninvestment grade (NIG) or speculative issuers. IG firms are relatively stable issuers with moderate default risk while bonds issued in the NIG category, often called "junk bonds," are much more likely to default.

The credit quality of firms is best for Aaa/AAA ratings and deteriorates as ratings go down the alphabet. The coarse grid AAA, AA, A, . . . CCC can be supplemented with plusses and minuses in order to provide a finer indication of risk.

The Rating Process

A rating agency supplies a rating only if there is adequate information available to provide a credible credit opinion. This opinion relies on various analyses[†] based on a defined analytical framework. The criteria according to which any assessment is provided are very strictly defined and constitute the intangible assets of rating agencies, accumulated over years of experience. Any change in criteria is typically discussed at a worldwide level.

---

[*] A notching-down may be applied to junior debt, given relatively worse recovery prospects. Notching up is also possible.

[†] Quantitative, qualitative, and legal.

FIGURE 2.1

Moody's and S&P's Rating Scales.

Description	Moody's	S&P	
Investment grade			
	Aaa	AAA	Maximum safety
	Aa	AA	
	A	A	
	Baa	BBB	
Speculative grade			
	Ba	BB	
	B	B	
	Caa	CCC	
			Worst credit quality

For industrial companies, the analysis is commonly split between business reviews (firm competitiveness, quality of the management and of its policies, business fundamentals, regulatory actions, markets, operations, cost control, etc.) and quantitative analyses (financial ratios, etc.). The impact of these factors depends highly on the industry.

Figure 2.2* is an illustration of how various factors may impact differently on various industries. It also reports various business factors that impact the ratings in different sectors.

Following meetings with the management of the firm asking for a rating, the rating agency reviews qualitative as well as quantitative factors and compares the company's performance to its peers (see the ratio medians per rating in Table 2.1). Following this review, a rating committee meeting is convened. The committee discusses the lead analyst's recommendation before voting on it.

The issuer is subsequently notified of the rating and the major considerations supporting it. A rating can be appealed prior to its publication if meaningful new or additional information is to be presented by the issuer. But there is no guarantee that a revision will be granted. When a rating is assigned, it is disseminated to the public through the news media.

---

*This figure is for illustrative purposes and may not reflect the actual weights and factors used by one agency or another.

FIGURE 2.2

An Example of Various Factors that May be Used to Assign Ratings.

Indicative averages	Retail	Airlines	Property	Pharmaceuticals
Investment and speculative grade(%)	Investment grade: 82% Speculative grade: 18%	Iinvestment grade: 24% Speculative grade: 76%	Investment grade: 90% Speculative grade: 10%	Investment grade: 78% Speculative grade: 22%
Business Risk Weight	heigh	low	high	high
Financial Risk Weight	low	high	low	low
Business Qualitative Factors	-Scale & Geographic profile -Position on price, value and service -Regulatory environment	-Market Position (share capacity) -Ultimation of capacity. -Aircraftfleet (type/age) -Cost control (labour fuel)	-Quality and location of the assets -Quality of tenarts -Lease structure -Country-specific criteria (laws, taxation, and market liquidity	-R&D Programs -Product portfolio -Patert expirations

TABLE 2.1

Financial Ratios per Rating (Three-Year Medians– 1998–2000) in U.S. firms

	AAA	AA	A	BBB	BB	B	CCC
EBIT int. cov. (x)	21.4	10.1	6.1	3.7	2.1	0.8	0.1
EBITDA int. cov. (x)	26.5	12.9	9.1	5.8	3.4	1.8	1.3
Free oper. cash flow/ total debt (%)	84.2	25.2	15.0	8.5	2.6	(3.2)	(12.9)
Funds from oper./ total debt (%)	128.8	55.4	43.2	30.8	18.8	7.8	1.6
Return on capital (%)	34.9	21.7	19.4	13.6	11.6	6.6	1.0
Operating income/ sales (%)	27.0	22.1	18.6	15.4	15.9	11.9	11.9
Long-term debt/ capital (%)	13.3	28.2	33.9	42.5	57.2	69.7	68.8
Total debt/capital (%)	22.9	37.7	42.5	48.2	62.6	74.8	87.7
Number of Companies	8	29	136	218	273	281	22

Source: S&P's.

All ratings are monitored on an ongoing basis. Any new qualitative and quantitative piece of information is under surveillance. Regular meetings with the issuer's management are organized. As a result of the surveillance process, the rating agency may decide to initiate a review (i.e., put the firm on Credit Watch) and change the current rating. When a rating comes on a Credit Watch listing, a comprehensive analysis is undertaken. After the process, the rating change or affirmation is announced.

More recently, the "outlook" concept has been introduced. It provides information about the rating trend. If, for instance, the outlook is positive, it means that there is some potential upside conditional to the realization of current assumptions regarding the company. If the opposite, a negative outlook suggests that the creditworthiness of the company follows a negative trend.

A very important fact that is persistently emphasized by agencies is that their ratings are mere opinions. They do not constitute any recommendation to purchase, sell, or hold any type of security. A rating in itself indeed says nothing about the price or relative value of specific securities. A CCC bond may well be under-priced while an AA security may be trading at an overvalued price, although the risk may be appropriately reflected by their respective ratings.

The Link between Ratings and PDs

Although a rating is meant to be forward looking, it is not devised to pinpoint a precise PD but rather to a broad risk bucket. Rating agencies publish on a regular basis tables reporting observed default rates per rating category, per year, per industry, and per region. These tables reflect the empirical average defaulting frequencies of firms per rating category within the rated universe. The primary goal of these statistics is to verify that better (worse) ratings are indeed associated with lower (higher) default rates. They show that ratings tend to have roughly homogeneous default rates across industries,* as illustrated in the Table 2.2.

Figure 2.3 displays cumulative default rates in S&P's universe per rating category. There is a striking difference in default patterns between investment grade and speculative grade categories. The clear link between observed default rates and rating categories is the best support

---

*For some industries, observed long-term default rates can differ from the average figures. This type of change can be explained as major business changes like, for example, regulatory changes within the industry. Statistical effects, such as too limited and nonrepresentative sample, can also bias results.

TABLE 2.2

Average One Year Default Rates Per Industry*

	Trans.	Util.	Tele.	Media	Insur.	Hightec	Chem	Build	Fin.	Ener.	Cons.	Auto.
AAA	0.00	0.00	0.00	0.00	0.00	0.00	0.00	0.00	0.00	0.00	0.00	0.00
AA	0.00	0.00	0.00	0.00	0.06	0.00	0.00	0.00	0.00	0.00	0.00	0.00
A	0.00	0.11	0.00	0.00	0.09	0.00	0.00	0.42	0.00	0.20	0.00	0.00
BBB	0.00	0.14	0.00	0.27	0.67	0.73	0.19	0.64	0.32	0.22	0.17	0.29
BB	1.46	0.25	0.00	1.24	1.59	0.75	1.12	0.89	0.86	0.98	1.77	1.47
B	6.50	6.31	5.86	4.97	2.38	4.35	5.29	5.41	8.97	9.57	6.77	5.19
CCC	19.40	71.43	35.85	29.27	10.53	9.52	21.62	21.88	24.66	14.44	26.00	33.33

*Default rates for CCC bonds are based on a very small sample and may not be statistically robust.

Source: S&P's CreditPro, over the period 1981–2001.

Abbreviations: Trans. = transportation; Util. = utilities excluding Energy comps.; Tele. = telecoms; Insur. = insurance; Hightec = High Technology; Chem = chemistry; Build = construction; Fin. = Financial companies excluding insurance companies; Ener. = Energy companies; Cons. = consumer products; Auto. = automotive companies..

Cumulative Default Rates per Rating Category (S&P's CreditPro).

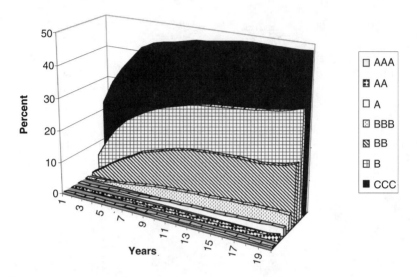

for agencies' claim that their grades are appropriate measures of creditworthiness.

Rating agencies also calculate transition matrices, which are tables reporting probabilities of migrations from one rating category to another. They serve as indicators of the likely path of a given credit up to a given horizon. Ex-post information, as that provided in default tables or transition matrices, does not guarantee provision of ex-ante insights regarding future PDs or migration. The stability over time of the PD in a given rating class and stability of rating criteria used by agencies, however, contribute to making ratings forward-looking predictors of default.

Estimating Cumulative Default Rates and Transition Matrices

Stability of Default Rates and Transition Matrices over the Cycle

Transition matrices appear to be dependent on the economic cycle, as downgrades and PDs increase significantly during recessions. Nickell et al. (2000) classify years between 1970 and 1997 in three categories (growth, stability, and recession), according to GDP growth for the G7 countries. One of their observations is that for IG counterparts, migration volatility is much lower during growth periods than during recessions. Their conclusion is that transition matrices unconditional on the economic cycle cannot be considered as Markovian.*

In another study based on S&P's data, Bangia et al. (2002) observe that the more the time horizon of an independent transition matrix increases, the less monotonic[†] the matrix becomes. Regarding its Markovian property, the authors tend to be less affirmative than Nickell et al. (2000), that is, their tests show that the Markovian hypothesis is not strongly rejected. The authors however acknowledge that one can observe path dependency in transition probabilities. For example, a past history of downgrades has an impact on future migrations. Such path dependency is significant as future PDs can increase up to five times for recently downgraded companies.

The authors then focus on the impact of economic cycles on transition matrices. They select two types of periods (expansion, recession) according to NBER indicators. The main difference between the two matrices corresponds mainly to a higher frequency of downgrades during recession periods. Splitting transition matrices in two periods is helpful, i.e., out of diagonal terms are much more stable. Their conclusion is that choosing two transition matrices conditional to the economic cycle gives much better results, in terms of Markovian stability, than considering only one matrix unconditional on the economic cycle.

In order to further investigate the impact of cycles on transition matrices and credit VaR, Bangia et al. (2002) use a version of CreditMetrics on a portfolio of 148 bonds. They show that during recession periods, the necessary economic capital increases substantially compared to growth periods (by 30 percent for a 99 percent confidence level of credit VaR or 25 percent for a 99.9 percent confidence level). Note that the authors ignore the increase in correlation during recessions.

Estimating Default and Rating Transition Probabilities via Cohort Analysis

A common approach for rated companies is to derive historic average default or rating transition probabilities by observing the performance of groups of companies—frequently called cohorts—with identical credit

---

*A Markov chain is defined by the fact that information known at time $t-1$, used in the chain, is sufficient to determine the probabilities at time t. In other words, it is not necessary the complete path till $t-1$ in order to obtain the probabilities at time t.

[†]Monotonicity rule: probabilities are decreasing when the distance to the diagonal of the matrix increases. This property is characteristic from the trajectory concept: migrations occur through regular downgrade or upgrade rather than through a big shift.

ratings. These estimates are particularly suitable in the context of long-term "through-the-cycle" risk management, which attempts to dampen fluctuations due to business cycle and other economic effects.

We start by considering all companies at a specific point in time t (e.g., December 31, 2000). We denote the total number of companies in the kth cohort at time t by $N_k(t)$, and the total number of observed defaults in period T (i.e., between time $t+T-1$ and time $t+T$) by $D_k(t, T)$. We then obtain an estimate for the (marginal) PD in year T (as seen from time t):

$$P_k(t, T) = \frac{D_k(t,T)}{N_k(t)}. \quad *$$

Repeating this analysis for cohorts created at M different points in time t allows us to obtain an estimate for the unconditional PD in period T,

$$\overline{P}_k(T) = \sum_{t=1}^{M} w_k(t) P_k(t).$$

These unconditional probabilities are simply weighted averages of the estimates obtained for cohorts considered in different periods. Typically, $w_k(t) = \dfrac{1}{M}$ (each period is equally weighted) or $w_k(t) = \dfrac{N_k(t)}{\sum_{m=1}^{M} N_k(m)}$ (weighted according to the number of observations in different periods).

One way to obtain unconditional cumulative PDs is to replace the (marginal) number of defaults in period T, $D_k(t, T)$, with the cumulative number of defaults up to period T, $D'_k(t, T) = \sum_{m=1}^{T} D_k(t, m)$.

Unfortunately, this estimator "loses" more and more information as T increases.[†] An alternative method, which incorporates all available information, is to calculate the unconditional (weighted average) cumulative probabilities $\overline{P}_k^{\text{cum}}(T)$ from the unconditional marginal probabilities $\overline{P}_k(T)$. This can be done by means of the following recursion:

---

[*] The cohort analysis outlined here is based on the global ratings performance data contained in S&P's CreditPro® Version 6.60 (http://creditpro.standardandpoors.com/).

[†] Some companies will have their rating withdrawn during the course of the year. It is common to treat these transitions to NR (not rated) as noninformative with respect to the credit quality. Hence, companies that have their rating withdrawn during the period of interest are ignored in the subsequent analysis.

$$\overline{P}_k^{cum}(1) = \overline{P}_k(1),$$

$$\overline{P}_k^{cum}(T) = \overline{P}_k^{cum}(T-1) + (1 - \overline{P}_k^{cum}(T-1))\overline{P}_k(T).$$

Table 2.3 and Figure 2.4 show the cumulative PDs for time horizons of up to 10 years, estimated from the S&P CreditPro® database. The database contains the ratings history of 9740 companies from December 31, 1981 to December 31, 2003, and includes 1386 defaults. Figure 2.4 plots the results for rating classes "AAA" to "B."

The estimates for "AAA" companies over short horizons reveal one of the main drawbacks of cohort analysis. The approach is not capable of deriving nonzero probabilities if no defaults have been observed in the past. However, it is clear that there is a chance (however small) that even a highly rated company will default within the course of one or two years.

The same approach can be taken for estimating probabilities for rating transitions. In this case, we have, for a given horizon, a matrix of probabilities (transition matrix) instead of a vector of probabilities. The entries of this matrix can be estimated using straightforward generalizations of the given equations. The corresponding rating transition matrix is given in Table 2.4.

TABLE 2.3

Cumulative PDs (in Percents) 1981–2003.

Rating	Y1	Y2	Y3	Y4	Y5	Y6	Y7	Y8	Y9	Y10
AAA	0.00	0.00	0.03	0.06	0.10	0.17	0.25	0.38	0.43	0.48
AA	0.01	0.04	0.10	0.19	0.31	0.43	0.58	0.71	0.82	0.94
A	0.05	0.15	0.28	0.45	0.65	0.87	1.11	1.34	1.62	1.95
BBB	0.37	1.01	1.67	2.53	3.41	4.24	4.94	5.61	6.22	6.93
BB	1.36	4.02	7.12	9.92	12.38	14.75	16.65	18.24	19.84	21.00
B	6.08	13.31	19.20	23.66	26.82	29.29	31.33	33.01	34.21	35.41
CCC/C	30.85	39.76	45.47	49.53	53.00	54.30	55.50	56.11	57.59	58.44

Source: S&P's.

---

*For $T=5$ years, e.g., the last cohort that can be considered is December 1998 if the last entry in the database corresponds to December 2003. This is because cohorts originating from later dates would not be not observed for the whole five years, they are "right-censored."

FIGURE 2.4

Cumulative Default Probabilities (AAA to B) 1981–2003. (S&P's).

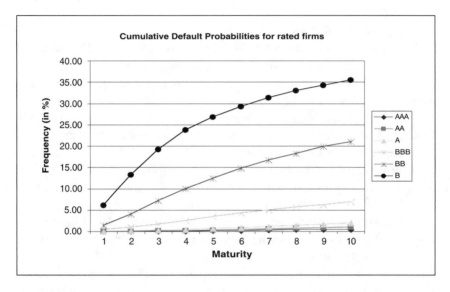

TABLE 2.4

One year Transition Matrix (Percents) in U.S. Industries (1981–2001)

Initial Rating	End rating							
	AAA	AA	A	BBB	BB	B	CC	D
AAA	89.41	5.58	0.44	0.08	0.04	0	0	0
AA	0.58	88.28	6.51	0.6	0.07	0.09	0.03	0.01
A	0.07	2.05	87.85	4.99	0.46	0.17	0.05	0.06
BBB	0.04	0.24	4.52	84.4	4.24	0.68	0.16	0.27
BB	0.03	0.07	0.43	6.1	75.56	7.33	0.82	1.17
B	0	0.09	0.25	0.32	4.78	74.59	3.75	5.93
CCC	0.13	0	0.25	0.75	1.63	8.67	51.01	25.25

D denotes default in this table.
Source: S&P's Credit Pro.

Adjusting for Withdrawn Ratings (NR).   Some firms that have a rating at the beginning of a given period may no longer have one at the end. This may be because the issuer has not paid the agency's fee or that it has asked the agency to withdraw its rating. These events are not rare and account for about 4.5 percent of transitions in the IG class and 10 percent in the speculative grade category over a given year.

When calculating probabilities, one needs to adjust the probabilities calculated earlier to take into consideration the possibility of withdrawn rating. Otherwise, the sum of transition probabilities to the n ratings would be less than one.

The adjustment is performed by ignoring the firms that have their rating withdrawn during a given period. The underlying assumption is that the withdrawal of a rating is a neutral event, i.e., it is not associated with any information regarding the credit quality of the issuer. One could, however, argue that firms that expect a downgrade below what they perceive is an acceptable level ask for their ratings to be withdrawn, whereas firms that are satisfied with their grade generally want to maintain it.

It is difficult to get information about the motivation behind a rating's withdrawal and, therefore, such adjustment is generally considered acceptable.

Table 2.5 shows the default table used in collateral debt obligations S&P CDO Evaluator version 2.4.1. In that version, the cohort analysis was the basis of the methodology used.

Estimating Default and Rating Transition Probabilities via a Duration Technique

The cohort approach outlined earlier is also frequently employed in the calculation of rating transition probabilities or transition matrices. Instead of counting the number of defaults, $D_k(t, T)$, we use the number of rating migrations from rating class k to a different class l, $N_{kl}(t, T)$. Although matrices can be obtained for different horizons T, it is common to focus on the average one-year transition matrix, denoted by $\bar{Q}$. Assuming that rating transitions follow a time homogeneous Markov process, the T-period matrix $\bar{Q}(T)$ is given by $\bar{Q}(T) = \bar{Q}^T$. The analysis does not take into account the exact timing of events and ignores multiple transitions between time t and the end of the observation period, $t + T$. The estimates may also vary with the exact choice of t and the number of cohorts considered within a fixed period of time (e.g., monthly or annual cohorts). One way to overcome these drawbacks is to work within a so-called *duration* (or hazard)

TABLE 2.5

Cumulative PDs per Rating Category (in Percents)–CDO Evaluator 2.41 Assumptions

	AAA	AA+	AA	AA-	A+	A	A-	BBB+	BBB	BBB-	BB+	BB	BB-	B+	B	B-	CCC+	CCC	CCC-	CC	SD	D
1	0.023	0.023	0.111	0.136	0.136	0.136	0.145	0.225	0.225	0.544	1.666	2.772	2.792	3.667	8.594	9.563	14.693	19.824	46.549	100.000	100.000	100.000
2	0.062	0.071	0.242	0.290	0.303	0.317	0.358	0.532	0.638	1.357	3.316	5.265	5.667	7.535	14.514	16.626	23.401	30.176	53.451	100.000	100.000	100.000
3	0.119	0.143	0.394	0.464	0.501	0.542	0.632	0.911	1.182	2.317	4.916	7.498	8.380	11.078	18.594	21.564	28.696	35.829	57.219	100.000	100.000	100.000
4	0.193	0.239	0.565	0.659	0.728	0.808	0.959	1.352	1.814	3.344	6.439	9.489	10.826	14.122	21.446	24.962	32.024	39.086	59.390	100.000	100.000	100.000
5	0.284	0.357	0.757	0.875	0.984	1.111	1.330	1.841	2.500	4.387	7.866	11.255	12.973	16.655	23.488	27.316	34.200	41.083	60.722	100.000	100.000	100.000
6	0.392	0.497	0.968	1.113	1.265	1.448	1.737	2.368	3.215	5.415	9.189	12.817	14.834	18.735	24.997	28.985	35.690	42.394	61.596	100.000	100.000	100.000
7	0.517	0.656	1.198	1.372	1.570	1.814	2.173	2.921	3.941	6.410	10.407	14.197	16.436	20.438	26.151	30.208	36.762	43.317	62.211	100.000	100.000	100.000
8	0.658	0.835	1.445	1.650	1.896	2.204	2.632	3.492	4.667	7.360	11.525	15.419	17.816	21.840	27.065	31.141	37.576	44.010	62.673	100.000	100.000	100.000
9	0.815	1.033	1.710	1.946	2.242	2.614	3.108	4.074	5.383	8.261	12.548	16.503	19.008	23.004	27.816	31.883	38.222	44.562	63.041	100.000	100.000	100.000
10	0.988	1.247	1.990	2.259	2.604	3.041	3.597	4.661	6.084	9.112	13.486	17.470	20.044	23.984	28.453	32.497	38.760	45.023	63.349	100.000	100.000	100.000
11	1.176	1.478	2.285	2.588	2.981	3.481	4.096	5.248	6.766	9.914	14.346	18.338	20.952	24.821	29.008	33.023	39.223	45.424	63.616	100.000	100.000	100.000
12	1.378	1.724	2.594	2.931	3.371	3.931	4.599	5.831	7.428	10.671	15.139	19.122	21.755	25.548	29.504	33.488	39.635	45.782	63.855	100.000	100.000	100.000
13	1.594	1.985	2.916	3.287	3.772	4.389	5.106	6.409	8.068	11.384	15.872	19.835	22.473	26.190	29.957	33.910	40.011	46.111	64.074	100.000	100.000	100.000
14	1.823	2.259	3.249	3.654	4.183	4.852	5.614	6.979	8.687	12.058	16.554	20.489	23.122	26.765	30.377	34.300	40.359	46.418	64.278	100.000	100.000	100.000
15	2.066	2.546	3.593	4.032	4.601	5.319	6.120	7.539	9.286	12.697	17.189	21.093	23.714	27.288	30.771	34.667	40.687	46.708	64.472	100.000	100.000	100.000
16	2.320	2.844	3.947	4.418	5.025	5.789	6.624	8.090	9.864	13.304	17.786	21.655	24.260	27.770	31.146	35.015	41.000	46.986	64.657	100.000	100.000	100.000
17	2.586	3.154	4.310	4.812	5.454	6.259	7.125	8.629	10.425	13.882	18.349	22.182	24.768	28.220	31.506	35.349	41.301	47.253	64.835	100.000	100.000	100.000
18	2.863	3.473	4.681	5.213	5.887	6.728	7.621	9.159	10.967	14.435	18.882	22.680	25.245	28.643	31.854	35.673	41.593	47.513	65.009	100.000	100.000	100.000
19	3.150	3.802	5.058	5.619	6.323	7.197	8.112	9.677	11.493	14.965	19.390	23.152	25.696	29.045	32.191	35.987	41.877	47.766	65.178	100.000	100.000	100.000
20	3.447	4.140	5.442	6.030	6.761	7.663	8.598	10.185	12.005	15.474	19.875	23.603	26.126	29.430	32.520	36.294	42.154	48.014	65.343	100.000	100.000	100.000
21	3.753	4.485	5.831	6.444	7.200	8.127	9.078	10.683	12.502	15.966	20.342	24.036	26.538	29.801	32.843	36.595	42.427	48.258	65.505	100.000	100.000	100.000
22	4.067	4.838	6.224	6.861	7.639	8.588	9.552	11.171	12.987	16.442	20.792	24.454	26.935	30.161	33.159	36.892	42.695	48.498	65.665	100.000	100.000	100.000
23	4.389	5.197	6.622	7.281	8.078	9.046	10.021	11.650	13.460	16.904	21.227	24.858	27.319	30.510	33.471	37.183	42.959	48.735	65.823	100.000	100.000	100.000
24	4.719	5.562	7.023	7.702	8.517	9.500	10.483	12.120	13.923	17.353	21.650	25.251	27.692	30.852	33.779	37.472	43.220	48.969	65.979	100.000	100.000	100.000
25	5.056	5.932	7.426	8.124	8.954	9.950	10.940	12.582	14.376	17.791	22.062	25.634	28.056	31.186	34.083	37.756	43.479	49.201	66.134	100.000	100.000	100.000
26	5.398	6.307	7.831	8.547	9.389	10.396	11.391	13.036	14.819	18.219	22.463	26.008	28.412	31.515	34.383	38.039	43.734	49.430	66.287	100.000	100.000	100.000
27	5.747	6.686	8.239	8.970	9.823	10.838	11.836	13.482	15.255	18.638	22.856	26.375	28.761	31.838	34.681	38.318	43.988	49.658	66.438	100.000	100.000	100.000
28	6.101	7.068	8.647	9.392	10.254	11.276	12.276	13.921	15.683	19.048	23.242	26.735	29.104	32.157	34.976	38.595	44.239	49.883	66.589	100.000	100.000	100.000
29	6.459	7.454	9.056	9.813	10.684	11.710	12.711	14.354	16.104	19.452	23.620	27.089	29.442	32.472	35.268	38.870	44.489	50.107	66.738	100.000	100.000	100.000
30	6.822	7.842	9.465	10.234	11.110	12.140	13.140	14.780	16.518	19.848	23.992	27.437	29.775	32.783	35.559	39.143	44.737	50.330	66.887	100.000	100.000	100.000

modeling framework, where the exact points in time of migrations are captured. In its simplest form, the duration analysis involves the estimation of a generator matrix of a Markov chain, which, for the time-homogeneous as well as time-inhomogeneous case, is only marginally more complex than a cohort analysis. Lando and Skodeberg (2002), Jafry and Schuermann (2003), and Jobst and Gilkes (2003) discuss these approaches in more detail. Another advantage of the duration framework is that the estimation process can be extended to incorporate state variables (economic variables or past ratings), in order to capture business cycle effects and ratings momentum. See, e.g., Kavvathas (2001), Christensen et al. (2004), and Couderc and Renault (2005).

Let us consider the simplest case of a time-homogeneous, constant intensity estimator. A transition matrix can be estimated in a straightforward manner. The maximum-likelihood estimator under the assumption of constant transition intensities is:

$$\lambda_{ij} = \frac{m_{ij}(0,T)}{\int_0^T n_i(u)du}$$

where $m_{ij}(0, T)$ corresponds to the total number of migrations from class i to class j with $i \neq j$ over the interval $[0, T]$; it includes firms that were not in rating class i initially, but have entered into this class i during the period $[0, T]$ and subsequently moved to class j during the same period. $n_i(u)$ is the total number of firms in class i at time u. As a consequence, $\int_0^T n_i(u)du$ represents the total number of firms in class i during the $[0, T]$ period weighted by the actual length of time each firm spent in this class.

We show in Tables 2.6A and B how the estimation of a one-year time-homogeneous transition matrix can differ whether it is computed with the duration method or with the cohort approach. We use S&P's Credit Pro over the period 1981–2002, adjusting for NRs.

A comparison of the matrices reveals three major differences:

1. AAA default probabilities and migration rates to B and CCC are nonzero for the duration method, despite the fact that no defaults were observed for highly rated issuers. Migrations of a firm from AAA to AA to A to a subsequent default are sufficient to contribute probability mass to AAA default probabilities (PD_{AAA}).

TABLE 2.6A

Duration Method: One-year (NR-adjusted) Transition Matrix (1981–2002)

	AAA	AA	A	BBB	BB	B	CCC	D
AAA	93.1178	6.1225	0.5736	0.1267	0.0536	0.0048	0.0006	0.0003
AA	0.5939	91.3815	7.3290	0.5600	0.0697	0.0527	0.0092	0.0040
A	0.0641	1.9125	91.9291	5.4793	0.4386	0.1514	0.0157	0.0093
BBB	0.0363	0.2314	4.0335	89.5775	5.0656	0.8554	0.0866	0.1137
BB	0.0299	0.0987	0.5407	5.0917	83.8964	8.8088	0.8564	0.6774
B	0.0043	0.0764	0.2531	0.4936	4.3764	83.4296	6.3009	5.0658
CCC	0.0595	0.0101	0.3169	0.4650	1.1593	7.0421	47.1048	43.8423
D	0.0000	0.0000	0.0000	0.0000	0.0000	0.0000	0.0000	100.000

2. In particular, IG (except AAA) PDs are significantly smaller for the time-homogeneous duration approach: the less-efficient cohort approach appears to overestimate default risk significantly. For example, PD_A is approximately six times higher in the cohort approach. These lower estimates are obtained when firms spend time in the A state during the year on their way up (down) to higher (lower) ratings from lower (higher) rating classes (passing through effects). Such moves reduce the default intensity of A-rated issuers (as the denominator increases) which in turn leads to lower PDs.

TABLE 2.6B

Cohort Method: Average One-year (NR-adjusted) Transition Matrix (1981–2002)

	AAA	AA	A	BBB	BB	B	CCC	D
AAA	93.0859	6.2624	0.4534	0.1417	0.0567	0.0000	0.0000	0.0000
AA	0.5926	91.0594	7.5372	0.6134	0.0520	0.1144	0.0208	0.0104
A	0.0538	2.0987	91.4858	5.6084	0.4664	0.1913	0.0419	0.0538
BBB	0.0324	0.2265	4.3362	89.2161	4.6355	0.9223	0.2751	0.3560
BB	0.0361	0.0843	0.4334	5.9595	83.0966	7.7173	1.2039	1.4688
B	0.0000	0.0830	0.2844	0.4029	5.2264	82.4484	4.8353	6.7196
CCC	0.1053	0.0000	0.3158	0.6316	1.5789	9.8947	56.5263	30.9474
D	0.0000	0.0000	0.0000	0.0000	0.0000	0.0000	0.0000	100.0000

3. For very low rating categories (CCC in the above coarse setup), the differences are also extreme; About 30 percent CCC default rates for the cohort approach compared to 44 percent for the duration method. Hence, using the less efficient (yet industry standard) cohort approach leads to 13 percent lower results. One explanation is that companies pass through CCC ratings on their way to default and if they do so, usually spend only little time there. This yields a small denominator and therefore higher PDs.

The use of this duration approach has had a significant impact on the default table embedded into CDO Evaluator version 3. The new default table (Table 2.7) is presented next, and changes can be seen from the table (Table 2.5) that corresponded to CDO Evaluator version 2.41. This new table is a result of a blend between the cohort approach, the duration approach, and empirically observed cumulative default rates.

STATISTICAL PD MODELING AND CREDIT SCORING

In order to quantify credit risk, practitioners often build models that provide PDs of specific obligors over a given period of time. Alternatively, one often assigns a so-called credit score to an obligor, e.g., a number between 1 and 10 with 1 corresponding to low risk and 10 corresponding to high risk of default.

There are two fundamentally different approaches to modeling PDs or assigning credit scores:

♦ Statistical approach
♦ Structural approach (also called Merton model)

Both types of approaches, along with a myriad of hybrids, are commonly used in practice. We shall review some popular examples for the former approach first, and we shall discuss the latter approach in a later section.

Some Statistical Techniques

In this section, we briefly discuss some statistical approaches to modeling PDs for a given period of time (typically one year) and deriving credit scores. Some of these approaches are based on techniques from classical statistics, whereas others resort to methods from machine learning

TABLE 2.7

Cumulative PD per Rating Category (in Percents)–CDO Evaluation 3 Default Rates

	AAA	AA+	AA	AA–	A+	A	A–	BBB+	BBB	BBB–	BB+	BB	BB–	B+	B	B–	CCC+	CCC	CCC–	CC	SD	D
1	0.000	0.001	0.008	0.014	0.018	0.022	0.033	0.195	0.294	0.806	1.484	2.296	3.457	4.100	5.295	8.138	23.582	45.560	66.413	100.000	100.000	100.000
2	0.005	0.009	0.039	0.048	0.064	0.080	0.121	0.427	0.684	1.805	2.915	4.506	6.624	8.124	10.833	16.559	38.046	59.087	79.205	100.000	100.000	100.000
3	0.016	0.027	0.085	0.102	0.138	0.172	0.262	0.701	1.162	2.899	4.312	6.597	9.516	11.903	15.940	23.729	46.605	64.704	82.840	100.000	100.000	100.000
4	0.034	0.056	0.144	0.178	0.240	0.298	0.451	1.023	1.713	4.034	5.681	8.567	12.164	15.388	20.479	29.578	52.040	67.875	84.478	100.000	100.000	100.000
5	0.061	0.098	0.219	0.276	0.371	0.459	0.686	1.391	2.323	5.179	7.020	10.424	14.595	18.571	24.463	34.333	55.809	70.042	85.513	100.000	100.000	100.000
6	0.097	0.153	0.310	0.397	0.531	0.655	0.966	1.805	2.980	6.316	8.327	12.175	16.832	21.462	27.947	38.234	58.626	71.685	86.285	100.000	100.000	100.000
7	0.144	0.224	0.420	0.543	0.719	0.887	1.287	2.261	3.672	7.434	9.598	13.826	18.895	24.083	30.999	41.476	60.850	73.005	86.907	100.000	100.000	100.000
8	0.204	0.311	0.549	0.713	0.937	1.152	1.648	2.756	4.390	8.529	10.831	15.387	20.800	26.457	33.680	44.209	62.672	74.105	87.429	100.000	100.000	100.000
9	0.276	0.414	0.700	0.909	1.184	1.451	2.047	3.284	5.127	9.598	12.025	16.862	22.563	28.610	36.046	46.543	64.204	75.041	87.877	100.000	100.000	100.000
10	0.362	0.536	0.872	1.130	1.458	1.782	2.479	3.842	5.876	10.637	13.179	18.258	24.197	30.565	38.145	48.559	65.517	75.853	88.268	100.000	100.000	100.000
11	0.463	0.678	1.066	1.377	1.761	2.143	2.943	4.425	6.634	11.649	14.295	19.580	25.717	32.346	40.016	50.320	66.657	76.565	88.614	100.000	100.000	100.000
12	0.581	0.839	1.284	1.650	2.092	2.534	3.434	5.029	7.396	12.631	15.371	20.834	27.132	33.973	41.694	51.871	67.659	77.197	88.921	100.000	100.000	100.000
13	0.715	1.020	1.525	1.947	2.448	2.952	3.952	5.651	8.160	13.587	16.410	22.025	28.453	35.463	43.206	53.248	68.548	77.762	89.197	100.000	100.000	100.000
14	0.867	1.223	1.790	2.270	2.830	3.396	4.491	6.287	8.923	14.515	17.414	23.157	29.689	36.832	44.575	54.481	69.343	78.271	89.447	100.000	100.000	100.000
15	1.037	1.447	2.078	2.617	3.237	3.864	5.051	6.936	9.684	15.418	18.383	24.234	30.849	38.096	45.822	55.592	70.060	78.732	89.674	100.000	100.000	100.000
16	1.225	1.693	2.389	2.988	3.666	4.353	5.628	7.593	10.441	16.296	19.320	25.262	31.940	39.265	46.962	56.599	70.710	79.154	89.882	100.000	100.000	100.000
17	1.433	1.961	2.724	3.382	4.117	4.862	6.221	8.258	11.193	17.152	20.226	26.243	32.969	40.351	48.009	57.517	71.304	79.541	90.074	100.000	100.000	100.000
18	1.661	2.250	3.080	3.798	4.588	5.390	6.826	8.928	11.940	17.985	21.103	27.181	33.941	41.363	48.976	58.359	71.848	79.898	90.250	100.000	100.000	100.000
19	1.908	2.561	3.458	4.234	5.078	5.934	7.442	9.602	12.680	18.798	21.952	28.081	34.862	42.310	49.872	59.134	72.350	80.229	90.414	100.000	100.000	100.000
20	2.175	2.893	3.858	4.690	5.586	6.493	8.068	10.279	13.414	19.591	22.777	28.944	35.737	43.198	50.706	59.851	72.816	80.538	90.568	100.000	100.000	100.000
21	2.462	3.246	4.277	5.165	6.110	7.065	8.701	10.957	14.142	20.365	23.577	29.773	36.570	44.034	51.486	60.517	73.249	80.827	90.711	100.000	100.000	100.000
22	2.769	3.619	4.715	5.657	6.648	7.648	9.340	11.636	14.862	21.123	24.355	30.572	37.365	44.824	52.216	61.140	73.654	81.099	90.845	100.000	100.000	100.000
23	3.095	4.012	5.171	6.164	7.200	8.241	9.985	12.314	15.575	21.863	25.112	31.343	38.126	45.571	52.904	61.723	74.035	81.355	90.973	100.000	100.000	100.000
24	3.440	4.423	5.644	6.687	7.763	8.844	10.633	12.991	16.281	22.589	25.850	32.087	38.855	46.281	53.554	62.271	74.394	81.593	91.093	100.000	100.000	100.000
25	3.804	4.853	6.133	7.223	8.337	9.454	11.284	13.667	16.980	23.300	26.570	32.808	39.556	46.958	54.169	62.789	74.733	81.828	91.207	100.000	100.000	100.000
26	4.187	5.300	6.638	7.772	8.921	10.070	11.937	14.340	17.671	23.997	27.272	33.506	40.230	47.604	54.754	63.280	75.055	82.048	91.316	100.000	100.000	100.000
27	4.586	5.763	7.156	8.331	9.513	10.692	12.591	15.010	18.356	24.682	27.959	34.184	40.881	48.222	55.311	63.746	75.362	82.258	91.419	100.000	100.000	100.000
28	5.003	6.241	7.686	8.901	10.112	11.318	13.245	15.678	19.033	25.354	28.630	34.842	41.510	48.815	55.844	64.190	75.655	82.459	91.519	100.000	100.000	100.000
29	5.436	6.735	8.229	9.480	10.718	11.947	13.900	16.342	19.704	26.015	29.288	35.483	42.118	49.386	56.355	64.615	75.935	82.653	91.614	100.000	100.000	100.000
30	5.885	7.241	8.781	10.066	11.329	12.580	14.553	17.003	20.367	26.665	29.933	36.108	42.709	49.936	56.845	65.022	76.205	82.839	91.706	100.000	100.000	100.000

(also called statistical learning). They share the common idea that the PD of an obligor is learned from the data with no or little input of knowledge about the mechanisms that lead firms to default.

In statistical learning, one often makes a distinction between supervised and unsupervised classification. These two approaches differ with respect to the data from which we learn. In the first case, so-called labeled training data are available, i.e., observations that provide a default indicator or a credit score along with the potential risk factors. In other words, a supervised algorithm learns from historical observations of firms for which we know the class labels (default indicator or credit score). Unsupervised learning algorithms, on the other hand, rely on so-called unlabeled data, i.e., observations for which the class labels are unknown. While this type of learning can be used for the assignment of credit scores, it is not commonly used for modeling PDs; we will not discuss unsupervised learning in this chapter.

Some approaches that can be used for modeling PDs or deriving credit scores are[*]:

1. Logistic regression and probit
2. Maximum-likelihood estimation
3. Bayesian estimation (e.g., naïve Bayes classifier)
4. Minimum-relative-entropy models
5. Fisher linear-discriminant analysis
6. k-Nearest neighbor classifiers
7. Classification trees
8. Support vector machines
9. Neural networks
10. Genetic algorithms

Some of the methods in this list are closely related to each other, and the methods in the list are not exclusive. For example, logistic regression can be viewed as a special case of methods 2, 3, or 4, and maximum-likelihood estimation can be interpreted in the Bayesian framework. However, all of these methods are interesting in their own right and are applied by practitioners.

The first four of these methods provide conditional probabilities for the classes (default or nondefault for PD modeling and the score for credit

---

[*] See, e.g., Mitchell (1997), Hastie et al. (2003), Jebara (2004), or Witten and Frank (2005).

scoring), given the values of the risk factors. The remaining methods in the list are classifiers by design, i.e., they assign a single class but no class probabilities to obligors. This makes these methods more relevant for credit scoring than for PD modeling. However, some of these methods can be generalized to provide conditional probabilities. One way for doing this is to apply multiple, slightly different, classifiers for a given obligor and assign class probabilities according to how often each class is assigned.

In what follows, we shall focus on PD modeling and restrict ourselves to logistic regression, which is perhaps the most popular method for PD modeling, and to a generalization that fits into frameworks 2, 3, and 4.

Let us consider a vector X of risk factors, with $X \in R^d$. In a logistic regression, the probability of a default (symbolized by a "1") in a given period of time (e.g., one year), conditional on the information X, is written as the logit transformation of a linear combination of the feature functions $f_j(X)$, $j = 1, \ldots, J$, i.e.,

$$P(1|X) = \frac{1}{1 + e^{-\left(\beta_0 + \Sigma_{i=1}^{j} \beta_j f_j(X)\right)}},$$

where the β_j are parameters. One can think of the feature functions as terms of a Taylor expansion of some appropriate function of X that reflects the dependency of the PD on the risk factors. The logit transformation* enables us to obtain a result located in the interval $]0, 1[$.

There are various choices one can make for the feature functions. The simplest choice, which is frequently used, is a set of linear functions. In this case, we obtain the so-called linear logit model, i.e.,

$$P(1|X) = \frac{1}{1 + e^{-\left(\beta_0 + \Sigma_{i=1}^{d} \beta_i x_i\right)}}.$$

Another occasionally used choice for feature functions is the set of all first- and second-order combinations of risk factors; it results in

---

*Other transformations such as the probit are possible; the probit is used by Moody's Riskcalc™, see Falkenstein (2000).
Another way to present it is to further reduce the residual or error term.

$$P(1|X) = \frac{1}{1 + e^{-\left(\beta_0 + \Sigma_{i=1}^d \beta_i x_i + \Sigma_{j=1}^p \Sigma_{k=j}^p \delta_{jk} x_j x_k\right)}}.$$

We have renamed some of the β_j as δ_{jk} here in order to simplify the notation.

Another choice made for S&P PD model, called Credit Risk Tracker (CRT) (see Zhou et al., 2006), is to include, besides the first- and second-order terms, additional cylindrical kernel features of the form $f_j(X) = \frac{(x_i - a_j)^2}{\sigma^2}$, a_j are the selected centers and σ is a bandwidth corresponding to the decay rate of the kernels.

In order to specify a model of any of these types, one has to estimate the model parameters, i.e., the β_j. The standard approach for doing so is to maximize, with respect to the β_j, the log-likelihood function

$$L(\beta) = \sum_{i=1}^N \{Y_i \log P(1|X_i) + (1 - Y_i) \log[1 - P(1|X_i)]\},$$

where the (X_i, Y_i), $i = 1, \ldots, N$, are observed pairs of risk factors and default indicators (1 for default and 0 for no default). This approach is often called logistic regression (see, e.g., Hosmer and Lemeshow, 2000). This maximum-likelihood approach is effective if there are relatively few feature functions and relatively many observations available for the model training. Otherwise, it can lead to overfitting, i.e., to a model that fits the training data well, but performs poorly on out-of-sample data. In order to mitigate overfitting, one can use so-called regularization, i.e., maximize a regularized likelihood that typically takes the form

$$L(\beta) + R(\beta).$$

Here, $R(\beta)$ is a regularization term that takes a large value for large absolute β_j and a small value for small absolute β_j. Since smaller β_j correspond to smoother (as a function of the risk factors) PDs, the above regularization term penalizes nonsmooth PDs. The result of the estimation is the PD that is smoother than the one we would obtain from the maximum-likelihood estimation. In practice, one uses regularization terms that are either quadratic or linear in the absolutes of the β_j. It is interesting to observe that regularization linear in the absolutes of the β_j leads to automatic feature selection.*

The above statistical methods are usually characterized as (possibly regularized) maximum-likelihood estimations of exponential probabilities. They can also be shown to be equivalent to minimum-relative-entropy methods (see, e.g., Jebara, 2004). Moreover, the resulting probabilities turn out to be robust from the perspective of an expected utility maximizing investor (see Friedman and Sandow, 2003b).

Performance Analysis for PD Models

There are a variety of measures that are commonly used to quantify the performance of PD models. Many, such as the Gini curve or cumulative accuracy curve (CAP) and receiver operator characteristic (ROC), which we shall discuss next, analyze how a PD model ranks individual obligors. Other performance measures, such as the likelihood, which we shall also discuss next, do not explicitly focus on ranks but rather depend on the PD values that are assigned to obligors.

The Gini/CAP and ROC Approaches[†]

A commonly used measure of classification performance is the Gini curve or CAP. This curve assesses the consistency of the predictions of a scoring model (in terms of the ranking of firms by order of default probability) to the ranking of observed defaults. Firms are first sorted in descending order of default probability as produced by the scoring model (horizontal axis of Figure 2.5). The vertical axis displays the fraction of firms that have actually defaulted.

A perfect model would have assigned the D highest PDs to the D firms that have actually defaulted out of a sample of N. The perfect model would therefore be a straight line from the point $(0, 0)$ to the point $(D/N, 1)$, and then a horizontal line from $(D/N, 1)$ to $(1, 1)$. Conversely, an uninformative model would assign randomly the PDs to high risk and low risk firms. The resulting CAP curve is the diagonal from $(0, 0)$ to $(1, 1)$.

---

*See Hastie et al. (2003) for the general idea of regularization, and Zhou et al. (2006) for an application in the PD context.
[†]A more formal presentation of the Gini is in Appendix 1. For a more detailed discussion of ROC, see, e.g., Hosmer and Lemeshow (2000).

Any real scoring model will have a CAP curve somewhere in between. The Gini ratio (or accuracy ratio), which measures the performance of the scoring model for rank ordering, is defined as: $G = F/(E+F)$, where E and F are the areas depicted in Figure 2.5. This ratio lies between 0 and 1; the higher this ratio, the better the performance of the model.

The CAP approach provides a rank-ordering performance measure of a model and is highly dependent on the sample on which the model is calibrated. For example any model calibrated on a sample with no observed default, which predicts zero default, will have a 100 percent Gini coefficient. However, this result will not be very informative about the "true performance" of the underlying models. For instance, the same model can exhibit an accuracy ratio under 50 percent or close to 80 percent, according to the characteristic of the underlying sample. Comparing different models on the basis of their accuracy ratio and calculated with different samples is therefore totally nonsensical.

A closely related approach is the ROC curve. Here one varies a parameter α and computes, for each α, the hit rate [percentage of correct default prediction assuming that $P(1|X) > \alpha$ predicts default] and the false alarm rate (percentage of wrong default prediction assuming that $P(1|X) > \alpha$ predicts default). The ROC curve is the plot of the hit rate

FIGURE 2.5

The CAP Curve.

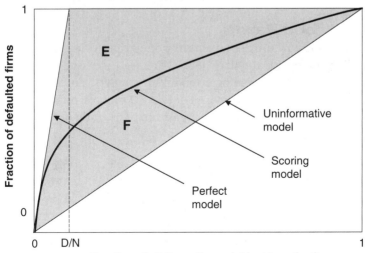

Fraction of all firms (from riskiest to safest)

against the false alarm rate. There exists a simple relationship between the area, ROC, under the ROC curve and the Gini coefficient, Gini, which is

$$\text{Gini} = 2(\text{ROC} - 0.5).$$

In order to give an idea of what ranges to expect for Gini or ROC, we quote Hosmer and Lemeshow (2000):

- If ROC = 0.5: this suggests no discrimination (i.e., we might as well flip a coin).
- If $0.7 < \text{ROC} < 0.8$: this is considered as an acceptable discrimination.
- If $0.8 < \text{ROC} < 0.9$: this is considered as an excellent discrimination.
- If ROC > 0.9: this is considered as an outstanding discrimination.
- In practice, it is extremely unusual to observe areas under the ROC curve greater than 0.9.

All of the model performance measures focus exclusively on how a model ranks the PDs of a set of obligors. They provide very valuable information and often work well in practice. However, they neglect the absolute levels of the PDs. That is, if, e.g., all PDs for a given set of obligors are multiplied by 10 (or any other monotone transformation is applied), the above performance measures do not change their values. So it seems advisable to supplement these measures, e.g., with the likelihood.

Log-likelihood Ratio

Among statisticians, the perhaps most popular performance measure for probabilistic models is the likelihood. We have discussed it in the previous section as a tool to estimate model parameters. For the purpose of measuring the relative performance of two PD models, one often uses the following log-likelihood ratio (the logarithm of the ratio of the two model likelihoods):

$$L(P_1, P_2) = \sum_{i=1}^{N} \left\{ Y_i \log \frac{P_1(1|X_i)}{P_2(1|X_i)} + (1 - Y_i) \log \frac{1 - P_1(1|X_i)}{1 - P_2(1|X_i)} \right\},$$

where the (X_i, Y_i), $i = 1, \ldots, N$, are observed pairs of risk factors and default indicators (1 for default and 0 for survival) on a test dataset (as opposed to the model training dataset) here.

The above log-likelihood ratio has a number of interpretations:

♦ It measures the relative probabilities the two models assign to the observed data (by construction).

♦ It is the natural performance measure from the standpoint of Bayesian statistics (see, e.g., Jaynes, 2003).

♦ It is the performance measure that generates an optimal (in the sense of the Neyman–Pearson Lemma) decision surface for model selection (see, e.g., Cover and Thomas, 1991).

♦ It is the difference in expected utility between a particular rational investor who believes the first model and such an investor who believes the second model, in a complete market with probabilities corresponding to the empirical ones of the test dataset (see Friedman and Sandow, 2003a).

Modeling the Term Structure of PDs

So far, we have discussed PDs for a fixed period of time. For many practical applications in Structured Finance, one needs to quantify the term structure of PDs, i.e., one needs to know the probability of default for a series of time intervals in the future. For example, in order to understand the credit risk associated with a typical CDO tranche, one has to be able to model the quantity and the timing of cashflows originated by the collateral, which requires a model for the term structure of PDs.

The most natural framework for modeling PD term structures is the so-called hazard rate framework. Perhaps, the easiest way to introduce hazard rates is to start with a set of consecutive discrete time intervals t_1, $t_2, \ldots, t_N$ that start at the current time. The discrete-time hazard-rate of a given obligor is then defined as

$$h(t_i, x, z(t_i)) = \text{Prob}(\text{default in } t_i \mid \text{no default before } t_i, X = x, Z(t_i) = z(t_i)),$$

where X is a set of risk factors at time zero (e.g., balance sheet information about an obligor) and $Z(t_i)$ is a set of risk factors at time t_i (e.g., the state of the economy). There are various choices one can make for the risk factors X and Z; in particular, one can omit variables of the Z-type or variables of the X-type.

Knowing the hazard rates of a given obligor, one can compute the probability of survival till the end of t_i as

$$S(t_i, x, z) = \prod_{j=1}^{i} [1 - h(t_j, x, z(t_j))]$$

and the probability of default at time t_i as

$$S(t_{i-1}, x, z) \, h(t_i, x, z(t_i)).$$

Unfortunately, the survival probability, $S(t_i)$, depends on the $Z(t_j)$ for all times upto t_i. which are unknown at the observation time. There are essentially two ways to deal with this issue: one can either build a model that does not include any Z-type factors, or one can build a time series model for those factors and average over their joint distribution.* Both approaches are viable and are used in practice.

Many models work with a continuous-time hazard rate $\lambda(t, x, z(t))$, which can be defined by letting the time-interval length, Δt, approach zero, i.e., as

$$\lambda(t, x, z(t)) = \lim_{\Delta t \to 0} \frac{h(t_i, x, z(t_i))}{\Delta t}.$$

The survival probability is then

$$S(t, x, z) = \exp\left(-\int_0^t \lambda(\tau, x, z(\tau) d\tau \right).$$

For both type of models, discrete or continuous, the hazard rates have to be estimated from data. This is typically done by assuming a parametric form and estimating the parameters by means of the (possible regularized) maximum-likelihood method.[†] One can also make use of nonparametric techniques, such as the Nelson–Aalen estimator (see, e.g., Klein and Moeschberger, 2003). However, these nonparametric techniques are not appropriate for directly deriving the conditional (on X and/or Z) hazard rates; one can use them in our context only for modeling the time dependence after separating out the time-dependence from the risk-factor dependence.[‡]

---

*Including, modeling, and averaging out Z-type factors (e.g., macroeconomic variables) that are common to all obligors in a portfolio provides a way to model default dependencies. Even if the individual hazard rates are independent given a realization of the Z-paths, after averaging out the Z-type variables, defaults become dependent.

[†]In a somewhat different approach, one can model the hazard rates as an affine stochastic processes of the type commonly used for interest rates (see, e.g., Lando, 2004).

[‡]The latter approach is usually taken to estimate the Cox proportional hazard model (see Cox, 1972, or Klein and Moeschberger, 2003).

An example for a model that contains only credit factors of X-type is the model by Shumway (2001). In this model, a discrete hazard rate of the form

$$h(t_i, x) = \frac{1}{1 + \exp(g(t_i)\theta_1 + x'\theta_2)}$$

is estimated, where θ_1 and θ_2 are parameters, and g is a function of time, which reflects the firm's age.

A model that includes Z-type variables, but no X-type variables, is the one from Duffie et al. (2005). Here, the Z-type variables describe macroeconomic as well as firm-specific information; e.g., each firm's distance to default (see the next section) and trailing one-year stock return are Z-type variables in the model. The model is formulated in the continuous-time setting.

Another, slightly different, approach is taken by Friedman et al. (2006), who incorporate firm-specific information in terms of X-type and macroeconomic information in terms of Z-type variables.

THE MERTON APPROACH

In their original option pricing paper, Black and Scholes (1973) suggested that their methodology could be used to price corporate securities. Merton (1974) was the first to use their intuition and to apply it to corporate debt pricing. Many academic extensions have been proposed and some commercial products use the same basic structure.

The Merton Model

The Merton (1974) model is the first example of an application of contingent claims analysis to corporate security pricing. Using simplifying assumptions about the firm value dynamics and the capital structure of the firm, the author is able to give pricing formulas for corporate bonds and equities in the familiar Black and Scholes (1973) paradigm.

In the Merton model, a firm with value V is assumed to be financed through equity (with value S) and pure discount bonds with value P and maturity T. The principal of the debt is K. The value of the firm is the sum of the values of its securities: $V_t = S_t + P_t$. In the Merton model, it is assumed that bondholders cannot force the firm into bankruptcy before the maturity

FIGURE 2.6

Payoff of Equity and Corporate Bond at Maturity T.

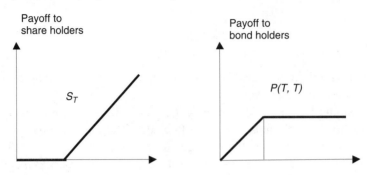

of the debt. At the maturity date T, the firm is considered solvent if its value is sufficient to repay the principal of the debt. Otherwise, the firm defaults.

The value of the firm V is assumed to follow a geometric Brownian motion* such that[†]: $dV = \mu V \, dt + \sigma_v V \, dZ$. Default happens if the value of the firm is insufficient to repay the debt principal: $V_T < K$. In that case, bond-holders have priority over shareholders and seize the entire value of the firm V_T. Otherwise (if $V_T > K$), bondholders receive what they are due: the principal K. Thus, their payoff is $P(T, T) = \min(K, V_T) = K - \max(K - V_T, 0)$ (see Figure 2.6).

Equity holders receive nothing if the firm defaults, but profit from all the upside when the firm is solvent, i.e., the entire value of the firm net of the repayment of the debt $(V_T - K)$ falls in the hands of shareholders. The payoff to equity holders is therefore $\max(V_T - K, 0)$ (see Figure 2.6).

Readers familiar with options will recognize that the payoff to equity holders is similar to the payoff of a call on the value of the firm struck at K. Similarly, the payoff received by corporate bond holders can be seen as the payoff of a risk-less bond minus a put on the value of the firm.

---

*A geometric Brownian motion is a stochastic process that results in a lognormal distribution for a fixed point of time. μ is the growth rate while σ_v is the volatility of the process. Z is a standard Brownian motion whose increments dZ have mean zero and variance equal to time. The term $\mu V \, dt$ is the deterministic drift of the process, and the other term $\sigma_v V \, dZ$ is the random volatility component. See Hull (2002) for a simple introduction to geometric Brownian motion.

[†]We drop the time subscripts to simplify notations.

Merton (1974) makes the same assumptions as Black and Scholes (1973), and the call and the put can be priced using Black–Scholes option prices. For example, the call (equity) is immediately obtained as:

$$S_t = V_t N(k + \sigma_V \sqrt{T - t}) - Ke^{-r(T-t)}N(k),$$

with $k = (\ln(V_t/K) + (r - \frac{1}{2}\sigma_V^2)(T - t))/(\sigma_V \sqrt{T - t})$ and $N(\cdot)$ denoting the cumulative normal distribution and r the risk-less interest rate.

The Merton model provides a lot of insight into the relationship between the fundamental value of a firm and of its securities. The original model, however, relies on very strong assumptions:

+ The capital structure is simplistic: equity + one issue of zero-coupon debt.
+ The value of the firm is assumed to be perfectly observable.
+ The value of the firm follows a lognormal diffusion process. With this type of process, a sudden surprise (a jump), leading to an unexpected default, cannot be captured. Default has to be reached gradually, "not with a bang but with a whisper," as Duffie and Lando (2001) put it.
+ Default can only occur at debt maturity.
+ Risk-less interest rates are constant through time and maturity.
+ The model does not allow for debt renegotiation between equity and debt holders.
+ There is no liquidity adjustment.

These stringent assumptions may explain why the simple version of the Merton model struggles to cope with the empirical spreads observed on the market. Van Deventer and Imai (2002) test empirically the hypothesis of inverse comovement of stock prices and of credit spread prices, as predicted by the Merton model. Their sample comprises First Interstate Bancorp two-year credit spread data and associated stock price. The authors find that only 42 percent of changes in credit spread and equity prices are consistent with the directions (increases or decreases) predicted by the Merton model.

Practical difficulties also contribute to hamper the empirical relevance of the Merton model:

+ The value of the firm is difficult to pin down, because the marked-to-market value of debt is often unknown. In addition, all that relates to goodwill or to out-of-the-balance-sheet elements is difficult to measure accurately.

♦ The estimation of assets volatility is difficult due to the low frequency of observations.

A vast literature has contributed to extend the original Merton model and lift some of its most unrealistic assumptions. To cite a few, we can mention:

♦ Early bankruptcy (default barrier) and liquidation costs have been introduced by Black and Cox (1976)

♦ Coupon bonds, e.g., Geske (1977)

♦ Stochastic interest rates, e.g., Nielsen et al. (1993) and Shimko et al. (1993)

♦ More realistic capital structures (senior and junior debt), e.g., Black and Cox (1976)

♦ Stochastic processes including jumps in the value of the firm, e.g., Zhou (1997)

♦ Strategic bargaining between shareholders and debtholders, e.g., Anderson and Sundaresan (1996)

♦ The effect of incomplete accounting information is analyzed in Duffie and Lando (2001)

♦ Uncertain default barrier, e.g., Duffie and Lando (2001)

♦ Endogenous default boundaries, e.g., Leland (1994) and Leland and Toft (1996).

Moody's KMV Credit Monitor® Model and Related Approaches

Although the primary focus of Merton (1974) was on debt pricing, the firm-value based approach has been scarcely applied for that purpose in practice. Its main success has been in default prediction.

Moody's KMV Credit Monitor® (see Crosbie and Bohn, 2003) applies the structural approach to extract probabilities of default at a given horizon from equity prices. Equity prices are available for a large number of corporates. If the capital structure of these firms is known, then it is possible to extract market-implied probabilities of default from their equity price. The probability of default is called expected default frequency (EDF) by Moody's KMV.

There are two key difficulties in implementing the Merton-type approach to firms with realistic capital structure. The original Merton model only applies to firms financed by equity, and one issue of zero-coupon debt is: how should one calculate the strike price of the call (equity) and put (default component of the debt) when there are multiple issues of debt? The estimation of the firm value process is also difficult: how to estimate the drift and volatility of the asset value process when this value is unobservable? Moody's KMV uses a "rule of thumb" to calculate the strike price of the default put and a "proprietary methodology" to calculate the volatility.

Moody's KMV assumes that the capital structure of an issuer is constituted of long-term debt (i.e., with maturity longer than the chosen horizon) denoted by LT and short-term debt (maturing before the chosen horizon) denoted by ST. The strike price default point is then calculated as a combination of short- and long-term debt: "We have found that the default point, the asset value at which the firm will default, generally lies somewhere between total liabilities and current, or short term liabilities" (see Crosbie and Bohn, 2003). The practical rule for choosing the default value, K, is

$$K = ST + 0.5 \, LT.$$

This rule of thumb is purely empirical and does not rest on any solid theoretical foundation. Therefore, there is no guarantee that the same rule should apply to all countries/jurisdictions and all industries. In addition, no empirical study has been shown to provide information about the confidence level associated with this default point.*

In the Merton model, the $PD^{\dagger}$ is

$$PD_t = N(-DD),$$

where $DD = (\ln(V_t) - \ln(K) + (\mu - \sigma_V^2/2)(T - t))/(\sigma_V \sqrt{T - t})$ is the so-called distance to default, and we have used the following notation:

$N(\cdot)$ = the cumulative Gaussian distribution
V_t = the value of the firm at t
X = the default threshold
σ_V = the asset volatility of the firm
μ = the expected return on assets

---

*Recent articles and papers focus on the stochastic behavior of this default threshold. See e.g., Hull and White (2000) and Avellaneda and Zhu (2001).
†This is the probability under the historical measure. The risk neutral probability is $N(-K) = 1 - N(K)$, as described in the equity pricing formula.

Example: Consider a firm with a market cap of $3 billion, an equity volatility of 40 percent, ST liabilities of $7 billion and LT of $6 billion. Thus $X = 7 + 0.5 \times 6 = \$10$ billion. Assume, further, that we have solved for $A_0 = \$12.511$ billion and $\sigma = 9.6$ percent. Finally $\mu = 5$ percent, the firm does not pay dividends, and the credit horizon is one year. Then $(\log(V_t/K) + (\mu - \sigma_V^2/2))/\sigma_V = 3$. And the "Merton" probability of default at a one-year horizon is $N(-3) = 0.13$ percent.

In order to use the Merton framework for practical ends, one needs to estimate the current asset value and the asset volatility from market data.* Moody's KMV does this by using the Black–Scholes option pricing framework, viewing equity as an option on the asset value. In this picture we have the following two equations:

$$\sigma_s = C'(V_t, \sigma_V)\sigma_V \frac{V_t}{S_t}, \quad \text{and} \quad S_t = C(V_t, \sigma_V, t, K, r),$$

where S_t is the equity value, σ_s its volatility, and C is the function that assigns the Black–Scholes value to a call option. The equity value is usually known (at least for publicly traded firms), and the equity volatility can be either estimated from historical data or implied from option prices if those are available. Knowing S_t and σ_s, one can solve the above equations for V_t and σ_V, which completes the calibration of the Merton model.

An alternative approach to the estimation of V_t and σ_V is the iterative scheme of Vassalou and Xing (2004). According to this scheme, a time series of asset values is computed from a times series of equity values by means of the Black–Scholes formula for call options, and σ_V is subsequently estimated from this time series.

Moody's KMV approximates the DD as

$$DD = \frac{V_t - K}{\sigma_V V_t}.$$

The EDF is then computed as

$$EDF_t = \Xi(-DD)$$

(see Crosbie and Bohn, 2003). Here, we denote by $\Xi(\cdot)$ the function mapping the DD to EDFs. Unlike Merton, Moody's KMV does *not* rely on the

---

*The PD actually depends, through the distance to default, on the asset value drift as well. However, this dependence is often neglected in practical approaches (see the approximative formula for the DD given herewith).

cumulative normal distribution $N(\cdot)$. PDs calculated as $N(-DD)$ would tend to be much too low due to the assumption of normality (too thin tails). Moody's KMV therefore calibrates its EDF to match historical default frequencies recorded on its databases. For example, if historically two firms out of 1000 with a DD of 3 have defaulted over a one-year horizon, then firms with a DD of 3 will be assigned an EDF of 0.2 percent. Firms can therefore be put in "buckets" based on their DD. What buckets are used in the software is not transparent to the user.

Figure 2.7 is a graph of the asset value process and the interpretation of EDF.

Once the EDFs are calculated, it is possible to map them to a more familiar grid, such as agency rating classes (see Table 2.8). This mapping, while commonly used by practitioners, makes little sense, since the EDFs are point-in-time measures of credit risk focused on default probability at the one-year horizon; while ratings are through-the-cycle assessments of creditworthiness, they cannot therefore be reduced to a one-year PD.

A similar approach is taken by S&P internal Merton model (see Park, 2006). Results from this model are demonstrated in Figure 2.8, which shows the one-year PD for the Delta Airline stock. This model is compared with S&P CRT for U.S. public firms (see Huang, 2006 and

FIGURE 2.7

The PD is related to the DD.

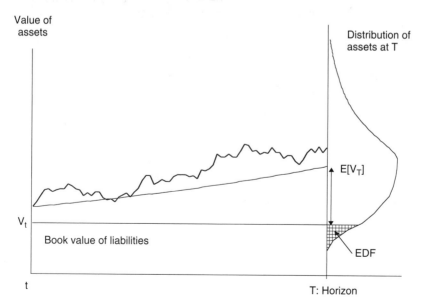

TABLE 2.8

EDFs and Corresponding Rating Class

EDF(%)	S&P
0.02–0.04	AAA
0.04–0.10	AA/A
0.10–0.19	A/BBB+
0.19–0.40	BBB+/BBB–
0.40–0.72	BBB–/BB
0.72–1.01	BB/BB–
1.01–1.43	BB–/B+
1.43–2.02	B+/B
2.02–3.45	B/B–

Source: Crouhy, Galai, and Mark (2000).

Zhou et al., 2006), which is a statistical model (see section "Some Statistical Techniques").

In Table 2.9, we compare S&P Merton model with S&P CRT for U.S. public firms. This Merton model ranks companies according to their

FIGURE 2.8

Evolution of the One-Year PDs from S&P's Merton Model and CRT for Delta Airlines. (S&P).

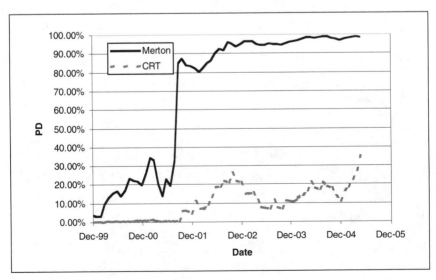

TABLE 2.9

ROCs for S&P's Merton Model (see Park, 2006) and S&P's CRT for U.S. Public Firms. ROCs were Computed for all Public U.S. Firms and for the Subset of the Largest 2000 Firms. In All Cases, a Five-Fold Cross-Validation was Applied.

	CRT	Merton model
ROC on all public U.S. firms	0.87	0.80
ROC on largest 2000 public U.S. firms	0.95	0.92

Source: S&P (see Zhou et al. 2006).

distance to default, which is sufficient to compute ROC without any mapping on a real-world PD. CRT uses the distance to default from the Merton model as one of its input variables. The results shown in the table are very interesting. One can see that both models perform much better on the largest 2000 firms than on the set of all public firms. One can also see that the Merton model rank-orders firms surprisingly well. In particular, for large firms, the ROC difference between the statistical model and the Merton model is only 3 percent; i.e., a large part of the explanatory power of the statistical model can be derived from the DD. Furthermore, the table seems to suggest that the Merton model is somewhat tuned toward large firms.

Uses and Abuses of Equity-Based Models for Default Prediction

Equity-based models can be useful as early warning systems for individual firms. Crosbie (1997) and Delianedis and Geske (1999) study the early warning power of structural models and show that these models can give early information about ratings migration and defaults.

There has undoubtedly been many examples of successes where structural models have been able to capture early warning signals from the equity markets. These examples, such as the WorldCom case, are heavily publicized by vendors of equity-based systems. What the vendors do not mention is that there are also many examples of false starts: a general fall in the equity markets will tend to be reflected in increases in all EDFs and many "downgrades" in internal ratings based on them, although the credit quality of some firms may be unaffected. False starts can be costly, as they often induce banks to sell the position in a temporary downturn at an unfavorable price.

Conversely, in a period of booming equity markets such as 1999, these models will tend to assign very low PDs to almost all firms. In short, equity-based models are prone to overreaction due to market bubbles.

Toward a Term Structure of Merton PDs: Use of Merton Model Results as an Input into CDO Models

In order to obtain a default term structure, one has to generalize the Merton model. One such generalization was proposed by Black and Cox (1976), who assume that default can occur at any time before the maturity of a particular bond, whenever the asset value hits a given barrier. This idea can be motivated if there are bond safety covenenants or in the context of a continuous stream of payments to be made by the obligor.

The basic idea of the Black–Cox model is that, as in the Merton model, the firm's value undergoes a geometric Brownian motion, i.e.,

$$dV = \mu V \, dt + \sigma_V V \, dZ.$$

Default occurs when V hits, for the first time, the barrier C, which undergoes the dynamics

$$C_t = C_0 \exp(\gamma t).$$

Computing the term structure of PDs in this setting amounts to solving a well-understood first passage time problem. This makes the Black–Cox model very attractive. Moreover, it is theoretically possible to generalize this model to a multivariate setting (see Zhou, 2001).

The default term structure one obtains from a Black–Cox model is not necessarily realistic. Although one can try to calibrate the parameters C_0 and γ to a term structure obtained from a statistical hazard rate model, the calibration is rarely very good, since there are only two parameters available. To avoid this problem, one can generalize the dynamics of the default barrier. One such generalization has been proposed by Hull and White (2001), who assume a very flexible dynamics that can be calibrated to an arbitrary term structure. This type of model, however, can hardly be viewed as a structural model anymore.

SPREADS (YIELD SPREADS AND CDS SPREADS)

Dynamics of Credit Spreads (Yield Spreads)

In this section, we review the dynamics of credit-spread series in the United States. The data consists of 4177 daily observations of Aaa and Baa average spread indices, from the beginning of 1986 to the end of 2001. Spread indices are calculated by subtracting the 10-year constant maturity treasury yield from Moody's average yield on U.S. long-term (>10 years) Aaa and Baa bonds.

$$S_t \text{Aaa} = Y_t \text{Aaa} - Y_t T, \quad \text{and} \quad S_t \text{Baa} = Y_t \text{Baa} - Y_t T.$$

All series are available on the Federal Reserve's web site,* and bonds in this sample do not contain option features.

Aaa is the best rating in Moody's classification with a historical default frequency over 10 years of 0.64 percent, whereas Baa is at the bottom of the IG category and have historically suffered a 4.41 percent default rate over 10 years (see Keenan et al., 1999). Both minima were reached in 1989 after two years of very low default experience. At the end of our sample, spreads were at their historical maximum, only matched by 1986 for the Aaa series. The rating agencies branded 2001 as the worst year ever in terms of the amount of defaulted debt.

Summary statistics of the series are provided in Table 2.10.

TABLE 2.10

Summary Statistics

	S_t^{Aaa}	S_t^{Baa}
Average	1.16%	2.04%
Standard deviation	0.40%	0.50%
Minimum	0.31%	1.16%
Maximum	2.67%	3.53%
Skewness	0.872	0.711
Kurtosis	3.566	2.701

---

*http://www.federalreserve.gov

FIGURE 2.9

U.S. Baa and Aaa spreads—1986 to 2001.

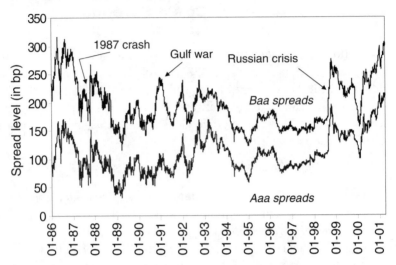

Figure 2.9 depicts the history of spreads in the Aaa and Baa classes whereas Figure 2.10 is a scatter plot of daily changes in Baa spreads, as a function of their level. The Aaa series oscillates around a mean of about 1.2 percent, whereas the term mean of the Baa series appears to be around 2 percent.

Several noticeable events have affected spread indices over the past 20 years. The first major incident occurred during the famous stock market crash of October 1987. This event is remembered as an equity market debacle, but corporate bonds were equally affected with Baa spreads soaring by 90 basis points (bp) over two days, the biggest rise ever (see Figures 2.10 and 2.11).

The Gulf war is also clearly visible on Figure 2.9. On the run-up to the war, Baa spreads rose by nearly 100 bp and started to tighten immediately after the start of the conflict and by the end of the war; they had narrowed back to their initial level. Aaa spreads were little affected by the event.

Finally, let us mention the spectacular and sudden rises which occurred after the Russian default of August 1998 and after September 11, 2001.*

---

*September 14 was the first trading day after the tragedy.

FIGURE 2.10

Daily Changes in U.S. Baa Spread Indices.

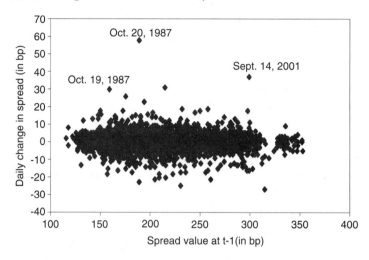

Explaining the Baa-Aaa Spread

We have noted earlier that some events such as the Gulf war did substantially impact on Baa spreads, whereas Aaa spreads were little affected. It is therefore interesting to focus on the relative spread between Baa and Aaa yields. Figure 2.11 is a plot of this differential.

FIGURE 2.11

Relative Spreads between Baa and Aaa Yields.

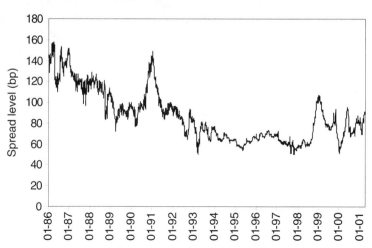

One can observe a clear downward trend between 86 and 98 only interrupted by the Gulf war. This contraction in relative spreads was due mainly to the improvement in liquidity of the market for lower-rated bonds.

We can observe three spikes in the relative spread (Baa–Aaa): 1991, 1998, and 2001. These are all linked to increases in market volatility, and the peaks can be explained in the light of a structural model of credit risk.

Recall that in a Merton (1974)-type model, a risky bond can be seen as a risk-less bond minus a put on the value of the firm. The put's exercise price is linked to the leverage of the issuing firm (in the simple case, where the firm's debt is only constituted of one issue of zero-coupon bond, the strike price of the put is the principal of the debt). Obviously the values of Baa firms are closer to their "strike price" (higher risk) than those of Aaa firms. Therefore, Baa firms have higher vega than Aaa issuers.* As a result, as volatility increases, Baa spreads increase more than Aaa spreads.

Determinants of Yield Spreads

Spreads should at least reflect the probability of default and the recovery rate. In a careful analysis of the components of corporate spreads in the context of a structural model, Delianedis and Geske (2001) report that only 5 percent of AAA spreads and 22 percent of BBB spreads can be attributed to default risk. We now turn in greater details to the possible components of an explanatory model for spreads.

Recovery

The *expected recovery rate* for a bond of given seniority in a given industry affects credit spreads and is therefore a natural candidate for inclusion in a spread model. Recoveries will be discussed in the forthcoming section. We shall see there that they tend to fluctuate with the economic cycle. So, ideally, a measure of expected recovery conditional on the state of the economy would be a more appropriate choice.

Probability of Default

Spreads should also reflect PD. The most readily available measure of creditworthiness for large corporates is undoubtedly *ratings*, and they are

---

*The vega (or kappa) of an option is the sensitivity of the option price to changes in the volatility of the underlying. The vega is higher for options near the money, i.e., when the price of the underlying is close to the exercise price of the option (see, e.g., Hull, 2002).

easy to include in a spread model. Figure 2.12 is a plot of U.S. industrial and treasury bond yields. Spreads are clearly increasing as credit rating deteriorates. The model by Fons (1994) provides an explicit link between default rates per rating class and the level of spreads. The main difficulty is to model the risk premium associated with the volatility in the default rate, as market spreads incorporate investors risk aversion.

A similar but dynamic perspective on the relationship between ratings and spreads is provided in Figure 2.13. We again observe what appears to be a structural break in the dynamics of spreads in August 1998. The post-1998 period is characterized by much higher mean spreads and volatilities for all risk classes. Although the event triggering the change is well identified (Russian default followed by flight to quality and liquidity), analysts disagree on the reasons for the persistence of high spreads in the markets. Some argue that investors risk aversion has durably changed and that each extra "unit" of credit risk is priced more expensively in terms of risk premium. Other put forward the fact that asset volatility is still very high and that default rates have increased steadily over the period. Keeping unchanged the perception of risk by investors, spreads merely reflect higher real credit risk.

An alternative explanation lies in the fact that the change coincided with the increasing impact of the equity market on corporate bond prices. The reasons for this are two-fold: the recent popularity of equity/

FIGURE 2.1 2

U.S. Industrial and Treasury Bond Yields. (*Riskmetrics*).

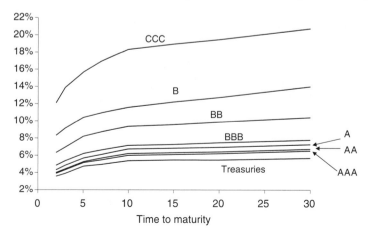

FIGURE 2.13

10Y Spreads per Rating. (*S&P Indices*).

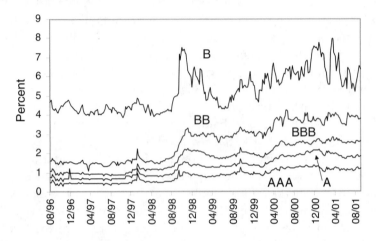

corporate bond trades among market participants and the common use of equity driven credit risk models.

PD Extracted from Structural Models

In many empirical studies of spreads, *equity volatility* often turns out to be one of the most powerful explanatory variables. This is consistent with the structural approach to credit risk, where default is triggered when the value of the firm falls below its liabilities. The higher the volatility, the more likely the firm will reach the default boundary and the higher the spreads should be. Several choices are possible: historical versus implied volatility, aggregate versus individual, etc. Implied volatility has the advantage of being forward looking (the trader's view on future volatility) and is arguably a better choice. It is, however, only available for firms with traded stock options. At the aggregate level, the VIX index, released by the Chicago Board Options Exchange VIX, is often chosen as a measure of implied volatility. It is a weighted average of the implied volatilities of eight options with 30 days to maturity.

The second crucial factor of PD in a structural approach is the *leverage* of a firm. This measures the level of indebtedness of the firm scaled by the total value of its assets. Leverage is commonly measured in empirical work, as the book value of debt divided by the market value of equity plus the book value of debt. The reason for the choice of book

FIGURE 2.14

Default rates and Economic Growth. (*S&P*).

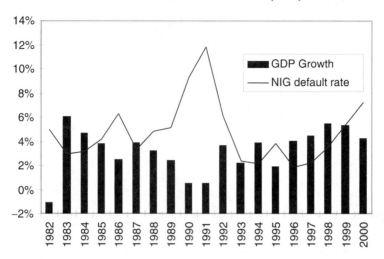

value in the case of debt is purely a matter of data availability: a large share of the debt of a firm will not be traded and it is therefore impossible in many cases to obtain its market value. This problem does not arise with the equity of public companies. If no information about the level of indebtedness is available or if the model aims at estimating aggregate spreads, then equity returns (individual or at the market level) can be used as a rough proxy for leverage. The underlying assumption is that book values of debt outstanding are likely to be substantially less volatile than the market value of the firms' equity. Hence, on average, a positive stock return should be associated with a decrease in leverage and in spreads.

At the macroeconomic level, the *yield curve* is often used as an indicator of the market's view of future growth. In particular, a steep yield curve is frequently associated with an expectation of growth whereas an inverted or flat yield curve is often observed in periods of recessions. Naturally, default rates are much higher in recessions (see Figure 2.14*); the slope of the yield curve can therefore be used as a predictor of future default rates and we can expect yield spreads to be inversely related to the slope of the term structure.

---

*GDP and NIG, respectively, stand for Gross Domestic Product and Non-Investment Grade.

Risk-less Interest Rate

There has been much debate in the academic literature on the interaction between the *risk-less interest rates* and spreads. Most papers (e.g., Duffee, 1998) report a negative correlation, implying that when interest rates increase (respectively decrease), risky yields do not reflect the full impact of the rise (fall). Morris et al. (1998) make a distinction between a negative short-term impact and a positive long-term impact of changes in risk-free rates on corporate spreads. One possible explanation for this finding would be that risky yields adjust slowly to changes in the treasury rate (short-term impact) but that in the long run, an increase in interest rates is likely to be associated with a slowdown in growth and therefore an increase in default frequency and spreads.

Risk Premium

The credit spread measures the excess return on a bond granted to investors as a compensation for credit risk. Measuring credit risk as the probability of default and recovery is insufficient. Investors' risk aversion also needs to be factored in.

If the purpose of the exercise is to determine the level of spreads for a sample of bonds, one can extract some information about the "market price of credit risk" from credit-spread indices. Assuming that the risk differential between highly rated bonds and speculative bonds remains constant through time (which is a strong assumption), changes in the difference between two credit-spread indices, such as those studied earlier in the chapter, should be the result of changes in the risk premium.

Is a Systemic Factor at Play? Many of the variables identified earlier are instrumental in explaining the levels and changes in corporate yield spreads. A similar analysis could be performed to determine the drivers of sovereign spread, such as that of Italy versus Germany or Mexico versus the United States. The fundamentals in these markets are however very different, and one could argue that trading or investment strategies in these various markets should be uncorrelated. This intuition would appear valid in most cases but spreads tend to exhibit periods of extreme comovement at times of crises.

To illustrate this, let us consider the Russian and LTCM crises in 1998. We have seen that the Russian default in August did push up corporate spreads dramatically. This was not an isolated phenomenon. Figure 2.15 jointly depicts the spread of the 10-year Italian government bond yield

FIGURE 2.15

Mexican Brady and ITL/DEM Spreads.

over the 10-year Bund (German benchmark) on the right-hand scale, and the spread of the Mexican Brady* discount bond versus the 30-year U.S. treasury on the left-hand scale.

Figure 2.15 is instructive on several counts. First, it shows that financial instruments on apparently segmented markets can react simultaneously to the same event. In this case, it would appear that the Russian default in August 1998 was the critical event.[†]

Secondly, it explains partly why hedging, diversification, and risk management strategies failed so badly over the period from August 1998 through February 1999. Typical risk management tools, including value at risk, use fixed correlations among assets in order to calculate the required amount of capital to set aside. In our case, the correlation between the two spreads from January to July 1998 was −11 percent. Then suddenly, although the markets are not tied by economic fundamentals and

---

*Brady bonds are securities issued by developing countries as part of a negotiated restructuring of their external debt. They were named after U.S. treasury secretary Nicholas Brady, whose plan aimed at permanently restructuring outstanding sovereign loans and arrears into liquid debt instruments. Brady bonds have a maturity of between 10 to 30 years and some of their interest payments are guaranteed by a collateral of high-grade instruments (typically the first three coupons are secured by a rolling guaranty). They are among the most liquid instruments in emerging markets.

[†]A more thorough investigation of this case can be found in Anderson and Renault (1999).

although the crisis occurred in a third market apparently unrelated, correlations all turned positive and very significantly so. In this example, the correlation over the rest of 1998 increased to 62 percent.

Some may argue that the Russian default may just have increased default risk globally or that market participants expected spill-over effects in all bond markets. Another explanation lies in the flight-to-liquidity and flight-to-safety observed over that period: investors massively turned to the most liquid and safest products, which were U.S. treasuries and German bunds. Many products bearing credit risk did not seem to find any buyer at any price in the immediate aftermath of the crisis.

From a risk management perspective, it is sensible to consider that a global factor (possibly investors' risk aversion) impacts across all bond markets and may lead to substantial losses in periods of turmoil.

Liquidity

Finally, and perhaps most importantly, yield spreads reflect the relative liquidity of corporate and treasury securities. Liquidity is one of the main explanations for the existence of corporate yield spreads. This has been recognized early (see, e.g., Fisher, 1959) and can be justified by the fact that government bonds are typically very actively traded large issues, whereas the corporate bond market is an over-the-counter market whose volumes and trade frequencies are much smaller. Investors require some compensation (in terms of added yield) for holding less liquid securities.

In the case of IG bonds, where credit risk is not as important as in the speculative class, liquidity is arguably the main factor in spreads. Liquidity is, however, a very nebulous concept and there does not exist any clear-cut definition for it. It can encompass the rapid availability of funds for a corporate to finance unexpected outflows or it can mean the marketability of the debt on the secondary market. We will focus on the latter definition. More specifically, we perceive liquidity as the ability to close out a position quickly on the market without substantially affecting the price. Liquidity can therefore be seen as an option to unwind a position.

Longstaff (1995) follows this approach and provides upper bounds on the liquidity discounts on securities with trading restrictions. If a security cannot be bought or sold for say seven days, it will trade at a discount compared to an identical security for which trading is available continuously. This discount represents the opportunity cost of not being able to trade during the restricted period. It should therefore be bounded by the value of selling* the position at the best (highest) price during the restricted period. The value of liquidity is thus capped by the price of a lookback put option.

Little research has been performed on the liquidity of nontreasury bonds. Kempf and Uhrig (1997) propose a direct modeling of liquidity spreads—the share of yield spreads attributable to the liquidity differential between government and corporate bonds. They assume that liquidity spreads follow a mean reverting process and estimate it on German government bond data. Longstaff (1994) considers the liquidity of municipal and other credit risky bonds in Japan. Ericsson and Renault (2001) model the behaviour of a bondholder who may be forced to sell his position due to and external shock (immediate need for cash). Liquidity spreads arise because a forced sale may coincide with a lack of demand in the market (liquidity crisis). Their theoretical model based on a Merton (1974) default risk framework generates downward sloping term structure of liquidity spreads as those reported in Kempf and Uhrig (1997) and also in Longstaff (1994). They also find that liquidity spreads should be increasing in credit risk: if liquidity is the option to liquidate a position, then this option is more valuable in presence of credit risk, as the inability to unwind a position for a long period may lead the bondholder to be forced to keep a bond entering default and to face bankruptcy costs. On a sample of over 500 U.S. corporate bonds, they find support for the negative slope of the term structure of liquidity premiums and for the positive correlation between credit risk and liquidity spreads.

On the empirical side, the liquidity of equity markets (and to a lesser extent also of treasury bond markets) has been extensively studied empirically, but very little has yet been done to measure liquidity premiums in default risky securities. Several variables can be used to proxy for liquidity. The natural candidates are the number of trades and the volume of trading on the market. The OTC nature of the corporate bond market makes this data difficult to obtain. As second best, the issue amount outstanding can also serve as proxy for liquidity. The underlying implicit assumption is that larger issues are traded more actively than smaller ones.

A stylized fact about bonds is that they are more liquid immediately after issuance and rapidly lose their marketability as a larger share of the issues becomes locked into portfolios (see, e.g., Chapter 10 in Fabozzi and

---

*We assume the investor has a long position in the security.

Fabozzi, 1995). The age of an issue could therefore stand for liquidity in an explanatory model for yield spreads. In the same spirit, the on-the-run/off-the-run spread (the difference between the yields of seasoned and newly issued bonds with same residual time to maturity) is frequently used as an indicator of liquidity. During the Russian crisis of 1998, which was associated with a substantial liquidity crunch, the U.S. long bond (30-year benchmark) was trading at a 35 basis point premium versus the second longest bond with just a few months less to maturity, while the historical differential was only 7 to 8 basis points (Poole, 1998).

Taxes

In order to conclude this nonexhaustive list of factors influencing spreads, we can mention taxes. In some jurisdictions (such as the United States), corporate and treasury bonds do not receive the same tax treatment (see Elton et al., 2001). For example, in the United States, treasury securities are exempt from some taxes while corporate bonds are not. Investors will of course demand a higher return on instruments on which they are taxed more.

We have reported that many factors impact on yield spreads and that spreads cannot be seen as purely due to credit. We will now focus more specifically on the ability of structural models to explain the dynamics and level of spreads.

CDS Rates

Another market quantity that provides default risk information is the CDS rate. Here, CDS stands for credit default swap. The credit default swap is the most commonly used credit derivative. In its most basic form, it works as follows: Party A, the so-called protection buyer, pays an annual or semi-annual premium to party B, the so-called protection seller. These payments end either after a given period of time (the maturity of the CDS) or at default of the reference entity. In the case of such a default, the protection seller compensated the protection buyer for the loss incurred due to the default. The CDS rate, also called credit-swap spreads or CDS premiums, is the premium paid by the protection buyer. Figure 2.16 illustrates the cashflows in a credit default swap.

It follows from a no-arbitrage argument that, under some idealized assumptions, the CDS rates are the same as the corresponding bond spreads (off LIBOR) for the same obligor, and are therefore determined by some of the same factors, such as default probability, risk premium, and recovery expectations. However, the assumptions underlying this relationship are often not accurate in practice, which can lead to differences between CDS rates and bond yields, i.e., between CDS spreads and yield spreads. We list a couple of reasons why such differences may appear:

♦ If the note that underlies a CDS is very illiquid, the no-arbitrage argument does not apply and CDS spreads can differ substantially from yield spreads.

♦ CDS usually have a cheapest-to-deliver option, which tends to increase CDS spreads with respect to bond spreads.

♦ CDS often have a wider definition of a credit event, which can increase CDS spreads with respect to bond spreads for long-dated bonds that trade below par.

♦ Shorting notes through a reverse repo is usually not cost-free, which increases CDS spreads with respect to bond spreads. The amount of increase is the so-called repo-special.

For empirical research on CDS rates, we refer to the reader to Houweling and Vorst (2002), Aunon-Nerin et al. (2002), and Nordon and Weber (2004). Examples for historical CDS spreads as a function of time are shown in Figure 2.17.

FIGURE 2.16

Cashflows for a Credit Default Swap (CDS) with Notional 100 in the Case where the Reference Entity Defaults at Some Time Before the Maturity of the CDS. Here, s Denotes in CDS Premium and V the Value of the Reference not at the Time of Default. In Case of No Default, the Payments of the CDS Premium Continue Until the CDS Expires.

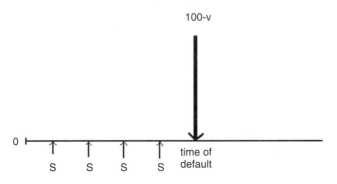

FIGURE   2.17

Five-Year CDS Spreads for General Motors as
Functions of Time. (*Markit Partners*).

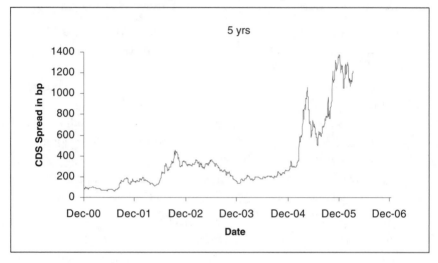

Extracting Default Information from
Spreads: Market-Implied Ratings

As we have seen in the previous section, spreads contain information
about default risk or rather about the market's perceived default risk.
There are various ways to extract this information from spread data; one
approach is to construct market-implied ratings. Moody's offers a product providing such ratings based on bond spreads and on CDS rates.

Some recent research conducted by S&P suggests that one approach
to constructing market-implied ratings can be from bond or CDS rates.
Since these spreads depend not only on default probabilities, but also on
other factors such as recovery expectations and liquidity, one has to
filter out some of these other factors in order to map spreads on ratings.
These other factors have market wide and idiosyncratic components.
One can filter out components of the first type by working with spreads
relative to average market spreads for the corresponding rating category. In order to do this, one constructs, at a given point of time, a
market spread curve for each (actual) rating. This can be done, e.g., by
applying joint Nelson–Siegel (see Nelson and Siegel, 1987) interpolations

FIGURE 2.18

Spread Curves for Rating Categories Constructed with U.S. Bond Spread Data Based on Nelson–Siegel Interpolations. (*S&P*).

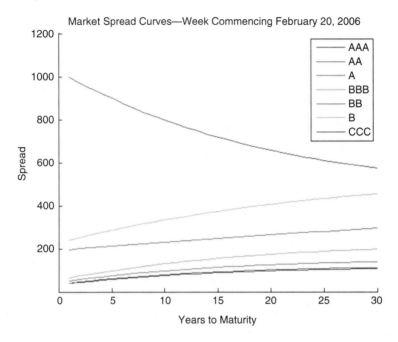

Market Spread Curves—Week Commencing February 20, 2006

to the spreads for each rating at a given date.* An example for a set of resulting spread curves is shown in Figure 2.18.

Having constructed a spread curve for each rating category at a given date, one can assign a spread-implied rating by comparing the spreads of a given obligor (again, after adjusting for idiosyncratic components of non-default-related factors) to the spread curves. A simple distance measure, e.g., the average square distance, can be used to identify the spread curve that is closest to the obligor of interest. The rating that corresponds to this closest spread curve is the spread-implied rating.

Another approach to implying ratings from spreads introduced by Breger et al. (2002). In this approach, optimal spread boundaries between

---

*Before the actual interpolation is done, one should remove outliers and adjust for idiosyncratic components of nondefault-related factors, such as recovery and liquidity. Such an adjustment can be done via regressions on historical data.

the rating categories are determined by means of a penalty function; these boundaries are subsequently used to imply ratings. Kou and Varotto (2004) use this approach to predict rating migrations.

RECOVERY RISK

In the previous sections, we have reviewed various approaches to assess default risk. However, the credit risk that an investor is exposed to consists of default risk and recovery risk. The latter, which reflects the uncertainty associated with the recovery from defaulted debt, is the topic of this section. To date, much less research effort has been made toward modeling recovery risk than toward understanding default risk. Consequently, the literature on this topic is fairly small in volume; the perhaps earliest works on recoveries were published by Altman and Kishore (1996) and Asarnow and Edwards (1995). A fairly comprehensive overview is provided by Altman et al. (2005).

The quantity that characterizes recovery risk is recovery given default (RGD) or equivalently loss given default (LGD). RGD is usually defined as the ratio of the recovery value from a defaulted debt instrument and the invested par amount, and LGD = 1 – RGD. There are various ways to define the recovery value; some people define it as the traded value of the defaulted security immediately after default, others define it as the payout to the debt holder at the time of emergence from bankruptcy (often called ultimate recovery). Which one of the recovery definition is the appropriate one, depends on the purpose of the analysis. For example, an investor (e.g., a mutual bond fund) who always sells debt securities immediately after they have defaulted should be interested in the first type of recovery value; whereas an investor (e.g., a bank that works out defaulted loans) who holds on to defaulted debt till emergence should care about the second type of recovery.

A prominent feature of RGD is its high uncertainty given the information a typical investor can obtain at a time before default. For example, an investor in bonds of large U.S. firms who has access to the obligor's balance sheet and is aware of the economic environment, but does not have any more detailed information about the debt, is only able to predict RGD with an uncertainty in the range of 30 to 40 percent, as measured by the standard deviation of a forecasting model (see Friedman and Sandow, 2005). For this reason, given relevant factors it is desirable to model the uncertainty associated with recovery and not just its expected value.

The perhaps most commonly used approach to modeling RGD is the beta-distribution. Here one assumes that RGD has the following conditional probability density function (pdf):*

$$p(r|D,x) = \frac{1}{B(\alpha(x),\beta(x))} \left(\frac{r - r_{min}}{r_{max}} \right)^{\beta(x)-1} \left(1 - \frac{r - r_{min}}{r_{max}} \right)^{\alpha(x)-1},$$

where r_{max} is the largest and r_{min} the smallest possible value of RGD,[†] B denotes the beta function, and α and β are parameterized functions of the risk factors x. The D in this equation indicates that we condition all PDs having happened. Often one assumes the α and β are linear in the risk factors x. It is then straightforward to estimate the model parameters via the maximum-likelihood method.

An RGD model that relies on this beta-distribution is Moody's KMV's LossCalc™ (see Gupton and Stein, 2002).[‡] This model, which predicts trading price recoveries of U.S. corporations, is commercially available. It was trained on data from Moody's recovery database.

Another commercially available RGD model is S&P's LossStats™ Model (see Friedman and Sandow, 2005). This model predicts ultimate recoveries and trading prices at arbitrary times after default for large U.S. corporations; it was built using data from S&P LossStats™ Database.[§] It is based on a methodology that is related to the one S&P's for PD modeling (see section "Some Statistical Techniques"). Specifically, for trading prices it is assumed that

$$p(r|D,x) = \frac{1}{Z(x)} \exp\{\alpha(x)r + \beta(x)r^2 + \gamma(x)r^3\}$$

---

*This conditional probability density function is interpreted as follows: for an obligor with risk factors x, the probability of recovering a value in the infinitesimal interval $(r, r+dr)$ is $p(r|D, x)dr$.

[†]One might think that $r_{max} = 1$, which corresponds to complete recovery. However, at least for ultimate recoveries of large U.S. firms, one can actually recover more than the invested par amount. This happens, e.g., if the investor recovers equity that has increased in value during the bankruptcy proceedings. The smallest possible recovery value, r_{min}, is zero, unless we include workout costs. In the latter case, r_{min} can be negative.

[‡]In LossCalc™, the parameters of the distribution are not estimated via the maximum-likelihood method, but rather by means of a linear regression after a transformation of the distribution into a normal distribution.

[§]See, e.g., Bos et al., 2002, for more details.

FIGURE 2.19

Conditional Probability Density Function (blue lines) of Trading Price Recovery from LossStats™ Model for Varying Debt Above Class. The Other Risk factors are kept fixed in the Middle of their Historical Ranges. The Red Dots are Actually Observed Data for Large U.S. Firms from the LossStats™ Database.

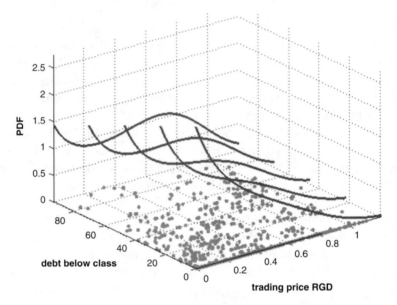

where $Z(x)$ is a normalization constant and α, β, and γ are linear functions of the risk factors x. In the case of ultimate recovery, additional point probabilities are added for $r=0$ and $r=1$ to account for the fact that there are substantial numbers of observations concentrated on these points. The parameters are estimated by means of a regularized maximum-likelihood method. As it was the case for S&P PD model, the resulting probabilities are robust from the perspective of an expected-utility maximizing investor.

The risk factors in S&P LossStats™ Model are

- ♦ Collateral quality. The collateral quality of the debt is classified into 16 categories, ranging from "unsecured" to "all assets."
- ♦ Debt below class. This is the percentage of debt on the balance sheet that is contractually inferior to the class of the debt instrument considered.

- ◆ Debt above class. This is the percentage of debt on the balance sheet that is contractually superior to the class of the debt instrument considered.
- ◆ Regional default rate. This is the percentage of S&P-rated U.S.-bonds that defaulted within the 12 months prior to default.
- ◆ Industry factor. This is the ratio of the percentage of S&P-rated bonds in the industry of interest that defaulted within the 12 months prior to default to the above regional default rate.

The risk factors in Moody's KMV's LossCalc™ are not the same, but capture similar characteristics of the balance sheet and the economy.

A typical model output is shown in Figure 2.19. The figure demonstrates how the probability density depends on one of the risk factors. It also shows that the probability density is fairly flat, i.e., is associated with a high uncertainty.

The models mentioned here approach recoveries from a statistical point of view: a probability density is learned from data without any assumptions about the underlying process, which leads to default. An alternative approach is taken by Chew and Kerr (2005), who approach recovery modeling from a fundamental perspective.

COMBINING PD AND RECOVERY MODELS

Investors in credit-risky debt are usually interested in the expected loss or the loss distribution of a given debt instrument. The latter one can be used, in its turn, as an input into a portfolio model for the computation of portfolio VaR, economic capital, or other risk characteristics of a credit portfolio. The loss distribution of a single credit can be computed by combining a PD model and a recovery model. Let us consider a debt instrument with risk factors x (this denotes the vector of all risk factors that affect either LGD or PD), and denote the PD by $P(D|x)$ and the probability density for LGD (which is $1 - \text{RGD}$) by $p(l|D, x)$, where l denotes a loss value and D denotes the default event. The loss distribution is then

$$p(l|x) = (1 - P(D|x))\delta(l) + P(D|x)p(l|D, x),$$

where δ is Dirac's delta function. This equation implies that

$$E[L|x] = P(D|x)E[L|D, x],$$

that is, that, for a debt instrument with known risk factors x, the expected loss is equal to the PD times the expected LGD. This formula is widely used by practitioners.

In many practical applications, however, the risk factors should be viewed as having a probability distribution, $p(x)$, rather than being given by a single value. Possible reasons for this are the following:

◆ The economic environment at the default time is uncertain.
◆ We are interested in a portfolio instead of in a single loan. The components of the portfolio are typically not identical with respect to their risk factor values.

In this case, the loss distribution is

$$p(l) = \int p(x)p(l|x)dx = \int p(x)[(1 - P(D|x))\delta(l) + P(D|x)p(l|D, x)]dx,$$

and the expected loss is

$$E[L] = \int p(x)E[L|x]dx = \int p(x)P(D|x)E[L|D, x]dx.$$

These expressions involve integrals over products. Therefore, if there are any risk factors that PD and LGD share,* one cannot simply calculate the loss distribution or the expected loss based on the formulae for given credit factors after averaging PD and LGD separately over x. This fact, which received some attention in the recent literature (see, e.g., Frye, 2003 or Altman et al., 2006), has important practical consequences. It has been shown that there are indeed joint risk factors, such as the economy-wide default rate, which typically drive PDs and LGDs in the same direction. Numerical experiments have shown (see Altman et al., 2006) that this leads to an expected loss; a VAR that is higher than the expected loss would be in the absence of such joint risk factors. These experiments are in line with what one would expect from the previous equation for $p(l)$; if those x-values with a higher PD have a greater probability for larger losses than those x-values with a lower PD, then $p(l)$ is more concentrated on higher loss values than it would be otherwise. In other words, in the case of common factors that drive PD and LGD in the same direction, if situations turn bad with regard to PDs they also turn bad with regard to LGDs, and the investor gets hit twice.

---

*Risk factors that affect either the PD or LGD only can be averaged out separately, and therefore do not affect the argument which follows.

CONCLUSION

In this chapter, we have reviewed some popular approaches to modeling PDs and RGD. Most practitioners analyze PDs from one of the following perspectives:

1. Ratings
2. Statistical modeling
3. Structural (Merton-type) models
4. Spreads

Interestingly enough, in the pricing world (risk-neutral), the dominant technique relies on spread, but we have seen that under the historical measure, it is very difficult to extract a probability of default from spread. This explains why the first three methods have been so dominant.

Going forward, we believe that the two dominant approaches that are going to be used are rating-based models and statistical models, i.e., approaches 1 and 2. We do not exclude structural models, but think that the refinements they go through these days increasingly bring them closer to statistical models. These two approaches usually provide different information. The first one, which is based to a large extent on expert judgement, gives a smoothed view over a longer horizon (through the cycle), whereas approach 2, which is usually used to derive a one-year PD from quantitative factors, gives a more precise but more volatile view of the term structure of the creditworthiness of an obligor. One can, however, use approach 2 to estimate long-term PDs, in which case its output resembles a rating-derived PD more closely.

RGD is rather difficult to predict. For this reason, it seems advisable to model its conditional probability distribution given a set of credit factors. Perhaps the most popular approach to doing so is to estimate a beta-distribution. More general families of distributions (e.g., exponential densities with point probabilities), however, can improve the performance of an RGD model substantially. An important feature, which any RGD model should reflect, is the empirical observation that RGD and PD share some credit factors, a fact which tends to increase the risk of high portfolio losses.

APPENDIX 1

Definition of the Gini Coefficient

Given a sample of n ordered individuals with x_i the size of individual i, in this specific case ordered by the PD with respect to the percentage of default events, and $x_1 < x_2 < \cdots < x_n$, the sample Lorenz curve is the polygon joining the points $(h/n, L_h, L_n)$, where $h = 0, 1, 2, \ldots, n$, $L_0 = 0$ and $L_h = \sum_{i=1}^{h} x_i$. If all the individuals are the same size, the Lorenz curve is a straight diagonal line, called the line of equality. The Lorentz curve can be expressed as $L(y) = \dfrac{\int_0^y x F(x)}{\mu}$, where $F(x)$ is a c.d.f. and μ is the mean size of x_i.

If there is any equality in size, the Lorenz curve falls below or above the line of equality.

The total amount of inequality can be summarized by the Gini coefficient, which is the ratio between the area enclosed by the line of equality and the Lorenz curve, and the total triangular area under the line of equality. The Gini coefficient G is a summary statistic of the Lorenz curve and a measure of inequality in a population. The Gini coefficient is most easily calculated from unordered size data as the "relative mean difference," i.e., the mean of the difference between every possible pair of individuals, divided by μ:

$$G = \frac{\sum_{i=1}^{n} \sum_{j=1}^{n} |x_i - x_j|}{2n^2 \mu}$$

Alternatively, if the data is ordered by increasing size of individuals, in this specific case ordered by PD with respect to the percentage of default events, G is given by:

$$G = \frac{\sum_{i=1}^{n} (2i - n - 1) x_i}{n^2 \mu}$$

The Gini coefficient ranges from a minimum value of zero, when all individuals are equal, to a theoretical maximum of one, in an infinite population in which every individual except one has a size of zero. In general, in the Credit universe, Gini coefficients are positioned in the 50 to 85 percent interval.

REFERENCES

Altman, E., B. Brady, A. Resti, and A. Sironi (2006), "The link between default and recovery rates: theory, empirical evidence and implications," *Journal of Business*, forthcoming, also: Working Paper Series #S-03-4, NYU Stern.

Altman, E., and V. Kishore (1996), "Almost everything you wanted to know about recoveries on defaulted bonds," *Financial Analyst Journal*, November/December, 57.

Altman, E., A. Resti, and A. Sironi (2005), *Recovery Risk: The Next Challenge in Credit Risk Management*, Risk Books.

Andersen, P. K., Ø. Borgan, R. D. Gill, and N. Keiding (1993), *Statistical Models Based on Counting Processes*, Springer.

Anderson, R., and O. Renault (1999), "Systemic factors in international bond markets," *IRES Quarterly Review*, December, 75–91.

Anderson, R., and S. Sundaresan (1996), "Design and valuation of debt contracts," *Review of Financial Studies*, 9, 37–68.

Asarnow, E., and D. Edwards (1995), "Measuring loss on defaulted bank loans: a 24-year study," *Journal of Commercial Lending*, 77, 11.

Aunon-Nerin, D., D. Cossin, T. Hricko, and Z. Huang (2002), "Exploring for the determinants of credit risk in credit default swap transaction data: Is fixed-income markets' information sufficient to evaluate credit risk?" FAME Research Paper No. 65, http://papers.ssrn.com/sol3/papers.cfm?abstract_id=375563

Avellaneda, M., and J. Zhu (2001), "Modeling the distance-to-default process of a firm," WP Courant Institute of Mathematical Sciences.

Bangia, A., F. Diebold, A. Kronimus, C. Schagen, and T. Schuermann (2002), "Rating migration and the business cycle, with application to credit portfolio stress testing," *Journal of Banking and Finance*, 26, 445–474.

Bielicki, T. R., and M. Rutkowski (2002), *Credit Risk: Modeling, Valuation and Hedging*, Springer.

Black, F., and J. Cox (1976), "Valuing corporate securities: Some effects of bond indenture provisions," *Journal of Finance*, 31, 351–367.

Black, F., and M. Scholes (1973), "The pricing of options and corporate liabilities," *Journal of Political Economy*, 81, 637–659.

Bos, R., K. Kelhoffer, and D. Keisman (2002), "Ultimate recovery in an era of record defaults," *Standard & Poor's CreditWeek*, August 7, 23.

Breger, L., L. Goldberg, and O. Cheyette (2002), "Market implied ratings," *Horizon, The Barra Newsletter*, Autumn.

Chew, W. H., and S. S. Kerr (2005), "Recovery ratings: A fundamental approach to estimating recovery risk", in E. Altman, A. Resti, and A. Sironi (eds.), *Recovery Risk: The Next Challenge in Credit Risk Management*, Risk Books.

Christensen, J., E. Hansen, and D. Lando (2004), "Confidence sets for continuous-time rating transition probabilities," working paper, Copenhagen Business School and University of Copenhagen.

Couderc, F., and O. Renault (2005), "Times-to-default: life cycle, global and Industry cycle impacts," WPFame.

Cover, T., and J. Thomas (1991), *Elements of Information Theory*, Wiley.

Cox, D. R. (1972), "Regression Models and Life-Time Tables (with discussion)," *J. R. Statist. Soc. B*, 34, 187–220.

Crosbie, P., and J. Bohn (2003), "Modeling default risk," Moody's KMV white paper, http://www.moodyskmv.com/research/files/wp/ModelingDefaultRisk.pdf

Crosbie, P. J. (1997), "Modeling default risk," KMV, June.

Davidson, R., and J. G. MacKinnon (1993), *Estimations and Inference in Econometrics*, Oxford University Press.

de Servigny, A., and O. Renault (2004), *Measuring and Managing Credit Risk*, McGraw Hill.

Delianedis, G., and R. Geske (1999), "Credit risk and risk neutral default probabilities: Information about default migrations and defaults," WP UCLA, May.

Duffee, G. (1998), "The relation between treasury yields and corporate bond yield spreads," *Journal of Finance*, 53, 2225–2242.

Duffie, D., and D. Lando (2001), "Term structure of credit spreads with incomplete accounting information," *Econometrica*, 69, 633–664.

Duffie, D., L. Saita, and K. Wang (2005), "Multi-period corperate default prediction with stochastic covariates," CIRJE-F-373, http://www.e.u-tokyo.ac.jp/cirje/research/03research02dp.html

Duffie, D., and K. J. Singleton (2003), *Credit Risk*, Princeton University Press.

Elton, E., M. Gruber, D. Agrawal, and C. Mann (2001), "Explaining the rate spread on corporate bonds," *Journal of Finance*, 56, 247–277.

Ericsson, J. and O. Renault (2001), "Liquidity and credit risk," working paper, London School of Economics.

Fabozzi, F., and T. Fabozzi (1995), *The Handbook of Fixed Income Securities*, Irwin.

Falkenstein, E. (2000), "Riskcalc™ for private companies: Moody's default model," Moody's Investor Service, May.

Fisher, L. (1959), "Determinants of the risk premiums on corporate bonds," *Journal of Political Economy*, 67, 217–237.

Fons, J. (1994), "Using default rates to model the term structure of credit risk," *Financial Analysts Journal*, 25–32.

Friedman, C., J. Huang, S. Sandow, and X. Zhou (2006), "An approach to modeling multi-period default probabilities," working paper, International Conference on Financial Engineering at the University of Florida in Gainesville, March 22–24.

Friedman, C., and S. Sandow (2003a), "Model performance measures for expected utility maximizing investors," *International Journal of Applied and Theoretical Finance*, 5(4), 335–401.

Friedman, C., and S. Sandow (2003b), "Learning probabilistic models: an expected utility maximization approach," *Journal of Machine Learning Research*, 4, 257–291.

Friedman, C., and S. Sandow (2005), "Estimating conditional probability distributions of recovery rates: A utility-based approach," in E. Altman, A. Resti, and A. Sironi (eds.), *Recovery Risk: The Next Challenge in Credit Risk Management*, Risk Books.

Frye, J. (2003), "A false sense of security," *Risk*, August, 63.

Gelman, A., J. B. Carlin, H. S. Stern, and D. B. Rubin (1995), *Bayesian Data Analysis*, Chapman & Hall/CRC.

Geske, R. (1977), "The valuation of corporate liabilities as compound options," *Journal of Financial and Quantitative Analysis*, 12, 541–552.

Greene, W. (2000), *Econometric Analysis*, Prentice Hall.

Gupton, G., and R. Stein (2002), "LossCalc™: Model for predicting loss given default (LGD)," Moody's Investors Service.

Hastie, T., R. Tibshirani, and J. H. Friedman (2003), *The Elements of Statistical Learning*, Springer.

Hosmer, D., and S. Lemeshow (2000), *Applied Logistic Regression*, 2nd ed., Wiley.

Hougaard, P. (2000), *Analysis of Multivariate Survival Data*, Springer.

Houweling, P., and A.C.F. Vorst (2002), "An empirical comparison of default swap pricing models," Research Paper ERS; ERS-2002-23-F&A, Erasmus Research Institute of Management (ERIM), RSM Erasmus University, http://ideas.repec.org/e/pho1.html

Huang, J. (2006), personal communication.

Hull, J. (2002), *Options, Futures and Other Derivatives*, 5th ed., Prentice Hall.

Hull, J., and A. White (2000), "Valuing credit default swaps I: No counterparty default risk," *Journal of Derivatives*, 8(1), 29–40.

Hull, J., and A. White (2001), "Valuing credit default swaps II: modelling default correlations," *Journal of Derivatives*, 8(3), 12–22.

Jafry, Y., and T. Schuermann (2003), "Measurement and estimation of credit migration matrices," working paper, Federal Reserve Board of New York.

Jaynes, E. T. (2003), *Probability Theory. The Logic of Science*, Cambridge University Press.

Jebara, T. (2004), *Machine Learning: Discriminative and Generative*, Kluwer.

Jobst, N., and K. Gilkes (2003), "Investigation transtition matrices: Empirical insights and methodologies," working paper, Standard & Poor's, Structured Finance Europe.

Journal of Commercial Lending, 77, 11.

Kavvathas, D. (2001), "Estimating credit rating transition probabilities for corporate bonds," working paper, Department of Economics, University of Chicago.

Keenan, S., I. Shtogrin, and J. Sobehart (1999), "Historical default rates of corporate bond issuers, 1920–1998," Special Comment, Moody's Investors Service.

Kempf, A., and M. Uhrig (1997), "Liquidity and its impact on bond prices," working paper, Universität Mannheim.

Kim, J. (2006), personal communication.

Klein, J. P., and M. L. Moeschberger (2003), *Survival Analysis*, Springer.

Kou, J., and S. Varotto (2004), "Predicting agency rating migration with spread implied ratings," working paper, http://ccfr.org.cn/cicf2005/paper/20050201065013.PDF

Lando, D. (2004), *Credit Risk Modeling*, Princeton University Press.

Lando, D., and T. Skodeberg (2002), "Analysing rating transitions and rating drift with continuous observations," *Journal of Banking and Finance*, 26, 423–444.

Leland, H. E. (1994), "Corporate debt value, bond covenenants, and optimal capital structure," *Journal of Finance* 49, 157–196.

Leland, H. E., and K. Toft (1996), "Optimal capital structure, endogenous bankruptcy, and the term structure of credit spreads," *Journal of Finance*, 51, 987–1019.

Longstaff, F. (1994), "An analysis of non-JGB term structures," Report for Credit Suisse First Boston.

Longstaff, F. (1995), "How much can marketability affect security values," *Journal of Finance*, 50, 1767–1774.

Merton R. (1974), "On the pricing of corporate debt: the risk structure of interest rates," *Journal of Finance*, 29, 449–470.

Mitchell, T. M. (1997), *Machine Learning*, McGraw-Hill.

Morris, C., R. Neal, and D. Rolph (1998), "Credit spreads and interest rates: A cointegration approach," working paper, Federal Reserve Bank of Kansas City.

Nelson, C., and A. Siegel (1987), "Parsimonious modelling of yield curves," *Journal of Business*, 60, 473–489.

Nickell, P., W. Perraudin, and S. Varotto (2000), "Stability of rating transitions," *Journal of Banking and Finance*, 24, 203–228.

Nielsen, L. T., J. Saa-Requejo, and P. Santa-Clara (1993), "Default risk and interest rate risk: the term structure of default spreads," WP Insead.

Nordon, L., and M. Weber (2004), "The comovement of credit default swap, bond and stock markets: an empirical analysis," CFS Working Paper No. 2004/20, http://www.ifk-cfs.de/papers/04_20.pdf

Poole, W. (1998), "Whither the U.S. Credit Markets?," Presidential Speech, Federal Reserve of St Louis.

Schönbucher, P. (2003), *Credit Derivative Pricing Models*, Wiley.

Shimko, D., H. Tejima, and D. Van Deventer (1993), "The pricing of risky debt when interest rates are stochastic," *Journal of Fixed Income*, September, 58–66,

Shumway, T. (2001), "Forecasting bankruptcy more accurately," *Journal of Business*, 74, 101–124.

Vassalou, M., and Y. Xing (2004), "Default risk in equity returns," *The Journal of Finance*, 59, 831–868.

Witten, H., and E. Frank (2005), *Data Mining*, Elsevier.

Zhou, C. (1997), "Jump-diffusion approach to modeling credit risk and valuing defaultable securities," WP Federal Reserve Board, Washington,

Zhou, C. (2001), "An analysis of default correlations and multiple defaults," *Review of Financial Studies*, 14, No. 2, 555–576.

Zhou, X., J. Huang, C. Friedman, R. Cangemi, and S. Sandow (2006), "Private firm default probabilities via statistical learning theory and utility maximization," *Journal of Credit Risk*, forthcoming.

CHAPTER 3

Univariate Credit
Risk Pricing

Arnaud de Servigny and Philippe Henrotte

INTRODUCTION

Univariate pricing is a key component to the pricing of structured credit vehicles. Several books like Bielecki and Rutkowski (2002) (BR) provide a detailed review of up to date modeling techniques.* In this chapter, we rather focus on giving an overview of the various possible pricing alternatives. We start with reduced-form models that have become the market standard. We then detail recent customizations in structural modeling, and we ultimately offer an example of a more advanced hybrid-modeling framework.

To date, credit is still very much an incomplete market. In addition, it is usually difficult to use a simple diffusion setup to model its dynamic, as default risk is usually perceived as an unexpected event, i.e., a jump. An incomplete market and the presence of jumps make the credit space a difficult market, where it is not always easy to derive prices from the cost of related replicating (hedging) strategies/portfolios.

Due to these characteristics, market participants have been trying hard to make the most of two alternatives:

---

*These authors spend some time on the definition of the appropriate reference filtration, more generally of the appropriate probability space and the uniqueness of martingale measures. We revert interested readers to them.

♦ Use the dynamics derived from the rating information in order to take advantage of the (more or less perfect) Markov chain properties of credit events.

♦ Use the information available in equity markets (stock and option prices) to improve the accuracy of the pricing of credit instruments. Interestingly, the structural approach has been rejuvenated mainly for this purpose. Unfortunately, its contribution in terms of calibration is generally poor and the incremental information it considers is limited, as these models mainly focus on the price of stocks and very little on equity option information.

We believe that further developments are required in this area. In this chapter, we therefore provide a discussion of joint calibration of various risks/underlyings, such as ratings and credit spreads, or debt and equity instruments.

REDUCED-FORM MODELS*

In structural models of credit risk, the default event is explicitly related to the value of the issuing firm. One of the difficulties with this approach lies in the estimation of the parameters of the asset value process and in the definition of the default boundary. For complex capital structures or securities with nonstandard payoffs such as credit derivatives, firm value-based models tend to be cumbersome to deal with. Reduced-form models aim at simplifying the pricing of these instruments by ignoring what the default mechanism is. In this approach, default is unpredictable and driven by a jump process: when no jump occurs, the firm remains solvent, but as soon as there is a jump, default is triggered.

In this section, we first review the usual processes used in the pricing literature to describe default, namely hazard rate processes. Once their main properties have been recalled, we give pricing formulae for default-risky bonds and explain some key results derived using the reduced-form approach.

In a second step, we build on continuous time transition matrices to cover rating-based pricing models for bonds and credit derivatives, before focusing on spread calibration.

---

*Also called intensity-based models.

At last, we focus on what tends to become a market standard: the combination of spread processes with migrations.

Pricing Based on Hazard Rate Models

The main approach to spread modeling (see Lando, 1998; Duffie and Singleton, 1999) consists of describing the default event as the unpredictable outcome of a jump process. Default occurs when a Poisson process with intensity λ_t jumps for the first time. $\lambda_t \, dt$ is the instantaneous probability of default. Under some assumptions, Duffie and Singleton (1999) establish that default risky bonds can be priced in the usual martingale framework* used for pricing treasury bonds. Hence the price of a credit risky zero-coupon bond is:

$$P(t,T) = E_t^Q\left[e^{-\int_t^T A_s ds} \right],$$

where $A_s = r_s + \lambda_s L_s$ and Q denotes the risk neutral probability measure (see Appendix 1 for further details).

L_s is the loss given default (LGD) and the second term therefore takes the interpretation of an expected loss (probability of default times loss given default). $\lambda_s L_s$ can also be seen as an instantaneous spread, the extra return above the risk-less rate. This approach is very versatile as it allows to price bonds and also credit-risky securities as discounted expectation under Q but with modified discount rate.

Standard Poisson Process

Let N_t be a standard Poisson process. It is initialized at time 0 ($N_0 = 0$) and increases by one unit at random times $T_1, T_2, T_3, \ldots$. Durations betweens jump times $T_i - T_{i-1}$ are exponentially distributed.

The traditional way to approach Poisson processes is to consider discrete time intervals and to take the limit to continuous time. Consider a process whose probability of jumping over a small time period Δt is proportional to time:

$$P[N_{t+\Delta t} - N_t = 1] = \lambda \Delta t \quad \text{and}^\dagger \quad P[N_{t+\Delta t} - N_t = 0] \approx 1 - \lambda \Delta t.$$

The constant λ is called the *intensity* or *hazard rate* of the Poisson process.

---

*See Appendix 1 for a brief introduction to this concept.
†For Δt sufficiently small, the probability of multiple jumps is negligible.

Breaking down the time interval $[t, s]$ into n subintervals of length Δt and letting $n \to \infty$ and $\Delta t \to dt$, we obtain the probability of the process not jumping:

$$P[N_s - N_t = 0] = \exp(-\lambda(s - t)),$$

and the probability of observing exactly m jumps is:

$$P[N_s - N_t = m] = \frac{1}{m!}(s - t)^m \lambda^m \exp(-\lambda(s - t)). \tag{0}$$

Finally, the intensity is such that: $E[dN] = \lambda\, dt$. These properties characterize a Poisson process with intensity λ.

Inhomogeneous Poisson Process

An inhomogeneous Poisson process is built in a similar way as the standard Poisson process and shares most of its properties. The difference is that the intensity is no longer a constant but a deterministic function of time $\lambda(t)$. Jump probabilities are slightly modified accordingly:

$$P[N_s - N_t = 0] = \exp\left(-\int_t^s \lambda(u)du\right) \tag{1}$$

and

$$P[N_s - N_t = m]\frac{1}{m!}\left(\int_t^s \lambda(u)du\right)^m \exp\left(-\int_t^s \lambda(u)du\right). \tag{2}$$

Cox Process

Cox processes or "doubly stochastic" Poisson processes go one step further and let the intensity itself to be random. Therefore, not only the time of jump is stochastic (as in all Poisson processes) but so is the conditional probability of observing a jump over a given time interval. Equations (1) and (2) remain valid but in expectation, that is,

$$P[N_s - N_t = 0] = E\left[\exp\left(-\int_t^s \lambda_u du\right)\right] \tag{3}$$

and

$$P[N_s - N_t = m] = E\left[\frac{1}{m!}\left(\int_t^s \lambda_u du\right)^m \exp\left(-\int_t^s \lambda_u du\right)\right] \tag{4}$$

where λ_u is a positive-valued stochastic process.

Default-Only Reduced-Form Models

We now study the pricing of defaultable bonds in a hazard-rate setting by assuming that the default process is a Poisson process with intensity λ. The case of Cox processes is studied afterwards. We further assume that multiple defaults are possible and that each default incurs a fractional loss of a constant percentage L of the principal (RMV).* This means that in case of default, the bond is exchanged for a security with identical maturity and lower face value.

In this section, we do not derive the equations of the pricing models for all the recovery options. For the RT and RFV cases, we revert the readers to Jobst and Schönbucher (2002).

Let $P(t, T)$ be the price at time t of a defaultable zero-coupon bond with maturity T.

Using Ito's lemma, we derive the dynamics of the risky bond price:

$$dP = \frac{\partial P}{\partial t} dt + \frac{\partial P}{\partial r} dr + \frac{1}{2} \frac{\partial^2 P}{\partial r^2} (dr)^2 - LP \, dN. \tag{5}$$

The first three terms in Equation (5) correspond to the dependence of the bond price on calendar time and on the risk-less interest rate. The last term translates the fact that when there is a jump $(dN = 1)$, the price drops by a fraction L.

Under the risk-neutral measure[†] Q, we must have $E^Q[dP] = rP \, dt$ and thus, assuming that the risk-less rate follows a stochastic process $dr = \mu_r \, dt + \sigma_r \, dw_r$, with a drift term μ_r and a volatility σ_r, under Q, we obtain:

$$0 = \frac{\partial P}{\partial t} + \frac{\partial P}{\partial r} \mu_r + \frac{1}{2} \sigma_r^2 \frac{\partial^2 P}{\partial r^2} - (r + L\lambda)P.^{‡} \tag{6}$$

Comparing this partial differential equation with that satisfied by a default free bond $B(t, T)$:

$$0 = \frac{\partial B}{\partial t} + \frac{\partial B}{\partial r} \mu_r + \frac{1}{2} \sigma_r^2 \frac{\partial^2 B}{\partial r^2} - rB, \tag{7}$$

---

*So far, we have not considered the case of uncertain recovery. Various options have been studied like (1) the recovery of treasury (RT), where a predefined fraction of the value of a comparable default-free bond is provided in the event of default, (2) the fractional recovery of face value immediately upon default (recovery of face value—RVF), (3) the fractional recovery of predefault value of the defaultable bond (recovery of market value—RMV), (4) the stochastic recovery, etc. We revert the readers to BR for further details.
[†]See Appendix 1.
[‡]Given that $E^Q[dN] = \lambda \, dt$ and $E^Q[dr] = \mu_r \, dt$.

one can easily see that the only difference is in the last term and that if one can solve Equation (7) for $B(t, T)$, the solution for the risky bond is immediately obtained as $P(t, T) = B(t, T)e^{-L\lambda(T-t)}$. The spread is therefore $L\lambda$, which is the risk-neutral expected loss.

Of course, this example is simplistic in many ways. The probability of default over an interval of given length is assumed to be constant as the intensity of the process is constant. In addition, default risk and interest rates are also not correlated.

We can consider a more the versatile specification of a stochastic hazard rate with intensity λ_t, such that under the risk-neutral measure:*

$$dr = \mu_r \, dt + \sigma_r \, dW_1,$$

$$d\lambda = \mu_\lambda \, dt + \sigma_\lambda \, dW_2,$$

The instantaneous correlation between the two Brownian motions W_1 and W_2 is ρ.

The derivation of the credit-risky zero-coupon bond follows closely that described earlier in the case of a Poisson intensity. We start by applying Ito's lemma to the dynamics of the bond price:

$$dP = \frac{\partial P}{\partial t} dt + \frac{\partial P}{\partial r} dr + \frac{\partial P}{\partial \lambda} d\lambda$$

$$+ \frac{1}{2}\left(\sigma_r^2 \frac{\partial^2 P}{\partial r^2} + \sigma_\lambda^2 \frac{\partial^2 P}{\partial \lambda^2} + 2\rho\sigma_r\sigma_\lambda \frac{\partial^2 P}{\partial r \partial \lambda} \right) dt - LP dN. \qquad (8)$$

We then impose the no arbitrage condition: $E^Q[dP] = rP \, dt$ which leads to the partial differential equation:

$$0 = \frac{\partial P}{\partial t} + \frac{\partial P}{\partial r}\mu_r + \frac{\partial P}{\partial \lambda}\mu_\lambda + \frac{1}{2}\left(\sigma_r^2 \frac{\partial^2 P}{\partial r^2} + \sigma_\lambda^2 \frac{\partial^2 P}{\partial \lambda^2} + 2\rho\sigma_r\sigma_\lambda \frac{\partial^2 P}{\partial r \partial \lambda} \right) - (r + L\lambda)P. \qquad (9)$$

The solution of this equation of course depends on the specification of the interest rate and intensity processes, but again one can observe that the spread is likely to be related to $L\lambda$.

Rather than setting up the dynamics of the credit-risky zero coupon bond through the stochastic differential equation (SDE) defined in

---

*We drop the time subscripts in r_t and λ_t to simplify notations.

Equation (9), it is possible to derive the solution using martingale methods. This is the approach chosen by Duffie and Singleton (1999).

From the FTAP* we know that the risk-less and risky bond prices must satisfy

$$B(t,T) = E_t^Q \left[1 \times \exp\left(-\int_t^T r_s \, ds \right) \right],$$ (10)

and

$$P(t,T) = E_t^Q \left[(1-L)^{N_T} \times \exp\left(-\int_t^T r_s \, ds \right) \right],$$ (11)

respectively.

Equation (10) corresponds to the discounted expected value of the $1 risk-free zero-coupon bond, given the paths of r_s. Equation (11) expresses the fact that the payoff at maturity is no longer always $1 as in the case of the risk-less security, but is reduced by a percentage L each time the process has jumped over the period $[0, T]$. N_T is the total number of jumps before maturity and the payoff is therefore $(1-L)^{N_T} \leq 1$.

Using the properties of Cox processes, one can simplify equation (11)[†] to obtain

$$P(t,T) = E_t^Q \left[\exp\left(-\int_t^T \left(r_s + L\lambda_s \right) ds \right) \right]$$

$$\equiv E_t^Q \left[\exp\left(-\int_t^T A_s \, ds \right) \right]$$ (12)

which corresponds to the discounted expected value of a defaultable bond, conditional on the paths of r_s and λ_s. This formulation is extremely useful, as it signifies that one can use the familiar Treasury bond pricing tools to price defaultable bonds as well. One just has to substitute the risk-adjusted discount rate $A_t \equiv r_t + L\lambda_t$ for the risk-less rate and all the usual formulas remain valid. Similar formulas can be derived for defaultable securities with more general payoffs by decomposing them into combinations/functions of defaultable zero-coupon bonds with different characteristics.

Obviously, the main practical challenge remains the appropriate calibration of the hazard rate process. Up to now, we have focused on a particular credit event: default. The next section focuses on multiple credit

---

*FTAP: first fundamental theorem of asset pricing, see Appendix 1.
[†]See Schönbucher (2000) for details of the steps.

events in an elegant setup based on the existence of multiple discrete intensity regimes related to rating migrations.

Defaultable HJM/Market Models

As in the interest rate universe, the natural next step is to move from the calibration of a unique hazard rate specification to the modeling of its entire term structure.

The Heath, Jarrow, and Morton (1992) (HJM) framework is therefore extended in order to model the dynamics of the defaultable forward rates:

- ♦ Schönbucher (2000) shows that under certain arbitrage free conditions, this model is applicable to the "zero recovery" situation and a multiple default setup that is (under certain assumptions) equivalent to the RMV assumption.

- ♦ Duffie and Singleton (1999) obtain similar results in the case of fractional recovery (RMV).

- ♦ Duffie and Singleton (1998) show that in the case of RT, it is still possible to refer to the HJM setup, provided that the usual conditions get customized.

These results are important from a methodological perspective. A practical limitation has, however, been so far the lack of data to calibrate such term structures appropriately.

Rating-Based Models

The idea behind this class of models is to use the creditworthiness of the issuer as a key state variable on which to calibrate the risk-neutral hazard rate.

The seminal article in this rating-based class is Jarrow, Lando and Turnbull (1997) (JLT). We review their continuous time pricing approach and discuss extensions that have lifted some of the original assumptions of the JLT model.

Key Assumptions and Basic Structure

The model by JLT considers a progressive drift in credit quality toward default and no longer a single jump to bankruptcy, as in many intensity-based models. Recovery rates are assumed to be constant and default is an absorbing state.

JLT assume the availability of risk-less and risky zero-coupon bonds for all maturities and the existence of a martingale measure Q equivalent to the historical measure P. In the sequel we work directly under Q.

The authors assume that the transition process under the historical measure is a time homogeneous Markov chain with K nondefault states (1 being the best rating and K the worst) and one absorbing default state $(K+1)$.

The risk-neutral transition matrix over a given horizon h is

$$Q(h) = \begin{pmatrix} q_h^{1,1} & q_h^{1,2} & \cdots & q_h^{1,K+1} \\ \cdots & \cdots & & \cdots \\ q_h^{K,1} & q_h^{K,2} & \cdots & q_h^{K,K+1} \\ 0 & 0 & \cdots & 1 \end{pmatrix}, \tag{13}$$

where for example $q_h^{1,2}$ denotes the risk-neutral probability to migrate from rating 1 to rating 2 over the time period h.

Transition matrices for all horizons h can be obtained from the generator* matrix Λ:

$$\Lambda = \begin{pmatrix} \lambda_1 & \lambda_{12} & \cdots & \\ \lambda_{21} & \lambda_2 & & \\ \vdots & & \ddots & \lambda_{K,K+1} \\ 0 & & 0 & 0 \end{pmatrix}, \tag{14}$$

via the relationship $Q(h) = \exp(h\Lambda)$. Over an infinitesimal period dt, $Q(dt) = I + \Lambda\, dt$, where I is the $(K+1) \times (K+1)$ identity matrix.

Pricing Zero-Coupon Bonds

Let $B(t, T)$ be the price of a risk-less zero-coupon bond paying \$1 at maturity T, with $t \leq T$. It is such that:

$$B(t,T) = E_t^Q \left[\exp\left(-\int_t^T r_s\, ds \right) \right],$$

$P^i(t, T)$ is the value at time t of a defaultable zero-coupon bond with rating i due to pay \$1 at T. In case of default (assumed to be absorbing in the JLT model), the recovery rate is constant and equal to $\delta < 1$. The default

---

*Loosely speaking the matrix of intensities.

process is assumed to be independent from the interest rate process and the time of default is denoted as τ. Finally, let $G(t) = 1, \ldots, K$ be the rating of the obligor at time t.

The price of the risky bond therefore is:

$$P^i(t,T) = E_t^Q\left[\exp\left(-\int_t^T r_s\, ds\right)(\delta 1_{(\tau \le T)} + 1_{(\tau > T)})|G(t) = i\right]. \tag{15}$$

Given that the default process is independent from interest rates we can split the expectations into two components:

$$\begin{aligned}
P^i(t,T) &= E_t^Q\left[\exp\left(-\int_t^T r_s\, ds\right)\right]E_t^Q\left[\delta 1_{(\tau \le T)} + 1_{(\tau > T)}|G(t) = i\right] \\
&= B(t,T)E_t^Q\left[1 - (1 - \delta)1_{(\tau \le T)}|G(t) = i\right] \\
&= B(t,T)\left(1 - (1 - \delta)q_{T-t}^{i,K+1}\right),
\end{aligned} \tag{16}$$

where $q_{T-t}^{i,K+1} = E_t^Q[1_{(\tau \le T)}|G(t) = i]$ is the probability of default before maturity T for an i-rated bond.

From Equations (10) and (16), one can observe that the term structure of spreads is fully determined by the changes in probability of default as T changes. We return to spreads a little later.

Pricing other Credit-Risky Instruments

The main comparative advantage of a rating-based model does not reside in the pricing of zero-coupon bonds for which the only relevant information is whether or not default will occur before maturity. JLT-type models are particularly convenient for the pricing of securities whose payoffs depend on the rating of the issuer. Some credit derivatives are written on the rating of specific firms, e.g., derivatives compensating for downgrades.* More commonly, step-up bonds whose coupon is a function of the rating of the issuer can also be priced using rating-based models.

We will consider a simple example of an European style credit derivative based on the terminal rating $G(T)$ of a company. We assume that its initial rating is $G(t) = i$ and that the derivative pays nothing in default. The payoff of the derivative is $\Phi(G(T))$ and its values are known conditional on the realization of a terminal rating $G(T)$.

---

*See Moraux and Navatte (2001) for pricing formulas for this type of options.

From the FTAP, the price of the derivative is:

$$C^i(t,T) = E_t^Q\left[\exp\left(-\int_t^T r_s\, ds\right)\Phi(G(T))|G(t) = i\right].$$ (17)

Given that the rating process is independent from the interest rate, we can write:

$$C^i(t,T) = E_t^Q\left[\exp\left(-\int_t^T r_s ds\right)\right]E_t^Q\left[\Phi(G(T))|G(t) = i\right]$$

$$= B(t,T)\sum_{j=1}^K q_{T-t}^{i,j}\Phi(j).$$ (18)

Deriving Spreads in the JLT Model

Let $f(t,T) = -\dfrac{\partial \log B(t,T)}{\partial T}$ be the risk-less forward rate agreed at date t for borrowing and lending over an instantaneous period of time at time T. It is such that: $f(t, t) = r_t$.

The risky forward rate for rating class i is:

$$f^i(t,T) = -\frac{\partial \log P^i(t,T)}{\partial T} = \frac{-\partial \log(B(t,T)(1-(1-\delta)q_{T-t}^{i,K+1}))}{\partial T}.$$

Hence,

$$f^i(t,T) = f(t,T) + 1_{\tau > t}\left[\frac{(1-\delta)\dfrac{\partial q_{T-t}^{i,K+1}}{\partial T}}{1-(1-\delta)q_{T-t}^{i,K+1}}\right].$$ (19)

The credit spread in rating class i for maturity T is defined as $f^i(t, T) - f(t, T)$. From Equation (19), one can indeed observe that spread variations reflect changes in the probability of default and changes in the steepness of the curve relating the probability of default to time T.

In order to obtain the risky short rate, one takes the limit as $T \to t$ and $f(t, T) \to r_t$:

$$r_t^i = r_t + 1_{\tau > T}(1-\delta)\lambda_{iK+1},$$

which immediately yields the spot instantaneous spread as $r_t^i - r_t$.

Calculating Risk-Neutral Transition Matrices from Empirical Ones*

For pricing purposes, one requires "risk-neutral" probabilities. A risk neutral transition matrix can be extracted from the historical matrix and a set of corporate bond prices.

$$
Q(h) = \begin{pmatrix} q_h^{1,1} & q_h^{1,2} & \cdots & q_h^{1,K+1} \\ \cdots & \cdots & & \cdots \\ q_h^{K,1} & q_h^{K,2} & \cdots & q_h^{K,K+1} \\ 0 & 0 & \cdots & 1 \end{pmatrix},
$$

where all q probabilities take the same interpretation as the empirical transition matrix that follows, but are under the risk-neutral measure.

$$
P(h) = \begin{pmatrix} p_h^{1,1} & p_h^{1,2} & \cdots & p_h^{1,K+1} \\ \cdots & \cdots & & \cdots \\ p_h^{K,1} & p_h^{K,2} & \cdots & p_h^{K,K+1} \\ 0 & 0 & \cdots & 1 \end{pmatrix}.
$$

Time Nonhomogeneous Markov Chain   In the original JLT paper, the authors impose the following specification for the risk premium adjustment, allowing to compute risk-neutral probabilities from historical ones:

$$
q^{i,j}(t, t+1) = \begin{cases} \pi_i(t)p^{i,j} & \text{for } i \neq j, \\ 1 - \pi_i(t)(1 - p^{i,i}) & \text{for } i = j. \end{cases} \tag{20}
$$

Note that the risk premium adjustments $\pi_i(t)$ are deterministic and do not depend on the terminal rating but only on the initial one. This assumption enables JLT to obtain a nonhomogenous Markov chain for the transition process under the risk-neutral measure.

The calculation of risk-neutral matrices on real data can be performed as follows. Assuming that the recovery in default is a fraction δ of a treasury bond with same maturity, the price of a risky zero-coupon bond at time t with maturity T is

$$
P^i(t, T) = B(t, T) \times (1 - q^{i,K+1}(1 - \delta)).
$$

---

*Some parts of the section come from de Servigny and Renault (2004).

Thus, we have

$$q^{i,K+1} = \frac{B(t,T) - P^i(t,T)}{B(t,T)(1-\delta)},$$

and thus the one-year risk premium is

$$\pi_i(t) = \frac{B(t,t+1) - P^i(t,t+1)}{B(t,t+1)(1-\delta)q^{i,K+1}}.$$

The JLT specification is easy to implement but often leads to numerical problems because of the very low probability of default of investment grade bonds at short horizons. In order to preclude arbitrage, the risk-neutral probabilities must indeed be non-negative. This constrains the risk premium adjustments to be in the interval:

$$0 < \pi_i(t) \le \frac{1}{1 - p^{i,i}}, \quad \text{for all } i.$$

From this we notice that the historical probability of an AAA bond defaulting over a one-year horizon is zero. Therefore, the risk-neutral probability of the same event is also zero.* This would however imply that the spreads on short dated AAA bond should be zero. (Why have a spread on default risk-less bonds?) To tackle this numerical problem, JLT assume that the historical one-year probability of default for an AAA bond is actually 1 basis point. The risk premium for the AAA row adjustment is therefore bounded above. This bound is, as we will see in the next equation, frequently violated on actual data.

Kijima and Komoribayashi (1998) propose another risk premium adjustment that guarantees the positivity of the risk-neutral probabilities in practical implementations.

$$\pi_{ij}(t) = l_i(t) \text{ for } j \ne K+1,$$

$$q^{i,j}(t,t+1) = \begin{cases} l_i(t)p^{i,j} & \text{for } i \ne K+1, \\ 1 - l_i(t)(1 - p^{i,i}) & \text{for } i = K+1. \end{cases} \tag{21}$$

where $l_i(t)$ are deterministic functions of time. Thanks to this adjustment, "negative prices" can be avoided.

Time-Homogeneous Markov Chain Unlike the precedent authors, Lamb, Peretyatkin, and Perraudin (2005) propose to compute a time-

---

*Recall that two equivalent probability measures share the same null sets.

homogeneous Markovian risk-adjusted transition matrix. They rely on bond spreads, thanks to the term structure of spreads per rating category.

$$\exp(-S_i(t)) = (\delta q_i^{K+1}(t) + (1 - q_i^{K+1}(t)).$$

where t corresponds to integer-year maturities.

In order to obtain the matrix, they minimize*

$$\min_{q_i^j(t)} \sum_{t=1}^{n} \sum_{i=1}^{K} \left[S_i(t) - (\delta q_i^{K+1}(t) + (1 - q_i^{K+1}(t))) \right]^2 \qquad (22)$$

knowing that q_i^{K+1} (t) is a function of the $q_i^j(\cdot)$.

A minor weakness of this approach is that it does not ensure that spreads are matching market prices for all maturities.

Some Extentions of JLT

Das and Tufano (1996)   The specificity of the model by Das and Tufano (1996) is to allow for stochastic recovery rates correlated to the risk-less interest rate. A wider variety of spreads can be generated due to this flexibility. In particular, features of the model include the following:

♦ Credit spreads can change although ratings are unchanged. In the JLT model, a given rating class is associated with a unique term structure of spreads, and all bonds with same maturity and rating are identical.

♦ Spreads are correlated with interest rates.

♦ Spreads are "firm specific" and not only "rating class specific."

♦ The pricing of credit derivatives is facilitated.

While the JLT model assumed that recovery in default was paid at the maturity of the claim,[†] Das and Tufano (1996) assume that recovery is a random fraction of par paid at the default time τ.

Arvanitis et al. (1999):   Arvanitis et al. (1999) extend the JLT model by considering nonconstant transition matrices. Their model is "pseudo

---

*Attaching penalties if entries in the transition matrix become negative in the course of the minimization.

[†]Or identically that recovery occurs at the time of default but is a fraction δ of a T-maturity risk-less bond.

nonMarkovian" in the sense that past ratings changes impact on future transition probabilities. This conditioning enables the authors to replicate much more closely the observed term structure of spreads.

In particular, their class of models allows for correlations between default probabilities and interest rate changes and for correlation of spreads across credit classes and spread differences within a given rating class for bonds that have been upgraded or downgraded.

Calibration of Spread Processes

Market practice is often to model spreads directly, which eliminates the need to make assumptions on recovery.

Spread modeling

Longstaff and Schwartz (1995) present a simple parametric specification and provide first empirical results on real market data. The main stylized fact incorporated in their model is the mean reverting behavior of spreads: the logarithm of the spread is assumed to follow an Ornstein-Uhlenbeck process under the risk-neutral measure Q:

$$ds_t = \kappa(\theta - s_t)dt + \sigma\, dW_t, \qquad (23)$$

where the log of the spread is s_t. The parameters are constant, with long-term mean θ, and volatility σ and a speed of mean reversion κ.

Mean reversion is an important feature in credit spreads and has been found in Longstaff and Schwartz (1995) and Prigent, Renault, and Scaillet (2001) (PRS). Interestingly the speed of mean reversion is not the same for Baa and Aaa spreads, for example. PRS provide a detailed parametric and nonparametric analysis of credit spread indices and find that higher rated spreads tend to revert much faster to their long-term mean than lower rated spreads. A similar finding is reported on a different sample by Longstaff and Schwartz (1995).

Another property of spreads is that their volatility tends to be increasing in level. This was not captured by the earlier model. To tackle this, Das and Tufano (1996) suggest an alternative specification, similar to the Cox–Ingersoll–Ross (1985) specification for interest rates:

$$ds_t = \kappa(\theta - s_t)dt + \sigma \sqrt{s_t}\, dW_t.{}^* \qquad (24)$$

---

*Their specification is actually in discrete time. This stochastic differential equation is the "equivalent" specification in continuous time.

Of course, various other stochastic processes can be considered. For example, a generalization of Equation (1) is given by

$$dx = (a + bx)dt + \sigma x^\gamma dW$$

where the mean reverting level is given by $\theta = -(a/b)$ and the mean reversion speed is given by $\beta = -b$, and γ is a scalar. PRS apply the model to credit spread data. Depending on the parameter γ (which measures the level of nonlinearity between the level and volatility), several commonly known models can be derived. For example, $\gamma = 0$ leads to the Vasicek (1977) process, while $\gamma = 1/2$ results in the Cox, Ingersoll, and Ross (1985) (CIR) process.

PRS also discuss a Jump-diffusion dynamics and support their claim by empirical evidence. They therefore extend the model of Longstaff and Schwartz (1995b) in a different direction and incorporate binomial jumps:*

$$ds_t = \kappa(\theta - s_t)dt + \sigma\, dW_t + dN_t, \tag{25}$$

where N_t is a compound Poisson process whose jumps take either the value $+a$ or $-a$ (given that the specification is in logarithm, they are percentage jumps).

Jumps are found to be significant in different rating series (Aaa and Baa), and a likelihood ratio test of the jump process versus its diffusion counterpart strongly rejects the assumption of no jumps at the 5 percent level. Note that the size of percentage jumps in Baa spreads is about half that of jumps in Aaa spreads. In *absolute* terms, however, average jumps in both series are approximately the same size, because the level of Aaa spreads is about half that of Baa spreads.

Calibration of Spreads Modeled as Jump-Diffusion Processes

The model specification we retain here corresponds to Equation (25)

Specification The discretization of Equation (25) leads to:

$$s_{t+1} - s_t = \kappa(\theta - s_t)dt + \sigma\sqrt{t}.N(0,1) + I_t.N_t(u,v) \tag{26}$$

The compound Poisson process specification means that the time-arrival of the jumps follows a Poisson process and that the size of the jumps

---

*Models estimated by PRS are under the historical measure and cannot be directly compared to the risk-neutral process mentioned earlier.

follows a normal distribution with parameters u and v. Practically, I_t is equal to 1 when there is a jump at time t and 0 otherwise. u is drawn from a standard uniform distribution and a jump takes place if $u < 1 - \exp(-\lambda\, dt)$.

MLE Calibration The common approach is to maximize the log-likelihood function. In order to build this function, we want to define the probability of obtaining a level of spread s_t, given a level of spread s_{t-1} in previous observation. We know from Ball and Torous (1983) that $p(ds_t)$ will follow a normal distribution weighted by the probability of a jump $(K = P(x = 1) \approx 1 - \exp(-\lambda t))$

$$p(ds_t) = p(s_t - s_{t-1}) = K \frac{1}{\sqrt{2\pi V_{jump}}} \exp\left(\frac{-(ds_t - E_{jump})^2}{2V_{jump}} \right)$$

$$+ (1 - K) \frac{1}{\sqrt{2\pi V_{no\_jump}}} \exp\left(\frac{-(ds_t - E_{no\_jump})^2}{2V_{no\_jump}} \right)$$

with the density of normally distributed spread changes being written as:

$$p(ds_t) = \frac{1}{\sqrt{2\pi V}} \exp\left(\frac{-(ds_t - E)^2}{2V} \right)$$

$E_{no\_jump} = \kappa(\theta - s)dt$ and $E_{jump} = \kappa(\theta - s)dt + u$ being the expectation of the spread process

$$V_{no\_jump} = \sigma^2 dt \quad \text{and} \quad V_{jump} = \sigma^2\, dt + v^2.$$

The Log-likelihood function to be maximized is then:

$$\underset{\kappa,\theta,u,v,\lambda}{\text{Max}(L)} \text{ with } L = \sum_{t=1}^{T} \log(p(s_t - s_{t-1})) \tag{27}$$

The tractability of the approach has been previously demonstrated, and the more data is available, the more the MLE estimators are close to the "true" parameters (i.e., there is a high confidence level).

More Advanced Calibration

A relatively recent trend in spread calibration has been to calibrate spread movements as the combination of a jump-diffusion process and a correlated migration process. This type of process can be seen as an advanced version of the CreditMetrics setup where instead of relying on deterministic spreads, we would add pure spread uncertainty. Such a framework has been considered in Kiesel et al. (2001) and Jobst and Zenios (2005), where the relative contribution of spread, (interest rate) and transition/default risk is explored for various bond portfolios.

The calibration of the two processes does not represent a serious issue as long as they are considered as independent from each other. The challenge becomes obvious when dealing with dependence between these two processes and when suggesting cocalibration. This topic seems to be open for research, See for example, Bielecki et al. (2005) who try to tackle the problem formally.

STRUCTURAL MODELS

Structural models have received some renewed consideration recently, as market participants investigate more thoroughly hybrid products as well as debt equity arbitrage, e.g., through credit default swap and equity default swap carry trades. In addition as the equity market is more complete than the credit market, credit pricing, and hedging solutions based on equity products receives ongoing market interest.*

The Merton Model

The Merton (1974) model is the first example of an application of contingent claims analysis to corporate security pricing. Using simplifying assumptions about the firm value dynamics and the capital structure of the firm, the author is able to give pricing formulae for corporate bonds and equities in the familiar Black and Scholes (1973) paradigm.

In the Merton model a firm with value V is assumed to be financed through equity (with value S) and pure discount bonds (with value P) and maturity T. The principal of the debt is K, and the value of the firm is given by the sum of the values of its securities: $V_t = S_t + P_t$. In the Merton model, it is assumed that bondholders cannot force the firm into bankruptcy before the maturity of the debt. At the maturity date T, the firm is

---

*Such models allow in particular to provide a "fair value" spread estimation on loans related to listed companies.

FIGURE 3.1

Payoff of Equity and Corporate Bond at Maturity T.

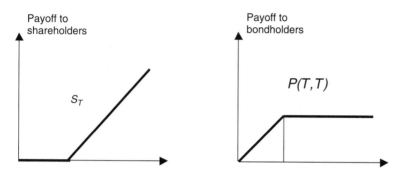

considered solvent if its value is sufficient to repay the principal of the debt. Otherwise, the firm defaults.

The value of the firm V is assumed to follow a geometric Brownian motion* such that[†] $dV = \mu V\,dt + \sigma_V V\,dZ$. Default happens if the value of the firm is insufficient to repay the debt principal: $V_T < K$. In that case, bondholders have priority over shareholders and seize the entire value of the firm V_T. Otherwise (if $V_T \geq K$), bondholders receive what they are due: the principal K. Thus, their payoff is $P(T, T) = \min(K, V_T) = K - \max(K - V_T, 0)$ (see Figure 3.1).

Equity holders receive nothing if the firm defaults, but profit from all the upside when the firm is solvent, i.e., the entire value of the firm net of the repayment of the debt $(V_T - K)$ falls in the hands of shareholders. The payoff to equity holders is therefore $\max(V_T - K, 0)$ (see Figure 3.1).

Readers familiar with options will recognize that the payoff to equity holders is similar to the payoff of a call on the value of the firm struck at X. Similarly, the payoff received by corporate bond holders can be seen as the payoff of a risk-less bond minus a put on the value of the firm.

---

*A geometric Brownian motion is a stochastic process with log-normal distribution. μ is the growth rate while σ_v is the volatility of the process. Z is a standard Brownian motion whose increments dZ have mean zero and variance equal to time. The term $\mu V\,dt$ is the deterministic drift of the process and the other term $\sigma_v V\,dZ$ is the random volatility component. See Hull (2002) for a simple introduction to geometric Brownian motion.
[†]We drop the time subscripts to simplify notations.

Merton (1974) makes the same assumptions as Black and Scholes (1973), and the call and the put can be priced using option prices derived in Black–Scholes.

For example, the call (equity) is immediately obtained as:

$$S_t = V_t N(k + \sigma_V \sqrt{T - t}) - Ke^{-r(T-t)}N(k), \tag{28}$$

with $k = (\ln(V_t / X) + (r - \frac{1}{2}\sigma_V^2)(T - t)) / (\sigma_V \sqrt{T - t})$ and $N(\cdot)$ denoting the cumulative normal distribution and r the constant risk-less interest rate.

From Risk-Neutral Probabilities to Spreads

The firm value approach suffers from several theoretical shortcomings like the fact that the evolution of the value of the firm usually follows a diffusion process that does not allow for unexpected default.

What is more important from the point of view of practitioners is to evaluate whether a structural model can help them to derive prices for credit instruments such as defaultable debt or credit default swaps (CDSs). A particular area of focus is short-term credit spreads, as in the traditional structural setup the probability of a firm to default in the short term is zero, leading to zero initial credit spreads. We review various approaches and assess whether they can provide realistic results.

The Capital Asset Pricing Model (CAPM) Approach

In Chapter 2, we have mainly focused on historical probabilities of default, i.e., probabilities estimated on historical data. However, for pricing purposes (for the calculation of spreads), one needs to estimate risk-neutral probabilities. Here, we show a customary way to obtain spreads from historical probabilities: a similar calculation is used by the firm MKMV (Moody's KMV) and many banks (see, e.g., McNulty and Levin, 2000).

Recall that the cumulative default probability (historical probability) for a firm i (HP^i_t) is defined as the probability of default at the horizon t under the historical measure P. In the MKMV (model, this corresponds to their expected default frequency.

We now introduce the risk-neutral probability, RNP^i_t, which is the equivalent probability under the risk-neutral measure Q (see Appendix 1). Under Q, all assets drift at the risk-free rate and therefore one should substitute r for μ_i in the dynamics of the value of the firm.*

---

*That is, we have $dA_t = rA_t\, dt + \sigma A_t\, dW_t$ under Q and $dA_t = \mu A_t\, dt + \sigma A_t\, dW_t^*$ under P.

The formulas for the two cumulative default probabilities are therefore:

$$HP_t^i = N\left(-\frac{(\ln(V_0^i) - \ln(X_i) + (\mu_i - \sigma_i^2 / 2)t)}{\sigma_i \sqrt{t}}\right), \text{ and}$$

$$RNP_t^i = N\left(-\frac{(\ln(V_0^i) - \ln(X_i) + (r - \sigma_i^2 / 2)t)}{\sigma_i \sqrt{t}}\right), \tag{29}$$

with:

$N(\cdot)$ = the cumulative standard normal distribution
V_0^i = the firm's asset value at time 0
X_i = the default point (value of liabilities)
σ_i = the volatility of asset values
μ_i = the expected return (growth rate) on asset values
r = the risk-less rate

The expected return on an asset includes a risk premium, leading to $\mu_i \geq r$, and hence:

$$RNP_t^i \geq HP_t^i.$$

Writing the risk-neutral probability of default as a function of HP_t^i, we obtain:

$$RNP_t^i = N\left(-\frac{\left(\ln(A_0^i) - \ln(X_i) + (\mu_i - \sigma_i^2 / 2)t - (\mu_i - r)t\right)}{\sigma_i \sqrt{t}}\right)$$

$$= N\left(N^{-1}(HP_t^i) + \left(\frac{\mu_i - r}{\sigma_i}\right)\sqrt{t}\right) \tag{30}$$

According to the CAPM (see, e.g., Sharpe et al., 1999), the risk premium on an asset should depend only on its systematic risk measured as the covariance of its returns with the returns on the market index.

More precisely for a given firm i with expected asset return μ_i we have:

$$\mu_i = r + \beta_i \left(E(r_m) - r \right)$$

$$\equiv r + \beta_i \pi_t,$$

with $E(r_m)$ the expected return on the market index and π_t, the market risk premium. $\beta_i = \sigma_{im} / \sigma_m^2 = \rho_{im} \sigma_i / \sigma_m$ is the measure of systemic risk of the firm's assets, where σ_m, σ_{im}, and ρ_{im} are, respectively, the volatility of the market, the covariance, and correlation of asset returns with the market.

Using these notations, the quasi probability becomes:

$$\mathrm{RNP}_t^i = N\left(N^{-1}(\mathrm{HP}_t^i) + \rho_{im} \left(\frac{\pi_t}{\sigma_m} \right) \sqrt{t} \right). \tag{31}$$

Corporate spreads are the difference between the yield on a corporate bond $Y(t, T)$ and the yield on an identical but (default) risk-less security $R(t, T)$. T denotes the maturity date while t stands for the current date.*

The spread is therefore: $S(t, T) = Y(t, T) - R(t, T)$. Recall that the price $P(t, T)$ at time t of a risky zero-coupon bond maturing at T can be obtained by:

$$P(t, T) = \exp(-Y(t, T) \times (T-t))$$

Similarly, for the risk-less bond $B(t, T)$:

$$B(t, T) = \exp(-R(t, T) \times (T-t)).$$

Therefore,

$$S(t, T) = 1/(T-t) \, \log(B(t, T)/P(t, T)). \tag{32}$$

Thus, all else being equal, the spread widens when the risky bond price falls.

For the sake of simplicity, assume for now that investors are risk neutral. In a risk-neutral world, an investor is indifferent between receiving \$1 for sure and receiving \$1 in expectation.

---

*We drop the superscript i in the probabilities for notational convenience.

Then: $B(t, T) = P(t, T)/(1 - \text{RNP}_{T-t} * L)$, where L is the loss in default (1 minus the recovery rate) and RNP_T the probability of default. Therefore, we get: $S(t, T) = -1/(T-t) \ln(1 - \text{RNP}_{T-t} * L)$.

The risk-neutral spread reflects both the probability of default and the recovery risk. In reality of course, investors exhibit risk aversion that will also be translated into spreads.

We now want to calculate the price of a defaultable bond using risk-neutral probabilities of default. Let $P^C(t, T)$ be the value at time t of a T-maturity risky coupon bond paying a coupon C (there are n coupon dates spaced by Δt years). We assume that the principal of the bond is 1 and that the value recovered in case of default is constant and equal to R. We have:

$$P^C(t,T) = \sum_{k=1}^{n} B(t, t + k\Delta t)\Big[C \times (1 - \text{RNP}_{k\Delta t}) + R \times (\text{RNP}_{k\Delta t} - \text{RNP}_{(k-1)\Delta t})\Big]$$
$$+ B(t,T) \times (1 - \text{RNP}_{T-t}) \tag{33}$$

An important point to notice is that this approach does not prove really satisfactory to cope with nonzero short-term credit spreads.

The Market Implied Volatility Approach

In a Merton setup, the value of the equity at time t is immediately obtained as:

$$S_t = V_t N(k + \sigma_V \sqrt{T - t}) - Ke^{-r(T-t)}N(k),$$

with $k = (\ln(V_t / X) + (r - \frac{1}{2}\sigma_V^2)(T - t)) / (\sigma_V \sqrt{T - t})$ and $N(\cdot)$ denoting the cumulative normal distribution and r the risk-less interest rate.

It can be rewritten at $t = 0$ as:

$$S_0 = (P_0 + S_0)N(k + \sigma_V \sqrt{T}) - Ke^{-r(T)}N(k) \quad \text{and}$$

$$k = \frac{\ln((P_0 + S_0) / X) + \left(r - \frac{1}{2}\sigma_V^2\right)(T)}{\sigma_V \sqrt{T}}.$$

If we assume that an implied volatility σ_V can be derived from the market, we can obtain P_0 as a function of S_0: $P_0 = F(S_0)$. For small t, we can assume: $P_t \approx F(S_t)$.

We also would like to infer the density of P_t from that of S_t. A standard assumption for the distribution of the equity is log-normality.

Let us call $\varphi(\cdot)$ the density function of S_t:

$$\varphi(S) = \frac{1}{\sigma_s S \sqrt{2\pi t}} \exp\left(-\frac{1}{2}\frac{(\ln(S_0) - \ln(S) + (\mu_s - \sigma_s^2/2)t)^2}{\sigma_s^2 t}\right) \tag{34}$$

where μ_s and σ_s are, respectively, drift and the volatility of the equity under the empirical measures.

The density function of P_t can now be inferred numerically from that of S_t as:

$$\text{Probability } (P_t) \in [P; P + dP] = \xi(P)dP = \varphi(F^{-1}(S))d(F^{-1}(S))$$

The expected return of the zero-coupon bond price can be written as:

$$\overline{R}_p(t) = E\left[\frac{1}{t}\ln\left(\frac{P_t}{P_0}\right)\right] = \frac{1}{t}\left(\int_0^\infty \ln(P)\xi(P)dP - \ln(P_0)\right) \tag{35}$$

and the bond spread can be derived as $\bar{s}_p(t) = |R_p(t) - r|$.

This type of analysis is typically used in the market by the financial institutions that want to obtain some indication of whether a bond is "cheap" or "expensive," based on a relative value assessment between the observed spread and the corresponding fair-value spread.

Obviously, the fair-value of the bond spread will depend on the specification of the dynamics of the equity price. As we have considered log-normal dynamics for the value of the firm $V(\cdot)$ over the period $[0, T]$, we cannot consider an arbitrary density for S over the corresponding period. As we are focusing on a very short time horizon, we could however consider a more complex pattern generating an implied volatility skew. There is a large range of possibilities based, for instance, on the use of standard CEV diffusion processes. One can even think of jumps in order to generate very steep volatility skews.

So far, we have not referred to a term structure of spreads, but only to an assessment of what the market value of the spread could be in the very short term. The way to obtain a term structure of spreads would be to rely on forward prices for the equity, the equity and the asset volatilities, the equity drift, and the risk-free rate, as well as on a specification of the forward density of the equity price. In the end, it is probably fair to say that the result will correspond to an art as much as to a scientific piece of work.

Extensions of the Merton Framework

First-Passage-Time Models

An important extension of the original Merton model consists of the "first-passage-time approach." The idea is introduced in Black and Cox (1976). It allows for default to occur prior to the maturity of the debt. This approach consists in including an early default time-dependent barrier as can be seen in Figure 3.2. Depending on the authors, the dynamics of the barrier (the barrier process) can be specified either endogenously or exogenously. For example, for a simple constant barrier K, the probability of default ("first passage time") is given in closed form:

$$P(\min_{[0,T]} V_t < K)$$

$$= 1 - \Phi\left(\ln\left(\frac{V_0}{K}\right) \middle/ (\sigma_V \sqrt{T}) + (\mu_V - 0.5\sigma_V^2)\sqrt{T}/\sigma_V \right)$$

$$+ \left(\frac{K}{V_0}\right)^{2(\mu_V - 0.5\sigma_V^2)/\sigma_V^2} \Phi\left(\ln\left(\frac{K}{V_0}\right) \middle/ (\sigma_V \sqrt{T}) + (\mu_V - 0.5\sigma_V^2)\sqrt{T}/\sigma_V \right).$$

In addition, the recovery upon default can be defined in various ways.

FIGURE 3.2

Introduction of a Time-Dependent Default Barrier.

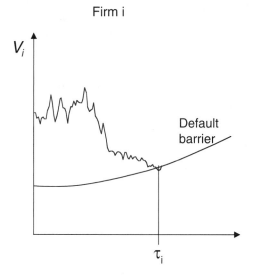

Firm i

The Effect of Incomplete Information   Duffie and Lando (2001) lay
stress on the fact that first-passage structural models are based on accounting information. This information to investors can be somewhat opaque
and sometimes insufficient, as we have observed recently with Enron,
Worldcom, Parmalat, and others. In addition, accounting practices lead to
the release of data with a time lag and in a discrete way. For all these reasons, part of the information used as an input in structural model (e.g.,
asset value and default boundary) can be imperfect.

Duffie and Lando (2001) suggest that if the information available to
investors was perfect, observed credit spreads would be closer to theoretical ones, as predicted by the Merton models. However, as the information available in the financial markets is not complete, observed spreads
exhibit significant differences (see Figure 3.3).

To summarize, the driving forces behind the dynamics of the Merton
approach, we can say that the risk on the debt of the firm, reflected in its
spread, largely depends on three key factors: the debt equity leverage, the
asset volatility, and the dynamics of the default barrier.

The Dynamic Barrier Approach

This class of model builds on the first-passage-time approach, where
default can happen before the maturity of the debt when the value of the
firm hits a time varying barrier. The problem with such models is to

FIGURE 3.3

Credit Spreads and Information.

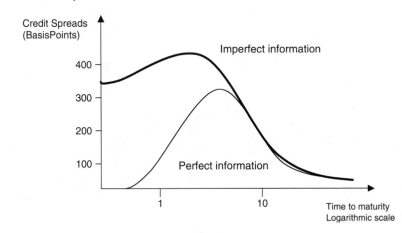

define a specification for the time-dependent barrier that allows for tractable pricing solutions.

The CreditGrades Approach   Finger et al. (2002) propose a fair value spread estimator (CreditGrades) more refined than the MKMV one. In order to allow for non-zero spreads at the beginning of the life of a CDS, the model assumes a stochastic barrier driven by a log-normally distributed stochastic recovery rate.

Assuming zero drift, the authors show that it is then possible to derive the risk-neutral probability of default of the obligor in a simple way:

$$
\text{RNP}_t^i = N\left(\frac{\left(\ln(V_0^i) - \ln(\hat{X}_i) \right)}{\sqrt{\text{var}_i}} - \sqrt{\text{var}_i}/2 \right)
$$

$$
- \frac{V_0^i}{\hat{X}_i} N\left(-\frac{\left(\ln(V_0^i) - \ln(\hat{X}_i) \right)}{\sqrt{\text{var}_i}} - \sqrt{\text{var}_i}/2 \right)
$$

with $\hat{X}_i$ being the mean value of the new barrier depending on the mean recovery value and var_i a time-dependent element derived from the variance term of the Brownian component of the geometric Brownian motion characterizing the asset value of the firm, complemented with the variance of the recovery. As a result, initially as time is zero or close to zero, the var_i term differs from zero and the risk-neutral probability remains strictly positive. This in turn justifies the existence of a nonzero initial spread.

The spread can be derived as in the previous paragraph. The authors describe a closed form solution in the case of a continuously compounded spread.

This model has become a market standard in particular because of its tractability. It however relies on an ad hoc hypothesis on recovery that is difficult to validate empirically and that positions the model at the boundary of structural models.

The Safety Barrier Approach   Brigo and Tarenghi (2005) suggest to consider a "safety barrier" that is defined as the product of the barrier at the maturity of the debt and a discount factor derived from an adjusted drift extracted from the geometric Brownian motion corresponding to the asset return of the firm. The risk-neutral drift is adjusted in the sense that it includes a parameter β whose main role is to vary the steepness of the safety barrier by reinforcing the effect of the volatility. Based on this choice, they derive analytically the risk-neutral survival probability of the firm. By assuming a deterministic risk-free rate and an equivalence between the equity and the firm value volatilities, they can ultimately infer in a straightforward manner the price of a CDS at time 0.

To start with, the authors assume a diffusion process for the dynamics of the value of the firm under the risk-neutral measure, with time-dependent risk-free rate, payout ratio, and asset volatility.

$$\frac{dV_t}{V_t} = (r_t - q_t)dt + \sigma_t dW_t$$

The expression of the "safety barrier" $\hat{H}(t)$ is related to the default threshold H

$$\hat{H}(t) = H \exp\left(-\int_0^t \left(q_s - r_s + (1+2\beta)\frac{\sigma_s^2}{2}\right)ds\right) \tag{36}$$

τ is the first time when V hits $\hat{H}$

$$\tau = \inf\{t \geq 0 : V_t \leq \hat{H}(t)\}.$$

The survival probability is given in a closed form way:

$$Q\{\tau > T\} = \left[\Phi\left(\frac{\ln\frac{V_0}{H} + \beta\int_0^T \sigma_s^2 ds}{\sqrt{\int_0^T \sigma_s^2 ds}}\right) - \left(\frac{H}{V_0}\right)^{2\beta}\Phi\left(\frac{\ln\frac{H}{V_0} + \beta\int_0^T \sigma_s^2 ds}{\sqrt{\int_0^T \sigma_s^2 ds}}\right)\right] \tag{37}$$

Under deterministic interest rates, the value at time 0 of a CDS between times T_a and T_b corresponding to two payment date of the installments, with a fixed running amount per period R and fixed LGD can easily be inferred as:

$$\text{CDS}_{T_a,T_b}(0,R,\text{LGD}) = -R\sum_{i=a+1}^{b} P(0,T_i)\alpha_i Q(\tau \geq T_i)$$

$$- \text{LGD}\int_{T_a}^{T_b} P(0,t)dQ(\tau > t)$$

with $P(0,t)$ the zero-coupon bond at time 0 for maturity t.

As can be seen, the pricing of the CDS will depend on the definition of V_0/H, the asset volatility that is approximated by the equity volatility and the barrier curvature parameter β.

The authors calibrate* their model with $V_0/H=2$ and $\beta=0.5$. With this calibration, they show that they are able to provide a calibration of the CDS on Vodafone with results quite close to those derived from an intensity model.

This paper looks quite promising in the sense that it leads to tractable results while providing some intuition in terms of rational economic interpretation.

The Structural Approach Blended with a Jump-Diffusion Process to Model the Evolution of the Firm

The pioneer article related to jump-diffusion structural models is Zhou (2001).

We can write the evolution of the value of the firm as the sum of a diffusion process and a compound Poisson jump process Z. c is the product of the arrival intensity of the Poisson process by the mean jump size.

$$\frac{dV_t}{V_t} = (r - \gamma - c)dt + \sigma\, dW_t + dZ_t \tag{38}$$

Zhou (2001) is able to derive a closed form expression of the risk-neutral probability of default.

There are some technical difficulties to calibrate such a model:

♦ Asset returns are not observable
♦ A proxy is to rely on equity return or on an index return, but this calibration needs to be transformed from the real to the risk-neutral probability measure and as the market is not complete, there is no unique solution to the problem.

Huang and Huang (2003) go through the process of calibrating a jump-diffusion process in a structural framework. Their finding is that even when introducing a jump term, pure credit risk cannot account for the observed level of credit spread. The only way to reach such level

---

*Brigo and Tarenghi (2005) suggest to link the ratio of the initial value of the firm to the barrier to expected recovery. I.e., we have $dA_t = rA_t\, dt + \sigma A_t\, dW_t$ under Q and $dA_t = \mu A_t + \sigma A_t dW_t^*$ under P.

would be by forcing parameters into the model that lack empirical support.

Hybrid Models: A Discussion Around the Equity-to-Credit Paradigm

In this section, we discuss new approaches to the pricing of credit instrument based on the cocalibration with equity products. This is summarized as the "equity-to-credit paradigm" that attempts to grasp the complexity of the full spectrum of securities issued by or related to a single name in a consistent framework. It results from the need to price consistently equity products such as options, credit instruments such as bonds and CDSs, and hybrid securities such as convertible bonds. The intuitive idea is simple. The prices of out-of-the-money put must say something about the probability of default of the issuer, and reciprocally the credit standing revealed by the term structure of CDS spreads should impact the implied volatility smile. The joint calibration of different classes of assets related to a single name is often viewed as a complex and distant challenge. We argue instead that a large set of available market data provides a great opportunity to extract precise information on a single name. This nice feature of single name modeling is in sharp contrast with multiname problems such as CDO pricing, where there is less hope of finding enough instruments to calibrate precisely a correlation structure for hundreds of names. As a result, multiname pricing is limited to educated guesses and statistical inference from past data. The calibration of single name models has the luxury to rely on a large set of forward looking derivative prices. The challenge is to propose models that are capable of handling this rich source of information. We review why both standard structural models and simple reduced-form models fail and propose a new class of regime-based models, versatile enough to handle most situations in a numerically tractable way.

Structural Models

As we have seen earlier, structural models attempt to explain the price dynamics of the instruments related to a single name, the so-called equity-to-credit universe, by making use of the available information on the capital structure of the firm. Default is triggered when the assets of the company fall below some critical threshold. The value of the company's assets is the only state variable, and the price of every security is derived from its process and its relation to the critical threshold. From their introduction by Merton in 1974, these models have been continuously refined but have kept the same philosophy. The most advanced refinements introduce complex joint dynamics for the value of the assets and the critical default threshold. Jumps for instance, either in the asset value or in the threshold itself, make it possible for a firm to fall into default at every instant. This is a much-needed feature as otherwise default would always be predictable and short-term CDS spread should consequently be close to zero, a clear empirical contradiction.

The main problem with structural models is their inability to reproduce the observed prices of the equity-to-credit instruments. By tweaking the volatility parameter of the asset value process, for instance, it is possible to account for the observed term structure of CDS spreads. Such calibration exercise is however limited to a single asset class. The tweaked model will, in general, fail to reproduce the observed term structure of at-the-money implied volatilities, let alone the entire smile across strikes and maturities or the prices of critical exotic derivatives such as barrier or forward starting options.

It is important to understand why the shortcoming of the structural model is not marginal. Its inability to calibrate the equity-to-credit universe is fundamental and cannot be dealt with by a few adjustments on the underlying process. The reason is rather obvious: corporate life is a complex process that cannot be summarized in a one-dimensional process. A trader with equity and credit exposures knows intuitively that the stock price is not the only variable which affects his P&L (Profit and Loss). At the minimum, he is equally concerned with the volatility and the evolution of the spread. These risk dimensions, although clearly correlated with the stock price, cannot be reduced to a one-dimensional problem. The critical weakness of structural models is to assume that the value of every security linked to an issuer is a function of the assets of the company alone. The empirical reality presents a much more complex picture.

Simple scatter plots of CDS spread or implied volatility against stock price show the gap that often exists between the structural theory and the empirical evidence. Figures 3.4 and 3.5 show, respectively, the five-year CDS spread and the one-year ATM implied volatility as a function of spot for the firm Accor from April 2003 to December 2005. Structural theory predicts that both the spread and the implied volatility should be decreasing functions of the spot price.

Not only is it clear that in many situations the price dynamics of equity-to-credit securities cannot be reduced to a one-dimensional manifold, but in some critical cases the structural models fail to grasp the sign of the correlations. Structural models view the equity as a call written on the assets of the company whose value decreases with the value of the assets. As the

FIGURE 3.4

CDS Spread vs Equity Spot Price.

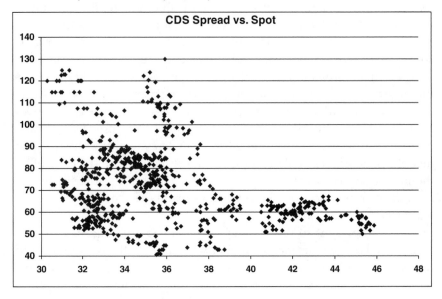

FIGURE 3.5

Implied ATM Volatility vs Equity Spot Price.

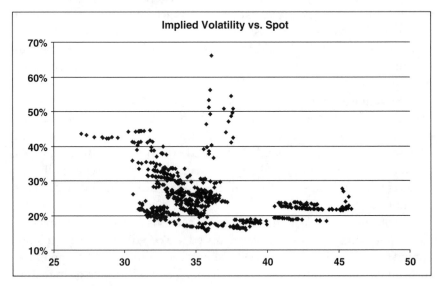

stock price falls with the value of the assets, leverage increases and the company becomes more risky resulting in larger spreads and higher stock price volatility levels. This intuitive behavior often fails to grasp the rich dynamics of the equity-to-credit universe.

Figure 3.6 examines in more detail a subset of the data presented earlier for Accor, from June 1, 2005 to December 8, 2005. It can be decomposed into three subperiods that correspond to three distinct regimes. Period 1 runs from June 1 to July 7 and is characterized by a low level of volatility. On July 8, the volatility suddenly increases and this regime lasts until August 10 (Period 2). On August 11, the volatility jumps again to a third regime until the end of the sample (Period 3). At each juncture, the spot price barely moves. The CDS spread scatter plot for the same period (see Figure 3.7) fails to reveal any clear regime or any correlation with the spot price. The regimes can therefore best be described as volatility regimes. They correspond to very real events affecting the life of the company or the business environment. The first regime change on July 7, 2005 was most probably triggered by the terrorist attacks in London, which ushered in a period of perceived instability, reflected in a larger implied volatility. The second regime switch corresponded to rumours in the press of manage-

FIGURE 3.6

Implied ATM Volatility vs Equity Spot Price: June 2005–December 2005.

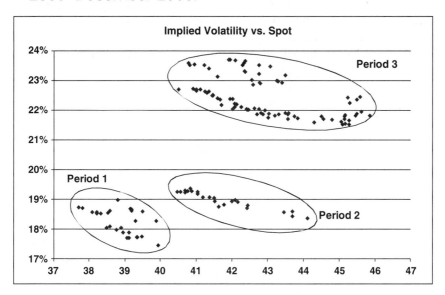

FIGURE 3.7

CDS Spread vs Equity Spot Price: June
2005–December 2005.

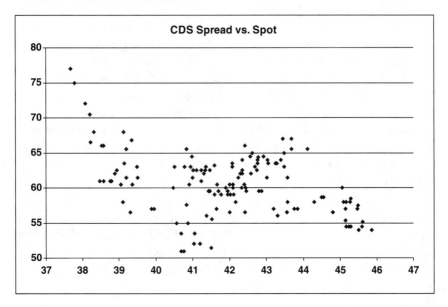

ment shakeout and potential buyout of Accor by the real estate fund Colony
Capital together with the company Starwood Hotels & Resorts Worldwide
Inc. The stock price increased first from 41.78 to 43.69 euros on Friday
August 5, and the implied volatility then jumped on August 11 from 18.4 to
21.9 percent. Needless to say that none of these changes of regime can be
accounted for by standard structural models. The potential buyout has log-
ically a positive impact on both the stock price and the implied volatility
while the structural model would imply a smaller risk as the price increases.

It could be argued however that the structural model remains a good
candidate within each regime in order to describe the day-to-day behavior
of the Equity-to-Credit universe. Figure 3.7 has already shown that it is difficult to believe that the CDS spread is a function of the spot price, even
within each regime. Figure 3.8 describes the joint behavior of the CDS
spread and the implied volatility over a small period of time from May 4 to
June 3, 2005 while Figure 3.9 tracks the spot price over the same period.

During that period, the stock remained virtually constant until May 18
at around 36 euros while both the spread and the implied volatility were
increasing significantly. The stock then jumped to around 37.5 euros while

FIGURE 3.8

Implied ATM Volatility (Left Axis) vs CDS Spread (Right Axis).

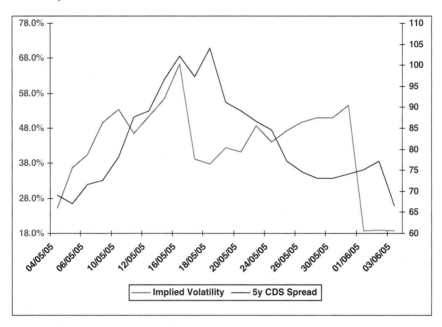

FIGURE 3.9

Accor Stock Price.

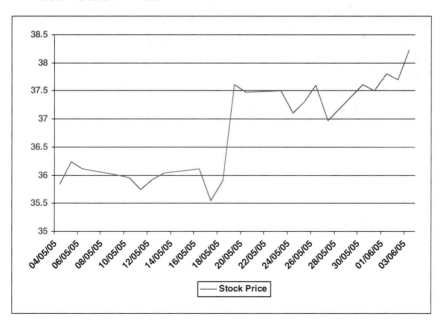

both the spread and the implied volatility went back to their original values. Traders who would have hedged their credits or volatility position on Accor in the first two weeks of May 2005 with the underlying alone according to a structural model would have been widely off the mark.

Reduced-form Equity to Credit Models

A reduced-form model is sometimes seen as an attempt to alleviate the most striking shortcoming of the structural model: the fact that the default event itself is triggered by the stock price. In its standard formulation, a typical reduced-form model often keeps the stock price as the only explanatory variable for the entire equity-to-credit universe but for one event, which is the time of default. Default is seen as an exogenous and unexplained event that may occur anytime according to a Poisson process. The intensity of this process, just like the instantaneous volatility of the stock price, may itself be a function of time and spot. The state space is therefore expanded from the stock price alone (as in structural models) to the stock price and the default event in the reduced-form model. The stock price S follows a stochastic differential equation under the risk-neutral probability:

$$dS_t / S_t = (r_t + \lambda(S_t, t))\, dt + \sigma(S_t, t)\, dW_t - dN_t$$

where r_t is the short-term risk-free rate at time t and N_t is a Poisson process with instantaneous intensity $\lambda(S_t, t)$, which triggers default. We assume here for simplicity that the stock price jumps to zero upon default. Notice that the drift is adjusted to make sure that the stock price follows a discounted martingale in the risk-neutral probability measure, as required by the absence of arbitrage opportunity. Any derivative instrument should also earn the risk-free rate on average under the risk-neutral measure and from this we derive the value V of any derivative security:

$$E[dV]/dt = r_t V = \partial V / \partial t + (r_t + \lambda(S_t, t)) S \partial V / \partial S + \tfrac{1}{2}\sigma^2 S^2 \partial^2 V / \partial S^2 + \lambda(S_t, t)\Delta V$$

The term ΔV describes the jump in value on the derivative caused by a jump to default of the underlying. Contrary to structural models, reduced-form models do not impose any a priori structure on the local default intensity and volatility parameters. In practice, one seeks to calibrate these functions to market data such as vanilla options and CDS.

The structural model setup fails to grasp the rich behavior of the equity-to-credit universe, because the spot price alone is too crudely a state variable. Adding the default event to the state space is certainly welcome but is unlikely to be sufficient. Standard reduced-form models are still unable to grasp regime changes, except in the most extreme case of default. As a result, even if they manage to reproduce a smile of vanilla options and a term structure of CDS at a given time, they will not properly account for the rich dynamics of these objects. This in turn implies that they will produce wrong hedges and that they will fail to correctly price exotic instruments.

Regime-Switching Models

The models that we have reviewed so far share the same drawback. They rely on a state space that is too restrictive to correctly handle the complex situations that are common in the corporate life of a firm. Expanding the state space from the stock price alone in the structural model to an additional default state variable in the standard reduced-form model goes in the right direction but is still too limited. Our choice of additional dimensions for the state space will be guided by two complementary sources, asset pricing theory on the one hand and corporate finance on the other hand.

From advanced asset pricing theory, we know that robust pricing and hedging of equity and credit derivatives require complex models for the stock price process with jumps, stochastic volatility with possibly jumps on the volatility, and finally a stochastic credit dimension with a rich correlation structure between these risk factors. This means that we need to keep track of at least two or more processes, in addition to the stock price and the default status: a process for the instantaneous volatility and another one for the instantaneous default intensity. A full-fledged three or more dimensional state variable is however extremely cumbersome to work with and such complex models have so far been confined to academic studies. Their calibration time is often too important to be of any value for practitioners, which explains the popularity of simpler models where the state space is essentially limited to the stock price. We face a disturbing contradiction. Asset pricing theory requires a rich state space while numerical tractability demands a limited number of risk dimensions.

Discrete regimes offer a nice way to solve this contradiction. We consider here a small number of abstract regimes: in practice, two are often enough and three is plenty. In each regime, the stock price follows a geometric jump-diffusion process with constant parameters. Each regime is defined by a distinct volatility, a distinct hazard rate, and distinct stock price jumps. The switch between regimes is driven by a Markov chain in continuous time. Default can be seen as an additional regime from which the firm does not recover. Formally, the state space is described by the stock price and an additional discrete variable that tracks the regime and default status. Finally, the much needed correlation between stock price, volatility, and default risk is obtained by allowing stock price jumps of various sizes when changes of regime occur. The proposed state space is both coarse enough to remain numerically tractable and rich enough to capture the risk dimensions called for by advanced pricing theory. It is crucial to remark that, contrary to the stock price or the default status, the volatility and the hazard rate are abstract variables, which are not directly observed. An elementary Markov chain is the simplest framework where these variables are stochastic with potentially rich correlation patterns.

One drawback of any regime-switching model is the absence of any closed form solution, which means that a calibration exercise must rely on fast numerical procedures. Luckily, the regime-switching model lends itself to fast numerical analysis through the use of coupled partial differential equations. We need to solve one backward one-dimensional grid per regime, which means that the pricing of an option with three regimes is only three times as costly as in the case of a standard jump diffusion, a far cry from the time needed to solve a full three-dimensional grid. In each regime i, the underlying price follows a jump-diffusion process in the risk-neutral probability with Brownian volatility σ_i and some jumps of percentage size y_{ij} and intensity λ_{ij}:

$$dS_t / S_t = (r_t - \Sigma_j \lambda_{ij} y_{ij})\, dt + \sigma_i\, dW_t + \Sigma_j\, y_{ij}\, dN_{ijt}$$

We distinguish three kinds of jumps: simple price jumps within each regime, a jump to default with a regime-dependent intensity or hazard rate, and jumps that occur together with a regime switch. The value V_i of a derivative in regime i is a solution to a one-dimensional evolution equation which results from the fact that in the absence of arbitrage every security must earn the risk-free rate in the risk-neutral probability:

$$E[dV_i]/dt = r_t V_i = \partial V_i/\partial t + (r_t - \Sigma_j \lambda_{ij} Y_{ij})S\partial V_i/\partial S + \frac{1}{2}\sigma_i^2\, S^2\partial^2 V_i/\partial S^2$$
$$+ \Sigma_j\, \lambda_{ij}\Delta V_{ij}$$

The last term ΔV_{ij} measures the jump on the value of the instrument implied by the corresponding jump of the underlying. For the jump to default, we need to input here the residual value of the instrument after default. In the case of a switch between regimes, ΔV_{ij} involves the value of the instrument in the new regime. This coupling jump term explains how the values of the derivative in the different regimes are interrelated.

Although apparently simple, the regime-switching model is quite versatile. Even with two regimes, it may give rise to very different interpretations depending on the values of its parameters. It can, for instance, reproduce the features of a stochastic volatility model or the ones of a credit migration model. Most interestingly, and unlike structural models, it can accommodate correlations of any sign and size between the stock price, the credit quality, and the volatility.

As predicted by asset pricing theory, the regime-switching model can successfully reproduce an entire smile of vanilla options and a term structure of CDS. We consider here the case of Tyco as of April 13, 2005 when its shares traded at US $33.64. We used a simple two-regime model. There are three sorts of jumps. First, the stock price jumps to zero upon default and this can occur in each regime with a different intensity. Second, the stock price jumps when the regime changes. And finally, we allow an additional stock price jump in the first regime only, which helps capture the options of very short maturities. Figure 3.10 describes the calibrated parameters while Figures 3.11 to 3.13 compare the market data with the option prices and CDS spreads produced by the model. The two regimes are solved by two-coupled one-dimensional PDE (Partial Differential Equation), essentially doubling the numerical effort needed to solve a standard jump-diffusion model. Calibration was obtained on a normal laptop in a few minutes.

The two regimes differ widely in terms of volatility or default intensity. The first regime has low volatility and no possibility of default while the second regime has a large volatility and a positive hazard rate. Switching from the first regime to the second is accompanied by a negative jump while reverting to the first regime occurs with a positive jump. This reproduces the

FIGURE 3.10

Model Calibration: A 2 State Regime Switching Approach.

	Brownian Volatility	Default Intensity
Regime 1	16.09%	0.000
Regime 2	66.17%	0.041

	Size	Jump Intensity
Regime 1	-15.96%	0.986
Regime 1-> 2	-44.58%	0.078
Regime 2 ->1	21.29%	0.020

FIGURE 3.11

Model Fit vs Market Data: Credit Spreads.

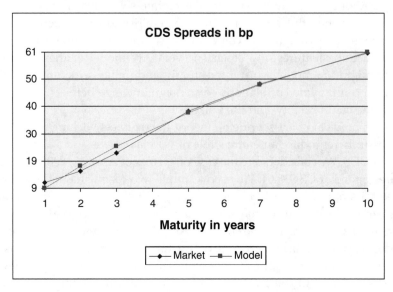

familiar correlation pattern of the structural model, where the volatility and the hazard rate increase as the price goes down. Notice, however, that the relation here is not functional but only probabilistic.

These regimes are not only a convenient way to tackle the asset pricing challenge of the Equity-to-Credit universe. They also offer a unique corporate finance perspective on the underlying firm. This is a second important source of inspiration for expanding the state space, this time

FIGURE 3.12

Model Fit vs Market Data: Implied Equity Options by Strike and Maturity.

Market Time Value

Strike / Maturity	15	20	22.5	25	27.5	30	32.5	35	37.5	40	42.5	45	50
21/05/05					0.12	0.19	0.25	0.68	0.56	0.18			
16/07/05				0.14	0.23	0.30	0.63	1.23	1.14	0.37	0.12		
22/10/05				0.19	0.40	0.67	1.15	1.90	2.02	1.05	0.43	0.22	0.13
21/01/06	0.15	0.25	0.33	0.56	0.96	1.54		2.59		0.85		0.18	0.14
20/01/07		0.74		1.58		2.91		4.55		3.10		1.84	1.10

Model Time Value

Strike / Maturity	15	20	22.5	25	27.5	30	32.5	35	37.5	40	42.5	45	50
21/05/05					0.06	0.10	0.24	0.59	0.41	0.03			
16/07/05				0.09	0.16	0.29	0.58	1.18	1.07	0.34	0.07		
22/10/05				0.23	0.38	0.65	1.11	1.86	2.00	1.07	0.50	0.21	0.08
21/01/06	0.08	0.24	0.38	0.61	0.97	1.52		2.69		1.01		0.29	0.07
20/01/07		0.75		1.50		2.82		4.85		3.05		1.78	1.00

FIGURE   3.13

Model Fit vs Market Data: Implied Equity Options by
Strike (Oct 2005).

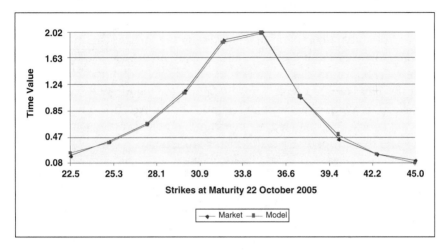

corporate finance point of view. While asset pricing theory views the regimes as a cheap and abstract expedient to produce stochastic volatility and stochastic hazard rate, corporate finance would want to name the regimes and to relate regime changes with the life of the firm.

This naming exercise is rather obvious in our example. The change of regime describes a likely deterioration in the credit standing of the company, and regimes can simply be interpreted here as proxy for credit rating. A downgrading is then associated with higher volatility and a large negative jump of −44 percent. Recovery from this bad state is possible and would be associated with a positive jump of 21 percent. It is interesting to note that these two regimes are enough to recover the entire term structure of CDS spreads quite accurately. This could certainly also be obtained in a model where the hazard rate is an increasing function of time but we would then have lost the underlying probabilistic interpretation.

The versatile nature of the regime-switching model means that it can morph to correspond to very different corporate finance stories. A company faced with the prospect of an LBO (Leveraged Buyout) will typically be described with a second regime with higher volatility and higher hazard rate, and reaching this regime will occur with a positive jump if the market sees the transaction as a creating value. This correlation pattern is at odds with the leverage story of the standard structural model.

Corporate restructuring may be another situation outside the reach of traditional models. The second regime would correspond to a successful restructuring of the balance sheet of the company. It would typically be associated with a smaller hazard rate and a smaller volatility. The stock price direction is unclear since it depends on the outcome of the negotiation between the various stakeholders.

Larger hazard rate should not automatically be associated with higher volatility. A company that is the target of an acquisition could see its shares swapped and the acquiring company may be less risky in terms of default, but more risky in terms of share price volatility. This would typically be associated with a positive jump for the target company, but this is certainly not a rule and no scenario should be a priori rejected.

In conclusion, the regime-switching model proposes an elegant answer to three apparently contradictory requests:

- Asset pricing theory needs a model complex enough to grasp the securities of the equity-to-credit universe
- Traders want quick numerical solutions
- Finally, corporate finance seeks to capture the significant events of the life of the company.

No doubt that in addition to its flexibility, this type model will generate heated debates between the derivatives experts and the capital structure specialists.

APPENDIX 1

Fundamental Theorems of Asset Pricing (FTAP) and Risk Neutral Measure

In many occasions in this book, we encounter the concept of risk-neutral measure and of pricing by discounted expectation. We will now summarize briefly the key results in this area. A more detailed and rigorous exposition can be found, for example, in Duffie (1996).

Intuitively, the price of a security should be related to its possible payoffs, to the likelihood of such payoffs, and to discount factors reflecting both the time value of money and investors risk aversion.

Standard pricing models such as the Dividend Discount Models use this approach to determine the value of stocks. For derivatives, or securities with complex payoffs in general, there are two fundamental difficulties with this approach:

1. To determine the actual probability of a given payoff
2. To calculate the appropriate discount factor.

The seminal papers of Harrisson and Kreps (1979) and Harrisson and Pliska (1981) have provided ways to circumvent these difficulties and have led to the so-called FTAP.

1st FTAP: markets are arbitrage free if and only if there exists a measure Q equivalent* to the historical measure P under which asset prices discounted at the risk-less rate are martingales.[†]

2nd FTAP: this measure Q is unique if and only if markets are complete.

A complete market is a market in which all assets are replicable. This means that you can fully hedge a position in any asset by creating a portfolio of other traded assets.

The first fundamental theorem provides a generic option pricing formula that does not rely either on a risk-adjusted discount factor or on finding out the actual probability of future payoffs. Assume that we want to price a security at time t whose random payoff $g(T)$ is paid at $T>t$. By no arbitrage, we know that at maturity the price of the security should be equal to the payoff $P_T=g(T)$. By the 1st FTAP, we immediately get the price:

$$P_t = E^Q[e^{-r(T-t)} P_T | P_t] = E^Q[e^{-r(T-t)}g(T)|P_t].$$

The probability Q can typically be inferred from traded securities. It is called the risk-neutral measure or the martingale measure.

The second theorem says that the measure Q (and therefore also security prices calculated as earlier) will be unique if and only if markets are complete. This is a very strong assumption, particularly in credit markets which are often illiquid.

REFERENCES

Arvanitis, A., J. Gregory, and J-P. Laurent (1999), "Building models for credit spreads," *Journal of Derivatives*, Spring, 27–43.

Ball, C., and W. Torous (1983), "A simplified jump process for common stock returns," *Journal of Financial Quantitative Analysis*, 18(1), 53–65.

Bielecki, T. and M. Rutkowski (2002), *Credit Risk: Modeling, Valuation and Hedging*, Springer-Verlag, Berlin.

---

*Two measures are said to be equivalent when they share the same null sets, i.e., when all events with zero probability under one measure has also zero probability under the other.

[†]A martingale is a drift-less process, i.e., a process whose expected future value conditional on its current value is the current value. More formally: $X_t = E[X_s | X_t]$ for $s \geq t$.

Black, F., and J. Cox, Valuing Corporate Securities (1976), "Some effects of bond indenture provisions," *Journal of Finance*, 31, 351–367.

Black, F., and M. Scholes (1973), "The pricing of options and corporate liabilities," *Journal of Political Economy*, 81, 637–659,

Brigo, D., and M. Tarenghi (2005), "Credit default swap calibration and equity swap valuation under counterparty risk with a tractable structural model," in Proceedings of the FEA 2004 Conference at MIT, Cambridge, Massachusetts, November 8–10, and in Proceedings of the Counterparty Credit Risk 2005 C.R.E.D.I.T. conference, Venice, September 22–23, 2005, Vol. 1.

Cox, J., J. Ingersoll, and S. Ross (1985), "A theory of the term structure of interest rates," *Econometrica*, 53, 385–407.

Das, S., and P. Tufano (1996), "Pricing credit sensitive debt when interest rates, credit ratings and credit spreads are stochastic", *Journal of Financial Engineering*, 5, 161–198.

Duffie D. (1996), 201cDynamic Asset Pricing Theory201d, Princeton University Press.

Duffie D., and Lando D. (2001), "Term structures of credit spreads with incomplete accounting information," *Econometrica*, 69, 633–664.

Duffie, D., and K. Singleton (1998), "Defaultable term structure models with fractional recovery at par," working paper, Graduate School of Business, Stanford University.

Duffie, D., and K. Singleton (1999), "Modeling term structures of defaultable bonds," *Review of Financial Studies*, 12, 687–720.

Finger, C., V. Finkelstein, G. Pan, J-P. Lardy, and T. Ta, (2002), *CreditGrades*™ *Technical Document*, RiskMetrics Publication.

Harrison J. and D. Kreps (1979), 201cMartingale and arbitrage in multiperiod securities markets201d, Journal of Economic Theory, 20, 348–408.

Harrison J. and S. Pliska (1981), 201cMartingales and stochastic integrals in the theory of continuous trading201d, Stochastic Processes and their Applications, 11, 215–260.

Heath, D., R. Jarrow, and A. Morton, (1992), "Bond Pricing and the term structure of interest rates: a new methodology for contingent claims valuation," *Econometrica*, 60, 77–105.

Huang, J. and M. Huang (2003), "How much of the corporate-treasury yield spread is due to credit risk?" working paper, Penn State University.

Hull J. (2002), Options, Futures and Other Derivatives, 5th edition, Prentice Hall.

Jarrow, R., D. Lando, and S. Turnbull (1997), "A Markov model for the term structure of credit risk spreads," *Review of Financial Studies*, 10, 481–523.

Jobst, N., and P. J. Schönbucher (2002) "Current developments in reduced-form models of default risk," working paper, Department of Mathematical Sciences, Brunel University.

Jobst, N., and S. A. Zenios (2005), "On the simulation of interest rate and credit risk sensitive securities," *European Journal of Operational Research*, 161, 298–324.

Kiesel, R., Perraudin, W., and Taylor, A. (2001), "The structure of credit risk: spread volatility and ratings transitions," technical report, Bank of England.

Kijima, Masaaki and Katsuya Komoribayashi, "A Markov chain model for valuing credit risk derivatives", Journal of Derivatives, Vol. 6, Kyoto University, (Fall 1998) pp. 97–108.

Lamb R., Peretyatkin V. and Perraudin W. (2005), 201c Hedging and asset allocation for structured products201d, Working Paper Imperial College.

Lando, D. (1998), "On Cox processes and credit risky securities," *Review of Derivatives Research*, 2, 99–120.

Longstaff, F., and E. Schwartz (1995) "Valuing credit derivatives," *Journal of Fixed Income*, 5, 6–12.

McNulty, C., and R. Levin (2000), "Modeling credit migration," Risk Management Research Report, J.P. Morgan.

Merton, R. (1974), "On the pricing of corporate debt: The risk structure of interest rates," *Journal of Finance*, 29, 449–470.

Moraux, F., and P. Navatte (2001), "Pricing credit derivatives in credit classes frameworks," in Geman, Madan, Pliska, and Vorst (eds.), *Mathematical Finance—Bachelier Congress 2000 Selected Papers*, Springer, 339–352.

Prigent, J-L., O. Renault, and O. Scaillet (2001), "An empirical investigation into credit spread indices," *Journal of Risk*, 3, 27–55.

Sharpe W., G. Alexander and J. Bailey (1999), Investments, Prentice-Hall.

Schönbucher, P. J., (2000), "A Libor market model with default risk", working paper, Department of Statistics, University of Bonn.

Valuation of Basket Credit Derivatives in the Credit Migrations Environment by Tomasz R. Bielecki of the Illinois Institute of Technology, St9c28ane Cr9c25y of the Universit9824'0276ry Val d'Essonne, Monique Jeanblanc of the Universit9824'0276ry Val d'Essonne, and Alexander McNeil of the University of New South Wales and Warsaw University of Technology, March 30, 2005.

Zhou, C., (2001), "The term structure of credit spreads with jump risk," *Journal of Banking and Finance*, 25, 2015–2040.

Modeling Credit Dependency

Arnaud de Servigny

INTRODUCTION

In this chapter,* we introduce multivariate effects, i.e., interactions between credit instruments or obligors.

The analysis of credit risk in a portfolio requires measures of dependency across assets. Individual spreads in the pricing world, probabilities of default (PDs) and loss-given-default in the risk universe, management world, are important but insufficient to determine the price/risk of multiname products and their entire distribution of losses. Because the diversification effects are related to dependency, neither the price of a portfolio can be defined as a linear combination of the price of its underlying components, nor its loss distribution can be the sum of the distributions of individual losses.

The most common measure of dependency is linear correlation. Figure 4.1 illustrates the impact of correlation on portfolio losses.[†] When default correlation is zero, the probability of extreme events in the portfolio (large number of defaults or zero default) is low. However, when correlation

---

*Some elements of this chapter have been extracted from "Measuring and Managing Credit Risk" by Arnaud de Servigny and Olivier Renault, Mc Graw Hill, 2004.
[†]Correlation here refers to factor correlation. This graph was created by using a factor model of credit risk and assuming that there are 100 bonds in the portfolio and that the probability of default of all bonds is 5 percent. Maturity is one year.

FIGURE 4.1

Effect of Correlations on Portfolio Losses.

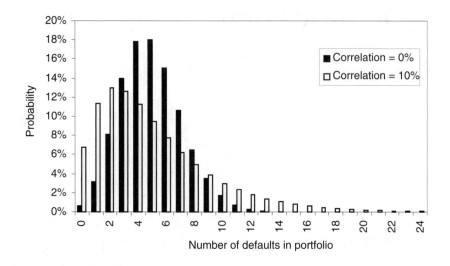

is significant, the probability of very good or very bad events increases substantially. Given that market participants and risk managers focus on tail measures of credit risk such as value at risk, correlation is of crucial importance. In addition, the constant development of derivative products that are priced and hedged depending on the joint default or survival behavior of portfolios, such as collateral debt obligation (CDOs), baskets, etc., has lead to a specific emphasis on dependence modeling.

Dependency is a more general concept than linear correlation over a predefined time period. For most marginal distributions, linear correlation is only part of the dependence structure and is insufficient to construct the joint distribution of losses. In addition, it is possible to construct a large set of different joint distributions from identical marginal distributions.

In structured credit markets, default correlation has given way to a more flexible approach in the form of the "time-to-default" survival correlation introduced by Li (2000). In addition, the need to account better for extreme joint events or comovements has led to focus on more customized dependence structures called copulas.

The copula approach is not really dynamic, in the sense that, for instance, there are no stochastic processes for the intensities or for the copulas. In this respect, the need for a more dynamic analysis has re-ignited the emphasis on joint intensity modeling.

Dependency includes effects more complex than correlation, such as the comovement of two variables with a time lag, or causality effects. Some recent research tries to express dependency as the consequence of a contagion of infectious events.

Sources of Dependencies

In this chapter, we will focus primarily on *measuring* default and spread dependencies rather than on *explaining* them. Before doing so, it is worth spending a little time on the sources of joint defaults and of joint price movements.

Defaults occur for three main types of reasons:

+ Firm-specific reasons: bad management, fraud, large project failure, etc.
+ Industry specific reasons: entire sectors sometimes get hit by shocks such as overcapacity, a rise in the prices of raw materials, etc.
+ General macroeconomic conditions: growth and recession, interest rate changes, and commodity prices affect all firms with various degrees.

Firm-specific causes do not lead to correlated defaults. Defaults triggered by these idiosyncratic factors tend to occur independently. On the contrary,

FIGURE 4.2

US GDP Growth and Aggregate Default Rates.
(Source: S&P and Federal Reserve Board)

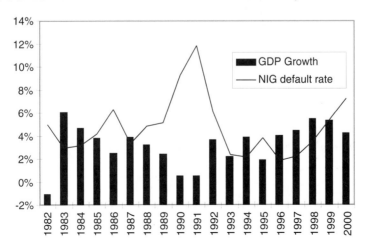

macroeconomic and sector specific shocks lead to increases in the default rates of entire segments of the economy and push up correlations.

Figure 4.2 depicts the link between macroeconomic growth (measured by the growth in gross domestic product) and the default rate of noninvestment grade (NIG) issuers. The default rate appears to be almost a mirror image of the growth rate. This implies that defaults tend to be correlated as they depend on a common factor.

Figure 4.3 shows the impact of a sector crisis on default rates in the energy and telecom sectors. The surge in oil prices in the mid-1980s and the telecom debacle starting in 2000 are clearly visible.

Prices, i.e., credit spreads, can move simultaneously for at least as many reasons:

♦ Default information that triggers prices on the basis of industry, macroeconomic, or idiosyncratic changes
♦ Common changes in the risk aversion of market participants due to changing economic conditions, such as the downgrade in May 2005 of General Motors (GM) and Ford (see Figure 4.4*).

FIGURE 4.3

Default Rates in Telecom and Energy Sectors. *(Source: S&P CreditPro)*

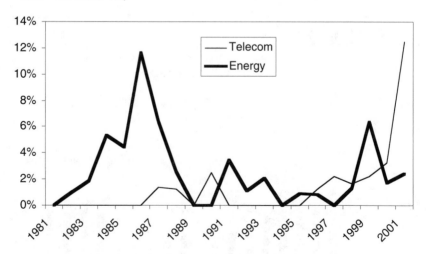

---

*In Figure 4.4, we show the impact of the downgrade of Ford and GM on the CDO prices. As a consequence, indicators such as spread and correlation level exhibit large movements during the period.

FIGURE 4.4

The Contagion Effect of General Motors and Ford Downgrades. *(Source: Citigroup 2005)*

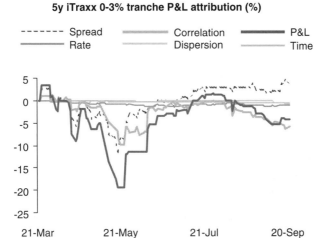

5y iTraxx 0-3% tranche P&L attribution (%)

The first part of this chapter (Part 1) reviews useful statistical concepts. We start by introducing the most popular measures of dependence (covariance and correlation) and show how to compute the variance of a portfolio from individual risks.

We then illustrate on several examples that correlation is only a partial and sometimes misleading measure of the comovement or dependence of random variables. We review various other partial measures. We continue and introduce default factor correlation and survival factor correlation and copulas, which describe more accurately multivariate distributions. We finally describe intensity-based correlation.

These statistical preliminaries are useful for the understanding of following part (Part 2), which deals with credit-specific applications of these dependence measures. Various methodologies have been proposed to estimate default correlation. These can be extracted directly from default data or derived from equity or spread information.

PART 1: CORRELATION METHODOLOGY

Correlation and Other Dependence Measures

Definitions

The covariance between two random variables X and Y is defined as:

$$\text{cov}(X, Y) = E(XY) - E(X)E(Y), \tag{1}$$

where $E(\cdot)$ denotes the expectation.

It measures how two random variables move together. The covariance satisfies several useful properties, including:

- $\text{cov}(X, X) = \text{var}(X)$, where $\text{var}(X)$ is the variance
- $\text{cov}(aX, bY) = ab\,\text{cov}(X, Y)$
- In the case X and Y are independent, $E(XY) = E(X)E(Y)$, and the covariance is 0.

The linear correlation coefficient, also called the Pearson's correlation measure, conveys the same information about the comovement of X and Y but is scaled to lie between -1 and $+1$. It is defined as the ratio of their covariance to the product of their standard deviations:

$$\text{corr}(X, Y) = \rho_{XY} = \frac{\text{cov}(X, Y)}{\text{std}(X)\,\text{std}(X)} \tag{2}$$

$$= \frac{E(XY) - E(X)E(Y)}{\sqrt{\left(E(X^2) - [E(X)]^2\right)\left(E(Y^2) - [E(Y)]^2\right)}} \tag{3}$$

In the particular case of two binary $(0, 1)$ variables A and B, taking value 1 with probability p_A and p_B, respectively, and 0 otherwise and given joint probability p_{AB}, we can calculate:

$$E(A) = E(A^2) = p_A, \quad E(B) = E(B^2) = p_B, \quad \text{and} \quad E(AB) = p_{AB}.$$

The correlation is therefore:

$$\text{corr}(A, B) = \frac{p_{AB} - p_A p_B}{\sqrt{p_A(1 - p_A)p_B(1 - p_B)}}. \tag{4}$$

This formula will be particularly useful for default correlation, as defaults are binary events. In Part 2, we will explain how to estimate the various terms in Equation (4).

Calculating Diversification Effect in a Portfolio

Two Asset Case   Let us first consider a simple case of a portfolio with two assets X and Y with proportions w and $1-w$, respectively. Their variance and covariance are σ_X^2, σ_Y^2, and σ_{XY}.

The variance of the portfolio is given by

$$\sigma_P^2 = w^2\sigma_X^2 + (1-w)^2\,\sigma_Y^2 + 2w(1-w)\sigma_{XY}. \tag{5}$$

The minimum variance of the portfolio can be obtained by differentiating Equation (5) and setting the derivative equal to 0:

$$\frac{\partial\sigma_P^2}{\partial w} = 0 = 2w\sigma_X^2 - 2\sigma_Y + 2w\sigma_Y^2 + 2(1-2w)\sigma_{XY} \tag{6}$$

The optimal allocation w^* is the solution to Equation (6):

$$w^* = \frac{\sigma_Y^2 - \rho_{XY}\sigma_X\sigma_Y}{\sigma_X^2 + \sigma_Y^2 - 2\rho_{XY}\sigma_X\sigma_Y}. \tag{7}$$

We thus find the optimal allocation in both assets that minimizes the total variance of the portfolio. We can immediately see that the optimal allocation depends on the correlation between the two assets and that the resulting variance is also affected by the correlation. Figures 4.5 and 4.6 illustrate how the optimal allocation and resulting minimum portfolio variance change as a function of correlation. In this example, $\sigma_X = 0.25$ and $\sigma_Y = 0.15$.

In Figure 4.5, we can see that the allocation of the portfolio between X and Y is highly nonlinear in the correlation. If the two assets are highly positively correlated, it becomes optimal to sell short the asset with highest variance (X in our example), hence W^* is negative. If the correlation is "perfect" between X and Y, that is, if $\rho=1$ or $\rho=-1$, it is possible to create a risk-less portfolio (Figure 4.6). Otherwise, the optimal allocation w^* will lead to a low but positive variance.

Figure 4.7 shows the impact of correlation on the joint density of X and Y, assuming that they are standard-normally distributed. It is a snapshot of the bell-shaped density seen in this figure. In the case where the correlation is zero (left-hand side), the joint density looks like concentric circles. When nonzero correlation is introduced (positive in this example), the shape becomes elliptical: it shows that high (low) values of X tend to be associated with high (low) values of Y. Thus there is more probability in the top-right

FIGURE 4.5

Optimal Allocation as a Function of Correlation.

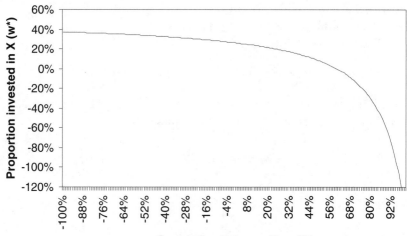

FIGURE 4.6

Minimum Portfolio Variance as a Function
of Correlation.

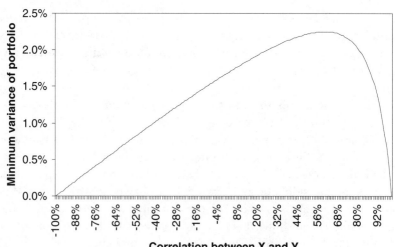

FIGURE 4.7

The Impact of Correlation on the Shape of the Distribution.

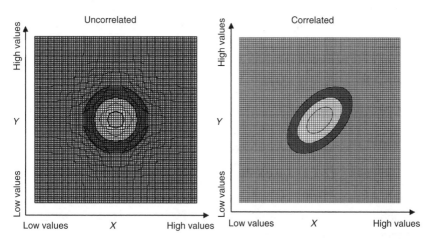

and bottom-left regions than in the top-left and bottom-right areas. The reverse would have been observed in the case of negative correlation.

Multiple Assets   We can now apply the properties of covariance to calculate the variance of a portfolio with multiple assets. Assume that we have a portfolio of n instruments with identical variance σ^2 and covariance $\sigma_{i,j}$ for $i, j = 1, \ldots, n$.

The variance of the portfolio is given by:

$$\sigma_P^2 = \sum_{i=1}^{n} x_i^2 \sigma^2 + \sum_{i=1}^{n} \sum_{\substack{j=1 \\ j \neq 1}}^{n} x_i x_j \sigma_{i,j}, \tag{8}$$

where X_i is the weight of asset i in the portfolio.

Assuming that the portfolio is equally weighted: $X_i = 1/n$, for all i, and that the variance of all assets is bounded, the variance of the portfolio reduces to:

$$\sigma_P^2 = \frac{\sigma^2}{n} + \frac{n(n-1)}{n^2} \overline{\text{cov}} \tag{9}$$

where the last term is the average covariance between assets.

When the portfolio becomes more and more diversified, i.e., when $n \to \infty$, we have $\sigma_P^2 \to \overline{\text{cov}}$. The variance of the portfolio converges to the average covariance between assets. The variance term becomes negligible compared to the joint variation.

For a portfolio of stocks, diversification benefits are obtained fairly quickly: for a correlation of 30 percent between all stocks and a volatility of 30 percent, one is within 10 percent of the minimum covariance with n around 20. For a pure default model (i.e., when we ignore spread and transition risk and assume 0 recovery) the number of assets necessary to reach the same level of diversification is much larger. For example, if the probability of default and the pair-wise correlations for all obligors are 2 percent, one needs around 450 counterparts to reach a variance that is within 10 percent of its asymptotic minimum.

Deficiencies of Correlation

As mentioned earlier, correlation is by far the most used measure of dependence in financial markets, and it is common to talk about correlation as a generic term for comovement. We will use it a lot in Section 3 of this chapter and in the following chapter on CDO pricing. In this section, we want to review some properties of the linear correlation that make it insufficient as a measure of dependence in general, and misleading in some cases. This is best explained through examples.*

- Using Equation (2), we see immediately that correlation is not defined if one of the variances is infinite. This is not a very frequent occurrence in credit risk models, but some market risk models exhibit this property in some cases.

  Example: see the large financial literature on α-stable models since Mandelbrot (1963), where the finiteness of the variance depends on the value of the α parameter.

- When specifying a model, one cannot choose correlation arbitrarily over [−1; 1] as a degree of freedom. Depending on the choice of distribution, the correlation may be bounded in a narrower range $\left[\underline{\rho}; \overline{\rho}\right]$, with $-1 < \underline{\rho} < \overline{\rho} < 1$.

  Example: if we have two normal random variable x and y, both with mean 0 and with standard deviation 1 and σ, respectively. Then $X = \exp(x)$ and $Y = \exp(y)$ are lognormally distributed. However, not all correlations between X and Y are attainable.

---

*Embrecht et al. (1999a,b) give a very clear analysis of the limitations of correlations.

One can show that their correlation is restricted to lie between:

$$\underline{\rho} = \frac{e^{-\sigma}-1}{\sqrt{(e-1)(e^{\sigma^2}-1)}} \quad \text{and} \quad \overline{\rho} = \frac{e^{\sigma}-1}{\sqrt{(e-1)(e^{\sigma^2}-1)}}.$$

See Embrecht et al. (1999a) for a proof.

♦ Two perfectly functionally dependent random variables can have zero correlation.

  Example: Consider a normally distributed random variable X with mean 0 and define $Y = X^2$. Although changes in X completely determine changes in Y, they have zero correlation. This clearly shows that while independence implies zero correlation, the reverse is not true!

♦ Linear correlation is not invariant under monotonic transformations.

  Example: (X, Y) and $(\exp(X), \exp(Y))$ do not have the same correlation.

♦ Many bivariate distributions share the same marginal distributions and the same correlation but are not identical.

  Example: See section on copulas.

All these considerations should make clear that correlation is a partial and insufficient measure of dependence in the general case. It only measures linear dependence. This does not mean that correlation is useless. For the class of elliptical distributions, correlation is sufficient to combine the marginals into the bivariate distribution. For example, given two normal marginal distributions for X and Y and a correlation coefficient ρ, one can build a joint normal distribution for (X, Y).

Loosely speaking, this class of distribution is called elliptical because when we project the multivariate density on a plane, we find elliptical shapes (see Figure 4.6). The normal and the t-distribution, among others, are part of this class.

Even for other nonelliptical distributions, covariances (and therefore correlations) are second moments that need to be calibrated. While they are insufficient to incorporate all dependence, they should not be neglected when empirically fitting a distribution.

Other Dependence Measures: Rank Correlations

Many other measures have been proposed to tackle the problems of linear correlations mentioned earlier. We only mention two here, but there are countless examples:

Spearman's Rho   This is simply the linear correlation but applied to the ranks of the variables rather than on the variables themselves.

Kendall's Tau   Assume we have n observations for each of two random variables, i.e., (X_i, Y_i), $i=1, \ldots, n$.

We start by counting the number of pairs of bivariate observations whose components are concordant, i.e., pairs for which the two elements are either both larger or both lower than the elements of another pair. Call that number N_c.

Then Kendall's Tau is calculated as:

$$\tau_K = \frac{(N_c - N_D)}{(N_c + N_D)},$$

where N_D is the number of discordant (nonconcordant) pairs.

Kendall's Tau shares some properties with the linear correlation: $\tau_K \in [-1, 1]$ and $\tau_K(X, Y) = 0$ for X, Y independent. However, it has some distinguishing features that make it more appropriate than the linear correlation in some cases. If X and Y are comonotonic,* then $\tau_K(X, Y) = 1$; whereas if they are counter-monotonic, $\tau_K(X, Y) = -1$. τ_K is also invariant under strictly monotonic transformations. To return to our earlier example, $\tau_K(X, Y) = \tau_K(\exp(X), \exp(Y))$.

An interesting feature of Kendall's tau is that it gives the opportunity to analyze comovement in a dynamic way (see Figure 4.8).

In the case of the normal distribution,[†] the linear and rank correlations can be linked analytically:

$$\tau_K(X, Y) = \frac{2}{\pi} \arcsin(\rho(X, Y)). \tag{10}$$

These dependence measures have nice properties but tend to be less used by finance practitioners. Again, they are insufficient to obtain the entire bivariate distribution from the marginals. We are now going to focus on a very important class of models that accounts for correlation: factor models.

Factor Models of Credit Risk

This approach underlies portfolio models based on a structural approach of the firm. It is used in commercial portfolio credit risk models such as those offered to the market by Risk Metrics, MKMV, and Standard &

---

*X and Y are comonotonic if we can write $Y = G(X)$ with $G(\cdot)$ an increasing function. They are countermonotonic if $G(\cdot)$ is a decreasing function.
[†]More generally, this result holds for elliptical distributions.

FIGURE 4.8

Comparing Defaults and Equity Default Swap Events
in the Compustat U.S. Universe.

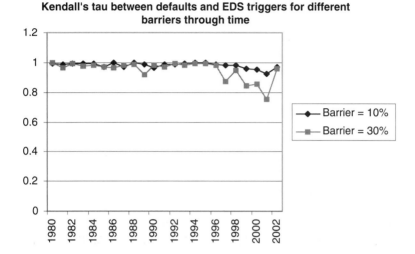

Kendall's tau between defaults and EDS triggers for different
barriers through time

Poor's (S&P) Risk Solutions. The main advantage of this setup is that it
reduces the dimensionality of the dependence problem for large portfolios.

In a factor model, a latent variable drives the default process: when
the value A of the latent variable is sufficiently low (below a threshold K),
default is triggered. It is customary to use the term "asset return" instead
of "latent variable," as it relates to the familiar Merton-type models where
default arises when the value of the firm falls below the value of liabilities.

Asset returns for various obligors are assumed to be functions of
common state variables (the systematic factors, typically industry and
country factors) and of an idiosyncratic term ε_i that is specific to each firm
i and uncorrelated with the common factors. The systematic and idiosyncratic factors are usually assumed to be normally distributed and are
scaled to have unit variance and zero mean. Therefore, the asset returns
are also standard normally distributed. In the case of a one-factor model
with systematic factor denoted as C, asset returns at a chosen horizon (say
one year), for obligors i and j, can be written as:

$$A_i = \rho_i C + \sqrt{1 - \rho_i^2}\, \varepsilon_i,$$ (11)

$$A_j = \rho_j C + \sqrt{1 - \rho_j^2}\, \varepsilon_j$$ (12)

such that:

$$\rho_{i,j} \equiv \mathrm{corr}(A_i, A_j) = \rho_i \, \rho_j. \tag{13}$$

In order to calculate default correlation using Equation (4), we need to obtain the formulas for individual and joint default probabilities at the one-year horizon. Given the assumption about the distribution of asset returns, we have immediately:

$$p_i^D = P(A_i \le K_i)$$
$$= N(K_i), \tag{14a}$$

and

$$p_j^D = P(A_j \le K_j)$$
$$= N(K_j), \tag{14b}$$

where $N(\cdot)$ is the cumulative standard normal distribution. Conversely, the default thresholds can be determined from the probabilities of default by inverting the Gaussian distribution: $K = N^{-1}(p)$.

Figure 4.9 illustrates the asset return distribution and the default zone (area where $A \le K$). The probability of default corresponds to the area below the density curve from $-\infty$ to K.

FIGURE 4.9

The Asset Return Setup.

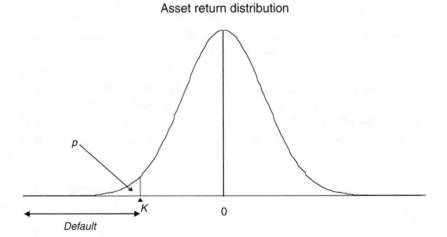

Asset return distribution

FIGURE 4.10

The Relationship Between Default Correlation
and Asset Correlation.

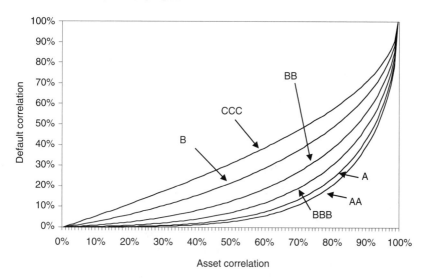

Assuming further that asset returns for obligors i and j are bivariate normally distributed,* the joint probability of default is obtained
using:

$$p_{i,j}^{D,D} = N_2(K_i, K_j, \rho_{ij}). \tag{15}$$

Equations (14) and (15) provide all the necessary building blocks to calculate default correlation in a factor model of credit risk.

Figure 4.10 illustrates the relationship between asset correlation and
default correlation for various levels of default probabilities, using
Equations (15) and (4). The lines are calibrated such that they reflect the
one-year probabilities of default of firms within all rating categories.[†]

It is very clear from the picture that as default probability increases,
default correlation also increases for a given level of *asset* correlation.

It is now possible to compute the full loss distribution of a portfolio.

Correlation between obligors stems from the realization of the latent

---

*From the section on copulas we know that we could choose other bivariate distributions
while keeping Gaussian marginals.
[†]The AAA curve cannot be computed as there has never been a AAA default within a year.

variable. It impacts asset values and therefore default probabilities. Conditional on a specific realization of the factor $C=c$, the probability of default of obligor i is:

$$P_i(c) = P_i(A_i < K_i \mid C = c) = N\left(\frac{K_i - \rho_i c}{\sqrt{1 - \rho_i^2}}\right). \tag{16}$$

Furthermore, conditional on c, defaults become independent Bernouilli events. This leads to simple computations of portfolio loss probabilities.

Assume that we have a portfolio of H obligors with same probability of default and same factor loading ρ. Out of these obligors, we may observe $X=0, 1, 2$ or up to H defaults before the horizon T. Using the law of iterated expectations, the probability of observing exactly h defaults can be written as the expectation of the conditional probability:

$$P[X = h] = \int_{-\infty}^{+\infty} P[X = h \mid C = c]\phi(c)\,dc, \tag{17}$$

where $\phi(\cdot)$ is the standard normal density.

Given that defaults are conditionally independent, the probability of observing h defaults conditional on a realization of the systematic factor will be binomial such that:

$$P[X = h \mid C = c] = \binom{H}{h}(p(c)^h(1 - p(c))^{H-h}). \tag{18}$$

Using Equations (17) and (18), we then obtain the cumulative probability of observing less than m defaults:

$$P[X \le m] = \sum_{h=0}^{m} \binom{H}{h} \int_{-\infty}^{+\infty} \left(N\left(\frac{K - \rho c}{\sqrt{1 - \rho^2}}\right)\right)^h \left(1 - N\left(\frac{K - \rho c}{\sqrt{1 - \rho^2}}\right)\right)^{H-h} \phi(c)\,dc \tag{19}$$

Figure 4.11 shows a plot of $P[X=h]$ for various assumptions of factor correlation from $\rho=0$ percent to $\rho=10$ percent. The probability of default is assumed to be 5 percent for all $H=100$ obligors.

The mean number of defaults is 5 for all three scenarios but the shape of the distribution is very different. For $\rho=0$ percent, we observe a roughly bell-shaped curve centered on 5. When correlation increases, the likelihood of joint bad events increase, implying a fat right-hand tail. The

FIGURE 4.11

Impact of Correlation on Portfolio Loss Distribution.

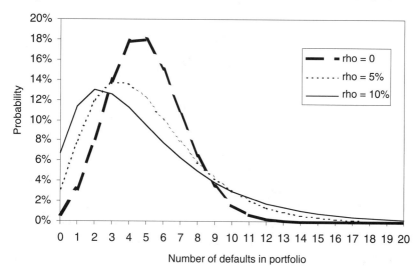

Number of defaults in portfolio

likelihood of joint good events (few or zero defaults) also increases and there is a much larger chance of 0 defaults.

The main drawbacks associated with this approach are that:

◆ It tells if default happens before the predefined time horizon, without specifying when.

◆ It can underestimate "tail dependence," given the assumption of normal asset returns.

From a Default Factor Model to A Survival Factor Model

This approach, usually called the "Gaussian copula" default time approach, has been introduced in Li (2000). It has become a market standard for the pricing of CDOs and baskets of credit derivatives. The key innovation is to question the fixed predefined time horizon described in the previous section and to define the correlation between two entities as the correlation between their survival times.

Let us define $S_i(t)$ the cumulative survival time function for obligor i, where τ_i is the time-until-default.

$$S_i(t) = P(\tau_i > t)$$

The related cumulative default probability for obligor i is expressed as:

$$F_i(t) = P(\tau_i \le t)$$
$$= 1 - S_i(t)$$

For two obligors i and j, with respective survival times T_i and T_j, we then define a survival time correlation:

$$\rho_{i,j} = \frac{\text{cov}(T_i, T_j)}{\sqrt{\text{var}(T_i)\,\text{var}(T_j)}} \tag{20}$$

The objective in this section is to obtain the cumulative survival distribution for a set of obligors included in an instrument such as a CDO, taking into account their correlated survival times. As in the previous section in Equation (11), we consider a factor model where the asset return of obligor i is defined both by a systematic risk factor and an idiosyncratic one.

The next step is to compute credit curves, i.e., the evolution of the probability of default or of survival of an obligor with time. We revert readers to the Chapters 2 and 3 on "Univariate Risk and Univariate Pricing" and give here a simplified view.

We first start with a simple stylized approach, using credit ratings.* In this case instead of computing a specific default curve for each obligor, we define standard ones per credit rating category. For a detailed methodology description of the estimation of cumulative rating curves (Figure 4.12), see Chapter 2.

Another way is to rely on market observable data as described in Chapter 3 [asset swap spreads, credit default swap (CDS) spreads, etc.]. The methodology corresponds, for instance, to defining a credit event as characterized by the first event of a Poisson process occurring at time t, with τ being the default time and h the hazard rate:

$$\Pr[\tau \le t + dt \mid \tau > t] = h(t)dt \tag{21}$$

We can then write and calibrate the survival probability over $[0, t]$ as

$$S(t) = \exp\left(-\int_0^t h(u)\,du\right) = \exp\left(-\sum_{t=1}^{n} h_i(t_i - t_{i-1})\right) \tag{22}$$

---

*It is also possible to obtain default curves using the Merton (1974) model and its extensions.

FIGURE 4.12

Cumulative Default Probabilities (AAA to B)
1981–2003. (Source: S&P's)

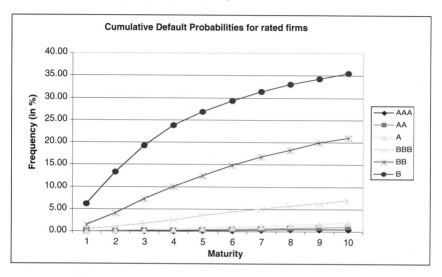

assuming that h is constant piecewise per interval (t_{i-1}, t_i). In fact, modeling the default or the survival curve properly is a source of competitive advantage for market participants.

By considering here a constant intensity of the hazard rate h over the life of the instrument, we can even simplify the equation to:

$$S(t) = e^{-ht} \qquad (23)$$

In the two instances, i.e., for a given rating or for a given obligor, there exists a unique link between the survival probability or the probability of default and a corresponding time. We can therefore obtain the default time τ for each obligor, depending on any selected random variable u on the default curve.

$$\tau = -\frac{\log(u)}{h} \qquad (24)$$

Survival probabilities can now be aggregated using the normal multivariate distribution also called "Gaussian copula" setup:

Based on an adjustment of Equation (16), using the copula mapping $F_i(t) = N(K_i)$ that is performed on a "percentile per percentile" basis,* any marginal conditional probability of survival $u_i = (S(\tau_i|C) = P(t < \tau_i|C)$ can be written as:

$$P(t < \tau_i|C) = N\left(\frac{\rho_i C - N^{-1}(F_i(t))}{\sqrt{1 - \rho_i^2}}\right) \tag{25}$$

Because of conditional independence, the joint conditional survival probability can be written as:

$$S(t_1, \ldots, t_n|C) = \prod_{i=1}^{n} S_i(t_i|C) \tag{26}$$

The joint unconditional survival probability can ultimately be expressed as:

$$S(t_1, \ldots, t_n) = \int_{-\infty}^{+\infty} S(t_1, \ldots, t_n|c)\frac{e^{-c^2/2}}{\sqrt{2\pi}}\,dc \tag{27}$$

The empirical mechanism to generate correlated survival default times from Excel is articulated here and summarized in Figure 4.13. We consider a portfolio of i obligors. Let us first consider **A** an $i \times j$ matrix of i uncorrelated uniform random variables of size j.

+ *Step* 1: Draw i random variables from a uniform [0, 1] distribution to obtain **A**.
+ *Step* 2: Invert the cumulative standard normal distribution function to obtain a new matrix **B** of i uncorrelated random variables from $N(0, 1)$.
+ *Step* 3: Impose the correlation structure by multiplying matrix B by the Cholesky decomposition of the covariance matrix. The new matrix **C** contains i correlated random variables from $N(0, 1)$.
+ *Step* 4: Use the cumulative standard normal distribution to obtain the new matrix of uniform random variables.
+ *Step* 5: From the default/survival curve, infer for each obligor i the series of j conditional survival times.

---

*This means that the closer the realization of the latent variable A_i is from the default threshold K_j, the sooner the default is going to occur.

FIGURE 4.13

Obtaining Univariate Survival Times from Realizations
of the Latent Variable at a Given Horizon.

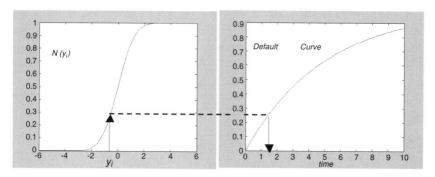

A More Advanced Multivariate Distribution: The Copula

A copula is a function that combines univariate density functions into
their joint distribution. We can in fact either extract copulas from multivariate distributions or create a new multivariate distribution by combining the marginal distributions with a selected copula. The interest with
copulas is that the marginal distributions and the dependence structure
can be modeled separately. An in-depth analysis of copulas can be found
in Nelsen (1999).

Applications of copulas to risk management and the pricing of
derivatives have soared over the past few years. An interesting feature of
copulas is the Sklar's theorem.

Definition and Sklar's Theorem   *Definition*: A copula with dimension
n is an n-dimensional probability distribution function defined on $[0, 1]^n$
that has uniform marginal distributions U_i.

$$C(u_1, \ldots, u_n) = P[U_1 \le u_1, U_2 \le u_2, \ldots, U_n \le u_n] \qquad (28a)$$

One of the most important and useful results about copulas is known as
Sklar's theorem (Sklar, 1959). It states that any group of random variables
can be joined into their multivariate distribution using a copula. More
formally:

FIGURE 4.14

The Marginal Distribution Function F_i,

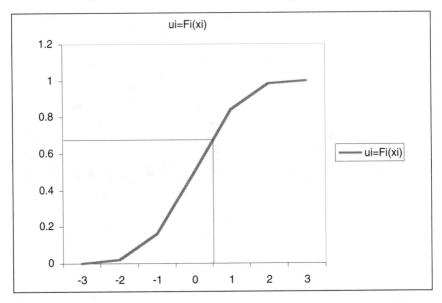

If X_i, $i=1, \ldots, n$ are random variables with respective marginal distributions F_i, $i=1, \ldots, n$, and multivariate probability distribution function F, then there exists an n-dimensional copula of F such that:

$$F(X_1, \ldots, X_n) = C(F_1(X_1), \ldots, F_n(X_n)) \quad \text{for all } (X_1, \ldots, X_n) \qquad (28b)$$

and

$$C(u_1, \ldots, u_n) = F(F_1^{-1}(u_1), \ldots, F_n^{-1}(u_n)). \qquad (28c)$$

With the pseudo-inverse F^{-1} defined as (see Figure 4.14):

$$x = F^{-1}(u) = \sup\{x / F(x) \le u\}$$

Furthermore, if the marginal distributions are continuous, then the copula function is unique.

Looking at Equation (28c), we clearly see how to obtain the joint distribution from the data. The first step is to fit the marginal distributions F_i, $i=1, \ldots, n$, individually on the data (realizations of X_i, $i=1, \ldots, n$). This yields a set of uniformly distributed random variables $u_1 = F_1(x_1), \ldots,$ $u_n = F_n(u_n)$.

FIGURE 4.15

The Shape of a Bivariate Frank Copula.

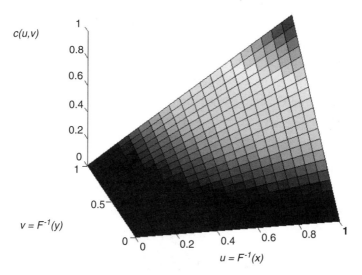

The second step is to find the copula function that appropriately describes the joint behavior of the random variables. There is a plethora of possible choices that make the use of copulas sometimes unpractical. Their main appeal is that they allow us to separate the calibration of the marginal distributions from that of the joint law. Figure 4.15 is a graph of a bivariate Frank copula (see next paragraph for an explanation).

Properties of The Copula: Copulas satisfy a series of properties including the four listed herewith. The first one states that for independent random variables, the copula is just the product of the marginal distributions. The second property is that of invariance under monotonic transformations.* The third property provides bounds on the values of the copula: these bounds correspond to the values the copula would take if the random variables were countermonotonic (lower bound) or comonotonic (upper bound). Finally, the fourth one states that a convex combination of two copulas is also a copula.

---

*This property is important to account for nonlinear dependencies and different time horizons. In particular, it is the reason why one-year correlation matrices can be used to derive multiple year portfolio loss distribution.

Using similar notations as earlier where X and Y denote random variables and u and v stand for the uniformly distributed margins of the copula, we have:

1. If X and Y are independent, then $C(u, v) = uv$.
2. Copulas are invariant under increasing and continuous transformations of marginals.
3. For any copula C, we have $\max(u+v-1, 0) \leq C(u, v) \leq \min(u, v)$.
4. If C_1 and C_2 are copulas, then $C = \alpha C_1 + (1-\alpha)C_2$ for $0 < \alpha < 1$ is also a copula.

Survival Copulas   As we have seen in the previous section, the CDO world focuses on joint survival times.

We can define $S_i(t)$ the cumulative survival time function for obligor i, where τ_i is the time until default.

$$S_i(t) = P(\tau_i > t)$$

The related cumulative default probability for obligor i is expressed as:

$$F_i(t) = P(\tau_i \leq t)$$
$$= 1 - S_i(t)$$

Let us now consider two obligors i and j. We call C as the copula that links τ_i and τ_j. The joint survival function can be written as $S(t_i, t_j) = P(\tau_i > t_i, \tau_j > t_j)$ and $S(t_i, t_j) = \tilde{C}(S_i(t_i), S_j(t_j)) = S_i(t_i) + S_j(t_j) - 1 + C(1 - S_i(t_i), 1 - S_j(t_j))$, where $\tilde{C}$ is called the survival copula of τ_i and τ_j.

We now briefly review three important classes of copulas which are most frequently used in risk management applications: Elliptical (Gaussian and Student-t) copulas, Archimedean copulas, and Marshall-Olkin copulas.

Important Classes of Copulas   There exists a wide variety of possible copulas. Many but not all are listed in Nelsen (1999). In what follows, we introduce briefly elliptical, Archimedean, and Marshall-Olkin copulas. Among elliptical copulas, Gaussian copulas are now commonly used to generate dependent random vectors in applications requiring Monte-Carlo simulations (see Bouyé et al., 1999, or Wang, 2000). The Archimedean family is convenient as it is parsimonious and has a simple additive structure. Applications of Archimedean copulas to risk management can be found in Das and Geng (2002) or Schönburcher (2002), among many others. The Marshall-Olkin copula has recently be used in the CDO world as an alternative way to compensate for the weaknesses of the Gaussian copula.

Elliptical Copulas: Gaussian and t-Copulas

The Gaussian Copula   As recalled earlier, copulas are multivariate distribution functions. Obviously, the Gaussian copula will be a multivariate Gaussian (normal) distribution.

Using the notations of Equation (28b), we can write C_Σ^{Gau}, the n-dimensional Gaussian copula with covariance matrix Σ*:

$$C_\Sigma^{Gau}(u_1, \ldots, u_n) = N_\Sigma^n (N^{-1}(u_1), \ldots, N^{-1}(u_n)), \qquad (29)$$

with N_Σ^n and N^{-1} denoting, respectively, the n-dimensional cumulative Gaussian distribution with covariance matrix, Σ and the inverse of the cumulative univariate standard normal distribution.

In the bivariate case, assuming that the correlation between the two random variables is ρ, Equation (29) boils down to:

$$C_\rho^{Gau}(u,v) = N_\rho^2(N^{-1}(u), N^{-1}(v))$$

$$= \frac{1}{2\pi(1-\rho^2)} \int_{-\infty}^{N^{-1}(u)} \int_{-\infty}^{N^{-1}(v)} \exp\left(-\frac{g^2 - 2\rho gh + h^2}{2(1-\rho^2)} \right) dg\, dh \quad (30)$$

The t-Copula   The t-copula (bivariate t-distribution) with v degrees of freedom is obtained in a similar way. Using evident notations, we have:

$$C_{\rho,v}^t(u,v) = t_{\rho,v}^2(t_v^{-1}(u), t_v^{-1}(v)), \qquad (31)$$

The bivariate t-copula can be defined as an independent mixture of a multivariate normal distribution N_Σ^2 and of scalar random $S = \sqrt{\dfrac{v}{W}}$, variable where W follows a chi-squared distribution with v degrees of freedom, with $\rho_{ij} = \sigma_{ij}/\sqrt{\sigma_{ii} * \sigma_{jj}}$ and $\Sigma = \lfloor \sigma_{ij} \rfloor$. Its usage for credit modeling purposes has been suggested by different authors such as Frey et al. (2001). t-Copulas generate "tail dependence," i.e., more extreme events than the Gaussian copulas.

---

*Also the correlation matrix in this case.

More recently, Hull and White (2004) have referred to double t copulas for the pricing of CDOs. In this case, the marginal probability distributions are not derived from a latent variable following a Student-t distribution but following a convolution of two Student-t distributions. This convolution is not a Student-t distribution itself and the copula is not a Student-t copula either.

Archimedean Copulas The family of Archimedean copulas is the class of multivariate distributions on $[0,1]^n$ that can be written as

$$C^{\text{Arch}}(u_1, \ldots, u_n) = G^{-1}(G(u_1) + \cdots + G(u_n)), \tag{32}$$

where G is a suitable continuous monotonic function from $[0, 1]$ to $\mathbb{R}^+$ satisfying $G(1) = 0$. $G(\cdot)$ is called the generator of the copula.

Three examples of Archimedean copulas used in the finance literature are the Gumbel, the Frank, and the Clayton copulas, for which we provide the functional form now. They can easily be built by specifying their generator (see Marshall and Olkin, 1988, or Nelsen, 1999).

♦ *Example 1: The Gumbel copula* (multivariate exponential)

The generator for the Gumbel copula is:

$$G_G(t) = (-\ln t)^\theta \tag{33}$$

with inverse: $G_G^{[-1]}(s) = \exp(-s^{1/\theta})$ and $\theta \geq 1$.
Therefore using Equation (29), the copula function in the bivariate case is:

$$C_G^\theta(u,v) = \exp\left(-\left[(-\ln u)^\theta + (-\ln v)^\theta\right]^{1/\theta}\right). \tag{34}$$

♦ *Example 2: The Frank copula*

The generator is:

$$G_F(t) = -\ln\left(\frac{e^{-\theta t} - 1}{e^{-\theta} - 1}\right), \tag{35}$$

with inverse $G_F^{[-1]}(s) = \frac{-1}{\theta} \ln[1 - e^s(1 - e^\theta)]$, and $\theta \neq 0$.
The bivariate copula function is therefore:

$$C_F^\theta(u,v) = \frac{-1}{\theta} \ln\left(1 + \frac{(e^{-\theta u} - 1)(e^{-\theta v} - 1)}{(e^{-\theta} - 1)}\right). \tag{36}$$

♦ *Example 3: The Clayton copula*
  The generator is:

$$G_C(t) = \frac{1}{\theta}(t^{-\theta} - 1),$$ (37)

with inverse: $G_C^{[-1]}(s) = (1 + \theta s)^{-1/\theta}$, and $\theta \geq 0$.
The bivariate copula function is therefore:

$$C_C^{\theta}(u, v) = \max([u^{-\theta} + v^{-\theta} - 1]^{-1/\theta}, 0).$$ (38)

Calculating a Joint Cumulative Probability Using an Archimedean Copula   Assume we want to calculate the joint cumulative probability of two random variables X and Y $P(X < x, Y < y)$. Both X and Y are standard-normally distributed. We are interested in looking at the joint probability depending on the choice of copula and on the parameter θ.

The first step is to calculate the margins of the copula distribution: $v = P(Y < y) = N(y)$ and $u = P(X < x) = N(x)$. For our numerical example, we assume $x = -0.1$ and $y = 0.3$. Hence $u = 0.460$ and $v = 0.618$.

The joint cumulative probability is then obtained by plugging these values into the chosen copula function [Equations (34), (36), and (38)]. Figure 4.16 illustrates how the joint probabilities change as a function of θ for the three Archimedean copulas presented earlier. The graph shows that different choices of copulas and theta parameters lead to very different results in terms of joint probability.

The Marshall-Olkin Copula   This type of copula has been promoted recently by several authors such as Elouerkhaoui (2003a,b) and Giesecke (2003). It can be useful to describe intensity-based models for correlated defaults in which unpredictable default arrival times are jointly exponentially distributed.

The bivariate survival copula is expressed as:

$$C_{MO}^{\theta_1, \theta_2}(u, v) = uv \min(u^{-\theta_1}, v^{-\theta_2})$$ (39)

where θ_1 and θ_2 are the controls for the degree of dependence between the default times of firms 1 and 2, respectively.

FIGURE 4.16

Examples of Joint Cumulative Probabilities Using Archimedean Copulas.

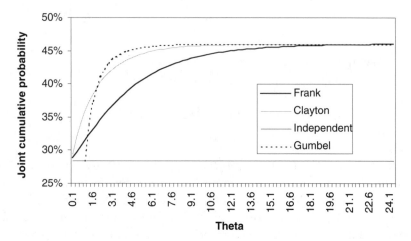

The "Functional Copula"   The definition of the "functional copula" is introduced by Hull and White (2005).

The "functional copula" approach is derived from the section "Factor Models of Credit Risk" described earlier.

The underlying idea is that in a factor model, what is simulated, is a distribution of adjusted probabilities of default [Equation (16)] conditional on the realization of the systematic factor c. Typically, because of an adverse realization of the common factor (e.g., a recession), the adjusted probability of default will be higher than the empirically estimated one. We can therefore consider that the distribution of the latent variable C corresponds to the description of the various static default environments until the horizon.

Moving from a default factor model to a survival factor model, and in the case of a constant hazard rate model, we can write the probability of default as:

$$F_i(t) = P(\tau_i \le t) = 1 - S_i(t) = 1 - e^{-ht} \qquad (40)$$

the conditional survival probability for obligor i being Equation (25), we can infer a conditional hazard rate, depending on the realization of the common factor C:

$$h_C = -\frac{1}{t} * \ln N\left(\frac{\rho_i C - N^{-1}(F_i(t))}{\sqrt{1 - \rho_i^2}} \right) \qquad (41)$$

The distribution of C, leads to a distribution of static pseudo-hazard rates h_C. These conditional hazard rates represent the range of possible expected hazard rates, depending on different realizations of the macroeconomic environment. Such conditional average hazard rates during the life of the instrument are not, however, currently observable.

Hull and White (2005) suggest that there is no reason to assume a normal distribution for the common factor C and the idiosyncratic term ε_i. Equation (41) can therefore be written in a more general way as:

$$h_C = -\frac{1}{t} * \ln H_i \left(\frac{\rho_i C - G_i^{-1}(F_i(t))}{\sqrt{1 - \rho_i^2}} \right) \tag{42}$$

where H_i is the cumulative probability distribution of ε_i and G_i the cumulative probability distribution of the latent variable A_i. In addition, of course, the conditional hazard rates can be considered as time-dependent.

The idea of the authors is in fact not to specify the parametric form for any variable, but to extract from empirical CDO pricing observations the empirical distribution of conditional hazard rates.

The empirical distribution can be inferred from a three-step process:

◆ *Step 1*: Assume a series of possible default rates at the horizon of the instrument and extract the corresponding pseudo-hazard rates.

◆ *Step 2*: Compute the cash inflows and outflows of the various market instruments (CDO tranches) for each pseudo-hazard rate extracted from step 1.

◆ *Step 3*: Write the unconditional expected value of the instruments as a linear combination of weighted step 2 conditional expected values. Estimate the weights by considering that the unconditional expected values of each instrument should be zero.

There is no single set of values, given the fact that there are usually more possible default rates than credit instruments, but results are stable when a regularization term is added in the optimization problem to maximize the smoothness of the distribution of conditional hazard rates.

Thanks to this approach, the fit with the observation is almost perfect at the time the distribution of pseudo-hazard rates is computed. This distribution is time-dependent and reflects the changes in the market expectation related to this multiple regime-switching pattern.

Copulas and Other Dependence Measures   Recall that we introduced earlier Spearman's Rho and Kendall's Tau as two alternatives to linear correlation. We mentioned that they could be expressed in terms of the copula. The formulas linking these dependence measures to the copula are:

- Spearman's rho:

$$\rho_S = 12 \int_0^1 \int_0^1 (C(u, v) - uv) \, du \, dv \tag{43}$$

- Kendall's tau:

$$\tau_K = 4 \int_0^1 \int_0^1 C(u, v) dC(u, v) - 1 \tag{44}$$

Thus, once the copula is defined analytically, one can immediately calculate rank correlations from it. Copulas also incorporate tail dependence. Intuitively, tail dependence will exist when there is a significant probability of joint extreme events. Lower (upper) tail dependence captures joint negative (positive) outliers.

If we consider two random variables X_1 and X_2 with respective marginal distributions F_1 and F_2, the coefficients of lower (LTD) and upper tail dependence (UTD) are*:

$$\text{UTD} = \lim_{z \to 1} \Pr\left[X_2 > F_2^{-1}(z) \big| X_1 > F_1^{-1}(z) \right] \tag{45}$$

and

$$\text{LTD} = \lim_{z \to 0} \Pr\left[X_2 < F_2^{-1}(z) \big| X_1 < F_1^{-1}(z) \right] \tag{46}$$

Figure 4.17 illustrates the asymptotic dependence of variables in the upper tail, using t-copulas. The tail dependence coefficient shown in the Figure 4.17 corresponds to UTD. As can be observed, Gaussian copulas exhibit no tail dependence.

Statistical Techniques Used to Select and Calibrate Copulas

In this section, we mainly focus on two sensitive issues related to the use of copulas: how to select the most appropriate copula and how to calibrate any selected copula.

In summary, copula estimation is still in its infancy, and so far there has not been any real way to define and estimate the "optimal parametric

---

*The UTD and the LTD depend only on the copula and not on the margins.

FIGURE 4.17

A Comparison of the Coefficient of Upper Tail
Dependence for the Gaussian and *t*-Copulas.

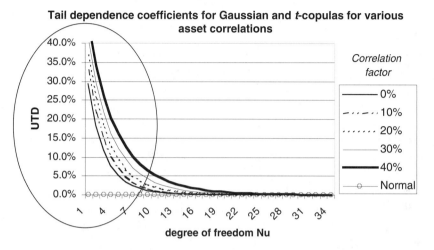

copula" from a multivariate set of observations. There are different reasons to account for such a situation:

♦ A copula summarizes in a stable way the dependencies between the margins. The existence of temporal dependencies in time series does not facilitate the identification of stable patterns. Longin and Solnik (2001), for instance, identify different dependencies during periods with large movements in returns and more stable periods.

♦ There is a large set of copula classes, with little evidence on how to select one class rather than another. A common market practice is to retain only those copulas that are widely spread or easily tractable (see earlier for a description).

♦ Once selected, a copula function is usually not easy to calibrate. Does a copula provide a good fit when it accounts for tail events or when it replicates reasonably well most joint observations?

The selection of an appropriate copula is usually dictated by the identification of some key features, such as:

♦ No asymptotic dependence (no fat tail) in the case of Gaussian copulas, except in the case of perfect correlation

+ Symmetric asymptotic dependence both for t-copulas and Frank copulas
+ Higher dependence in bear conditions when using Clayton copulas
+ Higher dependence in bull conditions with Gumbel copulas

Based on the selection of a class of copulas, we review how to calibrate and to measure subsequently the goodness-of-fit.

In terms of calibration, there is a first choice between parametric and nonparametric estimations.

We are presenting here the three most common parametric approaches: Full Maximum Likelihood (FML, a one-step parametric approach), Inference Functions for Margins (IFM, a two-step parametric approach) and Conditional Maximum Likelihood (CML, a two-step semiparametric approach). Fermanian and Scaillet (2004) show that there can be pitfalls attached to these different estimation techniques, either due to a misspecification of the margins or to a loss of efficiency when the margins do not require explicit specification.

We then introduce nonparametric estimation, based on the calculation of the "Empirical copula" defined in Deheuvels (1979).

Mapping the empirical copula to a well-known parametric one becomes a problem of goodness-of-fit in a multivariate environment. Classical statistical tests, such as the Kolmogorov-Smirnov, the Chi-square, or the Anderson-Darling tests, usually cannot be used in a straightforward manner.

There are mainly two types of approaches that are usually considered to obtain the best fit:

+ An approach based on a visual comparison, as suggested by Genest and Rivest (1993).
+ The selection of the copula that minimizes the distance with the empirical copula. Obviously, results will depend on the choice of such a distance. Scaillet (2000), Fermanian (2003), and Chen et al. (2004), among others, suggest the use of Kernels to smooth the empirical copula before fitting in order to obtain an explicit limiting law for the test statistic.

Full Maximum Likelihood Also Called Exact Maximum Likelihood

In this approach, the parameters of the copula and of the marginal distributions are estimated simultaneously. It is worth noting that both the univariate and multivariate distributions are assumed to correspond to some preselected parametric forms, hence the classification of FML in the parametric estimation category.

The density c of a copula C is defined as:

$$c(u_1, u_2, \ldots, u_n) = \frac{\partial C(u_1, u_2, \ldots, u_n)}{\partial u_1 \partial u_2 \cdots \partial u_n} = \frac{f(x_1, x_2, \ldots, x_n)}{\prod_1^n f_i(x_i)} \tag{47}$$

$$\text{and} \quad x_i = F_i^{-1}(u_i)$$

where f is the density of the joint distribution F and f_i the density of the margin F_i.

Let us define θ the vector of parameters to be estimated and $l_t(\theta)$ the log-likelihood for the n observations (x_i^t), with $i = 1$ to n, at time t. For the density function f, the canonical expression of the log-likelihood can be written as:

$$l(\theta) = \sum_{t=1}^{T} \ln c(F_1(x_1^t), \ldots, F_n(x_n^t)) + \sum_{t=1}^{T} \sum_{t=1}^{n} \ln f_i(x_i^t) \tag{48}$$

In the case of the Gaussian copula, the parameters that need to be estimated correspond the covariance matrix Σ: They can be obtained easily as the solution of the equation $\dfrac{\partial l(\theta)}{\partial \theta} = 0$, with $\hat{\theta} = \hat{\Sigma}$.

In the case of the t-copula, the solution is more complex to obtain as both Σ and v have to be estimated simultaneously.

Under the appropriate regularity assumptions, we know that the maximum likelihood estimator exists and that it is asymptotically efficient.

Inference Functions for Margins   The IFM approach, initiated by Joe and Xu (1996), takes advantage of the property of copulas via Sklar's representation: the disconnection between univariate margins and the multivariate dependence structure. It is worth noting that both the univariate and multivariate distributions are assumed to correspond to preselected parametric forms—hence the classification of IFM in the parametric estimation category.

The first step is to estimate the parameters for the univariate margins and then only to calibrate the copula parameters, using the estimators of the univariate margins.

Let us call $\theta = (\theta_1, \ldots, \theta_n, \alpha)$, with θ_i the parameters related to the marginal distributions and α the vector of the copula parameters. The log-likelihood expression [Equation (48)] can be written as:

$$l(\theta) = \sum_{t=1}^{T} \ln c(F_1(x_1^t, \theta_1), \ldots, F_n(x_n^t, \theta_n), \alpha) + \sum_{t=1}^{T} \sum_{t=1}^{n} \ln f_i(x_i^t, \theta_i) \qquad (49)$$

The two-step maximization process follows:

$$\hat{\theta}_i = \arg\max_{\theta_i} \sum_{t=1}^{T} \ln f_i(x_i^t, \theta_i) \qquad (50)$$

and subsequently

$$\hat{\alpha} = \arg\max_{\alpha} \sum_{t=1}^{T} \ln c[F_1(x_1^t, \hat{\theta}_1), \ldots, F_n(x_n^t, \hat{\theta}_n), \alpha] \qquad (51)$$

It is worth mentioning that the IFM estimation is computationally easier to obtain than the FML/exact maximum likelihood one.

Conditional Maximum Likelihood or Canonical Maximum Likelihood

With this approach presented inter alia in Mashal and Zeevi (2002), there is no parametric assumption related to the distribution of the margins.

The dataset of n sequences of observations $X = (X_1^t, \ldots, X_n^t)_{t=1}^{T}$ is transformed into discrete variates $\hat{u} = (\hat{u}_1^t, \ldots, \mu_n^t)_{t=1}^{T}$ through empirical distribution functions $\hat{F}_i(\cdot)$ defined as:

$$\hat{F}_i\left(\frac{\tau}{T}\right) = \frac{1}{T} \sum_{t=1}^{T} 1_{\{X_i^t \leq X_i^\tau\}}, \quad \text{and} \quad \hat{u}_i = (\hat{F}_i(X_i))_{t=1}^{T} \qquad (52)$$

This transformation is referred to as the "empirical marginal transformation." See Figure 4.18 for an example corresponding to two quarterly time series of default rates over 20 years corresponding to two groups of industry. Data has been retrieved from CreditPro.

In a second step, the copula parameters, corresponding to the parametric family that has been selected, can be estimated in a straightforward way as:

$$\hat{\alpha} = \arg\max_{\alpha} \sum_{t-1}^{T} \ln c(\hat{u}_1^t, \ldots, \hat{u}_n^t, \alpha) \qquad (53)$$

FIGURE 4.18

Plotting Two Times Series of Quarterly Default Rate Corresponding to Two Industry Groups, Using the Empirical Marginal Transformation Technique.

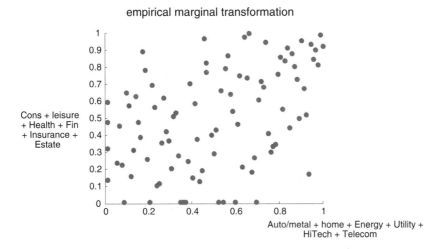

empirical marginal transformation

Definition of the Empirical Copula　With this approach, there is no parametric assumption neither on the marginal distributions, nor on the copula function itself. It has been introduced by Deheuvels (1979). Appropriate assumptions are summarized in Durrleman et al. (2000).

As in the precedent paragraph, let us consider the dataset of n i.i.d. sequences of T observations $X = (X_1^t,...,X_n^t)_{t=1}^T$, on which an empirical marginal transformation is performed.

Instead of selecting a parametric copula function, the next step is to observe the new uniform variates $\hat{u} = (\hat{u}_1^t,...,u_n^t)_{t=1}^T$ and to define an associated empirical copula $\hat{C}$:

$$\hat{C}_T\left(\frac{\tau_1}{T},\frac{\tau_2}{T},...,\frac{\tau_n}{T}\right) = \frac{1}{T}\sum_{t=1}^T 1_{\{X_1^t \le X_1^{\tau_1}, X_2^t \le X_2^{\tau_2},...,X_n^t \le X_n^{\tau_n}\}} \tag{54}$$

The introduction of T in the notation $\hat{C}_T$ defines the order of the copula, i.e., the dimension of the sample/time series used.

Deheuvels (1981) shows that the empirical copula converges uniformly to the underlying copula.

The empirical copula can be expressed based on its empirical frequency $\hat{c}_T$ (Nelsen, 1999):

$$\hat{C}_T\left(\frac{\tau_1}{T},\frac{\tau_2}{T},\ldots,\frac{\tau_n}{T}\right) = \sum_{t_1=1}^{\tau_1}\cdots\sum_{t_n=1}^{\tau_n}\hat{c}_T\left(\frac{t_1}{T},\frac{t_2}{T},\ldots,\frac{t_n}{T}\right) \tag{55}$$

where

$$\hat{c}_T\left(\frac{t_1}{T},\frac{t_2}{T},\ldots,\frac{t_n}{T}\right) = \begin{cases} \dfrac{1}{T} & \text{if}(X_1^{t_1},X_2^{t_2},\ldots,X_n^{t_n})\text{ are below the values} \\ & \text{defined by }(X_1^{\tau_1},X_2^{\tau_2},\ldots,X_n^{\tau_n}) \\ 0 & \text{otherwise} \end{cases}$$

A practical example is provided in Figure 4.19.

FIGURE 4.19

Plotting the Corresponding Empirical Copula.

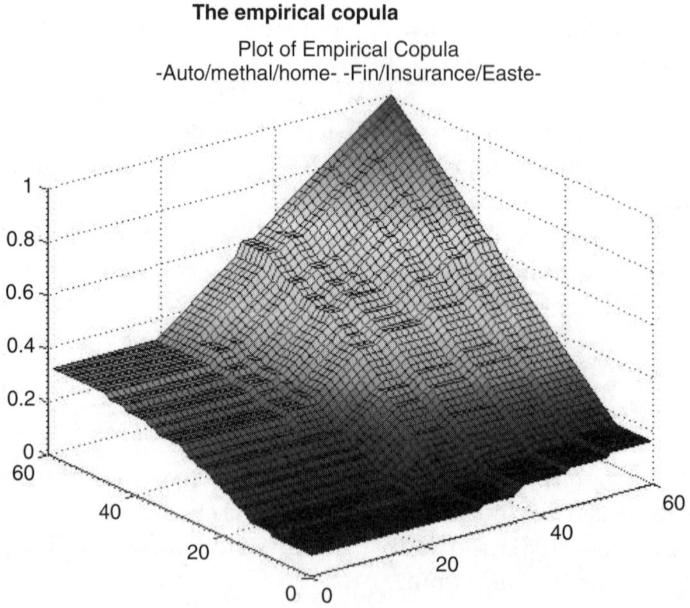

The empirical copula

Plot of Empirical Copula
-Auto/methal/home- -Fin/Insurance/Easte-

Goodness-of-Fit and Visual Comparison   Genest and Rivest (1993) propose a graphical technique to compare and fit a copula belonging to a parametric class **C**, like the class of Archimedean copulas, to the empirical one.

Let us define $K_\theta(y) = P\{C(U_1, U_2, \dots, U_n) \le y\}$, with $(U_1, U_2, \dots, U_n)$ being a random vector of uniform variables with copula C. A nonparametric estimate of K_θ, $\hat{K}_T$, can be written as a cumulative distribution function allocating a weight of $1/T$ to each pseudo observation.

$$\hat{K}_T(y) = \frac{1}{T} \sum_{\tau=1}^{T} (V_{\tau T} \le y), \quad \text{with } y \in [0,1] \text{ and} \tag{56}$$

$$V_{\tau T} = \frac{1}{T} \sum_{t=1}^{T} 1_{\{X_1^t \le X_1^\tau, X_2^t \le X_2^\tau, \dots, X_n^t \le X_n^\tau\}} \tag{57}$$

If we introduce R_i^t as the rank of X_i^t among $X_i^1, X_i^2, \dots, X_i^T$, then

$$V_{\tau T} = \frac{1}{T} \sum_{t=1}^{T} 1_{\{R_1^t \le R_1^\tau, R_2^t \le R_2^\tau, \dots, R_n^t \le R_n^\tau\}} \tag{58}$$

Figure 4.20 gives an example of $\hat{K}_T$ in the case described previously.

The graphical procedure for model selection is based on a visual comparison of the nonparametric estimate $\hat{K}_T$ to the parametric one K_θ. (see Figure 4.21)

A way to evaluate how close the graphs are is to measure the distance between them (see Figure 4.22). One distance can be defined as the sum of the weighted quadratic differences: $D_\theta^W = \sum_\theta [K_y(y) - \hat{K}_T(y)]^2\, W_y$.

There is of course, no unique definition of distance and no unique way to allocate weights. In particular, it could be tempting to attribute higher weights to extreme events rather than to equally split between observations and, in fact, calibrate the copula based on the bulk of the distribution. Ultimately, $\hat{\theta} = \arg\min_{\theta}(D_\theta^W)$.

One of the weaknesses of this approach, however, is that the definition of the univariate function $\hat{K}_T$ corresponds to the reduction of the n-dimensional copula problem. There cannot be any certitude that the choice of this $\hat{K}_T$ is optimal, leading to the selection of the most appropriate parametric copula.

FIGURE 4.20

A Visual Presentation of the Genest and Rivest (1993)
Estimator in the Case of the Two Default Rate Series.

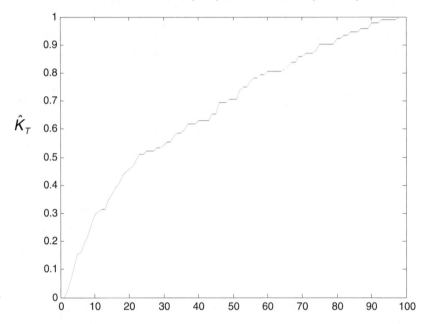

The Genest and Rivest (1993) estimator of the empirical copula

Goodness-Of-Fit and Distribution-Free Distance Minimization

One of the additional possible problems with the previous approach is
that the shape of the empirical copula can be far from smooth. As a consequence, goodness-of-fit results will depend very much on the set of
observations on which they are computed. By using a kernel-smoothed
estimator of the empirical copula density, Fermanian (2005) suggests that
the goodness-of-fit tests behave in a more stable manner with nice distribution asymptotic properties.

In what follows, the presentation is derived from Fermanian and
Scaillet (2004). Getting back to initial steps, a goodness-of-fit test is
designed to test a null hypothesis that in this case can be:

$$H_0: \hat{C} \in \mathbf{C} \text{ against } H_a: \hat{C} \notin \mathbf{C},$$

where $\hat{C}$ is the copula function to be tested and $\mathbf{C} = \{C_\theta, \theta \in \Theta\}$ represents
the parametric class of copulas.

FIGURE 4.21

A Comparison Between the Two Estimates (*t*-Copula, Empirical).

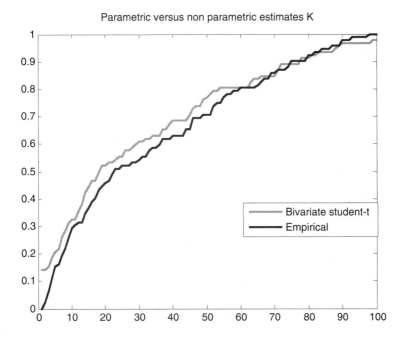

Let us define some p disjoint subsets of dimension n: $A_1, \ldots, A_p$, $\hat{u} = (\hat{u}_1^t, \ldots, \hat{u}_n^t)_{t=1}^T$ and

$$\chi^2 = T \sum_{l=1}^{p} \frac{[\hat{C}(\hat{u} \in A_l) - C_\theta(\hat{u} \in A_l)]^2}{C_\theta(\hat{u} \in A_l)}, \qquad (59)$$

with T representing the size of the sample. Under the null hypothesis, χ^2 tends in law toward a chi-squared distribution.

In order to obtain a tractable solution, let us consider the empirical copula and smooth it using a classic kernel estimator. Let us call g_T its density at point u:

$$\hat{g}_T(u) = \frac{1}{T h^n} \sum_{t=1}^{T} K\left(\frac{u - \hat{u}^t}{h}\right) \qquad (60)$$

FIGURE 4.22

Distance (Quadratic Difference) Between Parametric and Nonparametric Estimates of K. Case of the Two Default Rate Data Series Described Earlier.

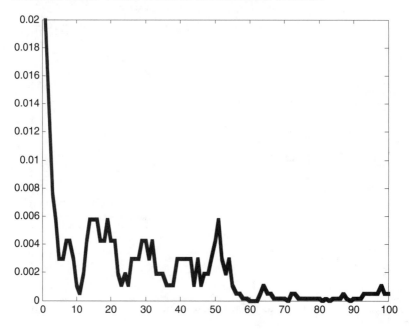

where $K(\cdot)$ is an n-dimensional kernel, with $h(T)$ being the bandwidth and vector $\mathbf{u}^t = (\hat{u}_1^t, \ldots, \hat{u}_n^t)$ being defined on the basis of the empirical marginal transformation Equation (52).

As usual, $\int K(\cdot) = 1$ and $\lim_{T \to \infty} h(T) = 0$.

Based on the definition of this kernel, we can now revert to the χ^2-test that can be written as:

$$\chi^2 = \frac{T h^n}{\int K^2} \sum_{l=1}^{p} \frac{[\hat{g}_T(\hat{u}^l) - g_{\hat{\theta}}(\hat{u}^l)]^2}{g_{\hat{\theta}}(\hat{u}^l)} \qquad (61)$$

where $g_\theta(\cdot)$ corresponds to the parametric copula density, $\hat{\theta}$ to the estimated parameter vector, and the p vectors $(\hat{\mathbf{u}}_l)_{l=1}^{p}$ to some arbitrary choice defined by where the tester wants to assess the quality of the fit.

Discussing the Estimation of Copulas for Time Series Copula estimation has been presented so far under the assumption of an environment of i.i.d. observable samples or time series. When dealing with partially autocorrelated time series displaying varying heteroscedasticity, we need to revisit the previous copula estimation techniques and to assess their robustness. This point is of particular importance, for instance, in the synthetic CDO world where samples typically correspond to spread prices.

Some initial transformation of the data at the univariate level may be needed in order to be able to rely on the i.i.d. assumption. Some techniques are available. Serial autocorrelation, nonstationarity, heteroscedasticity of the time series can be filtered through GARCH and ARMA processes.

Based on this transformation, we can focus on the residuals, as it is much more likely to be i.i.d. Parametric copulas can then be typically fitted on these residuals.

We revert readers to Scaillet and Fermanian (2003), Fermanian et al. (2004), Doukhan et al. (2005), and Chen and Fan (2006) on this topic of estimation of copulas on time series and of time-dependent copulas.

Correlation as a Result of Joint Intensity Modeling

In May 2005, the downgrade of Ford and GM by S&P lead to a widening of the spreads of almost all the components of the CDS indices. In a Credit Metrics setup, we could imagine that a shock on the automotive sector would lead to some rating actions on other corporate firms in the same industry and to a lesser extent on other firms in different sectors. In this case, no other significant rating change has occurred as a consequence. Thereby, the Credit Metrics approach proved unable to account for the changes in the prices of CDO tranches. The period was surprising in the sense that two investors holding exactly the same tranche of a CDO in their portfolio (assuming it did not include Ford and GM) could have completely different views about the quality of their asset, whether they would consider it from a market-to-market or from a traditional pure default risk perspective. The general trend, over the recent period, has been to take into account both default dependency and market price risk.

As Schönbucher and Schubert (2001) point out, the joint risk-neutral survival function of two obligors A and B will depend dramatically on a default event on any of them. Typically, the default probability of B will increase as soon as obligor A defaults. If we focus on the period bounded by the time just before default and the time of obligor A's default, we will observe a jump in the default intensity of B. Any substantial jump like the downgrade to a NIG level of some obligors can have the same effect as a default and entail price contagion for other obligors, which could not be easily explained by Gaussian copulas. The GM and Ford examples stand as a good illustration of the phenomenon.

All these classes of joint-intensity models start by focusing heavily on the estimation of the price or the creditworthiness (hazard rate) of each obligor considered separately. These approaches do not preclude then the use of copulas but tend to encourage the selection of a multivariate model based on some explicit rationale. One of the main reasons why these approaches have not been widely used by practitioners so far is probably because the estimation problems that arise are generally more complex than with the traditional Gaussian copula setup. There seems, however, to be growing interest for these types of models as they can represent observed prices quite accurately.

In this context, it is important to refer to intensity-based models when dealing with dependence. In order to summarize the evolution in this field, we can identify four parallel classes of joint intensity models:

+ The most traditional class initially corresponded to the introduction of some correlation in the dynamics of the default intensity of obligors. This approach had been widely used in the context of interest rates and FX modeling and has then been introduced in credit. These initial models are usually considered to underestimate observed correlation. Duffie (1998) and Duffie and Singleton (1999) have suggested that higher default dependencies could be obtained by increasing the likelihood of joint default events. In their model, when an obligor defaults, an enhancement in the intensity of the jump of the other obligors is observed. Obviously, with a large sample, calibration of intensities can be a problem. Since then, other models presenting jump-intensity correlation have been developed, allowing for idiosyncratic as well as systematic jumps, like Giesecke (2003) and dealing with calibration thanks to an exponential copula framework.

+ Another area of investigation has been in the direction of frailty models. These models are used in other fields like biology and medicine. In such a setup, individuals within different groups can be affected by common frailties. In credit, this translates into an extra stress factor due to unobserved risk factors (see Yashin and Iachine, 1995). In this case, a particular specification of the intensity for a Gamma frailty model can be expressed as:

$$\lambda_t(t, X, Z) = (Z_0 + Z_t)\lambda_0(t)\exp(\beta'X_t) \qquad (62)$$

With Z_0 an unobservable gamma random variable common to all obligors (the shared frailty component), Z_i an unobservable gamma random variable that is specific to obligor i, and the rest of the specifications corresponding to a classic proportional hazard rate model*; i.e., a combination of a simple time-dependent hazard rate function and of a multifactor model of additional explanatory variables. Fermanian and Sbai (2005) show that this class of models can provide realistic levels of dependence.

♦ Another class corresponds to default infection models. The original papers in this area are Davis and Lo (1999a,b, 2000) and Jarrow and Yu (2001). In this approach the default of an obligor will impact the default intensities of other obligors through a jump. Let us consider n obligors. The default intensity of obligor i at time t can be written as:

$$\lambda_i(t) = \alpha_i(t) + \sum_{j=1}^{n} \beta_{ij}(t)1_{(\tau_j \le t)} \qquad (63)$$

Calibration of this class of models may not prove straightforward.

♦ The last class we will mention here is the threshold copula approach presented by Schönbucher and Schubert (2001). A detailed description of the model is provided in Appendix A. It focuses particularly on the dynamic specification of the survival probabilities and hazard rates. The concept is that any default in a portfolio will create a threshold effect through a modified specification of the survival copula, due to additional information gained over time on the default status of the obligors in the portfolio. This threshold information can also be seen as modifying the individual pseudo-intensities over time. Though the equations in the model look complex, the intuition remains simple. The major constraint resides with its implementation, as it seems to be tractable mainly with Archimedean copulas.

---

*Also called Cox regression model.

Discussion on the Evolution of Dependency Modeling

This section completes our introduction to correlation, copulas, and other dependence measures. Looking backwards, we can see that dependence measurement has considerably gained inaccuracy but also in complexity in a short time span. From the initial linear correlation approach, the credit world has quickly moved toward static factor models at the end of the 1990s, with the Credit Metrics setup. The subsequent leap has been from default correlation toward survival correlation with Li (2000). It has enabled us to adopt a more flexible view of correlation, taking into consideration the timing of default. With an almost simultaneous access to various forms of copulas, market participants have also been able to account for dependence in a more refined way. Surprisingly, many practitioners have however not fully adopted these innovative solutions so far for several reasons. The most reasonable cause accounting for it is that the selection of an appropriate copula is not a fully objective process and its calibration is not immediate. A second one corresponds to the very practical fact that no common language, other than the Gaussian copula, has emerged among practitioners so far. A point to mention at this stage is that there seems to be an increasing view on credit markets that the copula approach has shown some limitations and that there may not exist any perfect solution or "the Perfect Copula" as Hull and White (2005) put it. Such limitations are to be related, among other things, to the incomplete treatment by copulas of dynamic aspects. The next frontier for dependence models would indeed be to account not only for the default dynamics but also for the price dynamics, following, for instance, credit event or credit contagion. Possible paths for the future could be to introduce regime-switching patterns associated with copulas in order to account better for temporal dependencies or to focus on the joint modeling of intensity-based models, and on finding, among other issues, new solutions to the inherent dimensionality problem related to this approach.

PART 2: EMPIRICAL RESULTS ON CORRELATION

Calculating Empirical Asset Implied Correlations

In order to compute the loss distribution of a portfolio, a traditional approach has been to assume that the general correlation process is driven by latent variables that partially drive the movement to default or the time to default of the corporate obligors in that portfolio. Such models belong to the category of factor models described in the section "Factor Models of Credit Risk" of the previous part. This class of models ultimately relies on an interpretation within the structural Merton framework. In this context, default correlation is derived indirectly from asset correlation, as the comovement of the asset value of different obligors, to a default threshold.

The usual approach in CDO pricing and risk management is to consider equity or credit spread correlation as proxies for asset correlation. In what follows, we focus on extracting asset correlation from empirical default observations. This will enable us later on to understand properly the arbitrage between ratings and prices of structures.

We describe three ways to estimate implied asset correlation. The first way in called the joint default probability approach (JPD). The second corresponds to a maximum likelihood approach (MLE). The third one is based on a Bayesian inference technique generalized linear mixed model (GLMM).

The Joint Default Probability Approach

In Equation (4) of the previous part, we have derived the correlation formula for two binary events A and B. These two events can be joint defaults or joint downgrades, for example. Consider two firms originally rated i and j, respectively, and let D denotes the default category. The marginal probabilities of default are P_i^D and P_j^D, while $P_{i,j}^{D,D}$ denotes the joint probability of the two firms defaulting over a chosen horizon. Equation (4) can thus be rewritten as:

$$\rho_{i,j}^{D,D} = \frac{p_{i,j}^{D,D} - p_i^D p_j^D}{\sqrt{p_i^D(1 - p_i^D)p_j^D(1 - p_j^D)}} \tag{64}$$

Obtaining individual probabilities of default per rating class is straightforward. These statistics can be read off transition matrices. The only unknown term that has to be estimated in Equation (64) is the joint probability.

Estimating the Joint Probability   Consider the joint migration of two obligors from the same class i (say, a BB rating) to default D. The default correlation formula is given by Equation (64) with $j=i$, and we want to estimate $p_{i,i}^{D,D}$.

Assume that at the beginning of a year t, we have N_i^t firms rated i. From a given set with N_i^t elements, one can create $(N_i^t\,(N_i^t-1))/2$ different pairs. Denoting by $T_{i,D}^t$ the number of bonds migrating from this group to default D, one can create $(T_{i,D}^t\,(T_{i,D}^t-1))/2$ defaulting pairs. Taking the ratio of the number of pairs that defaulted to the number of pairs that could have defaulted, one obtains a natural estimator of the joint probability. Considering that we have n years of data and not only one, the estimator is:

$$p_{i,i}^{D,D} = \sum_{t=1}^{n} w_i^t \frac{T_{i,D}^t (T_{i,D}^t - 1)}{N_i^t (N_i^t - 1)}, \tag{65}$$

where w are weights representing the relative importance of a given year. Among possible choices for the weighting schemes, one can find:

$$w_i^t = \frac{1}{n}, \tag{66a}$$

$$w_i^t = \frac{N_i^t}{\displaystyle\sum_{s=1}^{n} N_i^s}, \text{ or} \tag{66b}$$

$$w_i^t = \frac{N_i^t (N_i^t - 1)}{\displaystyle\sum_{s=1}^{n} N_i^s (N_i^s - 1)}. \tag{66c}$$

Equation (65) is the formula used by Lucas (1995) and Bahar and Nagpal (2001) to calculate the joint probability of default. Similar formulae can be derived for transitions to and from different classes. Both papers rely on Equation (66c) as weighting system.

Although intuitive, the estimator in Equation (65) has the drawback that it can generate spurious negative correlation when defaults are rare. Taking a specific year, we can indeed check that when there is only one default, $T(T-1)=0$. This leads to a zero probability of joint default. However, the probability of an individual default is $1/N$. Therefore, Equation (64) immediately generates a negative correlation as the joint probability is 0 and the product of marginal probabilities is $(1/N)^2$.

de Servigny and Renault (2002) therefore propose to replace the Equation (2) with:

$$p_{i,i}^{D,D} = \sum_{t=1}^{n} w_i^t \frac{(T_{i,D}^t)^2}{(N_i^t)^2}. \tag{67}$$

This estimator of joint probability follows the same intuition of comparing pairs of defaulting firms to the total number of pairs of firms. The difference lies in the assumption of drawing pairs with replacement. de Servigny and Renault (2002) use the weights in Equation (66b). On a simulation experiment, they show that formula (65) has better finite sample properties than (65), that is, for small samples (small N) using Equation (67) provides an estimate that is on average closer to the true correlation than using Equation (65).

Empirical Default Correlation   Using the S&P's CreditPro 6.20 database that contains about 10,000 firms and 22 years of data (from 1981 to 2002), we can apply formulas (4) and (1) to compute empirical default correlations. Results are shown in Table 4.1.

The highest correlations can be observed on the diagonal, i.e., within the same industry. Most industry correlations are in the range of 1 to 3 percent. Real estate and, above all, Telecoms stand out as exhibiting particularly high correlations. Out-of-diagonal correlations tend to be fairly low.

Table 4.2 illustrates pairwise default correlations per class of rating.*
From these results we can see that default correlation tends to increase substantially as the rating deteriorates. This is in line with results from various studies of structural models and intensity-based models of credit risk.

We will return to this issue later on when we investigate default correlation in the context of intensity models of credit risk.

From Default Correlation to Asset-Implied Correlation   The estimated joint default probabilities can be used to back out the latent variable correlation $\Sigma = [\rho_{ij}]$ within the factor model setup described in the previous part.

Let us consider two companies (or two industries) i and j. Their joint default probability P_{ij} is given by

$$P_{ij} = \Phi(Z_i, Z_j, \rho_{ij}), \tag{68}$$

where Z_i and Z_j correspond to the default thresholds for each of these companies (or the average default threshold for each industrial sector).

The asset correlation between the two companies (or between the two sectors) can be derived by solving:

$$\rho_{ij} = \Phi^{-1}(P_{ij}, Z_i, Z_j) \tag{69}$$

---

*One-year default correlation involving AAA issuers cannot be calculated, as there has never been any AAA-rated company defaulting within a year.

TABLE 4.1

One-Year Default Correlations, All Countries, All Ratings, 1981–2002 (%)

	Automobile	Construction	Energy	Finanance	Build	Chemical	High tech	Insurance	Leisure	Real estate	Telecom	Transpor-tation	Utility
Automobile	**2.44**	0.87	0.68	0.40	1.31	1.15	1.55	0.17	0.93	0.71	2.90	1.08	1.03
Construction	0.87	**1.40**	-0.42	0.44	1.45	0.96	1.07	0.27	0.79	1.93	0.34	0.95	0.20
Energy	0.68	-0.42	**2.44**	-0.37	0.01	0.19	0.27	0.26	-0.37	-0.27	-0.11	0.17	0.29
Finanance	0.40	0.44	-0.37	**0.60**	0.55	0.22	0.30	-0.05	0.52	1.95	0.30	0.23	0.23
Build	1.31	1.45	0.01	0.55	**2.42**	0.95	1.45	0.31	1.54	1.92	2.27	1.65	1.12
Chemical	1.15	0.96	0.19	0.22	0.95	**1.44**	0.84	0.12	0.67	-0.15	1.03	0.78	0.23
High tech	1.55	1.07	0.27	0.30	1.45	0.84	**1.92**	-0.03	0.94	1.27	1.25	0.89	0.20
Insurance	0.17	0.27	0.26	-0.05	0.31	0.12	-0.03	**0.91**	0.28	0.47	0.28	0.72	0.48
Leisure	0.93	0.79	-0.37	0.52	1.54	0.67	0.94	0.28	**1.74**	2.87	1.61	1.49	0.85
Real estate	0.71	1.93	-0.27	1.95	1.92	-0.15	1.27	0.47	2.87	**5.15**	-0.24	1.38	0.71
Telecom	2.90	0.34	-0.11	0.30	2.27	1.03	1.25	0.28	1.61	-0.24	**9.59**	2.36	3.97
Transportation	1.08	0.95	0.17	0.23	1.65	0.78	0.89	0.72	1.49	1.38	2.36	**1.85**	1.40
Utility	1.03	0.20	0.29	0.23	1.12	0.23	0.20	0.48	0.85	0.71	3.97	1.40	**2.65**

Source: S&P's CreditPro 6.20.

TABLE 4.2

One-Year Default Correlations, All Countries,
All Industries, 1981–2002 (%)

Rating	AAA	AA	A	BBB	BB	B	CCC
AAA	NA	NA	NA	NA	NA	NA	NA
AA	NA	0.16	0.02	−0.03	0.00	0.10	0.06
A	NA	0.02	0.12	0.03	0.19	0.22	0.26
BBB	NA	−0.03	0.03	0.33	0.35	0.30	0.89
BB	NA	0.00	0.19	0.35	0.94	0.84	1.45
B	NA	0.10	0.22	0.30	0.84	1.55	1.67
CCC	NA	0.06	0.26	0.89	1.45	1.67	8.97

Source: S&P's CreditPro 6.20.

In this particular context, as we compute pairwise industry default correlation, we are able to generate the corresponding pairwise industry asset
correlation.

The Maximum Likelihood Approach

The estimation of implied asset correlation can also be extracted directly
through a maximum likelihood procedure, as described originally in Gordy
and Heitfield (2002). Given the default data scarcity, the numerical tractability of this approach is however the major constraint. Demey et al. (2004)
suggest a simplified version of the previous estimation technique, where all
inter industry correlation parameters are assumed equal. Thanks to this
additional constraint, for each company or sector, the number of parameters to estimate is in fact limited to two.

In order to describe precisely the estimation technique, we first start
by displaying the latent variable (the asset value) for each obligor i in the
portfolio as the linear combination of a reduced number of independent
factors. Given the assumption of a unique correlation intensity across all
industries ($\rho_{cd} = \rho$ for all industries $c \neq d$), the asset value of any company i in
industry c can be written as a function of two independent common factors
C and C_c as:

$$A_i = \sqrt{\rho}C + \sqrt{\rho_c - \rho}C_e + \sqrt{1 - \rho_c}\varepsilon_i, \quad i \in c \qquad (69)$$

C can be considered as a factor common to the whole economy, whereas C_c is a more industry specific common factor and ε_j is the idiosyncratic term corresponding to obligor j.

The resulting asset correlation matrix can be written as:

$$
\Sigma_{\text{MLE}} = \begin{bmatrix}
\rho_1 & \rho & \cdots & & \rho \\
\rho & \rho_2 & \ddots & & \\
\vdots & & \ddots & & \vdots \\
& & & \ddots & \rho \\
\rho & \cdots & & \rho & \rho_C
\end{bmatrix}
$$

Assuming that the idiosyncratic factor ε_j is Gaussian, and that Z_c corresponds to the average, time invariant, default threshold of all companies in industry c, we can write the probability of default within industry c, conditional on the realization (f, f_c) of factors (F, F_c) as:

$$
P_c(f, f_c) = \Phi\left(\frac{Z_c - \sqrt{\rho}\, f - \sqrt{\rho_c - \rho}\, f_c}{\sqrt{1 - \rho_c}} \right) \tag{70}
$$

where Φ is the normal c.d.f.

Conditional on the realization of the factors, the number of defaults in a given industrial sector c has a binomial distribution, with parameters N_c, the number of firms in class c at time t, and D_c the default number in the same class.

$$
\text{Bin}_c(f, f_c) = \binom{N_c}{D_c} P_c(f, f_c)^{D_c} (1 - P_c(f, f_c))^{N_c - D_c} \tag{71}
$$

Due to the property of conditional independence, we can write the unconditional log-likelihood as:

$$
l_t(\theta) = \log \int \left(\prod_{c=1}^{C} \int_R \text{Bin}_c(f, f_c)\, \mathrm{d}\,\Phi(f_c) \right) \mathrm{d}\,\Phi(f) \tag{72}
$$

Demey et al. (2004) investigate the potential stability and bias problems in several bootstrap experiments. They obtain reasonably good performances, as the mean of the bootstrap distribution converges quickly to the true correlation for class samples as small as 50.

Computing the Asset-Implied Correlation Through JPD and MLE

de Servigny and Jobst (2005) use the S&P's Credit Pro 6.60 database over the period 1981 to 2003. It contains 66,536 annual observations and 1170 default events. On a yearly basis and for each of 13 industrial sectors c, they compute N_c and D_c.

The authors compare the value of the asset-implied correlation estimated under the JPD and the MLE techniques (Table 4.3 and Figure 4.23). They find a reasonably good match between the two approaches.

Regarding default based asset-implied correlation, it is worth mentioning that Gordy and Heitfield (2002) show that the slight positive relationship between credit quality and asset-implied correlation is not statistically significant and that there is no real value in terms of accrual precision to reject the hypothesis of constant implied asset correlation derived from default, across ratings.

TABLE 4.3

Comparison of Asset-Implied Correlation Using JPD and MLE

Industrial sector	Average N	Average PD	Implied asset correlation JPD	Implied asset correlation MLE
Automobile	297	2.17	11.80	10.84
Construction	354	2.48	6.80	7.63
Energy	149	2.20	12.60	19.06
Finance	530	0.60	9.40	15.93
Chemical	113	2.04	13.40	6.55
Health	149	1.25	10.00	8.44
High tech	97	1.84	9.60	6.55
Insurance	260	0.65	14.60	13.32
Leisure	169	3.07	8.60	9.16
Real estate	60	1.11	34.20	33.02
Telecom	119	1.97	27.80	30.32
Transportation	134	2.07	9.70	6.55
Utility	352	3.52	21.90	21.30
Average intra industry			14.65	14.51
Average inter industry			4.70	6.45

Abbreviations: JPD = joint default probability approach; MLE = maximum likelihood; PD = probability of default.

FIGURE 4.23

Quality of the Intra-Industry Estimation Match Using Maximum Likelihood Approach and Joint Default Probability Approach.

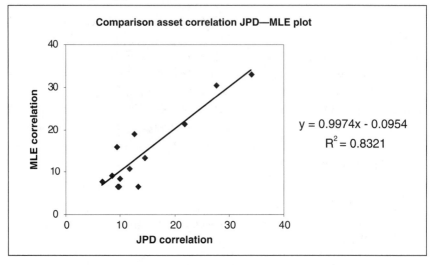

$y = 0.9974x - 0.0954$

$R^2 = 0.8321$

The Bayesian Estimation Approach—GLMM

This approach has been proposed recently by Mc Neil and Wendin (2005). The authors assume a multi time-step econometric model conditional on time varying predictive covariates. This model belongs to the class of GLMMs. In this setup, probabilities of default rely on some usual fixed covariates that are used in scoring,* but they also include one unobservable vector of random dynamic factors. Serial correlation is assumed for this vector, i.e., its current realization is partially conditioned by its past realizations through a serial dependence AR(1) specification.

The aggregation of the probabilities of default in a portfolio is performed assuming independence conditional on the realization of the paths of the common vector of random covariates. In order to resolve this dynamic estimation problem, the authors use a Bayesian computational technique.

The authors test their approach in an empirical study, using the rating database from S&P's Credit Pro 6.60 and selecting observations in the United States and Canada from 1981 to 2000.

---

*Typically company specific or macroeconomic covariates.

For an obligor i, at time t, the probability of default conditional on the realization of this systematic, unobserved, risk factor F_i is therefore:

$$P(Y_t^i = 1/F_t) = logit(\mu_t^i + \beta X_t + \gamma_t^j F_t)$$

where X_t corresponds to a vector of explainable common macroeconomic effects,* μ_t^i to the intercept,† and β_t^i and γ_t^i to related weights. The AR(1) process for the vector of latent systematic unobserved Gaussian random risk factors F_i can be written as: $F_t = \alpha F_{t-1} + \phi \varepsilon_t$.

At the portfolio level, the usual assumption of conditional independence leads to the calculation of the loss distribution in a straightforward manner.

In a first analysis, the authors assume that there is no fixed common variable X_t, but only one random unobservable variable F_t. Using the Bayesian technique, they observe that the hypothesis of an independent simulation of the factor at each step, i.e., $\alpha = 0$, is strongly rejected empirically. The estimation of α gives a mean value of around 0.65 with a standard deviation representing around 25 percent of the mean. In addition, the expected value of the implied asset correlation can be estimated. Practically it comes to 7.6 percent.

In a second step, the authors incorporate a fixed macroeconomic variable X_t corresponding to the Chicago Fed National Activity Index, published on a monthly basis. They also consider six broad industrial sectors:

- ◆ Aerospace, automotive, capital goods, and metal
- ◆ Consumer and service sector
- ◆ Leisure time and media
- ◆ Utility
- ◆ Health care and chemicals
- ◆ High tech, computers, office equipment, and Telecom

They show that the mean realization of the common random factor is depending very clearly on the economic cycle, as can be seen on Figure 4.24.

Results show that both the introduction of industrial sectors and of a macroeconomic factor reinforces the quality of the estimation. With this specification, average inter-industry asset-implied correlation comes to 6 percent and intra-industry correlation to 10.5 percent. These results are in line in terms of magnitude with the results provided by the previous MLE

---

*Let us think of the typical credit factors used in credit scoring models.
†Possibly derived from company specific factors and a true intercept.

FIGURE 4.24

A Clear Correlation of the Common Factor with the
Economic Cycle. *(McNeil and Wendin, 2005)*

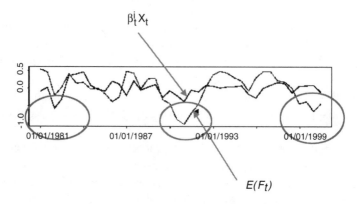

and JPD estimators, especially given the fact that we are now talking
about a less granular industry specification. We also note that asset correlation follows a cycle-dependent pattern.

Are Equity Correlations Good Proxies for Asset Correlations?

We have just seen that the formula for pairwise default correlation is quite
simple but relies on asset correlation, which is not directly observable. It has
become market practice to use equity correlation as a proxy for asset correlation. The underlying assumption is that equity returns should reflect the
value of the underlying firms and, therefore, that two firms with highly correlated asset values should also have high equity correlations.

To test the validity of this assumption, de Servigny and Renault (2002)
have gathered a sample of over 1100 firms for which they had at least five
years of data on the ratings, equity prices, and industry classification. They
then computed average equity correlations across and within industries.

These scaled equity correlations were inserted in Equation (68) to
obtain a series of default correlations extracted from equity prices. They
then proceeded to compare default correlations calculated in this way to
default correlations calculated empirically using Equation (69).

Figure 4.25A summarizes their findings. Equity-driven default correlations and empirical correlations appear to be only weakly related or, in
other words, equity correlations provide at best a noisy indicator of default
correlations. This casts some doubt on the robustness of the market standard

FIGURE 4.25A

The match between Default Correlation Derived from Equity and Empirical Default Correlation.

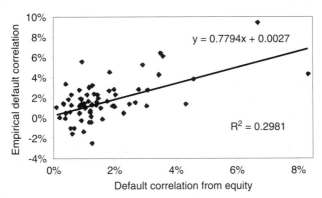

assumption and also on the possibility of hedging credit products using the equity of their issuer.

Although disappointing, this result may not be surprising: equity returns incorporate a lot of noise (bubbles, etc.) and are affected by supply and demand effects (liquidity crunches) that are not related to the firms' fundamentals. Therefore, although the relevant fundamental correlation information may be incorporated in equity returns, it is blended with many other types of information and cannot easily be extracted. Figure 4.25B confirms

FIGURE 4.25B

Two Proxies for Asset Correlation: Implied Asset Correlation from Default Events or Equity Correlation.

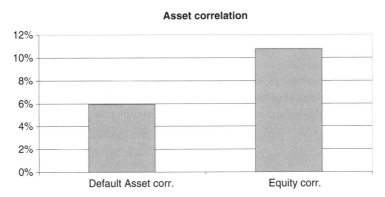

this fact in the sense that it shows that there is half of the equity correlation that is not coming from joint default events.

Describing the Behavior of Implied Asset Correlation

So far, we have observed that different default based asset-implied correlation estimators do give comparable results. In the light of the difference observed between asset-implied correlation and equity correlation, we would however like to reach a more in depth understanding of the issue. In this respect, we are testing for the stability of this asset-implied correlation based on different "default" events.

In this paragraph, we therefore compute implied asset correlation, using MLE, in two cases:

♦ We define an event as breaching an equity value barrier in the case of EDSs.*

♦ We can also consider pure credit event triggers that are different from default. We, for instance, consider rating based events like the joint downgrade to a predefined rating level (from CCC to BBB).

By backing out the implied asset correlation from different events like joint defaults, joint EDSs triggers, or joint downgrades, we would expect to obtain similar results. Whatever the instrument or event we consider, the underlying reference asset value is indeed unique for any obligor.

Extracting Asset-Implied Correlation from EDSs   Based on EDS events at different barrier levels, Jobst and de Servigny (2006) measure asset-implied correlation using JPD and MLE. The universe they work on represents 2,200 companies for which they have collected monthly equity time series, the corresponding ratings, and financial information from 1981 to 2003.

As can be observed in Figures 4.26 and 4.27, asset-implied correlation is far from being stable across barrier levels.

A correlation skew can be observed, whichever estimator is retained. Note that below the 50 percent barrier, EDSs can be considered more like debt products as shown in de Servigny and Jobst (2005). On the

---

*An EDS is a credit hybrid derivative, and more precisely a deep "out-of-the-money" long dated digital American put with regular installments. A barrier level such as 30 percent corresponds to a loss in value of 70 percent of the related equity share.

FIGURE 4.26

Intra-industry Implied Asset Correlation Backed out of
Equity Default Swaps with Different Barrier Level from
10 to 90 Percent.

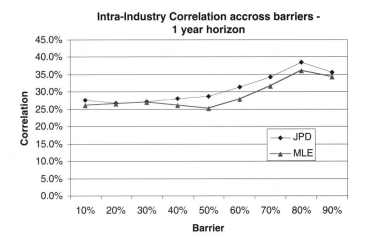

FIGURE 4.27

Inter-Industry Implied Asset Correlation Backed Out
of Equity Default Swaps with Different Barrier Level
from 10 to 90 Percent.

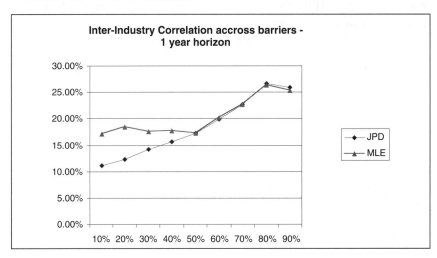

contrary, above the 50 percent barrier, EDSs typically look more like equity products.

To summarize the situation, we can observe distinctly three correlation states:

1. *Pure default:* (average intra-industry asset-implied correlation, average inter-industry asset-implied correlation) = (14.5, 5.5).

2. *EDS below 50 percent barrier:* (Average intra-industry asset-implied correlation, Average inter-industry asset-implied correlation) = (26.5, 15.5).

3. *EDS above 50 percent barrier:* (Average intra-industry asset-implied correlation, average inter-industry asset-implied correlation) = (31, 22.5)

Correlation in state (2) and to some extent in state (3) looks quite comparable with typical equity correlation. It differs significantly from the lower default levels observed in state (1).

In the next paragraph, we consider different credit event triggers rather than EDS barriers. By going this way, we will be able to assess whether asset-implied correlation extracted from default constitutes a singular, doubtful situation or a confirmed and robust observation.

Extracting Asset-Implied Correlation from Different Credit Events

de Servigny et al. (2005) now consider different credit triggers.* Instead of picking default as the only relevant event, they back out asset-implied correlation from different downward migrations toward a predefined rating level. They start by identifying all firms that move to default, as well as the firms that are downgraded to a rating level ranging from CCC to BBB during a given period of time, typically one year.

Using the JPD approach, we can obtain the joint probability of comovement to a rating level K from an adjustment of Equation (4):

$$p_{i,i}^{K,K} = \sum_{t=1}^{n} W_i^t \frac{(T_{i,K}^t)^2}{(N_i^t)^2}. \tag{73}$$

With K being defined as the credit event ranging from BBB to D. In addition, we introduce the condition $i > K$, in order to insure that we are capturing downgrades only.† We can then easily extract the asset-implied correlation using Equations (68) and (69).

---

*Using Credit Pro 6.60 between 1990 and 2003.
†When using both downgrades and upgrades, we obtain significantly lower asset-implied correlation levels.

Using the MLE approach, we derive the conditional probability of default from an adjustment of Equation (8):

$$P_c^K(f, f_c) = \Phi\left(\frac{Z_c^K - \sqrt{\rho}f - \sqrt{\rho_c - \rho}f_c}{\sqrt{1 - \rho_c}} \right) \qquad (74)$$

with Z_c^k being the credit event threshold associated with rating K. We then proceed with Equations (72) and (73).

The results are summarized in Figure 4.28. Interestingly, unlike what we would have expected from the experience derived from EDSs, here we cannot identify a clear skew effect.

To summarize, though the asset-implied correlation figures obtained from default events look significantly lower than those extracted from EDS events or equity prices, they do not correspond to any anomaly among credit events.

In reality, the latent variable we refer to as the asset-implied value for a given obligor is not unique whether we refer to credit events, to equity, or to EDS events. Unlike in the pure default/migration environment, the last two approaches contain a market component in the valuation of the

FIGURE 4.28

Assessing the Level of Asset Implied Correlation based on Different Credit Events: Not Only Joint Default, But Also Joint Down Grades (Intra=Intra-Industry Correlation, Inter=Inter-industry Correlation)

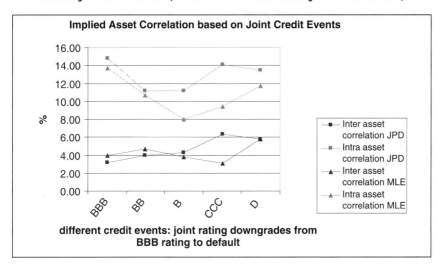

different credit events: joint rating downgrades from BBB rating to default

asset. This is the reason why in the pure credit situation asset-implied correlation is lower.

A similar conclusion applies when we compare CDO compound correlation with default implied asset correlation.

Correlations in an Intensity Framework

We have seen earlier in this book (in Chapter 3) that intensity-based models of credit risk are very popular among practitioners to price defaultable bonds and credit derivatives. This class of model, where default occurs as the first jump of a stochastic process, can also be used to analyze default correlations.

In an intensity model, the probability of default over $[0, t]$ for a firm i is:

$$PD_i(t) = P_0[\tau_i \leq t] = 1 - E_0\left[\exp(-\int_0^t \lambda_s^i \, ds)\right].$$ (75)

λ_s^i is the intensity of the default process and τ_i the default time for firm i. Linear default correlation [Equation (23)] can thus be written as:

$$\rho(t) = \frac{E(y_t^1 y_t^2) - E(y_t^1)E(y_t^2)}{\sqrt{E(y_t^1)(1 - E(y_t^1))E(y_t^2)(1 - E(y_t^2))}}$$ (76)

with

$$y_t^i = \exp(-\int_0^t \lambda_s^t \, ds) \quad \text{for } i = 1, 2.$$ (77)

In the remainder of this section, we show the findings that we have obtained in the previous section.

Testing Conditionally Independent Intensity Models

Yu (2005) implements several intensity specifications belonging to the class of conditionally independent models including those of Driessen (2002) and Duffee (1999), using empirically derived parameters.

The intensities are functions of a set of k state variables $X_t = (X_t^1, \ldots, X_t^k)$ defined below. Conditional on a realization of X_t, the default intensities are independent. Dependency therefore arises from the fact that all intensities are functions of X_t.

Common choices for the state variables are term structure factors (level of a specific Treasury rate, slope of the Treasury curve), other macroeconomic variables, firm-specific factors (leverage, book-to-market ratio), etc. For example, the two state variables in Duffee (1999) are the two factors of a risk-less affine term structure model (see Duffie and Kan, 1996). Driessen (2002) also includes two term structure factors and adds two further common factors to improve the empirical fit. In most papers, including those mentioned earlier, the intensities λ_s^j are defined under the risk-neutral measure and they therefore yield correlation measures under that specific probability measure. These correlation estimates cannot be compared directly to empirical default correlations as shown in Tables 4.1 to 4.3. The latter are indeed calculated under the historical measure.

Yu (2005) relies on results from Jarrow et al. (2001), who prove that asymptotically in a very large portfolio, average intensities under the risk-neutral and historical measures coincide. Yu argues that given that the parameters of the papers by Driessen and Duffee are estimated over a large and diversified sample, this asymptotic result should hold. He then computes default parameters from the estimated average parameters of intensities reported in Duffee (1999) and Driessen (2002), using Equations (77) and (78).

These results are reported in Tables 4.4 and 4.5. The model by Duffee (1999) tends to generate much too low default correlations compared to other specifications.

Table 4.6. [empirical default correlations using Equation (64)] and Table 4.7 (default correlations in the equity-based model of Zhou, 2001) are presented for comparative purposes. Driessen (2002) yields results that are comparable to those of Zhou (2001).

TABLE 4.4

Default Correlations Inferred from Duffee (1999)—In Percent

	1 year			2 years			5 years			10 years		
	Aa	A	Baa	Aa	A	Baa	Aa	A	Baa	Aa	A	Baa
Aa	0.00	0.00	0.00	0.01	0.01	0.01	0.02	0.02	0.03	0.03	0.03	0.05
A	0.00	0.00	0.00	0.01	0.01	0.01	0.02	0.03	0.04	0.03	0.06	0.06
Baa	0.00	0.00	0.01	0.01	0.01	0.02	0.02	0.04	0.06	0.05	0.06	0.09

Source: Yu (2005).

TABLE 4.5

Default Correlations from Driessen (2002)—In Percent

	1 year			2 years			5 years			10 years		
	Aa	A	Baa	Aa	A	Baa	Aa	A	Baa	Aa	A	Baa
Aa	0.04	0.05	0.08	0.17	0.19	0.31	0.93	1.04	1.68	3.16	3.48	5.67
A	0.05	0.06	0.10	0.19	0.32	0.35	1.04	1.17	1.89	3.48	3.85	6.27
Baa	0.08	0.10	0.15	0.31	0.35	0.56	1.68	1.89	3.05	5.67	6.27	10.23

Source: Yu (2005).

Both intensity-based models exhibit higher default correlations as the probability of default increases and as the horizon is extended.

Yu (2005) notices that the asymptotic result by Jarrow et al. (2001) may not hold for short bonds because of tax and liquidity effects reflected in the spreads. He therefore proposes an ad hoc adjustment of the intensity:

$$\lambda_t^{\text{adj}} = \lambda_t - \frac{a}{b+t},$$

where t is time and a and b are constants obtained from Yu (2002).

Tables 4.9 and 4.10 report the liquidity-adjusted tables of default correlations. The differences with Tables 4.4 and 4.5 are striking. First, the level of correlations induced by the liquidity-adjusted models is much higher. More surprisingly, the relationship between probability of default and default correlation is inverted: the higher the default risk, the lower is the correlation.

Modeling Intensities Under the Physical Measure

The modeling approach proposed by Yu (2005) relies critically on the result by Jarrow et al. (2001) about the equality of risk-neutral and historical intensities that only holds asymptotically. If the assumption is valid, then the risk-neutral intensity calibrated on market spreads can be used to calculate default correlations for risk management purposes.

Das et al. (2006) consider a different approach and avoid extracting information directly from market spreads. They gather a large sample of historical default probabilities derived from the Moody's RiskCalc™ model for public companies from 1987 to 2000. Falkenstein (2000) describes this model that provides one-year probabilities for a large sample of firms.

TABLE 4.6

Average Empirical Default Correlations [Using Equation (26)]–In Percent

	1 year			2 years			5 years			10 years		
	AA	A	BBB	AA	A	BBB	AA	A	BBB	AA	A	BBB
AA	0.16	0.02	–0.03	0.16	–0.03	–0.07	0.48	0.12	0.09	0.79	0.54	0.60
A	0.02	0.12	0.03	–0.03	0.20	0.23	0.12	0.32	0.23	0.54	0.54	0.61
BBB	–0.03	0.03	0.33	–0.07	0.23	0.78	0.09	0.23	0.82	0.60	0.61	1.17

Source: S & P's CreditPro 6.20—over 21 years.

TABLE 4.7

Default Correlations from Zhou (2001)—In Percent

	One year			Two years			Five years			Ten years		
	Aa	A	Baa	Aa	A	Baa	Aa	A	Baa	Aa	A	Baa
Aa	0.00	0.00	0.00	0.00	0.00	0.01	0.59	0.92	1.24	4.66	5.84	6.76
A	0.00	0.00	0.00	0.00	0.02	0.05	0.92	1.65	2.60	5.84	7.75	9.63
Baa	0.00	0.00	0.00	0.01	0.05	0.25	1.24	2.60	5.01	6.76	9.63	13.12

The authors show that in the Merton setup, the two drivers to the variation of PDs and to PD correlation changes are the debt ratio and the equity volatility of companies. In addition, they outline that volatility seems to be the dominant factor, having the largest impact on PDs.

They start by transforming the default probabilities into average intensities over one-year periods. Using Equation (76) and an estimate of default probabilities, they obtain a monthly estimate of default intensity by:

$$\lambda_t^i = -\ln(1 - PD_i^t).$$ (78)

The time series of intensities can be filtered for autocorrelation by being either derived from a mean value (Model 1) or modeled as a discrete AR(1) process (Model 2).

TABLE 4.8

Liquidity-Adjusted Default Correlations Inferred from Duffee (1999)—In Percent

	1 year			2 years			5 years			10 years		
	Aa	A	Baa	Aa	A	Baa	Aa	A	Baa	Aa	A	Baa
Aa	0.08	0.07	0.05	0.17	0.14	0.11	0.29	0.23	0.20	0.30	0.22	0.23
A	0.07	0.08	0.05	0.14	0.15	0.10	0.23	0.24	0.17	0.22	0.30	0.18
Baa	0.05	0.05	0.03	0.10	0.11	0.07	0.20	0.17	0.14	0.23	0.18	0.17

Source: Yu (2005).

TABLE 4.9

Liquidity-Adjusted Default Correlations from Driessen
(2002)—In Percent

	1 year			2 years			5 years			10 years		
	Aa	A	Baa	Aa	A	Baa	Aa	A	Baa	Aa	A	Baa
Aa	1.00	1.12	0.63	3.11	2.98	1.90	11.78	9.58	7.48	28.95	21.92	20.03
A	1.12	1.29	0.72	2.98	2.90	1.84	9.58	7.87	6.12	21.92	16.68	15.22
Baa	0.63	0.72	0.40	1.90	1.84	1.17	7.48	6.12	4.77	20.03	15.22	13.91

Source: Yu (2005).

$$\lambda^i_t = \lambda^i_{t-1} + \varepsilon^i_t = \overline{\lambda}^i + \xi^i_t \qquad (79)$$

$$\lambda^i_t = \alpha_i + \beta_i \lambda^i_{t-1} + \tilde{\varepsilon}^i_t \qquad (80)$$

The objective is to study the correlations between ε^i_t and ε^j_t, as well as between $\tilde{\varepsilon}^i_t$ and $\tilde{\varepsilon}^j_t$ for two firms i and j.

In the case of the AR(1) model, β_i ranges from 0.90 to 0.94.

Table 4.11. reports results for various time periods and rating classes. As can be seen in Figure 4.29, correlation of the residuals of default intensities appears to be less stable for high PDs than for low PDs.

In the case of low PDs, we can approximate: $\varepsilon^i_t = \lambda^i_t - \lambda^i_{t-1} \approx PD^t_i - PD^{t-1}_i$. This means that measuring the correlation of the change in intensities is close to measuring the correlation of the change in one-year PDs. Under the Merton assumption, the key driver for PD changes is equity volatility. These results cannot be directly compared with that related to rating based default correlation, as they clearly include a market component in addition to pure default event correlation.

Duration Models

The discussion about how much systematic and company specific covariates contribute to explain either spread, PD, or rating movements has gained some traction over the past five years. In the early 2000, Collin-Dufresne et al. (2001), Elton et al. (2001), and Huang and Huang (2003) reported that only a small fraction of corporate yield spreads could be

TABLE 4.10

Average Correlations Between Residuals of Default Intensities

Group	January 87 to June 90		July 90 to December 93		January 94 to June 97		July 97 to October 2000	
	Model 1	Model 2	Model 1	Model 2	Model 1	Model 2	Model 1	Model 2
HIGH GRADE Above A	0.36	0.37	0.10	0.10	0.02	0.01	0.37	0.38
MEDIUM GRADE Ba and Baa	0.22	0.23	0.10	0.10	0.03	0.02	0.24	0.25
LOW GRADE Single B and C	0.16	0.16	0.06	0.07	0.02	0.02	0.17	0.17

Source: Das et al. (2006).

FIGURE 4.29

The evolution of Correlation of Delta Default Intensities
through Time using Model 1.

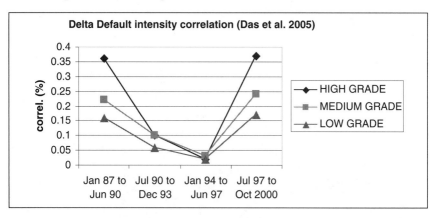

explained by default information.* Based on these findings, systematic
risk components, such as common factors, liquidity effects, and risk
aversion, can be considered as very important drivers to account for
spread changes. From an opposite perspective a legitimate question can
be: how much company specific are default intensities under the empirical measure?

In the research community, the first step has been to move from a
discontinuous rating based approach to a time continuous intensity one.
In the wake of Lando and Skodeberg (2002), Jafry and Schuermann (2003),
Jobst and Gilkes (2003), and several authors like Couderc and Renault
(2005) or Duffie et al. (2005), the model default intensity as a parametric
or semiparametric factor model derived from the Cox proportional hazard methodology (Cox, 1972 and 1975)[†] as follows:

$$\lambda^i(t) = \lambda^0(t) \exp (\beta' X^i(t)),$$

where $X^i(t)$ corresponds to the vector of covariates.

In Table 4.11, we draw a comparison between the categories of factors that have been tested, in order to explain default intensity changes.
Interestingly, at a rating category level, Couderc and Renault (2005) show
that contemporaneous financial market factors as well as past financial,

---

*Less than 25 percent Collin-Dufresne et al. (2001) and Elton et al. (2001).
[†]The former estimates the default intensity at a company level, the latter per rating category.

TABLE 4.11

The Table contains All Covariates that were Reviewed. In Italic, the Selected Covariates

	Data source	Bangia et al. (2002)	Koopman and Lucas (2005)	Couderc and Renault (2005)	Duffie et al. (2005)
Noncompany specific	*Credit market*		Spread of the LT Baa bond yields over LT U.S. Government bonds; U.S. business failure rate	Spread of LT BBB bonds over treasuries; Spread of LT BBB bonds over AAA bonds; Net issues of treasury securities	
	Business cycle	NBER growth/ recession monthly classification	GDP Index	M2–M1; Real GDP growth; Industrial production growth; Personal income growth; CPI growth	
	Financial market			Return on S&P's 500; Volatility of S&P's 500 returns; 10-year treasury yield; Slope of the term structure of interest rates	U.S. 3-month Treasury bill rate one-year return S&P's is 500
	Default Cycle			IG and NIG upgrade rates; IG and NIG downgrade rates	
	Lag effects			Mainly Financial Market series	
Company Specific	*Company specific*				Distance to default 1 year stock return

Abbreviations: LT = long term; NBER = _____; GDP = gross domestic product; CPI = _____; IG = investment grade; NIG = noninvestment grade.

credit market, and business cycle factors provide valuable explanatory power jointly. They find, based on principal component analysis, that the first five eigenvectors related to the above factors can explain 71 percent of the variance in the data. Figure 4.30, illustrates very clearly the impact of macroeconomic events on the default intensity.

Intensity models are usually undershooting the level of correlation generated by factor models, both under the empirical and the risk-neutral measure. Fermanian and Sbai (2005) try to reconcile the loss distribution of the portfolio models constructed based on a traditional factor model approach with intensity-based portfolio modeling. In order to reach similar levels of magnitude in the distribution of portfolio losses, they need to add to the Cox model defined earlier an unobservable random frailty term Z, common to all obligors.

$$\lambda^i (t) = Z \lambda^0 (t) \exp(\beta' X^i (t))$$

FIGURE 4.30

Changes in the Default Rate Intensity Over Time Based on S&P's Credit Pro 6.6 Database. A New Pool is Considered Each Quarter, Corresponding to the Incremental Rated Universe of the Year. (Couderc and Renault, 2005)

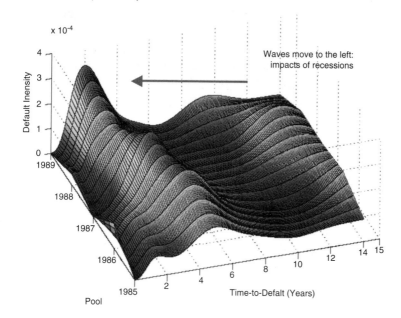

The calibration of this frailty term (typically a gamma distributed variable) enables us to obtain even more skewed loss distributions and thereby to avoid the underestimation problem that factor models usually face, due to the assumption of a Gaussian distribution of the common factors.[*]

Das et al. (2006) tend to provide some rationale for the use of a frailty term. They look at the same problem from a different perspective and esti-mate a default intensity model for each of the 2770 firms in their sample, according to the specification detailed in Duffie et al. (2005). Because some of the covariates in the estimation are common to all obligors, they ini-tially assume that it is possible to aggregate losses in the portfolio condi-tional on the realization of these factors. Based on the different tests they perform, they find that their model fails to fully match the tail of the true loss distribution of the portfolio. This could be because their intensity model is not capturing all the relevant common macrofactors at play. They focus on one extra covariate in particular: "the growth rate of the industrial production." It could also well be that more fundamentally, the assumption of conditional independence does not hold due to contagion (i.e., the presence of an unobservable variable common to all firms). As we know, contagion cannot be accounted for in a proper manner under the conditional independence assumption.

Implications for CDOs

Identifying How Sensitive CDO Tranches are to Empirical Correlation

In order to investigate the impact of correlation on CDO tranches, we con-sider the simple case of a well-diversified portfolio of 100 BB (or BBB) bonds with a nominal exposure of 1$ each. During growth periods we consider that the average default rate at a five-year horizon Q corre-sponds to P_{BB}^{gr}, and during recession periods the average default rate jumps to P_{BB}^{re}. In terms of correlation, we assume a one-factor model com-mon to all obligors. Based on empirical work, we consider that the aver-age asset-implied correlation ρ in a portfolio is in the range of ρ^{gr} during growth periods and moves up to ρ^{re} during recessions.

We focus on four scenarios:

- A growth scenario where the default rate and the correlation levels are, respectively, P_{BB}^{gr} and ρ^{gr}

---

[*]The point is to calibrate the frailty term properly.

- A recession scenario where the default rate and the correlation levels are P_{BB}^{re} and ρ^{re}
- A hybrid scenario with a default rate corresponding to the recession period (P_{BB}^{re}) and a correlation applicable to the growth period (ρ^{gr})
- An average scenario with a default rate corresponding to an average period (P_{BB}^{av}) and a correlation applicable to growth periods (ρ^{av})

The next step is to define the loss distribution of the portfolio in four different cases: growth, recession, hybrid, and average (i.e., one single average state of the world).

The probability of default conditional to the realization f of the common factor can be written as:

$$P(f) = \Phi\left(\frac{\Phi^{-1}(Q) - \sqrt{\rho}f}{\sqrt{1-\rho}} \right)$$

The function Φ typically corresponds to the Gaussian c.d.f.

The computation of the loss distribution of the portfolio is performed by drawing $N = 100$ binary variables (default or no default) from a binomial distribution, conditional on the realization f of the latent variable.

$$P(X = D/f) = \text{Bin}_D(f) = \binom{N}{D} P(f)^D (1 - P(f))^{N-D}$$

where D corresponds to the number of defaulters.

In order to obtain the unconditional loss distribution of the portfolio, we integrate on the density of the latent variable f. In this exercise, we assume that the law of the density of the latent variable corresponds to that of the PD.

$$P[X \leq D] = \sum_{d=0}^{D} \int \text{Bin}_d(f) \, d\phi(f)$$

Depending on the values we input for Q and ρ, we obtain one of the four loss distributions mentioned earlier.

An increase in portfolio losses from the growth scenario to the hybrid scenario is therefore purely due to the increase in default probability. The

TABLE 4.12

Default Rates Conditional on the Economic Cycle

Default rate	BB		BBB	
	Growth (%)	Recession (%)	Growth (%)	Recession (%)
1 Year	1.026	2.35	0.289	0.44
2 Years	2.51	5.93	0.69	1.17
3 Years	4.33	10.27	1.19	2.15
4 Years	6.37	15.01	1.78	3.79
5 Years	8.55	19.90	2.47	4.78

further increase in loss associated to the move from the hybrid scenario to the recession case is purely attributable to correlation.

Identifying the Impact of Cycles on the Tranching of Rated Transactions

Based on the work that has been performed in the past, we know from Bangia et al. (2002) that it is relevant to extract cumulative growth and recession default rates per rating category based on the approximation of first order Markovian transition matrices (see Table 4.12).

Based on empirical findings, on an average, default based asset-implied correlation during growth periods is found equal to 4.15 percent, correlation during recession periods amounts to 9.22 percent, and overall average correlation is 7.05 percent.

Based on the information related to the average PD and average correlation in the portfolio, we can define the initial tranching of the pool. We therefore obtain Scenario Loss Rates (SLR)* defining the attachment points related to the tranching, based on targeted ratings. For instance, in the average view of the world, a AAA tranche scenario can sustain D_{AAA} defaults and a BBB tranche scenario, D_{BBB} defaults. We then consider that we move to a world with three different states: growth, hybrid, and recession. We look at the new loss distribution of the pool depending on which state we are in and derive how many defaults we can now sustain with the initial SLR, given the fact that we are in a given state of the world.

---

*See Chapter 10.

FIGURE 4.31

Relative Sensitivity of Rated Tranches to Univariate and Multivariate Changes in the Cycle.

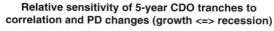

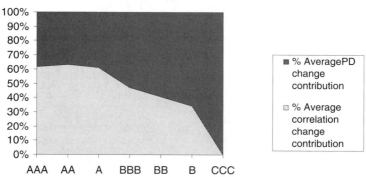

The increase in portfolio losses from the growth scenario to the hybrid scenario is therefore purely due to the increase in default probability. The further increase in loss associated to the move from the hybrid scenario to the recession case is purely attributable to correlation.

In a first step, we consider an underlying homogeneous BBB pool. In the growth and recession cases, the loss distribution of the portfolio is impacted by a change in PDs and a change in correlation. Based on the methodology described earlier, we know for each rated tranche what is the relative contribution of univariate (PD) and multivariate (correlation) changes. In Figure 4.31 we see that the more senior a tranche is, the more correlation matters.

In a second step, we use the earlier methodology. Practically, we consider two underlying portfolios constituted of BB and BBB bonds. We analyze the impact on the structured tranches of having one to five years of recession or growth after the deal is rated. We can observe in Figure 4.32 that the quality of the underlying pool makes a significant difference during the first year of recession: the lower the quality of the pool, the more sensitive to the cycle it is. When recession periods last more than one year, the quality of the underlying pool does not seem to matter anymore in a clear way.

FIGURE 4.32

Comparison of the Level of the Addition Enhancement Theoretically Relieved or Required to the Initial Level of Scenario Loss Rates, in Order to Keep an Identical Level of Risk in a Rated Tranches as a Result of One to Five Years of Recession (dark) or Growth (light), Following the Initial Tranching.

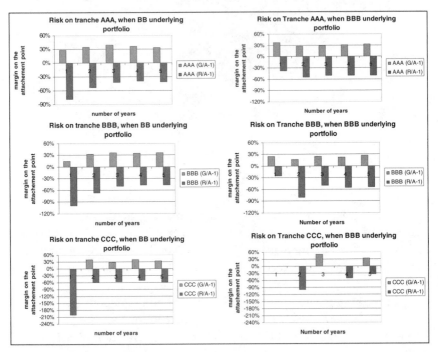

Identifying the Sources of the CDO Arbitrage Between Ratings and Prices

In this section, we investigate the impact of arbitrage between risk-neutral pricing and tranche ratings in a simple setup. We consider an underlying portfolio of 100 BBB bonds equally weighted in a five-year CDO.

In a layman's term, market prices include risk aversion and pure spread risk that the rating model doesn't consider. As a consequence, market quotes are typically higher than if prices were compared to prices made on a pure rating basis. In what follows we "project" the risk-neutral components in the empirical setup and analyze the change of enhancement levels that would be suggested by the change of measure, in order to match the empirical default rates per tranche. We then investigate whether this change in enhancement levels would be caused primarily by the multivariate or the univariate adjustment.

The model we use is the one described in the previous paragraphs. In addition, we consider a flat compound correlation of 14 percent that corresponds to the average level on the iTraxx on February 28, 2006. The average BBB bond spread that day was 67 bps, and we assume a 50 percent recovery rate.

We consider three scenarios:

♦ An Empirical scenario, where the default rate and correlation levels are historical ones.

♦ A Risk Neutral scenario, where the default rate and correlation levels are market ones

♦ A Hybrid scenario with a risk-neutral default rate and an empirical correlation.

The increase in portfolio losses from the first scenario to the hybrid scenario is therefore purely due to the change in default probability measure. The further increase in loss associated to the move from the hybrid

FIGURE 4.33

What is the Source of Arbitrage, Depending on the Rating of a CDO Tranche?

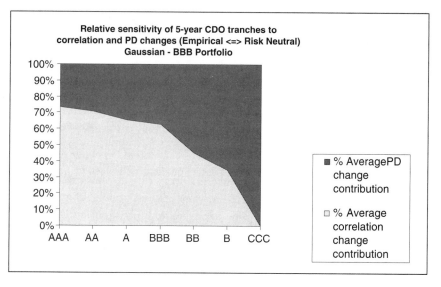

scenario to the risk-neutral case is purely attributable to a change in measure for correlation.

As can be seen in Figure 4.33, for investment grade tranches, it is the change from an average 7 percent correlation level to an average 14 percent, which explains the majority of the arbitrage. On the opposite, in the case of subinvestment grade tranches, it is the change, at a name level, from the empirical measure to the risk-neutral one, which explains the majority of the arbitrage.

When we run a similar exercise with a subinvestment grade underlying pool, we observe an increased contribution of the univariate component (change from the empirical to the risk-neutral measure) with respect to that of the change in correlation.

Of course, some precaution is required with all these results, as they do not factor in the correlation skew observed in the market.

CONCLUSION

Dependency is a vast and complex topic. A lot of progress has been made as the size of this chapter shows. There are still many problems to be solved in this field. An important area of investigation is undoubtedly around the dynamic dimension of comovements. Copulas have shown some limit in this respect.

REFERENCES

Bahar, R., and K. Nagpal (2001), "Measuring default correlation," *Risk*, March, 129–132.

Bangia, A., F. X. Diebold, A. Kronimus, C. Schagen, and T. Schuermann (2002), "Ratings migration and the business cycle, with application to credit portfolio stress testing," *Journal of Banking and Finance*, Elsevier, 26(2–3), 445–474, March.

Bouyé, E., V. Durrelman, A. Nikeghbali, G. Riboulet, and T. Roncalli (2000), "Copulas for finance: A reading guide and some applications," working paper, Credit Lyonnais.

Chen, X., and y. Fan (2006), "A model selection test for bivariate failure-time data," working paper NYU.

Chen, X., Y. Fan, and A. Patton (2004), "Simple tests for models of dependence between multiple financial time series, with applications to U.S. equity returns and exchange rates," working paper, LSE.

Collin-Dufresne, P., R. S. Goldstein, and S. J. Martin (2001), "The Determinants of Credit Spreads," *The Journal of Finance*, LVI (6), December.

Couderc, F., and O. Renault (2005), "Times to default: life cycle, global and industry cycle impacts," working paper, Fame.

Cox, D. R. (1972), "Regression models and life tables (with discussion)," *J. Roy. Statist. Soc B.*, 34, 187–220.

Cox, D. R. (1975), "Partial likelihood." *Biometrika*, 62, 269–276.

Das, S., D. Duffie, N. Kapadia, and L. Saita, (2006), "Common failings: How corporate defaults are correlated," Graduate School of Business, Stanford University, forthcoming in *The Journal of Finance*.

Das, S., L. Freed, G. Geng, and N. Kapadia (2002), "Correlated default risk," working paper, Santa Clara University.

Das, S., and G. Geng (2002), "Measuring the processes of correlated default," working paper, Santa Clara University.

Davis, M., and V. Lo (1999a), "Infectious defaults," working paper, Tokyo-Mitsubishi Bank.

Davis, M., and V. Lo (1999b), "Modelling default correlation in bond portfolios," working paper, Tokyo-Mitsubishi Bank.

Davis, M., and V. Lo (2000), "Infectious default," working paper, Imperial College.

de Servigny, A., R. Garcia-Moral, N. Jobst, and A. Van Lanschoot (2005), *Internal Document*. Standard & Poor's.

de Servigny, A., and N. Jobst (2005), "An empirical analysis of equity default swaps I: univariate insights," *Risk*, December, 84–89.

de Servigny, A., and O. Renault (2002), "Default correlations: empirical evidence," working paper, Standard & Poor's.

Deheuvels, P. (1979), "La fonction de dependance empirique et ses proprietes." *Acad. Roy. Belg., Bull.C1 Sci. 5ieme ser.*, 65, 274–292.

Deheuvels, P. (1981), "A nonparametric test for independence." *Pub. Inst. Stat. Univ. Paris.*, 26 (2), 29–50.

Demey, P., J.-F. Jouanin, and C. Roget (2004), "Maximum likelihood estimate of default correlations." *Risk*, November, 104–108.

Doukhan, P., J-D. Fermanian, and G. Lang (2005), "Copulas of a vector-valued stationary weakly dependent process," *Stat. Inf. Stoc. Pro.*

Driessen, J. (2002), "Is default event risk priced in corporate bonds?" working paper, University of Amsterdam.

Duffee, G. (1999), "Estimating the price of default risk," *Review of Financial Studies*, 12, 197–226.

Duffie, D. (1998), *Defaultable Term Structure Models with Fractional Recovery of Par*, Graduate School of Business, Stanford University,

Duffie, D., A. Berndt, R. Douglas, M. Ferguson, and D, Schranz (2005), "Measuring default-risk premia from default swap rates and EDFs," working paper, Graduate School of Business, Stanford University,

Duffie, D., and R. Kan (1996), "A yield-factor model of interest rates," *Mathematical Finance*, 6, 379–406.

Duffie, D., L. Saita, and K. Wang (2005), "Multi-period corporate default prediction with stochastic covariates" working paper.

Duffie, D., and K. Singleton (1999), "Modeling Term Structures of Defaultable Bonds" (with Ken Singleton), *Review of Financial Studies*, 12, 687–720.

Durrleman, V., A. Nikeghbali, and T. Roncalli (2000), "Which copula is the right one?" working paper, GRO Credit Lyonnais.

Elouerkhaoui, Y. (2003a), "Credit risk: correlation with a difference", working paper, UBS Warburg.

Elouerkhaoui, Y. (2003b), "Credit derivatives: basket asymptotics," working paper, UBS Warburg.

Elton, E., M. Gruber, D. Agrawal, and C. Mann (2001), "Explaining the rate spread on corporate bonds," *Journal of Finance*, 56, 247–277.

Embrecht, P., A. McNeil, and D. Strautmann (1999a), "Correlation and dependency in risk management: Properties and pitfalls," working paper, University of Zurich.

Embrecht, P., A. McNeil, and D. Strautmann (1999b), "Correlations: Pitfalls and alternatives," working paper, ETH Zurich.

Falkenstein, E. (2000), "RiskCalc™ for private companies: Moody's default model," Report, Moody's Investors Service.

Fermanian, J. D. (2005), "Goodness of fit tests for copulas," *Journal of Multivariate Analysis*, 95, 119–152.

Fermanian, J. D., D. Radulovic, and M. Wegkamp (2004), "*Weak convergence of empirical copula processes*," *Bernoulli*, 10(5), 847–860.

Fermanian, J-D., and M. Sbai (2005), "A comparative analysis of dependence levels in intensity-based and Merton-style credit risk models," working paper available on www.defaultrisk.com.

Fermanian, J. D., and O. Scaillet (2004), "Some statistical pitfalls in copula modeling for financial applications," FAME Research Paper Series rp108, International Center for Financial Asset Management and Engineering.

Frey, R., A. J. McNeil, and M. Nyfeler (2001), "Copulas and credit models," *Risk*, 14(10), 111–114.

Genest, C., and L-P. Rivest (1993), "Statistical inference procedures for bivariate Archimedean copulas," *J. Amer. Statist. Assoc.*, 88, 1034–1043.

Giesecke, K. (2003), "A simple exponential model for dependent defaults," *Journal of Fixed Income*, December, 74–83.

Gordy, M., and E. Heitfield (2002), "Estimating default correlations from short panels of credit rating performance data," working paper, Federal Reserve Board.

Harrison (1985), *Brownian Motion and Stochastic Flow Systems*, Wiley, New York.

Huang, J.Z., and M. Huang (2003), "How much of corporate-treasury yield spread is due to credit risk?: A new calibration approach," working paper.

Hull, J., and A. White (2004), "Valuation of a CDO and an nth to default CDS without Monte Carlo simulation," *Journal of Derivatives*, 2, 8–23.

Hull, J., and A. White (2005), "The perfect copula," working paper, J. L. Rotman School of Management, University of Toronto.

Jafry, Y., and T. Schuermann (2003), "Measurement and estimation of credit migration matrices," working paper, Federal Reserve Board of New York.

Jarrow, R., D. Lando and F. Yu (2001), "Default risk and diversification: Theory and applications," working paper, UC Irvine.

Jarrow, R., and F. Yu (2001), "Counterparty risk and the pricing of defaultable securities," *Journal of Finance*, 56, 1765–1800.

Jobst, N., and A. de Servigny (2006), "An empirical analysis of equity default swaps II: multivariate insights," *Risk*, January, 97–103.

Jobst, N., and K. Gilkes (2003), "Investigation transtition matrices: empirical insights and methodologies," working paper, Standard & Poor's, Structured Finance Europe.

Joe, H. and J. J. Xu (1996), "The estimation method of inference functions for margins for multivariate models," working paper, Department of Statistics, University of British Columbia.

Koopman, Siem Jan, and André Lucas (2005), "Business and default cycles for credit risk," *Journal of Applied Econometrics*, 20, 311–323.

Lando, D., and T. Skodeberg (2002), "Analysing rating transitions and rating drift with continuous observations," *Journal of Banking and Finance*, 26, 423–444.

Li, D. (2000), "On default correlation: a copula function approach," *Journal of Fixed Income*, 9, 43–54.

Longin, F., and B. Solnik (2001), Extreme correlation of international equity markets," *Journal of Finance*, 56, 649–676

Lucas, D. (1995), "Default correlation and credit analysis," *Journal of Fixed Income*, March, 76–87.

Mandelbrot, B. (1963), "The variation of certain speculative prices," *Journal of Business*, 36, 394–419.

Marshall, A., and I. Olkin (1988), "Families of multivariate distributions," *Journal of the American Statistical Association*, 83, 834–841.

McNeil, A. J., and Wendin, J. (2005): "Bayesian inference for generalized linear mixed models of portfolio credit risk," *working paper*, ETH.

Nelsen, R. (1999), *An Introduction to Copulas*, Springer-Verlag.

Scaillet, O. (2000), "Nonparametric estimation of copulas for time series," working paper, Departement des Sciences Economiques, Universite Catholique de Louvain, Belgium.

Scaillet, O., and J.D. Fermanian (2003). "Nonparametric estimation of copulas for times series," *Journal of Risk*, 5, 25–54

Schönbucher, P. (2002), "Taken to the limit: Simple and not-so-simple loan loss distributions," working paper, Bonn University.

Schönbucher, P. J. and D. Schubert (2001), "Copula-dependent default risk in intensity models," working paper, Department of Statistics, Bonn University.

Sklar, A. (1959), "Fonctions de répartition à n dimensions et leurs marges," *Publication de l'Institut Statistique Universitaire de Paris*, 8, 229–231.

Wang, S. (2000), "Aggregation of correlated risk portfolios: models and algorithm," working paper, Casualty Actuarial Society.

Yashin, A. I., and I. A. Iachine (1995), "Genetic analysis of durations: Correlated frailty model applied to survival of danish twins," *Genetic Epidemiology*, 12, 529–538.

Yu, F. (2002), "Modeling expected returns on defaultable bonds," *Journal of Fixed Income*, 12, 69–81.

Yu, F. (2005), "Default correlation in reduced-form models," *Journal of Investment Management*, 3(4), 33–42.

Zhou, C. (2001), "An analysis of default correlation and multiple defaults," *Review of Financial Studies*, 14, 555–576.

Rating Migration and Asset Correlation: Structured versus Corporate Portfolios*

Astrid Van Landschoot and Norbert Jobst

INTRODUCTION

This chapter investigates the differences in rating migration behavior of structured finance (SF) tranches and corporates and analyzes asset correlation within and between these groups. Although the market size of SF products such as asset-backed securities (ABS), collateralized debt obligations (CDO), residential-mortgage backed securities (RMBS), etc. has grown enormously over the past decade, only little is known about their behavior in terms of rating migration, especially default, compared to corporates. Credit risk portfolio models generally rely on the estimation of rating migration and/or default probabilities and asset correlation between exposures.[†] The latter significantly affects the portfolio loss distribution and in particular the tails of the distribution. Therefore, the accuracy of these parameter estimates is of vital importance.

---

*We would like to thank Arnaud de Servigny, Kai Gilkes, and André Lucas for very helpful comments and suggestions.
[†]The loss distribution also requires information on the recovery rate. However, the latter is not the focus of this chapter.

We use Standard & Poor's rating migration data to perform the analysis. Rating transition matrices are estimated using the cohort method, which corresponds to the industry standard, and the time-homogeneous duration method. For SF tranches, we focus on portfolios based on ratings and/or collateral types, whereas for corporates, we focus on portfolios based on ratings and/or industry classification. We then estimate asset correlation within and between portfolios using two methods. The first method derives implied asset correlation from joint default probabilities using historical transition data. [see, e.g., Bahar and Nagpal (2001) and de Servigny and Renault (2002)]. The second method uses a two-factor credit risk model to estimate asset correlation applying a maximum likelihood approach similar to Gordy and Heitfield (2002) and Demey et al. (2004).

DATA DESCRIPTION

We use Standard & Poor's rating performance data for SF and corporate tranches and the Standard & Poor's CreditPro dataset for corporates. The sample covers the period December 1989–December 2005. Since the SF market is much less mature than the corporate bond market. The reason for using this period is simply the availability of data. The SF (corporate) dataset consists of 71,646 tranches from 26,256 deals (11,436 corporate issuers, respectively) with at least one long-term Standard & Poor's rating during the sample period. Both datasets include U.S.-denominated as well as non-U.S.-denominated assets and only cover the assets with a long-term Standard & Poor's rating. For the SF tranches, similarly rated credit classes in the same deal are collapsed into a single tranche.*

As shown in Panels A and B of Table 5.1, the majority of SF tranches (83 percent) and corporates (69 percent) are issued in North America, especially in the United States. For corporates, the regional distribution of the financial sector is somewhat different from the other sectors. On average, 33 percent of the financials have their main office in Europe, which is high relative to the corporate average of 14 percent. For SF tranches, the regional distribution of CDOs is somewhat different from ABS, CMBS, and RMBS. An important percentage (39 percent) of CDOs is issued in Europe. Making a distinction between different types of CDOs, namely cash flow (CF) or synthetic (Synt), shows that the majority of U.S. CDOs are CF deals, whereas the majority of European CDOs are synthetic deals (see Panel B of

---

*Notice that corporate issuer ratings are based on senior bond ratings.

TABLE 5.1

Regional Distribution for SF Tranches and Corporates

	Total	United States/Canada (%)	Europe (%)	Asia/Japan (%)	Australia/New Zealand (%)	Latin America/Africa (%)
Panel A: SF tranches						
ABS	12,856	79	12	5	2	2
CDO	11,134	56	39	3	2	0
CMBS	8,657	84	9	5	2	0
RMBS	38,999	92	5	1	2	0
Total	71,646	83	12	2	2	0
Panel B: Corporates						
Auto	1,350	71	13	10	2	4
Cons	1,481	78	9	5	3	5
Energy	645	77	11	5	2	5
Fin	2,068	38	33	16	4	10
Home	465	73	11	5	3	9
Health	732	78	13	6	1	3
HiTech	462	82	6	10	1	1
Ins	921	66	17	7	3	6
Leis	922	83	9	3	2	3
Estate	351	70	10	9	8	3
Telecom	553	63	18	7	1	11
Trans	496	60	17	9	7	7
Utility	990	62	18	5	6	8
Total	11,436	69	14	7	3	6

Note: This table presents the number of SF tranches (Panel A) and corporates (Panel B) with at least one long-term Standard & Poor's rating between December 1989 and December 2005. SF tranches are classified by collateral type, whereas corporates are classified by industry.

FIGURE 5.1

Different Types of ABS and CDOs (Sample period: December 1989–December 2005)

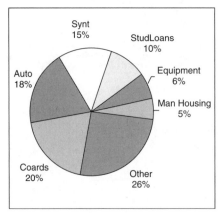 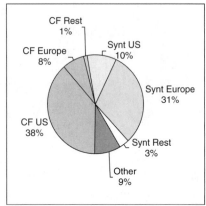

Note: Panel A and B give an overview of the different types of ABS and CDOs, respectively. The percentages are calculated as the total number observations for a specific subgroup of ABS and CDOs between December 1989–December 2005 divided by the total number of ABS and CDOs, respectively, between December 1989–December 2005. In Panel B, CF stands for cash-flow CDOs, whereas Synt stands for synthetic CDOs.

Figure 5.1). Panel A of Figure 5.1 shows the most common types of ABS included in the sample: auto loans or lease (18 percent), credit cards (20 percent), synthetic ABS (15 percent), student loans (10 percent), equipment (6 percent), and manufactured housing (MH) (5 percent). Even though the MH sector is relatively small compared to other sectors, it can significantly affect the results be discussing.

Making a distinction between different rating categories shows that the majority of SF tranches rated by Standard & Poor's between December 1989 and December 2005 are high quality, often AAA. Over the last decade, the number of rated SF tranches has grown enormously. To get an indication of the growth rate, we split the sample in two subperiods 1990–1997 and 1998–2005 (see Table 2). From the results, it is clear that the total number of observations between December 1997 and December 2005 is significantly higher than the number of observations between December 1989 and December 1997. For corporates, the most important rating categories in terms of number of observations are A and BBB. While the number of corporates has grown as shown in Table 5.2, the growth rate is much smaller relative to SF tranches.

TABLE 5.2

Average Number of SF Tranches and Corporates
by Rating

	AAA	AA	A	BBB	BB	B	CCC/C
SF tranches							
1990–2005	3,241	1,509	1,283	920	422	300	55
1990–1997	1,714	984	524	188	76	70	13
1998–2005	4,986	2,109	2,151	1,756	819	563	102
Corporates							
1990–2005	156	496	927	808	554	540	70
1990–1997	177	476	772	515	351	335	37
1998–2005	133	519	1103	1142	786	775	107

Note: This table presents the average number of observations between December 1989 and December 2005 for SF tranches and corporates by rating.

MIGRATION PROBABILITIES

In this section, we focus on the cohort and the time-homogenous duration method to estimate migration probabilities (see Chapter 2 of this book for more details). Using the cohort method, the average one-year unconditional migration probability from rating k to rating l can be written as follows

$$\bar{p}_{kl} = \sum_{t=0}^{T-1} w_k(t) \cdot \frac{N_{kl}(t, t+1)}{N_k(t)} \quad \text{for } k, l = 1, \ldots, K$$

$$\text{and } \sum_{t=0}^{T-1} w_k(t) = 1$$

(1)

where $N_{kl}(t, t+1)$ denotes the number of rating changes from rating k in year t to rating l in year $t+1$ and $N_k(t)$ the number of observations in rating k in year t. T represents the maximum number of years and $w_k(t)$ the weight for rating k at time t. For each rating, the weights sum to one. The unconditional migration probabilities $(\bar{p}_{kl})$ are weighted averages of yearly migration probabilities, with the weights being the relative size in terms of observations, that is $w_k(t) = \dfrac{N_k(t)}{\sum_{t=0}^{T-1} N_k(t)}$.

While the cohort method has become the industry standard, it ignores some potentially valuable information such as the timing of transition taking place during the calendar year and the number of changes that have led to a given rating at the end of the year. Furthermore, the cohort method is affected by the choice of observation times (See for example Lando and Skodeberg (2002), Schuermann and Jafry (2003)). An alternative approach that takes these issues into account is the time-homogeneous duration method, hereafter referred to as the duration method. The latter assumes that the transition probabilities follow a Markov process. Under the assumption of time-homogeneity, the transition probabilities can be described via a continuous time generator or matrix of transition intensities Λ.

$$\mathbf{P}(m) = \exp(\Lambda m) \quad \text{and } m \geq 0,$$

with $\mathbf{P}(m)$ the matrix of probabilities, Λ the generator, m the maturity (in years), and

$$\lambda_{kl} = \frac{N_{kl}(T)}{\int_0^T Y_k(s)ds} \quad \text{for } k \neq l$$

with N_{kl} the number of rating migrations from rating k to rating l over the interval $[0, T]$, Y_k the number of "firm years" spent in rating k. Λ is called a generator if $\lambda_{kl} \geq 0$ for $k \neq l$ and $\lambda_{kk} = -\Sigma_{k \neq l} \lambda_{kl}$. In the case of a homogeneous Markov chain, intensities are assumed to be constant. The denominator sums the number of "firm years" each tranche has spent in rating k.

While Table 5.3 presents the transition matrices for all SF tranches and corporates, Table 5.4 shows the transition matrices for ABS, CDO, CMBS, and RMBS.* Migration probabilities are estimated using the cohort method and are weighted averages of yearly probabilities from December 1989 until December 2005. Rating categories CC, C, and D are collapsed into one rating category D, which is absorbing. Migration probabilities are adjusted for transitions to NR.[†]

---

*The transition matrices for ABS, CDO, CMBS, and RMBS are in line with the transition matrices in Erturk and Gillis (2006). Notice that the latter have another approach for handling NR, which might cause slightly different results.
[†]NR stands for NonRated. Migration probabilities are adjusted as follows:

- ♦ a transition to NR is removed from the sample unless it is followed by a transition to a (nondefault) rating.
  - if a transition to NR is followed by a transition to the last rating before NR within three months, the transition to NR is assumed to be driven by noncredit related issues and therefore ignored.

TABLE 5.3

Transition Matrix for SF Tranches and Corporates Using Cohort Methods (NR Adjusted)

	AAA	AA	A	BBB	BB	B	CCC	D
Panel A: SF tranches								
AAA	99.2	0.65	0.11	0.06	0.01	0.01	0.01	0.005
AA	6.84	91.0	1.62	0.34	0.10	0.07	0.02	0.003
A	1.85	4.68	90.3	2.46	0.35	0.16	0.13	0.09
BBB	0.72	1.97	3.65	90.0	1.81	1.08	0.50	0.27
BB	0.17	0.27	1.73	5.13	87.4	2.56	1.67	1.09
B	0.05	0.09	0.11	1.13	4.05	87.3	4.00	3.24
CCC	0	0.10	0.20	0.10	0.51	2.95	64.8	31.4
Panel B: Corporates								
AAA	92.3	7.23	0.43	0.09	0	0	0	0
AA	0.43	90.7	8.36	0.43	0.01	0.05	0.01	0.01
A	0.04	1.68	92.2	5.65	0.27	0.07	0.01	0.08
BBB	0.01	0.14	3.50	91.2	4.09	0.60	0.14	0.35
BB	0.05	0.03	0.17	5.40	84.6	7.50	0.87	1.41
B	0	0.05	0.16	0.35	6.45	81.6	4.37	7.02
CCC	0	0	0.11	0.33	1.32	13.8	51.2	33.1

Note: Transition probabilities are weighted average probabilities over the period December 1989–December 2005. The weights are the number of observations in a particular rating category at time t divided by the total number of observations in that rating category over the sample period. The probabilities are presented in percent. Rating categories CC, C, and D are collapsed in one rating category D.

The estimates using the cohort and duration methods (not shown) allow us to draw the following main conclusions: Firstly, the one-year probability of staying in the same rating category is significantly higher for AAA SF tranches than for AAA corporates, 99 versus 92 percent. As shown in Table 5.4, this holds for all collateral types, especially CMBS and RMBS. Notice that the results for AAA CDOs are somewhat different from the other collateral types. The AAA CDO downgrade probability is high relative to

> – if a transition to NR is followed by a transition to a (nondefault) rating after three months or another rating than the rating just before NR within three months, the transition to NR is removed. However, later transitions are again taken into account.
> ♦ if a transition to NR is followed by a transition to default, the transition to NR and default are removed from the sample.

TABLE 5.4

Transition Matrix for Structured Products Using the Cohort Methods (NR adjusted)

	AAA	AA	A	BBB	BB	B	CCC	D
Panel A: Pure ABS								
AAA	98.6	1.08	0.21	0.08	0.01	0.01	0.01	0.02
AA	1.94	93.29	3.18	1.00	0.38	0.19	0	0.02
A	1.09	1.58	91.5	4.71	0.41	0.31	0.15	0.23
BBB	1.56	0.66	1.64	88.2	3.65	2.45	1.07	0.77
BB	0.29	0.38	2.58	2.96	74.8	9.16	6.20	3.63
B	0.23	0	0	0.23	3.42	59.7	18.0	18.5
CCC	0	0	0	0	0	4.41	61.0	34.6
Panel B: CDO								
AAA	97.6	1.69	0.38	0.28	0.03	0.03	0.03	0
AA	2.72	92.5	3.12	1.19	0.37	0.09	0.06	0
A	0.56	2.92	91.2	3.28	1.29	0.43	0.27	0.07
BBB	0.27	0.43	1.93	91.6	3.19	1.36	1.16	0.07
BB	0	0	0.06	1.68	90.4	3.07	3.59	1.22
B	0	0	0	1.11	2.77	79.8	10.6	5.82
CCC	0	0	0.41	0	0.41	2.48	73.6	23.1

Panel C: CMBS

AAA	99.6	0.33	0.03	0	0	0	0	0
AA	11.1	87.8	0.75	0.29	0	0.07	0	0
A	3.07	6.52	88.0	2.13	0.19	0.04	0.04	0.02
BBB	0.86	2.65	5.40	88.3	1.99	0.58	0.08	0.16
BB	0.25	0.22	0.57	4.77	90.4	2.51	0.60	0.72
B	0.04	0	0.04	0.30	3.16	90.8	3.75	1.94
CCC	0	0	0.40	0.40	1.61	4.42	75.9	17.3

Panel D: RMBS

AAA	99.8	0.18	0.01	0.01	0	0	0	0
AA	7.81	90.9	1.18	0.06	0.02	0.037	0.03	0
A	2.32	6.88	89.9	0.61	0.13	0.031	0.12	0.01
BBB	0.38	2.69	4.29	91.1	0.52	0.587	0.25	0.15
BB	0.15	0.38	2.94	7.10	87.1	0.95	0.69	0.71
B	0.05	0.17	0.17	1.69	4.74	88.9	2.12	2.17
CCC	0	0.457	0	0	0	0	47.0	52.5

Note: Transition probabilities are weighted average probabilities over the period December 1989–December 2005. The weights are the number of observations in a particular rating category at time t divided by the total number of observations in that rating category over the sample period. The probabilities are presented in percent. Rating categories CC, C, and D are collapsed in one rating category D.

CMBS, RMBS, and even ABS. This might be due to the relatively short rating history for CDOs and a higher downgrade probability at the end of our sample. Furthermore, the fact that there is a high degree of portfolio overlap between synthetic CDOs might cause higher downgrade probabilities (see, for example, South, 2005). For rating categories below AAA, the diagonal probabilities are very similar for SF tranches and corporates. Similarly to Schuermann and Jafry (2003), we estimate a mobility index (MI) or metric, which is the average of the singular values of the mobility matrix. The higher probability of staying in AAA for SF tranches is also reflected in a lower MI for SF tranches than corporates, 0.17 versus 0.12.

Secondly, the off-diagonal downgrade probabilities are significantly higher for corporates than for SF tranches. This holds for all rating categories, except for B and CCC. Thirdly, the upgrade probability for investment grade SF tranches, especially AA and A, is significantly higher than for corporates. As shown in Table 5.4, this is mainly driven by the results for CMBS and RMBS. Over the last few years, the MBS market could have benefited from a strong mortgage credit environment, including rapid industry wide prepayments, generally rising home prices and low interest rates.

Finally, the results using the cohort method seem to indicate that the default probabilities are higher for corporates than for SF tranches. However, using the duration method, the differences are much less pronounced and no clear conclusion can be drawn. Regarding the difference between the cohort and the duration methods, we find that default probabilities for high quality ratings (AAA and AA) are higher using the duration method, whereas for the below A rating assets, the probabilities are higher using the cohort method.

In Panels A and B of Figure 5.2, we present the distribution of notch-level rating migrations for SF tranches and corporates. For each product, we analyze the rating at the end of each year and compare it to the rating at the end of the previous year. The maximum notch-level downgrade is −19 (from AAA to D) and the maximum notch-level upgrade is 18 (from CCC–to AAA). The distributions are adjusted for migrations to NR (see footnote * on page 222). The following conclusions can be drawn from Figure 5.2: Firstly, for SF tranches, the number of rating migrations is clearly dominated by upgrades (64 percent), whereas for corporates, it is dominated by downgrades (63 percent).*

---

*This is even more pronounced when we focus on investment grade rating migrations (not shown).

FIGURE 5.2

Rating Migrations in Notches.

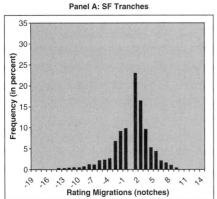

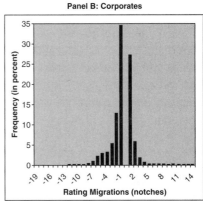

Note: This figure presents the percentage of rating migrations in notches. The maximum notch-level downgrade is −19 (from AAA to D) and the maximum notch-level upgrade is 18 (from CCC- to AAA). The distributions are adjusted for migrations to NR.

Given that the SF sample is clearly dominated by AAA tranches, the upgrade probability for SF tranches is likely to be even biased downwards. Secondly, for corporates, one- or two-notch-level rating migrations (up- or downgrades) represent 81 percent of all rating migrations. For SF tranches, however, the number of up-to-two notch-level rating migrations is significantly lower, 58 percent. As a result, the distribution of notch-level rating migrations is concentrated around the mean for corporates and more spread around the mean for SF tranches. Thirdly, the maximum notch-level downgrade is higher for SF tranches than for corporates, −19 and −16, respectively. Furthermore, on average 1.4 percent of the yearly rating migrations for SF tranches is a more than 10 notches (say from AAA to BB+) compared to 0.6 percent for corporates.

A general conclusion that can be drawn from Table 5.3 and Figure 5.2 is that there are less rating migrations for SF tranches than for corporates, but that the migrations are more significant in terms of notches for SF tranches.

So far, we have mainly focused on average probabilities over a period of 11 years. In what follows, we will briefly discuss the time-varying behavior of the downgrade probabilities for SF tranches and

FIGURE 5.3

Time-Varying Rating Downgrade Probabilities for
Investment and Speculative Grade Ratings
(NR adjusted)

Panel A: SF Tranches   Panel B: Corporates

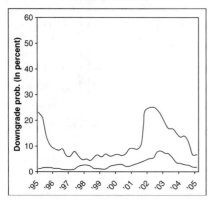
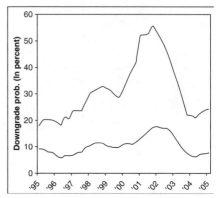

Note: This figure presents the downgrade probability (in percentage) for investment grade (pink line) and speculative
(blue line) grade ratings from December 1995 until December 2005. The probabilities are calculated as the number
downgrades at the end of each year divided by the total number of observations at the end of the previous year.
Probabilities are adjusted for migrations to NR.

corporates. As shown in Panels A and B of Figure 5.3, the downgrade
probabilities for investment grade (IG) and speculative grade (SG)
SF tranches and corporates vary substantially over time. The probability for corporates reaches a peak at the end of 2001 and remains
high for almost a year. This peak moment coincides with a very low
growth rate of the OECD U.S. leading indicator. For SF tranches, the
peak is reached mid-2003, which is somewhat later than for corporates.
Notice that the SG downgrade probability for SF tranches was high in
1995. This is mainly due to a very small number of SG observations for
SF tranches.

ASSET CORRELATION

An important input parameter for credit risk models is the correlation
between assets in the underlying portfolio (see Chapter 4 of this book
for more details on dependence). We use a non parametric and a parametric method to derive the (asset) correlation within and between

portfolios of assets from time series of default probabilities.[*],[†] The non-parametric method, which will hereafter be referred to as the joint default probabilities (JDP) approach, estimates JDP using historical transition data. Implied asset correlation is derived from JDP (see, for example, Bahar and Nagpal, 2001 and de Servigny and Renault, 2002). In the parametric approach, asset correlation is derived from a credit risk model. As suggested by Gordy and Heitfield (2002) and similar to Frey and McNeil (2003), Demey et al. (2004), Tasche (2005), Jobst and de Servigny (2006), and others, we use a two-factor model. The latter assumes that correlation between firm asset values is driven by two systematic risk factors, which could be thought of as an economic and a sector-specific factor. In the remainder of this chapter, we will create portfolios of assets based on sector classification, which implicitly assumes that sectors can be seen as homogeneous risk classes that are driven by similar factors.

Joint Default Probabilities (JDP) Approach

Based on the number of transitions to the default state D for sector i and j (M_D^i and M_D^j, respectively) and the total number of assets in sector i and j (N^i and N^j, respectively), the average JDP can be estimated as follows

$$\bar{p}_D^{i,j} = \sum_{t=0}^{T-1} w(t) \left(\frac{M_D^i(t,t+1)\, M_D^j(t,t+1)}{N^i(t)\, N^j(t)} \right) \tag{2}$$

with T the maximum number of years and $w(t)$ the weight at time t. To analyze the impact of the strong growth of the SF market, we estimate equally-weighted (that is, $w(t) = 1/T$) and size-weighted (that is, $w(t) = \sqrt{N^i(t)N^j(t)}/\sum_{t=0}^{T-1}\sqrt{N^i(t)N^j(t)}$) average JDP.

Implied asset correlation, which is the correlation needed in a typical credit risk model to recover or match the joint default events that have

---

[*]In this chapter, we focus on asset correlation derived from rating migrations to default. Alternatively, we could use credit spread data or equity data to obtain asset correlation. See Schönbucher (2003) (p. 297) for a detailed discussion of the advantages and disadvantages of the three approaches.

[†]See Van Landschoot (2006) for a detailed analysis of asset correlation estimates derived from default probabilities and rating transitions (including default) for SF tranches and corporates and a discussion of confidence intervals for correlation estimates based on a simulation analysis.

been observed, is derived from JDP. We start from a structural credit risk model, initiated by Merton (1974), and assume that default occurs when the firm's asset value falls below a threshold Z_D. The threshold is calibrated such that the default probability corresponds to the observed probability

$$p_D^i = \Phi(Z_D^i)$$

with $Z_D^i = \Phi^{-1}(p_D^i)$ and Φ the standard Gaussian cumulative distribution function (CDF).

The joint default probability for sector i and j is given by

$$\overline{p}_D^{\,i,j} = \Phi_2(Z_D^i, Z_D^j, \rho_{ij}) \tag{3}$$

with Φ_2 the bivariate standard Gaussian CDF. The implied asset correlation, ρ_{ij}, can be derived by solving Equation (3). Estimating asset correlation between I sectors results in the following estimator of the correlation matrix

$$\hat{\Sigma}_{\text{JDP}} = \begin{bmatrix} \hat{\rho}_1 & \hat{\rho}_{1,2} & \cdots & \hat{\rho}_{1,I} \\ \hat{\rho}_{2,1} & \hat{\rho}_2 & \cdots & \hat{\rho}_{2,I} \\ \vdots & \vdots & \vdots & \vdots \\ \hat{\rho}_{I,1} & \hat{\rho}_{I,2} & \cdots & \hat{\rho}_I \end{bmatrix} \tag{4}$$

with the elements being the intra (within sectors) and inter (between sectors) asset correlation. In what follows, we will only present the intra asset correlation (diagonals) and the average inter asset correlation (average of off-diagonal elements). The correlation structure $\hat{\Sigma}_{\text{JDP}}$ is the result of $I(I-1)/2$ pairwise estimations.

Two-Factor Model

In a two-factor model, the asset value V_i is driven by two common, standard normally distributed factors Y and Y_i and an idiosyncratic standard normal noise component ε_n

$$V_n^t = \sqrt{\rho}Y + \sqrt{\rho_i - \rho}Y_i + \sqrt{1 - \rho_i}\varepsilon_n \quad \text{for } n \le N \tag{5}$$

Y can be seen as a common (or economywide) factor that affects all assets at the same time and Y_i as a sector-specific factor. The asset values are correlated with correlation coefficients ρ and ρ_i. Default occurs when the asset value hits a threshold. An interesting feature of this model is that default events are independent conditional on the two common factors. The conditional default probability of sector i can be written as follows

$$p_D^i(y, y_i) = \Phi\left(\frac{Z_D^i - \sqrt{\rho}y - \sqrt{\rho_i - \rho}\, y_i}{\sqrt{1 - \rho_i}}\right)$$

with $Z_D^i = \phi^{-1}(\bar{p}_D^i)$ the default threshold for sector i, $\bar{p}_D^i$ the average (unconditional) default probability for sector i, and Φ the standard Gaussian CDF. This two-factor model implies the following correlation structure

$$\hat{\Sigma}_{\text{MLE}} = \begin{bmatrix} \hat{\rho}_1 & \hat{\rho} & \cdots & \hat{\rho} \\ \hat{\rho} & \hat{\rho}_2 & \cdots & \hat{\rho} \\ \vdots & \vdots & \vdots & \vdots \\ \hat{\rho} & \hat{\rho} & \cdots & \hat{\rho}_I \end{bmatrix}$$

with $\hat{\rho}$ the inter asset correlation (or the correlation between I sectors) and $\hat{\rho}_i$ the intra asset correlation (or the correlation within the ith sector). This two-factor model approach differs from the JDP approach in that the correlation structure ($\hat{\Sigma}_{\text{MLE}}$) is the result of one joint estimation. Default information for all sectors is considered at the same time. Similar to Demey et al. (2004), we apply the asymptotic maximum likelihood (ML) method to estimate the factor loadings and thus asset correlation.

Empirical Results: SF Tranches versus Corporates

In this section, we present the asset correlation estimates for different sectors defined by collateral type for SF and industries for corporates. We apply the JDP and the two-factor model approach. For each approach, we estimate asset correlation based on equally and size weighted default probabilities. We use time series of 3-monthly default probabilities for different sectors from December 1994 until December 2005.* In this chapter, we do not analyze the impact of country and/or regional differences.

---

*The reason for using a shorter sample period for asset correlation than for the transition matrices is because of a lack of default observations before December 1994.

In Table 5.5, we present the average yearly default probabilities based on historical data and the inter and intra asset correlation estimates for SF tranches. As shown in Panel A of Table 5.5, the intra asset correlation estimates are quite different for different collateral types, varying from on average 4 percent for RMBS to on average 17 percent for CDOs. To analyze the impact of regional differences on the estimations, we exclude all non-U.S. SF tranches from the sample. Although not reported the results are very similar. Again, we find that intra asset correlation estimates for CMBS and RMBS are somewhat below the estimates for ABS and especially CDOs. One could argue that the average intra asset correlation estimates, which are between 7 and 15 percent, are relatively low. However, one should bear in mind that SF rating performance histories

TABLE 5.5

Asset Correlation Estimates for SF Tranches

	$\bar{p}_k$		JDP		Two-factor model	
	Size	Equal	Size	Equal	Size	Equal
Panel A: SF tranches						
Inter correlation (ρ)			4.5	4.9	1.6	1.8
Intra correlation (ρ_i)						
ABS	0.74%	0.57%	9.1	11.6	12.4	19.7
CDO	0.19%	0.19%	15.0	20.2	16.9	17.6
CMBS	0.54%	0.43%	8.3	10.5	5.2	7.3
RMBS	0.32%	0.35%	5.0	5.0	3.2	3.5
			9.3	11.8	9.4	11.8
Panel B: SF tranches						
Inter correlation (ρ)			4.7	4.7	1.5	1.7
Intra correlation (ρ_i)						
ABS, excl MH	0.40%	0.34%	10.1	12.1	12.9	13.5
MH	3.88%	2.78%	20.7	24.1	26.7	37.5
CDO	0.19%	0.19%	15.0	20.2	13.1	13.5
CMBS	0.54%	0.43%	8.3	10.5	6.4	6.7
RMBS	0.32%	0.35%	5.0	5.0	4.4	5.2
			7.5	9.0	12.7	15.3

Note: This table presents average default probabilities ($\bar{p}_k$) and asset correlation estimates (ρ and ρ_i) for SF tranches. The latter are estimated using two methods: (1) Joint default probability (JDP) approach, and (2) a two-factor model approach. The latter is estimated using an asymptotic maximum likelihood (ML) technique. "Equal" refers to equally weighted results, whereas "Size" refers to size weighted results, with the weights in year t being the number of assets in year t relative to the number of assets over the total sample period (adjusted for NR).

are very short and only include one recession period.* As a result, the effect of (severe) several recession periods on rating transitions and default behavior has not been tested. Asset correlation is likely to be lower during economic growth periods.

The inter asset correlation estimates are always below 5 percent. However, they are significantly higher using the JDP approach than the two-factor model. An analysis of one-by-one inter asset correlation estimates using the JDP approach [see $\hat{\rho}_{i,i}$ in Equation (4)] shows that this is mainly driven by the inter asset correlation estimates with CDOs. Excluding CDOs from the sample (not shown) results in average inter asset correlation estimates just below 2 percent, which is very similar to the results based on a two-factor model. This shows that ABS, CMBS, and RMBS are very different and react differently to changes in a common factor, which could be seen as the business cycle.

Comparing equally- and size-weighted results indicates that the estimates for ABS and CDOs are most affected by the enormous growth in the SF market. However, when we split the ABS sector into two separate sectors, namely MH and ABS excluding MH, we find that the intra asset correlation estimates for ABS are much less affected by the methodology (see Panel B of Table 5.5). At the same time, it shows that the MH-sector is different from other ABS subsectors. In general, MH seems to be a risky sector in a sense that the behavior of MH tranches is substantially affected by sector-specific events, which results in a high intra asset correlation estimate. The average default probabilities are also substantially higher for MH than for other sectors. This is mainly due to an increasing trend in the delinquency rate for MH loans and the level of losses for MH pools over the last decade. As a result, the majority of MH issuers were affected by high levels of cumulative repossessions and losses.

In Table 5.6, we present the average annual default probabilities and asset correlation estimates for corporates. Similarly to the results for SF tranches, we find that intra asset correlation estimates differ substantially between sectors. However, average intra asset correlation estimates for SF tranches and corporates have more or less the same order of magnitude. This is somewhat surprising given the substantial differences between these markets. Comparing the default probabilities for SF tranches and corporates shows that the average default probability for ABS (excluding MH), CDO, CMBS, and RMBS are significantly below the average for corporates.

---

*A recession period is defined according to the NBER definition of a recession.

TABLE 5.6

Asset Correlation Estimates for Corporates

	$\overline{p}_k$		JDP		Two-factor model	
	Size	Equal	Size	Equal	Size	Equal
Inter correlation (ρ)			5.9	6.3	3.2	3.2
Intra correlation (ρ_c)						
Auto	3.45%	3.14%	9.8	10.6	8.6	8.7
Cons	3.35%	3.34%	5.1	4.9	6.7	6.8
Energy	1.70%	1.63%	14.4	14.7	9.7	9.6
Fin	0.51%	0.52%	18.0	17.6	10.0	9.9
Home	2.14%	2.07%	12.2	12.6	6.9	6.8
Health	2.08%	2.03%	9.6	9.9	7.1	7.3
HiTech	1.77%	1.66%	13.4	13.8	7.4	7.6
Ins	0.35%	0.36%	14.0	14.0	10.3	9.8
Leis	3.11%	2.92%	9.6	10.0	9.1	8.9
Estate	0.14%	0.13%	31.0	33.0	25.9	27.7
Telecom	5.87%	4.79%	17.0	18.7	18.4	16.7
Trans	2.94%	2.84%	8.5	8.9	7.0	6.9
Utility	0.83%	0.70%	21.1	22.3	10.8	10.3
			14.1	14.7	10.6	10.5

Note: This table presents average probabilities of default ($\overline{p}_k$) and asset correlation estimates (ρ and ρ_i) for corporates. The latter are estimated using two methods: (1) Joint default probability (JDP) approach. (2) Asymptotic maximum likelihood (ML). "Equal" refers to equally weighted results, whereas "Size" refers to size weighted results, with the weights in year t being the number of assets in year t divided by the number of assets over the total sample period (minus NR). The estimates are given in percent.

However, notice that the averages are calculated for the same short period (December 1994–December 2005).

The corporate bond market is more mature than the market for SF tranches, resulting in very similar results for size-weighted and equally-weighted estimates. Furthermore, when reestimating correlation for corporates using default probabilities from December 1981 until December 2005, we find that the average intra asset correlation estimates are between 13 and 16 percent for the two methods. Average inter asset correlation is between 4 and 6 percent. This is in line with the results in Jobst and de Servigny (2006).

In a final step, we combine the SF and corporate data and estimate inter and intra asset correlation for 13 corporate industries and 4 SF collateral types. Using a two-factor model, we assume that there is one factor that drives the results for SF tranches and corporates and a second factor that is specific for each sector/collateral type. Table 5.7 shows that adding SF data to the corporate dataset results in lower inter asset correlation and very similar average intra asset correlation. A few changes are worth mentioning. Firstly, intra asset correlation for ABS and RMBS is significantly higher once corporate default information is added. Secondly, intra asset correlation for automotive and consumer sector have gone up significantly, whereas the intra asset correlation for real estate and telecom has come down significantly. A possible explanation for these differences might be

TABLE 5.7

Asset Correlation Estimates for SF Assets and Corporates

	$\bar{p}_k$		JDP		Two-factor model	
	Size	Equal	Size	Equal	Size	Equal
Inter correlation (ρ)			4.3	4.69	2.37	2.41
Intra correlation (ρ_c)						
Auto	3.45%	3.14%	10.8	12.1	16.6	20.0
Cons	3.35%	3.34%	4.1	3.8	11.8	15.0
Energy	1.70%	1.63%	11.0	11.5	9.9	10.9
Fin	0.51%	0.52%	9.6	9.4	5.9	7.1
Home	2.14%	2.07%	9.5	10.0	7.2	8.4
Health	2.08%	2.03%	8.1	8.4	7.1	6.6
HiTech	1.77%	1.66%	13.7	13.9	8.2	8.9
Ins	0.35%	0.36%	10.0	9.7	8.9	9.5
Leis	3.11%	2.92%	8.5	8.8	6.3	6.0
Estate	0.14%	0.13%	17.8	18.6	6.0	6.8
Telecom	5.87%	4.79%	21.3	24.1	6.5	7.1
Trans	2.94%	2.84%	6.6	7.1	9.0	9.2
Utility	0.83%	0.70%	20.4	22.1	9.8	8.6
ABS	0.74%	0.57%	8.5	11.5	27.1	28.7
CDO	0.19%	0.19%	13.4	14.8	19.2	16.1
CMBS	0.54%	0.43%	5.4	7.8	5.7	5.6
RMBS	0.32%	0.35%	1.9	1.6	8.3	9.1
			10.6	11.5	10.2	10.8

Note: This table presents average probabilities of default ($\bar{p}_k$) and asset correlation estimates (ρ and ρ_c) for corporates and SF tranches. The latter are estimated using two methods: (1) Joint default probability (JDP) approach. (2) Asymptotic maximum likelihood (ML). "Equal" refers to equally weighted results, whereas "Size" refers to size weighted results, with the weights in year t being the number of assets in year divided by the number of assets over the total sample period (minus NR). The estimates are given in percent.

TABLE 5.8

Abbreviations for Corporate Sectors

Corporate Sectors	Abbreviations
Aerospace/automotive/capital goods/metal	Auto
Consumer/service sector	Cons
Energy and natural resources	Energy
Financial Institutions	Fin
Forest and building products/homebuilders	Home
Health care/chemicals	Health
High technology/computers/office equipment	HiTech
Insurance	Ins
Leisure time/media	Leis
Real estate	Estate
Telecommunications	Telecom
Transportation	Trans
Utility	Utility

For an overview of the different corporate industries, see Table 5.8.

that SF tranches and corporates are very different, in which case the sector and collateral specific factor partially captures the corporate common risk for corporate sector and the SF common risk for SF tranches. A possible solution, which has not been explored in this chapter, would be to use multi-factor extensions.

CONCLUSIONS

In this chapter, we investigate and compare transition probabilities and asset correlation estimates for SF tranches and corporates. We use Standard & Poor's rating transition data from December 1989 until December 2005 to perform the analysis. Rating transition probabilities are estimated using the cohort method, which is the industry standard, and the time-homogeneous duration method. Asset correlation within and between sectors of SF tranches and corporates are estimated using two methods. The first method, referred to as the joint default probability approach, derives implied asset correlation from joint default probabilities using historical transition data. The second method uses a two-factor credit risk model to estimate asset correlation. The latter is estimated using a asymptotic maximum likelihood. The following main conclusions can be drawn from the empirical analysis:

+ Over the past decade, AAA SF tranches show much higher rating stability than AAA corporates.

+ For SF tranches, the number of rating migrations is clearly dominated by upgrades (64 percent), whereas for corporates, it is dominated by downgrades (63 percent). This is even more pronounced when we focus on investment grade rating migrations.

+ One and two notch downgrades and upgrades represent a much higher percentage of the total number of migrations for corporates (81 percent) than for SF tranches (58 percent). This means that the distribution of notch-level rating migrations is concentrated around the mean, whereas for SF tranches, the distribution is more spread around the mean.

+ The distribution of notch-level rating migrations is also fatter tailed for SF tranches than for corporates. On average, 1.4 percent of the yearly rating migrations for SF tranches is more than 10 notches (say from AAA to BB+) compared to 0.6 percent for corporates.

+ Even though the SF and corporate markets are very different, the average intra asset correlation estimates within and between groups of SF tranches and corporates are comparable. Individual intra asset correlation estimates, however, can differ substantially.

+ The results seem to indicate that asset correlation within portfolios of CDOs and manufactured housing (MH) is higher than for other collateral types such as RMBS and CMBS.

REFERENCES

Bahar, R., and K. Nagpal (2001), "Measuring default correlation," *Risk*, 14(3), 129–132.

de Servigny, A., and O. Renault (2002), Default correlation: Empirical evidence. Standard & Poor's working paper.

Demey, P., J-F. Jouanin, C. Roget, and T. Roncalli (2004), "Maximum likelihood estimate of default correlations," *Risk*, 104–114.

Erturk, E., and T. G. Gillis (2006), Rating transitions 2005: Global structured securities exhibit solid credit behavior. Standard & Poor's Report.

Frey, R., and A. J. McNeil (2003), "Dependent defaults in models of portfolio credit risk." *Journal of Risk*, 6(1), 59–92.

Gordy, M., and E. Heitfield (2002), Estimating default correlations from short panels of credit rating performance data, Federal Reserve Board of Governers, mimeo.

Jobst, N., and de A. Servigny (2006), "An empirical analysis of equity default swaps: Multivariate insights," *Risk*, 97–103.

Lando, D., and T. M. Skodeberg (2002), "Analyzing rating transitions and rating drift with continuous observations," *Journal of Banking and Finance*, 26, 423–444.

Merton, R. C. (1974), "On the pricing of corporate debt: The risk structure of interest rates," *Journal of Finance*, 29(2), 449–470.

Schönbucher, P. J. (2003), *Credit Derivatives Pricing Models: Models, Pricing and Implementation*. John Wiley & Sons Ltd.

Schuermann, T. and Y. Jafry (2003), Measurement and estimation of credit migration matrices. Wharton Financial Institutions Center.

South, A. (2005), CDO spotlight: Overlap between reference portfolios sets synthetic CDOs apar Standard & Poor's Commentary.

Tasche, D. (2005), "Risk contributions in an asymptotic multi-factor framework," working paper, Deutsche Bundesbank.

Van Landschoot, A. (2006), "Dependent credit migrations: Structured versus corporate portfolios," working paper, Standard & Poor's.

CHAPTER 6

Collateral Debt Obligation Pricing

Arnaud de Servigny

INTRODUCTION

In this chapter, we present pricing techniques for Collateral Debt Obligation (CDO) tranches. As we will see, a very comprehensive toolbox has been recently developed, which enables us to quickly price standardized tranches. Prices in this market depend not only on pure credit and default risk but also significantly on market risk (spread movements and co-movements).

The first impression of the existence of a mature corpus of pricing techniques applicable to liquid synthetic CDO transactions is however somewhat deceiving. During the May 2005 crisis period, these models did not succeed in providing fully reliable pricing results and, in addition, the related hedging strategies did not prove very robust. The concept of correlation extracted from copulas,* on which these prices are typically based, has found some limitations. The main challenge for copulas is to account for a dynamic spread co-movement structure as well as to harness a robust hedging strategy.

The above mixed statement can look quite surprising as an introduction. In our view, it only reflects the fact that the segment of marked-to-market structured credit products corresponds to a very recent activity.

---

*See Chapter 4 for a definition of copulas.

The tools that have been developed so far are not perfect, but certainly facilitate the expansion of that market. In equity and fixed income pricing, it is agreed that the market standard Black and Scholes (1973) approach has a rather weak performance, everybody still uses it as the market standard. In a similar way, we have recently seen that copulas are not fully accurate in the fast growing credit space, but almost everybody keeps on using the paradigm for the sake of consolidating a common language.

In parallel to this liquid and traded market, there exists an important but less liquid bespoke synthetic market. The appropriate word used to describe these instruments is single tranche CDO (STCDO). The challenge here is to harness a pricing technique to an illiquid market.

In what follows, we focus at first on the synthetic CDO market, with some particular emphasis on "correlation trading" related to indices. We then discuss briefly the pricing techniques used for the more bespoke synthetic tranches.

The second type of instruments we will focus on in this chapter are cash CDOs. Pricing such instruments is not straightforward, especially when, on the asset side, there is no market price for the loans in the underlying pool. On the liability side, we need to be aware that the waterfall structure of cashflows has an effect on the value of tranches.

TYPOLOGIES OF CDOS

It is customary to classify CDOs depending on their function. In this case, usually consider CDOs are in balance sheets and arbitrage deals. The former type of transactions is typically used by financial institutions in order to rebalance their portfolio, whereas the latter focuses on the excess spread generated in the securitized pools because of diversification (see Chapter 10 for further details).

In the current analysis we focus on a different perspective, i.e., pricing techniques. As a consequence, it is more relevant to concentrate primarily on the way CDO instruments are structured. What really matters in order to differentiate CDO prices is the nature and the source of repayment of the collateral pool. We distinguish here between the two main categories of CDOs: synthetic and cashflow CDOs.

♦ *Synthetic CDOs*: These are based on a portfolio of Credit Default Swaps (CDSs) and constitute an alternative to the actual transfer of assets to the SPV, see Figure 6.1. These structures benefit from

FIGURE 6.1

Structure of a Synthetic CDO.

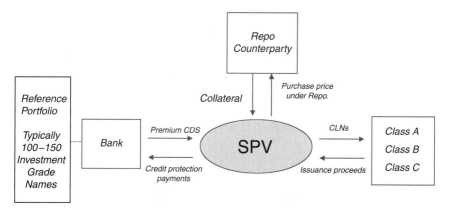

advances in credit derivatives and transfer the credit risk associated to a pool of assets to the SPV while not moving assets physically.* The SPV sells credit protection to the bank via credit default swaps.

Synthetic deals may be fully funded, through the recourse to CLNs (credit-linked notes), partially funded or totally unfunded. In the cases where the deals are partially funded or unfunded, counterparty risk needs to be mitigated.

Single tranches can be issued on their own, without the full CDO being placed in the market (STCDO). The issuing bank then performs the appropriate hedging of these tranches on its books.

♦ *Cashflow CDOs:* A simple cashflow CDO structure is described in Figure 6.2. The issuer (special purpose vehicle) purchases a pool of collateral (bonds, loans, etc.), which will generate a stream of future cash flows (coupon or other interest payment and repayment of principal). Standard cashflow CDOs involve the physical transfer of the assets.† This purchase is funded through the issuance of a variety of notes with different levels of seniority.

---

*The typical maturity for a synthetic CDO is five years, but has moved recently to longer ones like 7 and 10 years.
†The ramp up period can be quite lengthy and costly. In addition, loan terms vary. The lack of uniformity in the manner in which rights and obligations are transferred results in a lack of standardized documentation for these transactions.

FIGURE 6.2

The Structure of a Cashflow CDO.

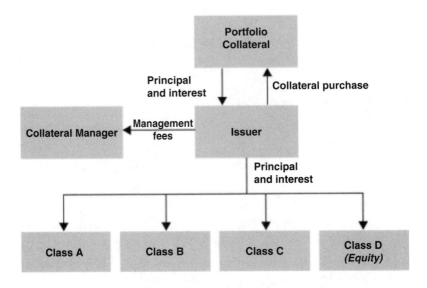

The collateral is managed by an external party (the collateral/
asset manager) who deals with the purchases of assets in the
pool and the redemption of the notes. The manager also takes
care of the collection of the cash flows and of their transfer to
the note holders via the issuer. The risk of a cashflow CDO
stems primarily from the number of defaults in the pool: the
more and the quicker obligors default, the thinner the stream of
cash flows available to pay interest and principal on the notes.
The cash flows generated by the assets are used to payback
investors in sequential order from senior investors (class A), to
equity investors that bear the first-loss risk (class D). The par
value of the securities at maturity is used to pay the notional
amounts of CDO notes.

PRICING SYNTHETIC CDOS

In this section, we focus on unfunded CDO transactions and articulate
the pricing techniques used in this market. We do not spend any time on

the related discussion on hedging, as this important topic will be dealt with in Chapters 7 and 8. In addition, it is one of the peculiarities of this somewhat incomplete market that the price of a tranche cannot always be related with the cost of hedging or a replicating portfolio.

There are many papers in the market to explain the most established pricing techniques, and we refer to a very pedagogical discussion by Gibson (2004).

Pricing a CDO tranche means being able to define the spread on the regular installments paid by the protection buyer to the protection seller. The central constituent necessary to define this spread on a tranche is the tranche-expected loss derived from the loss distribution of the underlying portfolio, as summarized in Figure 6.3. In this section, we detail successively all the building blocks necessary to compute a price.

We explain how to get to the tranche "Expected Loss," i.e., the average loss unconditional on systematic risk constituents. With this key input, we can move to the proper pricing of CDO tranches. We then focus more specifically on the traded market of tranches based on the CDS indices, also called "correlation trading." We ultimately focus on the new theoretical developments in this market, based on a more dynamic modeling of the portfolio loss and show how this may pave the way for advanced derivatives written on CDO tranches.

FIGURE 6.3

Main Steps to Price a CDO Tranche.

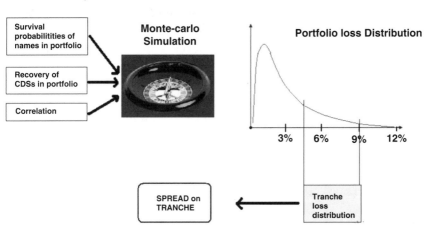

Generating the Loss Distribution
of the Portfolio

In the previous chapters, we have discussed in great detail how to estimate univariate survival probabilities (Chapters 2 and 3) as well as recovery rates (Chapter 3) and correlation (Chapter 4). Based on these three
constituents, we can generate the loss distribution of the portfolio at a
defined horizon. The loss distribution in the CDO portfolio is a key input
to obtain the tranche loss distribution and, subsequently, the expected loss
per tranche.

More generally, what we would like to generate is the continuum of
loss distributions in the portfolio at any point in time until the maturity of
the CDO. In order to reach this point, Li (2000) and Gregory and Laurent
(2003) have really been instrumental to orientate the market approach
towards the concepts of a default survival approach, copulas and conditional independence.

Basically, in order to obtain the portfolio loss distribution at any horizon, we need to know the survival probability of each obligor in the pool at
the corresponding time (step 1), as well as the nature of the dependence of
these probabilities on systematic risk factors (step 2). On the basis of these
constituents, we can identify the joint survival probability in the portfolio
conditional on the systematic risk factors (step 3). By blending it with recovery at default and simulating the behavior of the systemic risk factors, we
will be in a position to extract the portfolio loss distribution at the various
horizons (step 4) and the related term structure of expected losses per
tranche.

Step 1: Let us define $\tau_1, \ldots, \tau_n$ the default times of the n obligors in
the CDO portfolio.

For each obligor i, a risk-neutral survival probability function
$S(t_i) = Q(\tau_i > t_i)$ is defined and extracted from spreads as a result
from/credit curves.* It does not assume any dependence between
obligors.

Step 2: The joint probability cannot be computed directly. We need
to introduce a dependence structure. This joint survival probability
function is therefore written as a (survival) copula

$$S(t_1, \ldots, t_n) = Q(\tau_1 > t_1, \ldots, \tau_n > t_n)$$

---

*See Chapter 3 for a description of different methodologies.

In order to avoid dimensionality issues, dependence across obligors is typically modeled through a vector of latent factors V that is common to all obligors. The usual approach in the CDO world is to consider a single latent factor for ease of computation, but there is no theoretical restriction on the number.

Step 3: This step consists of expressing the joint survival probability conditional on the realization of the latent factor.

Let us denote the survival probability for obligor i, at time t, conditional on the factor V as:

$$q_i^V(t) = Q(\tau_i > t \mid V). \tag{1}$$

Based on the property of conditional independence, we can write the conditional joint survival probability in a simple way as:

$$S(t_1, \ldots, t_n \mid V) = \prod_{i=1}^{n} q_i^V(t_i) \tag{2}$$

Step 4: The unconditional joint survival probability distribution can then be obtained by integrating the conditional joint survival probability on the density of the common latent factor. In addition, by assuming a constant recovery level such as 40 percent, we obtain the portfolio loss distribution.

From this "recipe," it is clear that the key building block necessary to obtain the portfolio loss distribution, apart from the distribution of the latent factor V, is the conditional survival probability for each obligor [Equation (1)].*

We review different approaches based on copulas that have been used in the market.

Possible Candidates for Conditional Survival Probability

Gregory and Laurent (2003) and Burtschell et al. (2005) provide a taxonomy of possible candidates for conditional probabilities based on the choice of different copulas. Each of the options presented in this section are derived from the assumption of a deterministic asset correlation

---

*Or the univariate conditional risk neutral default probability for each obligor $p_i^V(t) = 1 - q_i^V(t)$.

structure. The selection of any one of them is usually driven by how well it can fit empirical evidence.*

We start with the Gaussian copula that corresponds by far to the market standard.

Gaussian Copula   The most established setup is the one factor Gaussian copula. That has been presented in the previous chapter on correlation. It can be interpreted as the asset value of the firm i being driven by a latent common factor and an independent idiosyncratic factor, both normally distributed:

$$A_i = \rho_i V + \sqrt{1 - \rho_i^2}\, \xi_i \tag{3}$$

If we define the cumulative default probability $p_i(t) = Q(\tau_i \leq t)$, ρ_i the factor loading corresponding to asset i and Φ, the normal c.d.f., the conditional default probability can be written as (Vasicek, 1987):

$$p_i^V(t) = \Phi\left(\frac{\Phi^{-1}(p_i(t)) - \rho_i V}{\sqrt{1 - \rho_i^2}} \right) \tag{4}$$

Student-t Copula   The Student-t copula is a natural extension of the Gaussian copula suggested by several authors, such as O'Kane and Schloegl (2001) and Frey and McNeil (2003). It is supposed to account for fat tails better than the Gaussian copula, but the drawback is its symmetry, leading to a high probability of zero losses, too.

The asset value of the firm i follows a Student-t distribution. It is, however, driven by a latent common factor and an independent idiosyncratic factor, both normally distributed:

$$A_i = \sqrt{W}(\rho_i V + \sqrt{1 - \rho_i^2}\, \xi_i),$$

where W is an inverse Gamma distribution with parameter equal to $(\nu/2)$, independent from the Gaussian factors.

The conditional default probability becomes:

---

*As a caveat though, we have seen in the previous chapter on correlation that a deterministic approach to correlation, whatever the circumstances, may not correspond to a fully appropriate representation of the reality.

$$p_i^{V,W}(t) = \Phi\left(\frac{W^{-1/2}t_v^{-1}(p_i(t)) - \rho_i V}{\sqrt{1-\rho_i^2}}\right) \tag{5}$$

Double-t Copula   This approach has been suggested in Hull and White (2004) in order to partially decouple the size and shape of the upper and lower tail of the loss distribution.

The asset value of the firm i does not follow a Student-t distribution, but is a convolution of a latent common factor and an independent idiosyncratic factor, both Student-t distributed, with respectively v and $\bar{v}$ degrees of freedom:

$$A_i = \left(\frac{v-2}{v}\right)^{1/2}\rho_i V + \left(\frac{\bar{v}-2}{\bar{v}}\right)^{1/2}\sqrt{1-\rho_i^2}\,\xi_i, \tag{6}$$

In this situation, the conditional default probability can be expressed as:

$$p_i^V(t) = t_{\bar{v}}\left(\sqrt{\frac{\bar{v}}{\bar{v}-2}} * \frac{H_i^{-1}(p_i(t)) - \rho_i\sqrt{\frac{v-2}{v}}V}{\sqrt{1-\rho_i^2}}\right) \tag{7}$$

where $H_i(A_i)=p_i(t)$ corresponds to the distribution function of A_i that has to be computed numerically as it is not a Student-t.

Normal Inverse Gaussian (NIG) Copulas   There are two rationales for using NIG Gaussian distributions:

♦ Fat tails: the fact that asset returns tend to exhibit more asymmetric, as well as fatter, tails than a Gaussian distribution supports the use of a NIG distribution.

♦ Tractability reasons: the point that a convolution of NIG distributions is a NIG distribution facilitates the computation of the pricing of tranches.

In Kalemanova et al. (2005), the asset value of the firm i is driven by a latent common factor and an independent idiosyncratic factor, both NIG distributed:

$$A_i = \rho_i V + \sqrt{1-\rho_i^2}\,\xi_i$$

If we define the NIG c.d.f. as:

$$F_{\mathrm{NIG}(s)}(x) = F_{\mathrm{NIG}}\left(x; s\alpha, s\beta, -s\frac{\alpha\beta}{\sqrt{\alpha^2 - \beta^2}}, s\alpha \right)$$

With s, α, and β the parameters of the NIG. The first one is related to correlation, whereas the next two are related to the mean and the variance.

Kalemanova et al. (2005) show that the conditional probability of default can be written as:

$$p_i^V(t) = F_{\mathrm{NIG}\left(\frac{\sqrt{1-\rho_i^2}}{\rho_i}\right)}\left(\frac{F^{-1}_{\mathrm{NIG}\left(\frac{1}{\rho_i}\right)}(p_i(t)) - \rho_i V}{\sqrt{1-\rho_i^2}} \right) \tag{8}$$

Archimedean Copulas   Archimedean copulas have been proposed in particular by Schönbucher and Schubert (2001) in the context of contagion models.

In the case of the Clayton copula, the conditional default probability can be expressed as:

$$p_i^V(t) = \exp(V(1 - p_i(t)^{-\theta})), \tag{9}$$

where θ is the parameter of the copula.

Marshall-Olkin Copula   Multivariate exponential spread modeling associated with the Marshall-Olkin copula is also called a "Poisson shock" model. It allows for simultaneous defaults and fat tails, as the default intensity for each obligor is split between a systematic and an idiosyncratic component. Several authors like Duffie and Singleton (1998), Lindskog and McNeil (2003), Elouerkhaoui (2003a,b), and Giesecke (2003) have suggested its use. Practical calibration can be challenging, as many parameters need to be calibrated. Figure 6.4 shows how this copula gives significant modeling flexibility.

In order to obtain a one factor representation of this approach, let us consider one latent common variable V and n obligor specific random variables $\bar{V}_i$, all independent and exponentially distributed with respective parameters α and $1 - \alpha$ and $\alpha \in [0, 1]$.* For each obligor i, we can

---

*α should be seen as describing the intensity of co-movement to default, $\alpha = 1$, meaning total comonotonicity.

FIGURE 6.4

The Flexibility Provided by the Marshall-Olkin
Copula—A Normalized Loss Distribution.

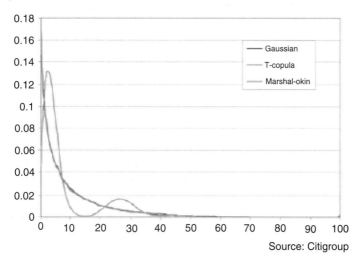

Source: Citigroup

define $V_i = \min(V, \overline{V}_i)$ and $S_i(t) = 1 - p_i(t)$, the marginal survival function.
We can then express the corresponding default time as: $\tau_i = S_i^{-1}\exp(-V_i)$.
Conditionally on V, τ_i are independent and the conditional default prob-
ability for obligor i can be expressed as:

$$p_i^V(t) = 1 - 1_{V > -\ln(1 - p_i(t))}(1 - p_i(t))^{1-\alpha} \tag{10}$$

The Functional Copula   The *functional copula* has been introduced by Hull and White (2005) and has been described in Chapter 4.

$$p_i^V(t) = -\frac{1}{t} * H_i\left(\frac{\rho_i V - G_i^{-1}(p_i(t))}{\sqrt{1 - \rho_i^2}}\right), \tag{11}$$

where H_i is the cumulative probability distribution of the idiosyncratic
term ε_i, and G_i is the cumulative probability distribution of the latent
variable A_i.

The idea of the authors is to eliminate the need for a parametric
form, but to extract the empirical distribution of conditional hazard rates
from empirical CDO pricing observations.

To date, the market standard remains the Gaussian copula. However, this Gaussian set-up does not prove very effective in pricing tranches. As an illustration of this problem, market participants have noted that a strong correlation skew is empirically observed based on market prices. This skew cannot be matched in a simple way with the Gaussian copula. As a result, finding a more accurate model has become the new frontier. In addition to the alternative copulae described previously, market practitioners have also tried to provide some extensions of the Gaussian copula in order to better match observed prices.

Possible Extensions of the Gaussian Copula: Relaxing Deterministic Assumptions

Gaussian copulas have such a footprint in the CDO market that it would be nice to be able to keep this framework while gaining accuracy in the valuation of tranches. Two related extensions have been suggested. They consist of either modifying the dependence structure of the asset value depending on different states of the world,* or considering that Loss Given Default is correlated to the realization of the common systematic factor.

Random Factor Loadings
The idea is that it is possible to approximate the apparently non-Gaussian behavior of an asset value as a convolution of Gaussian distributions.

In the correlation Chapter 4, it was noted that under the empirical measure there was evidence supporting a two-regime-switching approach depending on growth and recession periods in the economy. Andersen and Sidenius (2005) head towards this direction with "random factor loadings." Practically in their simplest setup, factor loadings depend on the realization of the common factor with respect to a barrier that can be seen as describing the state of the economy.

Burtschell et al. (2005) present the approach in a generic way under the wording of "stochastic correlation." Like in the simple Gaussian case, the asset value of the firm i is still driven by a latent common factor and an independent idiosyncratic factor, both normally distributed, but there are two possible states that come to play. In this respect, B_i is the Bernouilli distributed weight associated with the case where the factor-loading corresponding to company i is ρ_i, and a weight $(1-B_i)$ corresponds to a correlation of $\bar{\rho}_i$. As a result, asset value of the firm can be written as:

---

*Also, sometimes referred to as "local correlation."

$$A_i = (B_i\rho_i + (1 - B_i)\overline{\rho}_i)V + \sqrt{1 - (B_i\rho_i + (1 - B_i)\overline{\rho}_i)^2}\,\xi_i$$

Let us define the probability $b_i = Q(B_i = 1)$, the conditional default probability can be written as:

$$p_i^V(t) = b_i\Phi\left(\frac{\Phi^{-1}(p_i(t)) - \rho_i V}{\sqrt{1 - \rho_i^2}}\right) + (1 - b_i)\Phi\left(\frac{\Phi^{-1}(p_i(t)) - \overline{\rho}_i V}{\sqrt{1 - \overline{\rho}_i^2}}\right) \qquad (12)$$

Random Recovery The principle here is to have not only the asset value to be dependent on a vector of common factors, but also to have the recovery rate dependent on the same factors.

$$R_i = C(\mu_i + b_i V_i + \varepsilon_i), \qquad (13)$$

where C is a function on $[0, 1]$, such as a beta distribution function.

Increasing the dependency of the recovery on the common factors generates a fatter tail and therefore can account for some of the correlation skew observed for senior tranches. However, Andersen (2005) notes that when realistically calibrated, random recovery does not seem to be sufficient to explain the equity and the super senior correlation skews.

Assuming Homogeneity in the Portfolio

In an active market, traders require fast models and simple ways to communicate. Speed of computation and communication are often obtained at the expense of accuracy. Will a stylized model be sufficiently rich and robust to price and hedge transactions? This question represents a key challenge for the industry to date.

In addition to the assumption of the single factor copula framework, we mention below some other simplifications that are sometimes considered by market participants. Simplification can be obtained by assuming obligor homogeneity in the CDO portfolio. This leads to two simplifications:

♦ Factor loadings (i.e., the weight on the common factor, ρ_i) are independent from the obligors in the CDO portfolio. This means that we move from multiple, obligor dependent, factor loadings to a single one for the pool, ρ.

♦ Obligors can be considered as reasonably close in terms of creditworthiness and prices and as a result an average spread or probability of default is supposed to characterize the portfolio of obligors well. Practically, in all previous formulas, this assumption means that $p_i(t)$ can be turned into an average $p(t)$, independent from any name in particular. As shown in Figure 6.5, this assumption of homogeneity in the credit quality can prove hard to defend when dealing with the liquid indices.

Under these approximations, knowing factor loading (corresponding to the square root of what is defined in the market as the implied correlation) and given the corresponding average default probability is sufficient to obtain the loss distribution of the pool.

In addition to these approximations, some banks like JP Morgan have at some stage promoted the large pool approximation that facilitates the use of a limiting closed-form distribution described in Vasicek (1987, 1997).

$$P(L(t) \leq \alpha) = \Phi\left(\frac{1}{\rho}(\sqrt{1-\rho^2}\Phi^{-1}(\alpha) - \Phi^{-1}(p(t)))\right) \qquad (14)$$

with α a defined loss level, $L(t)$ the unconditional portfolio loss, and $p(t)$ the average probability of default of obligors in the pool.

As McGinty, Bernstein et al. (2004) from JP Morgan put it:

"The model we (JPM) use to imply correlations in tranches is known as the homogeneous large pool gaussian copula (the 'large pool model', or 'HLPGC'), which is a simplified version of the Gaussian copula widely used in the market.

FIGURE 6.5

Five-year CDS Spread-Based Distribution of the CDX.NA.IG.4.

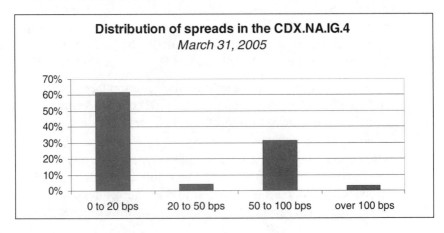

... The model is based on three major assumptions. First, default of a reference entity is triggered when its asset value falls below a barrier. Second, asset value of the portfolio is driven by a common, standard normally distributed factor M, which is often referred to as the 'Market,' and can be taken to imply the state of the overall business cycle. Finally, the portfolio consists of a very large number of credits of uniform size, which effectively cancels the effect of a single name's performance on tranche loss and is why the portfolio can be considered homogenous.

We believe that the fundamental benefits of the large pool model are transparency and replicability—we can provide our specific implementation of the model. The model also has the advantage that it requires few inputs–only the average level of market spreads and average recovery rate (which we define as 40%), rather than individual spreads for all of the credits in the portfolio, which would be impossible for a user to reproduce at any instant. The downside of course, is that the model does not consider single name blow-ups correctly. This manifests itself in two main ways: one, the model cannot differentiate between a single name widening by 10,000 bp and 100 names widening by 100 bp, and two, there is a discontinuity as credit spreads widen towards default. The model is unlikely to produce spreads consistent with market observations in these scenarios. . . ."

Such an approximation facilitates immensely the calculation of correlation and ultimately of prices. However, it can be very misleading when applied to a portfolio characterized by a low number of names and/or different profiles in terms of creditworthiness.

This fully granular model assumes full diversification of the idiosyncratic risk, but empirical evidence shows that full diversification in a credit portfolio is typically obtained with a minimum of 400–500 obligors. Indices like CDX, I-Traxx only contain up to 125 names. It can be therefore quite risky to apply the large pool model to index based correlation trading.

Pre-May 2005, Finger (2005) reported that the JP Morgan model had performed well for investment grade index tranches. This set-up is, however, no longer used by market participants, and other ways to reduce computational time are investigated next.

Getting to the Loss Distribution of the Portfolio: Monte-Carlo and Semi-analytical Techniques

Option 1: The Full Monte-Carlo Calculation* The Monte-Carlo approach is based on the random draw of realizations of the common systematic factor and for each realization, a portfolio loss can be computed as the sum of individual losses. The unconditional portfolio loss corresponds to the integration of the conditional losses on the distribution of the common factor.

This "brute force" approach is usually not selected by market participants, as it is time consuming.[†] Some techniques, often based on variance reduction, can help to speed-up the computation time.

Option 2: The Recursive Approach This approach has been suggested almost simultaneously by Andersen et al. (2003) and by Hull and White (2003). The principle is integration over a discretely approximated portfolio loss distribution.

In a portfolio of j names, the probability of observing exactly h defaults (with $h \leq j$) by time t, conditional on the realization of the common factor V can be written as $p_j^V(h, t)$. Furthermore, $p_{j-1}^V(t)$ is the conditional default probability of name $j-1$:

$$p_{j+1}^V(h, t) = p_j^V(h, t)(1 - p_{j+1}^V(t)) + p_j^V(h-1, t)p_{j+1}^V(t)$$

where, of course,

$$p_{j+1}^V(0, t) = p_j^V(0, t)(1 - p_{j+1}^V(t))$$

$$p_{j+1}^V(j+1, t) = p_j^V(j, t)p_{j+1}^V(t)$$

Based on the above recursion, we can obtain the unconditional probability of observing h defaults in a portfolio of n names by time t by integrating over the common factor with distribution function $f(V)$:

$$p_n(h, t) = \int_{-\infty}^{\infty} p_n^V(h, t) f(V) \, dV \qquad (15)$$

---

[*]See Rott and Fries (2005) regarding the use of variance reduction techniques.
[†]It is particularly cumbersome for CDO squared.

Option 3: Using Fourier Transform Techniques[*]

We consider the total accumulated loss of the reference pool at time t, and δ is the recovery fraction at default on each name. The default time for obligor j is τ_j. Once the nominal on each name j, N_j, is defined, we can write the accumulated loss at time t, $L(t) = \sum_{j=1}^{n} N_j (1 - \delta) X_j$, by calling the indicator function: $1_{\tau_i \leq t} = X_j$.

The Fourier transform of the accumulated loss function can be expressed as:

$$\varphi_{L(t)}(u) = E[\exp(-iuL(t)] = E[E(\exp(-iuL(t) \mid V)],$$

where V is the common systematic factor.

We can then introduce the expression of the Fourier transform of the loss

$$\varphi_{L(t)}(u) = E[e^{-iu(N_1(1-\delta)X_1 + N_2(1-\delta)X_2 + \cdots + N_n(1-\delta)X_n)}]$$

$$= E\left[\prod_{j=1}^{n} e^{-iuN_j(1-\delta)X_j}\right] \tag{16}$$

The Fourier transform of the conditional loss is more tractable, due to the possibility to permute the expectation under conditional independence. Based on the Bernoulli distribution of the indicator function X_j, we obtain:

$$\varphi^{V}{}_{L(t)}(u) = E\left[\prod_{j=1}^{n} e^{-iuN_j(1-\delta)X_j \mid V}\right] = \prod_{j=1}^{n} E[e^{-iuN_j(1-\delta)X_j \mid V}]$$

$$= \prod_{j=1}^{n} [q_j^{V}(t) + p_j^{V}(t)(e^{-iu(1-\delta)N_j})]$$

In turn, this can be written as

$$\varphi^{V}{}_{L(t)}(u) = \prod_{j=1}^{n} [q_j^{V}(t) + p_j^{V}(t)\, \varphi_{(1-\delta)N_j}(u)],$$

---

[*]We revert readers to the presentation on Fourier Transform techniques, by Debuysscher and Szego (2003). There are other possible convolution techniques, such as Laplace transforms and Moment Generating functions.

where $\varphi^V_{(1-\delta)}(N_j u)$ is derived from the Fourier transform of the Loss Given Default on asset j.

The unconditional Fourier transform is then obtained numerically by integrating on the distribution of the common systematic factor:

$$\varphi_{L(t)}(u) = \int_{-\infty}^{\infty} \prod_{j=1}^{n} [q_j^V(t) + p_j^V(t)\,\varphi_{(1-\delta)}(N_j u)] f(V) dV \qquad (17)$$

In a final step, the unconditional loss can be computed using the inverse Fourier transform by practically applying standard Fast Fourier transform algorithms.

Option 4: Proxy Integration   Proxy integration, presented in Shelton (2004), has gained traction in the market because of its simplicity.

The central limit theorem states that the sum of independent random variables with finite variance and arbitrary probability distribution converges to a normal distribution as the number of variables increases.

Shelton's approach is based on the idea that the convergence to a normal distribution might take place sufficiently quickly to allow for the approximation.

In the case of CDO pricing, we cannot consider the survival probability variables for each obligor to be independent, as obligor losses are typically correlated. We have seen though that conditional on a vector of latent risk factors, the portfolio loss distribution can be expressed as the weighted sum of conditionally independent random variables.

Let us consider again the total accumulated loss of the reference pool at time t, with δ the recovery fraction at default on each name. The default time for obligor j is τ_j. Once the nominal on each name j, N_j, is defined, we can write the accumulated loss at time horizon t, $L(t) = \sum_{j=1}^{n} N_j (1-\delta) X_j$, by calling the indicator function: $1_{\tau_j \le t} = X_j$.

We then consider various realizations of the common systematic latent factor V. Under the assumption of conditional independence, we can now easily compute the conditional loss distribution in the portfolio based on Equation (2). According to the Proxy integration approach, we assume that conditional on each realization of V, the joint distribution of losses in the portfolio converges to a normal distribution as shown in Figure 6.6. For each realization of the systematic factor, we can compute the mean and the variance of the approximated normal distribution.

FIGURE 6.6

Loss Distribution for Correlated Defaults. (*Citigroup*)

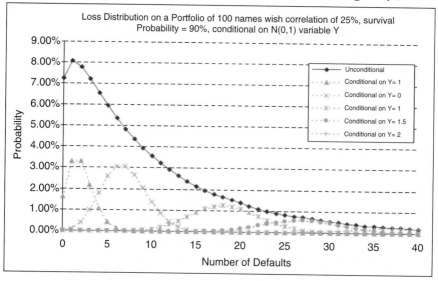

Loss Distribution on a Portfolio of 100 names wish correlation of 25%, survival
Probability = 90%, conditional on N(0,1) variable Y

Its mean is:

$$\mu_V(L(t)) = E[L(t) \mid V] = \sum_{j=1}^{n} N_j(1-\delta)\, p_i^V(t)$$

And, its variance is:

$$VAR_V(L(t)) = E[(L(t) - \mu_V(L(t)))^2 \mid V]$$

The unconditional portfolio distribution can be computed as a weighted mixture of Gaussian distributions, where the weights correspond to the distribution of the latent variable. This numerical integration problem can be solved by a simple algorithm like the trapezium rule.

For pools like the index pools, the degree of convergence proves satisfactory and the method typically delivers good results.

This approach is more straightforward than the option 2 (the recursive approach), in the sense that each conditional loss distribution is approximately characterized by only two parameters: the mean and the variance.

For CDO² trades, the proxy integration approach mentioned earlier can be generalized to a similar problem with a dimension corresponding to that of the number of underlying pools. Instead of computing a univariate normal integral, we now have to estimate a multivariate normal integral.

Pricing a CDO Tranche Once the Unconditional Portfolio Loss Distribution is Obtained

A synthetic CDO tranche can be valued like any other swap contract. There are two parties involved: the *issuer* who typically is the protection buyer and the *investor*, the protection seller. The investor receives from the issuer a regular "fee" or "premium." When default impacts the tranche, the investor has to pay a "contingent" amount, corresponding to the "contingent" or "default" leg. For the investor holding a tranche, there is a need to be compensated appropriately for bearing potential losses (the expected losses). The higher the seniority, the lower the fees.

Let us introduce the following notations:

In the CDO we consider, there are n different names with $i = \{1, \ldots, n\}$. A default time τ_t is associated to each name i.

We can now define $N(t) = \sum_{i=1}^{n} 1_{\tau_i \leq t}$, the counting process of the number of defaults at time t, T the maturity of the CDO, and δ the standard recovery fraction at default on each name. When conditioned on the common factor, these Bernouilli variables become independent and the conditional loss distribution at time t can be obtained easily. As a result, once the nominal on each name i, N_i, is defined, we can write the accumulated unconditional losses at time t, also called expected loss, as

$EL(t) = E[\sum_{i=1}^{n} N_i(1 - \delta)1_{\tau_i \leq t} | V]$, where V corresponds to the common systematic factor. Its practical computation has been described previously.

Computing the Value of the "Contingent Leg"*

We initially start with a three-tranche CDO with equity, mezzanine, and senior pieces, but nothing precludes us to consider more tranches in the remainder of this section. The subordination priority rule means that losses will be allocated first to the equity piece, then to the mezzanine, and the remainder to the senior tranche. The equity tranche corresponds to $[A_0 = 0, A_1 = A]$, the mezzanine to $[A, A_2 = B]$, and the senior to $[B, A_3 = \sum_{i=1}^{n} N_i]$, where A_j are agreed upon thresholds. Accumulated losses will therefore be successively absorbed by each of the tranches.

The next step is to measure explicitly overtime the unconditional average accumulated loss in each of the tranches $[A_j, A_{j+1}]$.

---

*Also called "protection leg" or "loss leg."

$$EL_j(t) = E(\max[\min((L(t) - A_j), (A_{j+1} - A_j)), 0]) \tag{18}$$

The discounted payout corresponding to contingent losses in tranche j during the life of the CDO can be written as:

$$C_j(t = 0) = \sum_{k=1}^{K} D(k)[EL_j(k + 1) - EL_j(k)] \tag{19}$$

where $D(k)$ is the discount factor term. We consider here the time series of the premium payment dates $k = \{1, \ldots, K\}$.

More rigorously, this contingent leg can be written as an integral and can be integrated by parts:

$$
\begin{aligned}
C_j(0) &= D(T)\, EL_j(T) + \int_0^T EL_j(t)\, dD(t) \\
&= D(T)\, EL_j(T) + \int_0^T EL_j(t)\, D(t)\, f(t)\, dt
\end{aligned}
\tag{20}
$$

where $f(t) = -(1/D(t))(dD(t)/dt)$ is the spot forward rate.

Computing the Value of the "Fee Leg"*

The expected present value of the fee leg on each tranche corresponds to the payment of regular installments at a predefined spread S_j applied to the principal exposure of the tranche outstanding at the date of payment of the premium.

$$F_j(0) = s_j \sum_{k=1}^{K} [(A_{j+1} - A_j) - EL_j(k)]\, D(k) \tag{21}$$

The initial mark-to-market value of the tranche is $C_j(0) - F_j(0)$. In the case that the CDO tranche is unfunded and fairly priced, this initial marked-to-market value is 0.

The value of the spread can be deducted in a straightforward way as:

$$s_j = \frac{C_j(0)}{\sum_{k=1}^{K} [(A_{j+1} - A_j) - EL_j(k)]D(k)} \tag{22}$$

---

*Also called "premium leg." For ease of presentation, we assume here that tranches are priced using spreads only, with no upfront payment.

During the life of a CDO, the balance between the value of the fee leg and that of the contingent leg usually vanishes. The marked-to-market value of a tranche is defined as the value difference between the two legs. One way to measure this value consists of defining the factor loading contributing to the expected loss as the unknown parameter. The factor loading corresponds to the square root of the correlation value that makes the fee leg break even with the contingent leg gives an equivalent of the price of the corresponding tranche. It is usually called the implied "compound correlation."

A Practical Example

We consider a synthetic CDO on a portfolio of 100 equally weighted names (Figure 6.7).

We assume that the size of the CDO is $100 million. The equity tranche corresponds to the usual 0 percent to 3 percent bucket. In addition, we consider a risk-neutral hazard rate of 100 bps for the CDSs on each underlying name, a factor-loading ρ_i equal to the square root of 0.2 and a standard recovery of 40 percent.

The premium fee for the equity tranche is 40 percent upfront payment plus a running fee of 500 bps.

In Table 6.1 we first look at the implication of the loss mechanism on the equity tranche for the protection seller.

In a second step, we consider the traditional one-factor approach. We can write the asset return as $A_i = \rho_i V + \sqrt{1 - \rho_i^2}\, \xi_i$.

FIGURE 6.7

A Stylized Synthetic CDO Structure.

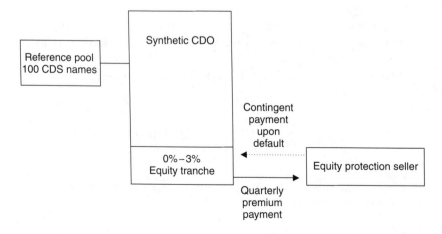

TABLE 6.1

Implication for the Protection Seller of Losses in the Portfolio Pool*

Number of defaulted names	Notional of the pool ($M)	Attachment point ($M)	Detachment point ($M)	Contingent payment by protection seller	Cumulative contingent payment by protection seller	Premium perceived by the protection seller (during 1 year assuming no additional default and without upfront fee)
0	100	0	3	0	0	0.15
1	99	0	2.4	0.6	0.6	0.12
2	98	0	1.8	0.6	1.2	0.09
3	97	0	1.2	0.6	1.8	0.06
4	96	0	0.6	0.6	2.4	0
5	95	0	0	0.6	3	0
6	94	0	0	0	3	0
7	93	0	0	0	3	0
8	92	0	0	0	3	0
9	91	0	0	0	3	0
10	90	0	0	0	3	0
.	.	.	.	.	.	.
.	.	.	.	.	.	.
.	.	.	.	.	.	.
100	0	0	0	0	3	0

*The recovery on the defaulted name is allocated to the most senior tranche holder as an early repayment.

We use the recursive methodology presented earlier in order to define the probability distribution of the number of defaults in the portfolio, given the distribution of the common factor, and then compute the unconditional default distribution. Results are summarized in Table 6.2.

By combining columns (A) and (B), we obtain the expected loss of the equity tranche at time $K=5$ years.

TABLE 6.2

Defining the Unconditional Loss Distribution of the Portfolio at any Time Horizon (in this case five years)

Number h of defaulted names (A)	Default distribution conditional on the realization of common factor V					Unconditional default distribution at a 5-year horizon $p_{100}(h, 5)$ (B)
	$V=...$	$V=-1$	$V=0$	$V=1$	$V=...$	
0		1.85×10^{-6}	0.007	0.210		0.109
1		2.6×10^{-5}	0.035	0.330		0.103
2		1.8×10^{-4}	0.088	0.257		0.093
3		8.4×10^{-4}	0.147	0.132		0.081
4		2.9×10^{-3}	0.183	0.051		0.070
5		7.8×10^{-3}	0.180	0.015		0.061
6		0.017	0.146	0.004		0.052
7		0.033	0.100	0.001		0.045
8		0.054	0.060	1.5×10^{-4}		0.039
9		0.078	0.031	2.4×10^{-5}		0.034
10		0.100	0.015	3.4×10^{-6}		.
.		.	.	.		.
.		.	.	.		.
.		.	.	.		.
.		.	.	.		.
100		1.6×10^{-91}	6.5×10^{-123}	1.1×10^{-181}		4.83×10^{-13}
Probability attached to each realization of the common factor		0.24%	0.39%	0.24%		100%

$$EL(5) = \sum_{h=0}^{n} P_{100}(h,5) \max(\min((h * 0.4), 3), 0)$$

The last necessary step in order to be able to obtain the value of the equity tranche is to compute the expected loss at all the time steps we are interested in. On the basis of this time series of expected losses, we can infer the contingent and the fee legs and easily deduct the par-spread from the computations.

Detailing Implied Correlation

Defining the Indices
The market of standardized tranches based on credit indices has grown tremendously over the past years. The market has benefited from the merger of the leading U.S. and European CDS indices in 2004. There are now the CDX indices in the United States and the iTraxx in Europe. The most important indices are the investment grade indices that include 125 CDS contracts corresponding to the most liquid names in each region.

The standardized tranches on the CDX.NA.IG* correspond to the equity tranche (0 to 3 percent), the junior mezzanine (3 to 7 percent), the mezzanine (7 to 10 percent), the senior (10 to 15 percent), and the junior super senior tranche (15 to 30 percent). On the European iTraxx index, attachment points differ slightly, with attachment points for the intermediary tranches at 6 percent, 9 percent, 12 percent, and 22 percent, respectively.

Implied Correlation
The idea behind the concept of an "implied correlation" is based on an analogy with the Black and Scholes formula for the valuation of options, where there is an equivalence between option prices and the definition of the corresponding "implied volatility." Similarly, in the case of CDO tranches, the knowledge of the price of a tranche as well as of the spread levels on the names of the underlying portfolio leaves only one degree of freedom, using a Gaussian copula: the value of the factor loading, called implied compound correlation. Given our past notations, $corr = \rho^2$.

Note that if the model was correct we should observe a flat level of correlation for all tranches, given that the asset value of the underlying pool we

---

*The CDX.NA.IG index corresponds to the Dow Jones North American Investment Grade index.

refer to is identical whatever the tranche. In general, however, implied compound correlation is higher for the equity and the more senior tranches than for the mezzanine tranche (Figure 6.8). This phenomenon is known as the "correlation smile." There are basically two ways to account for this smile:

 ♦ The first one focuses on market inefficiencies and segmentation. The market for junior tranches differs from that related to senior ones due to different investor preferences, with little "cross tranches" arbitrage.

 ♦ The second way to explain the skew is by considering that it corresponds to some model misspecification. According to this view, the true level of correlation cannot be captured in a stable way by the Gaussian copula due in particular to underestimation of the probability of extreme loss scenarios. This analysis explains why alternative copulas, or other extensions capturing random factor loadings and recoveries, have been introduced in the previous sections.

The use of compound correlation to quote tranches was the industry standard until spring 2004, but has been abandoned for three reasons. First, in

FIGURE 6.8

The Correlation Smile, 07/10/2004, Five-Year iTraxx Europe.

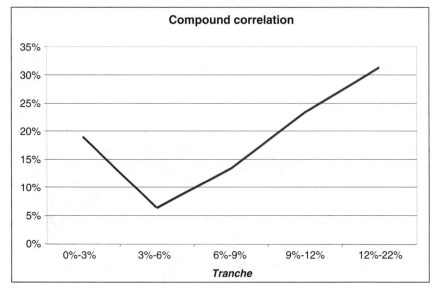

mezzanine tranches, there can be two solutions for the implied compound correlation.* In addition, for some spread levels (e.g., very high spreads on the mezzanine tranche), there can be no solution at all to the correlation problem using a Gaussian copula. Lastly, as compound correlation gives a "U-shaped" distribution, it is very difficult to infer from the correlation curve the interpolated prices on tranches that have nonstandard attachment points.

Since 2004, the market has moved to the quotation of equity tranches with different detachment points (0 percent to 3 percent, 0 percent to 7 percent, 0 percent to 10 percent, and so on). This is equivalent to pricing call options on the cumulative losses of the underlying portfolio up to a defined level (Figure 6.9). Such equity correlations are also called "base correlations." They are often (not always though) monotonically increasing with the level of detachment point. The price on a 3 to 6 percent tranche can be computed knowing the 0 to 3 percent and the 0 to 6 percent base correlations and considering that it corresponds to the combination of a long 0 to 6 percent tranche with a short 0 to 3 percent. Compared with compound correlation, base correlation offers the advantage of bringing a

FIGURE 6.9

Base Correlation, 07/10/2004, Five-Year iTraxx Europe.

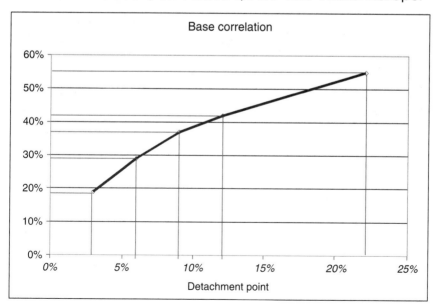

---

* Mezzanine tranche premiums are not monotonic in the compound correlation.

TABLE 6.3

Typical Market Quote on 28/02/06. Spreads are in bps, Except for the 0 to 3 Percent Equity Piece that is Defined as a % of the Notional Plus 500 bps.

	Spread	Delta	Base Corr	Impld Corr
iTraxx 5 year	(index 35 Mid)			
0–3%*	25.625/26.2	22.5×	10.9%	10.9%
3–6%	70/72	5.5×	22.0%	3.9%
6–9%	21/23	2.0×	29.9%	11.7%
9–12%	10/13	1.0×	36.3%	17.2%
12–22%	3.875/5.125	0.5×	53.6%	23.7%
iTraxx 7 year	(48 Mid)	Delta	Base Corr	Impld Corr
0–3%*	47.625/48.25	14.5×	7.2%	7.2%
3–6%	198/203	8.0×	19.9%	92.5%
6–9%	46/50	2.5×	30.3%	5.0%
9–12%	27/30	1.5×	38.2%	11.9%
12–22%	10.5/12.5	0.7×	59.1%	19.6%
iTraxx 10 year	(60 Mid)	Delta	Base Corr	Impld Corr
0–3%	58/58.75	8.0×	7.7%	7.7%
3–6%	590/610	11.0×	12.1%	19.0%
6–9%	126/131	4.25×	22.2%	na
9–12%	55/59	2.0×	30.8%	4.8%
12–22%	22/26	1.0×	53.0%	13.9%

unique solution to the pricing of Mezzanine tranches.* Some problem can however remain for the calibration of the most senior tranches, as reported in St-Pierre et al. (2004). Pricing tranches with bespoke attachment points is reasonably straightforward, by interpolation of the base correlation curve.† A practical example of market prices is provided in Table 6.3.

Base correlation can be seen as a way to represent the market perception relative to the underlying risk-neutral loss distribution of the collateral portfolio (Figure 6.10). Low-level losses and very high losses tend to exhibit higher probability in reality than anticipated by the Gaussian copula. This translates into the probability of losses in the equity and senior tranches being higher than expected and that in the mezzanine

---

*3 to 6 percent implied correlation for iTraxx 7 year in the table above illustrates the problem.
†One point to mention is that the pricing of equity tranchelets below the 3 percent detachment level is not possible by interpolation.

FIGURE 6.10

The c.d.f. of Conditional Portfolio Losses.

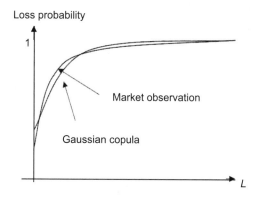

being lower. This phenomenon in turn accounts for the "correlation skew."

We can clearly see on Figure 6.10 why the Gaussian copula is not fully appropriate for pricing and leads to a correlation skew. Market participants have tried to find out if any of the other copulas introduced beforehand would perform better. We use for this comparison the results obtained by Burtschell et al. (2005), related to both compound (Figure 6.11) and base correlation (Figure 6.12).

FIGURE 6.11

Quality of the Fit Using Various Copulas Based on Compound Correlation.

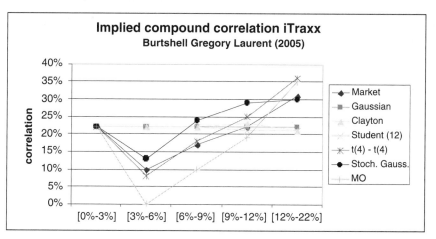

FIGURE 6.12

Quality of Fit of Various Copulas Based
on Base Correlation.

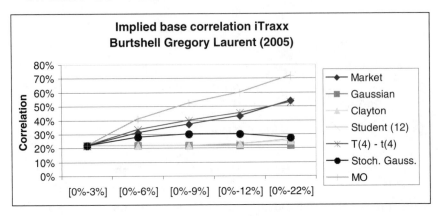

What we can see is that by trying to fit each copula* to the empirical
conditional losses in the portfolio, we obtain very different results. In particular, we can observe on Figure 6.11 that neither of the Gaussian, Student-
t, and Clayton copulas pick-up the skew and that only the Double-*t* and
the stochastic Gaussian copulas seem to be reasonably close in matching
the market skew. The picture looks identical when focusing on base correlation (Figure 6.9), with the Double-*t* being the closest to reality. Overall,
it is obvious that some of the copulas are doing a better job than others,
but that none of them can fully match market prices.

Practical Calibration of Base Correlation

From a practical perspective, base correlation can be derived from the
market quotes on the standardized tranches using a standard bootstrapping technique.

We want to price a 0 to 7 percent (T) tranche. This non-standard equity
tranche can be incorporated as the combination of two standard tranches
quoted in the market: the 0 to 3 percent (T_1) and the 3 to 7 percent (T_2).

$$C_{0,7} - C_{0,3} = (\bar{F}_{0,7} - \bar{F}_{0,3}),\qquad(23)$$

where the premium leg components $\bar{F}_{0,7}$ and $\bar{F}_{0,3}$ are computed using the
spread corresponding to tranche T_2.

---

*With one set of parameters only for all tranches. The Market correlation is using a Gaussian
copula with parameters adjusted for each tranche.

Let us decompose the process in three steps:

Step 1: We price T_1 and T_2 using the premium/fee (S_2) corresponding to T_2. We in fact only have to price T_1, given the fact that the price of T_2 given s_2 is zero. The price we compute for T_1 uses s_2 as the premium but the T_1 base correlation. It will always be positive, given the fact that the more senior the tranche, the lower the price. We can price tranche T_1 using $s_2 = s_{3,7}$

$$C_{0,3} = \sum_{k=1}^{K} D(k)[EL_{0,3}^{\rho_{0,3}}(k+1) - EL_{0,3}^{\rho_{0,3}}(k)] \qquad (24)$$

$$\overline{F}_{0,3} = s_{3,7}\sum_{k=1}^{K}[(A_3 - A_0) - EL_{0,3}^{\rho_{0,3}}(k)]\, D(k) \qquad (25)$$

$$P_{T_1} = C_{0,3} - \overline{F}_{0,3}$$

Step 2: All what we need is to price T, given the knowledge of T_1 computed in step 1. A rescaling operation has to take place at this stage, given the respective notional width of the two tranches T_1 and T_2:

$$P_T = P_{T_1}[(A_3 - A_0)/(A_7 - A_0)] \qquad (26)$$

Step 3: Once the value of tranche T is computed, the 0 to 7 percent base correlation can be inferred using the Gaussian copula approach.

$$\rho_{0,7} = \mathrm{Arg}(P_T = C_{0,7} - \overline{F}_{0,7}) \qquad (27)$$

With

$$C_{0,7} = \sum_{k=1}^{K} D(k)[EL_{0,7}^{\rho_{0,7}}(k+1) - EL_{0,7}^{\rho_{0,7}}(k)]$$

$$\overline{F}_{0,7} = s_{3,7}\sum_{k=1}^{K}[(A_7 - A_0) - EL_{0,7}^{\rho_{0,7}}(k)]\, D(k)$$

Pain et al. (2005) suggest that the estimation of base correlations can be further refined by the use of quotes at different horizons, typically 5, 7, and 10 years, hence moving from a single correlation term over the pricing period towards a term structure of correlations.

Massaging the Correlation Skew: Towards a Term Structure of Base Correlations

Many people have pointed out that the Gaussian copula model is not a dynamic model in the sense that spreads and correlation levels do not evolve through time. In addition it can be observed in the market that correlation is maturity dependent. This explains the attempt to build a more-time-dependent term structure of correlation. The principle of this more refined calibration is that the pricing of CDO tranches at different horizons gives some information about the dynamics of the expected loss over time, i.e., about the timing of defaults.

So far we have considered a unique premium payment date K, usually based on quarterly instalment over 5, 7, or 10 years and we have derived a unique base correlation over the life of the instrument. What we can do is to compute the term structure of base correlation over 10 years as a three-step process. We consider that from years zero to five we can rely on the price of the five-year tranche, from years five to seven we rely on the zero to five base correlation and on the price of the seven-year tranche, from years 7 to 10 we rely on the zero to five base correlation, on the five to seven adjusted base correlation, and on the price of the 10-year tranche.

Step 1: computing the five-year base correlation

We can rewrite the base correlation formula for a five-year tranche:

$$\rho_{0,7}^5 = \mathrm{Arg}(P_T = C_{0,7}^5 - \overline{F}_{0,7}^5) \tag{28}$$

With

$$C_{0,7}^5 = \sum_{k=1}^{K_5} D(k)[EL_{0,7}^{\rho_{0,7}^5}(k+1) - EL_{0,7}^{\rho_{0,7}^5}(k)]$$

$$\overline{F}_{0,7}^5 = s_{3,7}^5 \sum_{k=1}^{K_5} [(A_7 - A_0) - EL_{0,7}^{\rho_{0,7}^5}(k)] D(k)$$

Step 2: computing the base correlation between years five and seven

$$\rho_{0,7}^{5/7} = \mathrm{Arg}(P_T = C_{0,7}^7 - \overline{F}_{0,7}^7)$$ (29)

With

$$C_{0,7}^7 = \sum_{k=1}^{K_5} D(k)[EL_{0,7}^{\rho_{0,7}^5}(k+1) - [EL_{0,7}^{\rho_{0,7}^5}(k)]$$
$$+ \sum_{k=K_5+1}^{K_7} D(k)[EL_{0,7}^{\rho_{0,7}^{5/7}}(k+1) - EL_{0,7}^{\rho_{0,7}^{5/7}}(k)]$$

$$\overline{F}_{0,7}^7 = s_{3,7}^7 \left\{ \sum_{k=1}^{K_5} [(A_7 - A_0) - EL_{0,7}^{\rho_{0,7}^5}(k)] D(k) \right.$$
$$\left. + \sum_{k=K_5+1}^{K_7} [(A_7 - A_0) - EL_{0,7}^{\rho_{0,7}^{5/7}}(k)] D(k) \right\}$$

A more refined way to compute the base correlation between year five and year seven suggested by Pain et al. (2005) is to consider an interpolation, for instance, linear, for all the intermediary time steps.

Step 3: computing the base correlation between years 7 and 10.

The process is following the approach outlined in step 2.

Discussion on Implied Correlation

The CDO business had initially emerged as an illiquid activity helping in particular financial institutions to hedge their portfolio from a perspective of credit and default risk.

Little attention was paid at the time to the evolution of the price of a CDO tranche with respect to the movement of the credit spreads in the underlying pool. Factor models, whether they translate into a Gaussian copula or any more refined approach, provided results in terms of correlation or price without really integrating the dynamics of spread movements. The Gaussian copula model with the large portfolio approximation should be seen as the most extreme case of poor integration of the sensitivity to the dynamics of spreads.

With active trading on secondary markets, the focus has now changed dramatically towards an integration of market risk. Banks and investors are increasingly exposed to market risk in a way that is difficult to hedge. They are left with the traditional hedging techniques based on what is commonly called the "greeks,"* with the losses it may lead to when market shocks surge (see Chapter 8) translating into P&L damaging spread widening and contagion. Due to this problem, implied correlation, unlike implied equity volatility, looks like a poor instrument to work with. It offers limited security with existing instruments and is not the relevant parameter in order to price more complex instruments, such as options on tranches, or forward-starting CDOs that depend on the dynamics of the loss distributions of the CDO pool.

Currently, we observe a shift in the market, with banks keeping correlation as a pricing tool mainly for spot transactions and possibly gradually moving to a more robust framework for both, hedging and new CDO-related instruments. In this respect, two interesting theoretical papers have emerged in the second half of 2005: Sidenius et al. (2005) and Schönbucher (2005) suggesting the adoption of the whole loss distribution of the CDO portfolio and its dynamics as the underlying process to price CDO-based instruments. In what follows, we describe the methodology related to this change of paradigm and discuss related implications.

Dynamic Portfolio Loss Modeling

The idea behind this approach is to model the dynamics of portfolio losses directly and ensure an initial calibration to tranche prices for different seniorities and maturities (i.e., a calibration to a curve of tranche spreads). This is different to the Gaussian copula approach that focuses on correlated default times on a name-by-name basis and is not able to integrate the evolution of the univariate and multivariate parameters to future time under changing market conditions. Essentially, this is a result the static credit spread curve and constant correlation setup that is usually assumed. Here, we focus on a more macroscopic approach by specifying the dynamics of portfolio losses directly, motivated by the need to value advanced (hybrid) derivatives written on CDO tranches (e.g., options on tranches).

The SPA (Sidenius, Piterbarg, and Andersen) Model
The idea of Sidenius et al. (2005) is to consider the portfolio loss distribution corresponding to the underlying pool as the relevant variable. This

---

*Typically, "delta hedging," see Chapter 7 for a detailed introduction.

variable is considered in a dynamic way. The authors use a classical modeling technique that consists of splitting the modeling effort in two steps: the first one corresponding to the modeling of a diffusion process for the "smooth" portfolio loss probabilities (or forward rates), whereas the second focuses on the actual loss process consistent with, or conditional on, the loss probability or forward process.

In the first step, the authors define the variable they want to model as a diffusion. For any given level of loss considered in the portfolio initially, they consider the term structure of forward portfolio losses, in an analogy with the Heath, Jarrow, and Morton (HJM) approach for interest rates. The dynamics of the initial portfolio loss distribution can be inferred from the aggregation of the dynamics of the probability of portfolio losses* considered for any initial level of portfolio loss. The level of loss is assumed to remain stable over time in each forward process. From a technical perspective, as this first layer of modeling does not include any information about the dynamics of losses in the portfolio, they say that it is related to the "background filtration."

In a second step, the authors focus more precisely on the dynamics of defaults in the pool, thanks to a second layer of modeling based on proper information on default (i.e., under the loss filtration). The typical model considered is a one-step Markov chain. Transition probabilities are defined exclusively from the knowledge of the background forward loss rate at that time. Forward loss rates can in fact be seen as a way to describe the state of the market. In other words, the dynamics of losses in the portfolio at any time t will only depend on the situation in the market at that time, hence the view that we now have a much more dynamic set-up to assess CDO prices.

Portfolio Loss Probabilities and Forward Dynamics

In step 1, let us define first the loss probability

$$p_x(t, T) = P(\tau_x > T \mid M_t) = P[l(T) \leq x \mid M_t],$$

where $l(t)$ denotes the (nondecreasing) loss fraction at time t, and P is a martingale that corresponds to the risk-neutral measure with respect to the background filtration $\{M_t\}$, $x \in [0, 1]$ is a possible loss level in the portfolio and τ_x the corresponding stopping time. T corresponds to the horizon.

We can think of this stopping time as the first jump of a Cox process with intensity $\lambda_x(t)$, and we can write the loss probability as:

---

*Or from the forward loss rates defined from the probability of portfolio losses.

$$p_x(t, T) = E\left(\exp\left(-\int_0^T \lambda_x(s)\,ds \right) \mid M_t \right) = \exp\left(-\int_0^t \lambda_x(s)\,ds \right)$$
$$\times E\left(\exp\left(-\int_t^T \lambda_x(s)\,ds \right) \mid M_t \right)$$

By defining the compounded forward rates as:

$$f_x(t, T) = -\frac{(\partial/\partial T)p_x(t, T)}{p_x(t, T)}, \tag{30}$$

we can express the loss probability as:

$$p_x(t, T) = \exp\left(-\int_0^t f_x(u, u)\,du \right) \exp\left(-\int_t^T f_x(t, u)\,du \right)$$

with $f_x(t, t) = \lambda_x(t)$ \hfill (31)

Given the fact that $p_x(., T)$ is a martingale, and that we consider a diffusion process, we can write the process of the portfolio loss as:

$$dp_x(t, T)/p_x(t, T) = \Sigma_x(t, T)\,dW_x(t), \tag{32}$$

where $\Sigma_x(t, T)$ denotes a general stochastic process (in t) indexed by x, and T, and $W_x(t)$ is a Brownian Motion for each loss level x.

SPA outline a number of conditions a general loss process has to satisfy. For example, the probability of losses should be decreasing in maturity, and increasing in loss fraction, i.e., $P[l(T) \leq x] \leq P[l(T) \leq y]$, for all $x \leq y$. Essentially, this means that the probability of portfolio losses being lower than x has to be lower than the probability of losses being lower than y, and is denoted as "spatial order preservation" condition. Instead of working with portfolio loss probabilities, the first condition can be easily satisfied in terms of the forward loss rates, i.e., $f_x(t, T) \geq 0$. These forward loss rates $f_x(t, T)$ can naturally be derived from Equation (32) using the Ito's lemma.

Given this framework, SPA derive conditions for the dynamics of the processes to satisfy the necessary conditions (e.g., spatial ordering) under a dynamic loss probability, or instantaneous forward rate (HJM), or forward Libor (BGM) modeling framework. The advantage of the full modeling of a forward curve for each loss level (as in the HJM or BGM setup) is that it is very flexible and able to capture the full loss curve dynamics, whereas the "short-rate" loss probability modeling is less flexible but needs to propagate fewer variables.

Practically, this still means that in a portfolio of say 125 names like an index and assuming, homogenous recoveries across all names, we would need to calibrate up to 125 such diffusion processes for the loss probabilities in order to characterize all the realizations of x and be able to obtain the dynamics of the entire loss distribution. If idiosyncratic recoveries are assumed, the state space of x would further increase, which further increases the number of processes (and their interaction) to be considered. The only way to get there is to restrict the volatility process $\Sigma_x(t, T)$ to be a deterministic function of time t and of loss probabilities $\{p_x(t, s), s \geq t\}$. The SPA provide several examples of such functions, some of which are computationally challenging, while more tractable ones may lead to a violation of some of the conditions discussed beforehand.

Portfolio Loss Process Assuming that the dynamics of the loss probabilities is properly specified under the background filtration $\{M_t\}$, we can move to the second step, i.e., the calibration of the loss process under a broader filtration $\{L_t\}$, called the loss filtration.

We can now consider the intensity of the jump from the loss level x_i to the loss level x_{i+1}, conditional on the background filtration $\{M_t\}$ as:

$$K_{x_i}(t, T) \, dT = P[l(T + dT) = x_{i+1} \mid l(T) = x_i, M_t]$$

or

$$K_{x_i}(t, T) = \frac{(-\partial/\partial T)p_{x_i}(t, T)}{p_{x_{i+1}}(t, T) - p_{x_i}(t, T)} \tag{33}$$

The main contribution here is that SPA have constructed a one-step Markov chain ("one-step" as it is assumed that losses can take values on a finite grid $(0 = x_0 < x_1 < \cdots < x_N)$ and that loses can actually shift only by one step), i.e., a discrete one-step loss process on $\{x_i\}_{i=0}^N$ that is consistent with the loss probability process (32).

While the previous derivation is useful when a homogeneous portfolio (i.e., same recoveries) is considered, for idiosyncratic or stochastic recoveries, the state space needs to be extended to a much thin discretisation or to a continuous setup $x \in [0, 1]$, respectively.

In a more general setup using Markov processes, we can define a jump survival function: $m_{z, x}(t, T)$:

$$m_{z, x}(t, T)dT = P[l(T + dT) > x \mid l(T) = z, M_t]$$

and write, assuming that $l(t)$ is a nondecreasing pure-jump conditional Markov process on $[0, 1]$:

$$\frac{\partial}{\partial T} p_x(t, T) = -\int_0^x (m_{z,x}(t, T)\frac{\partial}{\partial z} p_z(t, T))\, dz \qquad (34)$$

It remains to define the actual dynamics of the loss process, given the knowledge of $p_x(t, T)$. This corresponds to the estimation of the jump survival process $m_{z,x}(t, T)$ itself.

In order to be able to estimate the latter process with sparse data, the only way is to specify more precisely a corresponding parametric function, and SPA motivate functions of the form $m_{z,x}(t, T) = \theta(T, x-z) \cdot v_x(t, T)$. Note that for $\theta(T, y) = 1_{\{y \in [0, 1/N]\}}$, a single one-step Markov chain is recovered. Then, even a more general setup where $\theta(\cdot)$ is given externally, $v_x(t, T)$ can be estimated from Equation (32).

Tranche Valuation   Assuming that the loss process is properly calibrated, we can reconsider the Equations (19) and (21) driving the price of any tranche j and write it for any starting time anterior to the first coupon date as:

$$C_j(t) = \sum_{k=1}^{K} D(t, k)[EL_j((k+1)|L_t) - EL_j((k)|L_t)]$$

$$F_j(t) = s_j \sum_{k=1}^{K} [(A_{j+1} - A_j) - EL_j((k)|L_t)] D(t, k)$$

Note that $EL(k|L_t)$ satisfies the following form $EL(k|L_t) = E[f(l(k))|M_t, l(t)]$, and it can be shown that this expectation can be decomposed into a linear combination of conditional loss probabilities:

$$p_{y,x}(t, k) = P[l(k) \leq x | M_t, l(t) = y] \qquad (35)$$

In other words, $p_x(t, T)$ provides an average default loss probability, and $p_{y,x}(t, T)$, is the loss probability conditional on a particular loss level y at time t.[*] It can be obtained by solving the following forward Kolmogorov equations in T and in x, with proper initial conditions (see SPA).

---

[*]Note that $p_{y,x}(t, T)$ is not observable from the background filtration.

$$\frac{\partial}{\partial T} p_{x,y}(t, T) = -\int_0^x (m_{z,x}(t, T) \frac{\partial}{\partial z} p_{z,y}(t, T)) \, dz \qquad (36)$$

This model is undoubtedly conceptually very attractive. In terms of tractability and practical implementation, it requires simplifying assumptions related to the volatility of the loss probability process. It also requires assumptions on the loss process through a tight characterization of the Markov chain (or Markov process). In order to be able to apply it for practical pricing purposes, three to four calibrations need to be undertaken with little data:

1. calibration of the loss probability processes (or?);
2. calibration of the compound forward rates;
3. calibration of the jump survival functions; and
4. calibration of the conditional loss probability processes.

The number of calibration steps involved requires a good understanding of the model behaviour, stability of parameterization and estimation, and the development of hedging strategies in order to mitigage the possibility of model risk and over fitting. If these issues can be addressed successfully, and if more market data becomes available, the model is capable of pricing options on tranches, forward starting tranches, and tranches with dynamic (loss dependent) attachment points, consistently.

Schönbucher's Model

Schönbucher's model does not differ very much from the SPA model. It does not go through a two-step model but models the loss distribution via time-inhomogeneous Markov chains.

Schönbucher calls $P(t, T)$ the transition probability matrix with a dimension corresponding to the number N of obligors in the underlying pool. $P(t, T)$ can be retrieved from a Kolmogorov equation with appropriate initial conditions:

$$\frac{d}{dt} P(t, T) = P(t, T) \cdot A(T),$$

with $A(T)$ being a generator function constituted of $N \cdot (N+1)/2$ elements $a_{nm}(T)$.

As with the previous model, the dynamic calibration of the generator function corresponds to the key challenge. Restrictions are required to be able to come with some tractable results. In our view, the SPA model might give more accurate results as it leads to a better understanding of the underlying processes and consequently perhaps to more realism regarding the simplifying assumptions required to be able to calibrate the model.

Pricing Based on a Dynamic Modeling of the Underlying Obligors

Given the tractability problems we think the dynamic loss distribution modelling approach might encounter, we believe it is important to mention alternative dynamic set-ups.

The most noticeable alternative is to simulate directly the dynamics of each exposure in the CDO pool. Duffie and Garleanu (2001) suggested to analyze the risk and valuation of CDOs in an intensity model where the issuers' hazard rates are assumed to follow correlated jump diffusion processes.

More recent approaches focus on less cumbersome solutions. Instead of describing the survival probability for a given obligor i over $[0, t]$ as $S_i(t) = \exp(-\int_0^t \lambda_i(u) du)$ and of thinking independently of correlation, di Graziano and Rogers (2005)* or Joshi and Stacey (2005) suggest to describe the survival probability as $S_i(t) = \exp(-\int_0^t \lambda_i(f(u)) du)$. For the former authors, the intensity is a deterministic function of a time continuous market chain common to all obligors, for the latter $f(u)$ is a Gamma process common to all obligors. In the two instances, the idea is to represent the dynamic time as a stochastic variable depending on market situations such as the state of the economy. With these specifications, correlation across the survival times of the obligors in the pool is coming naturally from the dependency on the state of the chain or from the calibration of the Gamma process and is not to be "forced" thanks to the use of a copula or by the calibration of a variance–covariance matrix.

In principle, the calibration of such processes looks reasonably tractable due to the recourse to conditional independence. Speed of computational calculation is most likely to be an issue as pointed out in the relevant papers.

---

*These authors suggest to add some jump terms too.

Pricing Bespoke CDO Tranches

Throughout this section, we consider two different types of "bespoke" tranches: first, bespoke tranches on traded indices and bespoke tranches based on a bespoke pool.

In the first case, we are typically talking about an investor who is considering, for example, a 5 to 8 percent five-year tranche on, say the iTraxx, for which there is no market price. Market practice is to use the levels of correlation at the bespoke attachment points from the interpolated base correlation curve to derive the price of the tranche. Recent practice has been to compute "centi-tranches" (1 percent tranchelets) as a building block to the pricing of bespoke tranches.

In the second case, the approach is cruder in the sense that banks tend to use internal recipes in order to get a sense of what the appropriate level of "market correlation" should be for the bespoke transaction, given correlation trends in the related index-based market.

Prince (2006) provides a review of three different valuation methodologies used in the industry and suggests to use a blend of them:

- ◆ *Net asset value*: The first one is the liquidation value (NAV). In this method, the first step is to measure the net market value of a CDO as the market value of the asset pool plus the value of the hedges minus all the liabilities. When the net market value is divided by the notional amount of the Equity, we have the liquidation value of the equity.

- ◆ *Cashflow analysis*: This approach is more forward looking, as it is based on the dynamics of the CDO collateral over time. It is in fact very close to what is presented in the following section of this chapter when dealing with cash CDOs.

- ◆ *Comparables*: This approach typically involves deriving prices from liquid tranches on indices.

PRICING CASH CDOS

In a cash CDO, loans and bonds in the asset pool are usually not traded actively. Price indications are therefore mainly related to ratings or to probabilities of default extracted from, e.g., a Merton type model. They will incorporate default risk, migration risk, and a component related to some average risk premium per rating category. However, these fair value prices cannot integrate idiosyncratic spread movements, as there is no market reference on which to rely.

In order to price a cash CDO, three constituents are necessary: a risk-neutral transition matrix, a risk-neutral asset correlation structure, and the knowledge of the waterfall structure. With these ingredients, it helps to have a multi-period rating-based portfolio model in order to be able to capture the dynamics of the waterfall structure that is conditioned by the performance of the asset pool, on the liability side.

Once these elements are defined, we detail various ways to obtain the fair value prices of the CDO tranches.

The numerical methodology presented next consists of simulating realizations of the value of the collateral pool and calculating the price of the CDO tranches by a technique similar to least square Monte-Carlo approach proposed by Longstaff and Schwartz (2001). The algorithm starts by calculating the payoff of each tranche at the maturity of the CDO and rolls backwards until the issuance of the notes by estimating the payoff of each tranche conditional on the performance of the pool of assets at each time step.

On the Asset Side

From Historical to Risk-Neutral Transition Matrices*

For pricing purposes, one requires "risk-neutral" probabilities. A risk-neutral transition matrix can be extracted from the historical matrix and a set of corporate bond prices.

$$\mathbf{Q}(h) = \begin{pmatrix} q_h^{1,1} & q_h^{1,2} & \cdots & q_h^{1,K+1} \\ \vdots & \vdots & & \vdots \\ q_h^{K,1} & q_h^{K,2} & \cdots & q_h^{K,K+1} \\ 0 & 0 & \cdots & 1 \end{pmatrix},$$

All q probabilities take the same interpretation as the empirical transition matrix below, but are under the risk-neutral measure.

$$\mathbf{P}(h) = \begin{pmatrix} p_h^{1,1} & p_h^{1,2} & \cdots & p_h^{1,K+1} \\ \vdots & \vdots & & \vdots \\ p_h^{K,1} & p_h^{K,2} & \cdots & p_h^{K,K+1} \\ 0 & 0 & \cdots & 1 \end{pmatrix}$$

*Some parts of the section are taken from de Servigny and Renault (2004).

Time Nonhomogeneous Markov Chain   In the original Jarrow-Lando-Turnbull (1997) (JLT) paper, the authors impose the following specification for the risk premium adjustment, allowing to compute risk-neutral probabilities from historical ones:

$$q^{i,j}(t, t+1) = \begin{cases} \pi_i(t)\, p^{i,j} & \text{for } i \neq j, \\ 1 - \pi_i(t)(1 - p^{i,i}) & \text{for } i = j. \end{cases} \tag{37}$$

Note that the risk premium adjustments $\pi_i(t)$ are deterministic and do not depend on the terminal rating but only on the initial one. This assumption enables JLT to obtain a nonhomogenous Markov chain for the transition process under the risk-neutral measure.

The calculation of risk-neutral matrices on real data can be performed as described below. Assuming that the recovery in default is a fraction δ of a treasury bond with same maturity, the price of a risky zero coupon bond at time t with maturity T is

$$P^i(t, T) = B(t, T) \times (1 - q^{i,K+1}(1 - \delta)).$$

Thus, we have

$$q^{i,K+1} = \frac{B(t, T) - P^i(t, T)}{B(t, T)(1 - \delta)},$$

and thus the one-year risk premium is

$$\pi_i(t) = \frac{B(t, t+1) - P^i(t, t+1)}{B(t, t+1)(1 - \delta)\, q^{i,K+1}}. \tag{38}$$

The JLT specification is easy to implement, but often leads to numerical problems because of the very low probability of default of investment grade bonds at short horizons. In order to preclude arbitrage, the risk-neutral probabilities must indeed be non-negative. This constrains the risk premium adjustments to be in the interval:

$$0 < \pi_i(t) \leq \frac{1}{1 - p^{i,i}}, \quad \text{for all } i.$$

As noticed above, the historical probability of an AAA bond defaulting over a one-year horizon is zero. Therefore, the risk-neutral probability of the same event is also zero.* This would however imply that the spreads on short-dated AAA bond should be zero (why have a spread on default risk-less bonds?). To tackle this numerical problem, JLT assume that the historical one-year probability of default for an AAA bond is actually 1 basis point. The risk premium for the AAA row adjustment is therefore bounded above. This bound is, as will be shown later, frequently violated on actual data.

Kijima and Komoribayashi (1998) propose another risk premium adjustment that guarantees the positivity of the risk-neutral probabilities in practical implementations.

$$\pi_{ij}(t) = l_i(t) \quad \text{for } j \neq K+1$$

$$q^{i,j}(t, t+1) = \begin{cases} l_i(t)p^{i,j} & \text{for } i \neq K+1, \\ 1 - l_i(t)(1 - p^{i,i}) & \text{for } i = K+1. \end{cases} \tag{39}$$

where $l_i(t)$ are deterministic functions of time. Thanks to this adjustment, "negative prices" can be avoided.

Time-Homogeneous Markov Chain   Unlike the precedent authors, Lamb et al. (2005) propose to compute a time-homogeneous Markovian risk-adjusted transition matrix. They rely on bond spreads, thanks to the term structure of spreads per rating category.

$$\exp(-S_i(t)) = (\delta \cdot q_i^{K+1}(t)) + (1 - q_i^{K+1}(t)). \tag{40}$$

where t corresponds to integer-year maturities.

In order to obtain the matrix, they minimize[†]

$$\underset{q_i^j(t)}{\text{Min}} \sum_{t=1}^{n} \sum_{i=1}^{K} [S_i(t) - (\delta \cdot q_i^{K+1}(t)) + (1 - q_i^{K+1}(t))]^2 \tag{41}$$

Knowing that $q_i^{K+1}(t)$ is a function of the $q_i^j(\cdot)$

A minor weakness of this approach is that it does not ensure that spreads are matching market prices for all maturities.

---

*Recall that two equivalent probability measures share the same null sets.
[†]Attaching penalties if entries in the transition matrix become negative in the course of the minimization.

Correlation

In a previous chapter, we have discussed correlation. An important question to answer here, in order to price tranches of a cash CDO, is what type of correlation to use.

There are basically three different options:

1. Using default implied asset correlation
2. Using equity correlation
3. Using correlation levels extracted from averaging the compound correlation on index tranches.

In option 1, the correlation we refer to only relates to credit events in the real world (rating downgrades and defaults). In option 2, we are capturing some market co-movement via equity price co-movements. What we can observe in Figure 6.13, however, is that equity correlation may be lower than average compound implied correlation retrieved from synthetic CDO index references. Equity correlation is commonly applied in software products comparable to Credit Metrics portfolio tool. This means that there could be some pricing mismatch between cash CDO and synthetic CDO pricing when equity correlation is used.

FIGURE 6.13

A Comparison between Different Asset Correlation Measures. Default-Based Asset Correlation is Based on Data from 1981 to 2005, Equity Correlation is Based on Data from 1998 to 2005, Compound Correlation Level is Based on Typical Recent History. (iTraxx 28/02/06).

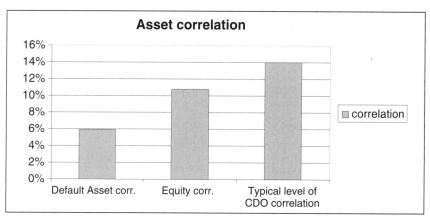

A related point to mention is that CPM* teams in commercial banks tend to rely primarily on models based on equity correlation, while the reference in the CDO market[†] may be closer to compound correlation levels. As a consequence, offloading exposures from the balance sheet of banks may turn out to be a costly exercise if the market grants less benefit to diversification than banks expect. The interest of obtaining a rating, from the perspective of a bank, is to counterbalance this mismatch with investors. Rating agencies, by using models that rely on default-based asset correlation, typically grant a higher benefit of diversification to offloaded tranches compared to the underlying assets staying on the portfolio of the bank. This situation, while it gives confidence to investors with respect to the risk/return of their structured investment, creates sufficient excess spread to facilitate disintermediation.

In what follows, we show how, in a portfolio model, correlation impacts the migration process. As we are considering a ratings-based model, the primary purpose of the simulation engine is precisely to generate migration events with the appropriate correlation structure.

Figure 6.14 illustrates the impact of asset correlations on the joint migration of obligors, assuming that there are two nondefault states (investment grade IG and noninvestment grade NIG) and an absorbing default state D.

The experiment uses a one-factor model. Similar results would be obtained in the multifactor setup. The tables are bivariate transition matrices for various levels of asset correlation under the assumption of joint normality of assets returns and using aggregate probabilities of transition extracted from CreditPro®.[‡] In order to reduce the size of the tables, we have assumed that the pair IG/NIG is identical from a portfolio point of view to the pair NIG/IG. Thus, each bivariate matrix is 6×6 instead of 9×9.

Taking, e.g., the case of two noninvestment grade obligors (row NIG/NIG) one can observe that, as the correlation increases, the joint default probability (as well as the joint probability of upgrades) increases significantly.

Multivariate transition probabilities cannot be computed for portfolios with reasonable numbers of lines. In a standard rating system with eight categories, a portfolio with N counterparts would imply an $8^N \times 8^N$ transition matrix that soon becomes intractable.

---

*Credit Portfolio Management.
[†]For instance, when investors try to assess the fair value of their investment on the basis of correlation trading-based prices.
[‡]A database from Standard & Poor's Risk Solutions.

FIGURE 6.14

Comparison of the Probability of Joint Migrations for Different Levels of Asset Correlation ρ.

$\rho=0$

	IG / IG	IG / NIG	IG / D	NIG / NIG	NIG / D	D / D
IG / IG	95.9%	3.9%	0.2%	0.0%	0.0%	0.0%
IG / NIG	3.6%	89.2%	5.2%	1.8%	0.2%	0.0%
IG / D	0.0%	0.0%	97.9%	0.0%	2.0%	0.1%
NIG / NIG	0.1%	6.7%	0.4%	82.8%	9.7%	0.3%
NIG / D	0.0%	0.0%	3.7%	0.0%	91.0%	5.3%
D / D	0.0%	0.0%	0.0%	0.0%	0.0%	100.0%

$\rho=20\%$

	IG / IG	IG / NIG	IG / D	NIG / NIG	NIG / D	D / D
IG / IG	96.0%	3.7%	0.2%	0.1%	0.0%	0.0%
IG / NIG	3.7%	89.2%	5.1%	1.7%	0.3%	0.0%
IG / D	0.0%	0.0%	97.9%	0.0%	2.0%	0.1%
NIG / NIG	0.3%	6.7%	0.1%	83.0%	9.3%	0.6%
NIG / D	0.0%	0.0%	3.7%	0.0%	91.0%	5.3%
D / D	0.0%	0.0%	0.0%	0.0%	0.0%	100.0%

$\rho=50\%$

	IG / IG	IG / NIG	IG / D	NIG / NIG	NIG / D	D / D
IG / IG	96.2%	3.3%	0.1%	0.3%	0.1%	0.0%
IG / NIG	3.7%	89.6%	4.7%	1.4%	0.7%	0.1%
IG / D	0.0%	0.0%	97.9%	0.0%	2.0%	0.1%
NIG / NIG	0.8%	5.8%	0.0%	84.1%	8.0%	1.3%
NIG / D	0.0%	0.0%	3.7%	0.0%	91.0%	5.3%
D / D	0.0%	0.0%	0.0%	0.0%	0.0%	100.0%

In a CreditMetrics type model, the process consists of simulating realizations of the systematic factors and the idiosyncratic components. As a consequence, given that firms all depend on the same factors, their asset returns are correlated and their migration events also exhibit co-movement. Joint downgrades for two obligors 1 and 2 will occur when the simulations return a low realization for both asset returns A_1 and A_2. This will be more likely when these asset returns are highly correlated than in the independent case.

Unlike the Gaussian copula model, based on survival probabilities, a CreditMetrics type model requires the specification of a targeted horizon. In risk management, the one-year horizon usually corresponds to the standard. However, it is an insufficient period to analyze CDO tranches with a five-year maturity. Two possibilities exist. The first one is to consider a single period model covering the five years. The issue with such a set-up is that it does not give sufficient visibility to assess the dynamics of cashflow allocation on the liability side (e.g., no collateralization test is possible during the life of the transaction). The second possibility is to rely on a multistep dynamic model. This latter type of model is obviously more relevant for cash CDO pricing.

However, one aspect related to multiple time-step models needs to be highlighted. A multi-period model with independence between the periods and a correlation level of ρ at each period will undershoot the corresponding single period model with a similar correlation level ρ. The difference can be explained intuitively, as in the case of a single period model, some autocorrelation prevails, whereas in a multi-period model, the assumption of independence between periods, there is essentially corresponds to no autocorrelation.

Computing the Price of Each Line in the Portfolio Depending on its Rating

In the previous paragraph, we have intuitively described how a CreditMetrics type model simulates all the ratings up to the horizon of interest t for any of the obligors in the portfolio.* The next step is to calculate the profits or losses arising from these risk-neutral migrations including defaults.

For "surviving" obligors, the value of the assets at time t is calculated using the risk free rate as observed at the time of calculation.

Let us consider a defaultable fixed rate bond with $j \in \{1, \ldots, N\}$ coupons c beyond the horizon t and with principal P. Its rating at the simulation horizon is i, its price $V_i(t)$, the spread level defined in Equation (40) from the risk neutral transition matrices is $S_i(j)$, and the forward risk free interest rate corresponding to the period $[t; t+j]$ is $r_{t, t+j}$.

$$V_i(t) = \sum_{j=1}^{N} \exp[-(r_{t,t+j}j + S_i(j))] + P \cdot \exp[-(r_{t,t+N}N + S_i(N))] \qquad (42)$$

The Monte Carlo simulation of the common and the idiosyncratic factors to which the latent variable (the asset value) of each exposure in the portfolio is tied enables us to draw many realizations of rating paths for each obligor at each future sub-period before the horizon. It ultimately allows us to price each of the exposures based on Equation (42).

On the Liability Side

A Brief Description of the Waterfall Structure

In this section, we describe briefly how the cashflows generated on the asset side are distributed on the liability side, thereby influencing the pricing of

---

*For a more refined description, see Chapter 4.

each tranche. Figure 6.15 provides an example of what a tranching exercise can look like.

The allocation of the proceeds from the asset side usually requires a relatively complex bespoke cashflow model. This type of model is designed to accurately reflect:

◆ The transaction capital structure
◆ The priority of payments
◆ Hedges
◆ The fee structures
◆ The coverage tests
◆ The collateral coupon spread
◆ The scheduled principal payments.

The Waterfall or priority of payments describes the flow of proceeds through the Special Purpose Vehicle to the note holders, hedge counterparties, and other agents participating in the CDO.

FIGURE 6.15

A Typical CDO Tranching.

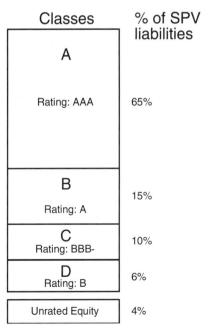

* Money flows into the CDO as asset interest proceeds and principal amortizations and hedge receipts.
* Money flows out of the CDO as fees, expenses, hedge payments and interests, and principal payments to the rated notes and preferred shares.

Coverage tests are ratios calculated in a CDO structure that alter the distribution priority of collateral proceeds by delevering the notes when the required ratio level is breached. There are two main tests:

* The over collateralization (OC) test. It is a ratio that tests the ability of the collateral balance (net of defaults and recoveries) to support the current liability balance (including deferred interest on the notes).
* The interest coverage (IC) test. It is a ratio that tests the ability of the collateral interest proceeds to support the current liability interest payouts (i.e., tests excess spread).

The dynamics of the waterfall structure is described in Figure 6.16 in a generic manner.

Impact on the Pricing of CDO Tranches

The payoff of a structured exposure depends in a complex way on the cashflows generated by the exposures on the asset side as well as on the way these cashflows are allocated to the tranches on the liability side, given the waterfall structure of the deal.

In practice, there are as many pricing models as there are different structures. Due to the Monte-Carlo approach, computational times are usually substantial.

Lamb et al. (2005) suggest an interesting shortcut consisting of the estimation of a pricing function by applying scoring techniques. More precisely, they show that it is possible to fit a regression-type function for each tranche that will give a price at the maturity of the CDO as a function of the realization of the vector of latent variables corresponding to the obligors in the CDO pool. As a result, any price of a tranche before maturity of the pool is easily obtainable by proper discounting. In terms of speed of calculation, the pricing functions for each deal typically require less than 10,000 Monte Carlo replications to provide accurate results. The tests performed by Lamb et al. (2005) show that this class of model performs well in terms of first moments, Value at Risk and Expected Shortfall. In terms of hedging, this model provides interesting and accurate strategies.

FIGURE 6.16

The Waterfall Structure Including Tests Extracted from Garcia et al. (2005).

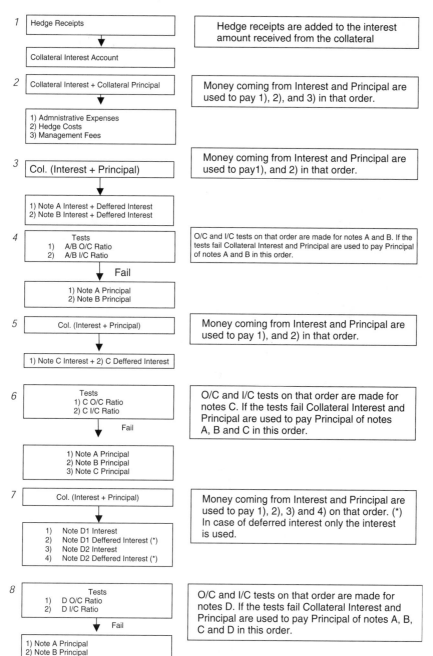

FIGURE 6.16 (Continued)

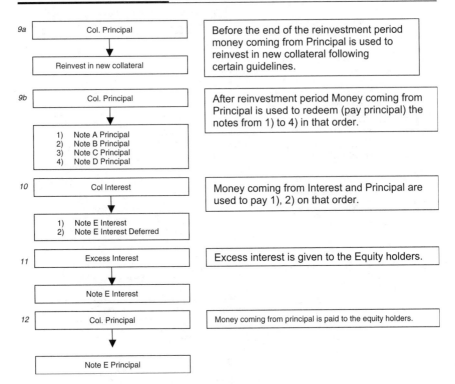

9a | Col. Principal |
    → Reinvest in new collateral

Before the end of the reinvestment period money coming from Principal is used to reinvest in new collateral following certain guidelines.

9b | Col. Principal |
    → 1) Note A Principal
       2) Note B Principal
       3) Note C Principal
       4) Note D Principal

After reinvestment period Money coming from Principal is used to redeem (pay principal) the notes from 1) to 4) in that order.

10 | Col Interest |
    → 1) Note E Interest
       2) Note E Interest Deferred

Money coming from Interest and Principal are used to pay 1), 2) on that order.

11 | Excess Interest |
    → Note E Interest

Excess interest is given to the Equity holders.

12 | Col. Principal |
    → Note E Principal

Money coming from principal is paid to the equity holders.

CONCLUSION

In this chapter, we have tried to provide some insight into the most prominent pricing techniques used in the synthetic and cash CDO markets. It is very difficult to offer a full coverage given the amount of academic as well as applied research that is continuously generated in this area.

The driving force in the efforts that we have reported is focused on generating accurate results while using data in a parsimonious way. We can see that the most recent techniques tend to be less parsimonious though. One question we might ask ourselves is: what is the appropriate minimum level of information (factors, and parameters) that is required to match market prices? In this respect, Longstaff and Rajan (2006) suggest that single factor models are too simplistic to price CDO tranches accurately. They advocate that the ideal number of common factors to consider should be 2 in order to allow for firm specific, industry, and economy-wide events to be explained. On the basis of this specification, they are able to identify three loss regimes on the CDX index. These regimes correspond to 0.4 percent, 6 percent, and 35 percent loss levels and take place respectively every 1.2, 41.5, and 763 years on average. The first firm-specific regime typically dominates 65 percent of the time, the second industry-specific regime is at play 27 percent of the time and the third regime, corresponding to catastrophic risk, accounts for the remaining 8 percent. The authors may not have a sufficiently large data sample yet to be too assertive on these results, with only two years of daily observations of the CDX index. There is, however, certainly an interesting aspect to these first statistical results.

REFERENCES

Andersen, L. (2005), "Base correlation, Models and Musings," in PPT presentation ICBI Credit Derivative Conference, Paris.

Andersen, L., and J. Sidenius (2005), "Extensions to the Gaussian copula: Random recovery and random factor loadings," *Journal of Credit Risk*, 1(1).

Andersen, L., J. Sidenius, and S. Basu (2003), "All your Hedges in One Basket," *Risk*, November, 67–72.

Black, F., and M. Scholes (1973), "The pricing of options and corporate liabilities," *Journal of Political Economy*, 81, 637–654.

Burtschell, X., J. Gregory, and J. P. Laurent (2005), "A comparative analysis of CDO pricing models," working paper.

Debuysscher, A., and M. Szego (2005), "Fourier Transform Techniques applied to Structured Finance," PPT presentation Moody's.

de Servigny, A., and O. Renault (2004) "Measuring and Managing Credit Risk," McGraw Hill book.

di Graziano, G., and L. C. G. Rogers (2005), "A new approach to the modelling and pricing of correlation credit derivatives," working paper Statistical Laboratory, University of Cambridge.

Duffie, D., and K. J. Singleton (1998), "Modeling the term structures of defaultable bonds," *Review of Financial Studies*, 12, 687–720.

Duffie, D., and N. Gârleanu (2001), "Risk and the valuation of collateralized debt Obligations," *Financial Analysts Journal*, 57, 41–59.

Elouerkhaoui, Y. (2003a), "Credit risk: Correlation with a difference," working paper, UBS Warburg.

Elouerkhaoui, Y. (2003b), "Credit Derivatives: Basket asymptotics," working paper, UBS Warburg.

Finger, C. C. (2005), "Issues in the pricing of synthetic CDOs," *Journal of Credit Risk*, 1(1).

Frey, R., and A. McNeil (2003). "Dependent defaults in models of portfolio credit risk," *Journal of Risk*, 6(1), 59–92.

Garcia, J., T. Dewyspelaere, R. Langendries, L. Leonard, and T. Van Gestel (2005), "On rating cash flow CDO's using BET technique," Dexia working paper.

Gibson, M. (2004), "Understanding the risk of synthetic CDOs," working paper FED.

Giesecke, K. (2003), "A simple exponential model for dependent defaults," *Journal of Fixed Income*, December, 74–83.

Gregory, J., and J.-P. Laurent (2003), "I Will Survive," *Risk*, June, 103–107.

Hull, J., and A. White (2003), "Valuation of a CDO and an nth to default CDS without Monte Carlo simulation," working paper J. L. Rotman School of Management, University of Toronto.

Hull, J., and A. White (2004), "Valuation of a CDO and an nth to default CDS without Monte Carlo simulation," *Journal of Derivatives*, 2, 8–23.

Hull, J., and A. White (2005), "The perfect copula," working paper J. L. Rotman School of Management, University of Toronto.

Jarrow, R. A., D. Lando, and S. M. Turnbull (1997), "A Markov model for the term structure of credit risk spreads," *The Review of Financial Studies*, 10, n. 2, 481–523.

Joshi, M., and A. Stacey (2005), "Intensity gamma: a new approach to pricing. portfolio credit derivatives," working paper.

Kalemanova, A., B. Schmid, and R. Werner (2005), "The normal inverse Gaussian distribution for synthetic CDO," working paper.

Kijima, M., and K. Komoribayashi (1998), "A Markov Chain Model for Valuing Credit Risk Derivatives," *Journal of Derivatives*, Fall, 97–108.

Lamb, R., V. Peretyatkin, and W. Perraudin (2005), "Hedging and asset allocation for structured products," working paper Imperial College.

Li, D. (2000), "On default correlation: a Copula approach," *Journal of Fixed Income*, 9, 43–54.

Lindskog, F., and A. McNeil (2003), "Common poisson shock models: Applications to insurance and credit risk modelling," *ASTIN Bulletin*, 33(2), 209–238.

Longstaff, F., and A. Rajan (2006), "An empirical analysis of the pricing of collateralized debt obligations," working paper.

Longstaff, F., and E. Schwartz (2001), "Valuing American options by simulation: a simple least-squares approach," *Review of Financial Studies*, 14(1), 113–147.

McGinty, L., E. Bernstein, R. Ahluwalia, and M. Watts (2004), "Introducing Base Correlations," JP Morgan.

O'Kane, D., and L. Schloegl (2001), "Modeling Credit: Theory and Practice," Lehman Brothers International.

Pain, A., O. Renault, and D. Shelton (2005), "Base correlation, The term structure dimension," Fixed Income Strategy and Analysis paper Citigroup, 09-12-05.

Prince, J. (2006), "A general review of CDO valuation methods," Global Structured Credit Strayegy paper Citigroup, 15-02-06.

Rott, M. G., and C. P. Fries (2005), "Fast and robust Monte Carlo CDO sensitivities," working paper.

Schönbucher, P., and D. Schubert (2001), "Copula dependent default risk in intensity models," working paper, Bonn University.

Schönbucher, P. J. (2005), "Portfolio losses and the term structure od loss transition rates: a new methodology for the pricing of portfolio credit derivatives," Working Paper.

Shelton, D. (2004), "Back to Normal," Global Structured Credit Research, 20-08-04.

Sidenius, J., V. Piterbarg, and L. Andersen (2005), "A new framework for dynamic portfolio loss modelling," Working Paper.

St Pierre, M., E. Rousseau, J. Zavattero, and O. van Eyseren (2004), "Valuing and hedging synthetic CDO tranches using base correlations"—Bear Stearns Credit Derivatives.

Vasicek (1987), "Probability of loss on loan portfolio," working paper, KMV Corporation.

Vasicek, O.A. (1997), "*An equilibrium characterization of the term structure,*" *Journal of Financial Economics*, 5, 1997–288.

CHAPTER 7

An Introduction to the Risk Management of Collateral Debt Obligations

Norbert Jobst

INTRODUCTION

In recent years, the market for collateral debt obligations (CDOs) and, in particular, the development of the synthetic CDO market and correlation trading has resulted in significant developments in valuation and risk management for such products. The market has been dominated by developments around the static Gaussian copula model, the introduction of base correlation as an alternative to the compound correlation, and extensions to better capture the observed correlation smile/skew, only recently more dynamic models that incorporate credit spreads—or other major modeling parameters—have been introduced by practitioners and academics (see Chapter 6). All valuation approaches are based on risk-neutral pricing principles and little focus has been given to replication-based arguments that would also lead to developments for practical hedging and risk management. Currently, risk management often focuses on static risk measures that address the likelihood of a CDO investor receiving full notional and actual interest in a timely manner (ratings perspective), or on mark-to-market (MtM) sensitivities and "the greeks" frequently employed by correlation investors and traders.

This chapter focuses on a MtM-based risk assessment. A brief and concise overview of static risk measures frequently employed by rating agencies or "buy-and-hold" investors is given in *the next* section. This chapter is complemented by Chapter 8, where many of the theoretical concepts introduced here are put into practice. Hence, whereas the focus in this chapter is on introducing "the greeks" conceptually and providing guidelines for practical implementation, the next chapter provides a critical discussion based on a number of popular synthetic CDO trading strategies. As with the chapter on valuation, many derivations evolve around the Gaussian copula model, and we provide implementation details on simulation-based and semianalytical techniques.

RISK MEASUREMENT I: A CREDIT RISK AND RATINGS PERSPECTIVE

Rating agencies (RAs), such as Standard & Poor's, Moody's, Fitch, or DRBS, are typically interested in the risk a CDO investor is facing, and base their opinions partly on model-based statistics. For example, Moody's rating is a so-called "expected loss" rating and, as a result, the expected loss on a CDO tranche is assessed and benchmarked to various rating-specific targets. Standard & Poor's, on the other hand, applies a "probability of default" (PD) or "first dollar of loss" rating and estimates the likelihood of an investor facing any loss at all.

Underlying such approaches is an assessment, in one form or another, of the (likelihood of) losses a CDO tranche investor may face over the life of the transaction. Traditionally, the definition of losses is restricted to a buy-and-hold perspective and hence to losses from default events only, but recently, RAs moved towards an assessment of the prevalent MtM risk (see Chapter 11 for a brief discussion). For now, we focus on potential losses from defaults that may occur until maturity T of a transaction.

More specifically, we consider a portfolio of N different names/obligors ($i=1, \ldots, N$) referenced by a CDO, and default times τ_i associated with each name. If τ_i is less than the maturity T of the CDO transaction, the loss L_i is determined as $L_i = N_i \times (1 - \delta_i)$, where N_i and δ_i are the exposure-at-default and recovery,* respectively for the ith asset. We can therefore write the portfolio loss up to time T, $L(T)$, as

---

*The recovery can either be assumed to be constant, or drawn from a distribution.

$$L(T) = \sum_i N_i \times (1 - \delta_i) \times 1_{\{\tau_i \leq T\}} \tag{1}$$

where $1_{\{\tau_i \leq T\}}$ is the default indicator for the ith asset.*

In practice, the distribution of portfolio losses can be determined with high accuracy, and various approaches capturing dependence in different ways have been discussed in Chapters 4 and 6.

Most rating agencies employ simulation-based approaches that generate correlated default times τ_i in which case the distribution of portfolio losses [Equation (1)] can be readily determined. Standard & Poor's simulation model, the CDO Evaluator, is outlined in Chapter 10 in further detail.

CDO Risk Measures and Rating Assignment

From now onwards, we assume that a model computing the loss distribution, $F_{L(T)}(l) = P(L(T) \leq l)$, and/or default times τ_i is available, and we introduce a few popular risk measures employed by "buy-and-hold" investors or RAs.

Tranche Default Probability
Given a CDO tranche T_j with attachment point A_j and detachment point D_j (i.e., a tranche thickness equal to $D_j - A_j$), the tranche default probability (PD) is the probability that portfolio losses at maturity T exceed A_j. This is given by

$$PD^{T_j} = 1 - F_{L(T)}(A_j) = P(L(T) > A_j) = E[1_{\{L(T) > A_j\}}], \tag{2}$$

where $E[]$ denotes the expectation. This measure forms the basis for assigning a rating to a synthetic CDO tranche for a PD-based rating, as provided for example by Standard & Poor's (see Chapters 10 and 11 for further details).

Expected Tranche Loss
Rather than focusing only on whether or not a single tranche (ST) CDO investor is facing a loss, we should also focus on the size of the losses. The cumulative loss on tranche T_j at time T, $L^{T_j}(T)$, is given by

$L^{T_j}(T) = (L(T) - A_j)1_{\{A_j \leq L(T) \leq D_j\}} + (D_j - A_j)1_{\{L(T) \geq D_j\}}.$ Then, the expected tranche loss is given by

---

*The default indicator equals 1 if the expression within parentheses is true, and 0 if it is false.

$$EL^{T_j} = E\Big[L^{T_j}(T)\Big] = E\Big[(L(T) - A_j)1_{\{A_j \le L(T) \le D_j\}} + (D_j - A_j)1_{\{L(T) \ge D_j\}}\Big]$$

$$= (D_j - A_j)Q_{L(T)}(D_j) + \int_{A_j}^{D_j} (l - A_j)\,\mathrm{d}F_{L(T)}(l) \tag{3}$$

which can be easily computed through Monte-carlo (MC) simulation. If the attachment probabilities $Q_{L(T)}(l) = 1 - F_{L(T)}(l)$ can be computed efficiently through (semi) analytic methods, we can show that integration by parts and $-Q_{L(T)}(l)/\mathrm{d}l = F_{L(T)}(l)/\mathrm{d}l$ enables us to rewrite Equation (3) as an integral over the attachment probabilities:

$$EL^{T_j} = \int_{A_j}^{D_j} Q_{L(T)}(l)\,\mathrm{d}\,l. \tag{4}$$

An expected loss rating assigned by rating agencies such as Moody's is partly based on this measure of tranche risk.

Tranche Loss-Given-Default

From the expected tranche loss and the tranche PD, the tranche loss-given-default (LGD)—assuming that LGD and PD are uncorrelated—is simply given by $\mathrm{LGD}^{T_j} = E(L^{T_j}(t)) / \mathrm{PD}^{T_j}$.

As discussed earlier, the typical RA assessment is based around a probabilistic view of tranche losses and is, as such, sensitive to the assumptions made in the underlying credit portfolio model (such as the Gaussian copula model). These assumptions are typically estimated from historic ratings and default data, and the probabilities and expectations considered are therefore taken under the "real world" or "historic" measure, whereas the assumptions throughout the next section are often denoted as "market implied" or "risk neutral." For corporate credit, for example, risk neutral default probabilities are on average two to five times observed default rates, thus embedding a risk premium taken by investors (see Berndt et al. (2005) for a empirical discussion on the credit risk premia). A good introduction to CDO risk management is also given in Gibson (2004).

RISK MEASUREMENT II: MARKET RISK, SENSITIVITY MEASURES, AND HEDGING

Correlation investors and traders are typically not only concerned with the pure credit or default risk of correlation products, but also with MtM risks such as spread, convexity, and correlation sensitivity, as well as volatility and relative value (risk/return) considerations. In addition, buy-and-hold investors, traditionally interested in the risk throughout the life of the transaction, also estimate their MtM exposures for internal risk reporting. Correlation traders, on the other hand, structure adequate hedging strategies and look for cheap convexity, volatility, and/or correlation from a relative value perspective. The sensitivity measures provide some insight into how the value of a CDO tranche may change when market factors, and therefore the valuation parameters, are changing. This is particularly important for CDO tranches, where the impact of such changes can be very different across tranches depending on tranche parameters such as seniority and thickness. Table 7.1 provides an overview of the measures that will be discussed throughout this section.

In the remainder of this section, we introduce these sensitivity measures from a conceptual perspective and discuss some computationally efficient approaches for practical implementation. In order to establish such

TABLE 7.1

MtM Sensitivity Measures ("Greeks").

Sensitivity Measure	Description
Spread sensitivity: Delta	Tranche price sensitivity to (small) changes in credit spreads. Frequently, the sensitivity to spread changes on individual names and/or to wider market movements (all names) is of interest.
Tranche Leverage: Lambda	Leverage effectively scales the DELTA of a tranche by the tranche notional and gives an indication of how the total spread risk is split across different tranches.
Spread Convexity: Gamma	Tranche price sensitivity to larger changes in credit spreads. Gamma is very important when considering delta-neutral positions as it gives some insight into the MtM changes when individual spreads or the market move significantly.
Time decay: Theta	Change in tranche value due to the passage of time. It is important as delta-neutral positions may become spread sensitive as time passes and no other parameters change.
Correlation sensitivity: Rho	Change in tranche value resulting from a change in "implied" compound or base correlation.
Default sensitivity: Omega	Change in tranche value resulting from an instantaneous default of one or more names in the portfolio. Omega is also denoted as "Value on Default" (VOD) or "Jump to default" (JTD), and is particularly interesting for delta-hedged positions.

sensitivities, a consistent valuation framework, as outlined in Chapter 6 on pricing, needs to be in place.

First Order Spread Sensitivity: Delta

In practice, the spread risk of a CDO tranche is managed by buying and selling single name CDS protection as an offsetting hedge. This, of course, is not addressing all risks inherent in ST CDOs and provides only a partial hedge (a spread hedge), compared to entering an offsetting but identical trade. Such an offsetting trade, however, is rarely possible due to the bespoke nature of many ST CDOs. With the recent growth in standardized index tranches—ST CDOs referencing the CDX indices in the United States and/or the ITraxx ones in Europe—such offsetting hedges are possible. Depending on how similar a bespoke tranche portfolio is to the composition of a CDS index, liquid tranches on that index can provide a good approximate hedge. In practice, instead of single name CDS, liquid indices can be used directly (in unlevered form) to manage spread sensitivity. We denote the sensitivity to single name spread movements by individual or microspread sensitivity (CS01), while the sensitivity to a broad move in the portfolio spread will be denoted by market or macrosensitivity (Credit01).*

Defining Single Name/Individual Delta

A widening in credit spreads (keeping everything else equal) leads to an increase in expected portfolio loss and, correspondingly, to the expected loss of all tranches. Hence, ST positions are subject to MtM movements as credit spreads in the underlying portfolio change. To hedge a long (short) position in a tranche requires buying (selling) protection on each of the underlying names according to the delta. We therefore define the delta $\Delta_i^{T_j}$ of a credit j in the underlying portfolio as the amount of protection the dealer sells (buys) on that name to hedge the MtM risk of a short (long) tranche position, denoted by T_j, due to credit spread change of name i. In practice, such a change in spreads will lead to MtM gains or losses on the tranche position $(\Delta \text{MtM}_i^{T_j})$ as well as on the single name CDS or hedge portfolio (ΔMtM_i). Hence, holding $\Delta_i^{T_j}$ amount of CDS on name i will lead to the same profit and loss (P&L) impact as holding the CDO tranche, if the credit spread of name i changes slightly. Formally,

$$\Delta_i^{T_j} \cdot \Delta \text{MtM}_i(\bar{x}) = \Delta \text{MtM}_i^{T_j}(\bar{x}),$$

---

*"01" in CS01 and Credit01 stands for a small, 1 bp shift in credit spreads.

and

$$\Delta_i^{T_j} = \frac{\Delta \, \text{MtM}_i^{T_j}(\vec{x})}{\Delta \, \text{MtM}_i(\vec{x})},$$ (5)

where $\vec{x}$ denotes the parameters necessary for valuation and MtM calculation. In the context of the Gaussian copula framework and compound correlations, $\vec{x}$ would contain the valuation time t, maturity T, a vector of credit spread curves $\vec{S}(t):=\vec{S}(t):=(S_1(t),\ldots,S_N(t))$ where $S_i(t)$ denotes the term structure of credit spreads of name i at time t, a vector of recovery rates $\vec{\delta}:=(\delta_1(t),\ldots,\delta_N(t))$, and the compound correlation (matrix) ρ. In the examples shown here, the maturity of the CDS position heding a CDO tranche spread sensitivity are taken to be identical. We only state the parameters of immediate interest in the remainder of this chapter, and assume that all other parameters remain unchanged, unless otherwise noted. In order to compute delta, the MtM of single name CDS and CDO tranches needs to be derived next.

MtM of a Single Name CDS

We denote by $Q(t, T, S_i(t))$, the risk neutral survival probability for obligor i:

$$Q(t, T, S_i(t)) = \exp\left(-\int_t^T \lambda_s(S_i(t))\,ds\right),$$

where $\lambda_s(S_i(t))$ denotes the hazard rate at time s bootstrapped from the credit spread curve $S_i(t)$ as seen at time t (see Chapter 3 for further details and Appendix A on the computation or bootstrapping of hazard rates from credit spread data).

The MtM of a default swap position, when the valuation date is on a premium payment date—thereby simplifying notation, as accrued interest and premium accrued can be ignored—is given for a long protection position by

$$\text{MtM}_i(t_v, T, S_i(t_v)) = (S_i(t_v) - S_i(t_0))\text{RiskyPV01}(t_v, T, S_i(t_v)),$$

where t_v denotes the valuation and premium payment date, and

$$\text{RiskyPV01}(t_v, T, S_i(t_v))$$

$$= \sum_{n=1}^{N} D(t_{n-1}, t_n)B(t_v, t_n)\left[Q(t_v, t_n, S_i(t_v)) + \frac{1_{\{PA\}}}{2}\left(Q(t_v, t_{n-1}, S_i(t_v))\right.\right.$$

$$\left.\left. - Q(t_v, t_n, S_i(t_v))\right)\right]$$ (6)

denotes the present value (PV) of one unit investment in a CDS written on obligor i that matures at time T. Here, $1_{(PA)} = 1$ if premium accrued is taken into consideration and 0 otherwise. $B(t,T)$ denotes the Libor discount factor, $D(t_{n-1}, t_n)$ the day count fraction between premium payment dates, and $t_N = T$ the deal maturity.

O'Kane and Turnbull (2003) show that Equation (6) provides a very good approximation to

$$\text{RiskyPV}01(t_v, T, S_i(t_v)) = \sum_{n=1}^{N} \int_{t_{n-1}}^{t_n} D(t_{n-1}, s) B(t_v, s) Q(t_v, s, S_i(t_v)) \lambda_s(S_i) \, ds,$$

where the premium accrued is modeled more accurately.

For the purpose of determining $\Delta_i^{T_j}$, the change in MtM, ΔMtM_i, caused by a 1 bp parallel shift in the credit spread of obligor i at the initial time $t = t_0$ is given by

$$
\begin{aligned}
\Delta \text{MTM}_i &:= \Delta \text{MTM}_i(t_0, T, S_i(t_0), S_i(t_0) + 1\,\text{bp}) \\
&= \text{MTM}_i(t_0, T, S_i(t_0) + 1\,\text{bp}) - \text{MTM}_i(t_0, T, S_i(t_0)) \\
&= \text{MTM}_i(t_0, T, S_i(t_0) + 1\,\text{bp}) \\
&= (S_i(t_0) + 1\,\text{bp} - S_i(t_0)) \, \text{RiskyPV}01(t_0, T, S_i(t_0) + 1\,\text{bp}) \\
&= (1\,\text{bp}) \, \text{RiskyPV}01(t_0, T, S_i(t_0) + 1\,\text{bp})
\end{aligned}
$$

Note that the third equality stems from the fact that at time $t = 0$, the PV of protection leg and premium leg are equal if the CDO is fairly priced. As a result, the MtM at that time is zero.

MtM of an ST CDO

In order to compute the delta of a tranche, we also need to derive the change in MtM on a specific tranche of a synthetic CDO resulting from the 1 bp parallel shift in credit spreads. At time $t_0 = 0$, the PV of the protection leg (PPV) of a synthetic CDO tranche T_j is given by

$$\text{PPV}^{T_j}(t_0, T, S(t_0)) = \sum_{k=1}^{K} B(0, t_k) \left(EL^{T_j}(t_k) - EL^{T_j}(t_{k-1}) \right) \tag{7}$$

where $EL^{T_j}(t_k) := EL^{T_j}(t_0, t_k, S(t_0)) = E(\max[\min(L(t_k) - A_j, D_j - A_j), 0])$ denotes the expected tranche loss cumulated until time t_k computed at time t_0 by employing the spread information (curve) available at that time $(S(t_0))$. Here, $S(t_0)$ denotes the vector of credit spreads (curves) for all names in the underlying portfolio. As before, the expected tranche loss can be computed from an adequate model, such as the Gaussian copula, and through various numerical techniques such as MC simulation, Fast Fourier Transform Methods, recursive schemes, or the proxy integration method. An overview of these approaches is provided in Chapter 6.

Given an estimate of expected tranche losses through time, we can also compute the PV of the fee or premium leg, that is,

$$FPV^{T_j}(t_0, T, S(t_0)) = S^{T_j}(t_0, T, S(t_0)) \sum_{k=1}^{K} \left[B(0, t_k) D(t_{k-1}, t_k) \right.$$

$$\left. \times \left(D_j - A_j - EL^{T_j}(t_k) \right) \right]. \qquad (8)$$

We also define the Tranche PV01 as the PV of 1 bp (unit) invested in tranche j as:

$$TrPV\,01^{T_j}(t_0, T, S(t_0)) := CS\,01(t_0, T, S(t_0)):$$

$$= \sum_{k=1}^{K} B(0, t_k) D(t_{k-1}, t_k) \times \left(D_j - A_j - EL^{T_j}(t_0, T, S(t_0)) \right).$$

Then, at time $t = 0$, the MtM for tranche j is defined as the difference in the fee and PPVs, which, assuming a fairly priced tranche, is zero at inception of a trade $(MtM^{T_j}(t_0, T, S(t_0)) = FPV^{T_j}(t_0, T, S(t_0)) - PPV^{T_j}(t_0, T, S(t_0)) = 0$. The fair tranche spread, $S^{T_j}(t_0, T, S(t_0))$, is therefore given by

$$S^{T_j}(t_0, T, S(t_0)) = \frac{PPV^{T_j}(t_0, T, S(t_0))}{TrPV\,01^{T_j}(t_0, T, S(t_0))}.$$

At a later date, say a premium payment date t_v (to keep the notation simple), the MtM is given by

$$\text{MtM}^{T_j}(t_v,T,S(t_v)) = S^{T_j}(t_0,T,S(t_0)) \, \text{TrPV}\,01(t_v,T,S(t_v))$$
$$- \text{PPV}^{T_j}(t_v,T,S(t_v)),$$

which is unequal to zero as time passes, and spreads and other pricing parameters may have changed. Hence, with

$$S^{T_j}(t_v,T,S(t_v)) = \frac{\text{PPV}^{T_j}(t_v,T,S(t_v))}{\text{TrPV}\,01^{T_j}(t_v,T,S(t_v))}$$

we obtain

$$\text{MtM}^{T_j}(t_v,T,S(t_v)) = \left(S^{T_j}(t_0,T,S(t_0)) - S^{T_j}(t_v,T,S(t_v)) \right) \text{TrPV}\,01(t_v,T,S(t_v)).$$

For the purpose of calculating $\Delta_i^{T_j}$, the change in tranche MtM for a 1 bp parallel shift in the credit spread term structure of name i is given by

$$\Delta\,\text{MtM}_i^{T_j} := \Delta\,\text{MtM}_i^{T_j}(t_0,T,S(t_0),S^{i01}(t_0))$$
$$= \text{MtM}^{T_j}(t_0,T,S^{i01}(t_0)) - \text{MtM}^{T_j}(t_0,T,S(t_0))$$
$$= \text{MtM}^{T_j}(t_0,T,S^{i01}(t_0))$$
$$= (S^{T_j}(t_0,T,S(t_0)) - S^{T_j}(t_0,T,S^{i01}(t_0))) \, \text{TrPV}\,01(t_0,T,S^{i01}(t_0))$$

where $S^{i01}(t) := (S_1(t),\dots,S_{i-1}(t),S_i(t)+1\,bp,S_{i+1}(t),\dots,S_N(t))$ denotes the vector of credit spreads and where the term structure of name i is shifted uniformly by 1 bp while all other term structures remain unchanged.

The approach just outlined is frequently denoted as "brute force" or "bumping," and is fairly flexible and independent of the actual valuation model employed. In order to compute the change in MtM, the expected tranche loss needs to be derived at different points in time efficiently. While simulation is in principle feasible, more efficient approaches are preferable, especially as calculations need to be repeated for each underlying name. Although there are generally no explicit analytical expressions for tranche deltas available, practitioners and academics have developed various approaches for determining tranche sensitivities more efficiently and accurately. These approaches are often developed for a specific pricing model or numerical implementation of such models and employ the exact definition $\partial \text{MtM}^{T_j}(t_0,T,S(t_0))/\partial S_i(t_0)$ rather than the approximate relationship

$$\frac{\partial \, \mathrm{MtM}^{T_j}(t_0, T, S(t_0))}{\partial S_i(t_0)} (1 \text{ bp}) \approx \Delta \, \mathrm{MtM}_i^{T_j}$$

$$= \mathrm{MtM}^{T_j}(t_0, T, S^{i01}(t_0)) - \mathrm{MtM}^{T_j}(t_0, T, S(t_0)).$$

Closed form or semi-closed-form solutions for the partial integral are frequently developed.

Appendix B outlines a semi-analytic computation of the sensitivity of the tranche value to small changes in PDs (spreads) within the commonly used recursive scheme of Andersen et al. (2003) as outlined in "Option 2: The recursive approach" of Chapter 6.

Appendix C reviews the LH+ model of Greenberg et al. (2004) where spread hedges are computed in closed form. The model is based on the large homogeneous portfolio (LHP) approximation with one additional asset, for which sensitivities are computed.

Additional insights into efficient and accurate computation of CDO and basket sensitivities, within a simulation framework can be found in Joshi and Kainth (2003), Rott and Fries (2005), and Glasserman and Li (2003). We provide some insight in appendix D on MC deltas, and also refer to Brasch (2004) who revisits analytic and semianalytic methods focusing on sensitivities for CDO and CDO^2 structures.

Practical Hedging and Delta Sensitivity

By definition, delta hedging immunizes the tranche against small changes in credit spreads. For larger spread movements, a significant amount of spread risk (spread convexity) prevails, resulting in a need to dynamically rebalance the hedges throughout the life of the transaction. Such a process may incur a significant amount of transaction costs, depending on the frequency of rebalancing actions and current bid–ask spreads. Furthermore, liquidity in some of the underlying names may be poor due to the bespoke nature of underlying assets in synthetic ST CDOs. Nevertheless, tranche deltas provide significant insight into the behavior of CDOs and are a major risk management tool. If the behavior of deltas is well understood, it is possible to design trading strategies with desired spread sensitivities over time. Similarly, strategies can be constructed with an initial delta-mismatch that become delta neutral when spreads move in line with one's expectations. We will therefore review the sensitivity of tranche deltas to various parameters that impact CDO performance.

Delta and the Capital Structure   Generally speaking, the delta of a single name increases as we move down the capital structure, i.e., the lower the level of subordination, the higher the tranche delta.

Delta and Credit Spread Levels   Credits with a higher spread are expected to default (in the risk neutral world) earlier than credits trading at a lower spread. The earlier a credit is expected to default, the higher the impact will be on the equity tranche, resulting in higher equity tranche deltas for wider trading names and vice versa. Similarly, lower spreads imply that the expected default time is later (than the average default time in the portfolio) and those names are more likely to impact the senior tranches. Hence, the delta for tight spread trading names is higher than the delta for wider trading names for senior tranches, and the reverse is true for junior positions (e.g., equity tranches). Figure 7.1 displays typical credit spread deltas expressed in percent of the names notional.* As we con-

FIGURE 7.1

Delta (in Percent of Reference Name Notional) as a Function of Credit Spread Level.

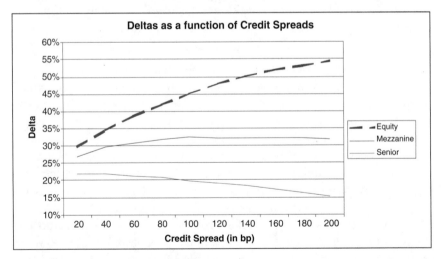

---

*The practical examples illustrating spread sensitivities are based on a homogeneous portfolio of 50 credits with a notional of 10 m each, trading at a spread of 100 bp under an assumed recovery of 38 percent. Furthermore, the compound correlation is assumed flat at 25 percent. The equity, mezzanine, and senior tranches are trached at 0 to 4 percent, 4 to 8 percent, and 8 to 12 percent, respectively.

sider a homogenous pool (same spreads, recoveries, and correlations), the delta is the same for each name. Figure 7.1 reveals that mezzanine tranches appear to have less directionality with respect to credit spread levels.

Deltas of individual credits will rise in time for the equity tranche if the spread on that name widens (assuming little change in average portfolio spread) as a result of an earlier expected default time for that name. For senior tranches, however, deltas will reduce as spreads widen on a single credit only, as this credit is expected to default earlier, impacting the equity tranche more than the senior exposures.

Of course, in practice, credit spreads on more than one name may widen, and one wants to consider how single name deltas change when all (or some) credits in the portfolio widen. A cumulative widening of all names in the portfolio leads to an increase in the chance of a high number of defaults and reduces the probability of a small number of defaults. Hence, the spread sensitivity of the value of an equity tranche reduces while the spread sensitivity of a senior tranche increases, leading to an increase in each individual senior tranche delta and a decrease in each individual equity tranche delta. The reverse holds when all spreads are tightening. A cumulative spread move also underlies the definition of Credit01, and is frequently used to estimate hedge ratios when liquid tranches are hedged with CDS indices, as further discussed in the section "Delta hedging with a CDS index: Credit01 sensitivity."

Delta as a Function of Time   Assuming there are no losses in the underlying portfolio, deltas will change due to the passage of time. The delta of the equity tranche will increase to 100 percent as time to maturity decreases. Mezzanine and senior tranches at the same time become less risky compared to the equity tranche, resulting in a decrease in their delta towards zero at maturity (see Figure 7.2 for a illustrative example).

Delta and Correlation   The MtM or fair spread on a CDO tranche within the usual Gaussian copula valuation framework depends on the current (observable) term structure of credit spreads on each of the underlying names, the maturity of the transaction, a recovery assumption for each name, and the correlation assumption (see Appendices B, C, and D for different numerical implementation techniques and Chapter 6 on pricing). Assuming that the first two sets of parameters are observable, (or can be at least implied from the single name CDS market) and a fixed maturity, the only variable left unspecified is the correlation applied in the pricing model. Then, given quoted tranche prices, one can compute the corresponding

FIGURE 7.2

Delta (in % of Notional) as a Function
of Time to Maturity.

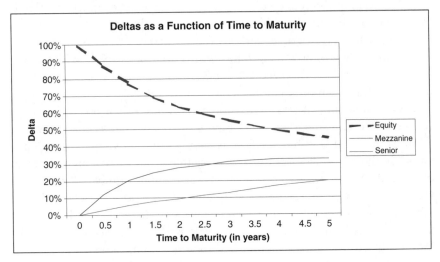

Deltas as a Function of Time to Maturity

"implied" or "compound" correlation that makes the model price consistent with market quotes.

If our valuation model could perfectly address replication dynamics, we could expect the same implied correlation for different tranches that reference the same portfolio. In practice, however, a correlation skew/smile is observed, where often implied correlations for equity and senior tranches are higher than for (junior) mezzanine tranches. Figure 7.3 shows the correlation smile for October 4, 2004 on standardized tranches on the ITraxx index.

Changes in the underlying compound (or implied) correlation also impacts tranche deltas. Typically, increased correlation leads to relatively more risk for senior tranches and relative less risk for the equity tranche, as large numbers of defaults are more likely for higher levels of correlation among credits. Therefore, as the implied correlation increases, the equity tranche deltas of credits decreases and the senior tranche deltas increase. Equity tranche deltas, however, are almost always above (very) senior tranche deltas independent of the actual level of correlation.

Delta and Upfront Payments Currently, the equity tranche for the investment grade DJ CDX index and the first two tranches of the high yield DJ CDX index trade with upfront payments. Upfront payments

FIGURE 7.3

Correlation Smile on 5 year 1Traxx Tranches
on October 7, 2004.

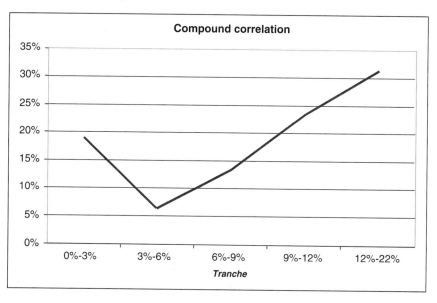

for tranches genuinely lowers their deltas compared to the same tranche that is valued with only a running spread (and no upfront payment). The reason is that if we have a significant amount of the tranche value paid up-front, any spread move thereafter only impacts a small amount of the pre-mium to be collected. On the contrary, upfront payments do not impact the protection leg of the CDO tranche, as higher spreads imply higher expected defaults. A tranche that has only running premium and no upfront pay-ments will be impacted much more by a spread widening as, in addition to more expected defaults, expected premium payments are also lower (as the notional is reduced), making it more sensitive to a spread move.

Delta Hedging with a CDS Index: Credit01 Sensitivity

In practice, an alternative to hedging each individual name by delta-amounts of single name CDS is to hedge by taking a position in a liquid index (such as the CDX or ITraxx indices). The advantage of hedging with an index is that liquidity is very high and bid–ask spreads (transaction costs) are tight. However, the quality of the hedge depends on how similar the portfolio referenced by the CDO tranche is to the computation of the index. Formally, we define the Credit01 as the change in MtM (dollar value) for a 1 bp parallel shift in credit spreads on all names in the portfolio. It can therefore be seen as a cumulative or aggregate (market) spread sensitivity measure:

$$\text{Credit01}^{T_j} := \Delta \text{MtM}^{T_j}(t_0, T, S(t_0), S^{01}(t_0))$$

$$= \left(S^{T_j}(t_0, T, S(t_0)) - S^{T_j}(t_0, T, S^{01}(t_0)) \right) \text{TrPV01}^{T_j}(t_0, T, S^{01}(t_0))$$

where $S^{01}(t_0) := (S_1(t) + 1\,\text{bp}, \ldots, S_{i-1}(t) + 1\,\text{bp}, S_i(t) + 1\,\text{bp}, S_{i+1}(t) + 1\,\text{bp}, \ldots, S_N(t) + 1\,\text{bp})$.

Credit01^{T_j} can therefore be used to estimate a hedge ratio when a standardized CDO tranche (e.g., ITraxx tranche) is hedged with the underlying CDS index (e.g., ITraxx), that is,

$$\Delta^{T_j} = \frac{\text{Credit01}^{T_j}(\vec{x})}{\cdot \Delta \text{MtM}_I(\vec{x})}$$

where $\cdot \Delta \text{MtM}_I \vec{x}$ corresponds to the change in MtM on the CDS index for a 1 bp spread widening on each of the underlying names (and hence on the overall index).*

Unlike individual spread sensitivity CS01, Credit01 increases for senior tranches as all spreads widen in parallel, whereas Credit01 of the equity tranche decreases if all spreads widen in a parallel move. This results from the fact that a widening in all spreads increases the risk of higher numbers of defaults shifting the risk from the equity to senior tranches.

Note, however, that an index hedge in practice provides only an approximate (or average) delta hedge when the underlying names in the portfolio are very dispersed, whereas it provides a perfect spread hedge if all names trade at the same spread. As a result, for an equity tranche in the index, a tighter name would be overhedged as the relative risk to the equity tranche of a low spread name is lower than that of a name with a (higher) average spread. Similarly, wider trading names would be underhedged as the deltas of the equity tranche are lower if the credits trade at a lower (average) level. The reverse behavior holds for hedging a senior tranche.

---

*In practice, an alternative way is to sum over all individual single name deltas and enter a CDS index position according to the resulting notional. The reason why there is hardly a difference in bumping all spreads at once or summing over all hedges when one spread is bumped at the time is that convexity is less of an issue for a small (typically 1 bp) spread move.

Tranche Leverage: Lambda

The leverage, or lambda, of a tranche is closely linked to tranche deltas and provides useful information as it effectively scales the delta by the tranche notional. Formally, we define leverage, or lambda, as

$$\text{Lambda}^{T_j} = \frac{N(\text{delta}-\text{hedge portfolio})}{N^{T_j}} = \frac{\sum_{n=1}^{N} \Delta_i^{T_j} N_i}{N^{T_j}} \approx \frac{\Delta^{T_j} \sum_{n=1}^{N} N_i}{N^{T_j}},$$

where $N^{T_j} = D_j - A_j$ denotes the tranche notional and N_i the notional of name i in the underlying portfolio.

Practically, leverage gives an indication of how the total risk is distributed between different tranches. Hence, the higher the leverage, the higher the spread risk in relation to the tranche notional. For example, consider a 7 to 10 percent tranche of a \$1 billion underlying portfolio with a notional of \$30 million. Assume an (average) hedge ratio of $\Delta^{T_j} = 15$ percent for this senior tranche resulting in a total notional of \$150 million for the hedge portfolio. The lambda, or leverage, for this tranche is therefore 5.

A super senior position (for example, 10 to 100 percent) usually results in a higher delta portfolio, but also a significantly lower leverage. Of course, given the leverage or lambda we can compute an average delta for an index tranche (as discussed in the previous section). Given the leverage and tranche size, the size of the underlying hedge portfolio can be computed and the index can be bought accordingly.

Credit Spread Convexity: Gamma

While first order spread sensitivity is a very important measure of risk, the sensitivity of credit product spread changes beyond 1 bp also needs to be considered. This is especially true when hedging instruments have different leverage, i.e. hedging a tranche with an index, or an equity tranche with a mezzanine or senior tranche. Spread convexity of credit products usually refers to the MtM behavior as a function of the underlying level of credit spreads. Spread convexity, or gamma, of various tranches can be very different, and particularly large compared to the convexity of single name CDS or CDS indices. A detailed understanding is therefore required, particularly when we want to implement various relative value or credit strategies.

As with first order sensitivity, we can differentiate between macro- and microspread convexity, and it is particularly important to understand the behavior of (delta-hedged) tranche products when individual spreads are moving (microconvexity), or when the overall market/portfolio spread is moving (macroconvexity).

Macroconvexity: Gamma

More formally, we define the macro spread convexity, gamma, as the additional MtM change on a tranche over that obtained by multiplying the Credit01 of that tranche by the parallel spread move for all of the underlying single name CDSs. Put another way, it is the difference between the linear approximation and the actual movement in market value. For example, assuming a 100 bp spread widening, gamma is given by:

$$\text{Gamma}_{100}^{T_j} := \Delta\,\text{MtM}^{T_j}(t_0, T, S(t_0), S^{100}(t_0))$$

$$- 100\,\text{Credit}\,01^{T_j}(t_0, T, S(t_0), S^{01}(t_0)) \tag{9}$$

where $S^{100}(t) := (S_1(t) + 100 \text{ bp}, \ldots, S_N(t) + 100 \text{ bp})$.

In practice, a relative spread shift factor is frequently introduced and gamma is calculated by bumping the underlying spreads uniformly by varying amounts (for example, in the range of 50 to 150 percent depending on the actual level of spreads). We therefore require efficient algorithms once again, as it requires a recalculation for various spread levels in a brute-force computation.*

Microconvexity: iGamma

Single name, or idiosyncratic convexity, iGamma, is defined as the convexity resulting from a single CDS spread moving independently of the others, i.e., one spread moves while the other names remain unchanged:

$$\text{iGamma}_{100}^{T_j} := \Delta\,\text{MtM}_i^{T_j}(t_0, T, S(t_0), S^{i100}(t_0)) - 100\Delta\,\text{MtM}_i^{T_j}(t_0, T, S(t_0), S^{i01}(t_0))$$

$$= \Delta\,\text{MtM}_i^{T_j}(t_0, T, S(t_0), S^{i100}(t_0)) - 100\Delta_i^{T_j}\,\text{RiskyPV}\,01(t_0, T, S^{i01}(t_0))$$

$$\tag{10}$$

where $S^{i100}(t) := (S_1(t), \ldots, S_{1i-1}(t), S_i(t) + 100 \text{ bp}, S_{i+1}(t), \ldots, S_N(t))$.

---

*While some of the efficient calculations of spread sensitivities outlined in the Appendix can be extended to higher order sensitivities, we are focusing on the most generic implementation through "brute-force" or "bumping" in the remainder of this chapter.

Convexity of Delta-Hedged Tranches

In practice, one is mostly concerned with the convexity of delta-neutral tranches, or portfolios of tranches, index, and single name positions when specific trading strategies are being developed. While a more elaborate discussion of specific strategies follows in the next chapter, we explore important convexity issues for simple delta-hedged equity and senior tranche positions next.

Similarly to the definitions in Equations (9) and (10), the convexity of a single name CDS can be defined as the difference between the RiskyPV100 and 100 times the RiskyPV01. For relatively simple credit exposures, multiplying the spread shift by the RiskyPV01 provides a good approximation of the true MtM impact, and while some level of convexity is present, the sign of the MtM impact is the same for various levels of spread widening. We will show that such consistency is not guaranteed for CDO tranches, highlighting the need to compute such higher order spread sensitivities. We will illustrate that the convexity of tranches can be very different to the convexity of single name CDS (and across tranches), which therefore expose delta-hedged or neutral portfolios to spread convexity. This not surprising, as the delta itself is a function of spread level and changes when spreads move. Again, in practice, the easiest way to observe convexity is to plot the P&L of a delta-hedged transaction. In particular, the change in tranche MtM, the change in hedge portfolio MtM, and the net P&L for a uniform and parallel shift in all (or a single) credit spreads provide some valuable insight into the likely MtM behavior of delta-neutral strategies.

Macroconvexity   In order to understand spread convexity and the resulting MtM of delta-hedged positions, we consider a delta-hedged equity tranche (long correlation) and a delta-hedged senior tranche (short correlation) when all spreads move together (macroconvexity/gamma) next.*

Delta-Neutral Long Equity Tranche   Selling protection on an equity tranche and buying delta-amounts of single name CDS results in an increase in expected tranche loss and a shift of the risk away from the

---

*A (delta-neutral) equity tranche is often denoted as a long correlation position as an increase in implied correlation leads to a decrease in tranche value. Similarly, a (delta-hedged) senior tranche is a short correlation as an increase in compound correlation implies an increase in tranche value.

TABLE 7.2

Delta-Neutral Portfolio MtM (Long Equity Tranche)
for a Change in ALL Spreads

	All Spreads Widen	All Spreads Tighten
Equity Tranche (protection sold)	–MtM	+MtM
Delta notional of CDS (protection bought)	+MtM	–MtM
Effective Hedge	Overhedged	Underhedged
Net MtM (net P&L)	+MtM	+MtM

equity tranche to mezzanine and senior tranches when all credit spreads widen. Essentially, this means that we are overhedged, as discussed in the previous section on first order sensitivity. Therefore, the MtM change on the delta portfolio is greater than the MtM on the equity tranche. Since the MtM on the hedge portfolio is positive, the net MtM, or P&L, is positive. Table 7.2 summarizes the behavior for both spread widening and tightening scenario, and Figure 7.4 shows a typical plot for such a long correlation trade.

FIGURE 7.4

Gamma for a Long Correlation Equity Tranche.

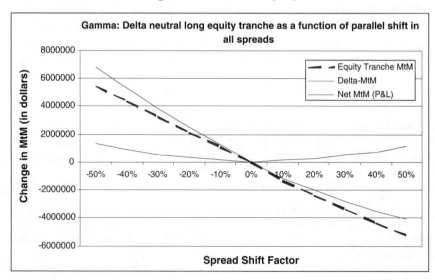

From an investor's perspective, in order to maintain a delta-neutral position, single name CDS contracts need to be sold at higher spreads, thus locking in a profit. However, if spreads are significantly tighter, the equity tranche becomes relatively more risky, implying higher deltas, i.e., the portfolio is underhedged. Put another way, the change in equity tranche position MtM is higher than the change in the current hedge portfolio, which implies again a positive net position.

Delta-Neutral Long Senior Tranche   For an investor who is short correlation by selling protection on a senior tranche and buying underlying CDS, the net MtM behaves the opposite. If all portfolio spreads are widening, the risk shifts towards the senior tranche, which implies that senior tranche deltas need to increase: the tranche is underhedged. With the MtM of the tranche decreasing (the tranche is worth more, but we sold protection) and the delta MtM increasing, further CDS contracts need to be bought at a higher spread. This means a net loss to the portfolio. The reverse holds for the tightening scenario and is further illustrated in Table 7.3 and Figure 7.5.

Microconvexity   Perhaps counter-intuitive, the iGamma or micro-convexity of a tranche is generally the opposite to macroconvexity. For example, a spread widening on a single CDS implies, for the long equity tranche, a positive MtM on the hedge portfolio and a negative MtM on the equity tranche. The equity delta for that name increases as, relative to the other credits, this name becomes more risky. Hence, the MtM of the hedge portfolio increases as all other spreads remain unchanged, leading to an

TABLE 7.3

Delta-Neutral Portfolio MtM (Long Senior Tranche) for a Change in ALL Spreads

	All Spreads Widen	All Spreads Tighten
Senior Tranche (protection sold)	−MtM	+MtM
Delta notional of CDS (protection bought)	+MtM	−MtM
Effective Hedge	Underhedged	Overhedged
Net MtM (net P&L)	−MtM	−MtM

FIGURE 7.5

Gamma for a Long Senior Tranche.

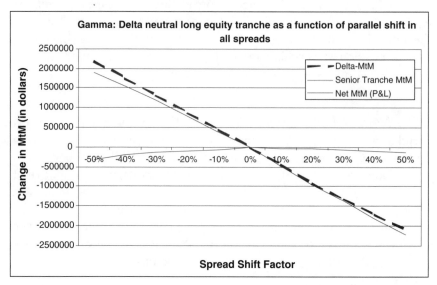

MtM change on the hedge portfolio due to changes only in credit i's spread (despite changes in all other deltas). In such a situation, we need to buy more CDS on name i at a higher spread (as we are underhedged), implying a negative net MtM or P&L.

For a delta-neutral senior tranche, a spread widening of only a single credit implies that we are essentially overhedged, as this credit becomes relatively more risky for the equity tranche and relative less risky for the senior tranche. As a result, this CDS needs to be sold at a higher spread, implying a positive net MtM. Table 7.4 illustrates the P&L impact further for a long correlation hedged equity tranche and a short correlation hedged senior tranche.

Figure 7.6 illustrates graphically iGamma for both hypothetical trades, also highlighting the significant assymmetry (difference in absolute MtM) for different delta-neutral CDO tranches. The difference in MtM behavior of different tranches also provides opportunities for hedging some tranches by shorting others. In order to do so, of course, the tranche spread, correlation, and default sensitivity need to be well understood.

Realized Correlation

The previous examples and definitions of macro- and microconvexity are of course not unique. One could also consider situations where a fraction

TABLE 7.4

Delta-Neutral Portfolio MtM for a Change in ONE Spread

	One Spread Widens	One Spread Tightens
Equity Tranche (protection sold)	–MtM	+MtM
Delta notional of CDS (protection bought)	+MtM	–MtM
Effective Hedge	Underhedged	Overhedged
Net MtM (net P&L)	–MtM	–MtM
Senior Tranche (protection sold)	–MtM	+MtM
Delta notional of CDS (protection bought)	+MtM	–MtM
Effective Hedge	Overhedged	Underhedged
Net MtM (net P&L)	+MtM	+MtM

of the portfolio (e.g., n obligors) spreads are moving, while the rest of the portfolio spreads remain unchanged. Another way of describing these spread movements is in terms of correlation. Clearly, the situation where one spread blows out significantly while the others remain unchanged can be seen as a low correlation environment, whereas all spreads widening

FIGURE 7.6

Delta-Neutral Long Equity or Senior Tranche.

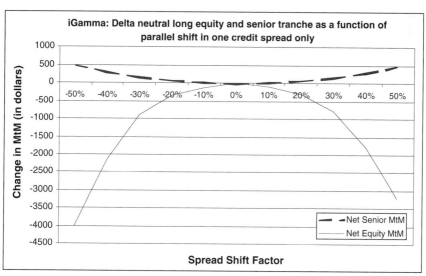

together corresponds to very high correlation. Frequently, realized correlation is defined as the observed spread correlation between the credits in the portfolio relative to the assumed (or implied/compound) correlation. Realized correlation can be positive or negative: positive if observed correlation is above the compound correlation and negative if observed correlation is lower.

Generally, a delta-hedged tranche that is a long correlation generates a profit for a positive realized correlation and a loss for a negative realized correlation (see, e.g., Kakodkar et al., 2003). For example, investors holding delta-hedged equity (that are long correlation) hold long gamma (positive MtM and positive realized correlation) and short iGamma positions (negative MtM and negative realized correlation). Similarly a delta-neutral tranche that is a short correlation will generate a loss for a positive realized correlation and a profit for a negative realized correlation. For example, a delta-hedged senior investor (who is short correlation) holds short Gamma (negative MtM and positive realized correlation) and long iGamma positions (positive MtM and negative realized correlation).

Time Decay: Theta

The value and spread on a CDS converges to zero with its maturity approaching, but the rate of decline is determined by the slope of the credit curve or spread term structure. For example, consider an upward sloping (index) credit curve, where a significant amount of defaults is expected towards, say, the last year of the transaction. If no defaults occur during the first year of the transaction, the protection buyer faces a substantial MtM loss as a significant amount of losses "disappear," leading to a significantly lower valuation after a year. With junior tranches being levered investments on default, their value (to the protection buyer) declines faster than the index value declines as time passes. Looking at the absolute tranche value, tranches with index deltas higher than one lose value faster than the index, whereas senior tranches with deltas lower than one lose value much slower than the index or portfolio.

Formally, time decay is frequently defined as the change in MtM or total return that a tranche position generates when time passes, all other parameters remaining unchanged (i.e., credit spread term structure, compound or base correlation, no defaults, etc.). Theta is usually computed by simply valuing a tranche with different time horizons (maturities) and taking the difference. For example, from a protection seller's viewpoint,

FIGURE 7.7

Total Return of CDO Tranches for Different
Time Horizons.

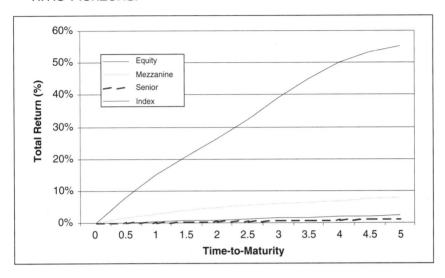

$$\text{Theta}^{T_j}(v) = S^{T_j}(t_0, T, S(t_0)) \text{TrPV } 01^{T_j}(t_0, T, S(t_0))$$
$$- S^{T_j}(t_0, T - v, S(t_0)) \text{TrPV } 01^{T_j}(t_0, T - v, S(t_0)),$$

where v denotes the time that has passed since inception of the transaction.*

For a typical equity, mezzanine, and senior tranche backed by an investment grade (IG) portfolio or index, the total return is shown for various tranches from the protection seller's viewpoint in Figure 7.7. Theta would therefore be the difference between the values at two points along these curves.

It is also interesting to consider the speed of time decay, i.e., how much of the total value is realized every year. It is not unusual for IG tranches to observe that only the equity tranche value decays slower than the index, whereas the other tranches decay faster. Looking at the expected premium received and the expected tranche loss through the life of the transaction gives further insight into the theta of different tranches. While at inception of a trade, expected premium PVs and expected tranche loss PVs are equal, as time evolves, the premium received will not exactly offset tranche losses in each period.

---

*An alternative view of time decay can be obtained by rolling down the transaction on the interest rate and credit spread forward curves.

FIGURE 7.8

Expected Premium and Loss for Mezzanine Tranche.

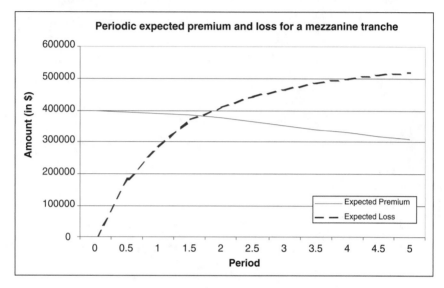

Figure 7.8 plots the expected tranche loss and expected premium for a typical IG mezzanine tranche.

We can observe that protection buyers pay more than required over the first few month of the transaction and the relationship reverses at a later point in time. From a protection seller's viewpoint this implies a negative theta (negative MtM).

For a senior tranche, expected premiums are flat in each period, which reflects the small incremental loss over each period. Similar to the mezzanine tranche, losses are initially significantly below periodic spread or premium expectations.

Only equity tranches may have periodic losses exceeding the expected premium received initially. Figure 7.9 illustrates this for a typical tranche when all premium payments occur periodically, with no upfront payments. Here, theta is initially positive from a protection seller's viewpoint, but negative thereafter.

Correlation Sensitivity: Rho

As previously discussed, different CDO tranches have different sensitivity to changes in correlation. Junior tranches are typically long correlation as

FIGURE 7.9

Expected Premium and Loss for Equity Tranche.

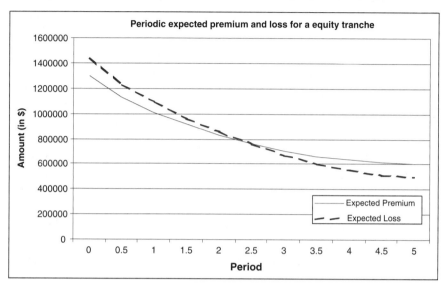

the value of protection decreases (from a protection buyer's perspective), when correlation increases, causing the trance value to decrease correspondingly. Senior tranches, on the other hand, are short correlation (value increases in correlation) for investors who bought protection. Mezzanine tranches are typically relatively insensitive to changes in correlation. In today's credit markets, compound or base correlations are quoted daily on liquid index tranches and severe changes have been observed in the past. Given the sensitivity of tranche positions to changes in implied correlation, an understanding of the correlation sensitivity is essential in managing the risk in ST CDOs. Over time, however, the sensitivity of various tranches can change, particularly if credit spreads in the underlying CDOs move significantly or if losses occur and diminish subordination.

Formally, we define Rho as the MtM change of a tranche for a small (typically 1 percent) change in the compound correlation that is used to price the tranche, that is:

$$\text{Rho}^{T_j} = \text{MtM}^{T_j}(t_0, T, S(t_0), \rho) - \text{MtM}^{T_j}(t_0, T, S(t_0), \rho + 1\%)$$

$$= \left(S^{T_j}(t_0, T, S(t_0), \rho) - S^{T_j}(t_0, T, S(t_0), \rho + 1\%) \right)$$

$$\times \text{TrPV}\,01^{T_j}(t_0, T, S(t_0), \rho + 1\%)$$

In practice, Rho is once again computed by bumping the correlation parameters and tranche revaluation.

In general, long equity or short senior tranches have positive Rho (long correlation positions), while long senior or short equity postitions have negative Rho (short correlation positions). For example, Figure 7.10 plots Rho as a percentage of the tranche size for a typical (and risky) CDO portfolio with a fixed tranche size of 1 percent and varying attachment points (or levels of subordination).

The figure reveals that Rho tends to zero for very high levels of subordination (senior positions) but there is also a correlation neutral point between the senior and equity tranches. It is therefore possible to construct a correlation neutral mezzanine tranche around this point. For example, in a tight spread environment, junior mezzanine tranches tend to be correlation neutral. Indeed, we can try to construct tranches (e.g., two mezzanine tranches, one at each side of the correlation neutral point) such that the portfolio of tranches is correlation neutral, particularly as the change in expected tranche loss due to a correlation move from ρ to $\bar{\rho}$ can be derived as an integral over changes in the attachment probabilities:

$$\Delta EL^{T_j}(T) = \int_{A_j}^{D_j} Q_{L(T),\rho}(l)\,\mathrm{d}l - \int_{A_j}^{D_j} Q_{L(T),\bar{\rho}}(l)\,\mathrm{d}l = \int_{A_j}^{D_j} \Delta Q_{L(T),\rho,\bar{\rho}}(l)\,\mathrm{d}l.$$

FIGURE 7.10

Correlation Sensitivity as a Function of Subordination.

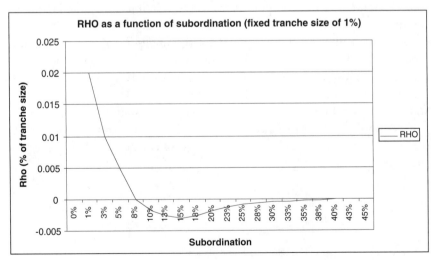

In practice, of course, correlation may change by more than 1 percent, which means that a "correlation hedged" tranche is still exposed to possible losses from more severe correlation movements. Furthermore, correlation may depend on spreads, which would also imply an imperfect correlation hedge (see Chapter 8 for further details).

Base Correlation

The computations so far have considered only compound correlation, and similar steps are required when base correlation is employed instead (refer to the chapter on CDO pricing for further details). There, one assumes frequently that the base correlation skew moves in parallel, i.e., for all tranches the attachment and detachment point correlations change by the same amount. In practice, of course, this base correlation skew may change. For example, the skew tends to rise as spreads fall to very low levels, and flatten as spreads widen. Similarly, the skew tends to steepen when correlation increases and it tends to flatten with decreasing correlation.

Delta-Hedging and Rho

It is worth mentioning that a single name CDS, or a portfolio of CDS (and hence a CDS index), is insensitive to correlation changes. As a result, a delta-neutral tranche has the same correlation sensitivity as the tranche itself. This allows us to combine tranches with CDS and index positions without altering the correlation behavior of the credit strategy.

Default Sensitivity: Omega

Another very important risk factor in correlation products is the default sensitivity, Omega, which we will define as the change in MtM of a tranche position (hedged or unhedged) as a result of an instant default of one underlying, keeping spreads on the surviving names unchanged. Although default events occur relatively rarely, the impact of "the unexpected" should be measured. Furthermore, a default can be viewed as the most severe form of iGamma where spreads widen unboundedly. We define iOmega formally as:

$$iOmega^{T_j} := \Delta MtM^{T_j}(t_0, T, S(t_0), S^{i\infty}(t_0)).$$

Omega is often also denoted as VOD (value on default) or JTD (jump to default), and we will use these terms interchangeably. The impact of an instantaneous default is genuinely high for unhedged tranches, whereas the level of risk for hedged strategies depends on the tranche seniority and thickness. The impact of a sudden default on the performance of credit strategies is important, particularly when comparing different strategies with similar expected returns (or carries) at the outset. This section only provides some conceptual discussion, and a more detailed insight into the performance/relative value of popular trading strategies is given in Chapter 8.

Multiple Defaults (Omega)

In practice, it is not only interesting to consider the MtM change as a result of a single default, but also as resulting from multiple defaults. We define the default sensitivity, when the n-widest trading names are defaulting, as $\text{Omega}_n^{T_j}$.* The n names with the highest credit spreads are chosen as these are the most likely defaulters, but many different combinations of n defaulters could be chosen. In reality, of course, a probabilistic view can be imposed and a distribution of Omega, and tranche P&L more generally, can be derived for different trading strategies (see Chapter 8).

iOmega and Omega for Hedged and Unhedged Tranche Positions

Figures 7.11 and 7.12 show iOmega (VOD) and Omega (RVOD), respectively, for a delta hedged equity and senior tranche. It is apparent that the default sensitivity is significantly reduced for the delta-neutral strategy up to a point where the sign of the sensitivity even reverses.

We can observe the maximum loss for six defaults in the case of equity tranche and five defaults for the delta-neutral equity strategy. Furthermore, Omega reduces for more than five defaults again and becomes neutral around the breakeven scenario of eight defaults. Beyond that, Omega is positive. It is also worth pointing out that due to upfront payments (typical for equity tranches), losses amount to less than the total tranche notional (<100 percent).

The (delta neutral) senior position reveals quite a different behavior. The Omega of the delta-hedged position is significantly higher for the hedge position for the first few defaults, compared to the senior tranche. The hedged senior positions Omega is positive for the first 11 defaults, and becomes negative thereafter.

---

*In Chapter 8, this measure will be denoted as Running VOD (RVOD).

FIGURE 7.11

Default Sensitivity for Delta Hedged Equity Tranche.

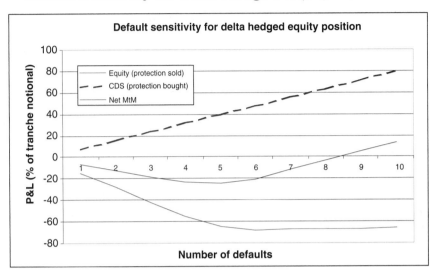

FIGURE 7.12

Default Sensitivity for Delta Hedged Senior Tranche.

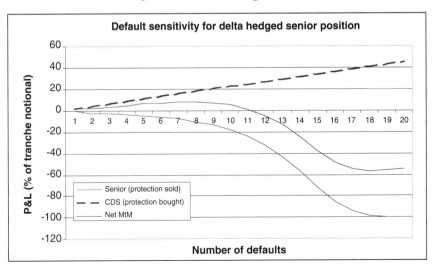

By focusing once again on just a single default, i.e., iOmega, we can say that a long correlation delta hedged tranche has a negative MtM as a result of default, is short iGamma, and also short iOmega. A short correlation delta-hedged tranche (e.g., delta-neutral senior tranche) has positive MtM after a single default, positive MtM is long iGamma and long iOmega.

(i)Omega and Spread Widening

In practice, it is also interesting to consider situations where spreads on the surviving names widen as a result of one or more defaults. For a delta hedged equity tranche that is long correlation, a widening of spreads on the surviving names implies that the realized correlation increases. This has a positive MtM impact and would therefore reduce the level of default sensitivity (iOmega). Similarly, a short correlation position suffers an MtM loss if all spreads widen and hence, the positive iOmega reduces.

Omega behaves in a similar way, e.g., a delta hedged equity tranche's default sensitivity reduces if all surviving spreads in the portfolio would widen.

Of course, this last example highlights the possibility of interaction between various (pricing) variables or risk factors and, as a result, highlights the need for more advanced sensitivities. For example, time decay in the "Time decay-Theta" section is simply computed as the difference in MtM when we reduce maturity while keeping all the other parameters unchanged. Essentially, we ignore the impact of the new, shorter maturity on other inputs, most notably correlation. If the correlation skew is different for different maturities, the MtM calculation for a one-year time decay of a five-year tranche should use the four-year base correlation. Similarly, if we calculate spread sensitivity (convexity) and bump spreads up significantly, we should use the correlation assumption applied for a more junior tranche. Essentially, these are all higher order effects that can be quite significant and would need to be addressed in more advanced sensitivity calculations. We address such issues in Chapter 8 by motivating a more flexible (and computationally demanding) MC framework for CDO risk management.

SUMMARY AND CONCLUSIONS

This chapter forms the first part of our discussion on CDO risk management. After a very brief introduction of risk measures important to buy-and-hold investors and rating agencies, we focus on popular MtM sensitivity measures. We start with first order spread sensitivity and delta hedging, by capturing the conceptual paradigm as well as practical implementation. Delta hedging gained widespread acceptance in credit markets, partially because many (fixed-income) risk management systems were initially designed for single name exposures such as corporate bonds or single name CDSs. For such products, delta hedging has proven adequate and at first sight it seems plausible to introduce synthetic CDOs into such a risk management framework through their delta-exposures. However, the nonlinearity inherent in tranched products necessitates a closer look into the likely MtM sensitivity to additional risk factors. We introduce micro- and macrospread convexity, and show that the sign of the MtM impact changes when the overall market is moving instead of one individual spread. Similarly, the concepts of correlation and instantaneous default sensitivity are introduced, highlighting—once again—that synthetic tranche positions, even when delta-hedged, exhibit significant MtM risk.

Furthermore, spread, correlation, and default risk between various tranches on the same reference portfolio can vary substantially, providing opportunities to create hedging strategies that immunize against some (or all) of the risks prevailing. For example, equity tranches exhibit substantial default risk as well as spread risk, whereas the default risk of senior tranches is much smaller when some spread risk still prevails. A delta-neural combination of equity and senior tranches (has positive carry and) compensates investors for taking default risk without having spread exposure (at least to first order). The resulting hedge is cheaper than buying protection on all single names; however, residual higher order spread and correlation risk exist (in addition to the default risk). For example, the straddle outlined above has significant correlation risk, as changes in correlation have an impact on both the long equity and the short senior exposure.

In the next chapter, the practical aspects of many of these concepts are put into practice by analyzing several popular CDO strategies. By investigating the performance of real trades, we shed some further light onto the inadequacy of pure delta-hedging for synthetic tranche products. In addition, we are take a detailed look at risk/return characteristics of such trades.

A P P E N D I X   A

Building a Hazard Rate Term Structure

The standard assumption in credit markets is to assume that the hazard rate is a piecewise flat function of maturity, which is sensible given the limited number of observable points on the term structure of credit spreads.

Given 1-, 3-, 5-, 7-, and 10-year default swap spread values, we would build a hazard rate term structure with five sections λ_{01}, λ_{13}, λ_{35}, λ_{57}, and λ_{710} where λ_{kl} is a short form of $\lambda_{kl}(S(t))$ in which t denotes the time when the credit spread curve is available. Bootstrapping the term structure of hazard rates is an iterative process, where we start by taking the shortest maturity contract and use it to calculate the first survival probability. In this case, the one-year default swap has to be used to calculate the value λ_{01}. Assuming quarterly premium payment frequency, using a value of $M = 12$ (monthly frequency), and assuming that premium accrued is not paid, λ_{01} is found by solving:

$$\frac{S(t_v, t_v + 1y)}{(1 - R)} \sum_{m=3,6,9,12} D(t_{m-3}, t_m) B(t_v, t_m) e^{-\lambda_{01}\tau_m}$$

$$= \sum_{m=1}^{12} B(t_v, t_m)(e^{-\lambda_{01}\tau_{m-1}} - e^{-\lambda_{01}\tau_m}),$$

where a monthly discretization means $\tau_0 = 0$, $\tau_1 = 0.0833$, ..., $\tau_{12} = 1$ and R denotes the assumed recovery rate.

This procedure is the repeated to solve for λ_{13} and the other sections of the hazard curve until final maturity. Beyond that, a flat hazard rate is frequently assumed. Defining $\tau = T - t_v$, we obtain the (risk neutral) survival probabilities implied from the term structure of credit spreads:

$$Q(t_v, T) = \begin{cases} \exp(-\lambda_{01}\tau) & 0 < \tau \le 1 \\ \exp(-\lambda_{01} - \lambda_{13}(\tau - 1)) & 1 < \tau \le 3 \\ \exp(-\lambda_{01} - 2\lambda_{13} - \lambda_{35}(\tau - 3)) & 3 < \tau \le 5 \\ \exp(-\lambda_{01} - 2\lambda_{13} - 2\lambda_{35} - \lambda_{57}(\tau - 5)) & 5 < \tau \le 7 \\ \exp(-\lambda_{01} - 2\lambda_{13} - 2\lambda_{35} - 2\lambda_{57} - \lambda_{710}(\tau - 7)) & \tau > 7 \end{cases}$$

APPENDIX B

Efficient Computation of Tranche Sensitivities within the Gaussian Copula Recursive Scheme

The Gaussian copula model, as introduced in the chapters on correlation and pricing, is most commonly implemented through a one-factor model, and interpreted as the asset value of firm i, A_i, driven by a normally distributed latent common factor V, and an normally distributed independent idiosyncratic factor ε_i: $A_i = \rho_i V + \sqrt{1 - \rho_i^2}\, \varepsilon_i$.

In Andersen et al. (2003), quasi-analytical techniques are developed for the computation of the conditional loss distribution over a time interval $[0, t]$ by simple recursion since defaults, when conditioned on the outcome of the factors, are independent. In order to do so, an arbitrary loss unit, u, is required such that loss amounts l_i can be well approximated by integer multiples of u, say $l_i = k_i u$. Now let L_n, $1 \leq n < N$, be the loss measured in loss units in the subportfolio consisting of the first n obligors (ordered arbitrarily). We then have the following recursive relationship between the conditional distributions of L_n and L_{n+1}:

$$p_{n+1}^V(L_{n+1} = K,\, t) = p_{n+1}^V(t) p_n^V(L_n = K - k_{n+1}, t) + (1 - p_{n+1}^V(t)) p_n^V(L_n = K, t) \quad (11)$$

where $p_n^V(L_n = K, t) = \mathrm{Prob}(L_n(t) = K | V)$ denotes the probability of L_n units of loss at time t conditional on factor V, and $p_n^V(t)$ denotes the PD for name n by time t conditional on the common factor outcome. This relationship can then be used to compute the portfolio loss distribution starting from an empty portfolio.

Andersen et al. (2003) show that sensitivities of expectations over the loss distribution can be efficiently computed using the recursive relationship (10). Let $F(L(t))$ be some function of the portfolio loss. If we consider the sensitivity of its expectation to PD p_i, that is, $\partial E(F(L))/\partial P_i(t)$, it can be shown that

$$\frac{\partial E(F(L))}{\partial p_i(t)} = \int \frac{\partial E(F(L) \mid V)}{\partial p_i(t)} d\Phi(V)$$

$$= \int \frac{dp_i^V(t)}{dp_i(t)} \frac{\partial E(F(L) \mid V)}{\partial p_i^V(t)} d\Phi(V)$$

$$= \int \frac{dp_i^V(t)}{dc_i(t)} \left(\frac{dp_i(t)}{dc_i(t)} \right)^{-1} \frac{\partial E(F(L) \mid V)}{\partial p_i^V(t)} d\Phi(V) \qquad (12)$$

where Φ denotes the cumulative Gaussian distribution function and $c_i(t) := \Phi^{-1}(p_i)$ denotes the default threshold of asset i.

The first two factors of the integrand can be easily computed analytically, and the last factor can be derived from the recursive relationship:

$$\frac{\partial E(F(L) \mid V)}{\partial p_i^V(t)} = \sum_K F(K) \frac{\partial p_N^V(L_N = K, t)}{\partial p_i^V(t)}$$

$$= \sum_K F(K) \left[p_{N-1}^V(L_{N-1}^i = K - k_i, t) - p_{N-1}^V(L_{N-1}^i = K_i, t) \right].$$

Here, L_{N-1}^i is the loss of the portfolio with the ith obligor removed and can be obtained from the recursive relationship very efficiently.

Within the context of the computation of spread sensitivities for CDO tranches, we are interested in the computation of $(\partial \mathrm{MtM}^{T_j}(t_0, T, S(t_0)) / \partial S_i(t_0))(1 \text{ bp})$.

Hence, $E(F(L(t))) = \mathrm{MtM}^{T_j}(t_0, t, S(t_0)) = \mathrm{FPV}^{T_j}(t_0, t, S(t_0)) - \mathrm{PPV}^{T_j}(t_0, t, S(t_0))$, where the fee PV and protection PV are functions of the expected tranche loss $EL^{T_j}(t) = E(\max[\min(L(t) - A_j, D_j - A_j), 0])$, and are given by Equations (7) and (8). As a result, the sensitivity of the MtM with respect to changes in the underlying PD, $(\partial \mathrm{MtM}^{T_j}(t_0, T, S(t_0)) / \partial p_i(T))(1 \text{ bp})$ of name i requires the calculation of sensitivities of form Equation (12), that is:

$$\frac{\partial \mathrm{MtM}^{T_j}(t_0, T, S(t_0))}{\partial p_i(T)} = \frac{\partial \mathrm{FPV}^{T_j}(t_0, T, S(t_0))}{\partial p_i(T)} - \frac{\partial \mathrm{PPV}^{T_j}(t_0, T, S(t_0))}{\partial p_i(T)}, \quad \text{with}$$

$$\frac{\partial \mathrm{FPV}^{T_j}(t_0, T, S(t_0))}{\partial p_i(T)} = S^{T_j}(t_0, T, S(t_0)) \sum_{k=1}^K B(0, t_k) D(t_{k-1}, t_k)$$

$$\times \left(D_j - A_j - \frac{\partial EL^{T_j}(t_k)}{\partial p_i(T)} \right), \quad \text{and}$$

$$\frac{\partial \text{PPV}^{T_j}(t_0,T,S(t_0))}{\partial p_i(T)} = \sum_{k=1}^{K} B(0,t_k)\left(\frac{\partial \text{EL}^{T_j}(t_k)}{\partial p_i(T)} - \frac{\partial \text{EL}^{T_j}(t_{k-1})}{\partial p_i(T)}\right).$$

Clearly, the RHS of both equations contains expressions of type Equation (12).

Hazard rate, or credit spread sensitivities, are related to these PD sensitivities by simple Jacobian factors. For example, assuming a constant hazard rate λ_i, $p_i = g(\lambda_i) = 1 - \exp\{\lambda_i t\}$, therefore

$$\frac{\partial \text{MtM}^{T_j}(t_0,T,S(t_0))}{\partial \lambda_i}(1\text{ bp}) = \frac{\partial \text{MtM}^{T_j}(t_0,T,S(t_0))}{\partial p_i(T)} \cdot \frac{d\,p_i(T)}{d\,\lambda_i}.$$

$$= \frac{\partial \text{MtM}^{T_j}(t_0,T,S(t_0))}{\partial p_i(T)} T \cdot \exp\{\lambda_i T\}.$$

Credit spread sensitivities can be computed similarly. Assuming that $p_i \approx 1 - \exp\left\{-\dfrac{S_i(t_0)t}{1-R_i}\right\}$, we obtain

$$\frac{\partial \text{MtM}^{T_j}(t_0,T,S(t_0))}{\partial S_i(t_0)}(1\text{ bp}) = \frac{\partial \text{MtM}^{T_j}(t_0,T,S(t_0))}{\partial p_i(T)} \cdot \frac{d\,p_i(T)}{d\,S_i}.$$

$$= \frac{\partial \text{MtM}^{T_j}(t_0,T,S(t_0))}{\partial p_i(T)} \frac{T}{1-R_i} \cdot \exp\left\{-\frac{S_i(t_0)T}{1-R_i}\right\}.$$

APPENDIX C

A Fast Analytical Model for CDO Sensitivities (LH+)

While the approach in Appendix B outlines a computationally efficient and exact way of computing spread sensitivities based on the commonly used recursive scheme, this section outlines an alternative based on an extension of the asymptotic LHP approach first introduced by Vasicek (1987). The advantage of this approach, developed by Greenberg et al. (2004), is ease of implementation and computational speed as, essentially, a closed-form solution for spread hedges can be derived; however, it only provides an approximate solution. The authors show, however, that the size of the error is small for realistic portfolios and recommend this approach for those looking for a fast, simple, and suitably accurate tool.

The main idea is to single out the credit for which we want to compute a particular sensitivity, and to treat the remaining names in the portfolio asymptotically, i.e., we consider an LHP plus one additional asset, which allows us to address both idiosyncratic and market wide risks in a tractable way.

Model Setup

The asset values or latent variables of the homogeneous part of the portfolio are assumed to follow $A_i = \rho V + \sqrt{1-\rho^2}\,\varepsilon_i$, where common factor and idiosyncratic terms are defined as before. Because all factor loadings are identical we can write the conditional default probability of an asset in the homogeneous portfolio as: $p^V(t) = \Phi((C - \rho V)/\sqrt{1-\rho^2})$, where $C := \Phi^{-1}(p(t))$ and $p(t)$ corresponds to the average default probability of an obligor in the homogeneous pool. Assuming a total notional N and a (average) recovery rate of R, we can write the expected conditional loss on the homogeneous part of the portfolio as

$$EL^{V,\ \mathrm{LHP}}(t) = (1-R)Np^V(t).$$

In addition we assume there is a single asset (with notional N_0 that evolves as $A_0 = \rho_0 V + \sqrt{1-\rho_0^2}\,\varepsilon_0$ and defaults when the latent variable falls below $C_0 := \Phi^{-1}(p_0(t))$. Then, the default probability of this single asset, conditional on the market factor V is given by

$$p_0^V(t) = \Phi\left(\frac{C_0 - \rho_0 V}{\sqrt{1-\rho_0^2}}\right).$$

The total portfolio loss is then given by

$$EL = \begin{cases} (1-R_0)N_0 + EL^{V.\mathrm{LHP}} & \text{with probability} \quad p_0^V(t) \\ EL^{V.\mathrm{LHP}} & \text{with probability} \quad 1 - p_0^V(t) \end{cases}.$$

PORTFOLIO LOSS DISTIRBUTION

Greenberg et al. (2004) show that the conditional loss distribution, $p^V(L(t) \geq K) = \text{Prob}(L(t) \geq K | V)$,

is given by $p^V(L(t) \geq K) = \mathbf{1}_{\{V \leq X\}} + p_0{}^V(t)\mathbf{1}_{\{X < V \leq Y\}}$, where

$$X(K) = \frac{1}{\rho}\left[C - \sqrt{1-\rho^2}\,\Phi^{-1}\left(\frac{K}{(1-R)N} \right) \right]$$

and

$$Y(K) = \frac{1}{\rho}\left[C - \sqrt{1-\rho^2}\,\Phi^{-1}\left(\frac{K - (1-R_0)N_0}{(1-R)N} \right) \right].$$

Integrating over the common factor V enables us to derive the unconditional loss distribution in terms of the bivariate normal distribution $p(L(t) \geq K) = \Phi(X) + \Phi_2(C_0, Y; \rho_0) - \Phi_2(C_0, X; \rho_0)$, which can be very easily and accurately evaluated numerically and is essentially a closed-form approach.

TRANCHE LOSSES

Rewriting the tranche loss $L^{T_j}(t) = \max[\min(L(t) = A_j, D_j - A_j), 0] = [L(t) - A]^+ - [L(t) - D]^+$, is, beneficial as it can be shown that the expectation $E[L(t) - K]^+$ can also be computed very efficiently within the current model setup:

$$E([L(t) - K]^+) = K\Big(\Phi_2(C_0, X; \rho_0) - \Phi(X)\Big) + \Big((1 - R_0)N_0 - K\Big)\Phi_2(C_0, Y; \rho_0)$$
$$+ \Big((1 - R)N\Big)\Big[\Phi_2(C, X; \rho) + \Phi_3(C_0, C, Y; \Sigma) - \Phi_3(C_0, C, X; \Sigma)\Big]$$

where $\Sigma = \begin{pmatrix} 1 & \rho\rho_0 & \rho_0 \\ \rho\rho_0 & 1 & \rho \\ \rho_0 & \rho & 1 \end{pmatrix}$ denotes the covariance matrix used in the

evaluation of the trivariate normal distribution that can also be evaluated very efficiently, see, e.g., Genz (2002).

CREDIT SPREAD SENSITIVITY

Calculation of credit spread sensitivities

$$\frac{\partial \text{MtM}^{T_j}(t_0, T, S(t_0))}{\partial S_i(t_0)} = \frac{\partial \text{FPV}^{T_j}(t_0, T, S(t_0))}{\partial S_i(t_0)} - \frac{\partial \text{PPV}^{T_j}(t_0, T, S(t_0))}{\partial S_i(t_0)}$$

requires the efficient computation of $\dfrac{\partial EL^{T_j}(t_k)}{\partial S_i(t_0)}$, as

$$\frac{\partial \mathrm{FPV}^{T_j}(t_0, T, S(t_0))}{\partial S_i(t_0)} = S^{T_j}(t_0, T, S(t_0)) \sum_{k=1}^{K} B(0, t_k) D(t_{k-1}, t_k)$$

$$\times \left(D_j - A_j - \frac{\partial EL^{T_j}(t_k)}{\partial S_i(t_0)} \right) \quad \text{and}$$

$$\frac{\partial \mathrm{PPV}^{T_j}(t_0, T, S(t_0))}{\partial S_i(t_0)} = \sum_{k=1}^{K} B(0, t_k) \left(\frac{\partial EL^{T_j}(t_k)}{\partial S_i(t_0)} - \frac{\partial EL^{T_j}(t_{k-1})}{\partial S_i(t_0)} \right).$$

Greenberg et al. (2004) show that $\dfrac{\partial EL^{T_j}(t)}{\partial S_i(t_0)}$ can be computed very efficiently as

$$\frac{\partial EL^{T_j}(t)}{\partial S_i(t_0)} = T \frac{1 - p_0}{1 - R_0} \left\{ A_j \Phi \left(\frac{X(A_j) - \rho_0 C_0}{\sqrt{1 - \rho_0^2}} \right) \right.$$

$$+ [(1 - R_0)N_0 - A_j]\Phi\left(\frac{Y(A_j) - \rho_0 C_0}{\sqrt{1 - \rho_0^2}} \right)$$

$$+ (1 - R)N \left[\Phi_2 \left(\frac{C - \rho\rho_0 C_0}{\sqrt{1 - (\rho\rho_0)^2}}, \frac{Y(A_j) - \rho_0 C_0}{\sqrt{1 - \rho_0^2}}; \rho \right) \right.$$

$$\left. - \Phi_2 \left(\frac{C - \rho\rho_0 C_0}{\sqrt{1 - (\rho\rho_0)^2}}, \frac{X(A_j) - \rho_0 C_0}{\sqrt{1 - \rho_0^2}}; \rho \right) \right]$$

$$- D_j \Phi \left(\frac{X(D_j) - \rho_0 C_0}{\sqrt{1 - \rho_0^2}} \right) - [(1 - R_0)N_0 - D_j]\Phi\left(\frac{Y(D_j) - \rho_0 C_0}{\sqrt{1 - \rho_0^2}} \right)$$

$$- (1 - R)N \left[\Phi_2 \left(\frac{C - \rho\rho_0 C_0}{\sqrt{1 - (\rho\rho_0)^2}}, \frac{Y(D_j) - \rho_0 C_0}{\sqrt{1 - \rho_0^2}}; \rho \right) \right.$$

$$\left. \left. - \Phi_2 \left(\frac{C - \rho\rho_0 C_0}{\sqrt{1 - (\rho\rho_0)^2}}, \frac{X(D_j) - \rho_0 C_0}{\sqrt{1 - \rho_0^2}}; \rho \right) \right] \right\}$$

Although this expression looks quite involved, its computation for a set of different valuation dates is straightforward, as the only numerical effort lies in the evaluation of the bivariate normal distribution function. We have therefore obtained an algorithm where tranche deltas can be computed almost analytically, which offers a considerable advantage in computation time and effort compared to the "brute-force" or bumping approach, and is also less implementation intense than the recursive derivation. All this comes at the cost of accuracy; however, Greenberg et al. (2004) show that the relative error is less than 5 percent.

A P P E N D I X   D

CDO Valuation and Sensitivities Through MC Simulation

MC simulation still provides one of the most flexible platforms for product valuation and risk management. However, the advantages of flexibility and ease of implementation come at the cost of computational efficiency and accuracy, especially when sensitivities have to be computed. While variance reduction techniques such as importance sampling, control variates, or stratified sampling [see Glasserman (2003) and Jaeckel (2002) for a general overview] may be applied with some benefit, more direct approaches focusing particularly on the problem of sensitivity estimation appear more promising and can be combined with variance reduction techniques in many cases.

MC VALUATION: BRUTE FORCE

In the following, we stay within the framework of the standard Gaussian copula model, where the latent variable is given by $A_i = \rho\, V + \sqrt{1 - \rho^2}\,\varepsilon_i$ as introduced earlier. Using standard notation, portfolio losses can be simulated by generating independent, standard normal random numbers for the common and idiosyncratic factors, and extracting the time of default as outlined in chapters on correlation and pricing.

For a standard ST CDO, the portfolio loss in each simulation ω, $\omega = 1, \ldots, W$, at time t is given by

$$L(t, \omega) := L(t_0, t, \lambda(S(t_0)), \omega) = \sum_{i=1}^{N} (1 - R_i) N_i 1_{\{\tau_i \leq t\}}$$

$$= \sum_{i=1}^{N} (1 - R_i) N_i 1_{\left\{ \varepsilon_i \leq \frac{\Phi^{-1}(p_i(t)) - \rho V}{\sqrt{1 - \rho^2}} \right\}}$$

where $p_i(t) = 1 - \exp[\int_0^t \lambda_i(s) ds]$ denotes the unconditional PD of name i. Then, for each simulation ω the tranche loss can be computed as

$$L^{T_j}(t, \omega) = \max \left[\min \left(L(t, \omega) - A_j, D_j - A_j \right), 0 \right],$$

and the PV of protection and premium leg, $\mathrm{PPV}^{T_j}(t, \omega) = \mathrm{PPV}^{T_j}$ $(t_0, t, \lambda(S(t_0)), \omega)$ and $\mathrm{FPV}^{T_j}(t, \omega) = \mathrm{FPV}^{T_j}(t_0, t, \lambda(S(t_0)), \omega)$, can be easily computed along the lines of Equations (7) and (8).

Repeating the simulation W times allows us to estimate the expected values of protection and premium legs as

$$\mathrm{PPV}^{T_j}(t_0, t, \lambda(S(t_0))) = \sum_{\omega=1}^{W} \mathrm{PPV}^{T_j}(t, \omega) \text{ and}$$

$$\mathrm{FPV}^{T_j}(t_0, t, \lambda(S(t_0))) = \sum_{\omega=1}^{W} \mathrm{FPV}^{T_j}(t, \omega), \text{ respectively.}$$

Then, the fair tranche spread can be computed, or the MtM can be estimated as

$$\mathrm{MtM}^{T_j}(t_0, t, \lambda(S(t_0))) = \sum_{\omega=1}^{W} \mathrm{MtM}^{T_j}(t, \omega) = \sum_{\omega=1}^{W} \mathrm{FPV}^{T_j}(t, \omega) - \mathrm{PPV}^{T_j}(t, \omega).$$

MC SENSITIVITIES: BRUTE FORCE

Computation of spread or hazard sensitivities involves once again the finite difference approximation

$$\Delta \mathrm{MtM}_i^{T_j} = \mathrm{MtM}^{T_j}(t_0, T, S^{i01}(t_0)) - \mathrm{MtM}^{T_j}(t_0, T, S(t_0))$$

$$\approx \frac{\partial \mathrm{MtM}^{T_j}(t_0, T, S(t_0))}{\partial S_i(t_0)} (1bp)$$

within the MC framework. The brute force computation of sensitivities proceeds by bumping of the spread curve and re-evalution; i.e.,

$$\Delta \mathrm{MtM}_i^{T_j} = \frac{1}{W} \sum_{\omega=1}^{W} \left[\mathrm{MtM}^{T_j}(t_0, T, \lambda(S^{i01}(t_0)), \omega) - \mathrm{MtM}^{T_j}(t_0, T, \lambda(S(t_0)), \omega) \right].$$

Of course, the problem with this MC simulation is that the sensitivity is mainly determined by just a few MC paths. Shifting the spread curve of name i by 1 bp will increase this PD slightly, and hence decrease the default time. The sensitivity is therefore mainly determined by the few paths that result in additional defaults, and only when this additional default results in an additional payout of the default leg of the CDO. In general, it is obvious that such a solution is highly unstable, and approaches focusing more directly on MC sensitivities need to be considered.

MC Sensitivities: Likelihood Ratio Method

One such approach that greatly enhances computation and accuracy is the likelihood ratio method. Rott and Fries (2005) show that we can approximate the derivative by

$$\frac{\partial \mathrm{MtM}^{T_j}(t_0, T, S(t_0))}{\partial \lambda_i(t_0)} (1\,bp) \approx \frac{1}{W} \sum_{\omega=1}^{W} \left[\mathrm{MtM}^{T_j}(t_0, T, \lambda(S(t_0)), \omega)(\mathrm{LR}_i(\omega) - 1) \right],$$

where LR_i denotes the likelihood ratio for the change of measure from the original to the shifted default intensities for the underlying credit i. If we denote by τ_i and $\bar{\tau}_i$ the random default times corresponding to the intensities $\lambda_i(S_i)$ and $\lambda_i(S_i + 1\,bp)$, respectively, and by $d_i(t) = \lambda_{it}(S_i + 1\,bp) - \lambda_{it}(S_i)$, the difference in intensities at time t, it can be shown that within each MC simulation, this likelihood ratio is given by

$$\mathrm{LR}_i(\omega) = \frac{\phi\left([\Phi^{-1}(P(\bar{\tau}_i \leq \tau_i(\omega)) - \rho V] / \left(\sqrt{1-\rho^2}\right)\right)}{\phi\left([\Phi^{-1}(P(\tau_i \leq \tau_i(\omega)) - \rho V] / \left(\sqrt{1-\rho^2}\right)\right)} \frac{\phi\left(\Phi^{-1}(P(\tau_i \leq \tau_i(\omega)))\right)}{\phi\left(\Phi^{-1}(P(\bar{\tau}_i \leq \tau_i(\omega)))\right)}$$

$$\times \left(1 + \frac{e(\tau_i(w))}{\lambda_i(\tau_i(w))}\right) \exp\left(-\int_0^{\tau_i(w)} d_i(s)\,ds\right).$$

Here, $\tau_i(\omega)$ denotes the simulated default time in iteration ω, and ϕ denotes the density of the standard normal distribution function, while Φ denotes the cumulative distribution functions of the standard normal distribution.

From this expression, it is apparent that only the default times $\tau_i(\omega)$ are simulated from the original spread or hazard curve, and each simulation path contributes to the computation of the hazard sensitivity. This method depends purely on the density of the default times and not on the payoff as such; hence, once implemented for ST CDOs, it also works for all other credit products where a valuation code is available. Further details on the likelihood ratio method within the Gaussian copula framework can be found in Rott and Fries (2005) and Joshi and Kainth (2003).

An alternative to the previous method is the pathwise method, which is often the most efficient, but the payoff of each product must be differentiated analytically, which makes it more difficult to implement. We refer the reader to Joshi and Kainth (2003) and Glasserman (2003) for further details.

REFERENCES

Andersen, L., J. Sidenius, and S. Basu (2003), "All your Hedges in One Basket," *Risk*, November, 67–72.

Berndt, A., R. Douglas, D. Duffie, M. Ferguson, and D. Schranz (2005), "Measuring Default Risk Premia from Default Swap Rates and EDFs," working paper, Tepper School of Business, Carnegie Mellon University.

Brasch, H-J. (2004), "A note on efficient pricing and risk calculation of credit basket products," working paper.

Genz. (2002), "Numerical Computation of Rectangular Bivariate and Trivariate Normal and t Probabilities," Department of Mathematics, Washington State University.

Gibson, M. (2004), "Understanding the risk of synthetic CDOs," working paper.

Glasserman, P. (2003), *Monte Carlo Methods in Financial Engineering*, Springer.

Glasserman, P., and J. Li (2003), "Importance sampling for portfolio credit risk," working paper.

Greenberg, A., D. O'Kane, and L. Schloegl (2004), "LH+: A fast analytical model for CDO hedging and risk management," *Quantitative Credit Research Quarterly*, Lehman Brothers, Q2.

Jaeckel, P. (2002), *Monte Carlo Methods in Finance*, Wiley Interscience.

Joshi, M., and D. Kainth (2003), "Rapid and accurate development of prices and greeks for nth to default credit swaps in the Li model," working paper.

Kakodkar, A., B. Martin, and S. Galiani (2003), "Correlation trading," *Fixed-Income Stategy*, Merrill Lynch.

O'Kane, D., and S. Turnbull (2003), "Valuation of Credit Default Swaps," *Quantitative Credit Research Quarterly*, Lehman Brothers, Q1/Q2.

Rott, M. G., and C. P. Fries (2005), "Fast and Robust Monte Carlo CDO sensitivities," working paper.

Vasicek, O. (1987), "Probability of loss on loan portfolio," working paper, Moody's KMV.

A Practical Guide to CDO Trading Risk Management

Andrea Petrelli, Jun Zhang, Norbert Jobst,
and Vivek Kapoor

INTRODUCTION AND MOTIVATION

The collateral debt obligations (CDO) modeling framework with static spread term structures and employing copula functions (see Chapters 4 and 6 for further details) is taking hold in the accounting of synthetic CDO trading profit and loss (P&L). This has been spurred by tranches on standardized credit indexes (e.g., CDX.NA.IG, CDX.NA.HY, ITRAXX Eur, etc.) that have provided a calibration target for pricing models. There are ongoing discussions on different ways of fitting prices across the capital structure (e.g., "compound correlation," versus "base correlation") as discussed in Chapter 6. Less understood are hedging strategies and their cost and effectiveness, and the basic risk-reward profiles of popular CDO trading strategies and the associated capitalization needs for banks. The two main reasons for this state of affairs are:

1. The popular emphasis and practical techniques for pricing CDO tranches have not addressed replication and hedging errors (accounting for spread diffusion, spread jumps, and jumps to default with uncertain recovery) and therefore have not resulted in a commensurate maturing of the hedging and risk management paradigm.

2. Risk aggregation regimes that are based merely on marginal and linear spread sensitivities are rendered ineffective and misleading due to the nonlinearity created by tranching (i.e., payoff is non linear in reference asset performance). These linear risk aggregation regimes are deeply entrenched in risk management circles that have not effectively participated in the revolution of structured credit products.

The practical task of assessing risk and developing a hedging strategy involves delineating probabilistic descriptions of the variables that the prevalent pricing models depend upon, and assessing a probabilistic description of the P&L associated with the trading strategy. While Chapter 7 focused on the conceptual framework and practical computation of popular risk measures, this Chapter is focused on assessing credit related risks and P&L performance. It can, therefore, be seen as part two of our discussion of CDO risk management.

The risks in one elementary long-only credit trade (sell protection on a credit index) and three popular synthetic CDO strategies are compared throughout this chapter. We will illustrate how marginal spread and default sensitivities are insufficient for the CDO trading strategies on account of the nonlinearities created by tranching credit exposures, despite providing a good description of the elementary credit strategy (sell protection on pool of names). In addition, we will compare the carry at inception with the downsides of popular CDO trades and provide a comparison of the carry and value on default (VOD) probability distributions for different CDO strategies.

After analyzing the risk characteristics of static portfolios in terms of default, spread, and correlation as introduced in Chapter 7, we provide an exposition of dynamic hedging and risk management. Specifically, we explore the equity trade (sell equity protection and buy index protection) and show how the trading P&L evolves and can be attributed to different market variables. We therefore go beyond the static risk measures previously described.

OVERVIEW OF SOME POPULAR TRADING STRATEGIES

Throughout this chapter, we will investigate a number of popular CDO trading strategies by using the tools introduced in Chapter 7, and by providing a probabilistic P&L exposition. The trading strategies considered are outlined next:

Elementary Portfolio

Selling protection on an index of credit default swap (CDS) is an example of an elementary credit portfolio. For example, the credit index, CDX.NA.IG, consisting of 125 North American credits, will be used to provide sample calculations. The risk-profile for the CDO trades will be compared with risks incurred in simply selling protection on the index.

CDO Portfolios

Quotes on tranches referencing credit indices and market participants' estimates of associated deltas (CS01 or Credit01 hedges)* are widely available on at least a daily frequency. These trades are sometimes based on delta-exchanges, which are ostensibly CS01 "hedges" for the tranches, which can, in certain strategies, be the long credit risk driver. We focus on three CDO trades based on such an indexed product:

I. Positive Carry Equity Tranche Trade
Sell protection on the 0 to 3 percent tranche referencing the CDX.NA.IG index and hedge CS01 exposure by buying protection on the index.

II. Positive Carry Straddle Trade
Sell protection on 0 to 3 percent of the CDX.NA.IG index and hedge CS01 exposure by buying protection on the 7 to 10 percent tranche.

III. Positive Carry Senior Mezzanine Tranche Trade
Buy protection on the 7 to 10 percent tranche of the CDX.NA.IG index and hedge CS01 exposure by selling protection on the index.

In these CDO *strategies*, at execution, the premium received as a result of selling credit protection exceeds the premium paid to immunize small

---

*CS01 and Credit01 terminology was introduced in Chapter 7 to denote single name and broad market sensitivity, respectively. Throughout this chapter, we will mostly use CS01 notation, for both, single name and market spread sensitivity. Unless otherwise stated, we are mostly concerned with hedging strategies that employ a credit index.

TABLE 8.1

Quote and Comparison of CDX.NA.IG.4 Tranche Trade
Carry at Inception on March 31, 2005. The Carry
for the CDO Strategies is Expressed in Terms of the
Tranche Notional, and for the Straddle (that Involves
Two Tranches), It is Expressed in Terms of the Equity
Tranche Notional

CDX.NA.IG.4	6/20/2010		49 bps
Tranche	Price	Correlation	Delta
0–3%	500 bps +33.5%	19%	17×
3–7%	199 bps	5%	7×
7–10%	64 bps	16%	2.8×
10–15%	25 bps	21%	1.1×
15–30%	10 bps	32%	0.3×
Strategy	Description		Carry
Linear	Long CDS index		49 bp/pa
CDO-I	Delta-hedged equity tranche		457 bp/pa
CDO-II	Straddle		1149 bp/pa
CDO-III	Delta-hedged senior mezzanine tranche		116 bp/pa

Abbreviations: CDO, collateral debt obligations.

spread changes (where upfront payments are amortized over the tranche duration and added to the running premium to provide an estimate of the net *carry*). The carry for these trades is computed by adding the running coupon rates to the time-decay of the trade mark-to-market. At inception the carry is close to a no-default cash flow found by simply amortizing the upfront payments over the tranche duration. Table 8.1 compares the carry at inception for the three trading strategies on March 31, 2005. It reveals that the Straddle (II) had the highest carry followed by the delta-neutral equity tranche (I) and the delta-hedged senior mezzanine tranche (III).

PRACTICAL RISK MANAGEMENT I: PITFALLS OF MONITORING CREDIT DELTA ALONE

The trading strategies introduced above are particularly interesting in the view of traditional risk management systems. Such systems typically do not address structured credit capital structures and the ensuing credit non-linearity. These risk systems were built for aggregating risks from vanilla credit products, such as corporate bonds or single name CDS, and are designed to monitor delta exposures ("bond equivalent market values" as customary in big bond shops, or delta-notional, respectively). These risk management systems typically monitor CS01: i.e., the change in mark-to-market (mtm) due to an issuer spread widening by 1 bps. Even for a single CDS, this is a simplification because the duration over which premiums are *expected* to be paid depends on the issuer risk-neutral default probability and then non linearly on the issuer spreads. As a consequence, the P&L impact of spreads changing by more than 1 bps doesn't have to be the product of CS01 and the spread move (in bps). Indeed, if an issuer, on which a trading book has sold default protection, was to suddenly approach default (say by an unbounded spread rise), the loss is bounded above by the notional amount (minus recovery and adjusting for mtm). Such non-linearity is endemic to credit instruments and it renders the results of sensitivity based risk management systems as approximations of the true risks. However for vanilla credit, such approximations are not pernicious. A book that is a net CDS protection purchaser will have its losses under spread tightening understated in a CS01 based system. A book that is a net CDS protection seller will have its losses under extreme moves somewhat exaggerated in a CS01 based system. In either situation, the sign of the mtm move incurred due to the extreme spread widening or tightening is captured by the spot CS01 of a vanilla credit book.

In the presence of such risk management regimes, the chosen CDO strategies can be particularly popular as they essentially provide positive cash flows (carry) with no delta exposure (widely regulated and monitored risk). In addition, if risk capital requirements are explicitly driven by, or proportional to, delta exposures, as they have been traditionally and continue to be, trading desks can essentially book positive-carry without having to set aside anticipatory risk capital.

Unless risk management systems and risk capital models capture credit spread-default convexity (single name and marketwide), and correlation risk measures, the risk–return characteristics of CDO trading strategies illustrated here can be quite different compared to risk management rendition based on the equivalent "delta-portfolio." We show here how the "delta-portfolio" can miss both the risks and the opportunities in CDO trading. In the next section, we shed some light on the sensitivities introduced in Chapter 7 for the three CDO strategies, before providing a full P&L (back-testing) case study thereafter.

Credit Spread Sensitivity

As previously discussed, a CS01 based risk management framework can provide a good approximation for vanilla credits, while the nonlinearity introduced through tranching creates non monotonic mtm changes for spread changes (e.g., market moves versus single-name, idiosyncratic moves). Here, we put the machinery developed in Chapter 7 into practice and examine model CDO trades. At inception, there is little or no "CS01 risk," yet if spreads were to blowout on any issuer name, the trade incurs a mtm loss. Figures 8.1 to 8.3 show the mtm impact when spreads on multiple names are widening-tightening for the three trading strategies, respectively. For each figure, the bottom panel provides a "zoom-in" for spread shifts from −20 to 40 bps.

We can clearly see that the mtm impact of spread widening on multiple names is certainly not the same as the sum of mtm impacts when individual names widen, and that the impact is amplified for larger spread changes. In fact, the simultaneous widening of spreads on many names could result in an mtm gain for the strategies shown here. This is referred to as having "positive index gamma." The positive index gamma can be of a local nature (e.g., if all names widen by 100 bps the mtm impact is positive), and the event of the spreads of all names increasing unboundedly could still be a loss event as shown in Figure 8.3 for the delta-neutral senior mezzanine tranche. It is also interesting to note that all trades appear to incur a positive mtm impact when spreads blow out enormously on somewhere between 5 and 10 names. However, while a further widening on even more names leads to larger and larger gains for the first two strategies, Figure 8.3 reveals that large "blowouts" may reduce the mtm gain again or even cause losses if the number of blowouts is too large.

While some of these spread shock scenarios are quite unlikely, it is interesting to note that when considering more realistic market changes (e.g., a large number of assets moving by moderate amounts, or the spreads of a few names widening modestly, as shown in the lower panels of Figures 8.1 to 8.3), the mtm sensitivity of the CDO trades is an increasing function of the initial trade carry (Table 8.1). The highest carry trade, the straddle (II), has the highest spread sensitivity, while the lowest carry trade, the senior mezzanine trade (III), has the lowest, when considering a spread shock scenarios in the range of −20 to +50 basis points. For the straddle, this is caused by the higher convexity causing larger losses (in the event of the spread of a handful of names widening) on both sides of the trade (i.e., long equity and short senior tranche).

FIGURE 8.1

Spread Sensitivity of Delta-Hedged Equity Tranche (0 to 3 percent). The Issuers are Arranged in a Decreasing Spread Order and the top 1,2,..., N Names are Applied a Parallel Spread Shock (Amount Depicted on Horizontal Axis). (CDX. NA. IG.4, March 31, 2005)

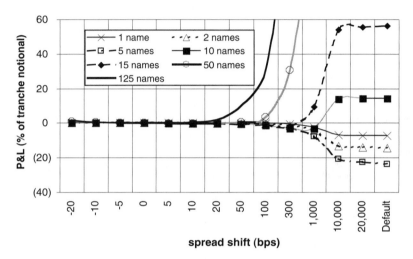

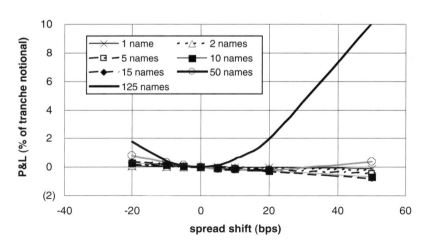

FIGURE 8.2

Spread Sensitivity of Straddle (0 to 3 Percent and 7 to 10 Percent). The Issuers are Arranged in a Decreasing Spread Order and the Top 1,2,..., N Names are Applied a Parallel Spread Shock (Amount Depicted on Horizontal Axis). (CDX. NA. IG.4, March 31, 2005)

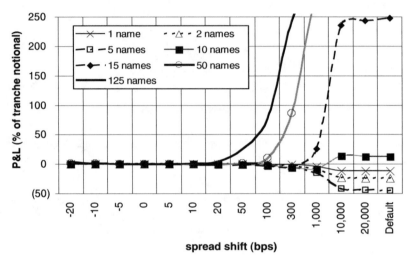

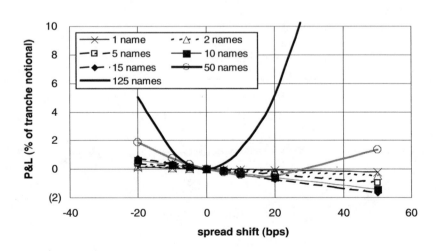

FIGURE 8.3

Spread Sensitivity of Delta-Hedged Senior Mezzanine Tranche (7 to 10 Percent). The Issuers are Arranged in a Decreasing Spread Order and the Top 1,2,..., N Names are Applied a Parallel Spread Shock (Amount Depicted on Horizontal Axis). (CDX. NA. IG.4, March 31, 2005)

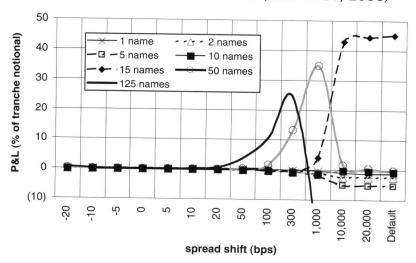

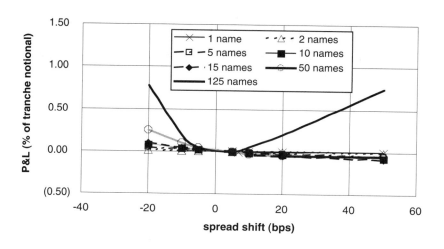

Hence, the carry may be seen as compensation for the idiosyncratic and systematic spread risk inherent in the corresponding CDO strategies. These examples highlight how a marginal CS01 based risk management framework does not effectively capture risks prevailing in popular CDO strategies. The spread sensitivity computations show that the popular CDO strategies are susceptible to idiosyncratic spread move risks, and any effort to "bucket" spread moves by ratings or sectors and potentially perturb many issuers simultaneously in the same direction is a poor way to assess CDO trading "market risks." The market risk of these CDO strategies can be controlled by the propensity of spreads to not move together and, therefore, the broad-brush coherent moves based on either sector or ratings are misleading.

In practice, when interested in synthetic CDO trading Value at Risk (VaR), both CS01 based VaR and/or VaR based on broad market moves are troublesome. While a CS01 based "VaR" can be completely uninformative for synthetic CDOs (by not addressing convexity and correlation risk), a "VaR" based on broad index moves can be even more misleading, because the positive carry strategies encounter losses under spread twists and not necessarily under coherent parallel shocks that are more amenable to traditional "market-risk" scenarios.

As a result, while there can be index or sector factor drivers for spread moves, a name specific spread time series (modeled or historically sampled) is a prerequisite for articulating a hedging strategy and for assessing a synthetic CDO trading VaR. Hence, good risk management requires a reasonable (probabilistic) description of possible future outcomes including a "real world" description of the credit spread environment.

The actual hedging, of course, still employs liquid indices because of ease–efficiency of execution. Periodic single name hedging can be undertaken as an overlay on top of the index hedging if one desires to maintain a small CS01 exposure per name. As the index is equally weighted, and the hedge ratios per name (found by bumping individual spreads one at a time) are not identical, employing the index as a CS01 hedge results in slight residual negative and positive CS01 exposures to individual names.*

---

*Note that whether one bumps all the names 1 bps simultaneously and finds the overall index hedge ratio (in terms of notional), or one bumps individual names to assess individual hedge ratios and hedges using the index with a notional that equals the sum of the individual hedge notionals, one arrives at the same point (because convexity does not manifest strongly at 1 bps).

Correlation Sensitivity

For illustration purposes all of the sensitivities shown above did not involve any changes to the implied correlation of the tranches. The tranche implied correlation reflects how the market views interact with model assumptions, which are: (1) static spread term structure; (2) normal copula; (3) fixed recovery; (4) deterministic asset-correlation structure. Indeed, there is no way to separate the effect of all of these assumptions once they have been thrown into the *kitchen sink* of implied correlation. Correlation is not the only uncertain variable in portfolio credit derivative pricing. Recovery uncertainty and recovery-default correlation are long outstanding features that do not find systematic treatment even in single name CDS pricing practice, to date.

The need for different implied correlation values to be used in pricing different tranches across the capital structure is referred to as the correlation skew. The correlation skew can be at least qualitatively *explained* with even a small set of the *kitchen sink* ingredients.

In the standard pricing model with static spreads, the asset correlation input controls the correlation between the times to default of different issuers. The value of buying protection on a tranche is a nonlinear function of the input correlation as shown in Figure 8.4. Therefore if one hypothesizes a correlation uncertainty band and assesses the expectation of the tranche value under uncertain correlation, one gets a price that is possibly quite different from what one gets by simply inputting the average correlation (Jensen's inequality). As value of default protection in different tranches have different degrees of dependence on the correlation input parameter, the *implied* correlation that produces the same price, as found under a correlation uncertainty band, is tranche-dependent. These rudimentary correlation convexity arguments are sufficient to explain the correlation skew qualitatively. Of course, asset and default correlation are not deterministically knowable parameters. Under significant correlation convexity, it is inconceivable for the market to price different tranches of the same structure at the same implied correlation.

As correlation is a pricing variable, CDO trades are exposed to the market risk of that pricing parameter changing. Interestingly, just like for spread-convexity for small to medium spread movements the correlation sensitivity is also an increasing function of the initial trade carry (see Figure 8.4 for the three CDO trades analyzed here). The highest carry trade, the straddle, has the highest correlation sensitivity (moving both the equity and senior mezzanine tranche correlation simultaneously in the same direction which is not guaranteed to occur). The equity tranche

FIGURE 8.4

Correlation Sensitivity. For the Straddle, the P&L
Impact is Plotted as a Percentage of Equity Tranche
Notional. (CDX. NA. IG.4, March 31, 2005)

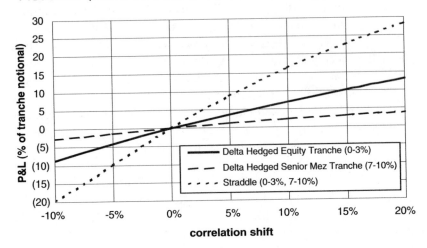

trade has the second highest correlation sensitivity and the second highest carry. The senior mezzanine tranche trade has the lowest carry and the
lowest correlation sensitivity. One reason for the higher correlation sensitivity of the straddle (II) is that an increase (decrease) in implied equity
and senior correlation leads to an mtm decline (increase) on the equity,
and a mtm increase (decline) on the senior tranche, respectively. Hence,
the long equity and the short senior tranche position suffer a double mtm
impact, while the hedging portfolio in the other two trades (I and III) is
insensitive to changes in correlation. Again, the carry seems to be a compensation for the additional correlation risk inherent in CDO positions.
Managing the risk by only looking at the spot delta-equivalent portfolio
would totally miss these risks, as the delta-portfolio is correlation neutral.
Later we show the connection between spread risks and implied correlation risk when we look at the evolution of the trading P&L.

Default Sensitivity

Marginal Value On Default (iOmega)

As with almost all credit risky instruments, default of one or several names
in the portfolio referenced by the CDO tranches may have a significant

FIGURE 8.5

Marginal Value on Default (VOD) Sensitivity for Three CDO Strategies and the Long Credit Index Trade. There are 125 Issuers in the Credit Index and Associated CDO Analyzed here. The Horizontal Axis is the Credit Spread Level of the Distinct Issuers, and the Vertical Axis is the Marginal P&L Impact of Default (VOD) of Distinct Issuers. (CDX. NA.IG.4, March 31, 2005)

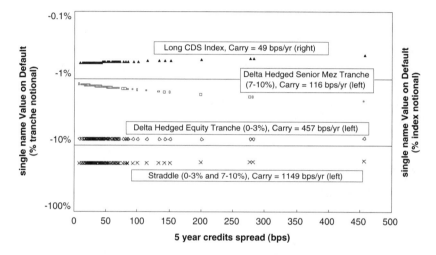

impact on the model trades. As introduced in Chapter 7, the change in mtm due to an issuer spread widening unboundedly (referred to as the VOD or iOmega) provides important insight into the risk inherent in CDO tranches. Figure 8.5 shows the mtm impact on the vanilla credit portfolio and the three CDO trades if one obligor in the portfolio is defaulting. Hence, each "dot" in Figure 8.5 shows the mtm loss for a specific credit defaulting.

For the long credit index trade, the sign of the VOD is negative: the spread on the index is the price of taking on default risk. The "delta-hedged" CDO trades also have negative marginal VODs to each reference entity in the pool. Within each positive carry CDO strategy on CDX.NA.IG.4, the marginal VODs (iOmega) themselves do not vary a great deal in this largely BBB pool. For different trading strategies, however, iOmega is ordered by the carry (computed at inception) of the strategy, i.e., the greater the carry; the more negative is the marginal VOD. Once again, the carry associated with the "delta-hedged" CDO trade is clearly a compensation for taking on credit event risks. Whether the carry provides a trading book any *excess* spread over what is *fair* to take on credit risk is an interesting question that will be addressed by comparing the default risk and carry of these strategies with the elementary credit strategy further below.

Running Value On Default (Omega)

By simultaneously defaulting multiple issuers, the running VOD of a trade can be computed. As there are many possible 2-tuples, 3-tuples, etc., there is no unique running VOD unless we are dealing with a homogeneous portfolio. As in Chapter 7, the running VOD shown here is based on sorting the issuers in the order of decreasing spreads and defaulting the top n names simultaneously as outlined in Chapter 7. Figures 8.6 to 8.8 show the running VOD for the three different CDO strategies. The entire strategies exhibit a "positive index gamma" type profile in the running VOD, i.e., the losses due to a few defaults is less than the sum of the corresponding marginal VODs.

FIGURE 8.6

Default Sensitivity of Delta-Hedged Equity Tranche (0 to 3 Percent).

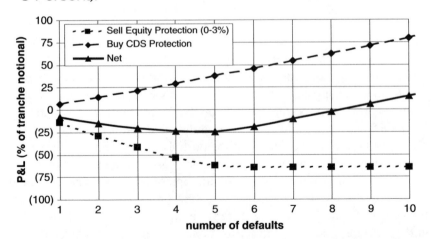

(The cumulative MtM impact due to defaults for the Equity Tranche Strategy is shown here. The issuers are sorted by their five year credit spread and the highest 1, 2,. . . . *N* names are defaulted. The MtM changes can be decomposed into those arising from the CDO Tranche and from the single name CDS. Due to upfront payments received for selling equity protection, the losses incurred due to defaults for the tranche level out at amounts less than the tranche notional. The CDS protection purchased via the index results in payoffs that grow linearly with the number of defaults. The net running default P&L impact is non-monotonic, with the maximum loss scenario corresponding to five defaults (24 percent of equity tranche notional) and the breakeven scenario corresponding to eight defaults (CDX. NA. IG.4, March 31, 2005)).

FIGURE 8.7

Default Sensitivity of Straddle (0 to 3 Percent and 7 to 10 Percent Tranche).

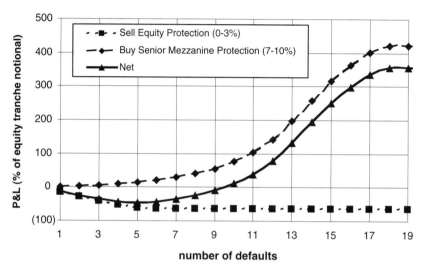

(The cumulative MtM impact due to defaults for the straddle strategy is shown here. The net running default P&L impact is non-monotonic, with the maximum loss scenario corresponding to six defaults (47 percent of mezzanine tranche notional) and the breakeven scenario corresponding to ten defaults (CDX. NA. IG.4, March 31, 2005)).

In fact all the strategies show a gain after the number of defaults exceeds a certain level.

For the positive carry equity tranche trade or straddle, the concept of maximum loss is useful because there is a clearly defined maximum loss for any sequence of defaults (Figures 8.6 and 8.7). The concept becomes less clear for the positive carry senior mezzanine tranche trade (Figure 8.8). After a certain number of defaults, the senior mezzanine strategy shows a reversal of the P&L gains associated with an increasing number of defaults. This feature arises because after the CDO tranche is eaten through by defaults, there is no short exposure left.

In general, the notion of a "maximum loss" associated with portfolio of CDO trades is not always a viable risk management target because the maximum loss scenario can be wildly unrealistic (e.g., all the names in the pool defaulting). Also, if we do not need to worry about defaults beyond the first maximum loss scenario, then carry versus maximum loss provides important bounds on CDO pricing with "arbitrageurs" (more

FIGURE 8.8

Default Sensitivity of Delta-Hedged Senior Mezzanine
Tranche (7 to 10 Percent).

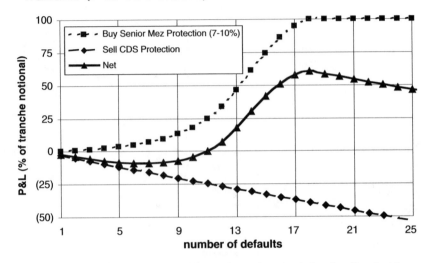

(The cumulative MtM impact due to defaults for the mezzanine tranche strategy is shown here. The net running
default P&L impact is nonmonotonic, with the first maximum loss scenario (9 percent mezzanine tranche notional)
corresponding to nine defaults and the first breakeven scenario corresponding to eleven defaults (CDX. NA. IG.4,
March 31, 2005)).

appropriately "relative value traders") stepping in when the carry to maximum loss ratio is out of line with other credit opportunities (i.e., the carry
to maximum loss ratio of a trade strategy can exert a "good-deal bound"
on CDO tranche pricing).

The positive carry CDO trades tend to exhibit positive P&L under
sufficiently large (or intermediately large) numbers of default within the
pool. Therefore, when considering a portfolio of positive carry CDO
trades with non overlapping pools, the worst P&L outcome associated
with a small number of defaults is likely to be when those defaults occur
in non overlapping pools.

VOD Risk Per Unit Carry

An extension to the computation of Omega is to actually simulate defaults
of the underlying issuers in a Monte-Carlo (MC) setting, which will generate many possible running VOD scenarios, and the associated mtm
impact. We will therefore be able to look at a distribution of mtm changes
resulting from a plausible default simulation. In particular, when the

FIGURE 8.9A

One-Year Default Risk. (CDX. NA. IG.4, March 31, 2005)

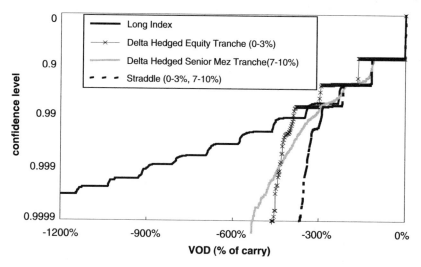

VOD losses are compared as multiples of the carry of trades (for positive carry trades), interesting insights and relative value comparisons can be obtained.

In the following we look at such VOD/carry distributions when "real measure" defaults are simulated using a normal copula with 25 percent asset correlation and Standard & Poor's 2004 corporate default table.* The P&L impact of the issuers that default over a time horizon less than one year is found by repricing the portfolio under that scenario. This is repeated 50,000 times and the one-year distribution of default sensitivity as a fraction/multiple of carry (annual cash flow associated with the trade) can be investigated. Figure 8.9a shows such carry-default statistics at different confidence levels, which will be valuable when comparing different trades.

The figure reveals the positive index gamma nature of the CDO strategies, i.e., the loss stemming from many defaults is lower for the CDO strategies compared to the index itself. Hence, the tail for the long short strategies

---

*Of course, one could employ Moody's MKMV expected default frequency, Kamakura default probabilities, or impose a proprietary view on the issuer's balance sheets and default probabilities.

FIGURE 8.9B

One-Year Default Risk of Equity Tranche Trade.
(CDX. NA. IG.4)

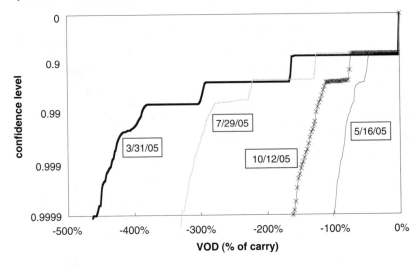

is relatively thin (at high confidence levels) compared to the index for the same amount of initial carry. Such a view is quite different from simply looking at the absolute carry. For instance, the carry-default profile of the different CDO strategies come out to be quite similar (on the specific date shown here), despite the absolute carry numbers being widely different. Hence, a proper risk capital calculation based on default risk would render the carry per unit risk capital for these strategies to be quite similar. Put in another way, at the 99 percent confidence level, the carry of the CDO strategies is not particularly attractive compared to a long credit index (on March 31, 2005), while at higher confidence levels the CDO strategies exhibit less default risk per unit carry compared to the long credit index strategy.

The observations made in Figure 8.9A are of course tied to the market data (issuer spreads, tranche pricing) and will change as the market spreads and pricing correlations change as the credit-cycle evolves and as market participants learn more about their risk–reward profiles, as shown in Figure 8.9B.

The residual VOD risk (expressed as a multiple of the trade carry) may be altered by hedging differently than an index-CS01 hedge. In some instances, buying more index protection for the equity trade reduces the VOD risk per unit carry (implying a cheap index protection and rich compensation for taking on equity tranche risk) and in other instances buying less protection reduces the VOD risk per unit carry (implying an expensive index protection and poor compensation for taking on equity tranche risk) as illustrated in Figure 8.10. This should not be surprising because the delta found by perturbing the spreads by 1 bps is not addressing hedge error minimization or elimination (in fact the standard CDO model does not address any dispersion in spreads either), therefore, the residual VOD risk (which is not zero even in theory) can be altered by changing the hedging strategy. Of course, such an alteration of hedging will end up producing credit-delta exposure, which will then show up in traditional risk management system radars.

Throughout this section, we have shown that a CS01-only based risk management system is particularly inadequate because of the potential of creating positive carry trades with little CS01 and with significant negative VOD sensitivity. A trading book with long and short positions on CDOs and CDS (e.g., the three model trades analyzed here) can become a seller of default protection on the issuers in the CDO reference pools (i.e., exhibit negative VOD to reference names), yet not exhibit any negative CS01 to those issuers, and under extreme spread widening for any of

FIGURE 8.10

One-Year Default Risk Versus Hedge Ratio for Equity Tranche Trade. (CDX.NA.IG.4)

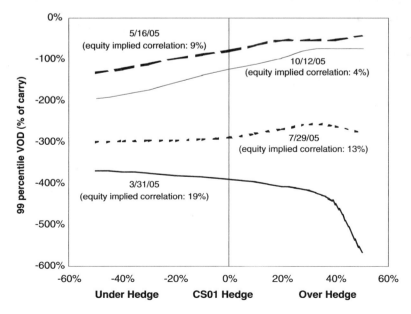

those issuers can incur a significant loss. If all risk management is doing is staring at credit delta or CS01 (or equivalent bond market value exposure), then CDO trading can simply become a pretext to sell default protection without any limit, or recognition of opportunities and risks.

PRACTICAL RISK MANAGEMENT II: TRADING P&L CASE STUDY

The Trade: Sell Equity Tranche Protection Position on CDX.NA.IG.4

While the previous analysis dissects the residual risks in CS01 or delta-hedged trades, and presents interesting risk–return tradeoffs (carry versus VOD, spread, and implied correlation sensitivity), it does not show how different components of the P&L evolve over time in response to simultaneous changes in market variables: i.e., issuer spreads and implied correlations. To examine in greater depth how a combination of market variable changes influences the risk–return of synthetic CDO trades, we examine the components of the trading P&L (1) Cash component; (2) Mark-to-market component. The change in a trading book's wealth is given by the sum of these components: $\Delta W(t) = C(t) + \text{mtm}(t)$. Under the assumption that the cash flows received/incurred accrue at the short risk-free rate, we have

$$C(t) = \sum_{i;t_i \leq t} c_i \exp\left[\int_{t_i}^{t} r(\tau)d\tau\right]$$

The cash flows incurred at times t_i are denoted by c_i, and $r(\tau)$ is the risk-free short term interest rate. The mark-to-market component responds to evolving spreads, pricing model correlations, and defaults, as discussed in Chapter 7.

An equity tranche trade on the CDX.NA.IG.4 pool is initiated on March 22, 2005. Using historical time-series for on the run quotes on CDX.NA.IG.4, index spread, and single name spreads; we display the P&L of different types of trades (unhedged and delta-hedged) and the impact of rebalancing on P&L volatility. To interpret these results, we examine many different measures of credit spread (see Appendix A) in addition to the implied correlation time series for the equity tranche.

Time-Decay—Carry View at Execution

If there are no market moves, as time passes by and the trade matures, what would be the wealth of the trader at different points in time? The cash component of trader's wealth is made up of the initial payment received to sell protection and ongoing premium payments. If a hedge is in place then there are ongoing payments for the hedge. The upfront payment on the CDO tranche and the received running premium payments (netted with premium payments to purchase the hedge) are assumed to accrete and grow at short-term risk-free rates. The initial mtm on the CDO equity tranche is negative due to the upfront payment, but it decays with time due to the decreased expected contingent payments over smaller maturities. Figure 8.11 (top panel) depicts the time-decay view of P&L on a sell equity tranche protection position.

Figure 8.11 (middle panel) depicts the time-decay view of P&L on a buy CDS index protection, i.e., the CDS index position needed to delta hedge CDO equity tranche sell protection position at inception depicted in Figure 8.11 (top). The mtm component of the CDS index hedge is zero at inception (assuming a fairly priced contract with no upfront payment) and at maturity. The mtm of the CDS index hedge may not be zero in between inception and maturity, depending on the credit spread term-structure and the manner in which time-decay is assessed. For the combined CDO tranche with CDS index hedge position, the P&L components are shown in Figure 8.11 (bottom panel). These time-decay views of P&L are assessed by decreasing the maturity of the transaction (from five years at inception). Another view of time-decay is by rolling the transaction on the interest rates and credit spread forward curves.

Both the unhedged sell equity protection trade (Figure 8.11 top) and the CS01-hedged trade (Figure 8.11 bottom) are *positive carry* insofar as in the absence of market moves the protection seller's wealth increases with time. Both the unhedged sell equity protection trade and the CS01-hedged trade, have negative marginal VOD sensitivities (Figure 8.5), with the unhedged trade having larger carry and a more negative VOD sensitivity than the CS01-hedged trade. Therefore both the unhedged sell equity protection trade and the CS01-hedged trade represent long credit positions.

FIGURE 8.11

Time-Decay View on Trade Date for Sell Equity Tranche
Protection Position. (CDX.NA.IG.4, March 31, 2005)

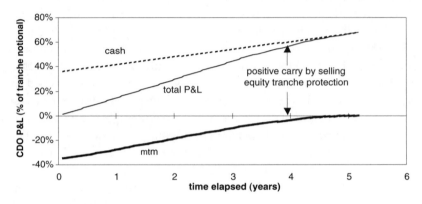

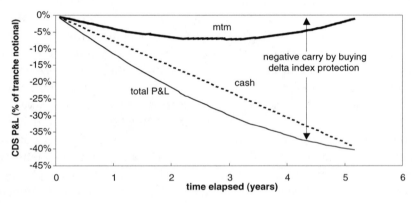

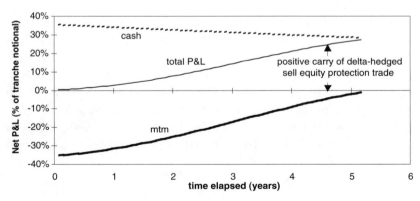

P&L Components With Market Moves: Back Testing Insights

We look at the P&L performance taking into account what actually happened in the market between March and December 2005 next. We dissect again the cash and mtm components in this exercise. In the long-only (sell equity tranche protection) trade or the statically delta-hedged trade, the cash component is not influenced by movements in credit spreads (Figure 8.12 top panel). A sell equity protection position results in receiving an upfront payment and ongoing running premium payments that have been accrued continuously here. Delta hedging of the equity tranche results in the running net premium to be negative (i.e., negative cash outflow) on top of the positive upfront payment. For the static hedge, the premium payments are also insensitive to spread moves after conducting the initial trade, while rebalancing introduces some spread sensitivity.

The mtm of the trade is influenced by movements in credit spreads and implied correlation, on top of time-decay (Figure 8.12 mid). The unhedged sell equity tranche protection position is an outright long credit-delta exposure and is also long correlation and therefore suffers a deep blow when spreads widen on the average and the equity tranche implied correlation falls. A short credit hedging position of course dampens the mtm fluctuations (and reduces the cash component of the P&L). The total P&L (cash plus mtm) is displayed in Figure 8.12 bottom panel.

Of course, as deltas change with changes in market variables, different hedging frequencies will impact the P&L differently. It turns out that a static hedge, i.e., a CS01 hedge using the index at inception, ends up performing not too different from a daily CS01-hedged trade employing the index to hedge. The less frequently hedged trade that involves delta hedging every two weeks or two months happens to perform better than the daily or statically hedged trade (Figure 8.12 bottom panel). In the following, we provide an interpretation of the P&L moves based on market variables attempting to gain further insight into the drivers of P&L performance.

Interpretation: Role of Index Spread, Spread Dispersion, & Implied Correlation

Figure 8.12 revealed that a sharp P&L drawdown event for the sell equity tranche trade (initiated in March 2005 on CDX.NA.IG.4) occurred in May 2005. Figure 8.13 shows that this was associated with a widening of the index average spread (top panel), a widening of the index cross-sectional

FIGURE 8.12

Components of P&L for Sample CDX.NA.IG.4 Sell Equity Protection Trade.

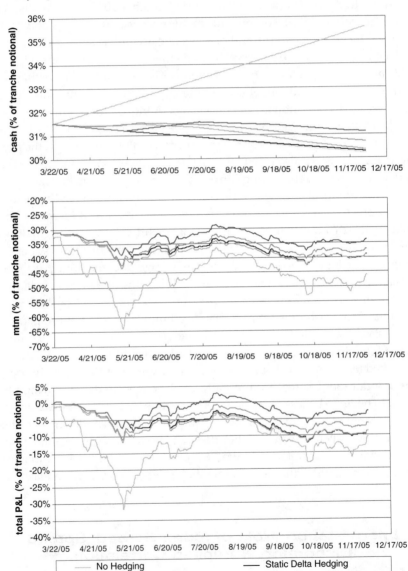

FIGURE 8.13

P&L and Risk Factors for Sample CDX.NA.IG.4 Sell Equity Protection Trade.

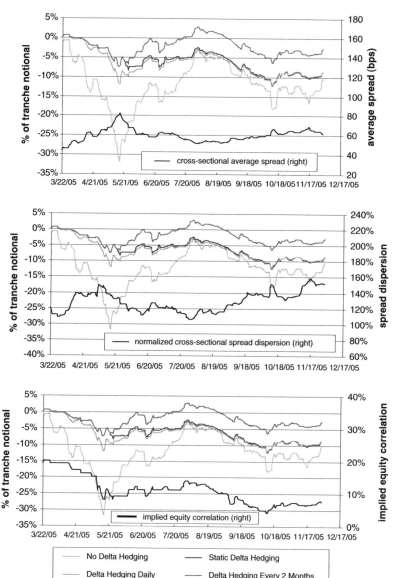

dispersion of spreads (middle panel), and a sudden drop in the implied correlation for the equity tranche (bottom panel). Both index spread widening and increase in dispersion had built up over April, and then in May there was a sharp drop in implied correlation.

Even the delta-hedged equity tranche trade experienced a significant P&L drawdown (10 to 15 percent of equity tranche notional) despite being CS01 hedged using the index, although delta hedging significantly reduces the negative P&L relative to naked long equity risk position (39 to 35 percent of equity tranche notional). This is because of the increase in cross-sectional spread dispersion in the index and the concomitant decrease in the equity tranche implied correlation. Index average spread widening, increase of cross-sectional dispersion, and drop of implied correlation tended to occur together (Figures 8.14 and 8.15).

The scatter plot of the equity implied correlation versus spread dispersion (Figure 8.15) suggests that the market developed a new realization of the vulnerability of the sell equity protection trade to pool idiosyncrasies in May 2005.

The response of the implied correlation pricing parameter to market spread moves can be interpreted as follows. As the index spread widens, those market players who have a leveraged long exposure to the index via an unhedged equity tranche protection sell position and those who have a heightened exposure to idiosyncratic spread moves via CS01 hedged sell equity tranche protection positions incur losses. In response to these losses they either try to close out their position by taking an opposing position, or demand greater compensation for taking on the risk. The increased demand for buying equity tranche protection and the higher asking price for selling equity tranche protection both manifest as a downward move in the equity tranche implied correlation parameter.

This empirical feature of spread dispersion being associated with index widening and equity implied correlation decreasing underlines the inadequacy of employing CS01 as the primary risk-monitoring tool for synthetic CDO trades. A delta-hedged trade will not exhibit any CS01 and not prepare anyone for losses that will occur when the index spread widens: These losses are inflicted by idiosyncratic spread-movements and the associated decrease in equity implied correlation which can be interpreted as an increase in risk-aversion to idiosyncratic credit impairments. If a CDO tranche is thought to simply be a collection of single name credit instruments (albeit with the correct individual CS01) one is not prepared for the downside risks associated with idiosyncratic spread flare-outs and implied correlation movements.

FIGURE 8.14

Time Series of Cross-Sectional Average Spread, Index Spread, Cross-Sectional Spread Dispersion (Normalized by Average Spread), and Equity Tranche Implied Correlation. (CDX.NA.IG.4)

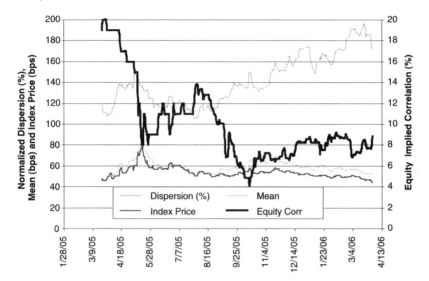

FIGURE 8.15

Equity Tranche Implied Correlation versus Normalized Spread Dispersion Scatter-Plot. (CDX.NA.IG.4)

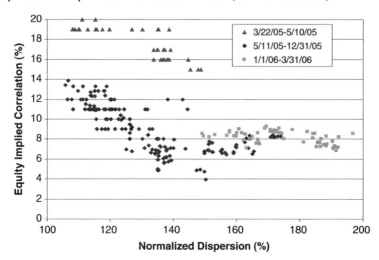

Tales of poor P&L attribution from credit-delta risk factors and elements of surprise and fear associated with P&L marking and risk-assessment abound the broker-dealer and hedge fund community transacting in synthetic CDOs. The experiences in 2005 have crystallized the fallacy of measuring synthetic CDO risk by systems that were built primarily for single name instruments and have also highlighted the importance of assessing P&L risk scenarios under a comprehensive set of spread moves, with single name granularity, and correlation move scenarios, in addition to the Monte-Carlo default risk described in previous sections.

Realized Correlation of Spread Moves and Hedging Frequency

A measure of the tendency of spreads to move together is expressed by the "realized correlation," which for a pair of names is the correlation of changes in spreads over different intervals. This measure is defined in Appendix A. To calculate the correlation between the changes of spreads for a pair of obligors from a time series requires a time window, which is taken to be the CDX.NA.IG.4 life (from March 22 onwards). This creates a pair-wise realized correlation matrix of spread change over different time intervals, and the average of those correlations (off-diagonal elements) is shown in Figure 8.16.

Spreads show a tendency to have more coherent moves over longer time-intervals (e.g., two months) compared to shorter time-intervals (daily). For example, the daily time-interval spread changes have an average correlation of about 16% whereas the correlation of spread changes over two weeks rises to 35 percent, and at two months it becomes ~ 40 percent. Beyond time-intervals of two months the realized correlation appears to fall (although that inference is relatively less reliable considering the time averaging window to infer correlations is approximately nine months long).

The relationship of realized correlation with time-interval helps to interpret the performance of the hedging strategy, where hedging every two weeks ends up with a more favorable P&L outcome relative to daily delta hedging, and hedging every two months ends up even better (Figure 8.12). This is a demonstration of monetization of positive index spread gamma when spreads move coherently over the hedging

FIGURE 8.16

Realized Correlation of Spread Moves over Different Time-Intervals, CDX.NA.IG.4 (March 22, 2005 to November 15, 2005).

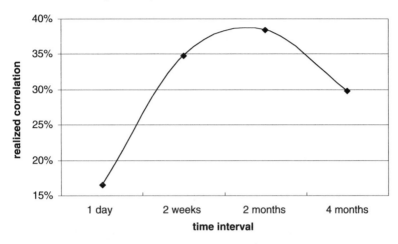

FIGURE 8.17

Impact of Spread Dispersion and Implied Correlation Fluctuations on P&L of a Daily-Hedged Sell Equity Protection Position on CDX.NA.IG.4 (March 22, 2005 to November 15, 2005).

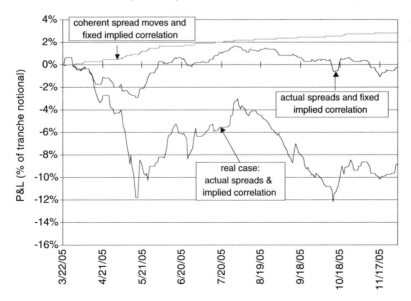

interval for the delta-hedged equity tranche. In the extremely artificial case where there is a perfect coherence of spread moves (i.e., all spreads move homogeneously) and no movement in implied correlation, the mere act of delta hedging would result in perpetual P&L gains (Figure 8.17).

In the more realistic case, idiosyncratic spread moves and the associated movements in the implied correlation parameters compete with coherent spread moves, thus more frequent CS01-hedging in itself does not guarantee the least volatile P&L profile and of course not the most favorable P&L outcome. Of course, the time window of this analysis is limited, and further analysis is needed in a framework that integrates market moves and default events to elucidate a definitive hedging strategy.

SUMMARY AND CONCLUSIONS

Throughout this chapter, we have investigated the P&L sensitivity of three popular, positive carry CDO trades. In particular, spread, correlation and default sensitivity highlighted the non linearity in tranche products and the fallacy of employing credit-delta as the primary risk measure for CDO trading. Furthermore, we show that within some popular CDO trading strategies, a higher carry is associated with higher mtm sensitivity to these additional risks.

Systematic Versus Idiosyncratic Risks

We have shown how the return of synthetic CDOs depends on spread movements throughout the life of the transaction and the interaction of hedging and realized spread correlation. Single name spread convexity, while providing an important measure of issuer risk, is not sufficient to fathom CDO trading risk–reward, as the mtm sensitivity to marketwide spread changes ("index spread convexity") can have a different sign from the "idiosyncratic spread convexity." If all spreads widen together by much more than 1 bps, a P&L gain is booked while independent spread moves (or single defaults) causes losses. Furthermore, pricing for the equity tranche appears to have a direct dependence on spread dispersion, which further exacerbates the losses experienced when spreads disperse, as experienced in 2005.

Tranche Pricing Correlation Risks

Positive carry CDO trades are in general long the correlation pricing parameter which can undergo sudden changes that can be caused—amongst other things—by sector credit quality moves (e.g., autos in May 2005) or specific trade flows (leveraged super senior trades—see Chapter 11—in September 2005). These fluctuations in implied correlation reflect an evolving market as it grapples with tranched credit risk in long-short portfolios. These fluctuations in implied correlation also reflect how the market becomes more or less risk averse depending on how coherently the spreads move, and a discernable correlation between the equity tranche pricing/correlation and the cross-sectional spread dispersion measure has been noted.

Credit Event Risk Versus Credit "Delta" Risk

We have also shown that the positive carry synthetic CDO trades in which the traders wealth increases with time in the absence of any market moves, can be created with little CS01 risk, yet being long credit exposures insofar as the trades have a marginal default sensitivity (VOD) that is negative, i.e., a loss in the event of a default, for all the names in the CDO reference pool. Additionally, for these positive carry CS01-neutral trades, the loss due to default sensitivity (VOD) tends to be an increasing function of the initial carry on the trade. This is different from traditional portfolio credit risk where the sign of the credit-delta exposure (CS01) and default exposure (VOD) tends to be the same. Similarly, the impact of multiple defaults is different from the sum of the impacts of single name defaults. For the delta-hedged CDO trades, multiple defaults can result in P&L gains despite the marginal impact of each individual default being a significant loss.

Risk Aggregation and Reporting Regimes

Marginal and linear sensitivity based risk aggregation provide risk management an appearance of sophistication insofar as every business line's marginal contribution to the overall risks and risk capital "can be" assessed. However such a risk management framework that is adequate for relatively linear credit instrument such as bonds, CDS, portfolios of bonds and CDS, has to evolve significantly to deal with a credit-type risk associated with synthetic CDOs as discussed above. Many popular synthetic CDO trades do not even show up on the radar of such traditional risk management schemes that are largely driven by *credit-delta* exposures—which provides the lowest common denominator of exposures than "can be aggregated." Risk reports will have to first stop equating credit-delta risk exposures with credit event risk exposures because CDO trades may not exhibit any credit-delta risk at inception (based on 1 bps spread moves) and yet be long all the credits underlying the CDO pool from a credit event perspective (i.e., negative VOD). The risk-systems challenge is to replace the highly convenient marginal and linear sensitivity based approaches, with the trade strategy cognizant approach that requires: (1) resolving single name credit description without any bucketing (or artificial separation of "index" and "specific" risks); and (2) a revaluation of the CDO positions under historical and/or simulated scenarios (including spread jumps and defaults) that explicitly describe the CDO reference pool at a constituent level and capture realistic spread dispersion, spread jumps, defaults, recovery, and correlation moves. Then, hedging strategies can be constructed that address all prevalent risks by minimizing P&L hedging-errors rather than only addressing spot spread delta sensitivity.

Models that explicitly capture the joint credit spread and default dynamics and directly address hedging costs provide a competitive advantage over the practice of just fitting static spread copula models to observed prices (without addressing replication-hedging challenges and costs) while accounting for synthetic CDO P&L. As the hedging and risk management strategy evolves, the correlation markets will "learn" to co-exist with the volatility markets (e.g., single name and index CDS swaptions) and the differences in index and single name implied volatilities should provide some constraint on the implied correlation markets. As these two markets start to transmit to each other, the credit modeling paradigm will be further pushed towards directly addressing hedging costs and hedging-errors while accounting for coherent and idiosyncratic spread moves and credit events, as an essential precursor to assessing *fair-value* rather than as an after thought.

APPENDIX A

Spread Measures

Item	Definition
Cross-sectional average spread for a CDO reference pool with N_n names for term T	$\tilde{s}(t_k, T) \equiv \dfrac{1}{N_n} \displaystyle\sum_{i=1}^{N_n} s_i(t_k, T)$
Cross-sectional spread dispersion	$\tilde{\sigma}_s(t_k, T) \equiv \sqrt{\dfrac{1}{N_n} \displaystyle\sum_{i=1}^{N_n} (s_i(t_k, T) - \tilde{s}(t_k, T))^2}$
Normalized cross-sectional spread dispersion	$\tilde{\sigma}_s(t_k, T) / \tilde{s}(t_k, T)$
Spread change over n days	$\Delta s_i(t_k, T; n) \equiv s_i(t_{k+n}, T) - s_i(t_k, T)$
Average of spread change over n days with N_d day dataset	$\overline{\Delta s_i}(T; n) = \dfrac{1}{(N_d - n)} \displaystyle\sum_{j=1}^{N_d - n} \Delta s_i(t_j, T, n)$
Standard deviation of spread change over n days with N_d day data	$\sigma_{\Delta s_i}(T; n) = \sqrt{\dfrac{1}{(N_d - n)} \displaystyle\sum_{j=1}^{N_d - n} \left(\Delta s_i(t_j, T, n) - \overline{\Delta s_i}(T; n) \right)^2}$
Pair-wise realized correlation of spread change over n days	$\rho_d(T; n)$ $\equiv \dfrac{\displaystyle\sum_{m=1}^{N_d - n} \left(\Delta s_i(t_m, T; n) - \overline{\Delta s_i}(T; n) \right)\left(\Delta s_j(t_m, T; n) - \overline{\Delta s_j}(T; n) \right)}{\sigma_{\Delta s_i} \sigma_{\Delta s_j} \times (N_d - n)}$,
Cross-sectional average realized correlation of spread change over n days	$\tilde{\rho}(T; n) = \dfrac{2}{N_n(N_n - 1)} \displaystyle\sum_{i=2}^{N_n} \sum_{i=1}^{i-1} \rho_{ij}(T, n)$

Disclaimer: The authors make no representation as to the accuracy or completeness of the information provided. The views expressed here are those of the authors, and do not necessarily represent those of their employers.

CHAPTER 9

Cash and Synthetic Collateral Debt Obligations: Motivations and Investment Strategies

Olivier Renault

In this chapter, we discuss the key motivations for investment in the structured credit's most popular product to date—collateral debt obligations (CDOs). We tackle this vast area by breaking it down into the two main structured credit markets: cash CDOs and synthetic CDOs. Although these two markets are broadly defined as CDOs, they are very different in terms of structure, underlying assets, and investor focus. Accordingly, we will deal with the motivations for both of these markets separately. First, we will discuss cash CDOs that are natural extension of asset-backed security (ABS) technology to more lumpy assets. Then, we will address synthetic CDOs that apply credit derivative technology to portfolios. Both markets share some of the same motivations for issuance, which we will discuss in the next section.

THE MOTIVATIONS OF A CDO ISSUER

The two main motivation for issuing CDOs are the need to free up capital or optimize return on capital, and rating arbitrage, i.e., the possibility to fund assets more cheaply in securitized format than by holding them on balance sheet.

Balance Sheet Optimization

Optimizing return on regulatory and economic capital is a key concern for bank portfolio managers. Reducing the capital backing existing holdings can help redeploy the capital to more profitable businesses, shrink the balance sheet, or boost returns.

One obvious way of reducing the capital held is to sell a particular set of assets that are capital-intensive. But these assets tend also to be the ones that yield more and selling them could harm the return on the banks portfolios. CDO technology enables banks to keep most of the returns while significantly reducing regulatory capital. The idea is to sell the assets to a separate bankruptcy-remote special purpose entity, thereby ridding the balance sheet of these assets and then buying back the equity tranche of the CDO, which has a levered first-loss exposure to the original assets and a correspondingly high yield.

Figure 9.1 provides an example of optimization of return on regulatory capital. Many regulators impose a one-for-one capital charge for holding the equity of a CDO but only an 8 percent capital charge for holding debt. This means that, should the bank decide to hold 2 percent of equity and 30 percent of the second loss (debt) of a CDO, it would have to hold a minimum of 2 percent $\times$ 1 + 30 percent $\times$ 8 percent = 4.4 percent of the notional in capital. In practice, the bank would usually *not* hold any of the debt but only retain the equity. Therefore, it would only have to hold

FIGURE 9.1

Example of a Bank's Strategy to Improve its Return on Capital using Cash CDOs. (*Citigroup*)

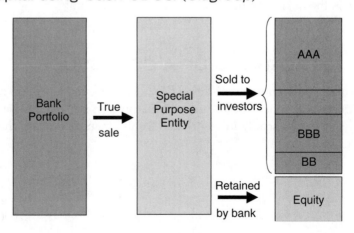

2 percent capital in our example. This contrasts with 8 percent capital to be held against the loans on the balance sheet. Thus, even with a first-loss piece requiring a one-for-one holding of capital, this strategy still typically can improve the return on the capital held against it. In our example, the capital drops by a factor of four, whereas the return may drop by only one half. Furthermore, the operation can drastically reduce the amount of assets on the balance sheet, and therefore help the bank extend new loans. The Balance sheet management was the original motivation behind cash CDOs, but balance sheet CDOs went out of fashion. They made a significant comeback in 2005.

By 2001, as the credit derivative market developed, banks were able to hedge credit exposure synthetically through the use of credit default swaps (CDSs) and, later, portfolio CDSs. The advantage of synthetic securitization is that the original assets are still owned by the bank, but because some of the credit risk is hedged, a reduction of capital can be achieved.

The rationale of the trade is the same as for cash CDO, but it does not involve a true sale of assets. The bank buys protection on the second loss piece of its loan book and retains the first loss. Because assets remain on the balance sheet, a full deduction of capital cannot be achieved but the hedged portion would typically benefit from a reduction of capital from 8 percent to 1.6 percent. The much lower costs involved in synthetic reduction of risk compared to a true sale partly offset the lower reduction in capital. The added benefit of synthetic balance sheet CDOs is that the risk transfer can occur without the original borrower's knowledge that the bank has hedged the credit risk. This enables banks to maintain or even increase relationships with borrowers while keeping the bank's risk exposures to individual borrowers under control (Figure 9.2).

Spread/Rating Arbitrage

Arbitrage CDOs, whether cash or synthetic, are motivated mainly by the mismatch between the return on assets (spread on loans or CDSs) and the cost of liabilities (spread on CDO notes). Because spreads on both sides are partly driven by ratings, it is often possible to tranche up a portfolio where the weighted average spread on rated liabilities is significantly lower than the spread generated by the assets. This enables to generate excess spread for equity holders who are often the arrangers of the transaction. The main difference between a balance sheet CDO and

FIGURE 9.2

Example of Improvement of Return on Capital Using Synthetic CDO Technology. (*Citigroup*)

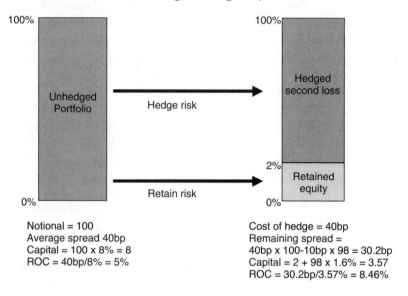

Notional = 100
Average spread 40bp
Capital = 100 x 8% = 8
ROC = 40bp/8% = 5%

Cost of hedge = 40bp
Remaining spread =
40bp x 100-10bp x 98 = 30.2bp
Capital = 2 + 98 x 1.6% = 3.57
ROC = 30.2bp/3.57% = 8.46%

an arbitrage CDO is the fact that assets for arbitrage deals are purchased specifically for the transaction rather than assets held on the arrangers books.

Often a manager is employed to manage the underlying collateral in order to satisfy rating agency criteria and to avoid defaults. The manager is incentivised by the fees he earns during the life of the transaction. Investors in the debt tranches of arbitrage-driven CDOs are motivated by a different type of "arbitrage": CDO tranches tend to offer more yield than cash assets (bonds and loans) with similar ratings. We will now describe investors' motivations in more detail.

MOTIVATIONS OF A CDO INVESTOR

Improving Returns Under Rating Constraints

Many fixed-income investors have strict rating constraints for their investments while also facing yield targets. The tightness of spreads prevailing over the last few years has made it hard for these investors to achieve their return targets while maintaining the risk of their portfolios within their risk limits. In order to achieve it, many have turned to CDOs that are typically higher yielding than cash assets. For example, in December 2005, AAA corporate bonds were trading at a spread of 5 basis points over Libor, whereas CDOs with comparable maturities were offering spreads between 25 basis points (AAA CLOs—Collateral Loan Obligations) and 50 basis points (AAA synthetic investment-grade CDOs).

There are several reasons for this rating arbitrage.

♦ First, the secondary market liquidity on tranches of CDOs is lower than that of corporate bonds. A higher spread is therefore justified to compensate for the lack of liquidity.

♦ Second, and related to the previous point, some portfolio managers are restricted from investing in structured credit, either by internal constraints or by guidelines determined by their investors or regulators. This creates market segmentation and a lower potential demand for CDOs than cash assets.

♦ Third, CDOs are leveraged investments and usually have higher mark-to-market volatility (or beta) than corporate bonds. This is particularly true of synthetic CDOs. Even buy-and-hold investors often mark their portfolios to market and require to be compensated for this extra volatility by means of a higher spread.

♦ Fourth, cash assets and CDOs have different recovery profiles. A corporate bond, in the event of default, is likely to have some nonzero recovery value. A common assumption in the investment-grade credit market is a recovery of 40 cents to the dollar. A tranche, however, has the potential to be completely wiped out if the number of defaults in the underlying pool is large enough.

♦ Lastly, there may be a perception among investors that CDOs are simply more risky than cash assets, despite having the same rating. This is difficult to judge historically as CDO rating histories are still relatively short and the type of products has evolved considerably over the years. The poor performance of high-yield CBOs (Collateral Bond Obligation) issued in the late nineties may however have contributed to this negative perception, although CBOs have now almost disappeared from the new issue market.

Diversified Exposure to Different
Underlying Asset Classes

Another reason for the success of CDOs is that they enable investors to access a large pool of underlying assets (Figure 9.3). This brings immediate diversification benefits and enables some investors to get exposure to assets they do not generally invest in.

For cash CDOs, the most popular asset classes are loans (for CLOs) and mezzanine or senior tranches of ABSs (CDOs of ABS). By buying a cash CDO, a corporate bond investor can enhance yield (as discussed earlier) while only bringing limited correlation in his portfolio as loans, and ABSs are typically not highly correlated with investment-grade corporate bonds.

CDO investors also benefit from the expertise of the collateral manager who often has a track record in managing loans or ABS assets. Furthermore, the manager brings his ability to source the assets, which can be difficult in periods of high demand as we saw in the last few years.

FIGURE 9.3

Average Spreads per Rating for Various Asset Classes. (*Citigroup*)

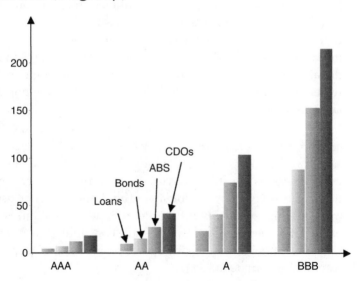

Tailored Risk and Return Profiles

CDOs are often said to have tailored risk return profiles. The "tailoring" can be performed in at least four ways: choice of underlying assets, choice of leverage, choice of rating, and choice of maturity.

One of the main advantages of CDOs is that they let investors disconnect their choice of risk from their choice of asset class. In a traditional bond portfolio, investors who are restricted to hold investment-grade paper will be forced to invest in well-rated bonds even if they believe the value is in noninvestment-grade issues. With CDOs, the same investor can access noninvestment-grade collateral while securing a high-grade rating for his investment.

Conversely, investors looking for high return may still want to have exposure to AAA ABS for diversification or value purposes. This can be achieved by buying an equity piece of a CDO of ABS.

SYNTHETIC CDOS

Synthetic CDOs are one of the key products in the structured credit world. They are portfolios of CDS that are tranched and sold on to investors based on their risk/reward preferences. Figure 9.4 illustrates the basic

FIGURE 9.4

Simple Synthetic CDO Structure and AAA Tranche Loss Mechanics. (*Citigroup*)

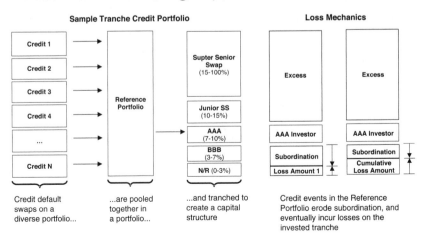

| Credit default swaps on a diverse portfolio... | ...are pooled together in a portfolio... | ...and tranched to create a capital structure | Credit events in the Reference Portfolio erode subordination, and eventually incur losses on the invested tranche |

setup of a standard synthetic CDO and how losses accrue up the capital structure, starting with the erosion of the most junior tranche (equity) and progressively affecting mezzanine and more senior tranches.

Over the last several years, synthetic CDOs have evolved through different stages, from full capital structure deals to single tranches. Today, they are firmly established as a credit investment and hedging tool. In the following sections, we will discuss the motivation behind synthetic CDOs and their main differences with cash products. We will also address who the participants to that market are and what are the main investment strategies followed by hedge funds and real money investors in the synthetic CDO market.

COMPARISON TO CASH CDOS

Synthetic and cash CDOs have many similarities as they offer leveraged exposures to a diversified basket of credits. Synthetic CDOs reference CDSs which are standardized bilateral contracts, whereas cash CDOs are more akin to a miniature bank, financing real assets, and distributing cash flows. Some of the main differences between the two types of products are listed below:

- *Separation of credit risk from other types of risk.* Synthetic structures are not exposed to interest rates, prepayments, and other types of risk that are common in cash CDOs. In particular, they allow investors to disconnect their choice of interest rate duration to that of credit duration.

- *Sourcing collateral: asset diversity and speed of ramp-up.* Using synthetic credit risk transfer technology, originators are not limited by the ability to physically source the collateral assets. Synthetic CDOs can be structured very fast as they do not require a ramp-up period. On the other hand, the need of dealers to hedge single-tranches restricts the universe of names that can be included in synthetic deals. These are normally only credits that are traded in the single-name CDS market.

- *Single-tranche versus full-capital structure deals.* Unlike cash CDOs where the entire capital structure is sold, synthetic CDOs are usually structured as single-tranche deals where only the risk of a limited part of the capital structure is sold to investors. Dealers hold the residuals risks (spreads, defaults, correlation, etc.) that are aggregated and hedged in their correlation book. Full-capital structure synthetic CDOs are rare but attractive for dealers as they prevent imbalances in their correlation books.

♦ *Simplified CDO structures.* Standard synthetic CDOs are much simpler than cash CDOs as they only involve the distribution of default losses. Cash CDOs rely on complex cash flow waterfalls and various technical features such as interest coverage and overcollateralization tests, prepayments, etc. The simplicity of synthetics have enabled structurers and investors to use simple models for pricing and risk management with only a limited number of inputs (CDS spreads, correlations, and tranching details). Proper modeling of cash CDOs require a detailed knowledge of the underlying pool of assets and of the cash flow distribution rules.

♦ *Customization and easy execution.* The simplicity of synthetic CDOs allows them to be customized in terms of size and attachment points for each individual tranche. Investors can select their reference portfolios and choose the credit exposure that best fits into their investment strategy.

♦ *Static versus managed structures.* Index-linked tranches are static in their nature, but bespoke tranches can be managed. In private transactions, investors can play the role of the manager if the structure includes credit substitution rights, and publicly placed synthetic deals usually include an external manager.

♦ *Liquid and transparent market for standard index-linked tranches.* Index-linked tranches are some of the most liquid products in the credit space. With the growth of CDS indices referencing new asset classes and the increasing number of liquid tenors, we expect that the index-linked tranche market will continue to expand. Derivatives referencing index-linked tranches are also likely to be introduced in coming years. No such benchmark exists for cash CDOs.

♦ *Shorting the credit risk in a leveraged form.* Unlike for cash CDOs that are primarily buy-and-hold investments, investors can take long or short positions in synthetic tranches. Synthetic CDO markets provide a variety of different directional and hedging investment opportunities. Short buckets can also be included in bespoke synthetic CDOs to mitigate the effect of a credit market selloff.

MOTIVATION BEHIND SYNTHETIC CDO INVESTORS

Synthetic CDOs gained their popularity from the variety of advantages they offer over cash CDOs or other related credit investments. These differences will be discussed in greater details next, but the advantages of synthetics are primarily their ease of structuring, their ability to separate funding (interest rate component) and risk transfer (credit risk component), and the ability they offer to investors to express views on the market.

Liquidity of Index Tranches and Flexibility of Bespokes

One of the most important motivations behind the use of synthetic structures is the flexibility and customization that can be achieved by the single-tranche technology. Instead of structuring a full-capital structure CDO, synthetic CDOs are issued in single-tranche form, where each transaction is a transfer of the credit risk between the seller and the buyer of protection on a specific part of the capital structure (e.g., from 3 to 7 percent on Figure 9.4). In that way, investors can target their specific risk/return profiles, and originators combine and manage outstanding positions in aggregated portfolios ("correlation books").

The synthetic CDO market is separated into flow tranche products, such as index-linked tranches that are primarily used as relative value and hedging tools, and bespoke (customized) tranches, which are private or publicly placed synthetic CDOs with a structure that is designed to fit investor needs. Liquidity and transparency in CDX/iTraxx index-linked tranches shaped the correlation market in the variety of ways. Credit investors can take on long or short leveraged positions, look for relative value trades, or express directional view strategies. On the other side, dealers are using index-linked tranches to hedge their positions in the bespoke products. In the recent past, we have experienced a significant improvement in liquidity of index-linked tranche across the term structure.

More Growth to Come

The development of synthetic indexes outside the corporate credit domain, in particular in ABS, should contribute to future expansion. The bespoke tranche market has also been developing at a rapid pace. Buy-and-hold investors, who focus on senior bespoke tranches, use these products not just as a leveraged investment, but also to achieve diversification of their positions. Leveraged accounts can find attractive investment opportunities in the junior and equity tranches of customized portfolios, as dealers are usually left with the overhang of bespoke equity positions from the process of placing customized senior tranches to traditional investors. In the past, credit hedge funds have been the natural buyers of the equity residual. As index-linked synthetic tranches become even more liquid and transparent, the key advantage of bespoke products is in customization: investors can select the credits in the reference pool and also customize the size and attachment point of the tranche.

Some Drawbacks as Well

Synthetic CDOs also have some drawbacks compared to cash products. The accounting treatment of derivatives and their perceived mark-to-market volatility can be major obstacles for certain types of investors. As synthetic tranches are marked-to-market and largely held by leveraged accounts, the tranche market can go through strong technical periods leading to significant repricings, as witnessed in May 2005. The relative youth of the synthetic CDO market compared to the seasoned cash CDO market may also be of concern to some investors. In particular, they may question the ability of single-tranche products to withstand a credit market downturn and a pick-up in default rates. CDS are bilateral contracts and not "real assets," and there is an element of legal risk whenever defaults occur in synthetic CDO pools.

SYNTHETIC CDOS: WHO BUYS WHAT AND WHY?

As mentioned previously, one of the main attractions of CDOs (cash or synthetic) is that they enable to split the choice of the credit risk of the actual investment (the tranche) from that of the underlying assets. For example, an investor may want to buy AAA paper but based on BB collateral. This property of CDOs makes them accessible to a very large section of the investment community, from risk averse pension funds to yield hungry hedge funds (Figure 9.5).

FIGURE 9.5

Schematic Distribution of Synthetic CDO Tranche Investors. (*Citigroup*)

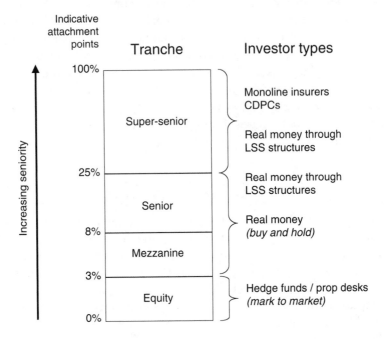

Hedge Funds and Proprietary Desks

Investors at the bottom end of the capital structure (equity and very junior mezzanine tranches) are primarily hedge funds and bank proprietary desks. These are investors willing to take first loss risk against the expectation of high returns, often in excess of ten percent per annum. These investors mark their positions to market and tend to delta-hedge them, either by buying single-name protection, by shorting an index, or a mezzanine tranche.

Real Money Investors

"Real money" investors (asset managers, banks, insurance companies, pension funds, etc.) primarily focus on mezzanine and senior tranches, which are safer than equity but offer lower returns. They tend to be buy-and-hold and often rating-sensitive investors who are attracted by the higher spread offered by synthetic CDOs compared to cash products with identical ratings.

Dealers and Other Market Participants

One of the key differences between cash and synthetic CDOs is that synthetics most often are not full-capital structure deals but single-tranche CDOs. This means that structurers do not sell all the risk of the underlying portfolio of CDS, but only a portion, e.g., the 3 to 9 percent tranche. Strong demand for mezzanine tranches risk from real money investors can lead dealers holding significant positions. Figure 9.6 illustrates schematically the residual position of a dealer after selling a mezzanine tranche to an investor in two extreme scenarios. In the first scenario, the dealer sells the mezzanine tranche risk to the investor and does not hedge its position, resulting in a net short mezzanine position. In the second scenario, the mezzanine is hedged with the full underlying portfolio of CDS, resulting in long equity and super senior positions. These positions (long equity, long super senior, and short mezzanine) are typical of the dealer community.

Dealers therefore hold significant positions in their correlation books and are not mere arrangers of deals, as is often the case for cash CDOs. Equity risk is either retained by dealers or passed on to hedge funds. Super senior tranches can also be retained by the bank or sold to monoline insurers (wrappers) or to Credit Derivative Product

FIGURE 9.6

Dealer's Residual Position After Selling Mezzanine Tranche Risk. (*Citigroup*)

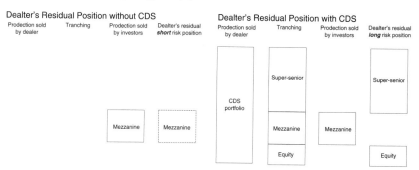

Companies (CDPCs). The risk on these tranches can also be transferred to real money investors in leveraged super senior (LSS) structures. LSS consists of recourse leverage notes referencing the super senior tranche, and levered several times to enhance return. They are usually designed to have a low probability of recourse (justifying a AAA rating) but their leverage makes them quite sensitive to mark-to-market fluctuations, hence their better suitability for buy-and-hold investors. We will return to LSS in the section on double leverage.

SYNTHETIC CDO STRATEGIES

Investment strategies in synthetic CDOs are as diverse as investors in tranches. Broadly speaking, we can split strategies into leverage trades, relative value trades, and directional trades. Tranches can also be used for hedging portfolios.

Taking Leverage

The tranching of CDS portfolios distributes the risk into the various tranches and introduces leverage. Recall that the delta of a tranche is the sensitivity of that tranche's spread to a one basis point change in the underlying portfolio. By definition, the delta of the portfolio itself (which can be seen as the 0 to 100 percent tranche) is equal to one. Junior tranches have deltas significantly higher than one and very senior tranches have deltas below one. The former are thus levered in spread terms and the latter de-levered. Tranching concentrates most of spread and default risks into the equity and junior mezzanine pieces but, although both sources of risk are higher at the bottom of the capital structure, the split between default risk and spread risk is very different to that of senior tranches. Thanks to their high degree of subordination, senior tranches bear very little default risk but they still suffer from some spread risk. In proportion, equity has more default risk than spread risk and vice versa for the senior. At this stage, it is useful to distinguish between idiosyncratic (single name) spread risk and market-wide spread risk. What we refer to as spread risk, unless clearly mentioned otherwise, is the widening of the entire market or underlying portfolio, not that of a single credit or group of credits. Equity tranches are more sensitive to high spread names, whereas senior tranches tend to react more to low spread names widening. They have different single-name deltas.

Figure 9.7 (right panel) illustrates a tranche combination that relies on these differences in default and spread risks. Assuming that the equity tranche has a delta 20 times higher than that of the senior, one can build a delta-neutral position by buying one unit of equity tranche and selling 20 units of the senior. The resulting position has positive carry to compensate investors for default risk but does not have spread exposure (ignoring convexity). This "bull-bear" trade (long default risk but spread-hedged) was popular with hedge funds but is very sensitive to changes in correlations. In particular, falls in correlations hurt the trade both on its long leg and on its short leg.

In summary, tranching distributes spread and default risks unequally across tranches. Investors can choose what type of risk they want to take and their degree of exposure by taking more or less senior tranches. The spreads paid on the tranches are compensation for both sources of risk. Through tranche combinations risk can be separated into a spread and a default component. Care should be taken not to consider that delta-neutral strategies are immune from all spread risk. Delta-hedging protects from small moves in the average spread of the portfolio, but not from large swings. Tranches exhibit convexity (second order spread sensitivities) that can be significant. Delta-hedging also relies on all spreads moving by an equal amount. We mentioned earlier that tranches have different micro-deltas. An uneven spread widening (with some names widening more than others) will not be perfectly hedge by traditional delta-hedging.

FIGURE 9.7

Indicative Risks and Returns of Tranches and Bull-Bear Combination. (*Citigroup*)

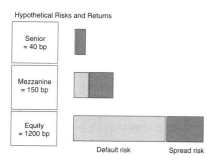

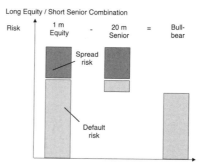

Relative Value Trades

Arguably the main motivation for real money investors for investing in tranches is their search of relative value. Value is present at two levels in synthetic CDOs. First, market segmentation, the lower liquidity of bespoke synthetic tranches compared to cash instruments and their higher mark-to-market sensitivity make them trade cheaper (offering higher spread) than cash products with identical ratings. Rating-sensitive investors, who are able to hold their positions to maturity and can withstand mark-to-market fluctuations, can thus find tranches attractive on a risk/reward basis. Second, as mentioned earlier, tranches enable investors to target underlying assets that they consider offer good relative value, irrespective of their ratings. They can thus extract the value of these underlying assets in levered form and benefit from the additional value brought by synthetic structures.

Directional and "Undirectional" Trades

Both the leverage and the relative value arguments apply equally to cash and synthetic CDOs. A peculiarity of synthetics is that they enable investors to go long or short risk, hence putting on directional trades. We have described long investment strategies earlier, including outright long positions or delta-hedged trades. Investors expecting spreads to widen can take short positions on mezzanine or senior tranches. These should benefit from a spread selloff, and the carry-to-delta ratio is often favorable to tranches compared to untranched portfolios. Investors who are bearish on default risk can buy equity risk protection, although the cost of this hedge is likely to be prohibitively high.

There are countless possible combinations of tranches offering different spread and default risk sensitivities. These enable savvy investors to express views on the direction of spreads and of default risk, possibly in different directions (e.g., bullish on default and bearish on spreads). This is not possible with cash products (bonds, cash CDOs, or even CDS) with which investors must either be long default and spread risk or, if at all possible, short both risks. Other trades do not take views on the direction of the market but rather on the behaviour of a subset of the market (sector, group of credits, etc.). For example, a dispersion trade consists of buying a senior tranche and delta-hedging the position by selling a more junior tranche on the same portfolio. If all spreads move by an equal small amount, the trade should be unaffected (but it suffers from negative convexity for large moves), but if a given subset suffers from a large spread widening while the overall market is unchanged, the trade should benefit. This is due to the greater sensitivity of more junior tranches to idiosyncratic (single name) risk.

Double Leverage

CDOs are leveraged products, as the risk of an entire portfolio is distributed among tranches of smaller size than the portfolio itself. However, structurers have created a newer generation of credit products that provide further leverage on CDOs. This is the case of CDO-squareds and LSS whose investors take exposure to a levered product referencing underlying tranches.

CDO-squareds leverage mezzanine tranches of CDOs (Figure 9.8). A portfolio of mezzanine tranches is collected and tranched again in equity, mezzanine, and senior tranches. This can be done in cash or synthetic formats and follows usually a rating arbitrage logic: more spread can often be achieved for a CDO-squared than with a CDO with same rating. A similar logic underlies CDOs of ABS where the underlying is also tranched.

LSS are levered positions on a very thick and senior tranche of a CDO. These are usually done in synthetic deals, but some form of LSS is also possible for cash CDOs. On the contrary to CDO-squared, the

FIGURE 9.8

Typical Collateral Debt Obligations-Squared Structure. (*Citigroup*)

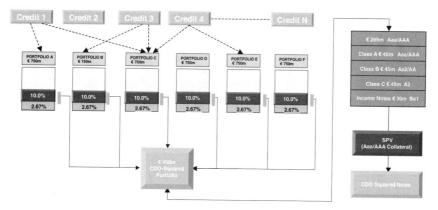

technology underlying LSS does not rely on further tranching but simply on the principle of recourse leverage. An investor can, e.g., take an exposure to a €500 million piece of the super senior tranche of a CDO (say, the 10 to 70 percent tranche), through a €50 million note. The leverage is 10 times (500/50) and the spread on the LSS is 10 times that on the unlevered super senior tranche. However, the contract is designed in such a way that if there are defaults in the portfolio or if spreads widen substantially, the protection buyer can ask the protection seller either to unwind the deal or post further collateral, on top of the initial €50 million.

Tranches as Hedging Vehicles

Although the vast majority of single tranche CDOs are issued to satisfy customer needs to take risk and receive premium, they are also used by some investors as hedging devices. Returning to Figure 9.7 (left panel), the advantage of hedging a portfolio with senior mezzanine tranches becomes apparent. Investors who are comfortable with the default risk on their portfolio can hedge their spread risk (delta-hedging) by buying protection on a mezzanine or senior tranche of a synthetic CDO, referencing the same or similar names. This hedge will offer little protection against default risk but should be significantly cheaper than single-name CDS protection or even index protection. Protection buyers thus only pay for the risk they want to hedge: spread risk in this example. The leverage of CDO tranches will often require hedgers to buy protection on a smaller tranche notional than that of the hedged portfolio, unless they use a very senior tranche (with delta lower than one).

As discussed at the beginning of this chapter, bank loan managers and insurance companies can also use tranche hedges to optimize their return on regulatory capital. Under the current banking regulations, which do not link regulatory capital based on the riskiness of exposures (e.g., all corporate loans and bonds have an 8 percent risk charge irrespective of maturity and default probability), the incentive has been for banks to buy protection on low risk and low yield exposures. These are cheaper to hedge and offer the same capital relief as more risky exposures. However, the new regulatory framework (Basel II) is about to change this (see the last section of this chapter).

MAY 2005: A TURNING POINT IN THE SYNTHETIC CDO MARKET

The May Events

In May 2005, the synthetic CDO market went through its first real crisis, with many tranches being repriced by over 20 percent and some of the most active players in tranche markets facing large losses (Figure 9.9). What did actually happen? The roots of the "crisis" can be found in the positions held by dealers and hedge funds at the time. As explained in a previous section, the natural position of dealers is short mezzanine, long equity, and long super senior, due to the relatively stronger demand for mezzanine (A to AAA rated) compared to other tranches. Hedge funds, on the other hand, have fairly little involvement in super senior, but were running large positions in the long equity/short mezzanine trade described earlier. The mezzanine pieces were in the hands of buy-and-hold investors such as pension funds or insurance companies.

On May 5, Standard & Poor's downgraded both General Motors (GM) and Ford (F) to noninvestment grade, prompting fears of a rapid default. While the downgrades were expected by most market participants, they came earlier than forecast by most and they led to a jump in

FIGURE 9.9

P&L of 5y iTraxx Equity Tranche (in Percent, Roll of March 20 to roll of September 20, 2005). (*Citigroup*)

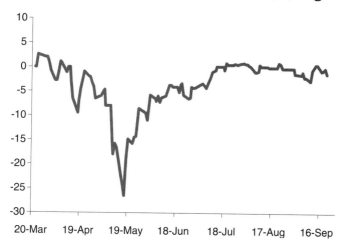

spreads of the two companies. GM and F are two of the most pervasive names in synthetic CDOs and their selling-off triggered a negative mark-to-market move in the price of equity tranches. Some hedge funds then hit their risk limits (value at risk constraints) and tried to close their positions. Unfortunately, because dealers were also long equity and were also facing losses on their positions, they had little appetite for buying the equity positions of hedge funds. The price of equities then started to plummet, resulting in a plunge in correlation (−10 percent in 5y iTraxx equity). The reallocation of losses into equity led to a relative outperformance of mezzanine, which was further fuelled by the unwinding of the equity/mezzanine trades.

Dealers who were caught short mezzanine tried actively to buy it back, but mezzanine tranches were held by long-term investors who did not intend to sell their positions early. This lack of paper led to a large drop in mezzanine spreads with the iTraxx 3 to 6 percent tranche, e.g., trading up to 120 basis points tighter than what its delta would have implied (Figure 9.10).

Mezzanines and equities were not the only tranches affected by the repricing. The tightening of the mezzanine was such that the

FIGURE 9.10

5y iTraxx 3–6% Tranche Spreads: Traded and Implied Spreads and Difference (Basis Points). (*Citigroup*)

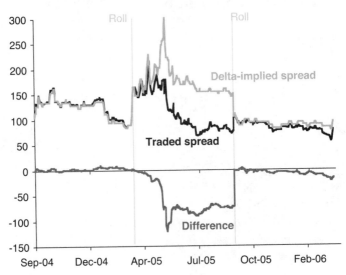

expected loss that came out of it could not be fully absorbed by the equity (which was saturated with risk). Some of it then spilled over to the super senior tranche (Figure 9.11), which, at the time, was neither closely traded nor even closely monitored. The super senior spread then doubled in a few days triggering interest from investors and spurring the growth of LSS.

Consequences

Market participants have reacted to these events by adjusting their trading and hedging behavior. Some of the trends that were started by the correlation turmoil include the following:

- Hedge funds have become significantly more cautious with their equity investments. Some have realized that parts of their losses were due to their high sensitivity to mark-to-market fluctuations and the possibility of hedge fund investors to withdraw their funds at short notice. They have tried to go round this problem by launching funds with longer lock-up periods or vehicles with permanent capital.
- Dealers have become a lot more reticent with issuing large single-tranche mezzanine deals. They are now increasingly trying to issue full capital structure CDOs. When they cannot do so, they try to fill up the capital structure by buying protection on liquid tranches (iTraxx or CDX).

FIGURE 9.11

Reallocation of Expected Losses Among Tranches in May 2005. (*Citigroup*)

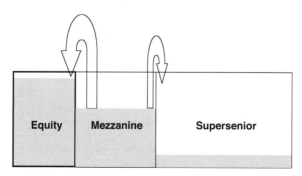

♦ Given the high demand for mezzanine, the main difficulty facing dealers since the May repricing is the placement of equity tranches, as placing the super senior is now straightforward with LSS. Equity tranches are more difficult to sell, as some of their natural holders (hedge funds and dealers) have shied away from them. Structurers have therefore developed new equity-linked products to broaden the investor base of equity. Buy-and-hold investors are particularly sought after, as they could bring more stability to the market and are less prone to overreaction linked to mark-to-market fluctuations. Rated equity and principal-protected structures such as simple combination securities, step-down coupon notes are CPPI (Constant Proportional Portfolio Insurance) referencing equity tranches, have now become mainstream.

♦ While the May events have led to financial innovation such as LSS and the equity-linked structures mentioned earlier, they have also led to the quasi-disappearance of CDO-squared, which were one of the most popular trades of 2004 and early 2005. The tightness of mezzanine spreads has made the rating arbitrage of CDO-squared less compelling, and dealers have become more wary of correlation risk inherent to those structures.

♦ Finally, buy-and-hold investors have moved their preferred maturity to seven year from five year because of the tightness of mezzanine spreads. Seven year is now the most common maturity for synthetic CDOs.

BASEL II–CHANGING THE RULES OF CDO ISSUANCE AND INVESTMENT

We have shown in this chapter how important banks are in the CDO market, both from an issuance perspective (balance sheet CDOs, synthetic hedging) and also as investors. Until now, no global set of regulation is available for banks with respect to CDOs and other securitizations. The current international regulatory framework (Basel I) does not cover CDOs, and each jurisdiction has its own local regulations.

However, this is about to change with the implementation of Basel II rules, from January 2007.*

---

*Banks opting for the standardized approach of Basel II will switch to the new rules in January 2007. Banks opting for the internal ratings-based approach have until January 2008.

For the first time, minimum capital requirements will be homogenized internationally, although local regulators will have significant scope for imposing more stringent rules on top of Basel II minimum standards. The main idea underlying Basel II is to better align capital with the riskiness of investments. For securitization tranches, the riskiness is assessed based on agency ratings, such that more capital is required, e.g., to hold a BB tranche than a AAA tranche of the same CDO. Figure 9.12 shows the capital requirement of the standardized and foundation IRB approaches of Basel II for CDOs. Clearly Basel II gives strong capital incentives for banks to buy well-rated tranches and avoid noninvestment-grade CDOs. The large jump in capital from 6 percent (75 percent × 8 percent) to 34 percent (425 percent × 8 percent) will induce some forced-selling by banks in case of downgrade below investment-grade. This should put some widening pressure on spreads of speculative-grade tranches.

Basel II also clarifies rules for hedging risk using CDOs, e.g., by buying protection on a portion of a bank's loan book. The proposed new banking regulatory framework indeed recognizes tranches as hedging tools, subject to their providing a "significant risk transfer."

FIGURE 9.12

Base Risk Weight for Securitization Tranches Under Basel II. (*BIS, Citigroup*)

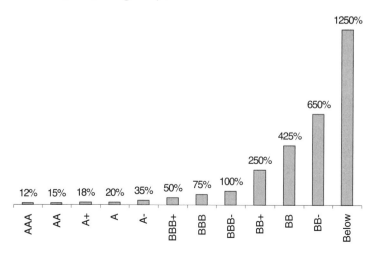

When buying protection on a tranche, the bank can replace the risk weight of the hedged portion of its portfolio with the risk weight of its hedge counterparty (another bank or an insurance company), as described at the begining of this chapter. We expect a lot of activity to take place in the junior mezzanine portion of the capital structure, as it is currently the most efficient in terms of improvement of return on capital.

The Collateral Debt Obligation Methodologies Developed by Standard and Poor's

This chapter consists of two parts. Part 1 describes the modeling of the credit behavior of the assets employed in Standard & Poor's Tool: "CDO Evaluator." Part 2 describes the modeling of the liabilities, i.e., the modeling of the cashflows of Cash CDOs. Both parts are retrieved from S&P criteria.

PART 1 DESCRIPTION OF S&P PORTFOLIO MODEL: CDO EVALUATOR VERSION 3* FOR SYNTHETIC SECURITIZATION

Standard & Poor's Ratings Service's CDO Evaluator is a portfolio credit risk model for analysis of CDO transactions. This document describes the theory, assumptions, and computational methods used by CDO Evaluator version 3.0 to simulate the portfolio loss distribution, which allows determination of the various portfolio risk measures we use in the CDO rating process. The application of the CDO Evaluator to different types of CDO transactions is also discussed.

---

*Extracted from the S&P criteria publication *CDO Evaluator Version 3.0: Technical Document* by Kai Gilkes, Norbert Jobst, and Bob Watson dated 19-12-05.

INTRODUCTION
CDO Market Developments

The collateral debt obligations (CDOs) are financial instruments that transfer the risk associated with a portfolio of assets to one or more investors. The first CDOs were issued as funded (cash) investments by a special purpose entity (SPE), collateralized by portfolios of bonds and loans. Over the past decade, the unfunded (synthetic) CDO market has grown rapidly, especially in Europe. Instead of purchasing a debt instrument of a given entity, the SPE enters into a credit default swap (CDS) that references the entity. This use of credit derivatives technology has greatly simplified the execution of CDO transactions, and has led to a market dominated by so-called "single-tranche" CDOs, bilateral contracts between a buyer and seller of default protection on a portfolio of entities. These can either take the form of a portfolio CDS between two counterparties or a credit-linked note (CLN).

While the rise of the synthetic CDO market has led to a simplification of the debt issuance, the composition of the asset portfolio has become more complex. In addition to corporate bonds and loans, CDO portfolios now routinely include sovereign bonds, loans to small- or mid-sized enterprises (SMEs), asset-backed securities (ABS), and other CDOs. More recently, equity default swaps (EDSs) and commodity options have also been included. The CDO risk transfer mechanism has also increased in complexity. In addition to referencing a single portfolio, a CDO transaction can also reference a number of bespoke CDO tranches, each of which in turn references a single portfolio. This leveraging creates an investment that is more isolated from small numbers of credit events within the underlying portfolio, but is also more likely to suffer large losses once its credit protection is eroded. The so-called "CDO-squared" transactions dominated synthetic CDO issuance in 2004 and in early 2005, partly due to the tightening of CDS spreads.*

In recent years, the synthetic CDO market has witnessed the proliferation of many innovative structures, including CDOs with short CDS positions, forward starting CDOs, nth-to-default baskets, leveraged super senior structures, and constant proportion portfolio insurance (CPPI) structures. These innovations typically arise from a variety of different

---

*These transactions often include a large proportion of ABS in addition to bespoke CDOs, and are therefore often referred to as "CDO of ABS" transactions.

incentives expressed by market participants: from the search by investors for yield in a tight spread environment to the need for investment diversification, from the quest for arbitrage to structures that can be used to express a view on either the credit cycle or idiosyncratic credit risk.

Portfolio Credit Risk Models

Models for CDO risk analysis are generally based on the estimation of transition/default probabilities and recoveries, and the linkage of these through a dependency model, which specifies the joint transition/default behavior. This allows simulation of the full loss distribution at maturity of a portfolio of assets. This loss distribution can then be used to determine a number of useful measures of portfolio risk.

Many portfolio credit risk models fall into the category of "structural" models, which assume that the default behavior of a firm can be determined from knowledge of the firm's assets and liabilities. These are based largely on a model originally proposed by Merton (1974), in which the asset value of a firm is assumed to follow a Geometric Brownian Motion characterized by the asset volatility. Default of the firm occurs when the asset value falls below a certain threshold.* Within this framework, the default correlation between pairs of firms will depend both on the correlation of asset value and the default threshold for each firm. For an excellent review of structural models, see de Servigny and Renault (2004).

In common with many other structural models, CDO Evaluator assumes that the transition/default probabilities, recoveries, and asset value correlations of all assets in the portfolio are exogenous variables, driven either by firm-specific (i.e., idiosyncratic) or systematic effects.[†] However, rather than using *market* data to estimate these parameters for each firm, we estimate these parameters from *historical* data.

For example, in the case of rated firms, we make use of our global CreditPro® database[‡] of rating transitions and defaults over the period

---

*In the Merton framework, this threshold is related to the value of the liabilities of the firm, and hence more highly leveraged firms will generally possess higher probabilities of default, assuming similar asset volatilities.

[†]Other models focus instead on the instantaneous default probability (also known as the "hazard rate" or "default intensity"), which is itself treated as a stochastic process.

[‡]For details, visit www.standardandpoors.com, run a search using "CreditPro," and scroll down to Products & Services.

1981–2003. This method assumes that the rating on a firm is a good proxy for the likelihood of the firm defaulting over a given horizon, when this firm is part of a portfolio.*

Technical Document Outline

The remainder of this part is divided into five sections. In the section "The CDO evaluator model," the underlying mathematical model for CDO Evaluator version 3.0 is outlined, along with the assumptions required by the model for computation of the portfolio loss distribution. The sections "Transition and default probabilities," "Recoveries," and "Correlation" outline the data and methods used to estimate these assumptions, which are the main inputs required by CDO Evaluator. The section "CDO risk analysis" describes the different CDO risk measures computed by CDO Evaluator and the application of CDO Evaluator to the risk assessment of various CDO transactions in the marketplace. Many of the detailed assumptions within CDO Evaluator are contained within the Appendices.

While this document addresses all of the technical aspects of the CDO Evaluator model and assumptions, it does not necessarily cover each and every aspect in full, as the purpose of this document is to provide a complete picture of CDO Evaluator to a wide range of market participants. Those readers interested in drilling down to a deeper technical or theoretical level should consult the references provided within the document.

THE CDO EVALUATOR MODEL

The main purpose of the CDO Evaluator model is the computation of the loss distribution of a portfolio of N assets. This is carried out by first simulating the *default time* of each asset. If the default occurs before the maturity of the CDO transaction, an asset-specific recovery is also computed. If the exposure to each asset at the time of default is known, then the complete distribution of portfolio losses can be computed.

In addition to modeling the individual (or *univariate*) default and recovery of each asset in the portfolio, the *dependency* between defaults of

---

*It is important that this method is used only for portfolios, not single firms. Given that ratings are ordinal measures of creditworthiness, a single rating cannot be uniquely linked to a default probability.

different assets must also be modeled. The standard dependency model in the marketplace is the *Gaussian copula* model, originally proposed by Li (2000). In this approach, a term structure of survival probabilities $S^i(t)$ is assumed for the ith asset. These survival probabilities can be obtained from the cumulative default probabilities for each asset, which we refer to as the *credit curves*. Dependency is then introduced via the Gaussian copula function $C(u_1, \ldots, u_N) = \Phi_\Sigma(y_1, \ldots, y_N)$, where Σ denotes the correlation matrix, Φ the univariate standard normal cumulative distribution function, and Φ_Σ the multivariate standard normal distribution function with correlation matrix Σ. The copula function therefore links together the standard normal variables y_1 to create a multivariate distribution of uniform random variables u_1. The standard normal variables y_i are often referred to as *latent variables* (analogous to asset values in the Merton model).

Correlated default times can therefore be simulated in the following order.

♦ Simulate a vector of N standard normal random variables y_i for each asset;[*]

♦ Impose a given correlation matrix Σ on the above vector.[†]

♦ Calculate $u_i = \Phi(y_i)$; and

♦ Calculate a default time $\tau_i = S^{-1}(u_i)$ for each asset. An example is shown in Figure 10.1 for a "BBB" rated asset.[‡]

If τ_i is less than the maturity T of the CDO transaction, the loss L_i is determined as $L_i = E_i \times (1 - \delta_i)$, where E_i and δ_i are the exposure-at-default and recovery,[§] respectively, for the ith asset. We can therefore write the portfolio loss up to time t, $L(t)$, as:

$$L(t) = \sum_i E_i \times (1 - \delta_i) \times 1_{\{\tau_i \leq t\}},$$

where $1_{\{\tau_i \leq t\}}$ is the default indicator for the ith asset.[‖]

---

[*] Standard normal random numbers are computed using the well-known Mersenne Twister algorithm. For details, see Matsumoto and Nishimura (1998).
[†] This is performed using *Cholesky factorisation*. See, e.g., Glasserman (2004), pp. 72–73.
[‡] S^{-1} is used to denote the quasi-inverse of the survival function.
[§] The recovery can either be assumed to be constant, or drawn from a distribution.
[‖] The default indicator equals 1 if the expression within parentheses is true, and 0 if it is false.

Simulation Procedure

There are two aspects of the simulation procedure worth discussing in more detail in order to understand the impact of different ratings, maturities, and correlation assumptions on the portfolio loss distribution.

Individual Asset Default Behavior

When assets are uncorrelated, the default time for each asset i is simply obtained by comparing a uniform random variable u_i with the credit curve for the asset, as shown in Figure 10.1 for a "BBB" rated asset. If the default time occurs before the asset maturity, a default is recorded. For example, if the "BBB" rated asset in Figure 10.1 has a maturity of seven years, a default is recorded halfway through year five. For the same rating, it is clear that high values of u_i will result in lower default times, whereas low values will result in higher default times. Also, for the same value of u_i, it is clear that higher ratings will experience higher default times.

Joint Default Behavior

When assets are correlated, the uniform random numbers for these assets are first correlated to the required level, as described above. For any pair of correlated assets, this produces values of u_i that tend to move together, i.e., are "clustered" around high or low values. As a result, the default times of the two assets will also move together, leading to more cases in which the assets survive or default together before their maturity.

Using the above Monte Carlo simulation procedure, the distribution of portfolio losses can be determined to a high level of accuracy by generating a sufficient number of default times to achieve satisfactory convergence, which depends on the shape of the credit curves and the degree of asset correlation. For example, highly rated assets will rarely generate low default times, requiring a larger number of simulation trials to generate a significant number of default events before maturity. For most portfolios, 500,000 simulation trials are sufficient to obtain satisfactory convergence.

FIGURE 10.1

An Example of the Use of a [0,1] Uniform Variable to Determine a Default Time from S&P's Credit Curves.

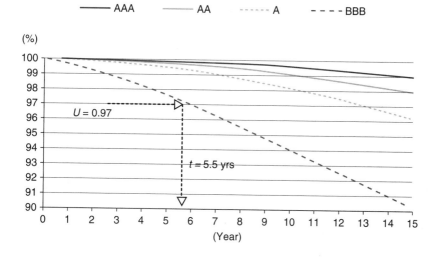

For a CDO linked to a single portfolio of assets, the portfolio loss distribution contains all of the information required to determine the performance of each CDO tranche. When a synthetic CDO references other synthetic CDOs, the model uses a "drill-down" approach to simulate the default times of the assets underlying each CDO. The drill-down approach is outlined in the section "Synthetic CDO squared transactions."*

TRANSITION AND DEFAULT PROBABILITIES
Rated Companies

For rated companies, we make use of our global CreditPro® database of rating transitions and defaults over the period 1981–2003, which contains a ratings history of 9740 companies from January 1, 1981 to December 31,

---

*See also *Drill-Down Approach for Synthetic CDO Squared Transactions*, Standard & Poor's Special Report, December 10, 2003, available to subscribers of RatingsDirect, our Web-based credit analysis system, at www.ratingsdirect.com. The criteria can also be found on our Web site at www.standardandpoors.com.

2003, including 1386 default events. The method used by Standard & Poor's to estimate credit curves involves two stages. The first stage is the estimation of the probabilities of transitions between different ratings—the *transition matrix*. The second stage is the repeated application of this matrix to determine the credit curves.* In both cases, rating transitions are assumed to follow a *Markov process*, in which transition probabilities are constant over time, and do not depend on the previous rating on the firm, e.g., whether the firm was recently upgraded or downgraded.[†]

A straightforward method for estimating a discrete transition matrix from empirical data involves observing the transition of cohorts of firms with the same initial rating. Indeed, our annual transition study[‡] is based on this cohort analysis. We denote the total number of firms in class k at time t by $n_k(t)$, and the total number of observed transitions from class k at time t to class l at time T by $n_{kl}(t, T)$. Assuming rating transitions follow a Markov process, the maximum likelihood estimator of the correspon-ding transition probability, $\hat{q}_{kl}(t, T)$, is $\hat{q}_{kl}(t, T) = (n_{kl}(t, T)/n_k(t))$, for all $k \neq l$. Denoting the average annual transition matrix by $\bar{Q}$, a T-period matrix $\bar{Q}(T)$ is obtained under the Markov assumption using $\bar{Q}(T) = \bar{Q}^T$. Credit curves can be directly extracted from this matrix.

An alternative to the cohort method, which compares the initial and final rating over a certain period, is the *duration* method, which takes into consideration the exact points in time at which rating transitions take place, using the instantaneous probability of transition, the *transition intensity*. We directly estimate transition intensities via the generator matrix $\hat{\Lambda}$ of the (time-homogenous) Markov chain. The off-diagonal transition intensities $\hat{\lambda}_{kl}$ are given by:

$$\hat{\lambda}_{kl}(t, T) = \frac{m_{kl}(t, T)}{\int_t^T n_k(s)ds}, \quad \text{for all } k \neq l,$$

---

*If only default probabilities are required, it is tempting to try to estimate cumulative default probabilities directly from the data. However, given the paucity of historical default data—especially for highly rated firms and/or long time horizons—this method can give unreliable results.

[†]While empirical data suggests that these assumptions do not always hold, they are nonetheless a very useful starting point for estimation purposes.

[‡]See, e.g., *Annual Global Corporate Default Study: Corporate Defaults Poised to Rise in 2005*, Standard & Poor's, January 31, 2005.

FIGURE 10.2

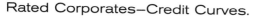

Rated Corporates–Credit Curves.

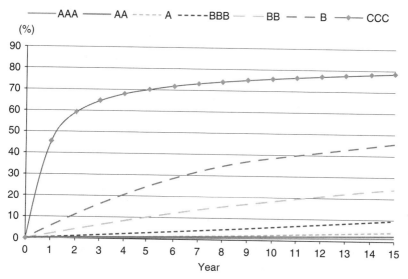

where $m_{kl}(t, T)$ is the total number of transitions from class k to class l ($k \neq l$) over the interval $[t, T]$. The denominator is the total time (in firm-years) firms spend in rating class k over the whole sample period. A T-year transition matrix is then calculated from the generator matrix (with diagonal elements $\lambda_{ll} = -\sum_{k \neq l} \lambda_{kl}$) using $\bar{Q}(T) = \exp\{T \cdot \tilde{\Lambda}\}$.*

By comparing the results of the two methods, and making certain qualitative adjustments,[†] we have derived a single one-year transition matrix that, in our view, produces the best agreement with the average long-term historical default behavior of rated firms. The full matrix is provided in *Appendix A*. The one-year transition matrix is then used to determine the long-term credit curves for each rating category.[‡] These are shown in Figure 10.2 for the major rating categories. The full table of credit curves is also provided in Appendix A.

---

*Further details can be found in Jobst and Gilkes (2003).

†For example, we adjust for certain "ratings momentum" effects reported in the literature. For details, see Fledelius et al. (2004).

‡This is done by raising the matrix to higher powers, and extracting the "default" column of each N-year matrix ($N = 1$–30).

Asset-Backed Securities

Given that structured finance securities themselves are often included in CDO portfolios, their transition and default behavior also needs to be estimated. On average, these securities have exhibited considerable ratings stability over the past two decades, and as a result there have been very few cases of default.* Given the relative paucity of default data, we have so far adopted a conservative treatment of these securities by using corporate default rates as proxies for their long-term default behavior.

In CDO Evaluator version 3.0, ABS default rates are determined using a transition matrix that is based on the average historical ABS transition matrix, with certain qualitative adjustments. These adjustments result in long-term ABS default rates that are approximately 55 and 75 percent of the corresponding default rates for rated firms at investment-grade and non-investment-grade, respectively (for maturities between five and seven years). The ABS credit curves are provided in Appendix A. Note that ABS maturities are capped at seven years for modeling purposes, as we consider that the probability of default of an ABS asset—conditional upon survival for seven years—is negligible.

Sovereign Securities

Given that transition and default data for sovereign debt securities are relatively sparse in comparison with rated firms, the credit curves used for rated firms are currently used as conservative proxies for sovereign default behavior.

Small- to Mid-sized Enterprises

The wealth of financial information obtained by Standard & Poor's Risk Solutions Group on SMEs has been used to create advanced "credit scoring" models for SME default prediction. For example, in Europe, the credit risk tracker (CRT) product can be used to obtain one-year default probability forecasts for more than 1 million SMEs across France, Germany, Italy, Spain, and the U.K. These models have also been used to analyze the historical volatility of default probabilities, in order to create

---

*See, e.g., *Global Structured Securities Rating Performance: 1978–2004*, Standard & Poor's, March 24, 2005.

"rating estimates" that combine one-year default probabilities and annu-alized default volatilities.* By analyzing the transition behavior across dif-ferent rating categories, we have created a one-year SME transition matrix and used it to create credit curves for SMEs. The credit curves are pro-vided in Appendix A. Note that while the rating identifiers are written in the same way as those for traditional Standard & Poor's ratings, they are not obtained through the normal rating analysis conducted by our ana-lysts. It is therefore not possible to make direct comparisons between the credit curves for SMEs and those for other rated entities.

Equity Default Swaps

An EDS is similar to a CDS, in that a protection seller agrees to pay the pro-tection buyer if the contract is triggered. However, as opposed to a credit event, an EDS is linked to the drop of the equity price of the reference entity below a certain barrier, typically 30 percent of the initial price. As a result of extensive analysis of historical equity price data from our Compustat® data-base, capturing approximately 12,000 companies trading in the United States or Canada between 1962 and 2003, we have developed new criteria for estimating the probability of an EDS contract triggering over a given time horizon. Using scoring techniques similar to those described in the pre-vious section, we have identified five variables that are very informative:

- The credit rating;
- The historical equity volatility;
- The market capitalization;
- The historical equity return; and
- The general level of the equity market measured by the current value of the S&P500 compared with the highest value of the pre-vious 10 years.

The resulting EDS scoring models are used to derive a risk score between one and five for each EDS. These scores can then be mapped to an EDS default curve, i.e., the cumulative probability of the EDS contract breach-ing its price barrier.† Further technical details can be found in de Servigny and Jobst (2005). An overview of our criteria for CDOs containing EDS

---

*For example, in the case of two SMEs with low one-year default probabilities but very dif-ferent volatilities, the one with the lower volatility is likely to be assigned a higher rating.
†We can provide these scoring models upon request.

can be found in a forthcoming criteria article, and Appendix A contains further details of the EDS default curves.

RECOVERIES

In general, the level of recovery achieved following a default is uncertain, or *stochastic*. For a debt instrument, such as a bond or loan, recovery depends on a number of factors, for instance, the seniority of the instrument and the economic environment in which the default occurred. However, in the context of synthetic CDOs, recovery can be determined in different ways, including the specification of a fixed level that does not depend on these factors.

In order to properly model the different types of recovery mechanisms included in CDOs, CDO Evaluator treats recoveries in two ways: *fixed* and *variable*. This section outlines the two different methods, both in terms of the rationale for using each method, and the underlying data used to estimate recoveries in each case.

Fixed Recoveries

Although recoveries are usually uncertain, there are two main reasons for using fixed recovery assumptions. First, recovery can in certain transactions be set at a fixed percentage of the amount at risk, e.g., 50 percent.* Secondly, historical data is not always sufficient to allow precise determination of the degree of variability in recoveries. For this reason, a fixed recovery that incorporates some degree of conservatism can be the best compromise. As this clearly involves some level of qualitative judgment, these assumptions are normally determined through a committee process.

Variable Recoveries

In some cases, sufficient historical data exists to allow the degree of variability in recoveries to be explicitly modeled. For example, our LossStats® database† contains recovery information for more than 500 non-financial

---

*This is the recovery level typically used for EDSs.
†For details, visit www.standardandpoors.com, run a search using "LossStats," and scroll down to Products & Services.

public and private U.S. companies that have defaulted since 1988. It contains information on more than 2,000 defaulted bank loans and high-yield bonds, and other debt instruments. This extensive data has allowed us to create recovery distributions for certain types of assets, based on the *beta* distribution, a well-known two-parameter distribution. Specification of the mean and standard deviation of the beta distribution is sufficient for CDO Evaluator version 3.0 to simulate the full range of potential recoveries for each type of asset. These assumptions are provided in Appendix B.

CORRELATION

In addition to specifying the univariate default probabilities and recovery assumptions for each asset in the portfolio, the correlation between pairs of assets must also be specified. As explained in the section "The CDO evaluator model," this is assumed to be the *asset value* correlation between each pair of assets, which is not directly observable in the market. In principle, there are several ways to estimate asset value correlation:

♦ Regression analysis of equity returns within a factor model;
♦ Using equity return correlations as proxies for asset value correlation;
♦ Using credit spread correlations as proxies for asset value correlation;
♦ Inferring asset value correlations from rating migrations; and
♦ Estimating asset value correlations from empirical default observations.

We have chosen to use empirical default observations to estimate the correlation assumptions within CDO Evaluator, as this estimation method is likely to be less prone to the "noise" within equity return data, and the limited time period of credit spread data. In addition, unlike rating migrations, it can be used consistently for a wide range of different rated and non-rated assets, such as corporates, ABS, SMEs, and EDS. In order to determine correlation assumptions for rated firms and EDSs, we have undertaken an extensive analysis of historical data, making use of the CreditPro® and Compustat® databases mentioned earlier. For SMEs, the CRT database mentioned earlier has been used.

We consider several statistical techniques which ensures a good degree of stability, ranging from maximum likelihood methods and factor models, to simple methods based on empirical joint default events. While a detailed overview of these techniques for corporate defaults and EDS can be found in Jobst and de Servigny (2006), the latter approach—frequently referred to as joint default probability (JDP) method—is outlined next, given the significance of correlation estimates for CDO risk analysis.

The JDP method involves two stages. The first is the estimation of the JDP $P_{ij}(t)$ between pairs of companies, either in the same industry or different industries. If pairs of companies are drawn (with replacement) from the database, an estimate of the JDP within an industry is given by:

$$P_{ij}^c(t) = \frac{(D_t^c)^2}{(N_t^c)^2},$$

and between industries by:

$$P_{ij}^{cd}(t) = \frac{D_t^c D_t^d}{N_t^c N_t^d}.$$

In these expressions, D_t^c, D_t^d and N_t^c, N_t^d are the number of defaulted companies and total number of companies in industries c and d, respectively, observed over a time period t. The empirical *default correlation* ρ^{cd} can easily be obtained from the standard correlation equation:

$$\rho^{cd} = \frac{\overline{P}^{cd} - \overline{P}^c \overline{P}^d}{\sqrt{\overline{P}^c(1 - \overline{P}^c)}\sqrt{\overline{P}^d(1 - \overline{P}^d)}}.$$

In this formula, $\overline{P}^k$ denotes the average default probability of companies in industry k.

The second stage of the JDP method is the calculation of the implied asset correlation from the JDPs. This is done using the Gaussian copula model described in the section "The CDO evaluator model" by calculating the asset correlation required to recover the empirically observed JDPs. For two companies, the JDP P_{ij} is given within the model by $P_{ij} = \Phi(Z_i, Z_j, \rho_{ij})$, where $Z_i = \Phi^{-1}(P_i)$ and $Z_j = \Phi^{-1}(P_j)$ are "z-scores" indicating the default threshold for each company. This means that the implied asset correlation ρ_{ij} can be determined by solving $\rho_{ij} = \Phi^{-1}(Z_i, Z_j, P_{ij})$.* In all cases, correlations were estimated within and between different industry sectors. The average intra-industry and inter-industry correlations across

---

*For further details, see Jobst and de Servigny (2006).

the entire datasets were then used to create the assumptions used in CDO Evaluator. These assumptions are contained in Appendix C.

CDO RISK ANALYSIS

This section describes how CDO Evaluator can be applied to different CDO transactions, in order to analyze the risk exposure of each CDO tranche. First, we discuss the different risk measures that can be computed for each CDO transaction, and then go on to show how the model is used in the risk analysis and rating of different CDO transactions. The emphasis here is on synthetic CDO transactions, as these can be completely analyzed by CDO Evaluator, whereas cash CDO transactions require some additional steps, such as modeling the impact of interest rate and currency risk on the interest payments made to each CDO tranche.

Scenario Loss Rate

The primary risk measure used in our analysis of CDO transactions is the scenario loss rate (SLR), which is a quantile of the portfolio loss distribution consistent with a given rating and maturity.* For example, if the rating quantile corresponding to a certain rating and maturity is 0.5 percent, the required percentile of the loss distribution will be 99.5 percent. It is important to note that the rating quantiles have been developed specifically for CDO tranches and are not identical to the corporate credit curves as in previous versions of CDO Evaluator. This is mainly due to the fact that both the corporate credit curves and CDO rating quantiles were highly "idealized" in previous versions, due to a lack of historical data. As described earlier, the corporate credit curves are now based on a more extensive analysis of historical corporate transition and default data, and have therefore been de-linked from the CDO rating quantiles.

Given that there is much less historical performance data for CDOs than the underlying corporates, the CDO rating quantiles have not been determined purely from historical data. In this case, we have used a number of quantitative and qualitative considerations, including the avoidance of potential instability in high investment-grade SLRs when very low CDO quantiles are imposed, and the observation that high degrees of

---

*The mean and standard deviation of the loss distribution are also computed by the CDO Evaluator.

leverage in CDO tranches tend to result in higher average rating volatility than investment-grade corporates. As a result, the CDO rating quantiles are higher than the corporate credit curves at investment-grade rating levels, and converge to the corporate credit curves at low, speculative-grade rating levels. The CDO rating quantiles are provided in Appendix A.

For a synthetic CDO, the SLR is equivalent to the *attachment point* (or credit enhancement) required for a tranche with the relevant rating and maturity. For cash CDOs, the credit enhancement is determined through a cash flow modeling exercise, in which the default times of the asset portfolio are combined with interest rates and currency exchange rates (if required) to determine the overall credit performance of each rated CDO tranche.

Rated Overcollateralization

Once a CDO transaction has been structured, it is possible to determine the extent to which available credit enhancement exceeds the required level. This can be done either for a cash or synthetic tranche. In the latter case, the SROC (synthetic rated overcollateralization) is given simply by:

$$SROC = \frac{PortfolioNotional - SLR}{PortfolioNotional - CreditEnhancement}$$

In the case of cash CDO tranches, the value of any excess spread must also be included, which requires the additional modeling of the transaction cash flows.

Synthetic CDO Tranche Risk Measures

The SLR is a *portfolio* risk measure. There are also several useful CDO *tranche* risk measures, such as the tranche default probability, expected loss, and the loss-given-default.* For a synthetic CDO tranche, these can all be computed by "overlaying" the tranche on the portfolio loss distribution, as shown schematically in Figure 10.3. Here, the tranche has an attachment point equal to 4 percent of the total notional amount of the

---

*Clearly these measures also exist for cash CDO tranches. However, their determination requires the additional step of modelling time-dependent cash flows.

FIGURE 10.3

Hypothetical CDO Portfolio Loss Distribution.

Showing the position of a 4%-8% CDO tranche

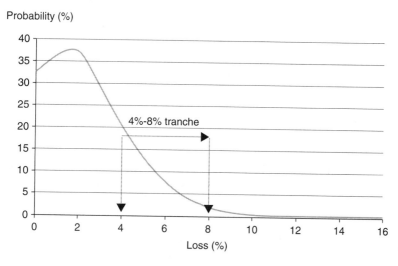

portfolio, and a thickness also equal to 4 percent. This means that the tranche will no longer suffer losses above 8 percent of the portfolio notional amount, and, for this reason, this upper loss level is referred to as the *detachment point* of the tranche.

Tranche Default Probability

Given an attachment point A and detachment point D (i.e., a tranche thickness equal to D−A), the tranche default probability is the probability that portfolio losses at maturity T exceed A. This is given by: $PD^{\text{Tranche}} = P(L(T) \geq A) = E[1_{\{L(t) \geq A\}}]$, where $L(t)$ is the portfolio loss up to time t (see section "The CDO evaluator model"), $1_{\{\}}$ is the indicator function,* and $E[]$ denotes the expectation. This forms the basis for assigning a rating to a synthetic CDO tranche.

In the above expression for the tranche default probability, we assumed that the attachment point A is constant over time. This can easily be generalized to cases where the attachment point is a function of time t, so that the above expression becomes $PD^{\text{Tranche}} = P(L(t) \geq A(t)) = E[1_{\{L(t) \geq A(t)\}}]$.

---

*This equals 1 if the expression within parentheses is true, and 0 if it is false.

In this case, we evaluate the loss distribution at all points in time at which the attachment point changes. As an example, consider a hypothetical seven-year synthetic CDO transaction. If the attachment point is initially set at 3 percent of the portfolio notional balance, but then increases to 5 percent after three years and remains at this level until maturity, we need to evaluate the loss distribution at years three and seven. The cumulative default probability of the tranche is therefore the probability that losses exceed 3 percent by year three, plus the probability that losses exceed 5 percent by year seven, *conditional* upon losses not exceeding 3 percent by year three.

Finally, the time dependency of the attachment point can even be made conditional upon certain levels of loss being reached within the portfolio. For example, it is possible to model transactions in which the attachment point "resets" according to the cumulative loss experienced by the portfolio by a certain date. This dynamic behavior is easily modeled by keeping track of the portfolio loss paths during simulation.

Expected Tranche Loss

The cumulative loss on the tranche at time t, $M(t)$, is given by: $M(t) = (L(t) - A)1_{\{A \le L(t) \le D\}} + (D - A)1_{\{L(t) \ge D\}}$. The expected tranche loss is therefore given by $E[M(t)] = E\lfloor (L(t) - A)1_{\{A \le L(t) \le D\}} + (D - A)1_{\{L(t) \ge D\}} \rfloor$.

Tranche Loss-Given-Default

The tranche loss-given-default is given simply by:

$$LGD^{\text{Tranche}} = \frac{E(M(t))}{PD^{\text{Tranche}}}.$$

Other Tranche Risk Measures

The tranche leverage $\left(\text{Leverage}^{\text{Tranche}} = \dfrac{E(M(t))}{E(L(t))} \right)$ and hedge ratio $\left(HR^{\text{Tranche}} = \dfrac{\text{Leverage}^{\text{Tranche}}}{\text{TrancheNotional}} \right)$ are also useful in quantifying implied tranche performance.

Synthetic CDO-Squared Transactions

Synthetic CDO-squared transactions have now become an established feature of the global CDO marketplace. Rather than referencing secondary market CDO tranches, these transactions typically use portfolio CDSs to create so-called "bespoke" CDO tranches, each referencing a single underlying corporate portfolio. In this way, additional leverage is created above and beyond the leverage already present in each bespoke CDO, resulting in a yield pickup of these structures relative to similarly rated synthetic CDOs.

While some CDO-squared transactions reference only CDOs, many recent CDO-squared transactions have referenced portfolios containing a mixture of CDO and ABS tranches, where the proportion of ABS is typically in the range of 70 to 90 percent by reference notional amount. The ABS component normally consists of funded tranches that exist in the secondary market, whereas the CDO tranches are often tailor-made for the CDO-squared investor. A CDO-squared typically references between 5 and 15 different bespoke CDOs, each of which may reference between 100 and 200 corporate names. At first sight, this might suggest that the underlying corporate reference portfolio could be as large as 3000 names! However, this is not the case, given that the liquid corporate names in the CDS market number between 400 and 600. For this reason, there is normally a significant overlap between the reference portfolios of different bespoke CDOs, ranging from 20 to 30 percent in most cases. The basic structure of a typical CDO-squared transaction is shown schematically in Figure 10.4.

Should a credit event occur on an underlying corporate name, a bidding process is used to establish a recovery, and the resulting loss is allocated to each bespoke CDO that references this name. The overall impact

FIGURE 10.4

Structure of a Typical CDO-Squared Transaction.

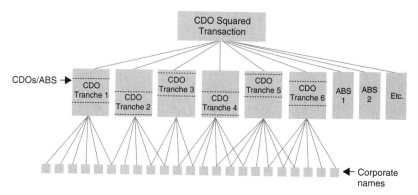

of the credit event will therefore clearly depend on the overlap among the underlying CDO tranches. When the loss allocated to a bespoke CDO exceeds the attachment point of the CDO tranche, the loss is passed through to the CDO-squared transaction. Bespoke CDOs therefore act as "loss filters" between the underlying corporate assets and the CDO-squared. This is very different to the ABS tranches, where a credit event in general triggers a bidding process, the ABS tranche is removed from the CDO-squared reference portfolio, and the resulting loss is allocated to the CDO-squared transaction.

While each bespoke CDO tranche can be analyzed using the approach described earlier, CDO-squared transactions require additional modeling, such as the ability to "drill down" to the corporate names underlying each CDO tranche included within the CDO-squared portfolio. In this way, losses are modeled "from bottom to top," flowing through each bespoke CDO before being allocated to the CDO-squared tranche. This allows the overlap between pairs of bespoke CDO tranches to be explicitly modeled, in addition to their individual default and loss-given-default characteristics.*

Cross-Subordination

One of the innovations in the CDO-squared market has been the introduction of so-called "cross-subordination." This mechanism allows different bespoke CDOs to share the total subordination provided by all bespoke CDOs. For example, eight CDOs with attachment points and thicknesses of €10 million would create a total cross-subordination of €80 million. During the life of the transaction, if any CDO experiences losses greater than €10 million, these losses are not passed through to the CDO-squared until the total aggregate losses exceed €80 million. In this way, the CDO-squared investor is protected from the risk of a small number of CDOs experiencing losses, but is exposed to the risk that a large number of CDOs experience losses.†

This is easily modeled within CDO Evaluator by "tracking" the losses experienced by each bespoke CDO in each simulation step, and

---

* See *Drill-Down Approach for Synthetic CDO Squared Transactions*, Standard & Poor's Special Report, December 10, 2003.
† Another way of stating this is that cross-subordination reduces the idiosyncratic risk specific to each CDO, but increases the systematic risk common to all CDOs.

only passing through the aggregate loss if it exceeds the total available subordination. This can also be extended to cases in which the subordination is only "partially" cross-subordinated (e.g., the CDO-squared transaction is insulated from only 75 percent of the total aggregate subordination of the bespoke CDOs).

Consider a hypothetical CDO-squared with the following characteristics:

♦ The CDO-squared references a portfolio containing eight bespoke CDO tranches and 50 "AAA" rated ABS tranches, with an average asset correlation of 10 percent.

♦ Each bespoke CDO tranche references a portfolio of approximately 100 "A" rated names with 5 percent average asset correlation, equal reference notional amounts of euro;10 million, and assumed recoveries of 35 percent.

♦ Each bespoke CDO tranche has an attachment point of €40 million (consistent with a CDO rating at the "A" rating level) and a detachment point of €0 million, i.e., a tranche thickness of €10 million.

♦ The average overlap between pairs of bespoke CDOs is 33 percent.

♦ Each ABS tranche has a reference notional amount of €10 million and an assumed recovery of 90 percent.

♦ The CDO-squared has a maturity of five years.

The CDO-squared portfolio therefore has a total reference notional amount of €580 million. Of this amount, the ABS portion makes up 86 percent, and the bespoke CDOs 14 percent.

Figure 10.5 shows the loss distribution of the CDO-squared portfolio. In one case, the CDOs are assumed to contribute losses to the CDO-squared without cross-subordination, as described earlier. In the other case, all eight bespoke CDOs are assumed to be cross-subordinated, as described above. In both cases, the probability of zero or small losses is very high, while there is a "tail" of higher losses. However, in the case of the cross-subordinated transaction, the probability of zero/small losses increases significantly, with a corresponding decrease in the probability of larger losses. This means that a senior CDO-squared tranche with a relatively high attachment point has a lower probability of default in the case of cross-subordination, as the total area of the distribution above 6 percent

FIGURE 1 0 . 5

Loss Distribution for Two Hypothetical CDO-Squared Transactions.

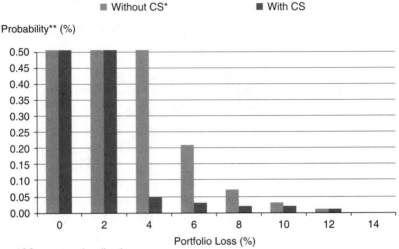

■ Without CS*   ■ With CS

Probability** (%)

Portfolio Loss (%)

*CS - cross-subordination.

**When portfolio loss is assumed to be 0%,those transactions without CS, probability is 86.0%, those with CS, is 88.9%. When protfolio loss is assumed to be 2% probability is 13.0% for those without CS and 10.9% for those with CS. When portfolio loss is assumed to be 4% probability is 0.89% for those without CS and 0.05% for those with CS.

loss is lower. However, this tranche is likely to exhibit a higher loss-given-default.

Long/Short CDS

The CDSs behave in a similar fashion to bilateral insurance contracts. One party (the protection seller) agrees to pay another party (the protection buyer) an amount equal to the reference notional amount of the contract minus a recovery amount in the event of a default of a given reference entity on one or more of its obligations. The recovery amount is normally determined either by physical delivery of a specified obligation or by cash settlement. The details of allowable obligations and settlement procedures are not discussed in any detail here.

In exchange for this contingent payment, the protection buyer pays the protection seller a premium. A CDS therefore consists of two cash

FIGURE 10.6

CDS Payment Mechanics.

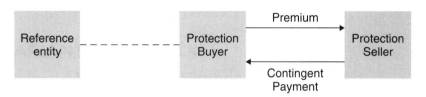

flows: the premium flow and the contingent payment. The "fair value" of the CDS is that which makes the net present value (NPV) of the premium flow exactly equal to the NPV of the contingent payment. Figure 10.6 illustrates the CDS payment mechanics.

When an entity sells protection in CDS form, it is said to take a "long" position, as it receives the same economic loss/benefit as owning a bond issued by the reference entity. Conversely, when an entity buys protection, it takes a "short" position. The CDO Evaluator models a short CDS simply by reversing the sign of the loss (i.e., making it a gain) in the event of default of the reference name, conditional upon the survival of the protection seller. This is one example of the way in which CDO Evaluator treats counterparty risk, which requires additional information on the CDS counterparty when short CDSs are included within the portfolio.

Long/Short CDO Tranches

Using CDS technology, it is also possible to take a short position on an underlying CDO tranche within a CDO-squared transaction. In this case, the CDO-squared buys protection on an underlying CDO tranche, so that if losses exceed the attachment point of the tranche the CDO-squared receives a payment equal to the difference between the net portfolio loss and the tranche attachment point, up to a maximum of the size of the tranche.

Nth-to-Default Baskets

The mechanics of these transactions are similar to those of a CDS (Figure 10.6), except that the reference entity is replaced by a basket of reference entities, and the seller of protection is exposed to the risk of the nth default within the basket. An nth-to-default basket can be treated as a special case of a synthetic CDO containing a small number of equal exposures (typically three to five). As described earlier, the tranche default probability is the probability that portfolio losses at maturity T exceed the attachment point A. For an nth-to-default basket with a fixed recovery δ, the attachment point is clearly equal to $(n-1)\delta$.

APPENDIX A

Transition Matrices and Credit Curves for CDO Evaluator Assets

Rated Firms—One-Year Transition Matrix

(%)	AAA	AA+	AA	AA-	A+	A	A-	BBB+	BBB	BBB-	BB+	BB	BB-	B+	B	B-	CCC+	CCC	CCC-	D
AAA	83.32	8.92	5.20	1.01	0.53	0.25	0.38	0.09	0.17	0.02	0.05	0.05	0.00	0.00	0.00	0.00	0.00	0.00	0.00	0.00
AA+	1.06	78.41	13.10	4.72	1.06	0.84	0.25	0.14	0.20	0.10	0.09	0.01	0.01	0.00	0.00	0.00	0.00	0.00	0.00	0.00
AA	0.58	0.56	77.07	13.10	4.26	2.68	0.68	0.54	0.31	0.03	0.01	0.04	0.04	0.01	0.01	0.03	0.00	0.03	0.00	0.01
AA-	0.09	0.22	1.28	75.53	13.57	6.78	1.31	0.44	0.26	0.15	0.09	0.06	0.02	0.05	0.12	0.01	0.00	0.00	0.00	0.01
A+	0.02	0.10	0.57	2.46	76.39	13.05	4.74	1.25	0.69	0.20	0.07	0.14	0.08	0.08	0.12	0.01	0.01	0.00	0.00	0.02
A	0.07	0.09	0.49	0.87	2.13	79.20	11.75	3.17	1.20	0.35	0.19	0.20	0.13	0.08	0.04	0.01	0.00	0.00	0.01	0.02
A-	0.14	0.05	0.21	0.39	1.17	2.81	77.11	13.52	3.21	0.75	0.20	0.15	0.06	0.11	0.03	0.03	0.00	0.00	0.00	0.03
BBB+	0.09	0.08	0.12	0.26	1.01	3.37	2.64	75.69	14.09	1.56	0.36	0.28	0.08	0.08	0.05	0.02	0.00	0.01	0.00	0.20
BBB	0.04	0.03	0.19	0.22	0.62	1.50	2.92	8.87	71.49	11.42	1.08	0.72	0.22	0.17	0.15	0.03	0.01	0.02	0.00	0.29
BBB-	0.12	0.01	0.12	0.28	0.38	1.01	1.30	3.87	12.81	64.39	4.87	5.67	2.26	1.15	0.45	0.37	0.09	0.05	0.02	0.81
BB+	0.19	0.01	0.02	0.20	0.17	0.47	1.00	1.16	4.83	11.79	68.09	8.24	1.24	0.64	0.27	0.13	0.03	0.03	0.01	1.48
BB	0.01	0.04	0.09	0.06	0.03	0.32	0.24	0.51	1.41	3.96	13.35	69.32	6.02	1.48	0.47	0.21	0.09	0.08	0.02	2.30
BB-	0.00	0.01	0.01	0.06	0.12	0.20	0.35	0.49	1.01	1.60	4.85	12.37	66.63	7.08	1.08	0.38	0.16	0.10	0.04	3.46
B+	0.00	0.07	0.02	0.13	0.06	0.11	0.31	0.41	0.24	0.42	0.93	3.40	14.42	68.09	5.66	0.92	0.35	0.24	0.10	4.10
B	0.01	0.00	0.13	0.02	0.06	0.36	0.37	0.30	0.28	0.16	0.71	1.49	3.58	16.42	63.13	5.08	1.44	0.79	0.36	5.29
B-	0.02	0.00	0.01	0.01	0.19	0.18	0.19	0.36	0.22	0.17	0.40	0.59	1.32	6.81	15.08	58.99	4.60	2.00	0.72	8.14
CCC+	0.02	0.00	0.01	0.02	0.86	0.09	0.08	0.62	0.35	0.05	0.17	0.19	1.20	3.64	7.00	15.58	40.65	4.20	1.70	23.58
CCC	0.36	0.01	0.01	0.01	0.04	0.38	0.39	0.73	0.43	0.12	1.06	1.09	0.68	2.09	8.08	6.87	12.57	17.02	2.51	45.56
CCC-	0.01	0.00	0.00	0.00	0.01	0.02	0.02	0.04	0.04	0.06	0.71	0.20	2.08	2.36	1.79	2.71	1.72	12.48	9.34	66.41
D	0.00	0.00	0.00	0.00	0.00	0.00	0.00	0.00	0.00	0.00	0.00	0.00	0.00	0.00	0.00	0.00	0.00	0.00	0.00	100.00

Rated Firms—Credit Curves

(%)	AAA	AA+	AA	AA-	A+	A	A-	BBB+	BBB	BBB-	BB+	BB	BB-	B+	B	B-	CCC+	CCC	CCC-	AAA
Year																				
1	0.0002	0.001	0.008	0.014	0.018	0.022	0.033	0.195	0.294	0.806	1.484	2.296	3.457	4.100	5.295	8.138	23.582	45.560	66.413	
2	0.005	0.009	0.039	0.048	0.064	0.080	0.121	0.427	0.684	1.805	2.915	4.506	6.624	8.124	10.833	16.559	38.046	59.087	79.205	
3	0.016	0.027	0.085	0.102	0.138	0.172	0.262	0.701	1.162	2.899	4.312	6.597	9.516	11.903	15.940	23.729	46.605	64.704	82.840	
4	0.034	0.056	0.144	0.178	0.240	0.298	0.451	1.023	1.713	4.034	5.681	8.567	12.164	15.388	20.479	29.578	52.040	67.875	84.478	
5	0.061	0.098	0.219	0.276	0.371	0.459	0.686	1.391	2.323	5.179	7.020	10.424	14.595	18.571	24.463	34.333	55.809	70.042	85.513	
6	0.097	0.153	0.310	0.397	0.531	0.655	0.966	1.805	2.980	6.316	8.327	12.175	16.832	21.462	27.947	38.234	58.626	71.685	86.285	
7	0.144	0.224	0.420	0.543	0.719	0.887	1.287	2.261	3.672	7.434	9.598	13.826	18.895	24.083	30.999	41.476	60.850	73.005	86.907	
8	0.204	0.311	0.549	0.713	0.937	1.152	1.648	2.756	4.390	8.529	10.831	15.387	20.800	26.457	33.680	44.209	62.672	74.105	87.429	
9	0.276	0.414	0.700	0.909	1.184	1.451	2.047	3.284	5.127	9.598	12.025	16.862	22.563	28.610	36.046	46.543	64.204	75.041	87.877	
10	0.362	0.536	0.872	1.130	1.458	1.782	2.479	3.842	5.876	10.637	13.179	18.258	24.197	30.565	38.145	48.559	65.517	75.853	88.268	
11	0.463	0.678	1.066	1.377	1.761	2.143	2.943	4.425	6.634	11.649	14.295	19.580	25.717	32.346	40.016	50.320	66.657	76.565	88.614	
12	0.581	0.839	1.284	1.650	2.092	2.534	3.434	5.029	7.396	12.631	15.371	20.834	27.132	33.973	41.694	51.871	67.659	77.197	88.921	
13	0.715	1.020	1.525	1.947	2.448	2.952	3.952	5.651	8.160	13.587	16.410	22.025	28.453	35.463	43.206	53.248	68.548	77.762	89.197	
14	0.867	1.223	1.790	2.270	2.830	3.396	4.491	6.287	8.923	14.515	17.414	23.157	29.689	36.832	44.575	54.481	69.343	78.271	89.447	
15	1.037	1.447	2.078	2.617	3.237	3.864	5.051	6.936	9.684	15.418	18.383	24.234	30.849	38.096	45.822	55.592	70.060	78.732	89.674	
16	1.225	1.693	2.389	2.988	3.666	4.353	5.628	7.593	10.441	16.296	19.320	25.262	31.940	39.265	46.962	56.599	70.710	79.154	89.882	
17	1.433	1.961	2.724	3.382	4.117	4.862	6.221	8.258	11.193	17.152	20.226	26.243	32.969	40.351	48.009	57.517	71.304	79.541	90.074	
18	1.661	2.250	3.080	3.798	4.588	5.390	6.826	8.928	11.940	17.985	21.103	27.181	33.941	41.363	48.976	58.359	71.848	79.898	90.250	
19	1.908	2.561	3.458	4.234	5.078	5.934	7.442	9.602	12.680	18.798	21.952	28.081	34.862	42.310	49.872	59.134	72.350	80.229	90.414	
20	2.175	2.893	3.858	4.690	5.586	6.493	8.068	10.279	13.414	19.591	22.777	28.944	35.737	43.198	50.706	59.851	72.816	80.538	90.568	
21	2.462	3.246	4.277	5.165	6.110	7.065	8.701	10.957	14.142	20.365	23.577	29.773	36.570	44.034	51.486	60.517	73.249	80.827	90.711	
22	2.769	3.619	4.715	5.657	6.648	7.648	9.340	11.636	14.862	21.123	24.355	30.572	37.365	44.824	52.216	61.140	73.654	81.099	90.845	
23	3.095	4.012	5.171	6.164	7.200	8.241	9.985	12.314	15.575	21.863	25.112	31.343	38.126	45.571	52.904	61.723	74.035	81.355	90.973	
24	3.440	4.423	5.644	6.687	7.763	8.844	10.633	12.991	16.281	22.589	25.850	32.087	38.855	46.281	53.554	62.271	74.394	81.598	91.093	
25	3.804	4.853	6.133	7.223	8.337	9.454	11.284	13.667	16.980	23.300	26.570	32.808	39.556	46.958	54.169	62.789	74.733	81.828	91.207	
26	4.187	5.300	6.638	7.772	8.921	10.070	11.937	14.340	17.671	23.997	27.272	33.506	40.230	47.604	54.754	63.280	75.055	82.048	91.316	
27	4.586	5.763	7.156	8.331	9.513	10.692	12.591	15.010	18.356	24.682	27.959	34.184	40.881	48.222	55.311	63.746	75.362	82.258	91.419	
28	5.003	6.241	7.686	8.901	10.112	11.318	13.245	15.678	19.033	25.354	28.630	34.842	41.510	48.815	55.844	64.190	75.655	82.459	91.519	
29	5.436	6.735	8.229	9.480	10.718	11.947	13.900	16.342	19.704	26.015	29.288	35.483	42.118	49.386	56.355	64.615	75.935	82.653	91.614	
30	5.885	7.241	8.781	10.066	11.329	12.580	14.553	17.003	20.367	26.665	29.933	36.108	42.709	49.936	56.845	65.022	76.205	82.839	91.706	

ABS—Credit Curves

Year	AAA	AA+	AA	AA-	A+	A	A-	BBB+	BBB	BBB-	BB+	BB	BB-	B+	B	B-	CCC+	CCC	CCC-
1	0.000	0.001	0.004	0.008	0.010	0.012	0.018	0.107	0.162	0.443	1.113	1.722	2.593	3.075	3.971	6.104	17.687	34.170	49.810
2	0.003	0.005	0.021	0.026	0.035	0.044	0.067	0.235	0.376	0.993	2.186	3.380	4.968	6.093	8.125	12.419	28.535	44.315	59.404
3	0.009	0.015	0.047	0.056	0.076	0.094	0.144	0.386	0.639	1.595	3.234	4.948	7.137	8.927	11.955	17.797	34.954	48.528	62.130
4	0.019	0.031	0.079	0.098	0.132	0.164	0.248	0.562	0.942	2.219	4.261	6.426	9.123	11.541	15.359	22.184	39.030	50.906	63.359
5	0.033	0.054	0.120	0.152	0.204	0.252	0.377	0.765	1.278	2.848	5.265	7.818	10.946	13.928	18.347	25.750	41.857	52.532	64.135
6	0.053	0.084	0.171	0.219	0.292	0.360	0.531	0.993	1.639	3.474	6.245	9.131	12.624	16.097	20.960	28.676	43.970	53.764	64.714
7	0.079	0.123	0.231	0.299	0.396	0.488	0.708	1.243	2.020	4.089	7.198	10.370	14.171	18.062	23.249	31.107	45.638	54.754	65.180

SMEs—Credit Curves

(%) Year	A+	A	A-	BBB+	BBB	BBB-	BB+	BB	BB-	B+	B	B-	CCC+	CCC	CCC-
1	0.049	0.067	0.110	0.196	0.238	0.441	0.442	1.020	1.711	2.980	8.495	12.138	31.592	31.592	31.592
2	0.130	0.184	0.276	0.459	0.596	0.953	1.038	2.150	3.486	6.077	15.082	22.373	46.180	46.180	46.180
3	0.244	0.345	0.497	0.786	1.039	1.546	1.756	3.351	5.277	9.048	20.311	29.758	54.423	54.423	54.423
4	0.393	0.551	0.772	1.174	1.552	2.209	2.572	4.592	7.043	11.802	24.508	35.127	59.634	59.634	59.634
5	0.578	0.799	1.096	1.618	2.123	2.928	3.462	5.852	8.758	14.318	27.929	39.162	63.185	63.185	63.185
6	0.800	1.088	1.466	2.112	2.742	3.690	4.407	7.115	10.406	16.603	30.770	42.301	65.747	65.747	65.747
7	1.059	1.416	1.877	2.651	3.401	4.486	5.391	8.367	11.979	18.679	33.171	44.821	67.684	67.684	67.684
8	1.354	1.782	2.327	3.230	4.092	5.306	6.401	9.602	13.478	20.571	35.237	46.900	69.205	69.205	69.205
9	1.685	2.182	2.812	3.842	4.811	6.145	7.425	10.814	14.906	22.303	37.042	48.655	70.440	70.440	70.440
10	2.049	2.615	3.328	4.484	5.550	6.995	8.456	11.998	16.265	23.896	38.640	50.168	71.470	71.470	71.470
11	2.446	3.078	3.872	5.151	6.306	7.854	9.487	13.155	17.561	25.369	40.072	51.493	72.348	72.348	72.348
12	2.874	3.570	4.441	5.839	7.075	8.716	10.512	14.282	18.799	26.739	41.369	52.670	73.111	73.111	73.111
13	3.330	4.088	5.033	6.545	7.855	9.580	11.528	15.380	19.984	28.020	42.555	53.729	73.785	73.785	73.785
14	3.814	4.629	5.645	7.264	8.641	10.444	12.533	16.450	21.121	29.223	43.648	54.692	74.388	74.388	74.388
15	4.323	5.193	6.275	7.996	9.433	11.304	13.524	17.491	22.213	30.358	44.663	55.576	74.934	74.934	74.934
16	4.855	5.776	6.920	8.737	10.227	12.160	14.500	18.506	23.264	31.433	45.610	56.393	75.434	75.434	75.434
17	5.410	6.377	7.580	9.485	11.023	13.011	15.461	19.495	24.278	32.456	46.501	57.154	75.894	75.894	75.894
18	5.983	6.995	8.251	10.238	11.819	13.856	16.405	20.459	25.258	33.431	47.341	57.867	76.322	76.322	76.322
19	6.575	7.628	8.932	10.996	12.614	14.695	17.333	21.399	26.206	34.365	48.138	58.539	76.722	76.722	76.722
20	7.184	8.273	9.623	11.756	13.408	15.526	18.245	22.317	27.126	35.261	48.896	59.175	77.098	77.098	77.098

EDSs

(%)	Barrier (10%) EDS score				
	1	2	3	4	5
0	0.000	0.000	0.000	0.000	0.000
1	0.008	0.018	0.056	0.154	1.721
2	0.028	0.059	0.238	0.717	4.477

(%)	Barrier (20%) EDS score				
	1	2	3	4	5
0	0.000	0.000	0.000	0.000	0.000
1	0.011	0.037	0.141	0.693	4.532
2	0.035	0.120	0.413	2.044	9.830
3	0.088	0.386	0.888	3.608	14.278
4	0.177	0.584	1.621	5.168	17.766
5	0.354	0.905	2.615	6.564	20.725
6	0.443	1.356	3.296	8.129	22.636
7	0.535	1.788	3.759	9.510	24.283
8	0.732	2.071	4.592	10.296	25.802
9	0.947	2.432	5.308	11.408	27.048
10	1.203	2.770	5.759	12.300	28.273
3	0.070	0.117	0.428	1.469	7.114
4	0.124	0.196	0.694	2.317	9.180
5	0.177	0.316	1.049	3.131	11.463
6	0.266	0.480	1.390	3.981	13.096
7	0.358	0.696	1.558	4.901	13.896
8	0.400	0.838	1.836	5.463	14.656
9	0.572	0.992	1.989	6.142	15.340
10	0.828	1.105	2.383	6.554	16.089

(%)	Barrier (30%) EDS score				
	1	2	3	4	5
0	0.000	0.000	0.000	0.000	0.000
1	0.026	0.146	0.395	1.463	8.484
2	0.088	0.452	1.423	4.588	16.460
3	0.265	1.152	2.435	7.264	21.918
4	0.531	1.745	3.868	9.807	26.184
5	0.885	2.147	5.608	11.824	29.463
6	1.242	2.885	6.441	13.747	31.614
7	1.516	3.964	7.155	15.333	33.685
8	2.010	4.483	8.313	16.568	35.638
9	2.332	5.153	9.234	18.050	36.945
10	2.715	5.773	9.853	18.942	38.239

CDOs Tranches—Credit Curves and Rating Quanties

(%)	AAA	AA+	AA	AA-	A+	A	A-	BBB+	BBB	BBB-	BB+	BB	BB-	B+	B	B-	CCC+	CCC	CCC-
1	0.0004	0.002	0.013	0.024	0.027	0.033	0.049	0.234	0.353	0.967	1.632	2.525	3.803	4.510	5.824	8.138	23.582	45.560	66.413
2	0.009	0.017	0.062	0.078	0.097	0.121	0.185	0.514	0.825	2.142	3.211	4.946	7.260	8.885	11.751	16.674	38.104	59.145	79.233
3	0.030	0.050	0.135	0.166	0.212	0.263	0.396	0.850	1.405	3.415	4.758	7.230	10.401	12.960	17.152	24.004	46.752	64.835	82.905
4	0.065	0.104	0.232	0.290	0.372	0.459	0.676	1.246	2.073	4.728	6.276	9.380	13.265	16.694	21.921	30.025	52.288	68.078	84.581
5	0.118	0.182	0.356	0.452	0.578	0.709	1.020	1.704	2.812	6.046	7.763	11.403	15.886	20.087	26.089	34.945	56.158	70.313	85.650
6	0.190	0.287	0.512	0.654	0.830	1.013	1.424	2.221	3.607	7.352	9.216	13.310	18.291	23.156	29.725	38.996	59.071	72.019	86.454
7	0.285	0.420	0.701	0.897	1.128	1.368	1.883	2.792	4.443	8.635	10.632	15.110	20.503	25.929	32.903	42.374	61.383	73.396	87.105
8	0.405	0.584	0.927	1.182	1.472	1.774	2.395	3.413	5.310	9.891	12.007	16.810	22.544	28.435	35.692	45.227	63.284	74.546	87.653
9	0.552	0.781	1.191	1.509	1.859	2.226	2.954	4.076	6.198	11.116	13.340	18.418	24.432	30.702	38.151	47.666	64.886	75.529	88.124
10	0.728	1.013	1.493	1.876	2.290	2.724	3.557	4.777	7.103	12.309	14.631	19.941	26.182	32.760	40.331	49.776	66.261	76.383	88.535
11	0.934	1.280	1.833	2.285	2.762	3.263	4.198	5.510	8.017	13.471	15.881	21.386	27.809	34.633	42.275	51.620	67.459	77.133	88.899
12	1.173	1.583	2.213	2.733	3.273	3.841	4.873	6.269	8.937	14.602	17.091	22.758	29.326	36.343	44.018	53.245	68.512	77.799	89.223
13	1.445	1.923	2.631	3.219	3.822	4.454	5.578	7.050	9.860	15.704	18.261	24.064	30.744	37.910	45.589	54.691	69.448	78.396	89.515
14	1.750	2.300	3.086	3.742	4.404	5.099	6.309	7.850	10.783	16.776	19.394	25.307	32.073	39.353	47.014	55.985	70.287	78.935	89.779
15	2.089	2.712	3.577	4.299	5.018	5.773	7.063	8.664	11.704	17.822	20.491	26.494	33.323	40.685	48.313	57.154	71.045	79.426	90.020
16	2.463	3.160	4.102	4.887	5.662	6.473	7.836	9.490	12.621	18.841	21.555	27.629	34.501	41.920	49.504	58.214	71.733	79.875	90.241
17	2.870	3.643	4.659	5.506	6.332	7.195	8.624	10.325	13.534	19.836	22.587	28.716	35.614	43.070	50.600	59.183	72.363	80.288	90.445
18	3.311	4.158	5.247	6.152	7.026	7.937	9.426	11.167	14.441	20.808	23.589	29.759	36.670	44.145	51.614	60.073	72.943	80.671	90.634
19	3.784	4.704	5.863	6.823	7.741	8.696	10.238	12.013	15.342	21.757	24.563	30.761	37.674	45.153	52.557	60.895	73.479	81.028	90.810
20	4.289	5.281	6.506	7.516	8.475	9.470	11.059	12.862	16.235	22.686	25.510	31.727	38.630	46.102	53.438	61.658	73.978	81.362	90.974
21	4.823	5.885	7.172	8.229	9.225	10.256	11.886	13.713	17.121	23.596	26.434	32.658	39.545	46.998	54.263	62.370	74.445	81.675	91.129
22	5.386	6.514	7.860	8.961	9.989	11.053	12.718	14.563	17.999	24.487	27.334	33.558	40.420	47.848	55.040	63.036	74.883	81.971	91.275
23	5.975	7.168	8.567	9.707	10.765	11.857	13.552	15.413	18.869	25.361	28.213	34.429	41.261	48.655	55.774	63.663	75.296	82.252	91.413
24	6.590	7.843	9.292	10.468	11.552	12.668	14.389	16.261	19.731	26.218	29.071	35.273	42.070	49.426	56.470	64.256	75.686	82.518	91.544
25	7.229	8.538	10.032	11.240	12.346	13.484	15.226	17.105	20.584	27.060	29.911	36.093	42.851	50.162	57.132	64.817	76.057	82.773	91.670
26	7.889	9.250	10.786	12.022	13.147	14.303	16.062	17.947	21.428	27.887	30.733	36.890	43.605	50.868	57.764	65.351	76.411	83.017	91.789
27	8.568	9.979	11.550	12.811	13.954	15.125	16.897	18.784	22.264	28.700	31.538	37.667	44.335	51.546	58.369	65.860	76.750	83.251	91.904
28	9.266	10.721	12.325	13.608	14.764	15.947	17.729	19.616	23.092	29.499	32.327	38.423	45.043	52.200	58.950	66.348	77.074	83.476	92.015
29	9.980	11.475	13.108	14.409	15.576	16.770	18.559	20.443	23.911	30.286	33.102	39.162	45.731	52.832	59.508	66.816	77.386	83.693	92.121
30	10.708	12.240	13.897	15.213	16.390	17.591	19.385	21.265	24.721	31.061	33.863	39.884	46.400	53.443	60.047	67.266	77.687	83.903	92.224

APPENDIX B

Recovery Assumptions for CDO Evaluator Assets

	Corporate						Sovereign	
	Senior secured		Senior unsecured		Subordinate		—	
	Mean (%)	Standard deviation (%)	Mean (%)	Standard deviation (%)	Mean (%)	Standard deviation (%)	Mean (%)	Standard deviation (%)
United States	50.0	20.0	38.0	20.0	19.8	15.0	25.0	12.0
Isle of Man	15.0	8.0	10.0	5.0	5.0	3.0	25.0	12.0
Liechtenstein	15.0	8.0	10.0	5.0	5.0	3.0	25.0	12.0
Canada	50.0	20.0	38.0	20.0	19.8	15.0	25.0	12.0
Egypt	15.0	8.0	10.0	5.0	5.0	3.0	25.0	12.0
Morocco	15.0	8.0	10.0	5.0	5.0	3.0	25.0	12.0
Algeria	15.0	8.0	10.0	5.0	5.0	3.0	25.0	12.0
Tunisia	15.0	8.0	10.0	5.0	5.0	3.0	25.0	12.0
Senegal	15.0	8.0	10.0	5.0	5.0	3.0	25.0	12.0
Ghana	15.0	8.0	10.0	5.0	5.0	3.0	25.0	12.0
Nigeria	15.0	8.0	10.0	5.0	5.0	3.0	25.0	12.0
Gabonese Republic	15.0	8.0	10.0	5.0	5.0	3.0	25.0	12.0
Barbados	15.0	8.0	10.0	5.0	5.0	3.0	25.0	12.0
Botswana	15.0	8.0	10.0	5.0	5.0	3.0	25.0	12.0
South Africa	15.0	8.0	10.0	5.0	5.0	3.0	25.0	12.0
Greece	40.0	20.0	29.0	15.0	14.0	11.0	25.0	12.0
The Netherlands	47.0	20.0	31.0	15.0	16.0	12.0	25.0	12.0
Belgium	40.0	20.0	29.0	15.0	14.0	11.0	25.0	12.0
France	40.0	20.0	29.0	15.0	14.0	11.0	25.0	12.0
Spain	40.0	20.0	29.0	15.0	14.0	11.0	25.0	12.0
Portugal	40.0	20.0	29.0	15.0	14.0	11.0	25.0	12.0
Luxembourg	40.0	20.0	29.0	15.0	14.0	11.0	25.0	12.0
Ireland	60.0	20.0	32.5	15.0	17.0	13.0	25.0	12.0
Iceland	15.0	8.0	10.0	5.0	5.0	3.0	25.0	12.0
Albania	15.0	8.0	10.0	5.0	5.0	3.0	25.0	12.0

Recovery Assumptions For CDO Evaluator Assets

Recovery Assumptions For CDO Evaluator Assets							
	Corporate						Sovereign
	Senior secured		Senior unsecured		Subordinate		—
	Mean (%)	Standard deviation (%)	Mean (%)	Standard deviation (%)	Mean (%)	Standard deviation (%)	Mean (%)	Standard deviation (%)
Malta	15.0	8.0	10.0	5.0	5.0	3.0	25.0	12.0
Cyprus	15.0	8.0	10.0	5.0	5.0	3.0	25.0	12.0
Finland	37.4	20.0	24.3	15.0	12.7	9.0	25.0	12.0
Bulgaria	15.0	8.0	10.0	5.0	5.0	3.0	25.0	12.0
Hungary	15.0	8.0	10.0	5.0	5.0	3.0	25.0	12.0
Lithuania	15.0	8.0	10.0	5.0	5.0	3.0	25.0	12.0
Latvia	15.0	8.0	10.0	5.0	5.0	3.0	25.0	12.0
Estonia	15.0	8.0	10.0	5.0	5.0	3.0	25.0	12.0
Moldova	15.0	8.0	10.0	5.0	5.0	3.0	25.0	12.0
Monaco	15.0	8.0	10.0	5.0	5.0	3.0	25.0	12.0
Ukraine	15.0	8.0	10.0	5.0	5.0	3.0	25.0	12.0
Croatia	15.0	8.0	10.0	5.0	5.0	3.0	25.0	12.0
Slovenia	15.0	8.0	10.0	5.0	5.0	3.0	25.0	12.0
Bosnia & Herzegovina	15.0	8.0	10.0	5.0	5.0	3.0	25.0	12.0
Macedonia	15.0	8.0	10.0	5.0	5.0	3.0	25.0	12.0
Italy	40.0	20.0	29.0	15.0	14.0	11.0	25.0	12.0
Romania	15.0	8.0	10.0	5.0	5.0	3.0	25.0	12.0
Switzerland	47.0	20.0	31.0	15.0	16.0	12.0	25.0	12.0
Czech Republic	15.0	8.0	10.0	5.0	5.0	3.0	25.0	12.0
Slovak Republic	15.0	8.0	10.0	5.0	5.0	3.0	25.0	12.0
Austria	37.4	20.0	24.3	15.0	12.7	9.0	25.0	12.0
United Kingdom	60.0	20.0	32.5	15.0	17.0	13.0	25.0	12.0
Bermuda	15.0	8.0	10.0	5.0	5.0	3.0	25.0	12.0
Denmark	37.4	20.0	24.3	15.0	12.7	9.0	25.0	12.0
Sweden	37.4	20.0	24.3	15.0	12.7	9.0	25.0	12.0
Norway	37.4	20.0	24.3	15.0	12.7	9.0	25.0	12.0
Grenada	15.0	8.0	10.0	5.0	5.0	3.0	25.0	12.0
Poland	15.0	8.0	10.0	5.0	5.0	3.0	25.0	12.0
Germany	47.0	20.0	31.0	15.0	16.0	12.0	25.0	12.0
Belize	15.0	8.0	10.0	5.0	5.0	3.0	25.0	12.0
Guatemala	15.0	8.0	10.0	5.0	5.0	3.0	25.0	12.0
El Salvador	15.0	8.0	10.0	5.0	5.0	3.0	25.0	12.0
Honduras	15.0	8.0	10.0	5.0	5.0	3.0	25.0	12.0
Nicaragua	15.0	8.0	10.0	5.0	5.0	3.0	25.0	12.0

	Corporate						Sovereign	
	Senior secured		Senior unsecured		Subordinate		—	
	Mean (%)	Standard deviation (%)	Mean (%)	Standard deviation (%)	Mean (%)	Standard deviation (%)	Mean (%)	Standard deviation (%)
Costa Rica	15.0	8.0	10.0	5.0	5.0	3.0	25.0	12.0
Panama	15.0	8.0	10.0	5.0	5.0	3.0	25.0	12.0
Peru	15.0	8.0	10.0	5.0	5.0	3.0	25.0	12.0
Mexico	15.0	8.0	10.0	5.0	5.0	3.0	25.0	12.0
Argentina	15.0	8.0	10.0	5.0	5.0	3.0	25.0	12.0
Brazil	15.0	8.0	10.0	5.0	5.0	3.0	25.0	12.0
Chile	15.0	8.0	10.0	5.0	5.0	3.0	25.0	12.0
Colombia	15.0	8.0	10.0	5.0	5.0	3.0	25.0	12.0
Venezuela	15.0	8.0	10.0	5.0	5.0	3.0	25.0	12.0
Bolivia	15.0	8.0	10.0	5.0	5.0	3.0	25.0	12.0
Ecuador	15.0	8.0	10.0	5.0	5.0	3.0	25.0	12.0
Paraguay	15.0	8.0	10.0	5.0	5.0	3.0	25.0	12.0
Suriname	15.0	8.0	10.0	5.0	5.0	3.0	25.0	12.0
Uruguay	15.0	8.0	10.0	5.0	5.0	3.0	25.0	12.0
Malaysia	25.0	15.0	16.2	10.0	8.5	6.0	25.0	12.0
Australia	37.4	20.0	24.3	15.0	12.7	9.0	25.0	12.0
Indonesia	18.0	10.0	11.7	5.0	6.1	3.0	25.0	12.0
Philippines	18.0	10.0	11.7	5.0	6.1	3.0	25.0	12.0
New Zealand	40.0	20.0	29.0	15.0	14.0	11.0	25.0	12.0
Singapore	34.6	20.0	22.5	12.5	11.7	8.0	25.0	12.0
Thailand	25.0	15.0	16.2	10.0	8.5	6.0	25.0	12.0
Papua New Guinea	15.0	8.0	10.0	5.0	5.0	3.0	25.0	12.0
Cook Islands	15.0	8.0	10.0	5.0	5.0	3.0	25.0	12.0
Russia	15.0	8.0	10.0	5.0	5.0	3.0	25.0	12.0
Kazakhstan	15.0	8.0	10.0	5.0	5.0	3.0	25.0	12.0
Dominican Republic	15.0	8.0	10.0	5.0	5.0	3.0	25.0	12.0
Japan	21.0	10.0	13.5	8.0	7.0	5.0	25.0	12.0
South Korea	25.0	15.0	16.2	10.0	8.5	6.0	25.0	12.0
Vietnam	15.0	8.0	10.0	5.0	5.0	3.0	25.0	12.0
North Korea	15.0	8.0	10.0	5.0	5.0	3.0	25.0	12.0

Recovery Assumptions For CDO Evaluator Assets

Recovery Assumptions For CDO Evaluator Assets							
	Corporate					Sovereign	
	Senior secured		Senior unsecured		Subordinate		—	
	Mean (%)	Standard deviation (%)	Mean (%)	Standard deviation (%)	Mean (%)	Standard deviation (%)	Mean (%)	Standard deviation (%)
Hong Kong	34.6	20.0	22.5	12.5	11.7	8.0	25.0	12.0
China	25.0	15.0	16.2	10.0	8.5	6.0	25.0	12.0
Trinidad & Tobago	15.0	8.0	10.0	5.0	5.0	3.0	25.0	12.0
Jamaica	15.0	8.0	10.0	5.0	5.0	3.0	25.0	12.0
Taiwan (Republic of China)	25.0	15.0	16.2	10.0	8.5	6.0	25.0	12.0
Turkey	15.0	8.0	10.0	5.0	5.0	3.0	25.0	12.0
India	15.0	8.0	10.0	5.0	5.0	3.0	25.0	12.0
Pakistan	15.0	8.0	10.0	5.0	5.0	3.0	25.0	12.0
Sri Lanka	15.0	8.0	10.0	5.0	5.0	3.0	25.0	12.0
Lebanon	15.0	8.0	10.0	5.0	5.0	3.0	25.0	12.0
Jordan	15.0	8.0	10.0	5.0	5.0	3.0	25.0	12.0
Syrian Arab Republic	15.0	8.0	10.0	5.0	5.0	3.0	25.0	12.0
Kuwait	15.0	8.0	10.0	5.0	5.0	3.0	25.0	12.0
Saudi Arabia	15.0	8.0	10.0	5.0	5.0	3.0	25.0	12.0
Oman	15.0	8.0	10.0	5.0	5.0	3.0	25.0	12.0
United Arab Emirates	15.0	8.0	10.0	5.0	5.0	3.0	25.0	12.0
Israel	15.0	8.0	10.0	5.0	5.0	3.0	25.0	12.0
Bahrain	15.0	8.0	10.0	5.0	5.0	3.0	25.0	12.0
Qatar	15.0	8.0	10.0	5.0	5.0	3.0	25.0	12.0
Mongolia	15.0	8.0	10.0	5.0	5.0	3.0	25.0	12.0

APPENDIX C

Correlation Assumptions for CDO Evaluator Assets

Rated Securities

	Sovereign vs. Sovereign
Within region	0.2
Between regions	0.0

	Obligor vs. Obligor								
	Between sectors				Within sector				
	Corp	ABS	Muni	SME	Corp	ABS	Muni	CDO	SME
Within country	0.05	0.10	0.00	0.04	0.15	0.30	0.30	0.15	0.10
Within region****	0.05	0.10	—	0.04	*0.00 **0.15 ***0.15	0.20	0.30	—	0.10
Between regions****	0.00	0.00	—	0.04	*0.00 **0.00 ***0.15	0.00	0.00	—	0.10

*Local

**Regional

***Global

****If any correlation is without local, regional, or global classifications, then correlation applies to asset pairs regardless of classifications.

EDSs

	0.1	0.2	0.3	0.4	0.5	0.6	0.7	0.8	0.9	1.0
Barrier										
Within sector	0.27	0.27	0.27	0.27	0.27	0.29	0.33	0.37	0.37	0.37
Between sectors	0.18	0.18	0.18	0.18	0.18	0.2	0.23	0.26	0.26	0.26

PART 2   CASH FLOW METHODOLOGY*

In this part, we present S&P methodology related do cashflow modeling for cash CDOs.

This part provides a detailed insight into the analytics we employ in the cash flow modeling of CDO transactions. It expands upon our global criteria for cash flow and synthetic CDO transactions, which were published in 2002. Specifically, this article augments the section in the global criteria that covers the cash flow analytics performed as part of the rating process. Transaction arrangers should also use this as a guideline with which to structure a CDO transaction to achieve the desired ratings.

These criteria are relevant to both cash flow and synthetic CDO transactions. Besides being an integral part of the rating process for all cash flow CDOs, cash flow analytics is also employed in the quantitative analysis of synthetic CDO transactions that generate excess spread to reduce the subordination requirement for the rated notes.

CDO transaction structures and collateral eligibility can vary significantly from transaction to transaction. We modify the general assumptions that follow to fit the unique circumstances of each transaction. While comprehensive, this part does not attempt to cover all the cash flow modeling stresses that might be applied to any particular transaction. Sponsors and arrangers are encouraged to work with us as early as possible in the structuring process of the transaction to ensure that appropriate cash flow modeling parameters are used.

Our published criteria, entitled *Global Cash Flow and Synthetic CDO Criteria*, were published on March 21, 2002 and are available on RatingsDirect, our Web-based credit analysis system, at www.ratings direct.com.

OVERVIEW OF ANALYSIS

Our CDO quantitative analysis consists of two components: a default analysis and a cash flow analysis.

---

*This section is extracted from the S&P Structured Finance publication called *General Cash Flow Analytics for CDO Securitizations*, by K. Cheng, J.C. Martorell, D. Tescher, P. Inglis, H. Abulescu, K. Van Acoleyen, and B. Radicopoulos dated 25-08-04.

Default Analysis

The default analysis uses CDO Evaluator to determine the default rate expected on a defined portfolio at each rating level. This default rate is referred to as the scenario default rate (SDR).

The CDO Evaluator uses "Monte Carlo" statistical methodology to evaluate the credit quality of a portfolio. The basic information required of each asset is the issuer ID, the par amount, the maturity date, the industry group, and the corporate issuer credit rating or ABS rating. These asset attributes are superimposed upon the model parameters—sector correlation coefficients, the table of default probabilities for assets, and the table of default probabilities for CDO classes—to determine a probability distribution of potential default rates for the portfolio in the aggregate. The set of SDRs at each rating level is then derived from this distribution.

Our published criteria, *Global Cash Flow and Synthetic CDO Criteria*, give a detailed description of CDO Evaluator and how we estimate SDRs.

Cash Flow Analysis

The second component of the CDO quantitative analysis, the cash flow analysis, evaluates the availability of funds for full payment of interest and principal in accordance with the terms of each rated class of notes. For transactions with multiple classes, the cash flow analysis is run for each class to assess whether the level of credit support provided is consistent with the rating sought on each class. Cash flow modeling is also used to size liquidity and other reserves.

The analysis is transaction-specific and takes into account the structural elements of a transaction, including:

- The principal and interest priority of payment;
- Overcollateralization and interest coverage tests;
- Reinvestment of proceeds;
- Early amortization, fast pay, or redemption events;
- Excess spread accumulation; and
- Reserve levels.

In assessing a CDO class's ability to meet the desired ratings level, the flow of proceeds from the assets to cover the payments due on the liabilities is subjected to a series of stress scenarios. The severity of these stress scenarios depends on the desired rating as well as transaction-specific factors like the quality of the portfolio and the liability payment sequence. The result of this analysis is a series of breakeven default rates (BDRs), one for each stress scenario.

Each BDR is the default rate the portfolio can withstand and still be able to generate adequate cash flow to meet contractual payments of interest and principal on the CDO class when subjected to the particular stress scenario. The lowest of these BDRs is compared with the SDR generated by CDO Evaluator for the portfolio at the desired rating level.

Achieving the Desired Rating

The desired rating is achieved when the BDR, i.e., the level of defaults the portfolio can withstand at the rating level, is the same or higher than the SDR, i.e., the level of defaults expected for the portfolio at that rating level. The excess of the BDR above the SDR is commonly referred to as the "cushion." It reflects the ability of the portfolio to withstand the combination of additional defaults beyond the SDR and still pay out the notes.

Approach to Cash Flow Modeling

This article details our analytical guidelines for the cash flow analysis of CDO transactions. Central to these guidelines are the stress elements that form the scenarios used to test the ability of the cash flow generated by the assets to cover payment obligations on the CDO liabilities. Many of these elements, such as the timing and pattern of defaults, timing and extent of recovery, and interest-rate movements, are difficult to model because they are historically variable.

To tackle this problem, we have established a set of basic default paths for each variable. We pay particular attention to the nature of the assets eligible for inclusion in the portfolio and the jurisdictions from which they are issued. Where appropriate, adjustments are made to the cash flow modeling stresses to account for asset-specific characteristics and legal requirements.

Accurate cash flow modeling of the transaction, as dictated in the governing legal documentation, is crucial to our analysis. Proper representation of the characteristics of the asset pool in all material aspects is also critical.

THE MEANING OF THE RATING

The combination of default patterns and timing sequences, interest-rate paths, and various additional stresses applied in the cash flow modeling lead to a multitude of scenarios, each of which has a separate BDR. To achieve the desired rating on a specific class of notes, we compare the lowest of these BDRs for the class with the corresponding SDR generated by CDO Evaluator.

For "AAA" to "A" rated CDO classes, we generally rate to the timely payment of interest and ultimate payment of principal by the legal final maturity date. The cash flow model at these ratings levels should demonstrate that interest and principal are paid when due and there is no deferral of interest payments.

At the "A−" rating level, our cash flow model allows for the deferral of interest for no more than three consecutive years. After the interest deferral period, interest payments should resume as scheduled.

At the "BBB+" rating level and lower, we allow for the deferral of interest until the legal final maturity date. However, all current and past interest, along with interest on interest, due must be paid by that date.

If the interest cannot be paid within the required time frame for the desired rating, it is still possible for the notes to achieve the rating but the legal name of the notes must specify "deferred interest." This is also to avoid any confusion among the investors.

In all cases, interest incurred on all accrued and unpaid interest should also be incorporated into the cash flow model. The applicable interest rate is typically the same as that on the subject notes.

DEFAULTS

Although CDO Evaluator estimates the magnitude of defaults expected in the portfolio at each rating level, a lack of empirical loss curves leaves the pattern or timing of these defaults unclear. This problem is addressed in our cash flow models by testing the sensitivity of the transaction to a variety of default patterns. Four standard default patterns—which are each shifted in accordance with the expected life of the transaction—and a few other default patterns designed to stress certain cash flow behavior, form the core of our established default stresses.

Details of these patterns and timings follow. These core default stresses are conceived to address the risks inherent in most of the sequential pay senior/subordinated structures common to the CDO marketplace. Where appropriate, we modify or request additional patterns or timings to fit the unique circumstances of a transaction.

Standard Default Patterns

The four standard default patterns are shown in Table 10.1.

These patterns are expressed as a percentage of the cumulative portfolio default rate occurring every year once defaults start. For example, applying the 40/20/20/10/10 default pattern to a cumulative default rate of 40 percent, the original par balance of the portfolio experiences defaults of 16 percent, 8 percent, 8 percent, 4 percent, and 4 percent, respectively, in the five years covered by the pattern.

The default patterns are applied to the original par balance of the portfolio. This is the target balance at the effective date for transactions that have a ramp-up period. Staying with this example, for any original par balance of $500, the defaulted balance in absolute dollar terms would be $80, $40, $40, $20, and $20, respectively, in the five years.

Front-loaded default patterns, such as the 40/20/20/10/10 pattern, tend to stress a transaction's dependence on excess spread. Defaults in the early life of the transaction lead to fewer interest-generating assets and result in less excess spread for credit support. The 20/20/20/20/20 pattern focuses more on the back end of a transaction, when a combination of amortizing assets and cumulative defaults may make a transaction more sensitive to late-period defaults.

Timing of the Standard Default Patterns

To capture the sensitivity of the transaction to defaults across the entire life of the transaction, each of the four standard patterns is started in the

TABLE 10.1

Standard & Poor's Standard Default Patterns

	Annual defaults as percentage of cumulative defaults (%)				
	Year 1	Year 2	Year 3	Year 4	Year 5
Pattern I	15	30	30	15	10
Pattern II	40	20	20	10	10
Pattern III	20	20	20	20	20
Pattern IV	25	25	25	25	—

first year, then started in the second year, and so on. The start times of the patterns are pushed back to the point where the final default in the pattern occurs in the same year that the balance of the portfolio are expected to mature. That is, the starting points continue to be shifted as long as adequate assets remain in the portfolio. This is dictated by the length of the reinvestment period and the weighted-average expected life (WAL) of the collateral. The maximum WAL at the end of the reinvestment period is generally the appropriate measure for the WAL because it reflects the tenor of the portfolio when it becomes static.

If the collateral manager is allowed to buy assets during the amortization period, the trading constraints are assessed to gauge the need for additional timing shifts beyond those dictated by the maximum WAL covenant. Some transactions have a maximum WAL covenant at the effective date that does not reduce during the reinvestment period. For these transactions, we generally use the effective date WAL covenant as the WAL at the end of the reinvestment period to determine the appropriate timing shifts.

As an example, take a transaction with a five-year reinvestment period, a maximum WAL covenant of four years at the end of the reinvestment period, and trading activities permitted only during the reinvestment period. Because the balance of the portfolio does not mature until the end of year nine (four years after the end of the reinvestment period), the start of the default patterns can be pushed back to year five, which spreads defaults across years five through nine. The constraints in this example dictate the use of the standard default patterns beginning in years one through five.

If the WAL covenant is two years at the end of the reinvestment period, rather than four years as in the previous example, there would not be adequate assets remaining after year seven. We would run the default patterns from years one through three so that the last default would occur in year seven.

Modifying the Timing Based on Liability Ratings

The stress elements must reflect the difference between each rating category. Different default timing stresses are applied in the cash flow modeling according to which rating is sought on the notes. Although each of the four standard default patterns is run beginning in year one, we delay the start of these patterns by a longer period to capture the effect of later defaults at the higher liability ratings.

For example, the reinvestment period and WAL covenant of a transaction might dictate stressing the transaction with default patterns beginning as far out as year five at the "AAA" rating level. At the "BBB" rating level, we might require default patterns to begin only as far out as year three.

Guidelines for the required timing shift of the standard default patterns for ratings below "AA−" are described below. The required timing shift at the "AA" liability level is identical to that required at the "AAA" level. The requirements at the lower liability ratings change according to these shifts.

For "A+" to "A−" rated classes. The standard default patterns start at the end of year one and last until one year less than the period required for "AAA" and "AA" rated notes. For example, if the applicable starting years for the default patterns for the "AAA" and "AA" rated notes are one through five years, then the starting years for the "A" rated notes are up to four years.

For "BBB+" to "BBB−" rated classes. The standard default patterns start at end of year one and last until two years less than the period required for "AAA" and "AA" rated notes. In the example above, the starting years for the "BBB" rated notes are up to three years.

For "BB+" to "BB−" rated classes. The standard default patterns start at end of year one and last until three years less than the period required for "AAA" and "AA" rated notes. In the example above, the starting years for the "BB" rated notes are up to two years.

For "B+" and below. The standard default patterns start at end of year one and last until four years less than the period required for "AAA" and "AA" rated notes. In the example above, the default patterns are required to begin only in year one for the "B" rated notes.

The examples provided in Table 10.2 further illustrate the starting years required. For fractions of years, the determining point is the half-year mark (see the last two examples in the table).

Additional Core Default Patterns

In addition to the four standard default patterns covered above, "saw-tooth" default patterns and expected-case default patterns are also required.

Saw-Tooth Patterns

The saw-tooth patterns are used to stress transactions that use principal to pay deferred interest on subordinate classes before amortizing the senior class. By deferring interest, then paying it back, deferring interest again, and paying it back, these patterns test the transaction's ability to pay out

TABLE 10.2

Example of Starting Years for Standard Default Patterns

Reinvestment period	WAL covenant at end of reinvestment period	AAA tranche	AA tranche	A tranche	BBB tranche	BB tranche	B tranche
5	4	1 to 5	1 to 5	1 to 4	1 to 3	1 to 2	1
5	6	1 to 7	1 to 7	1 to 6	1 to 5	1 to 4	1 to 3
4	4	1 to 4	1 to 4	1 to 3	1 to 2	1	1
4	6	1 to 6	1 to 6	1 to 5	1 to 4	1 to 3	1 to 2
5	4.5	1 to 6	1 to 6	1 to 5	1 to 4	1 to 3	1 to 2
5	4.3	1 to 5	1 to 5	1 to 4	1 to 3	1 to 2	1

all the required principal on the rated notes after principal proceeds are diverted to pay interest on these liabilities.

For ratings of "BBB–" and above, the saw-tooth patterns are as follows.

Pattern 1. Defaults occur in alternating years, beginning in year 1 and ending in the last year that adequate assets remain in the portfolio. Defaults are lumped at the end of the year. In a transaction with a five-year reinvestment period and a minimum WAL covenant of four years at the end of the reinvestment period, the saw-tooth pattern requires that 20 percent of total defaults are modeled to occur in each of years 1, 3, 5, 7, and 9.

Pattern 2. Defaults occur every three years, beginning in year one and ending in the last year that adequate assets remain in the portfolio. Defaults are lumped at the end of the year. In the example above, this pattern requires that 25 percent of total defaults are applied in each of years 1, 4, 7, and 10.

For ratings of "BB+" and below, the saw-tooth pattern is as follows.

Pattern 3. Defaults occur in alternating years, beginning in year one and ending in year seven. Defaults are lumped at the end of the year. Thus 25 percent of total defaults are modeled to occur in each of years 1, 3, 5, and 7.

Expected Case Patterns

There are two expected-case patterns:

- The low pro rata default pattern: Defaults should be distributed evenly across $(n-2)$ years, where n is the number of years to legal final maturity. The annual default rate should be calculated as the gross default rate/$(n-2)$. For example, defaults are modeled to occur evenly at the end of years 1 to 10 for a transaction with a 12-year legal final maturity.
- Zero defaults: no defaults are applied in the modeling. Excess spread flows down the priority of payments for the benefit of the equity. This tests the ability of the transaction structure to adequately support the rated notes without trapping excess spread to pay down principal on the liabilities upon breach of an overcollateralization test. It also helps make our cash flow model comparable to that of the transaction arranger.

Smoothing the Patterns

Defaults are more likely to be spread throughout a given year than occur at one specific time (at year end, for instance). We allow the annual defaults on the standard default patterns to be modeled to occur as frequently as quarterly for transactions where at least 80 percent of the assets pay not less frequently than quarterly, after taking into account any basis swaps. In this manner, annual defaults are spread evenly across the four quarters with defaults occurring on the last day of each quarter. Given that transactions typically have a 5 to 10 percent allowance for less frequent pay assets, most quarterly pay transactions would qualify for the smoothing of annual defaults. The transaction arranger also has the option of modeling defaults less frequently. Regardless, in all cases, assets maturing in any period remain subject to defaults in that period.

The entire default amount in the first year, however, should be modeled to occur on the last day of the year. This reflects our opinion that, in most instances, some time lapses before defaults occur on a recently assembled portfolio. An exception to this is when the targeted portfolio consists of an abnormally high concentration of low credit quality assets. In these cases, we may request that the model begin defaults earlier during the first year.

Defaults clearly affect the interest received from the defaulted assets—interest is earned only on the performing pool balance. During the liability payment period when the asset is assumed to default, credit is given for the interest earned only if the asset pays interest more frequently than the liabilities. For example, in a transaction paying semi-annually, an asset that receives quarterly interest payments is modeled to receive interest for the first, but not the second, quarter of the default period. In contrast, an asset that receives semi-annual interest payments is not given credit for interest in the modeling for that default period.

We assume a lag period from the time the asset defaults to the time recoveries are realized on defaulted assets and the money is available for reinvestment in substitute collateral. During this period (which is addressed in the section "Recoveries"), no interest is received on the defaulted assets. Following the lag period, recovery proceeds are modeled to occur on the last day of the payment period that recovery is realized. Redeployment of the proceeds in interest income-generating assets does not occur until the first day of the subsequent period.

Adjustments to Default Patterns and Timing

The default patterns and timings that form the core of our default stresses are designed to address the risks common in many of the traditional sequential pay senior/subordinated CDO transaction structures.

TABLE 10.3

Standard & Poor's Additional Default Patterns
for Low Quality Pools

	Annual defaults as percentage of cumulative defaults (%)			
	Year 1	Year 2	Year 3	Year 4
Pattern I	50	25	25	—
Pattern II	60	20	10	10
Pattern III	70	10	10	10

Variations, such as certain asset characteristics or transactional mechanisms, introduce risks that sometimes necessitate the use of alternative or additional stresses. Several are now covered.

Low Credit Quality Portfolios

Several CDO transactions backed by portfolios with a high concentration of very low credit quality assets have already entered the marketplace. Although the increased default probability of these portfolios is captured by the ratings on the assets and the default tables embedded within CDO Evaluator, an adjustment to the established default patterns is warranted to cover the possibility that the defaults would occur earlier in the transaction's life cycle, and be lumpier. In general, three additional default pattern stresses, all beginning in year one, are required and applied to the entire portfolio (Table 10.3).

Short Legal Final Maturity Transactions

Most cash flow CDO transactions issue liabilities with legal final maturities of 10 years or longer. However, a few CDO transactions have been brought to the market that are a hybrid of synthetic and cash flow structures. These have relatively short maturities, typically five years. Applying the standard default patterns and timings on these transactions is inappropriate. Instead, the following two default patterns are generally used (Table 10.4).

The first default pattern is applied five times with the 50 percent shifted to each of the five years (e.g., 50/10/10/10/20, 10/50/10/10/20, etc.). The second default pattern does not change.

TABLE 10.4

Standard & Poor's Default Patterns for Shorter
Maturity Transactions

	Annual defaults as percentage of cumulative defaults (%)				
	Year 1	Year 2	Year 3	Year 4	Year 5
Pattern I	10	10	10	50	20
Pattern II	33	33	34	—	—

Default Bias For Interest Mismatches

Most CDO transactions are modeled based on the general pool characteristics, with pro rata defaults applied across all assets. However, when
there is a significant mix of fixed- and floating-rate assets, the bias of
defaults makes it more appropriate to stress the shift of portfolio composition over time. The bias of default that follows is applied at the "AAA"
through "A–" rating levels.

In a high interest-rate environment, obligors paying a floating rate
might be under greater pressure to meet their payment obligations due to
rising interest rates. In this scenario, a larger percentage of floating-rate
obligors might default. Conversely, in a low interest-rate environment,
obligors that pay high fixed-interest rates might be more likely to default.
In this second scenario, a larger proportion of the fixed-rate obligors
might default.

To test for this phenomenon we usually request certain cash flow
runs where defaults are biased toward the fixed-rate assets during low
interest-rate environments and, conversely, towards floating-rate assets
during high interest-rate environments. The goal of this analysis is to test
the rated class's ability to pay out even if defaults shift within the collateral pool.

For all ratings where the mix is greater than 10 percent, the formula
generally applied for biasing defaults is as follows:

$$\text{Default Bias} = 2x/(1+x)$$

where x is the initial percentage of fixed-rate bonds or floating-rate loans
in a pool.

For example, if the collateral portfolio has a mix of 30 percent fixed-rate assets and 70 percent floating-rate assets, the applicable fixed-rate default bias would be:

$$\text{Fixed-Rate Default Bias} = 2(0.3)/(1+0.3) = 0.46$$

In this case, the cash flow model would be adjusted to default 46 percent of the fixed-rate assets and 54 percent of the floating-rate assets, instead of the actual 30 percent/70 percent split. This fixed-rate default bias is generally applied only to the dominant run in the Index Down interest-rate stresses.

In the same example, the applicable floating-rate default bias would be:

$$\text{Floating-Rate Default Bias} = 2(0.7)/(1+0.7) = 0.82.$$

In this case, the cash flow model would default 18 percent of the fixed-rate assets and 82 percent of the floating-rate assets. This floating-rate default bias is generally applied only to the dominant run in the Index Up interest-rate stresses.

RECOVERIES

Loss severity and recovery timing assumptions are another intrinsic part of CDO transaction analyses. These aim to estimate the loss on an asset upon default and when the recovery is realized.

Recovery Rates

Recoveries specify the amount of money realized on a defaulted obligation after it has defaulted. Factors such as the breadth and depth of the secondary market profoundly influence recovery rates realized. These factors differ across markets, so recovery rates must be assigned by asset type and domicile.

Within each asset type, additional influences affect recovery rates. In the case of corporate obligations, recoveries are not dependent on the rating on the obligor or on the notes in the transaction. Instead, they depend on the type, seniority, domicile, and security of the obligation. The recovery rates that are ultimately realized are further influenced by the actions of the collateral manager. Thus, two collateral managers, following different workout strategies, may realize significantly different recoveries for the same assets under identical market environments. We use an established range of recovery rates for each classification of corporate asset and assign transaction-specific recovery rates within these ranges based on a review of the collateral manager.

The recovery rates applied for assets governed by one jurisdiction are not necessarily appropriate for other jurisdictions. The recovery ranges also differ across governing domicile. The *Global Cash Flow and Synthetic CDO Criteria* book shows the various recovery ranges for corporate bonds and loans issued under U.S. and European jurisdictions, and recovery assumptions for defaulted emerging market assets. These recovery assumptions are generally lower and reflect the relative lack of liquidity in the secondary market for emerging market obligations.

In contrast to corporate obligations, the ratings on structured finance securities—as a reflection of position in the capital structure—influence recovery prospects, as does the seniority of an asset. The recovery rates assigned are also tiered across economic conditions, using the rating on the CDO notes as the proxy for those conditions. The resultant recovery matrices for structured finance securities under U.S. and European jurisdictions are shown in the *Global Cash Flow and Synthetic CDO Criteria* book.

It is critical to note that the recovery ranges and tables are applicable to many, but not all, assets that fall within the collateral classifications identified in those tables. Recoveries may be adjusted based on characteristics or mechanisms particular to any asset. Assets not covered by the existing recovery tables (e.g., project finance bonds, operating company obligations, and distressed-debt CDOs) are assigned recoveries on a case-by-case basis.

Although recoveries are assigned to each asset, we use the minimum weighted-average recovery rate covenant (as defined by the transaction's portfolio eligibility criteria) in cash flow modeling for CDO transactions that allow for reinvestment of proceeds.

The CDO transactions that prohibit reinvestment of proceeds and are fully ramped up on the closing date have no need to incorporate minimum weighted-average recovery rate tests. In these transactions, the actual weighted-average recovery rate at closing is generally used in the cash flow modeling. However, a "bar-belled" portfolio might necessitate the use of a recovery rate lower than the weighted-average or a bias of defaults toward the lower recovery assets.

In all instances, recovery rates are applied to the par balance of the asset without accounting for any deferred and capitalized portion of par outstanding.

Recovery Timing

Recovery timing specifies the time it takes to achieve recoveries once an obligation defaults. Time to recovery is influenced by the type of asset, the form of the obligation, the actions of the collateral manager, the liquidity of the market, the governing legal jurisdiction, and the requirements of the transaction with regard to forced sale or settlement. In most cases, two general assumptions are made for the timing of recoveries on defaulted assets, as follows:

- ♦ Recoveries on defaulted sovereign, corporate, and structured finance securities are assumed to occur one year after default through secondary market liquidation.
- ♦ Recoveries on defaulted loans are assumed to occur over a three-year workout period, with one-half of the recovery received at the end of the second year and the remaining half at the end of the third year.

The above assumptions are consistent across many jurisdictions. A longer recovery horizon is assumed on defaulted loans because loan markets are not generally as liquid as bond markets. These recovery horizons are consistent with the holding periods that we consider sufficient to allow the manager to maximize recoveries on defaulted securities. The recovery levels in our recovery rate ranges and tables are reflective of this holding period.

When modeling recoveries, the model should show recoveries realized at the end of the appropriate period. In this manner, recovery proceeds are not available for reinvestment and, therefore, no interest income is earned on these proceeds during this period. Earning of interest begins in the subsequent period.

INTEREST RATE STRESSES

The CDO transactions often have a fixed-to-floating interest-rate mismatch between the assets and the liabilities. To mitigate this risk, transactions are commonly structured with interest-rate hedges. In the absence of a balanced guaranteed hedge, mismatches between the notional of the hedge and the liabilities might develop as the magnitude or bias of defaults between fixed- and floating-rate assets diverge from projected levels. Testing of the transaction under several distinct interest-rate paths is performed to gauge the effectiveness of the hedge structure in a variety of interest-rate environments.

TABLE 10.5

Standard & Poor's Interest Rate Paths

Index Up
Index Down
Index Down/Up
Current Index Forward Curve
At Swap
At Cap

Stresses

In general, transactions are stressed under the index scenarios listed in Table 10.5. In addition, the "At Swap" and "At Cap" rates are typically run to test the transaction's ability to perform without depending on the hedges for additional credit support.

The interest rate curves for each transaction are adjusted to match the length of the transaction and the index used. They may also vary by rating level. We provide to the arranger the curves applicable to the transaction early in the rating process. General details of our interest-rate assumptions are provided in the *Global Cash Flow and Synthetic CDO Criteria* book.

Adjustments to Interest Rate Sensitivity Analysis

These interest rate paths or the manner in which they are applied are sometimes adjusted to address peculiarities of a transaction. Additional adjustments to other aspects of the cash flow modeling are sometimes also necessary to address interest rate related risks. Several are now covered.

Fixed-Rate/Floating-Rate Asset Mix

Transactions that allow for reinvestment of proceeds typically contain investment guidelines that allow for a range of asset mix between fixed- and floating-rate collateral. When the mix is heavily concentrated toward one or the other of these possibilities (either at least 95 percent fixed or 95 percent floating), the transaction can be modeled in one of two ways at the discretion of the transaction arranger:

- ◆ Model either as 100 percent fixed or floating; or
- ◆ Model at a maximum percentage of fixed or floating.

For transactions that allow for greater flexibility between the mix of fixed- and floating-rate assets, disparities in the minimum weighted-average coupon and spread covenants could lead to pronounced differences in the cash flow performance along the fixed/floating-rate asset mix continuum. In these circumstances, the mix of fixed/floating-rate assets must be modeled at the maximum and minimum levels to capture the extremes in the spectrum of possibilities.

When a transaction is stressed to the maximum allowance for floating-rate assets, it often leads to a high concentration of loans. Since higher recoveries are generally extended to loans relative to bonds, it is possible that the weighted-average recovery for the portfolio in this scenario could be higher than the minimum weighted-average recovery rate covenant typically used in the cash flow modeling exercise. We take this into consideration when stressing the transaction for the fixed/floating-rate asset mix.

Loan Basis Risk

The floating-rate liabilities of CDO transactions and the floating-rate assets in the portfolio typically use the same repricing index. Often, the index is LIBOR or EURIBOR. Occasionally, there is a mismatch between these indices due to the payment frequencies. The ability of the assets to adequately cover the interest due on the liabilities is strained when the movement of the indices between any two points in time is different.

The additional stress required to capture this risk depends on the magnitude of the difference between the two indices' movements. In general, we apply a five basis point haircut to the weighted-average spread above the index when the mismatch is greater than 5 percent and the gap in rate movements between the pair of indices has historically exhibited significant variability.

Multiple Liability Indices

The presence of floating-rate liabilities tied to more than one index raises questions regarding the appropriate interest-rate stresses. In this situation, we apply the interest-rate curves commensurate with the dominant index. For example, if 60 percent of floating-rate liabilities are based on EURIBOR and 40 percent are based on LIBOR, then the EURIBOR interest-rate stress scenarios generated by our LIBOR/EURIBOR curve dynamic model prevail.

PORTFOLIO CONSIDERATIONS

Factors such as the composition of a portfolio or specific asset characteristics introduce risks that might necessitate the use of additional or alternative stresses. Several are now covered.

Prepayment Sensitivities

Most structured finance products are collateralized by loans or mortgages that include provisions, allowing the borrower to make unscheduled payments without a penalty. These prepayments affect the timing and magnitude of the cash flow available to cover the liabilities on the structured finance securities. In turn, this affects the cumulative excess spread generated by the securities. Since excess spread is often used to cover losses, prepayments affect the ability of the transaction to support losses and must be considered in the cash flow modeling.

To capture the effect of these prepayment provisions, we impose prepayment stress scenarios on those assets that exhibit elastic prepayment sensitivities to interest-rate movement, including RMBS and home equity line of credit (HELOC) securities. We should be consulted to help identify these asset types. The prepayment stresses are applied to those CDO transactions in which these assets make up more than 5 percent of the portfolio in aggregate par balance. When the permitted concentration exceeds this threshold, the entire bucket is stressed to test the impact of prepayments.

The three scenarios typically modeled include:

+ The market (base) prepayment speed;
+ An accelerated prepayment speed of 150 percent of the market prepayment speed; and
+ A decelerated prepayment speed of 50 percent of the market prepayment speed.

For new issuance, the market prepayment speed is the expected prepayment speed of the transaction. For seasoned issuance, it is the average of actual market prepayment speeds during the previous six months.

When applying the accelerated and decelerated prepayment speed stresses, consideration is given to the relationship between prepayment behavior of the asset and interest-rate movements in determining the appropriate accompanying interest-rate stresses. For example, prepayment of fixed-rate mortgages is apt to pick up when interest rates are declining and likely to slow down when they are increasing. Thus, the accelerated prepayment speed stress would be applied in conjunction with the interest-rate index down stress, and the decelerated prepayment speed stress would be applied in conjunction with the interest-rate index up stress. Regardless, we should be consulted to determine the appropriate prepayment speed/interest-rate stress pairings based on the mix of these assets.

When the mix of prepayment-sensitive assets cuts across national markets subject to different prepayment behavior (e.g., U.K. vs. Italian RMBS), we should be consulted for guidance on the appropriate base prepayment speed to apply. In general, this is the prepayment speed prevailing in the market where most of the assets are expected to be purchased.

Foreign Currency Risk

Some CDO transactions, particularly those issued out of Europe, allow for a bucket of assets denominated in a currency different from that of the notes issued. The currency mismatch introduced is best hedged with a balance-guaranteed foreign exchange swap, but the cost of entering into these swaps is often prohibitive. The most common way to address this risk is to use a natural hedge or asset-specific foreign exchange swaps based on set notional balances. In both of these cases, the foreign exchange risk is not fully hedged throughout the life of the transaction, thus necessitating additional cash flow stresses to capture the foreign exchange risk.

A natural foreign exchange hedge exists when both the assets and liabilities denominated in each currency make up the same proportion of a given pool. For instance, the collateral pool may have 70 percent euro-denominated and 30 percent U.S. dollar-denominated assets matched to 70 percent euro-denominated and 30 percent U.S. dollar-denominated liabilities, thereby creating a natural hedge. However, this natural hedge often does not immunize the CDO against foreign exchange risk. This hedge remains perfectly balanced so long as defaults to the assets occur pro rata across the currency denominations. If defaults do not occur in proportion (the more likely scenario), the resultant imbalance would throw the natural hedge askew. The balance of the natural hedge could also be upset by prepayments on the assets or diversion of principal proceeds to pay down liabilities in a sequential pay structure triggered by the breach of a coverage test.

The effectiveness of a natural hedge is also dependent upon its position in the capital structure. Segregating the most senior class of notes across the currencies is more effective than segregating a more junior class.

The other common strategy for addressing foreign exchange risk is to use asset-specific foreign exchange swaps. The issuer of the securities enters into a foreign exchange swap, often for a set notional balance or a schedule of notional balances. This hedging strategy is likewise susceptible to hedging imbalances due to the bias of defaults or prepayments on the asset balance.

In the absence of a strategy that adequately addresses foreign exchange risk over the life of the transaction, we typically employ a two-part analysis to test for the potential effect of this risk. First, the cash flow is subjected to additional stresses that bias defaults toward each of the currency denominations. The magnitude of the bias is dictated by factors that include the position of the natural hedge in the capital structure, the proportion of assets denominated in each currency, and the disparity of the credit risk profiles between each currency-denominated sub-portfolio. Currency devaluation factors, calculated using a currency devaluation model, are then applied to the resultant hedge imbalance to size the extent of the currency mismatch.

The presence of different indices (e.g., LIBOR and EURIBOR) in transactions with multiple currencies might also necessitate additional analysis to capture the mismatch of indices. The empirical relative movement of the indices and the magnitude of the mismatch determine this need.

We should be consulted for the default bias, currency devaluation stresses, and index mismatch stresses applicable to each particular transaction.

In addition to hedging the periodic payments, the foreign exchange strategy should remain in place to cover the recoveries realized on defaulted securities. Automatic termination of the foreign exchange swap upon default of an asset exposes the recoveries to foreign exchange risk. We typically adjust the recovery rate assigned when the swap is required to terminate before the base recovery delay assumptions. The magnitude of this adjustment is determined according to factors such as the length of time the defaulted asset is exposed to foreign exchange risk and the particular currencies involved.

Foreign exchange risk also arises when an asset is sold, but the asset-specific foreign exchange swap is not automatically retired or, conversely, the foreign exchange swap terminates before the asset matures. In the first instance, the collateral manager is likely to include the economic effect of the swap in making its sell decision and, in the latter, the manager might sell the unhedged asset to eliminate foreign exchange concerns. In both cases, noncredit-based considerations are factored into the decision process and we consider adjusting the recovery rate assigned.

Coupon on Assets

We base our cash flow analysis on a portfolio that generates interest income at the minimum coupon/spread dictated by the collateral pool eligibility criteria. This assumes that market conditions prevent the collateral manager from purchasing collateral at spreads or coupons higher than the minimum weighted-average spread or coupon.

However, if the portfolio is fully ramped up at closing and trading is allowed, credit is afforded to the actual weighted-average coupon/spread of the pool at the start of the transaction. The pool coupon/spread migrates down to the minimum levels over two years on a straight-line basis. The form of this migration is dictated by the frequency of payments on the liabilities. For example, take a transaction that covenants to a minimum weighted-average coupon of 6 percent but has an actual weighted-average coupon of 8 percent, and pays out on its liabilities quarterly. The appropriate cash flow modeling allows interest to be earned at an 8 percent coupon between closing and the first payment period, with the coupon reduced by 25 bps each subsequent payment period until it reaches 6 percent after the eighth payment period.

It is important to note that the cash flow should be modeled at the coupon and not the stated yield rate.

Interest Income on Eligible Investments

Proceeds received from assets in the form of scheduled principal and interest payments and recovery proceeds are held in eligible investments before being reinvested in substitute collateral or being used to pay liabilities on a payment date.

In the cash flow model, the analysis should assume that scheduled principal and interest proceeds are held in eligible investments for one-half of the payment period of the collection before it is reinvested in substitute collateral. Also, in the analysis, recoveries should be assumed to occur at the end of a payment period. Therefore, interest is not earned on recovery proceeds held as eligible investments during the period in which it is recovered.

Interest earned on the regular payments received from the eligible investments is modeled at the index referenced minus 100 bps.

Payment Timing Mismatch

It is common for transactions to include a bucket for assets that pay less frequently than the payment terms of the liabilities. In many instances, the transaction uses an interest reserve mechanism or enters into a basis swap to address this mismatch. In the absence of an adequate mitigant, the modeling should reflect the mismatches in payment timing, as they actually occur, to allow for accurate testing of cash flows. There should be no "smoothing" of asset payments to match liability payments.

Pay in Kind (PIK) Assets

When more than 5 percent of the assets in a portfolio by par balance have the ability to pay in kind, we apply a PIK stress test to ensure that the liquidity facility can cover interest shortfalls from the assets. The PIK stress applied is determined after taking into account the transaction structure and targeted portfolio profile. We typically ask that this is done only for the most severe stress case to verify if it can pass; BDRs may be set without this stress.

It is important to note that some transactions treat assets that pay in kind for a defined time period as defaulted assets. The defaulted balance of the PIK assets should be marked as the original par principal balance, not its principal plus accrued interest balance.

Long-Dated Corporate Assets

The inclusion of corporate assets that mature on a date beyond the legal final maturity date of the liabilities requires the CDO transaction to sell these assets before this date. This exposes the transaction to the noncredit-related risk of loss of par and is particularly troublesome for corporate bonds and other types of instruments that return all or substantially all of the par balance at the asset's legal final maturity date.

We address this concern by limiting the concentration of assets in the long-dated bucket to 5 percent. When the allowance for this bucket exceeds 5 percent, the par credit for each long-dated asset is reduced by applying a present value of 10 percent per year to each principal payment due on the asset beyond the legal final maturity date of the transaction. This adjustment reflects a potential par loss incurred for the forced sale of the asset under less than ideal market conditions.

Note that this approach applies only to corporate assets. Long-dated structured finance assets raise different issues that are beyond the scope of this chapter.

Corporate Mezzanine Loans

Corporate mezzanine loans are common to many European leveraged loan CDO transactions. These loans have a junior secured position and typically have two components to their interest payments: a current-pay coupon and a PIK coupon. The latter coupon is structured in the loan documents to pay in kind from day 1 and accrues to principal; in effect, it behaves like a zero coupon bond.

Although a mezzanine loan typically has a 10-year tenor, it is quite likely that it will be refinanced within two to three years. The ability of a CDO manager to reinvest in new mezzanine loans depends upon the length of the reinvestment period, the ability of the manager to reinvest unscheduled principal proceeds after the end of the reinvestment period, and any maturity restriction imposed on each new loan. Given the current lack of a secondary market for European mezzanine loans, it is unlikely that a manager will be able to maintain its desired/covenanted mezzanine loan balance throughout the transaction.

We give credit to the accrued portion of the PIK coupon component in the cash flow modeling, subject to the following conditions:

♦ Credit for the accrual of PIK coupon is typically allowed for the reinvestment period plus an additional 2.5 years. The amount of credit would have to be reduced if the maturity of the CDO notes or the WAL test of the assets would prevent reinvestment of mezzanine loans during the reinvestment period. Conversely, if the CDO transaction is structured with a long note maturity and unscheduled proceeds can be reinvested after the reinvestment period, then we consider extending the credit given to the PIK coupon.

♦ For the purpose of the coverage tests, credit is extended to the accrued PIK interest in the overcollateralization test so long as the accrued interest is treated as principal proceeds; credit is not given in the interest coverage test because it is not interest that is received in cash during the payment periods.

♦ The asset eligibility guidelines for the transaction should include covenants for a minimum mezzanine loan bucket and a minimum PIK interest-rate for the mezzanine loans. This is needed to size aggregate credit to extend to the accrued PIK interest.

♦ For purposes of default and recovery, the defaulted balance is calculated as the product of the default probability and the par balance inclusive of the accrued PIK interest. The recovery balance is calculated as the product of the recovery rate and the base par. Accrued PIK balance is excluded.

The recovery range for corporate loans is used in the assignment of recovery rates to mezzanine loans.

Amortizing Assets

The CDO portfolios often include assets that pay back principal according to an amortization schedule rather than as a single bullet payment at maturity. Difficulty in modeling this amortization arises when the full portfolio has not been identified and "dummy" assets are used or when the portfolio is actively managed. We scrutinize the reasonable nature of the assumptions used. As a guideline, the amortization schedule should generally coincide with the minimum WAL covenant of the transaction.

OTHER STRUCTURAL CONSIDERATIONS

Transactional mechanisms and features also vary across transactions, often necessitating the use of alternative or additional cash flow stresses to properly address the risks specific to the transaction. Some of the more common mechanisms and features are discussed as follows.

Forced Sale of Defaulted Assets

Although we do not require the forced sale of defaulted assets within a defined period, and often discourage it, this feature is included in some transactions. When the terms of the transaction require the sale of defaulted assets more quickly than we would ideally assume, the manager's ability to maximize recoveries is potentially inhibited. In these cases, we generally apply a haircut to the recovery rate assigned to the transaction. The magnitude of the haircut is generally the present value at 10 percent per year based on the differential between the transaction's required sale time limit and the idealized recovery timing that we use.

Static Transactions

Although most CDO transactions to date have been structured as managed CDOs, several transactions backed by static collateral portfolios have entered the marketplace. These transactions eliminate the manager's ability to purchase assets after the closing date (or after the effective date in some cases) and significantly limit the manager's ability to sell assets. Some transactions limit the sale of collateral to defaulted securities and credit-impaired securities, with all proceeds received used to pay down the outstanding liabilities. Pure static transactions go even further by completely eliminating both sales and purchase of assets.

The elimination of the reinvestment period in these transactions allows for the application of shorter default timing stresses in the cash flow modeling. While the established default patterns remain the same, the default pattern starting times are truncated to match the life of assets in a portfolio without reinvestment. For example, a static transaction backed by assets with a WAL of eight years is subjected only to the standard default patterns beginning in years one through three at the "AAA" rating level (Table 10.6).

Because the "fixed" collateral portfolio is identified at the start of the transaction, it is possible to scrutinize the expected payment characteristics of the asset pool more closely. Defaults are typically applied pro rata across asset pools in revolving CDO transactions, but we might bias defaults toward specific assets in a static portfolio when additional concerns are identified.

For example, concerns might be raised about a portfolio with some relatively low-rated assets that pay a significantly higher-than-average coupon. The default of these assets could result in inadequate interest

TABLE 10.6

Example of Starting Years for Standard Default Patterns in Static Transactions

WAL of actual portfolio	AAA tranche	AA tranche	A tranche	BBB tranche	BB tranche	B tranche
7	1 to 2	1 to 2	1 to 2	1	1	1
8	1 to 3	1 to 3	1 to 3	1 to 2	1 to 2	1
9	1 to 4	1 to 4	1 to 4	1 to 3	1 to 2	1

TABLE 10.7

Annual Senior Collateral Manager Fees

Corporate CBO/CLO	15 bps
ABS CDO	15 bps
CSOs (collateralized swap obligations)	10 bps

cash flow from the remaining assets. This scenario is not tested by the standard application of pro rata defaults. In this situation, bias of defaults toward these assets could be warranted.

Senior Collateral Manager Fees

Senior collateral manager fees should be at market levels to provide adequate incentive for a replacement manager to take over the transaction, should the need arise. In general, these fees are modeled at the higher of the contractual fee and the minimum fees listed in Table 10.7 to ensure that the transaction can support such fees.

Factors such as other forms of compensation to the collateral manager, the responsibilities of the manager, and the size of the transaction are considered when determining the appropriate senior fee. For instance, a contractual senior fee of 10 bps could be sufficient when the notional balance of the portfolio of a corporate CLO transaction is $1 billion. Lower fees might also be adequate in static transactions where the activities of the collateral manager are limited.

Equity

One challenge confronted in the cash flow analysis for rating equity or combination notes that include equity as an asset is the sizing of unknown and uncapped administrative expenses senior in the priority of payments. For the purposes of cash flow modeling, we assume that these additional expenses are equal to the capped expenses located near the top part of the priority of payments (Table 10.8).

In addition, the cash flows are also stressed with the three additional default patterns employed for low credit quality portfolios. These patterns are applied to the equity analysis even if the credit quality of the portfolio is not necessarily low.

TABLE 10.8

Standard & Poor's Additional Default Patterns
for Equity

	Annual defaults as percentage of cumulative defaults (%)			
	Year 1	Year 2	Year 3	Year 4
Pattern I	50	25	25	—
Pattern II	60	20	10	10
Pattern III	70	10	10	10

COVERAGE TEST CONSIDERATIONS

Most transactions contain certain structural features aimed at limiting par
building trades and improving rating stability. These features often go
beyond the stressing of defaults and recoveries that we employ in assigning ratings. Many of these features are tied to the overcollateralization
test. Several are now covered.

Breach of Coverage Tests

Upon breach of an overcollateralization or interest coverage test, most
CDO transactions divert interest, scheduled principal, and/or realized
recoveries to pay down the notes sequentially, beginning with the most
senior outstanding class, until the breached test is brought back into compliance. If the transaction documentation dictates this, then it should be
properly modeled in the cash flow exercise.

However, the documentation for some CDO transactions incorporates "maintain or improve" language upon breach of a coverage test. In
these cases, cash is not diverted to pay down the notes. Instead, reinvestment of proceeds is allowed within the maintained or improved constraint. To properly reflect this in the cash flow modeling, the delevering
mechanism for the coverage tests should be shut off (i.e., breach of test
does not cause diversion of proceeds to pay down the notes).

Furthermore, we subject all recoveries that are reinvested in securities to additional defaults based on the SDR of the original asset pool. This
increases the total default amount modeled in the transaction.

Haircut for Low-Rated Collateral

While a certain concentration of "CCC" rated assets is not necessarily bad, especially if factored into the original class sizing of the transaction, "CCC" rated assets have a tendency to be downgraded more quickly. Most transactions include a value haircut to "CCC" rated assets to capture this increased proclivity to default in the overcollateralization test. This causes it to breach earlier as the "CCC" asset concentration increases, allowing for faster paydown of the rated debt. We generally look for the overcollateralization test haircut when the percentage of assets in the pool with a rating of "CCC" or less exceeds the original amount by 5 percent. Any amount over the original amount plus the 5 percent threshold is then carried at either 70 percent of its par value or at the market value of the asset in the numerator of the test. The collateral manager before the closing date of the transaction makes the choice between treatment at 70 percent of par or market value. When the market value treatment is chosen, the rating analyst should be consulted to determine the proper market value treatment.

Overcollateralization Reinvestment Test

In addition to the "CCC" haircut in the overcollateralization tests, many transactions also include a reinvestment overcollateralization test with a "CCC" haircut. This latter test is lower in the priority of payments, and, if breached, requires the manager to start reinvesting all or part of the excess interest proceeds. The overcollateralization reinvestment threshold is typically set higher than the minimum class overcollateralization threshold, thus allowing for reinvestment of interest proceeds before any delevering overcollateralization trigger is breached.

As the portfolio starts losing par from credit-impaired sales, the reinvestment trigger would be breached before the class overcollateralization trigger is breached. This would allow the transaction to start purchasing new collateral to improve the overcollateralization reinvestment test. This test works best for transactions that incur slow, gradual declines in collateral values. If the transaction experiences large asset defaults in a short period, the delevering overcollateralization test would likely be tripped simultaneously. Even under these circumstances, the overcollateralization reinvestment test is likely to bring some benefits, as it should force additional reinvestments, once the delevering overcollateralization test is brought back into compliance.

Current-Pay Collateral

A "current-pay" security is defined as an obligation that continues to pay interest or principal payments even though the obligor has defaulted on other obligations. In general, the collateral manager cannot purchase current-pay assets into the transaction, because these assets are credit-impaired obligations that they are typically prohibited from purchasing.

However, if the transaction holds an asset that then becomes a current-pay obligation, the collateral value is reduced to reflect the higher rating volatility. We use a market value test for this, giving full par value if the security trades at 80 percent or better, and the assigned recovery if it trades below. This haircut also reduces the numerator of the overcollateralization test, causing faster paydown of the rated debt.

Value of Defaulted Securities

Other than the current-pay securities valuation, all defaulted securities should be carried at the lower of their assigned recovery rate or current market value for the purpose of the overcollateralization test. In certain instances, however, we may assign instrument-specific recoveries. Equity securities received as part of a workout can be held in the CDO transaction, but are given no value.

REQUIREMENTS FOR RUNNING THE CASH FLOW MODEL

In order to ensure timely completion of the cash flow analysis, we ask that the arranger provide:

- ♦ A summary of all assumptions used in the cash flow modeling;
- ♦ A summary of the cash flow model results showing BDRs. We request the BDRs for all classes (rated and unrated) be provided;
- ♦ Detailed printouts of at least the two most stressful cash flow model runs for each rating level;
- ♦ A working, Excel-based cash flow model;
- ♦ A reliance letter from an accountant for each substantially different transaction structure or model; and

♦ A listing of failed scenarios, if any, including a present value calculation (discounted at the coupon rate of the applicable class).

APPENDIX A

Examples for Default and Recovery Modeling

Clarification of the application of the default and recovery modeling assumptions is provided by way of example (see Table A.1). Modeling assumptions applied include the following:

♦ Recoveries for defaulted bonds are assumed to have a one-year lag.
♦ Defaults are caused by nonpayment of interest. As such, no interest payment is received during and after the period that the asset defaults.
♦ Reinvestment of recovery proceeds from defaulted assets is assumed to occur at the end of the period that the recovery is realized. As such, the reinvested proceeds do not earn interest during the recovery period.
♦ Coverage tests are not breached—recovery proceeds are reinvested and not used to pay down liabilities.

There are two ways to model defaults in this scenario—the defaults can be modeled to occur at the end of each year or they can be smoothed out

TABLE A.1

Scenario Analyzed

Default pattern	40/20/20/10/10 beginning in year 1
Cumulative defaults (%)	30
Weighted-average recovery rate (%)	40
Asset type	Bonds
Liability payment frequency	Semi-annually

semi-annually. During the first year, defaults are usually modeled to occur at the end of the year. An initial portfolio with a high concentration of low-rated assets is one exception where defaults might be modeled to begin earlier.

First Method

All defaults occur at the end of the year (Table A.2).

Key Observations for First Method

Defaults are lumped together at the end of each year. For assets paying semi-annually, the defaulting assets earn interest during the first payment period, but not the second period, of the year. Thus, for the 6 percent of the portfolio that defaults (20×30 percent) in year 2, these assets receive credit for interest payments in period 3 but none beginning in period 4. Assets paying annually, however, would not earn interest in either of these periods.

Recovery of defaulted bonds occurs after a one-year lag. Again taking the 6 percent of the portfolio that defaults in year 2 (at end of period 4) and applying a 40 percent recovery rate to the defaulted balance, recoveries equating to 2.4 percent of the portfolio balance ($40 \times 20 \times 30$ percent) is realized at the end of period 6. If these recoveries occur during the reinvestment period, the recovery proceeds are reinvested and begin to earn interest starting in period 7.

Second Method

Annual defaults are separated into two semi-annual periods, starting after the first year. During first year, all defaults occur at the end of the year (Table A.3).

Key Observations for Second Method

Beginning with the second year, defaults are smoothed semi-annually. Thus, for the 6 percent of the portfolio that defaults (20×30 percent) in year 2, 3 percent occurs in period 3 and the remaining 3 percent occurs in period 4. For assets paying semi-annually, those defaulting in period 3 do not earn interest in that period; those defaulting in period 4 earn interest in period 3, but not in period 4. Assets paying annually do not receive interest in either of these periods.

TABLE A.2

Default and Recovery Scenario: Annual Defaults Modeled at End of Year

| | Application of default and recovery patterns (%) | | | | | | | | | | | |
| | Year and period | | | | | | | | | | | |
	Year 1 1st	Year 1 2nd	Year 2 3rd	Year 2 4th	Year 3 5th	Year 3 6th	Year 4 7th	Year 4 8th	Year 5 9th	Year 5 10th	Year 6 11th	Year 6 12th
Effective default pattern	—	40.0	—	20.0	—	20.0	—	10.0	—	10.0	—	—
Effective recovery pattern	—	—	—	40.0	—	20.0	—	20.0	—	10.0	—	10.0
Modeled default scenario (assuming 30% defaults)	—	12.0	—	6.0	—	6.0	—	3.0	—	3.0	—	—
Modeled recovery scenario (assuming 30% defaults and 40% recoveries)	—	—	—	4.8	—	2.4	—	2.4	—	1.2	—	1.2

TABLE A.3

Default and Recovery Scenario: Annual Defaults Modeled Semi-Annually

	Application of default and recovery patterns (%)											
	Year and period											
	Year 1 1st	Year 1 2nd	Year 2 3rd	Year 2 4th	Year 3 5th	Year 3 6th	Year 4 7th	Year 4 8th	Year 5 9th	Year 5 10th	Year 6 11th	Year 6 12th
Effective default pattern	—	40.0	10.0	10.0	10.0	10.0	5.0	5.0	5.0	5.0	—	—
Effective recovery pattern	—	—	—	40.0	10.0	10.0	10.0	10.0	5.0	5.0	5.0	5.0
Modeled default scenario (assuming 30% defaults)	—	12.0	3.0	3.0	3.0	3.0	1.5	1.5	1.5	1.5	—	—
Modeled recovery scenario (assuming 30% defaults and 40% recoveries)	—	—	—	4.8	1.2	1.2	1.2	1.2	0.6	0.6	0.6	0.6

Recovery of defaulted bonds occurs after a one-year lag. Recoveries on the 3 percent balance defaulting in period 3 are realized at the end of period 5 and begin to earn interest in period 6 (if the reinvestment period has not lapsed).

REFERENCES

de Servigny, A., and O. Renault (2004), *Measuring and Managing Credit Risk*, McGraw-Hill.

de Servigny, A., and N. Jobst (2005), "An empirical analysis of equity default swaps I: Univariate insights," *Risk*, December.

Fledelius, P., D. Lando, and J. P. Nielsen (2004), "Non-parametric analysis of rating transition and default data," working paper, Copenhagen Business School.

Glasserman, P. (2004), *Monte Carlo Methods In Financial Engineering*, Springer-Verlag.

Jobst, N., and A. de Servigny (2006), "An empirical analysis of equity default swaps II: Multivariate insights," RISK, January.

Jobst, N., and K. Gilkes (2003), "Investigating transition matrices: Empirical insights and methodologies," working paper, Standard & Poor's.

Li, D. (2000), "On default correlation: A copula function approach," *Journal of Fixed Income*, 9, 43–54.

Matsumoto, M. and Nishimura, T. (1998). Mersenne twister: A 623-dimensionally equidistributed uniform pseudo-random number generator, *ACM Transactions on Modelling and Computer Simulation*, 8(1), 3–30.

Merton, R. (1974), "On the pricing of corporate debt: The risk structure of interest rates," *Journal of Finance*, 29, 449–470.

Recent and Not So Recent Developments in Synthetic Collateral Debt Obligations

Norbert Jobst

INTRODUCTION

Collateralized debt obligations (CDOs) are designed to transfer the risk inherent in a portfolio of (credit) risky assets to one or more investors. Although the first CDOs were "cash"-funded and backed by portfolios of bonds and loans, in recent years the unfunded "synthetic" CDO market has grown enormously. Instead of purchasing a debt instrument of a given entity, the special purpose vehicle (SPV) enters into a credit default swap (CDS) that references the entity. This use of credit derivatives led to a European market dominated by "single-tranche" (ST) CDOs, bilateral contracts between a buyer and seller of default protection on a portfolio of entities. The U.S. market is currently evolving toward a blend of cash and synthetic transactions in a more gradual way.

Since 2004, the pace of innovation in structured credit markets, and particularly in synthetic CDOs, has increased significantly. The rise to prominence of ST synthetic CDOs stems from ease of execution, providing the flexibility of expressing various views on (credit) markets, and enabling the separation of funding and risk (see Chapter 9). In recent years, investor demands for higher yielding products in a extremely tight spread environment, combined with (various) market events, have led to financial innovations addressing higher structural complexity and nontraditional (noncredit) risks. Throughout this chapter, we provide an overview of a number of these developments mainly from a rating agency perspective where the risk assessment usually involves an estimate of the expected loss to the investor, or an estimate of the likelihood of principal and interest being paid in a timely manner.* The genesis of these innovations, as almost any in the synthetic CDO market, comes from a mixture of different drivers from the market participants: from investors' search for new yield in a tight spread environment to the need to investment diversification, and from arbitrage exploitation to structures that can be used to express a view on the systemic credit cycle as well as idiosyncratic credit risk.

We start in the following section by discussing various extensions or variants of ST CDOs where the main risks (from a rating agency perspective) are still default events and subsequent losses. We will discuss CDO squared transactions that were very popular in 2004/2005 with demand drying up after the downgrade of Ford and General Motors (GM) in May 2005. Forward-starting transactions, long/short structures, and ST CDOs with time varying attachment points are further examples that will be briefly introduced. In addition to these "add-ons" to traditional synthetic CDOs, investors frequently seek to try and take advantage from developments in noncredit markets.

In section "Beyond Credit Risk: Hybrid Structured Products," we focus on the most significant developments in alternative asset classes that find their way into so-called hybrid transactions. We also focus on equity risk via so-called equity default swaps (EDSs) and commodity risk in its subsections.

In section "Structural Innovations: Introducing MtM Risk," we focus on some of the latest developments caused by changes in the market participants' trading and hedging behavior, following the May 2005 events. These new structures aim at placing equity and/or super senior risk to "hedge" the high demand of mezzanine tranches and go beyond a pure default risk assessment of the underlying pool of assets by taking into account the risk of mark-to-market (MtM) changes. We start by discussing leveraged super senior (LSS) transaction in the first subsection, a product that is very popular since 2005. In the second subsection, a very recent development, the so-called credit constant propostional portfolio insurance (CPPI) transaction, which addresses guaranteed principal and interest payments and involves automatic portfolio rebalancing depending on portfolio performance,

---

*The focus lies therefore on a discussion (and modeling overview) of the main risk factors, rather than on valuation and relative-value considerations. References on the latter will be provided when available and adequate.

followed by a brief discussion of the latest innovation in rated structured credit markets: Constant Proportion Debt Obligation (CPDO). The last section summarized current trends and future modelling challenges.

VARIANTS OF ST CDOs

ST CDOs: A Ratings Perspective

Before moving to the evolution on ST synthetic CDOs, we start by reviewing typical risk assessments conducted in a similar way by most rating agencies (RAs) on the standard, vanilla ST CDO product. RAs, such as Standard & Poor's, Moody's, Fitch, or DBRS, are typically interested in the risk a CDO investor is facing throughout the life of the transaction and base their opinions partly on model-based statistics. For example, Moody's rating is a so-called "expected loss" rating and, as a result, the expected loss on a CDO tranche is estimated and benchmarked to various rating specific targets. Standard & Poor's, on the other hand, applies a "probability of default" rating and estimates the probability of the investor to face a "first dollar of loss" using its CDO Evaluator (see Chapter 10 for further details).

RAs, to date, mostly employ simulation methodologies in order to estimate the relevant risk measures. For example, Standard & Poor's models the dependency between defaults of different assets through the Gaussian copula approach, as introduced in the Chapters 4 and 6. For this model, correlated default times can be easily simulated by

1. Generating N standard multivariate normal random variables y_i admitting a correlation matrix Σ,
2. Calculating $u_i = \Phi(y_i)$, and
3. Calculating a default time $\tau_i = S^{-1}(u_i)$ for each asset.*

If τ_i is less than the maturity T of the CDO transaction, the loss L_i is determined as $L_i = N_i \times (1 - \delta_i)$, where N_i and δ_i are the exposure-at-default and recovery,[†] respectively, for the ith asset. We can therefore write the portfolio loss up to time t, $L(t)$, as

$$L(t) = \sum_i N_i \times (1 - \delta_i) \times 1_{\left\{ \tau_i \leq t \right\}},$$

---

*S^{-1} is used to denote the quasi-inverse of the survival function.
†The recovery can either be assumed to be constant or drawn from a distribution.

where $1_{\{\tau_i \leq t\}}$ is the default indicator for the ith asset.*

Using this Monte-Carlo simulation framework, the distribution of portfolio losses can be determined with high accuracy by generating a sufficient number of default times while maintaining a good level of flexibility. In practice, of course, this loss distribution can be generated through a number of different numerical techniques or models, as outlined in the Chapters 4, 6, and 7. In any case, each assets' default probability and recovery rate as well as the dependency behavior (correlation) across all asset types are required, and we refer to Chapter 10 for a detailed discussion of Standard & Poor's modeling assumptions.

CDO Risk Measures and Rating Assignment

From now onwards, we assume that correlated default times and the portfolio loss distribution are simulated efficiently, and introduce a few typical risk measures computed by RAs (see also Chapter 7 for further details).

Tranche Default Probability (Tranche PD)   Given an attachment point A and detachment point D (i.e., a tranche thickness equal to $D-A$), the tranche default probability is the probability that portfolio losses at maturity T exceeds A.† This is given by

$$PD^{Tj} = P(L(t) \geq A) = E[1_{\{L(t) \geq A\}}],$$

where $L(t)$ is the cumulative portfolio loss up to time t, $1_{()}$ is the indicator function,‡ and $E[]$ denotes the expectation that is determined by averaging the over all simulation paths. This forms the basis for assigning a rating to a synthetic CDO tranche for a PD-based rating. For example, in order to assign a tranche "AAA" rating, the tranche PD needs to be sufficiently low, and RAs frequently provide detailed tables (Target Probabilities or "CDO cutpoints") for different rating classes and maturities.

Expected Tranche Loss   Instead of only focusing on the likelihood of losses, the actual size of all losses may also be of interest. The cumulative loss on tranche j at time t, $L^{Tj}(t)$, is given by

$$L^{Tj}(t) = (L(t) - A)1_{\{A \leq L(t) \leq D\}} + (D - A)1_{\{L(t) \geq D\}}.$$

---

*The default indicator equals 1 if the expression within parentheses is true, and 0 if it is false.
†Note that in order to compute the tranche probability, the detachment point D is not required in the anlaysis.
‡This equals 1 if the expression within parentheses is true, and 0 if it is false.

The expected tranche loss is therefore given by

$$E[L_j^T(t)] = E[(L(t) - A)1_{\{A \le L(t) \le D\}} + (D - A)1_{\{L(t) \ge D\}}],$$

which is computed easily by simulation. An expected loss rating assigned by RAs, such as Moody's, is partly based on this measure of tranche risk.

Tranche Loss-Given-Default From the expected tranche loss and the tranche PD, the tranche loss-given-default is simply given by $LGD_j^T = \left(E[L^{T_j}(t)]\right)/PD^{T_j}$ under the assumption of independence between tranche PD and LGD.

With ST CDOs and several risk measures introduced earlier, we will now start to discuss evolutions of standard tranche products and assess the risks prevalent within the framework presented earlier. Unless otherwise stated, all numerical examples are based on Standard & Poor's modeling assumptions, as outlined in Chapter 10.

CDO Squared Transactions: Extending Leverage

Synthetic CDO squared transactions have become an established feature of the global CDO marketplace in 2004/2005. Since May 2005, however, demand has reduced significantly, as a result of MtM losses caused by many market participants following the downgrade of Ford and GM by Standard & Poor's (see Chapters 8 and 9 for further details). CDO squared transactions typically reference other "bespoke" CDO tranches, each referencing a single underlying corporate portfolio. In this way, additional leverage is created, resulting in a yield pick-up of these structures relative to similarly rated synthetic CDOs. This leveraging creates an investment that is less sensitive to small numbers of credit events within the underlying portfolio, but is also more likely to suffer large losses once its credit protection is eroded. Within the framework of the risk measures presented earlier, this implies very small tranche PDs but high tranche LGDs, hence, keeping expected tranche losses balanced. While some CDO squared transactions reference only CDOs, others have referenced portfolios containing a mixture of CDO and asset-backed securities (ABS) tranches, where the proportion of ABS is typically in the range of 70 to 90 percent by reference notional amount. The basic structure of a typical CDO squared transaction is shown schematically in Figure 11.1.

FIGURE 11.1

Schematic Diagram of a CDO Squared Transaction.

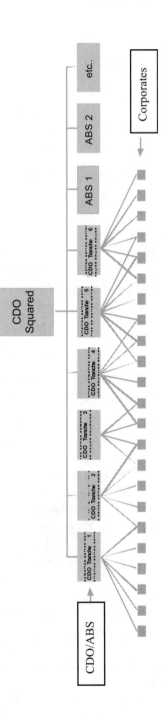

A CDO squared typically references between five and 15 different bespoke CDOs, which may lead to relatively large asset portfolios. Normally, there is a significant overlap between the reference portfolios of different bespoke CDOs, ranging from 20 to 30 percent in most cases, which also stems from the fact that only 600 to 800 CDSs trade liquidly in the market.

When the loss allocated to a bespoke CDO exceeds the attachment point of the CDO tranche, the loss is passed through to the CDO squared tranche. Bespoke CDOs therefore act as "loss filters" between the underlying corporate assets and the CDO squared. Of course, if a single CDS is referenced in multiple CDOs, this "overlap" creates "extra" correlation that can have a significant impact on CDO squared tranches. Mathematically, we can write the loss or protection payoff of a CDO squared tranche with attachment point $\tilde{A}$ and detachment point $\tilde{D}$ as:

$$L^{\text{CDO}^{\text{squared}}}(t) = (\tilde{L}(t) - \tilde{A})1_{\{\tilde{A} \le \tilde{L}(t) \le \tilde{D}\}} + (\tilde{D} - \tilde{A})1_{\{\tilde{L}(t) \ge \tilde{D}\}},$$

where

$$\tilde{L}(t) = \sum_{j=1}^{J} L^{T_j}(t) + \sum_{k=1}^{K} (1 - \delta_k)N_k 1_{\{\tau_{k_j} \le t\}}$$

$$= \sum_{j=1}^{J} \left[(L_j(t) - A_j)1_{\{A_j \le L_j(t) \le D_j\}} + (D_j - A_j)1_{\{L_j(t) \ge D_j\}} \right] + \sum_{k=1}^{K} (1 - \delta_k)N_k 1_{\{\tau_{k_j} \le t\}}$$

denotes the total portfolio loss resulting from J underlying "bespoke" CDO tranches and K additional assets (e.g., ABS or corporates). A_j and D_j denote the attachment and detachment point of bespoke tranche j, and $L_j(t)$ the portfolio loss at time t of the portfolio that backs (or is referenced by) tranche j. From that, tranche PD and expected tranche loss can be computed easily within the simulation framework.

An example of a typical CDO squared transaction, taken from Gilkes (2005), and illustrating the impact of overlap is presented next. Consider a hypothetical CDO squared with the following characteristics:

+ The portfolio contains eight bespoke CDO tranches and 50 "AAA" ABS tranches, with an average asset correlation of 10 percent.

+ Each bespoke CDO tranche references a portfolio of approximately 100 "A" names with 5 percent average asset correlation,

472   CHAPTER 11

equal reference notional amounts of €10 million, and assumed
recoveries of 35 percent.

+ Each bespoke CDO tranche has an attachment point of €40 million (consistent with a CDO rating at the "A" level) and a
detachment point of €50 million; i.e., a tranche thickness of
€10 million.

+ The average overlap between pairs of bespoke CDOs is 33 percent (or 66 percent).

+ Each ABS tranche has a reference notional amount of €10 million and an assumed recovery of 90 percent.

+ The CDO squared has a maturity of five years.

We consider three different CDO squared tranches. Each tranche is
assumed to reference the same portfolios as the ones described in the previous section, containing 33 percent and 66 percent CDO overlap. The
tranches are assumed to attach at 0 percent, 3 percent, and 6 percent loss,
and are therefore equivalent to equity, mezzanine, and senior tranches
with ratings in the "BB," "AA," and "AAA" range, respectively. Each CDO
squared tranche is assumed to have a thickness of 4 percent of the portfolio, i.e., €23.2 million. The results are shown in Tables 11.1 and 11.2.

In both sets of results (Tables 11.1 and 11.2), the tranche PD decreases
with increasing attachment point as expected. However, changing the
overlap from 33 to 66 percent has different effects, depending on the level
of seniority of the tranche. For example, the equity tranche PD decreases
with increasing overlap, whereas the mezzanine and senior tranche PDs
increase. The same is true of the expected tranche losses. As mentioned

TABLE 11.1

Tranche Risk Measures for a Hypothetical CDO
Squared with 33 Percent Overlap Between Bespoke
CDO Tranches

AP (%)	DP (%)	Tranche PD (%)	Tranche LGD (%)	Expected tranche loss (%)
0	4	12.67	11.39	1.44
3	7	0.35	50.89	0.18
6	10	0.11	45.34	0.05

Abbreviations: AP-attachment point; DP-detachment point.
Source: Standard & Poor's.

TABLE 11.2

Tranche Risk Measures for a Hypothetical CDO
Squared with 66 Percent Overlap Between Bespoke
CDO Tranches

AP (%)	DP (%)	Tranche PD (%)	Tranche LGD (%)	Expected tranche loss (%)
0	4	12.01	10.56	1.27
3	7	0.44	64.72	0.29
6	10	0.22	59.29	0.13

Appreviations: AP-attachment point; DP-detachment point.
Source: Standard & Poor's.

previously, this is a result of the increased correlation between CDO
tranches, which makes extreme losses more likely, without changing the
expected loss of the portfolio.

The tranche LGDs can be seen to first increase and then decrease,
with increasing attachment point. The relatively low LGD of the equity
tranche results from the high probabilities of low/zero loss associated
with the ABS tranches. These are the same factors that cause this tranche
to have a much higher PD. In the case of the more senior tranches, the
much lower PDs, combined with the more extreme "tail" losses associated
with the bespoke CDO tranches, result in significantly higher LGDs.

Cross Subordination

Following the growth of the CDO squared market in 2004/2005, a so-
called "cross subordination" feature has been introduced. This mechanism allows different bespoke CDOs to share the total subordination
provided by all bespoke CDOs. For example, eight CDOs with attachment
points and thicknesses of €10 million would create a total cross subordination of €80 million. During the life of the transaction, if any CDO experiences losses greater than €10 million, these losses are not passed through
to the CDO squared until the total aggregate losses exceed €80 million. In
this way, the CDO squared investor is protected from the risk of a small
number of CDOs experiencing losses, but is exposed to the risk that a large
number of CDOs experience losses.* This can also be extended to cases in

---

*Another way of stating this is that cross subordination reduces the idiosyncratic risk spe-
cific to each CDO, but increases the systematic risk common to all CDOs.

which the subordination is only "partially" cross-subordinated (e.g., the CDO squared tranche is only insulated from 75 percent of the total aggregate subordination of the bespoke CDOs).

The payoff of such a cross subordination feature (assuming only bespoke CDO tranches and no other assets in the underlying pool of assets) can be represented as follows.

$$L^{CS}(t) = (\tilde{L}^{CS}(t) - \tilde{A}^{CS})1_{\{\tilde{A}^{CS} \le \tilde{L}^{CS}(t) \le \tilde{D}^{CS}\}} + (\tilde{D}^{CS} - \tilde{A}^{CS})1_{\{\tilde{L}^{CS}(t) \ge \tilde{D}^{CS}\}},$$

where

$$\tilde{L}^{CS}(t) = \left(\sum_{j=1}^{J} L^{T_j}(t) - A\right)1_{\{A \le \sum_{j=1}^{J} L^{T_j}(t) \le D\}} + (D - A)1_{\{\sum_{j=1}^{J} L^{T_j}(t) \ge D\}},$$

where $A = \Sigma_{j=1}^{J}A_j$ denotes the total amount of cross subordination available and $D = \Sigma_{j=1}^{J}D_j$. With credit spreads at some of their tightest levels in recent years and the respective vanishing of "rating arbitrage" and a raised awareness of correlation/overlap risk of CDO squared transactions, demand has dried up subsequently. Further details can be found in Gilkes (2005), and a discussion of CDO squared valuation and risk management is given in Metayer (2005).

Forward Starting CDOs

Also in 2005, ST CDOs evolved to incorporate so-called forward starting features, i.e., the risk horizon of the CDO only starts after time v. Losses due to defaults prior to v are not accounted for in the payoff and portfolio loss calculation:

$$L(t) = \sum_{i} N_i \times (1 - \delta_i) \times 1_{\{v \le \tau_i \le t\}}.$$

This feature allows investors to express their specific, short-term default views into the CDO product, or take advantage of favourable divergences between the credit curve perceived by RAs (under the real measure) and that of the market (implied, risk-neutral measure).

Of course, such a forward starting feature essentially impacts all tranches along the capital structures as the overall default rate reduces,

TABLE 11.3

Risk Measures for Forward Starting Equity Tranche
(in Percent)

	Equity tranche (0–3%)				
	Current	1y forward	2y forward	3y forward	4y forward
Expected portfolio loss	1.67	1.48	1.22	0.91	0.55
Expected tranche loss	48.70	44.25	37.73	28.95	17.94
Tranche PD	82.61	79.29	73.68	64.21	48.05

but the relative impact can vary across different tranches as illustrated in Tables 11.3 and 11.4 for an equity and a senior tranche backed by a portfolio of 100 BBB rated assets in 10 sectors.

Similarly, the relative impact of forward starting features also depends on the credit quality of the underlying pool and the shape of the term structure of default probabilities. From a modeling perspective, just ignoring the forward starting period implicitly assumes that in future periods, (forward) losses will prevail (in expectation) as given by current credit curves. In doing so, we essentially ignore the forward dynamics of portfolio losses, an area that has received some attention recently, see Schönbucher (2005) and Sidenius et al. (2005). Furthermore, forward starting transactions highlight an interesting question when monitoring it. As time passes, one can either rerun the analysis by assuming a shorter maturity and forward starting period with default probabilities, as seen at time

TABLE 11.4

Risk Measures for Forward Starting Senior Tranche
(in Percent)

	Senior tranche (7–10%)				
	Current	1y forward	2y forward	3y forward	4y forward
Exp portfolio loss	1.67	1.48	1.22	0.91	0.55
Exp tranche loss	0.23	0.14	0.06	0.01	0.00
Tranche PD	0.47	0.30	0.14	0.04	0.00

0 on the credit curve. That means, for future time s, we assume default probabilities $P_i(0, T-s)$, where T denotes the time maturity, and ignore defaults in the simulation between 0 and $v-s$. Alternatively, we can roll the transaction down the credit curve by assuming forward starting probabilities, i.e., use $P_i(s, T) \approx P_i(0, T) - P_i(0, s)$. Each approach has got drawbacks if static credit curves are assumed, and a detailed forward loss modeling is avoided. For example, in the former approach, we would essentially assume that noninvestment grade (NIG) companies have always the same default risk over the next year, despite the common opinion that credit risk is declining if an NIG firm stays in a specific rating for a significant period of time. The latter approach, on the other hand, is clearly based on the assumption that the forward expectation will prevail, and carries the problem that we would need to monitor the duration a company is/was in a given rating category prior to the risk assessment, unless a Markov assumption can be empirically justified.* Hence, this approach would be heavily dependent on the Markov property that has previously been questioned in empirical studies (see, e.g., Lando and Skodeberg, 2002).

Long/Short Structures

In a CDS, the protection seller agrees to pay the protection buyer the reference notional amount of the contract minus a recovery amount, in the event of default of a given reference entity. In exchange for this contingent payment, the protection buyer pays the protection seller a premium. When an entity sells protection in CDS form, it is said to take a "long" position, whereas buying protection corresponds to entering a "short" position. For loss computations, we can simply change the sign of the loss (i.e., making it a gain) in the event of default of the reference name, conditional upon the survival of the protection seller.†

The impact of shorting assets in the underlying portfolio depends, amongst other factors, on the credit quality of the long positions, the credit quality of the short positions, and the target rating that one wants to achieve (i.e., the level of subordination). We illustrate this on the following examples. First, we consider a portfolio of 100 long "A" rated

---

*Here we assume a typical RA approach, where default probabilities are directly linked to the rating of a company.
†Hence, there is some additional counterparty risk, which requires additional information on the CDS counterparty when short CDS are included within the portfolio.

FIGURE 1 1 . 2

Impact of Short Positions on "A" Quality Portfolio.

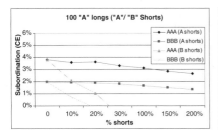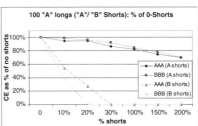

assets in 10 sectors. We then gradually add buckets of short positions, from 10 percent of the long notional amount up to 200 percent of the long notional amount. We consider "A" and "B" quality assets for the short buckets. Figure 11.2 shows the impact of adding short positions on the credit enhancement (CE) required, in order to achieve a "AAA" and "BBB" rating from Standard & Poor's. The left exhibit shows the absolute CE, whereas the right exhibit shows the relative CE as a fraction of the long only "A" rated portfolio notional (put another way, the right panel shows the CE with shorts scaled by the CE needed without shorts).

The grey line shows the CE required to achieve an "AAA" rating when different amounts of "A" shorts are added, whereas the greyline shows the same statistic when "B" shorts are added instead. The dotted and dashed line shows the same statistic for a target "BBB" rating. What is apparent is that the required CE reduces with the introduction of a short bucket and, as expected, that this reduction depends highly on the credit quality of the short portfolio. When "B" quality short positions are added, we see a stark decline in required subordination, resulting from significantly higher PDs of NIG assets compared to investment grade, (IG) ones.

Figure 11.3 repeats this exercise, but now for a long portfolio of "BB" quality, and we consider shorting "BB" and "B" quality assets this time.

Although the observations of Figure 11.2 also hold for this experiment, we can further observe that the relative decline in CE when shorts of the same credit quality as longs are introduced is higher for low credit quality portfolios.

In addition to shorting single-name exposures, short positions can also be taken in synthetic CDO tranches. Going long and short tranches allows one to execute directional trades where a (speculative) view is taken

FIGURE 11.3

Impact of Short Positions on "BB" Quality Portfolio.

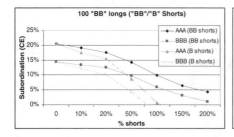 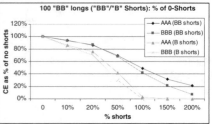

on future credit markets (see Chapters 7, 8, and 9, for further details). From a (loss) modeling perspective, CDO squared technology can be used to adequately implement short tranche positions.

Variable (Time-Dependent) Subordination: "Step-up" Transactions

In the earlier expression for the tranche default probability, we assumed that the attachment point A is constant over time. This can easily be generalized to cases where the attachment point is a function of time t, so that the earlier expression becomes $PD^{\text{Tranche}} = P(L(t) \geq A(t)) = E[1_{\{L(t) \geq A(t)\}}]$. In this case, we evaluate the loss distribution at all points in time at which the attachment point changes. As an example, consider a hypothetical seven-year synthetic CDO transaction. If the attachment point is initially set at 3 percent of the portfolio notional balance, but then increases to 5 percent after three years and remains at this level until maturity, we need to evaluate the loss distribution at years 3 and 7. The cumulative default probability of the tranche is therefore the probability that losses exceed 3 percent by year 3 plus the probability that losses exceed 5 percent by year 7, *conditional* upon losses not exceeding 3 percent by year 3.

In the market place, such transactions are often denoted as "step-up" deals and extensions where the time-dependent attachment point also depends on certain levels of losses being reached are feasible. For example, it is possible to model transactions in which the attachment point "resets" according to the cumulative loss experienced by the portfolio at a certain date. This dynamic behavior is easily modeled by keeping track of the portfolio loss path during simulation.

BEYOND CREDIT RISK: HYBRID STRUCTURED PRODUCTS

In recent years, structured credit products, and in particular synthetic CDOs, evolved toward referencing a variety of asset types. Routinely, ST CDOs reference corporate CDSs, ABS tranches, other CDOs, or loans given to small and medium enterprises. When included in a CDO, common to all these assets is the risk of default or credit risk of the underlying reference obligation. More recently, several noncredit derivatives have been introduced to the synthetic CDO market in a search for higher yielding instruments in a very tight credit environment.

In 2004, an upsurge in interest in so-called EDSs took place. EDSs are long-dated, deep out-of-the-money equity puts that are similar to CDS, in which a contingency payment takes place if the equity price of a specific entity breaches a low barrier (typically 30 percent). The reason for these developments was the search for higher yield in a tight spread environment, but also a general trend towards the convergence of credit and equity markets. Frequently, CDOs of EDS (or CEOs) reference both, CDS and EDSs. In the next section, we review a number of developments on EDS, as well as CDOs of EDS.

At the same time, dealers started to consider the introduction of deep out-of-the-money (European) commodity options into ST CDOs. The interest in this product has also increased toward the end of 2005, as a result of steadily rising commodity markets. Again, the incorporation of credit and commodity (and potentially equity) risk within an ST CDO comes with a number of modeling challenges. Dependence issues, e.g., the link between large oil corporations and oil prices, need to be carefully addressed. The section "CDOs: Commodity Transactions" reviews some recent developments by Standard & Poor's in modeling collateralized commodity obligations.

In addition to these developments, some general interest on multiasset-class products has been noted. Such transactions aim to transfer various other risks such as interest rate or FX risk, in addition to commodity, equity, and credit risk, via synthetic CDO technology.

When dealing with the problem of modeling ST CDOs backed by various (noncredit) asset types, one has the choice of staying within (and extending) the common framework used for ST CDOs or to develop a new methodology. Throughout this chapter, we focus on developments within the usual copula framework, offering a brief discussion of alternatives in the last section. For now, when looking at alternative asset types and risks, we focus on univariate and multivariate aspects separately, focusing on the Gaussian copula framework discussed in the "Variants of ST CDOs" section previously and in various other chapters.

Equity Default Swaps

Over the last two years, there has been some interest in CDOs referencing portfolios of EDS. These contracts trigger a payment when the underlying equity price falls below a predetermined level. This price decline is often referred to as an "equity event" (or interchangeably as "equity default," or "EDS default") analogous to a credit event within a CDS contract. As the trigger price is set closer to zero, these contracts can be expected to become more "credit-like," and EDS/CDS spreads should start to converge.

In a CDO that references a pool of equities under an EDS contract, the same basic roles exist as for a typical CDO referencing CDSs. The seller is paid a premium in exchange for a principal commitment when losses exceed the threshold amount. In this case, however, losses are defined as the notional amount of equities whose prices fall to the trigger level, minus a predetermined recovery rate. Although any combination of trigger level and recovery rate could be considered, EDS contracts are typically structured in the market with a trigger level set at 30 percent and a fixed recovery rate of 50 percent. For some investors, the risk–return characteristics of portfolios of these deep "out-of-the-money," long-dated digitals offer relative value, especially given the recent tightening of CDS spreads.

Introducing EDSs into ST CDOs within the current copula framework requires an assessment of the (univariate) likelihood of equity prices on individual names to breach the barrier (hit the strike), as well as an assessment of joint equity behavior, and potentially the link between credit and equity. All analysis conducted herewith are based on Standard and Poor's CreditPro® ratings and default database linked to Standard & Poor's Compustat® (North America) data. CreditPro contains the ratings history of approximately 9740 companies from December 31, 1981 to December 31, 2003 and includes 1170 default events. The Compustat database contains approximately 56,500 corporations trading in the United States or Canada between 1962 and 2003, of which, up to 12,240 equity time series or over 128,000 yearly observations are analyzed herewith.

Equity Events: Empirical Insights and Univariate Modeling

In the following, we review three different types of analysis. First, a pure cohort analysis, second, a direct modeling of equity prices via stochastic processes; and lastly, a statistical credit scoring approach.

Equity Default Events: Cohort Results Jobst and Gilkes (2004) present a cohort analysis (see Chapter 2 for further details) that is commonly used to derive historic average default or rating transition probabilities. We start by considering all companies at a specific point in time t (e.g., December 31, 2000). We denote the total number of companies in the kth cohort at time t by $N_k(t)$, and the total number of observed events (e.g., default or equity price decline) in period T (i.e., between time $t+T-1$ and time $t+T$) by $D_k(t, T)$. We then obtain an estimate for the (marginal) probability of default in year T (as seen from time t):*

$$P_k(t, T) = \frac{D_k(t, T)}{N_k(t)}.$$

Repeating this analysis for cohorts created at M different points in time t allows us to obtain an estimate for the unconditional probability of default in period T,

$$\overline{P}_k(T) = \sum_{t=1}^{M} w_k(t)P_k(t,T).$$

These unconditional probabilities are simply weighted averages of the estimates obtained for cohorts considered in different periods. Typically, $w_k(t)=1/M$ (each period is equally weighted) or $w_k(t) = N_k(t)/\Sigma_{m=1}^{M}N_k(m)$ (weighted according to the number of observations in different periods).

Unconditional (weighted average) cumulative probabilities $\overline{P}_k^{\,cum}(T)$ capturing defaults over T periods can be calculated from the unconditional marginal probabilities $\overline{P}_k(T)$:

---

*Some companies will have their rating withdrawn during the course of the year. It is common to treat these transitions to NR (not rated) as noninformative with respect to the credit quality. Hence, companies that have their rating withdrawn during the period of interest are ignored in the subsequent analysis.

$$\overline{P}_k^{\text{cum}}(T) = \overline{P}_k^{\text{cum}}(T-1) + \left(1 - \overline{P}_k^{\text{cum}}(T-1)\right)\overline{P}_k(T).$$

Jobst and Gilkes (2004) apply this cohort approach and estimate the unconditional long-term average probability of an equity price decline to a level of b percent of the initial price. This probability is referred to as the equity event probability (EEP), which obviously depends on the value of b. For each company in a given cohort at a specific point in time t (e.g., December 1980), we register the price P_t by comparing the running minimum monthly price between time $t+T-1$, P_{t+T-1}^-, and time T, P_{t+T}^-, to the EDS barrier $B_t = b \cdot P_t$. In practice, we can group companies with similar financial ratios (such as market capitalization or leverage), companies with similar equity performance (such as historic return or volatility), or by credit characteristics (such as credit rating).

The main finding of Jobst and Gilkes (2004) is that the likelihood of severe equity price declines is strongly linked to the historic equity price volatility of the equity issue and to the credit quality of the underlying corporation. This relationship holds across all barrier levels in the range of [0, 100 percent] and for a wide range of maturities. The relative importance of each of these factors varies by barrier and maturity. The link between EEPs and volatility is displayed in Figure 11.4 based on data from 1963 to 2003. Firms are grouped into different volatility bands by creating quintiles, i.e., the 20 percent of firms with the highest volatility

F I G U R E   1 1 . 4

Cumulative EEPs for 30 Percent Barrier by Volatiltiy (Left Panel) and Five-Year Equity Event Probabilities by Volatility for Different Barriers (Right Panel).

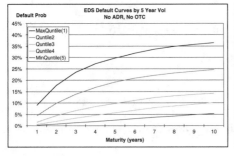
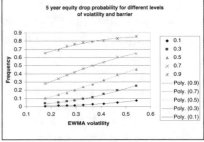

FIGURE 11.5

Equity Event Probabilities by Rating Category (Left Panel) and "A" Rated Firms by Volatility (Right Panel).

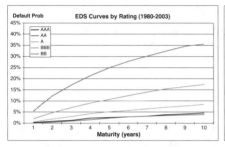
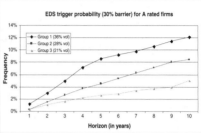

are grouped into Quintile 1, whereas the 20 percent of firms with the lowest volatility result in Quintile 5.

Occasionally, an equity price decline of 70 percent is denoted as "credit-like" or "default-like" event, which motivates the use of credit-related variables in empirical studies. We consider therefore a subset of rated firms over the period 1981 to 2003 and create cohorts by rating class. The cumulative equity drop probabilities are shown in Figure 11.5.

Although the cohort approach provides a first indication of EDS riskiness when the factors/groups are known, a more systematic approach is presented further next.

Direct Modeling of Equity Price Dynamics An alternative to a statistical counting approach is to apply stochastic models for equity prices. There are several models for equity prices that can be used in the analysis of EDS. Usually, research on equity returns or equity risk measurement focuses on horizons much shorter (typically a few days) than the standard five-year EDS maturity (e.g., a few days). Hence, it is necessary to gain insight into the performance of these approaches for extended horizons, an area that has received very little attention by (academic) researchers so far. An exception* is Kaufmann and Patie (2004) who discuss quantile risk measures estimated from lognormal (LN) models, generalized autoregressive conditional

---

*In addition, Christoffersen et al. (1998) and Morillo and Pohlman (2002) discuss long-term risk management.

heteroscedastic (GARCH) models, and heavy-tailed distributions for a one-year horizon. Bayliffe and Pauling (2003) also study long-term equity returns, focusing on the issue of mean reversion in equity markets, and compare several models, including mean-reverting (MR), index MR, and regime-switching models.

Jobst and Gilkes (2004) also present some insights into practical application and performance of two of the most common models—the LN and GARCH(1,1) models.

Lognormal Model with Constant Drift   The standard LN model with constant volatility is given by $dP_t = \mu_E P_t dt + \sigma_E P_t dW_t$, where μ_E and σ_E are constants denoting the drift and volatility. The great advantage of this model is its analytical tractability, which can lead to closed-form results for EEPs:

$$P(\min_{[0,T]} P_t < B) = 1 - \Phi\left(\frac{\ln(P_0/B)}{\sigma\sqrt{T}}\right) + \left(\frac{(\mu_E - 0.5\sigma^2)\sqrt{T}}{\sigma_E}\right)$$

$$+ \left(\frac{B}{P_0}\right)^{2(\mu_E - 0.5\sigma_{E^2})/\sigma^2} \Phi\left(\frac{\ln(P_0/B)}{\sigma_E\sqrt{T}}\right) + \left(\frac{(\mu_E - 0.5\sigma_{E^2})\sqrt{T}}{\sigma_E}\right),$$

where $B = b \cdot P_0$ denotes the EDS barrier.

In principle, the model parameters can easily be estimated from historic equity returns. Because the data generating process frequently does not follow Geometric Brownian Motion (GBM), a straightforward application of the model to real life data may need to overcome several difficulties.

Jobst and Gilkes (2004) conduct a back-testing experiment within the EDS framework on a very large number of companies over the period 1967 to 2003. A LN model with constant drift is calibrated to five years of historic data for each company in our database. The companies are grouped into volatility quintiles in the usual way, and we calculate the average EEP for a 30 percent barrier over maturities of 1 to 10 years by averaging the relevant probabilities derived for each company. The resulting weighted average EEPs derived by the model are compared to the historic average EEPs from the cohort analysis in Figure 11.6.

The outcome of this analysis is quite encouraging, in that the model estimates (dashed lines) are quite close to the unconditional

FIGURE 1 1 . 6

Backtesting Results: Unconditional Cohort Estimates
versus LN Model.

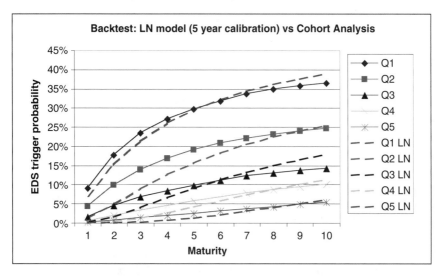

cohort estimates (solid line with markers), in particular for extended
horizons. For short horizons, the models seem to underestimate the risk
consistently.

Unfortunately, these results do not hold when a smaller sample is
considered (e.g., a narrower volatility band). One reason for the instability is the model sensitivity to the constant drift, which starts to dominate
the volatility term for extended horizons.* Figure 11.7 shows the EEPs for
varying values of the drift as a function of time to maturity, assuming a
constant 35 percent annualized volatility.

These results indicate that a name-by-name estimation may be troublesome, and that swings in stock markets would lead to rapidly changing EEPs. In order to dampen these effects, we need to derive adjustments
to the model inputs or outputs similar in nature to the adjustments necessary in the application of structural (Merton-type) models for PD estimation (see, e.g., Sobehart and Keenan, 2004). These amendments should

---

*The same problem needs to be addressed for structural (Merton-type) credit risk models.
There, the impact of the drift is also significant in near default situations and for medium to long
horizons. Because of the estimation difficulties for the asset drift term, the information added is
assumed to be noninformative and frequently ignored (see Lando, 2004 for a discussion).

FIGURE 1 1 . 7

EEPs for Different Drift Assumptions.

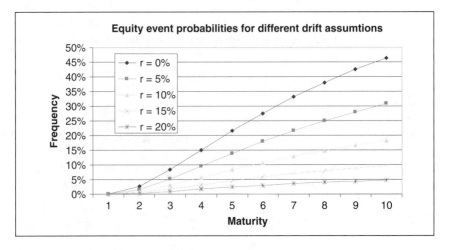

result in a better agreement between model performance and empirical evidence.

GARCH(1,1) Model with Constant Drift A simple extension of the LN model is based on the observation that volatility in financial markets is usually not constant. Indeed, clustering of volatility can be frequently observed, where tranquil periods of low returns are interspersed with volatile periods of high returns. Technically, this is known as autoregressive conditional heteroscedasticity (ARCH), and generalized ARCH (GARCH) models—first developed by Bollerslev (1986)—attempt to capture this behavior. In a simple GARCH(1,1) model with constant drift, the return of an equity is given by $r_t = \mu + \varepsilon_t$, where $\varepsilon_t \sim \Phi(0, \sigma_t)$. The conditional variance σ_t is modeled as $\sigma_t^2 = \omega + \alpha \varepsilon_{t-1}^2 + \beta \sigma_{t-1}^2$, and the model calibration is usually performed within a maximum likelihood framework.

The calibration of the GARCH parameters turns out to be quite sensitive to the chosen time series, in particular when a long time series (advisable for long-term risk management) are considered. Stărică (2003) provides a very useful discussion on GARCH parameter estimation and stability for large amounts of historic data.

Nevertheless, the more realistic specification of the volatility dynamics makes GARCH models suitable for EDS modeling. Compared to LN models, EEPs tend to be higher for short horizons (the first few years) while the estimates converge for longer horizons. As a result, some of the underestimation of the models compared to empirical evidence shown in Figure 11.6 would be reduced, and a further improvement may be achieved by introducing non-normal residuals. Equity time-series data usually exhibits fatter tails that the normal distribution is able to capture, and other distributions are employed to capture these tail events more adequately, see, e.g., McNeil and Frey (2000). The most common extensions of the GARCH(1,1) model involve non-normal residuals, higher order GARCH models, and extended GARCH models that focus on asymmetry in observed equity returns (see, Alexander, 2001 for an overview). The insights of Kaufmann and Patie (2004) on the choice of data frequency for estimation and on the adequacy of the "square-root-of time" scaling rules are also very relevant within our context of EDS modeling. Further details on the application of GARCH models for EDS ratings purposes can be found in Standard & Poor's (2004), and Fitch (2004).

A Statistical Credit Scoring Approach   Although the first cohort results illustrate the importance of ratings and volatility when assessing the performance of EDSs, several other variables could be informative, too. de Servigny and Jobst (2005) adapt commonly used credit scoring models for EDS. There, up to 23 variables—ranging from market variables (such as the S&P 500 volatility) and equity performance variables (e.g., equity specific mean return, volatility, or higher moments), to firm-specific accounting information (e.g., debt-to-equity ratio)—are considered in the scoring exercise.

In the credit world, this is one of the most widespread techniques to assess the risk on a large population, for which discrete information is available. Among the various scoring techniques, logistical regressions (logit models) correspond to a standard approach. These scoring techniques deliver point-in-time information in the sense that they enable us to assess default or event risk at a targeted and explicitly defined horizon. The results they provide are usually less informative before or beyond this horizon.

Overview of Methodology   de Servigny and Jobst (2005) use advanced logit techniques described in Cangemi et al. (2003). Let us consider a vector X of risk factors, with $X \in R^d$. The probability of a default or of an equity event (symbolized by a "1"), conditional on the information X, can be written as the logit transformation of a feature function, $F(X)$, maximizing the combined predictive power of the factors. The logit transformation* enables us to obtain a result located in the interval $]0,1[$:

$$P(1|\mathbf{X}) = \frac{1}{1 + e^{-F(\mathbf{X})}}.$$

The specification of $F(\mathbf{X})$ can be simple, corresponding to the first order of the Taylor expansion of the "true," unobservable, underlying feature function. In this case, we have a linear logit model. The specification can be more refined, including the quadratic terms too, leading to a quadratic logit. In order to better account for higher power terms[†] without having to estimate too many weights, we can include some additional cylindrical kernel features of the form

$$f_k(\mathbf{X}) = \sum_{i=1}^{p} \sum_{\theta=1}^{n} \varepsilon_{i\theta} \frac{(x_i - a_\theta)^2}{\sigma^2},$$

where $\varepsilon_{i\theta}$ are weights, a_θ the selected centers, and σ a bandwidth term corresponding to the decay rate of the kernel.

Practically, the models we run can be described as follows:

♦ A linear logit model

$$P(1|\mathbf{X}) = \frac{1}{1 + \exp(-(\beta + \sum_{i=1}^{p} \delta_i x_i))}$$

♦ A quadratic logit model

$$P(1|\mathbf{X}) = \frac{1}{1 + \exp(-(\beta + \sum_{i=1}^{p} \delta_i x_i + \sum_{j=1}^{p} \sum_{k=1}^{p} \gamma_{jk} x_j x_k))}$$

♦ A Full logit model, i.e., a combination of linear + quadratic + Kernel features

$$P(1|\mathbf{X}) = \frac{1}{1 + \exp\left(-\left(\beta + \sum_{i=1}^{p} \delta_i x_i + \sum_{j=1}^{p} \sum_{k=1}^{p} \gamma_{jk} x_j x_k + \sum_{i=1}^{p} \sum_{\theta=1}^{n} \varepsilon_{i\theta} \frac{(x_i - a_\theta)^2}{\sigma^2}\right)\right)}$$

By using different logit specifications, we reduce model risk and can better analyze the real predictive power of the data. The calibration of the

---

*Other transformations are possible such as the Probit one.
[†]Another way to present it is to further reduce the residual or error term.

models by maximum likelihood includes a regularization feature that helps to reduce overfitting when having to calibrate many weights related to corresponding terms, see Chapter 2 for further details.

Empirical Results de Servigny and Jobst (2005) show once again that rating and one-year historic volatility have consistently high factor loadings, which confirms our initial variable choice (see Figure 11.8, top panel). The genuine picture we obtain is that the explanatory power of credit variables decreases with rising barriers, whereas the impact of market variables such as volatility increases in barrier level. For example, the most important factor for barriers above 50 percent is volatility followed

FIGURE 11.8

Relative Contribution of Various Risk Factors (Top Panel) Aggregated by Credit or Equity Factors (Bottom Panel).

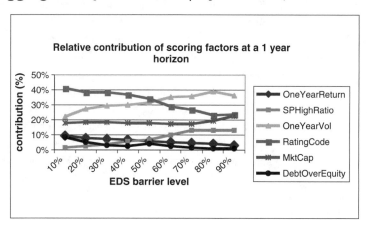

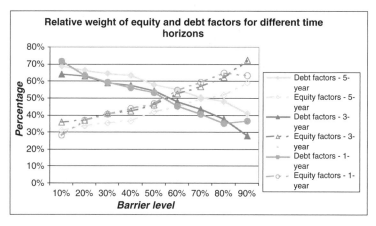

TABLE 11.5

Rank Ordering of Categories—Performance
Measurement (in Percent)

EDS categories	10% barrier			30% barrier			50% barrier		
Horizon	1 year	3 years	5 years	1 year	3 years	5 years	1 year	3 years	5 years
Gini coefficient	91.97	83.98	80.88	82.79	75.34	69.86	73.47	63.08	57.53

by credit rating, whereas for barriers below 50 percent the rank ordering is reversed. For extended horizons, however, the explanatory power of credit variables still appears most significant (Figure 11.8, bottom panel).

After identifying important factors using simple linear logit models, de Servigny and Jobst (2005) apply the advanced credit scoring models in order to improve the already encouraging performance of the scoring methodology. Using models estimated for 10 percent, 30 percent, and 50 percent barriers and 1-, 3-, and 5-year maturities, a filtering system is developed that allows us to classify EDSs into risk categories I to V.

The performance of this risk classification is reported through rank ordering statistics—so-called Gini coefficients (see Appendix A)—in Table 11.5. Basically, Gini coefficients give an indication whether or not the risky EDSs predicted by the model are indeed the ones that trigger EDS events. The same statistic is frequently applied for PD models, where Gini coefficients vary between 50 percent and 90 percent, depending on dataset and application. As can be seen from Table 11.5, the performance of the proposed EDS classification is very encouraging, supporting the choice of models and classification. For further details, we refer to de Servigny and Jobst (2005).

Although the section presented several ways of measuring the likelihood of equity events, many interesting valuation issues are addressed in Medova and Smith (2004) and Albanese and Chen (2005).

Dependent Events: Multivariate Aspects of EDS Modeling

The interpretation of the Gaussian copula model within the structural—Merton—framework indicates that all securities are functions of the firms asset value process. Therefore, all securities will move comonotonically with that process suggesting the adequacy of using equity or credit spread data for calibration. The advantage of correlations from equity prices is clearly data availability and the ability to estimate issuer specific comovements. Although this is true for corporate assets, the generalization to other structured finance assets that are frequently contained in CDOs [such as residential-mortgage backed securities (RMBS), ABS, etc.] and the exposure of equity prices to trends and market movements independent of the credit quality changes produce at best very noisy estimates (de Servigny and Renault, 2003). Similarly, credit spreads are likely to be influenced by market trends or liquidity issues. Unlike equity- and spread-based correlations, an approach that directly employs actual (observed) default events reduces the possibility of spurious correlation caused by unrelated external factors. Because event-based correlations usually require large samples spanning at least 20 years of data, they are frequently seen as long-term estimates that should dampen the fluctuations due to business cycle and economic effects. Jobst and de Servigny (2006) focus on empirical event-based correlations, where both default and equity events are considered (within the same analytic framework). They employ, once again, methods developed in the credit risk arena to EDSs. Stability of estimation is addressed by considering three different correlation estimators, all of which can produce estimates for industry- (or more generally risk-class-) specific correlations that would need to be used within the Gaussian copula model to reproduce average historic joint default/equity default behavior. First, joint (pairwise) event probabilities are estimated and transformed into empirical event and implied asset correlations, following the approach of de Servigny and Renault (2003). In order to mitigate bias due to (unknown) properties of certain estimators, we also consider the Binomial maximum likelihood estimator (MLE) and Asymptotic MLE of Demey et al. (2004) based on a factor modeling approach and conditional independence. While the first estimator is capable of producing correlations between all industry combinations, the second estimator produces industry specific correlations only within a certain industry. Correlations between two industries are constant and, hence, independent of the specific industries.

Constraint Factor Structure in MLE Approach

Having a very large number of firms to cope with in practice, it is usual to assume that we have identified a (lower) number of factors and rewrite the latent random variables/asset values $(V_1, \ldots, V_N)$ as a linear function of the factors:

$$V_i = \sqrt{\rho}F + \sqrt{\rho_c - \rho}F_c + \sqrt{1 - \rho_c}\varepsilon_i \quad i \in c$$

The resulting restricted correlation dynamics (with constant and indentical correlation between different groups),

$$
\sum\nolimits_{\mathrm{MLE}}^{\mathrm{Ind}} = \begin{bmatrix} \rho_1 & \rho & \cdots & \rho \\ \rho & \rho_2 & \ddots & \vdots \\ \vdots & \ddots & \ddots & \rho \\ \rho & \cdots & \rho & \rho_I \end{bmatrix}
$$

implies efficient numerical optimization of the MLE compared to the unconstrained model, as default probabilities conditional on the common factors can be computed in closed form. Then, the distribution of defaults/events follows a binomial distribution with known parameters, and the MLE is determined by integrating over the common factor (see Demey et al., 2004 or Jobst and de Servigny, 2006).

EDS Correlations: Empirical Insights

The Standard 30 Percent Barrier   Table 11.6 shows industry specific correlation estimates obtained form the EDS database for a 30 percent barrier. Column AvgN contains the average number of firms in each year in each industry; DefCorr and ImpAssCorr contain the empirical EDS event and implied asset correlation according to the de Servigny and Renault (2003) approach; and AsyMLE and BinMLE contains the Asymptotic MLE and Binomial MLE results of Jobst and de Servigny (2006). The last row contains the (average) correlation between two industries, and the average intra-industry correlation is reported in the row above.

This table (Table 11.6) reveals several interesting insights. First, the EDS correlations for 30 percent barriers appear to be significantly higher than the default correlations. The average intra- and inter-industry correlations are approximately 27 percent and 15 to 17 percent, respectively, which compares to 14 to 18 percent and 5 to 6 percent for (credit) default data (see Jobst and de Servigny, 2006 for results on credit defaults).

EDS Correlations for Different Barriers   In the following, we calculate intra- and inter-industry correlations based on all three estimators for barriers of 10 percent (corresponding to a 90 percent drop) to 90 percent (corresponding to a 10 percent drop). Figures 11.9A and 11.9B plot the corresponding intra-industry and inter-industry correlations for different barriers, respectively.

TABLE 11.6

Empirical Equity Event and Resulting Asset Correlations

	Avgn	DefCorr (%)	ImpAssCorr (%)	AsyMLE (%)	BinMLE (%)
Auto	113	5.8	23.0	15	20.3
Cons	115	3.0	17.0	18	22.5
Ener	58	8.1	28.0	28	36.1
Fin	85	2.5	16.0	13	17.7
Chem	46	4.2	21.0	16	18.0
Health	72	3.6	17.0	16	20.0
HiTech	55	22.1	44.0	28	36.3
Ins	44	2.3	14.0	18	17.7
Leis	60	5.3	19.0	16	18.2
RealEst	27	22.5	47.0	53	40.1
Telecom	22	34.4	61.0	39	52.9
Trans	24	1.5	19.0	23	24.6
Util	55	2.2	27.0	19	24.8
Avg(Ind) = Intra		8.5	27.2	23.2	26.9
Inter-Industry		3.7	14.2	9	17.6

Within a certain industry, the Binomial MLE and implied asset correlation estimators seem to be in good agreement, whereas for barriers below 50 percent, the small sample bias of the asymptotic estimator becomes apparent. For inter-industry correlations, the underestimation of the asymptotic estimator becomes even more apparent. In addition, we believe that the implied asset correlations are also biased downwards for barriers below 50 percent.*

The most interesting observation, however, is the behaviour of correlation below and above the 50 percent barrier levels. Although correlations appear to be almost constant for barriers below 50 percent, we observe a steep increase for barriers above 50 percent. This means that correlation appears to be issue-dependent, which highlights a inconsistency between empirical findings and the general theoretical assumptions made in Merton-type models.

---

*This conclusion is mainly drawn from the good agreement of the Binomial MLE and implied asset correlation estimators for defaults, where larger samples are available.

FIGURE 11.9A

Intra-Industry EDS Correlation by Barrier.

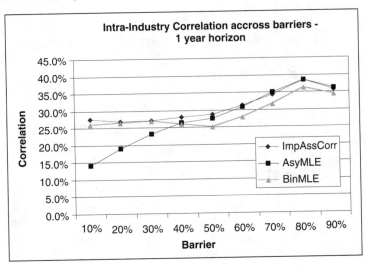

FIGURE 11.9B

Inter-Industry EDS Correlation by Barrier.

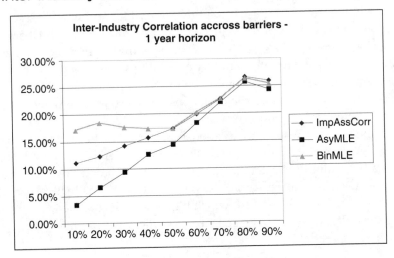

FIGURE 11.10

EDS Score Distribution of S&P100 in August 2000.
1 = Low Risk, to 5 = High Risk.

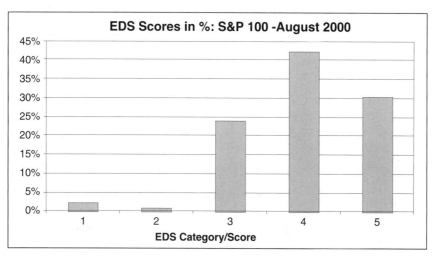

EDS Scores in %: S&P 100 -August 2000

EDS Category/Score

Case Study: A Hybrid CDO of EDS and CDS

Throughout this section, we employ the classification based on statistical scoring models, and the correlation findings to analyze several sample transactions, based on the S&P100 index. In a first case study, we analyze EDSs written on all S&P rated obligors in the S&P100 at two different points in time; just before the burst of the bubble in August 2000 and in November 2004.

For 92 names in the S&P100 in August 2000, S&P rating, industry, and regional information is available. The EDS analysis uses an advanced statistical scoring model (Standard & Poor's EDS Evaluator based on the methodology outlined in "Equity Events" section) to determine the EDS categories, an overview of the outcome is shown in Figure 11.10.

As we can see, the high volatility observed in equity markets during this period results in relative low scores across the index. A subsequent analysis at the portfolio level using the Gaussian copula model (e.g., CDO Evaluator), and assuming zero recovery, produces levels of subordination or scenario default rates (SDRs) shown in Table 11.7.*

By comparing these results to the SDRs for a portfolio of CDSs written on the same names, we can observe the overall increase for CDOs

---

*See Chapter 10 for further details on SDRs.

TABLE 11.7

SDRs for CDOs of CDS (Left Panel) and EDS (Right Panel) in August 2000

	CDS portfolio				EDS portfolio		
Desired rating	Rating quantile (%)	Scenario default rate (%)	Monetary loss	Desired rating	Rating default probability (%)	Scenario default rate (%)	Monetary loss
AAA	0.114	7.61	7	AAA	0.114	59.78	55
AA+	0.170	7.61	7	AA+	0.170	57.61	53
AA	0.354	6.52	6	AA	0.354	53.26	49
AA−	0.445	6.52	6	AA−	0.445	52.17	48
A+	0.584	6.52	6	A+	0.584	50.00	46
A	0.727	6.52	6	A	0.727	48.91	45
A−	1.036	5.43	5	A−	1.036	46.74	43
BBB+	1.731	5.43	5	BBB+	1.731	43.48	40
BBB	2.805	4.35	4	BBB	2.805	39.13	36
BBB−	6.059	3.26	3	BBB−	6.059	33.70	31
BB+	7.915	3.26	3	BB+	7.915	31.52	29
BB	11.571	3.26	3	BB	11.571	28.26	26
BB−	16.567	2.17	2	BB−	16.567	25.00	23
B+	22.035	2.17	2	B+	22.035	21.74	20
B	31.986	1.09	1	B	31.986	18.48	17
B−	42.293	1.09	1	B−	42.293	15.22	14
CCC+	57.946	1.09	1	CCC+	57.946	11.96	11
CCC	68.885	0.00	0	CCC	68.885	8.70	8
CCC−	84.129	0.00	0	CCC−	84.129	5.43	5

FIGURE 11.11

EDS Score Distribution of S&P100 in November 2004.
1 = Low Risk, to 5 = High Risk.

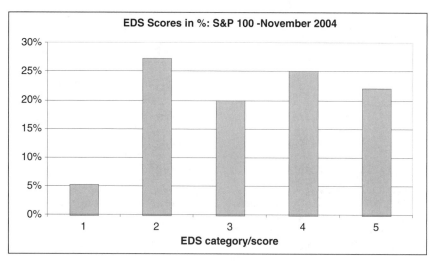

of EDS due to the higher probability of events and higher correlation assumptions. Assuming no recovery allows the identification of the number of defaults or trigger events in, say, an "AAA" environment. According to our analysis, more than half of the pool (55 names) would trigger the 30 percent barrier in such an environment, and this compares to 21 empirically observed events between August 2000 and November 2004. Out of the 21 equities dropping by 70 percent, 12 were classified as category 5, eight as category 4, and only 1 as category 3, which indicates that the proposed classification system is valuable.

In a next experiment, we repeat the analysis for November 2004. The new EDS score distribution is shown in Figure 11.11 followed by updated SDRs (Table 11.8).

The figures (Table 11.8) reveal a significant improvement in EDS scores, which translates into significantly lower levels of subordination. Overall, however, we can still see that there is a significant number of EDSs falling in categories 4 or 5 leading to higher SDRs, compared to a comparative CDO of CDS.

In a final experiment, we assume that a CDO, referencing CDS and EDS, are structured in a way that only includes EDSs belonging to categories 1 or 2. All other EDSs are replaced by their CDS counterparts,

TABLE 11.8

SDRs for CDO of EDS in November 2004

	EDS portfolio: November 2004		
Desired rating	Rating default probability (%)	Scenario default rate (%)	Monetary loss
AAA	0.114	47.37	45
AA+	0.170	45.26	43
AA	0.354	42.11	40
AA–	0.445	41.05	39
A+	0.584	38.95	37
A	0.727	37.89	36
A–	1.036	35.79	34
BBB+	1.731	32.63	31
BBB	2.805	30.53	29
BBB–	6.059	25.26	24
BB+	7.915	24.21	23
BB	11.571	21.05	20
BB–	16.567	18.95	18
B+	22.035	16.84	16
B	31.986	13.68	13
B–	42.293	11.58	11
CCC+	57.946	8.42	8
CCC	68.885	6.32	6
CCC–	84.129	4.21	4

which leaves in total 31 EDSs and 64 CDSs. Table 11.9 shows a significant reduction is subordination levels.

COOs: Commodity Transactions*

Recently, commodity linked CDO structures have also been introduced, motivated by steeply rising commodity prices (see Figure 11.12), and the historically low correlation to other asset classes.

The opportunity of higher yields and good diversification appear attractive to some investors. Commodity risk is introduced into CDOs in a similar form as equity risk is introduced via EDSs. Essentially, out of

---

*The author would like to thank Kimon Gkomozias from Standard & Poor's for insightful discussions and computational support.

TABLE 11.9

SDRs for Hybrid CDO of CDS/EDS in November 2004

	Hybrid CDS/EDS portfolio: November 2004		
Desired rating	Rating quantile (%)	Scenario default rate (%)	Monetary loss (%)
AAA	0.114	17.89	17
AA+	0.170	16.84	16
AA	0.354	14.74	14
AA–	0.445	14.74	14
A+	0.584	13.68	13
A	0.727	13.68	13
A–	1.036	12.63	12
BBB+	1.731	11.58	11
BBB	2.805	10.53	10
BBB–	6.059	8.42	8
BB+	7.915	7.37	7
BB	11.571	7.37	7
BB–	16.567	6.32	6
B+	22.035	5.26	5
B	31.986	4.21	4
B–	42.293	3.16	3
CCC+	57.946	3.16	3
CCC	68.885	2.11	2
CCC–	84.129	1.05	1

the money European options on the spot (or futures) price of the commodity with a strike price set at a predetermined "trigger level" are referenced. In contrast to CDOs of EDS where typically only one strike (barrier level) per name is referenced, when considering a CDO of commodity options, typically several options on a single commodity struck at different trigger levels (20 to 60 percent of the initial price) are considered in the underlying portfolios. Of course, there are many more equities to choose from than commodities, when attempting to construct a sizeable portfolio. Another difference is that EDS have usually American option features.

These differences have important modeling implications. Although statistical cohort and credit scoring approaches are performing well for EDSs, the adequacy of such techniques for commodity modeling purposes

FIGURE 11.12

Historic Commodity Prices.

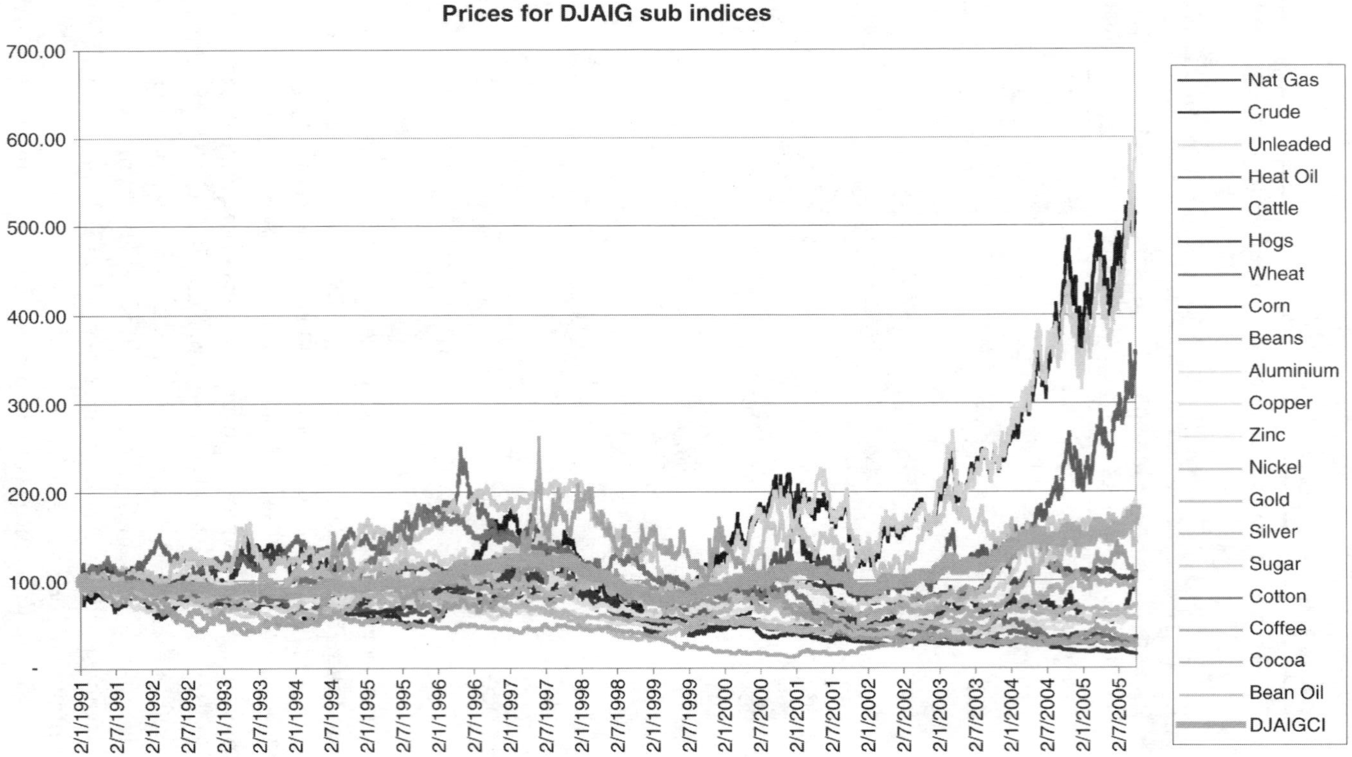

Prices for DJAIG sub indices

is questionable. The number of commodities considered, and the number of commodities with similar characteristics in general, is typically not large (usually, between 10 and 15 different commodities are referenced in a CDO). As a result, one needs to assess whether or not commodities could be grouped into meaningful categories (e.g., energy, metals, etc.) and/or if a sufficient number of commodities is available in order to conduct an analysis based on discrete events (e.g., historic strike hits). Similarly, for a correlation or dependence analysis, the number of commodity events is significantly smaller compared to thousands of events observed for a large number of equities, resulting in difficulties when attempting to apply estimation techniques based on discrete events as outlined in "Equity Default Swaps" section.

Modeling Individual Commodity Prices

Frequently, the commodity price dynamics are modeled through stochastic models (processes), see, e.g., Eydeland and Wolyniec (2003) or Geman (2005). For example, we recently considered the modeling of commodity spot prices using an arithmetic MR process based on the logarithm of prices. The model is discussed in detail in Schwartz (1997) and Geman (2005) and has the following form:

$$\frac{dS}{S} = \beta(\xi - \ln S)dt + \sigma\, dW.$$

Here, the spot price, S, mean reverts to the long-term level of e^{ξ} at a speed β. Introducing the new variable $x = \ln(S)$, leads to

$$dx = \beta(\theta - x)dt + \sigma dW \tag{1}$$

where $\theta = \xi - (\sigma^2/2\beta)$ and the long-term spot price is given by $\bar{S} = \exp(\theta + (\sigma^2/2\beta))$.

The solution to the stochastic process in Equation (1) is given by:

$$x(t) = x(s)e^{-\beta(t-s)} + \theta\left(1 - e^{-\beta(t-s)}\right) + \sigma\int_{u=s}^{t} e^{-\beta(t-u)}\, dW(u),$$

and the discrete form solution

$$x_{i+1} = x_i\, e^{-\beta\left(t_{i+1}-t_i\right)} + \theta\left(1 - e^{-\beta\left(t_{i+1}-t_i\right)}\right) + \sigma\sqrt{\frac{1}{2\beta}\left(1 - e^{-2\beta\left(t_{i+1}-t_i\right)}\right)}Z_i,$$

is very useful for simulation purposes when Z_i's are sampled from the standard normal distribution.

Of course, various other stochastic processes can be considered. For example, a generalization of Equation (1) is given by

$$dx = (a + bx)dt + \sigma x^\gamma\, dW \tag{2}$$

where the MR level is given by $\theta = -(a/b)$ and the MR speed is given by $\beta = -b$, and γ is a scalar. Prigent et al. (2001) apply the model to credit spread data. Depending on the parameter γ (which measures the level of nonlinearity between the level and volatility), several commonly known models can be derived. For example, $\gamma = 0$ leads to the Vasicek (1977) process, whereas $\gamma = \frac{1}{2}$ results in the Cox, Ingersoll, and Ross (1985) (CIR) process. Prigent et al. (2001) also discuss a specific jump-diffusion model, and the adequacy of introducing jump terms for modeling commodity prices needs to be investigated further.

Empirical Results and Model Calibration   Before estimating a parametric model for various commodities, it is useful to apply nonparametric techniques to gain some insight into the possible specification of the drift and diffusion terms. Appendix B outlines first-order approximations for the drift μ and diffusion term σ, where the stochastic process follows a general diffusion of type

$$dS_t = \mu(S_t)dt + \sigma(S_t)dW_t.$$

Figures 11.13 and 11.14 display the drift term as a function of prices, for silver and crude oil, respectively, estimated on daily data from 1991 to 2004.

It is apparent from both figures that the drift is not constant in the level of the price of the relevant commodity, especially when commodity prices are high. This gives a strong indication of an MR behavior, and therefore helps in the choice of a appropriate parametric model.

Similarly, the diffusion term can be estimated as outlined in Appendix B. For silver and crude oil, we obtain the following Figures 11.15 and 11.16, respectively.

For both commodities, the diffusion is almost linear in the price level; i.e., when prices are low, volatility is low, and when prices are high, volatility is high. Given these findings on drift and volatility, the choice of process presented earlier seems reasonable, at least for these commodities. For further results, we refer to Standard and Poor's (2006).

FIGURE 11.13

Drift as a Function of Price for Silver.

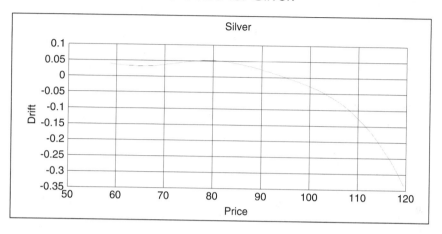

Appendix C outlines the parametric estimation of stochastic process [Equation (2)], and we present some of the estimation results on a set of five commodities next.

The results of an unconstrained estimation are shown in Table 11.10, while we constrain the model to the Brennan and Schwartz (1980) model ($\gamma = 1$) in Table 11.11.

FIGURE 11.14

Drift as a Function of Price for Crude Oil.

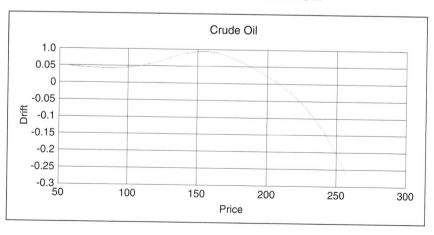

FIGURE 11.15

Volatility as a Function of Price for Silver.

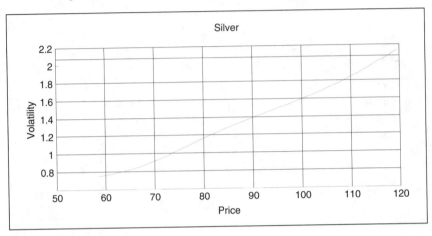

The parametric estimation (Table 11.10) also shows the high nonlinear relationship between prices and volatilities and confirms the MR behavior of the chosen commodities as $a>0$ and $b<0$ in all cases. The estimation of γ also indicates that very popular short-rate models, such as Vasicek or CIR, are less suitable for commodity prices. By constraining the model to $\gamma=1$, we observe only minor changes in mean reversion level and speed, however, the volatility changes significantly. For the commodities

FIGURE 11.16

Volatility as a Function of Price for Crude Oil.

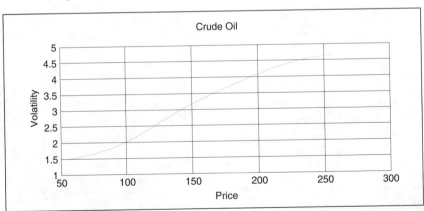

TABLE 11.10

Parametric Estimation of Commodity Prices
(1991–2004)

	Alpha	Beta	Gamma	Sigma	Volatility (%)
Nat gas	0.28	–0.0035	1.08	0.0196	31
Crude	0.10	–0.0004	1.18	0.0086	14
Aluminium	0.12	–0.0021	1.32	0.0028	4
Nickel	0.06	–0.0007	1.16	0.0090	14
Copper	0.10	–0.0008	1.47	0.0016	3

exhibited, the parametric (model) volatility is very much in line with the empirical volatility for $\gamma = 1$.

After choosing an adequate model and calibrating it to historic data, Monte-Carlo simulation allows us to estimate the probability of the commodities prices hitting the predetermined barrier (strike).

Dependence in a Portfolio of Commodities

Considering a portfolio of commodity options referenced within a CDO also requires the specification of the joint dynamics. As previously discussed, an approach based on discrete (default) events may be less suitable, and one can proceed, e.g., with the estimation of the linear correlation between different commodities from the price time-series information. We essentially estimate the correlation ρ_{ij} between the Brownian motions W^i and W^j that are specified in the dynamics of commodities i and j, respectively:

TABLE 11.11

Constrained Parametric Estimation of Commodity
Prices (1991–2004)

	Alpha	Beta	Gamma	Sigma	Volatility (%)
Nat gas	0.28	–0.0035	1.00	0.0282	45
Crude	0.09	–0.0004	1.00	0.0203	32
Aluminium	0.12	–0.0022	1.00	0.0104	16
Nickel	0.06	–0.0006	1.00	0.0182	29
Copper	0.08	–0.0005	1.00	0.0138	22

$$dS_t^i = \mu^i(S_t^i)dt + \sigma^i(S_t^i)dW_t^i,$$

for all $i = 1, \ldots, C$. C denotes the number of commodities (not options) considered.

Table 11.12 shows the resulting correlation matrix for the five commodities outlined earlier.

Whether or not such linear correlation estimates derived from commodity prices are adequately reflecting dependence in the context of sharp price declines (extreme events) awaits further research. Results for EDSs have shown that discrete event-based correlations are quite different to correlation estimates derived from price time-series at industry level granularity (see Jobst, 2004). As for commodities, the former estimates are not available; a more detailed inspection of the dependence structure during periods of high volatility and extreme commodity returns may provide interesting insights. Longin and Solnik (1999), e.g., study the dependence structure of international equity returns during extremely volatile bear and bull markets, using extreme value theory. They show that correlation of large positive returns is not inconsistent with multivariate normality, whereas correlation of large negative returns is much greater than expected. Although the existence of a "correlation breakdown" or changes in correlation through time has been frequently noted, Boyer et al. (1999) and Loretan and English (2000) argue that conditional correlation changes can be (theoretically) justified by time-varying sample volatility, rather than significant changes in the dependence behaviour itself. Although most discussions on extreme correlation focus on equity data, the relevant statistical techniques can provide valuable insights for commodities. The impact of such dependence effects on portfolios of deep out-of-the-money options obviously needs to be assessed in more detail.

TABLE 11.12

Correlation Between Commodity Spot Prices (in Percent)

	Nat gas	Crude	Aluminium	Nickel	Copper
Nat gas	100	65	-3	-2	4
Crude	65	100	6	8	8
Aluminium	-3	6	100	32	39
Nickel	-2	8	32	100	18
Copper	4	8	39	18	100

Given some indication of the dynamics of individual commodities, and the correlation across commodities, a portfolio can be simulated and the number of times the price breaches the barrier can be estimated. For a given tranche referencing commodity options, tranche PD and expected loss can then be easily estimated. For further details, outlining Standard & Poor's approach to employ the standard copula model for commodity portfolios, see Standard & Poor's (2006).

Of course, the models and developments outlined earlier can also be extended to portfolios of out-of-the-money interest rate and FX products, introducing new challenges for single-asset level, as well as dependence, modeling.

STRUCTURAL INNOVATIONS: INTRODUCING MtM RISK*

In May 2005, the synthetic CDO market experienced difficult times following the downgrade of Ford and GM by Standard & Poor's. The large demand for mezzanine tranches in recent years left dealers exposed to large short mezzanine positions that were hit hard during May 2005 (see Chapters 8 and 9 for further details). As a result of this experience, dealers are now trying to place full capital structure CDOs or employ (approximate) index hedges to reduce the prevalent risk. In order to place super senior risk, LSS transactions, one of the most successful products of 2005, have been introduced. We will discuss such transactions in the next section, highlighting the MtM component new to rated CDO tranches. Toward the end of 2005, and in early 2006, CPPI entered the structured credit market in an attempt to reduce MtM risk by guaranteeing principal while offering potential upside to investors. We will provide a brief overview of credit CPPI, as well as CPDOs-the latest innovation in the structured credit market.

Leverage Super Senior Transactions

LSS structures are relatively new products offered in the synthetic CDO market.[†] Their development in 2005 has resulted from a desire by protection

---

*The author would like to thank Sriram Rajan, Derek Ding, Benoit Metayer, Lapo Guadagnuolo, and Cian Chandler from Standard & Poor's for many interesting discussions and numerical support.
[†]LSS could be cash funded, too, in which case a detailed modeling of excess spreads and IC/OC tests would be required.

buyers in the credit market to transfer super senior risk more efficiently, accompanied by tightening spreads for super senior risk.

Unlike a typical super senior CDS, LSS notes contain both credit and market value risk. The latter in the form of triggers are based on the market value of the underlying reference assets. These triggers therefore expose the note holder to decreases in the market value of the LSS tranche. Three basic trigger types have been seen in the market, each of which offers a different aspect of market risk. Triggers can be based on losses, portfolio spreads, and MtM values and, if breached, may cause the transaction to unwind. Most transactions to date are based on spread triggers.

Basic Structure

A leverage super senior note is a credit-linked note in a synthetic CDO transaction. Its attachment point (subordination) is usually higher than that required for an "AAA" rated mezzanine notes. As in a typical super senior swap, LSS swaps usually cover all or most of the senior exposure. The difference, though, is that in a LSS structure only a fraction of the exposure is directly hedged—through funding—whereas in a super senior swap structure the entire notional value is funded. The funded amount is the lower portion of the senior exposure, which is also the riskiest portion of the super senior tranche (see Figure 11.17).

FIGURE   1 1 . 1 7

Basic Structure of a LSS Transaction.

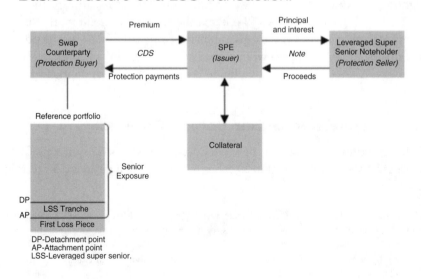

DP-Detachment point
AP-Attachment point
LSS-Leveraged super senior.

Hedging the entire super senior portion of the reference portfolio by funding only a fraction of it creates a "leverage," which is a distinguishing feature of this product. The number of times that the senior exposure is leveraged is equal to the senior exposure divided by the funded notional. Initially, most transactions had tenors of between five and seven years and were leveraged between 10 and 15 times, with portfolios typically referencing between 100 and 200 corporate and financial entities. More recently, LSS transactions reference ABS, including portfolios of RMBS and commercial mortgage backed securitization tranches.

Perspective of Protection Buyers and Sellers In a LSS structure, the protection seller earns the risk premium associated with selling protection on the entire senior exposure when the protection it provides is limited to only the principal amount that is funded, which is just a fraction of the entire exposure. For example, take a senior exposure (10 to 100 percent) of a portfolio with a notional equal to €100 million that pays 5 bp. If the funded portion of the resultant €90 million exposure is €6 million, the tranche is 15 times leveraged earning a spread of 75 bps per year on the funded notional.

The protection buyer on the other hand does not only protect oneself from the credit risk, but also from market value risk in the structure in form of MtM losses in excess of the principal amount funded by the protection seller. The combination of these risks justifies the return that the seller earns. From a protection buyer's point of view, the unwind event and the subsequent MtM payment means that it is effectively hedging the full senior portion of the portfolio even though only a fraction of the exposure has been funded. On a trigger being breached and the transaction terminating, the buyer has the MtM amount that it needs to purchase protection on the rest of the structure.

From a protection buyer's perspective, the most attractive structure would be the MtM trigger on the tranche value, because this would provide it with exact protection on the tranche (i.e., perfect hedge). However, the subjectivity associated with valuing bespoke tranches makes this less attractive to the protection seller. Both, the loss and spread triggers are "only" proxies for the market value of the tranche, and we will mostly focus on the spread trigger for the remainder of this chapter.

LSS with Spread Triggers

The rationale behind the spread trigger is that the market value of the LSS tranche is heavily dependent on the spread level of the portfolio. While

TABLE 11.13

Example of a Typical Spread Trigger Matrix as
of December 20, 2004 (in bp)

Losses (%)	Time to maturity (years)				
	5.00	4.92	4.83	4.75	4.67
0.0	267	271	275	279	283
0.5	258	262	267	271	275
1.0	250	254	258	**262**	266
1.5	247	251	254	258	262
2.0	238	242	246	250	253
2.5	232	236	240	244	248
3.0	226	230	234	237	241

the market value of the issued tranche is dependent on more than just the underlying asset values, spread triggers that provide a good (conservative) proxy to MtM movements can be constructed. This is normally done by the arranging bank that employs typical tranche pricing methodologies with conservative valuation assumptions to determine various average portfolio spreads that would cause specific MtM losses.

These trigger spreads are given in the transaction documents in the form of a trigger matrix, an example of which is shown in the extract in Table 11.13. This matrix tells us the level that the average portfolio spread would have to widen to for a trigger event to be caused. For example, presuming a closing date of December 20, 2004, if the transaction is three months into its life and 1 percent portfolio losses have occurred, spreads would need to widen to 262 bps to breach the spread trigger.

Modeling LSS Notes with Spread Triggers

RAs, such as Standard & Poor's, Moody's, and Fitch have developed methodologies to assess the risk in LSS transactions, see, e.g., Standard & Poor's (2005). We will provide a brief overview of the approach developed by Standard & Poor's, and provide a discussion of possible extensions. The methodology used in rating LSS transactions with a spread trigger involves an evaluation of both the credit risk on the reference portfolio and the risk that a spread trigger is breached.

Standard & Poor's LSS Model The matrix in Table 11.13 shows that we need to address two (inter-linked) risks in our analysis:

first, the default risk of the LSS note due to portfolio defaults, and second, the risk of spread widening to a level that would cause an unwind event. We address these risks by modeling the evolution of portfolio losses until maturity, and combining these loss scenarios with an assessment of whether portfolio spreads are likely to widen sufficiently to breach the maturity- and loss-dependent barrier.

Portfolio loss paths are determined from the default time simulation as outlined in "ST CDOs: A Ratings Perspective" section. For each simulation, after determining the percentage losses along each path, the barrier is calculated from the trigger matrix at fixed time-steps (usually one month) until maturity. End-of-month cumulative losses are used to determine the barrier for the beginning-of-month to end-of-month period, or linear interpolation is applied occasionally.

Modeling the Average Portfolio Spread Standard & Poor's models the average portfolio spread directly by focusing on systematic spread risk and considers idiosyncratic spread risk of secondary importance. As for commodities, there is a vast number of models to be considered, and the techniques outlined in Appendices B and C can be applied to gain some insight into drift and diffusion restrictions.

Prigent et al. (2001), e.g., show that both "AAA" and "BBB" corporate bond yield spreads show MR behavior. However, only the "BBB" volatility appears to scale linearly with the level of spreads while it oscillates around a constant mean for "AAA" data. S&P has chosen to estimate the diffusion model outlined in Appendix C and restricted the diffusion scalar $\gamma \leq 1$ for daily time series data on IG ("AAA," "AA," "A," and "BBB") option adjusted spreads (OAS) over the period 1997 to 2004. The resulting parameters shown in Table 11.14 confirm the MR behavior for all ratings (as $a > 0$ and $b < 0$ in each case).*

The diffusion estimates also confirm Prigent et al. (2001), indicating that the relationship between the spreads and volatility is stronger for lower ratings and weaker for higher ones. This indicated that a Brennan and Schwartz model ($\gamma = 1$) may be adequate for "AA" and "BBB" spreads, and a CIR or Vasicek process may be more suitable for "A" and "AAA" spreads, respectively. Of course, one can always estimate the same model for all IG spreads. For example, for $\gamma = 1$, we obtain the parameters shown in Table 11.15.

The results reveal a very systematic behaviour of IG credit spreads. Volatility appears to be decreasing in ratings, long-term MR levels increasing, and the MR speed also increases with decreasing ratings.

---

*Thanks to Astrid van Landschoot for empirical support.

TABLE 11.14

Parametric Estimation Results for IG OAS
(1997–2004)

	a	b	Gamma	Sigma	Volatility (%)
AAA	0.0048	–0.0067	0.29	0.0194	31
AA	0.0024	–0.0031	0.84	0.0223	36
A	0.0026	–0.0024	0.61	0.0187	30
BBB	0.0038	–0.0021	1.00	0.0151	24

It is apparent that the models presented earlier try to capture the most important time-series properties, without gaining further insight into the factors driving various spread level and volatility. Incorporating more explanatory power into the spread modeling exercise may prove a valuable extension. For further details, see Collin-Dufresne et al. (1999), Delianedis and Geske (2001), or Hull et al. (2004).

Standard & Poor's LSS Spread Model   Looking at the results presented earlier, Standard & Poor's choice of an MR model, where the log of the average portfolio spread follows an Ornstein-Uhlenbeck process—Equation (1)—appears justified, given that the average portfolio quality is usually around "BBB" for most transactions.

Figure 11.18 shows the average simulated portfolio spread and the 95th and 99th percentiles using a typical parameterization (mean reversion speed of 40 percent, LT spread of 100 bp, and volatility of 35 percent) of the model, assuming a starting spread of 39 bps. The maximum spread simulated after one, three, and five years is 150 bps, 250 bps, and 390 bps, respectively.

TABLE 11.15

Parameters of Restricted Model ($\gamma = 1$) for IG OAS
(1997–2004)

	a	b	Gamma	Sigma	Volatility (%)
AAA	0.0083	–0.0115	1.00	0.0273	44
AA	0.0026	–0.0033	1.00	0.0235	38
A	0.0032	–0.0030	1.00	0.0190	31
BBB	0.0038	–0.0021	1.00	0.0151	24

FIGURE 11.18

Percentiles of a Simulated Spread Process.

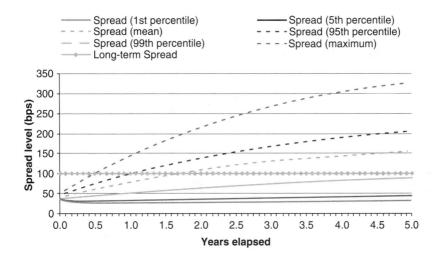

Simulated Spread Percentiles

——— Spread (1st percentile)   ——— Spread (5th percentile)
‑ ‑ ‑ ‑ Spread (mean)   ‑ ‑ ‑ ‑ Spread (95th percentile)
— — Spread (99th percentile)   ‑ ‑ ‑ ‑ Spread (maximum)
——+—— Long-term Spread

Although in this approach, no ratings migrations are explicitly taken into consideration, the portfolio spread is modeled on a constant maturity basis which means that "rolling down the curve" effects (the term-structure of spreads) are not explicitly modeled. While Standard & Poor's (2005) argues that the effects of decreasing maturities has a greater impact than a stressful ratings environment, Fitch, e.g., takes ratings migrations into consideration. There, spread processes for different rating classes are perfectly correlated, and ratings migrations are explicitly modeled leading to a jump in spreads at the time of a ratings migration. This is in the spirit of the model presented in Chapter 3, where more elaborate implementations are discussed. Such extensions should evolve toward capturing the correlation between credit spreads more adequately (than considering perfect correlation). For example, considering yield spread data for 1988 to 2005, we observe pretty strong (but not perfect) correlation between IG spreads, see Table 11.16.

Determining a PD-Rating on a LSS Note   Assessing the risk of LSS notes requires the determination of the likelihood of breaching the attachment point, as well as the probability of breaching a specific spread barrier.

TABLE 11.16

Correlation Between the Residuals of the Brennan & Schwartz Model Calibrated to IG Yield Spreads (1988–2005)

	AAA	AA	A	BBB
AAA	1	0.6924	0.7664	0.7266
AA	0.6924	1	0.7853	0.6996
A	0.7664	0.7853	1	0.8074
BBB	0.7266	0.6996	0.8074	1

In mathematical terms, we observe/simulate a loss path $\tilde{l} = l_\tau$, $\tau \in [0, T]$, where T denotes the transaction's maturity. We then need to estimate the probability of breaching the corresponding barrier $s(l_\tau)$ for the first time ("first passage time"), conditional on the loss path $\tilde{l}$:

$$P(\min_{[0,T]} S_t > s(l_t)|\tilde{l}).$$

By simulating N loss paths $\tilde{l}$ and subsequently simulating the portfolio spread, the required probability can be easily derived as:

$$P(\text{LSS default}) = \frac{1}{N} \sum_{\tilde{l}=1}^{N} 1_{\{\min_{[0,T]} S_t > s(l_t)|\tilde{l}\} \text{ or} \{l_T > A\}},$$

where A denotes the attachment point for this transaction.

Model Extension: Correlating the Default and Spread Process Incorporating ratings migrations and credit spreads as outlined earlier essentially presents one way to capture dependence between the credit spread and default process. Although intuitive, detailed empirical evidence is still outstanding (see, e.g., Hull et al., 2004 for initial results). Another way to quantify the effect of negative correlation is to extend the Black and Cox (1976) structural model to a large number of obligors. In Black and Cox, the firm's asset value follows a standard lognormal process

$$dV_i = \mu_i V_i \, dt + \sigma_i V_i \, dZ_i.$$

Hence, $V_i(t) = V_i(0) \exp((\mu_i - 0.5\sigma_i^2)t + \sigma_i Z_i(t))$, and default occurs when the firm value, V, hits the default barrier H_i for the first time (first passage time). The parameters of this stochastic process and/or the default barrier H can be calibrated to a given term structure of default probabilities (or hazard rates), see Hull et al. (2005) for further details.

When a portfolio of entities is considered, a factor model correlating the Wiener terms, such as

$$dZ_i(t) = \sqrt{\rho} \, dF(t) + \sqrt{\rho_c - \rho} \, dF_c(t) + \sqrt{1 - \rho_c}\, \varepsilon_i(t) \quad i \in c,$$

where F can be interpreted as a global factor and F_c can be interpreted as an industry or risk-class factor, can be applied. The actual correlation structure corresponds to a correlation of ρ_c between two entities in the same industry or risk-class c, and ρ between two firms in different industries or risk-classes. In practice, of course, any other (multi) factor model can be applied.

Defaults in this framework are determined by simulating the factors and idiosyncratic random terms through time, calculating the corresponding asset values $V_i(t)$, and comparing it to the default barriers $H_i(t)$.

The advantage of this structural factor model for LSS is that the factors driving the firms value can be correlated to the Brownian motion, driving the average portfolio spread process. This can be either done by setting up the Brownian motion $W(t)$ driving the spread process as a function of $F(t)$ and $F_c(t)$, or by simply imposing a linear correlation between the Wiener terms and simulating the factors and spread term from a multivariate normal distribution. Although the estimation and calibration of such a correlated default and spread model needs to be conducted carefully and the assumption of linear dependence is rather restrictive, the impact of simulating correlated asset values (default processes) and credit spreads can be assessed.

Table 11.17 shows the impact of increasing negative correlation between portfolio spreads and asset values by assuming some level of correlation between the average portfolio spread process and the global and industry specific factors, driving the firm's asset values (and therefore defaults).

In Table 11.17, we determine factor weights that are consistent with an assumption of 30 percent correlation between two obligors in the same industry, and 0 percent between obligors in different industries. The first row shows the results if we assume, in addition, a 30 percent

TABLE 11.17

LSS Default Probability as a Function
of Spread/Default Correlation

Correlation of spread process to the global and industry factors (%)		Probability of LSS tranche default (bps)
Global factor	Industry factor	
30	10	11
10	0	14
0	0	15
(20)	0	16
(30)	0	17
(20)	(7)	19
(30)	(7)	20

correlation between the spread process and the global factor, and a 10 percent correlation between the spread process and the industry specific factor.
In this typical case, the LSS note is expected to default with a probability
of 11 bps.

The table (Table 11.7) reveals overall that imposing negative correlation increases the risk to LSS investors. This makes intuitive sense as negative correlation implies that decreasing asset values (or nonfavorable factor
outcomes) lead to increasing spread levels; however, the impact of this correlation appears to be moderate, which becomes even more apparent when
we are looking at Table 11.18.

TABLE 11.18

LSS Default Probability as a Function
of Spread Volatility

Correlation of spread process to the global and industry factors (%)		Spread volatility (%)	Probability of LSS tranche default (bps)
Global factor	Industry factor		
0	0	25	0.16
0	0	30	2.70
0	0	35	15.00
0	0	40	47.00

TABLE 11.19

Correlation of spread process to the global and industry factors (%)		Probability of LSS tranche default (bps)
Global factor	Industry factor	
30	10	295
10	0	301
0	0	305
(20)	0	313
(30)	0	318
(20)	(15)	316
(30)	(15)	320

Here, we are assuming no correlation between the spread process and the factors but vary the volatility in the underlying spread model. As we can see, the probability of the LSS note defaulting reduces to 0.16 bps from 15 bps when considering a volatility of 25 percent instead of 35 percent, whereas it is more than triples when volatility is increased by 5 percent. Hence, the sensitivity to volatility seems to be higher than the effect of correlation between losses and spreads can have, but further work is needed on such dependence issues.

Although it is apparent that the risk in LSS transactions stems to a large extent from spread widening, the quality and concentration in the underlying asset pool is also very important. For example, imposing a higher asset correlation of 30 percent between all obligors leads to a steep increase in tranche default probabilities (see Table 11.19). Again, the sensitivity to changes in spread-to-factor correlation seems quite modest. Similarly, the impact of more "aggressive" spread triggers may have to be assessed.

Of course, the approach outlined here only provides first insights into dependence issues and is still quite restrictive in that spread dispersion, a possible jumps in asset values and/or credit spreads, the impact of defaults on spreads, and a more elaborate dependence structure still need to be explored. Despite some of these outstanding modeling challenges, LSS transactions have become an important part of synthetic CDO markets to date, by offering a vehicle to place the top end of the capital structure, which was previously dominated by (a limited number of) monoline insurers, to real-money investors (in leveraged form).

Credit Constant Proportional
Portfolio Insurance*

Following the development of the CDO squared market in 2004, LSS in 2005, the early part of 2006 was driven by a large interest in so-called credit CPPI. CPPI is a rules-based portfolio management framework where the portfolio allocation changes dynamically between a risky subportfolio and a risk-free subportfolio. The aim of this rebalancing exercise is to maximize return while guaranteeing (partial) principal protection. This is in stark contrast to typical ST CDOs where a fixed upside (premium) is countered by unlimited downside and a turn away from aggressive structures that focus on maximizing yield toward more defensive structures. CPPI is not new to capital markets; the concept of CPPI goes back to Black and Jones (1986), who consider this Portfolio Insurance mechanism in the context of equities. Perold (1986) and Perold and Sharpe (1988) apply the concept to fixed income instruments (see also Black and Rouhani, 1989; Rouman et al., 1989). Similarly to LSS, the rise in prominence of CPPI stems partially from the events of May 2005. Although higher leverage was achieved at the cost of significantly higher correlation sensitivity (e.g., CDO squared transactions) before May 2005, most CPPI transactions to date introduce leverage (or higher sensitivity) to an overall credit portfolio (or index), and hence, eliminates the direct exposure to (base) correlation risk.

A Typical Credit CPPI Structure

The basic idea of CPPI is that at any time, the investors principal investment can be repaid at maturity. In order to do so, the portfolio value $P(t)$ needs to be maintained above a minimum value, denoted as the floor or cost of guarantee $F(t, T)$. Hence, the floor if invested at the current risk-free rate will allow repayment of the guaranteed principal. More formally, the following condition needs to be satisfied for all $t \geq T$: $P(t) \geq F(t, T)$, where $F(t, T) = \overline{P}_T E\left(\exp - \int_t^T r(s)\,ds \right)$ denotes the present value of the final principal at time T, $\overline{P}_T$, discounted at the current risk-free rate r.

The difference between the portfolio value (the sum of the initial investment plus the MtM of the risky exposure) and the floor is usually denoted as the reserve or cushion, $C(t)$. This cushion is invested in risky assets, which within the framework of credit CPPI usually comprises of single-name CDS or CDS indices. Usually, at this part of the structure,

---

*Thanks to Benoit Metayer and Sriram Rajan for their contribution to this topic.

FIGURE 11.19

Typical Structure of a CPPI Transaction.

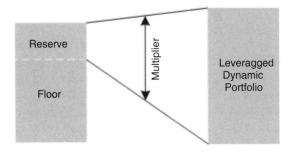

leverage is introduced. Practically, a "gearing factor" or "multiplier" m is applied to the reserve that determines the proportion of assets allocated to the risky portfolio, denoted as "risky exposure," RE. The multiplier is generally applied in some variation of the following basic formula:

$$RE = mC(t) = m(P(t) - F(t)).$$

Assuming a fixed multiplier, as the portfolio value increases, the reserve and RE increase (buying high), whereas a decrease leads to reduction in the RE (selling low). In practice, the maximum size of the RE (or leverage) is usually restricted. For example, the risky portfolio cannot exceed a fraction l of the current total portfolio value (RE and risk-free investment), i.e., RE = min[max($mC(t)$, 0), l $P(t)$].* Figure 11.19 shows the typical structure of a CPPI transaction.

The higher the multiplier, the higher is the risk that the portfolio value may fall below the bond floor. This risk is usually denoted by "gap risk" and is illustrated in the following idealized examples.

A Simplified CPPI Case Study

Consider a initial investment of $P(0) = 100$, a time horizon of $t = 10$ years, and a muliplier of $m = 5$. Current market conditions assume a risk-free yield of 2 percent throughout the life of the transaction, and the risky investment is assumed to be a credit risky portfolio, which pays a protection premium of 5 percent per annum. We start by calculating the bond floor as the value of the risk-free zero-coupon bond (ZCB) that matures at the end of the investment horizon. Table 11.20 shows a detailed example

---

*Alternatively, leverage may be dynamically adjusted, e.g., by the ratio of the current RE to the size of a possible overnight MtM loss, see Whetten and Jin (2005) for further details.

TABLE 11.20

A Typical Dynamic CPPI Example

Time	Bond floor	Losses from Defaults	Risky portfolio value	Total portfolio value	Reserve	Maximum RE	Purchase/ sale of credit risk	Risk-free asset
0	81.87	—	—	100.00	18.13	90.63	90.63	9.37
1	83.53	0.00	95.17	106.62	23.10	106.62	11.46	0.00
2	85.21	20%	90.63	92.44	7.23	36.14	−54.49	56.31
3	86.94	0.00	37.94	96.13	9.20	45.99	8.04	50.15
4	88.69	0.00	48.29	100.40	11.71	58.55	10.26	41.85
5	90.48	0.00	61.47	105.40	14.91	74.56	13.08	30.84
6	92.31	0.00	78.29	111.31	18.99	94.97	16.68	16.34
7	94.18	0.00	99.72	118.38	24.20	118.38	18.66	0.00
8	96.08	0.00	124.29	126.78	30.70	126.78	2.49	0.00
9	98.02	0.00	133.12	135.78	37.76	135.78	2.66	0.00
10	100.00	0.00	142.57	145.42	45.42	145.42	2.85	0.00

of the CPPI dynamics, when RE is restricted to the current portfolio value ($l = 1$), and the spreads received from the risky portfolio are reinvested.*

In this illustrative example, we also assume that the portfolio value is readjusted by (annual) spread payments and losses from defaults, only, rather than by "true" MtM changes of the portfolio value. Changes in spreads (and other relevant pricing variables) typically causes MtM gains and losses that need to be addressed. Despite this simplification, the general mechanics illustrated here is still reflective of CPPI. This means that a portfolio rebalancing takes place when the MtM value of the portfolio changes significantly as a result of changes in credit spreads and/or dependence behaviour, in addition to credit events/defaults.

At trade initiation, the bond floor is 81.87 resulting in a reserve of 18.13 and an RE of 5 times that value (90.63). Hence, 9.37 is invested in the risk-free portfolio,† whereas 90.63 is invested in the risky portfolio. After one year, the ZCB value increased, leading to an increased bond floor. Since the risky portfolio earned 5 percent spread, the total portfolio value increased to 106.62 [= (90.63 + 9.37) * (1 + 0.05 + 0.02)]. This results in a higher reserve of 23.1 and a subsequent purchase of 11.46 of the risky portfolio and a reduced risk-free investment. Repeating these calculations until maturity reveals that the overall portfolio value far exceeds the bond floor at any point in time, despite 20 percent losses in the risky portfolio in year 2. These losses lead to a significant reduction in the risky investment and a shift towards the risk-free portfolio, as shown in the Table 11.20.‡ It is also worth noting that the overall RE in this example is restricted to be at most the total portfolio value. In the example, this constraint is hit in year 2 and from year 7 onwards.

Sensitivity to Defaults and Default Timing

Table 11.21 shows the performance of the CPPI transaction introduced earlier for various loss scenarios. In loss scenario 1, 30 percent and 20 percent losses are assumed in the risky portfolio in years 5 and 8, respectively.

---

*Alternatively, spreads could be passed to investors, which would lead to very different transaction dynamics and performance (Internal rate of return IRR).
†Note that in real transactions, specific investment rules may require a minimum holding in the risk-free investment to further ensure market volatility. For example, in "static hedge" CPPI structures, a portion of the initial investment is allocated to a risk-free asset that accrues to return full-rated principal at maturity.
‡As indicated earlier, investment guidelines in real-world transactions would result in portfolio rebalancing subject to MtM changes. These MtM changes are often less severe than indicated here in the case of default. Hence, the situation where the portfolio composition changes as a result of defaults, only, as outlined in this case study, is highly illustrative and should not be misinterpreted.

TABLE 11.21

Sensitivity of CPPI Transaction to Defaults and Default Timing

| | | Loss scenario 1 | | Loss scenario 2 | | Loss scenario 3 | |
Time	Bond floor	Losses from defaults	Total portfolio Value	Losses from defaults	Total portfolio value	Losses from defaults	Total portfolio value
0	81.87	0	100	0	100		100
1	83.53	0%	106.62	0%	106.6224	10%	97.38
2	85.21	0%	114.19	0%	114.19	10%	95.79
3	86.94	0%	122.30	0%	122.30	10%	95.01
4	88.69	0%	130.98	20%	106.03	10%	94.85
5	90.48	30%	100.20	30%	86.04	10%	95.18
6	92.31	0%	104.68	0%		10%	95.88
7	94.18	0%	109.93	0%		10%	96.89
8	96.08	20%	100.08	0%		10%	98.14
9	98.02	0%	103.10	0		10%	99.57
10	100.00	0	106.46	0		10%	101.17

Despite these losses, the CPPI investor receives full principal at maturity, which essentially means that the return generated in the initial years was sufficient to repay full principal. In loss scenario 2, the same amount of default occurs (in percent terms), however, losses occur in two successive years and in reverse order. We can observe that in year 5, the overall portfolio value falls below the bond floor—the "gap risk" scenario occurred. This highlights that the timing and clustering, and therefore correlation, of defaults can impact CPPI transactions significantly.

In loss scenario 3, 10 percent losses are observed in every year of the transaction. Although this results in absolute losses higher than in the previous two scenarios, the full principal investment can still be repaid. This results from the fact that the RE is steadily reduced and shifted toward the risk-free investment. In doing so, the total amount in the risky portfolio is not very high after a few years running, leading to a lower impact of defaults/losses.

Sensitivity to Gearing/Leverage

Changing the constant multiplier has a significant impact on the performance of the dynamic CPPI transaction, as shown in Table 11.22. Loss scenarios 2 is considered once again illustrating that a leverage of $m = 3$ leads to a full repayment of principal, compared to $m = 4$ and $m = 5$, respectively.

We also consider loss scenario 3 with significantly higher leverage of $m = 15$. The higher RE due to higher gearing leads to large year on year losses, resulting in a gapping out of the transaction in year 7. Although the sign of the impact of leverage depends on may factors, these simple examples show that CPPI transactions are very sensitive to the multiplier.

Sensitivity to Interest Rates and Credit Spreads

Apart from losses and leverage, two other factors—interest rates and credit spreads—are very important for Credit CPPI.* Assuming a multiplier of $m = 4$ and loss scenario 2, Table 11.23 reveals the impact of increasing interest rates systematically until a maximum of 6 percent over the first four years of the transactions life. Higher interest rates imply a lower cost of guarantee, but also higher returns from the risk-free investment. Although for a constant 2 percent interest rate environment the transaction "gapped out" (Table 11.21) under loss scenario 2, the full principal can now be repaid at any point in time.

The table (Table 11.23) also reveals that a tightening in credit spreads has a massive impact on the transaction, leading to the portfolio value

---

*Note that in a real transaction, spread risk also enters the MtM calculations.

TABLE 11.22

Sensitivity of CPPI Transaction to Gearing Factor

Time	Bond floor	Loss scenario 1 (Leverage=3)		Loss scenario 2 (Leverage=4)		Loss scenario 3 (Leverage=15)	
		Losses from Defaults	Total portfolio value	Losses from Defaults	Total portfolio value	Losses from defaults	Total portfolio value
0	81.87	0	100	0	100		100
1	83.53	0%	104.77	0%	105.70	10%	96.90
2	85.21	0%	110.12	0%	112.33	10%	93.90
3	86.94	0%	116.13	0%	120.11	10%	90.99
4	88.69	20%	105.05	20%	104.14	10%	89.71
5	90.48	30%	94.64	30%	90.47	10%	90.72
6	92.31	0%	97.17	0%		10%	92.35
7	94.18	0%	99.85	0%		10%	94.17
8	96.08	0%	102.72	0%		10%	
9	98.02	0	105.79	0		10%	
10	100.00	0	109.09	0		10%	

TABLE 11.23

Sensitivity of Dynamic Credit CPPI to Interest Rates and Credit Spreads

Time	Loss Scenario 2 (Leverage = 4) Rising Short Rate				Loss Scenario 2 (Leverage = 4) Spread tightening				
	Short rate	Bond floor	Losses from defaults	Total portfolio value	Losses from defaults	Short rate	Bond floor	Spreads	Total portfolio value
0	0.02	81.87		100		0.02	81.87	0.05	100
1	0.03	76.34	0	105.70	0	0.02	83.53	0.04	104.96
2	0.04	72.61	0	114.31	0	0.02	85.21	0.03	109.68
3	0.05	70.47	0	124.83	0	0.02	86.94	0.02	113.87
4	0.06	69.77	0.2	111.41	0	0.02	88.69	0.02	96.37
5	0.06	74.08	0.3	88.57	0	0.02	90.48	0.02	89.53
6	0.06	78.66	0%	96.96	30%	0.02	92.31	0.02	
7	0.06	83.53	0%	106.65	35%	0.02	94.18	0.02	
8	0.06	88.69	0%	117.95	0%	0.02	96.08	0.02	
9	0.06	94.18	0	131.24	0	0.02	98.02	0.02	
10	0.06	100.00	0	146.06	0	0.02	100.00	0.02	

falling significantly below the bond floor in year 5. In this example, the spread income from the risky investment reduced from 5 percent per annum initially to 2 percent in year 3 and stays at 2 percent until maturity.

Overall, these illustrative examples reveal the sensitivity of CPPI transactions to various risk factors, which are summarized herewith.

Risks in CPPI Transactions

- *Structural factors*   such as investment guidelines and rebalancing rules (e.g., maximum RE restrictions).
- *Leverage*   introduced via a multiplier. In practice, upper or lower limits on leverage, or dynamic multipliers that react to market conditions are feasible.
- *Credit risk*   in form of the likelihood and timing of defaults and/or the erosion in credit quality.
- *Market risk*   in form of MtM changes on the risky portfolio and market value triggers that may drive the asset allocation and limit the ability to "ride out" temporary swings in prices. For simple credit indices, MtM is mostly a result of changes in credit spreads, and the term structure of credit spreads more generally.
- *Interest rate risk*   in form of sensitivity of the risk-free investment return and the change in bond floor.

Expected Performance

The nature of dynamically shifting the portfolio between the risky and risk-free investment depending on the performance of the credit risky portfolio, aims toward achieving a stable MtM profile, whereas guaranteeing principal investment and taking advantage of potential upside. When the credit market performs well, the pure credit portfolio can be expected to outperform the CPPI strategy, as the latter is only partially exposed to high yield. However, the impact of a sudden downturn in credit markets on the CPPI trade is somewhat reduced. When the credit portfolio performs badly (high losses and wide spreads), the CPPI strategy shifts exposure toward risk-free assets and, hence, significantly reduces downside risk for CPPI.

More generally, CPPI strategies are known to perform poorly when markets are very volatile. Under high volatility, gains and losses may quickly follow each other, resulting in exactly the "wrong" rebalancing actions guided by the CPPI trading rules. For further details, see Whetten and Jin (2005). As previously mentioned, CPPI has been an integral part of hedge fund activities for equity and fixed-income markets. Although credit CPPI introduces some new idiosyncracies (e.g., sudden severe MtM losses due to defaults), the CPPI framework can be applied to portfolios of complex credit exposures (e.g., portfolios of ST CDOs) or alternative asset classes (hybrids). Particularly, if credit CPPI could be referencing (synthetic) CDO equity tranches, and efficient framework for transferring CDO equity risk and, hence, another efficient hedging tool could be developed.

Modeling CPPI Transactions

Assessing the risk in credit CPPI transactions requires a comprehensive modeling of the risk factors outlined earlier. Such models are required by traders and risk managers for assessing the gap risk and for forming relative value views. RAs are getting involved in providing an assessment of a minimum coupon (or minimum IRR) that can be guaranteed with a desired (rating specific) certainty, in addition to a typical gap risk analysis. In order to compute such statistics, one needs to develop a probabilistic description of all underlying risk factors and address their interaction or joint behaviour adequately.

Although we are not describing a detailed approach to CPPIs due to the bespoke nature of transactions (and rules) and the high level of complexity it becomes apparent that many of the modeling approaches and challenges discussed throughout this chapter apply to credit CPPI.

Of course, the complexity of assessing MtM changes on a portfolio of (credit) exposures depends highly on the nature of the underlying portfolio. For a relatively homogeneous portfolio of CDS, a straightforward model for portfolio losses and spreads may be sufficient to gain some interesting insights, whereas high spread dispersion or low quality credits may require a more refined approach to modeling the interaction between spread and default risk. Similarly, when CDO tranches are also considered in reference portfolio, the quantitative complexity increases significantly as the sensitivity to base or compound correlation changes also needs to be assessed (see Chapter 7 for further details) in MtM computations. At the same time, there is scope for credit CPPI to move toward "hybrid CPPI," where equity, real estate, FX, or commodity risk may also be repackaged. For such problems, the approaches outlined in "Beyond Credit Risk: Hybrid Structured Products" section may provide some guidelines, however, the integration of all risks in a common modeling platform presents a big challenge.

In summary, although, in some instances, a (independent) modeling of portfolio defaults, average portfolio spreads (and interest rates) may provide some viable results—more complex structures need a fully integrated, dynamic, multiasset class framework in place. Ideally, such an environment does not only combine different asset classes, but also addresses the risks under the risk-neutral (pricing) measure and real (historical) measure consistently.

Constant Proportion Debt Obligations (CPDO)

Constant Proportion Debt Obligations (CPDOs) are the latest innovation in the rated structured credit market and we only intend to give a short summary of the risks and mechanics following Gilkes et al. (2006) from which parts of the presentation is taken.

CPDOs are similar to Credit CPPI in that it involves a leveraged exposure to a credit-risky portfolio to provide increased returns to investors. The mechanics of CPDOs are very different, however, and in some ways the exact reverse of credit CPPI. For example, CPDOs typically do not provide any principal protection, and a fall in the value of the strategy tends to lead to increases in leverage, whereas the opposite is true for credit CPPI structures.

Figure 11.20 below shows the main features of a typical CPDO.

FIGURE 11.20

Structure at Closing of a Typical CPDO Transaction.

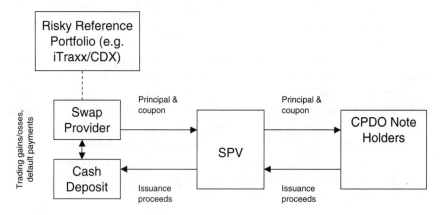

At trade inception, CPDO issuance proceeds are held in a deposit account that earns interest at the risk free rate. The SPV (Special Purpose Vehicle) enters into a total return swap with the arranging bank, which simultaneously sells protection on a certain (leveraged) notional amount of a risky reference portfolio (typically a combination of the main credit indices, CDX and iTraxx, but as for CPPI, bespoke portfolios, hybrid assets or more complex credit products my be also referenced). Over time, credit default swap (CDS) premium payments and mark-to-market (MtM) gains are paid into the deposit account, while MtM losses and default payments are taken out of the cash deposit. Principal and coupon payments are made to CPDO note holders subject to sufficient funds being available in the deposit account. In contrast to Credit CPPI, at inception the arranging bank does not enter a ZCB that guarantees principal investment, and hence, investors relay—amongst other things—on CPDO credit ratings to assess the likelihood of full principal and interest payments.

CPDOs provide returns to note holders through leverage, namely the selling of protection on a much larger notional amount than the note proceeds. The leverage factor is essentially a multiple of the difference— or *shortfall*—between the net asset value (NAV) of the CPDO strategy (the sum of the value of the cash deposit and the mark-to-market (MtM) value of the risky portfolio) and the present value of all future payments (Target Value) to be made by the SPV, including fees.* The portfolio is "rebalanced" when the calculated or required leverage differs from the current leverage by a certain preset amount.

A so called "Cash-in" event takes place when the shortfall decreases to zero, in which case the strategy is unwound completely, and the proceeds are held in the deposit account in order to make all future payments promised by the SPV. On the contrary, if the NAV falls below a certain threshold (typically 10% of the notional of the reference portfolio) the strategy is unwound, and the proceeds are distributed to CPDO note holders.

The first CPDOs referenced "on-the-run" IG (investment grade) credit indices, which means that on or close to each roll date (March 20 and September 20) the arranging bank must buy protection on the "off-

---

*Leverage is therefore purely formulaic (as opposed to discretionary), but will clearly vary over time depending on the performance of the strategy. Leverage is typically capped at around 15 to prevent unacceptably high leverage in periods of poor strategy performance.

the-run" indices (up to the full leveraged notional amount) and sell protection on the new "on-the-run" indices. Hence, index dynamics around roll periods and roll mechanics (e.g., replacement of NIG (non-IG) assets through IG ones) are very important.

Similarly to CPPI, the NAV of the CPDO strategy depends on the MtM of the risky portfolio, which evolves based on changes in index spreads and the term structure of the index credit curves. For example, spread widening/tightening between roll dates result in MtM losses/gains. Similarly, an adjustment of leverage (rebalancing) leads to MtM gains/losses that will affect level of the cash deposit. On roll dates, the CPDO buys back protection on the off-the-run index and contracts at the new on-the-run index spread. The difference in off-the-run index spread compared to the contractual spread entered at the previous roll date determines the MtM gain or loss experienced by the strategy. Contracting at a new (on-the-run) index spread also has an impact on CPDO performance due to the new CDS premium the SPV earns over the next roll period. This impact may be positive if is the new spread is high enough to offset unwind costs.

Key Risks in CPDOs

- Leverage mechanics and structural features
- Credit/default risk: see section on Credit CPPI
- Market Risk/Spread risk.: The MtM of the risky portfolio (and hence the NAV) is very sensitive to changes in index spreads. Although credit spreads depend on many factors such as expected default losses as well as default risk and liquidity premiums, it is also crucial how much benefit the strategy receives from "rolling down" the credit curve as the maturity of the contract shortens. Hence changes in constant maturity spreads and the slope of the term structure of credit curves are very critical. Again, as for Credit CPPI, more complex credit products or non-credit risky assets (e.g., equities or commodities) in the underlying risky portfolio leads to more complex market-risk assessments.
- Interest rate risk: Compared to Credit CPPI, interest rate sensitivity is lower (although not fully eliminated). This stems from the fact that there is no ZCB investment whose value depends significantly on interest rate moves. For CPDOs, interest rates influence on the one hand the interest earned on the cash deposit, and on the other hand, MtM calculations.

An Illustrative CPDO Case Study

The following example illustrates the evolution of the strategy NAV, Target Value, and Leverage for different credit spread and default scenarios throughout the live of the transaction. We consider a notional investment of $100 whereby the (leveraged) proceeds are invested a simple credit portfolio comprising of 250 assets with a initial weighted average spread of 30 bp, and a initial average maturity of 5.25 years. The maturity of the CPDO notes is 10 years, no fees, a bid-offer spread of 1 bp, and a initial as well as maximum leverage of 15 are assumed. The initial investment in the risky portfolio is therefore $1500. The CPDO note holder (investor) wants to be paid a coupon of 150 bp over the risk free rate which is assumed to be flat 2% throughout the live of the transaction. We consider three credit spread (term structure) and default scenarios outlined in Table 11.24.

Scenario A illustrates the CPDO performance in an environment where spreads will widen by 3 bp pa over the next five years and a single default occurs pa in the reference portfolio. Figure 11.21 reveals that the transaction cashes in after eight years guaranteeing the investor full repayment of principal and interest. The figure also reveals that the strategy runs on full leverage from years 1 to 7, as a result an increase in shortfall stemming from defaults and MtM losses caused by spread widening.

Scenario B considers the opposite credit environment, that is, five more years of tight spread environment (at constant 30 bp) followed by five years of annual spread widening combined with one default pa. Figure 11.22 reveals that the investor would not receive full principal at the end of the 10 year holding period. Again, the leverage mechanism is clearly visible. During the first five years without defaults and MtM losses (as spreads are not widening), the NAV increases. This clearly reduces the shortfall leading to a reduction in leverage. When spreads start to widen (casing MtM losses) and defaults occur, higher leverage is imposed. As defaults continue to occur and spreads continue to widen, the effect of higher leverage leads to further reductions in the NAV.

Scenario C illustrates the sensitivity of the CPDO performance to the slope of the credit spread term-structure (time-decay). We are reducing the assumed difference between the 5.25 year maturity spread and the 4.75 year maturity spread of 4% (relative) down to 1% when spreads (constant maturity) and defaults prevail as in scenario A. While the transaction cashed in under scenario A, the flatter term-structure of credit spreads assumed in scenario C leads to a very small loss in principal to the CPDO investor at maturity.

TABLE 11.24

Spread and Default Scenarios Considered in Illustrative CPDO Analysis. Time-Decay=x% Corresponds to the "Roll-Down" Component in Credit Spreads as We Move Forward in Time Within a Roll-Period (i.e., the Difference Between a 5.25 Year Spread and a 4.75 Year Spread).

Year	Scenario A: Time-decay = 4%		Scenario B: Time-decay = 4%		Scenario C: Time-decay = 1%	
	Spread	Defaults	Spread	Defaults	Spread	Defaults
0	30		30		30	
0.5	33	1.00	30	0.00	33	1.00
1	36	1.00	30	0.00	36	1.00
1.5	39	1.00	30	0.00	39	1.00
2	42	1.00	30	0.00	42	1.00
2.5	45	1.00	30	0.00	45	1.00
3	48	1.00	30	0.00	48	1.00
3.5	51	1.00	30	0.00	51	1.00
4	54	1.00	30	0.00	54	1.00
4.5	57	1.00	30	0.00	57	1.00
5	60	1.00	33	1.00	60	1.00
5.5	57	0.00	36	1.00	57	0.00
6	54	0.00	39	1.00	54	0.00
6.5	51	0.00	42	1.00	51	0.00
7	48	0.00	45	1.00	48	0.00
7.5	45	0.00	48	1.00	45	0.00
8	42	0.00	51	1.00	42	0.00
8.5	39	0.00	54	1.00	39	0.00
9	36	0.00	57	1.00	36	0.00
9.5	33	0.00	60	1.00	33	0.00
10	30	0.00	63	1.00	30	0.00

FIGURE 11.21

CPDO Performance Under Scenario A.

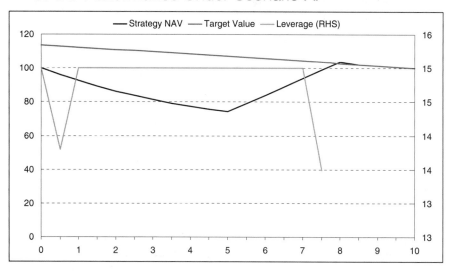

FIGURE 11.22

CPDO Performance Under Scenario B.

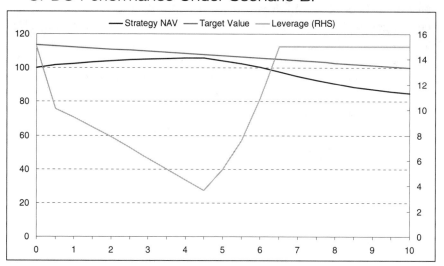

FIGURE 11.23

Sensitivity of CPDO Performance o Steepness of the Term-Structure of Credit Spreads.

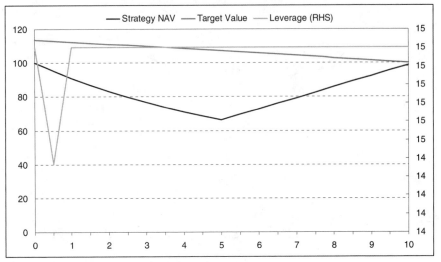

In order to model the time evolution of spreads, a mean-reverting stochastic spread process is typically assumed for a constant maturity credit index, which requires the estimation of spread volatility, speed of mean reversion and long-term mean level of spreads. Given the lack of a long time series of index spread data, reliable estimation of these parameters is difficult. Bond indices provide a richer data set, but create other challenges, such as establishing a reliable methodology for implying CDS spreads from bond spreads.

Modeling the evolution of the CDS index term-structure presents further challenges, as recent trends have been observed in a very low spread environment, and it is difficult to estimate how the slope of the credit curve will change as spreads revert to levels significantly above those currently observed. In addition, the impact of CPDO issuance and other structured credit market innovations on the "local" slope of the term structure around the roll date may be significant.

Modeling CPDO Transactions

Overall, the modeling requirement are similar as outlined for Credit CPPI transactions above. In the example transaction considered above, a default, credit spread, and interest rate modeling paradigm needs to be implemented. In order to model the time evolution of spreads, a mean-reverting stochastic spread process is typically assumed for a constant maturity credit index as outlined, for example, in the section on LSS transactions. Given the lack of a long time series of CDS index spread data, reliable estimation of these processes is difficult. Modeling the evolution of the CDS index term-structure presents further challenges, as recent trends have been observed in a very low spread environment, and it is difficult to estimate how the slope of the credit curve will change as spreads revert to levels significantly above those currently observed. Bond prices may provide a richer data set, but create other challenges, such as establishing a reliable methodology for implying CDS spreads from bond spreads (see, e.g., O'Kane and Sen, 2004 for further details).

Overall, a detailed, fully integrated modeling of various credit and market risks in a consistent framework, combined with a robust statistical analysis and parameter estimation are necessary, in order to gain a good understanding of risk/return opportunities offered by CPDO transactions. In the future, structural innovations and a move towards bespoke portfolios or more complex risk portfolios can be expected.

SUMMARY AND MODELING CHALLENGES

Since its inception, the synthetic CDO market has experienced an enormous growth, fuelled by ease of execution/structuring and the ability to implement specific credit market views via tailor made solutions. The strong growth in bespoke ST CDOs was supported by the development of liquid credit indices and index-linked tranches. Accompanied with a growth in volume of typical ST synthetic CDOs was an enormous drive in innovation in underlying asset classes and new products (structures).

Typical synthetic CDOs reference a pool of CDS written on corporations and financial institutions, and sometimes are combined with cash-funded assets such as corporate bonds or loans, or ABS. The recent tight spread environment, and the events of May 2005 that highlighted concerns of correlation risk and overlap (see South, 2005) given that a limited number of liquidly trading CDSs, resulted in a search for diversification opportunities and higher yields by introducing new risks and asset classes to ST CDO investors. Since 2004, EDSs have been considered as investment alternatives from time to time, leading to a need to integrate credit and equity risk in a consistent yet practical manner. More recently, ST CDOs have been suggested as vehicles to transfer commodity risk requiring yet another need to adequately model and integrate such products. In general, we expect these developments towards hybrid transactions to continue and, linked with further growth in noncorporate synthestic indices (e.g., ABSX), expect further growth in synthetic CDO markets.

Events like May 2005 have lead to changes in market participants trading behaviour, and fuelled the desire and need to place whole capital structure CDOs, as well as the need to develop structures aiming to reduce MtM volatility, too. LSS transactions allowed to sell super senior risk to real-money investors in leveraged form where in addition to credit risk, MtM risk is explicitly taken into consideration. While 2005 was the year of LSS, 2006 and 2007 are expected to be interesting due to further developments of credit CPPI and CPDO transactions. Such defensive trades are based on dynamic asset allocation to protect principal investment yet providing potential for substantial upside. We expect these developments to continue to evolve toward more complex credit and hybrid portfolios and toward their application as new, innovative structures for efficient risk transfer.

Hand in hand with these developments is the need for quantitative models that are capable of capturing univariate risks and dependence aspects inherent in such structures. Although the standard copula framework has the advantage of separating the marginal risk factors from portfolio aspects, further research on viable alternatives is required. For example, the recently renewed interest in structural—Merton type—models for consistent pricing of single-name credit and equity products (see Chapter 3) could lead to extensions where portfolios of equities, debt instruments and, hence, credit spread sensitive and default sensitive products are consistently integrated. Alternatively, practical development of stochastic intensity/hazard models appears to provide room for further research and application toward multiple asset classes. Both of these developments require further research, bearing in mind that consistency to current methodologies is frequently required.

In summary, we believe that developments in synthetic CDOs provide exciting opportunities for the convergence of various financial risks and markets, as well as further opportunities for innovative risk transfer. This is accompanied by a number of quantitative challenges and should provide room for further growth in coming years.

A P P E N D I X   A

Gini Coefficient (Gini)

The Gini/Lorenz curve measures the quality of the rank ordering of a model. A very good model should identify all defaults or events with the higher PDs/EEPs.

In Figure 11.24, the X-axis corresponds to the PDs/EEPs or ratings/categories ranked from highest percentages to lowest. The Y-axis reports the cumulative observed default/event rate corresponding to the observations ranked from highest score to lowest on the x-axis.

The Gini coefficient represents two times the grayshaded surface under the Gini/Lorenz curve. Gini coefficients are sample dependent. In general, in the credit universe, Gini coefficients are positioned in the 50 to 90 percent interval. Results are usually measured out-of-sample. When the size of the dataset is sufficiently large, which is the case in this paper, out-of-sample and in-sample performance results converge. Gini coefficients are sample dependent.

F I G U R E   1 1 . 2 4

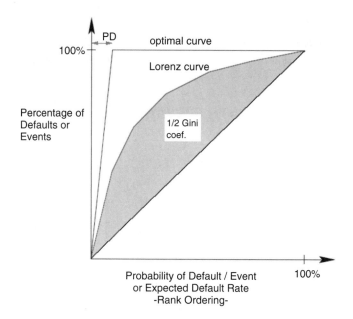

A P P E N D I X   B

Nonparametric Estimation

Before estimating a parametric model for a general diffusion process of type $dS_t = \mu(S_t)dt + \sigma(S_t)dW_t$, it is useful to apply nonparametric techniques to gain some insight into the possible specification of the drift μ and diffusion term σ. Here, S could denote the price of a specific commodity, the level of interest rates, or the level of credit spreads. Stanton (1997) proposes first- and higher-order approximations to the drift and diffusion term, and the first-order approximations are outlined next.

DENSITY ESTIMATION

The first step is to estimate the density of the data generating process, through a Gaussian kernel estimator. That is,

$$f(x) = \frac{1}{nh} \sum_{t=1}^{n} \phi\left(\frac{x - S_t}{h}\right),$$

where ϕ denotes the standard normal density, n is the number of observations, and the window or band width is given by $h = c\tilde{\sigma}n^{-1/5}$, where c is a constant and $\tilde{\sigma}$ the empirical standard deviation from the data. The level of smoothness of the density depends significantly on the choice of c. Prigent et al. (2001) and Stanton (1997) propose a value close to 3.

DRIFT AND VOLATILITY/DIFFUSION ESTIMATION

The drift term at a level of x can be estimated to first order, using

$$\tilde{\mu}(x) = \frac{\sum_{t=1}^{n-1}(S_{t+1} - S_t)\phi\left(\dfrac{x - S_t}{h}\right)}{\sum_{t=1}^{n-1}\phi\left(\dfrac{x - S_t}{h}\right)},$$

and the corresponding first-order approximation for the diffusion is given by

$$\tilde{\sigma}(x) = \left(\frac{\sum_{t=1}^{n-1}[S_{t+1} - S_t - \tilde{\mu}(x)]^2 \phi\left(\dfrac{x - S_t}{h}\right)}{\sum_{t=1}^{n-1}\phi\left(\dfrac{x - S_t}{h}\right)} \right)^{1/2}.$$

For higher-order estimators, we refer the reader to Stanton (1997).

APPENDIX C

Parametric Estimation by Chan et al. (1992)

Chan et al. (1992) propose to estimate the discrete time version of equation (2) that is given by:

$$S_{t+1} - S_t = a + bS_t + \sigma|S_t|^{\gamma}\varepsilon_{t+1},$$

where ε_{t+1} are assumed to be i.i.d. normal variables. The Markovian property of the process and the assumption of normality enable the derivation of the log-likelihood function that can be maximized thereafter:

$$L = -n\,\ln(\sqrt{2\pi}\sigma) - \sum_{t=1}^{n}\ln\left(\left|S_{t-1}\right|^{\gamma}\right) - \sum_{t=1}^{n}\left(\frac{S_t - a - (b+1)S_{t-1}}{\sigma|S_{t-1}|^{\gamma}}\right)^2.$$

As an assymptotically unbiased estimator with minimum variance, MLE is often preferred to alternative approaches such as method of moments, see Broze, Scaillet, and Zakoian (1995) for a discussion.

REFERENCES

Albanese, C., and O. Chen (2005), "Pricing equity default swaps," *Risk*, June.
Alexander, C. (2001), *Market Models: A Guide to Financial Data Analysis*, John Wiley & Sons.
Bayliffe, D., and B. Pauling (2003), "Long term equity returns," working paper, Tower Perrin.
Black, F., and R. Jones (1986), "Simplifying portfolio insurance," *Journal of Portfolio Management*.

Black, F., and R. Rouhani (1989), "Constant proportion portfolio insurance and the synthetic put option: a comparison," in F. J. Fabozzi (ed.), *Institutional Investor Focus on Investment Management*, Cambridge, Massachusetts: Ballinger, 695–708.

Boyer, B., M. S. Gibson, and M. Loretan (1999), "Pitfalls in tests for changes in correlation," International Finance discussion papers, Number 597, Board of Governors of the Federal Reserve System.

Cangemi, B., A. de Servigny, and C. Friedman (2003), "Standard & Poor's credit risk tracker for private firms, technical document," working paper, Standard & Poor's, Risk Solutions.

Christoffersen, P. F., F. X. Diebold, and T. Schuermann (1998), "Horizon problems and extreme events in financial risk management," working paper prepared for the Federal Reserve Bank of New York Economic Policy Review.

Collin-Dufresne, Goldstein, and Martin (1999), "The determinants of credit spread changes," working paper, Carnegie Mellon University.

Cox, J., J. Ingersoll, and S. Ross (1985), "A theory of the term structure of interest rates," *Econometrica*, 53, 385–407.

de Servigny, A., and N. Jobst (2005), "An empirical analysis of equity default swaps (I): Univariate insights," *Risk*, December.

de Servigny, A., and O. Renault (2003), "Correlations evidence," *Risk*, 90–94.

Delianedis, G., and R. Geske (2001), "The components of corporate credit spreads," Technical Report, The Andersen School, UCLA.

Demey, P., J.-F. Jouanin, and C. Roget (2004), "Maximum likelihood estimate of default correlations," *Risk*, November, 104–108.

Eydeland and Wolyniec (2003), "Energy and Power Risk Management."

Fitch (2004), "Equity Default Swaps in CDOs," Fitch Ratings, *www.fitchratings.com*.

Geman (2005), "Commodities and commodity derivatives."

Gilkes, K. (2005), "Modelling credit risk in synthetic CDO squared transactions," in *Securitisation of Derivatives and Alternative Asset Classes*, Kluwer Law International.

Gilkes, K., Jobst, N., Wong, J., and Xuan, Y. (2006) "Constant Proportion Debt Obligations—The DBRS Perspective", DBRS CDO Newsletter.

Hull, J., M. Predescu, and A. White (2004), "The relationship between credit default swap spreads, bond yields, and credit rating announcements," working paper, University of Toronto.

Hull, J., M. Predescu, and A. White (2005), "The valuation of correlation-dependent credit derivatives using a structural model," working paper, University of Toronto.

Jobst, N. (2004), "CDS/EDS correlation: Empirical insights," unpublished internal document, Standard & Poor's.

Jobst, N., and A. de Servigny (2006), "An empirical analysis of equity default swaps (II): Multivariate insights," *Risk*, January.

Jobst, N., and K. Gilkes (2004), "Risk analysis of CDS/EDS correlation products," in [A. Batchvarov (ed.),] *Hybrid Products: Instruments, Applications and Modelling*.

Kaufmann, R., and P. Patie (2004), "Strategic long-term financial risks: Single risk factors," working paper, ETH Zürich.

Lando, D. (2004), "Credit risk modelling: Theory and applications," in *Princeton Series in Finance*, Princeton University Press.

Longin, F., and B. Solnik (1999), "Correlation structure of international equity markets during extremely volatile periods," working paper, Department of Finance, ESSEC Graduate Business School.

Loretan, M., and W. B. English (2000), "Evaluating correlation breakdowns during periods of market volatility," International Finance discussion papers, Number 658, Board of Governors of the Federal Reserve System.

McNeil, A. J., and R. Frey (2000), "Estimation of tail-related risk measures for heteroscedastic financial time series: an extreme value approach," working paper, Department of Mathematics, ETH Zürich.

Medova, E., and R. G. Smith (2004), "Pricing equity default swaps using structural credit models," working paper, University of Cambridge.

Metayer, B. (2005), "CDO^2, correlation, overlap and subordination: Implication for pricing and risk management," working paper, Swiss Banking Institute, University of Zurich.

Morillo, D., and L. Pohlman (2002), "Large scale multivariate GARCH risk modelling for long-horizon international equity portfolios," working paper, Panagora Asset. Management.

Perold, A. F. (1986), Constant portfolio insurance," Harvard Business School, Unpublished manuscript.

Perold, A. F., and W. F. Sharpe (1988), "Dynamic strategies for asset allocation," *Financial Analysts Journal*, 44, 16–27.

Prigent, Renault, and Scaillet (2001), "An empirical investigation into credit spread indices," *Journal of Risk*, 3, Spring.

Roman, E., R. Kopprash, and E. Hakanoglu (1989), "Constant proportion portfolio insurance for fixed-income investment," *Journal of Portfolio Management*.

Schönbucher, P. J. (2005), "Portfolio losses and term structure of loss transition rates: A new methodology for pricing of portfolio credit derivatives," Working paper.

Schwartz (1997), "The stochastic behaviour of commodity prices: Implication for valuation and hedging," *Journal of Finance*, 52.

Sidenius, J., V. Peterbarg, and L. Andersen (2005), "A new framework for dynamic portfolio loss modeling," working paper.

Sobehart, J. R., and S. C. Keenan (2004), "Hybrid probability of default models— A practical approach to modeling default risk," Citigroup, The Quantitative Credit Analyst, Issue 3, 5–29.

South, A. (2005), "CDO spotlight: Overlap between reference portfolios sets synthetic CDOs," Standard & Poor's Commentary.

Stărică, C. (2003), "Is GARCH(1,1) as good a model as the Nobel prize accolades would imply?", working paper, Department of Mathematical Statistics, Chalmers University of Technology, Gothenburg.

Standard & Poor's (2004), "Global methodology for portfolios of credit and equity default swaps," Standard & Poor's, Criteria.

Standard & Poor's, (2005), "CDO spotlight: Approach to rating leveraged super senior CDO notes," Standard & Poor's Criteria.

Standard & Poor's (2006), "Collateralized Commodity Obligations (CCO): CDOE modelling methodology overview," Internal Document, Structured Finance Ratings.

O'Kane, D. and S. Sen, (2004) "Credit spreads explained", Lehman Brothers, Quantitative credit research quarterly, March 2004.

Vasicek, O. (1977), "An equilibrium characterization of the term structure," *Journal of Financial Economics*, 5, 177–188.

Residential Mortgage-Backed Securities

Varqa Khadem and Francis Parisi

INTRODUCTION

In this chapter, we start with a detailed presentation of the approach, followed by a rating agency. This approach looks simple, but is important to understand the more recent developments in the residential mortgage-backed securities (RMBS) sector. In a second stage, we focus on the more advanced modeling techniques that have emerged among the most active market participants.

From an historical perspective, the structured finance market began with the issuance of the first mortgage-backed security in the U.S. by the Government National Mortgage Association (Ginnie Mae) in 1968. Soon after, the Federal Home Loan Mortgage Corporation (Freddie Mac) introduced its mortgage participation certificates in 1970, and, by 1977, the Federal National Mortgage Association (Fannie Mae) was in the game. Loans eligible for sale to one of these agencies must satisfy specific criteria; such loans are *conforming* mortgages. Loans not eligible for sale to the agencies, or *nonconforming* mortgages, needed another way to the capital markets. Around that time, Standard & Poor's rated the first U.S. private issue mortgage-backed bond. This was the beginning of one of the fastest growing and most innovative sectors of the global capital markets. Today, Standard & Poor's rates transactions are backed by a wide variety of assets, including residential and commercial mortgages, credit cards, auto loans, and small business loans, to name a few. While historically the RMBS sector has dominated with respect to overall issuance volume, the collateral debt obligation (CDO) market currently is the fastest growing sector.

Standard & Poor's global criteria for rating structured finance transactions have their basis in the U.S. criteria developed for RMBS in the mid-1970s. The U.S. RMBS criteria also served as the starting point for developing criteria for other asset classes. All structured finance securities are either cash flow or synthetic securitizations. Simply put, in a cash flow structured finance transaction, an issuer conveys ownership of the assets to a special-purpose entity (SPE), which then issues the rated debt. Principal and interest related to those assets are conveyed along with the risks. In synthetic securities, only the risk is transferred. Standard & Poor's role is to evaluate the risk, assess the likelihood of repayment according to the terms of the transaction, and assign a rating to reflect the level of risk. Within this structural framework it is apparent that structured finance securities are generally the *same* so as the market evolved into other assets and then other regions of the world, this common ground was the starting point. The legal aspect of these transactions is also a key component and the criteria evolved to accommodate the local laws.

The U.S. RMBS sector has evolved quite a bit from those early days from the typical nonconforming prime mortgage pool to over a dozen different types of underlying assets. One of the fastest growing RMBS sectors is the sub-prime market. Sub-prime RMBS represent about a third to a half of the volume of Standard & Poor's-rated RMBS, and prime is about 20 percent. The remaining securities include home-equity, Alt-A, hi-LTV, scratch-n-dent, and net interest margin securities (NIMs). Interestingly, the European RMBS market has grown rapidly over the recent years and represents a non-negligeable proportion of the U.S. structured finance market.

Lastly, the banking industry has considerably developed the modeling techniques applicable to the RMBS sector and more generally to the asset-backed securities (ABS) sector. Talking about mortgage risk without describing the modeling of the broad prepayment and credit risks of underlying assets backing structured finance bonds is not possible any more. Cash flow statistical modeling is another area of focus for market participants.

The remainder of this chapter is as follows. In Part 1, we describe Standard & Poor's analytical methods for rating U.S. RMBS. Part 2 presents the analytical approach for European RMBS. Finally, Part 3 provides an overview of the quantitative methods used in structured finance with a particular focus on European transactions.

PART 1: ANALYTICAL TECHNIQUES TO RATE RMBS TRANCHES IN THE UNITED STATES

The rating process for RMBS begins when a banker or issuer contacts Standard & Poor's to discuss a proposal. This beginning phase usually takes place through a conference call or brief meeting, where an overview of the transaction is presented. The purpose of this discussion is to identify any unusual or complicated structural, credit, or legal issues that may need to be ironed out before a formal rating process can begin. If no such complication exists, the rating process proceeds according to an agreed-upon time schedule.

When the issuer decides to proceed, a complete analysis of the transaction begins. Rating analysts meet on-site with management of the originator or seller of the receivables. This exercise enables analysts to expand their understanding of the issuer's strategic and operational objectives. It also provides a more defined level of familiarity with underwriting policies, contractual breach procedures, and operational controls. In addition, a detailed discussion of the characteristics of the originator's collateral, the repayment pattern of the obligors, and the performance history of the assets, as well as an examination of prior transactions, is typically undertaken. These discussions are often complemented by walk-through tours of the originator and servicer. It is important to note that the review does not include an audit. Instead, the rating is based on the representations of the various parties to the transaction, including the issuer and its counsel, the investment banker and its counsel, and the issuer's accountants.

Overview: Collateral, Legal, and Structural Analysis

As with any structured finance rating, the analysis focuses primarily on the credit, structural, and legal characteristics of the transaction. The legal criteria for U.S. structured finance ratings were developed in the mid-1970s for RMBS and served as a launching point for criteria development in other asset classes and in other countries. The fundamental tenet of these criteria is to isolate the assets from the credit risk of the seller or originator.

The collateral analysis involves an in-depth review of historical asset performance. Analysts collect and examine years of data on the performance variables that affect transaction credit risk. In the United States, credit risk in RMBS pools is sized using Standard & Poor's LEVELS™, a loan-level model that evaluates the foreclosure frequency (FF) (risk of default) and loss severity (LS) (loss given default) for each loan in the pool. LEVELS is used internally by Standard & Poor's analysts and licensed externally to mortgage originators, issuers, and investors. In the United Kingdom, analysts use a similar model that is not yet commercially available.

The structural review involves an examination of the disclosure and contractually binding documents for the transaction. The criteria cover many aspects of the structure, from the method of conveyance of mortgage loans to the trust, to the method of security payment and termination. The analysis also considers the payment allocation and what is being promised to security holders.

After a rating is assigned, it is monitored and maintained by Standard & Poor's surveillance analysts. The purpose of surveillance is to ensure that the rating continues to reflect the performance and structure of the transaction, as it was analyzed at transaction closing. Performance information is disclosed in a report prepared monthly by the servicer of the transaction. Before a transaction's closing date, analysts review the data itemized in the servicing report to ensure that all necessary information is included.

Credit Analysis

Quantifying the amount of loss that a mortgage pool will experience in all economic scenarios is the key to modeling credit risk for ratings. To achieve this, analysts use varying stress assumptions to gauge mortgage pool performance in all types of economic environments. The basis for the stress scenario applied to each rating category can be found in the historical loss experience of the mortgage market. Based on studies of historical data, Standard & Poor's developed the criteria embedded in LEVELS.

The great depression of the 1930s provided what many consider the most catastrophic environment for mortgages in the United States in this century. While no one expects a repeat of a 1930s depression, it is an excellent case study of how unemployment and falling property values can impact mortgage losses. Loss data on individual loans vary from one to another, depending on the characteristics of the mortgages. A combination of historical evidence along with strong analytical judgment is used in determining loss criteria. The individual risk characteristics usually have an affect on one of the two factors that determine the overall risk of loss on a loan, although some characteristics affect both factors. These factors are:

◆ FF, which is the probability that a loan will default; and

◆ LS, which is the amount of loss that will be realized on a defaulted loan.

Foreclosure Frequency

Standard & Poor's LEVELS™ model determines the risk associated with a mortgage loan or a portfolio of mortgage loans. LEVELS uses standard mortgage and credit file data to compute credit enhancement requirements for residential mortgage loans based on the rating criteria. These individual loan analyses are then aggregated to provide credit enhancement levels needed to assign the appropriate ratings to a portfolio of mortgage loans. The FF reflects the borrower's ability and willingness to repay the mortgage according to the terms of the loan.

In 1996, the use of credit scores became commonplace in the residential mortgage industry. Used for many years in unsecured consumer lending, the credit score assesses the default risk based on a borrower's credit history. A credit score is a numerical summary of the relative likelihood that an individual will pay back a loan. As an index, the score reflects the relative risk of serious delinquency, foreclosure, or bankruptcy associated with a borrower. Although widely used in the U.S. consumer credit market, credit scores are still emerging in Europe. Based on research done, Standard & Poor's found that the use of consumer credit scores enhances the ratings process. Therefore, when loan level information regarding the mortgage loans is sent in for analysis, the consumer credit score should be included. Credit scores, in addition to other loan characteristics, are used to derive loan-level FF. The base FF assumptions for each rating category are affected by loan characteristics such as:

◆ Borrower credit quality (credit score)
◆ Loan-to-value (LTV) ratio
◆ Property type
◆ Loan purpose
◆ Occupancy status
◆ Mortgage seasoning
◆ Pool size

- ◆ Loan size
- ◆ Loan maturity
- ◆ Loan documentation
- ◆ Adjustable-rate mortgages (ARMs)
- ◆ Balloon mortgages
- ◆ Lien status.

The default and loss models embedded in LEVELS were estimated based on these variables. From these models, we can estimate the effect each variable has on the likelihood of borrower default, and the LS on a defaulted loan. For example, LTVs historically have proven to be key predictors of the likelihood of foreclosure. The LTV of a loan is defined as the mortgage loan balance divided by the lower of the home's purchase price or appraised value, expressed as a percentage. The higher the LTV ratio, the greater the risk of mortgage foreclosure, and the greater the expected loss after foreclosure; thus, these loans require more loss coverage than lower LTV loans.

Similarly, the type of property pledged to secure a mortgage loan also affects the borrower's likelihood of default. A loan secured by a single-family home generally has a lower risk of default than say a three-to-four family home. In the latter, the mortgagor most likely will rely on rental income to meet monthly obligations. This same phenomenon is observed with mortgages on non-owner-occupied homes. Here too, the mortgagor is relying on rental income in the case of an investment property. And, a homeowner is more likely to forfeit a second home or an investment property than their primary residence.

With the extremely low interest rates observed since 2001, the U.S. RMBS market witnesses record breaking origination volume. Borrowers refinancing their homes fueled a large portion of that volume. The purpose of any mortgage loan impacts the risk of default. A "purchase mortgage" is the term used to describe the typical mortgage transaction where a buyer is funding a portion of the acquisition price for a new home. The collateral value pledged to the lender is strongly supported by both the purchase price and an appraisal. In a rate/term refinancing, the mortgagor replaces an existing loan with a new, shorter maturity or lower interest rate loan, thereby decreasing the term or lowering the monthly payments. Cash-out refinance loans have a higher risk profile because of the difficulty in measuring actual market value without a sales price. LEVELS adjusts the expected loss on a cash-out loan to reflect this added risk.

Generally, default risk is diminished as a loan seasons. Thus, for seasoned pools, Standard & Poor's will make adjustments to the default and loss assumptions, reducing the credit enhancement needed for a similar but unseasoned pool of loans. The rationale is that as loans season and the borrower makes payments, the outstanding loan balance is amortizing; thus reducing the principal at risk. Additionally, in the past decade, home prices in the United States have grown at a steady rate, in some areas at double-digit rates, further reducing the exposure relative to the home's value. While we cannot guaranty house price appreciation, loan amortization is a sure bet (except, of course, in some ARMs where the balance negatively amortizes). Also dependent on the idea of building equity reduces risk is the relationship between mortgage term and default risk. By their very nature, mortgages with 15-year terms are less risky than comparable 30-year mortgages. The "shorter term" means that the 15-year mortgage amortizes faster, allowing for a quicker build-up of owner-equity. Industry data show that 15-year mortgages default less frequently than 30-year mortgages, as this equity build-up increases the borrower's incentive to keep the loan current.

As in any statistical sample, the number of loans in a pool is important in determining risk. The reason for this is that LEVELS was developed based on data on millions of loans, and the criteria represent law of large numbers properties. Any given pool under review for a rating is a subset of this larger universe. Based on research, Standard & Poor's found that pools with at least 250 loans are of sufficient size to ensure diversity and the accuracy of loss assumptions. Pools with fewer than 250 loans are ratable and an adjustment is made in pool credit quality analysis. The analysis focused on the observed variability in the default rate for thousands of samples of loans drawn randomly from a larger population. The distribution of the sampled default rates was compared and were not found to have a statistically significant difference until the sample sizes fell below 250. Estimating the coefficient of variation for each sample size and fitting a robust (M-estimate) regression, Standard & Poor's derived a relationship of the form

$$f(n) \propto \frac{\hat{\beta}}{\log(n)},$$

where n is the number of loans in the pool.

Another factor relating to concentration of risk is loan size. Higher balance loans are considered higher risk. In an economic downturn, "jumbo loans" are more likely to suffer greater market value decline (MVD) as a result of a limited market for the underlying properties. This would increase the LS on the mortgage. LEVELS default equation reflects this risk and adjusts accordingly. An important point to note in developing criteria for loan size is that in the United States, mortgage purchase entities Fannie Mae and Freddie Mac publish annually their guidelines for conforming loan balances to reflect the change in home prices across the country. What would have been a jumbo loan five years ago is most likely conforming today.

Besides establishing loan balance criteria, the agencies have standards for loan documentation requirements. In its research, Standard & Poor's found that reduced loan documentation may introduce additional risk, and an assessment must be made whether total credit risk has increased. Many accelerated underwriting programs aim to offset potentially higher credit risk by increasing the required size of the mortgagor's down payment. Intuitively, there is a point at which a certain level of risk is offset by an increased down payment. Therefore, a loan having a low LTV with limited documentation may have the same loss coverage requirement as a higher LTV loan with full documentation.

In analyzing ARM credit risk, the rating analysis focuses on the following additional factors to determine the level of credit enhancement needed for the various ratings: the frequency of interest rate changes; the amount of the potential rate increase per period; the interest rate life-cap, or the amount of rate increase over the life of the mortgage; the amount of negative amortization, if any; and the volatility of the underlying interest rate index. Similar in risk is the balloon mortgage. A balloon mortgage is a loan with principal payments that do not fully amortize the loan balance by the stated maturity. One common form of balloon mortgage offered in the U.S. residential market is a fixed-rate loan with level principal and interest payments calculated on the basis of a 30-year amortization schedule. After a specified term (usually 5, 7, 10, or 15 years), the remaining unpaid principal balance is due in one large payment. In light of this added credit risk, Standard & Poor's looks for higher levels of loss protection for rated transactions involving balloons.

Loss Severity

Standard & Poor's has LS assumptions for residential mortgages based on studies of historical data. The LS is made up of several components. Upon a mortgage foreclosure, the lender often takes title to the property and re-sells the property at auction to recover the loan amount. Quite often, properties sold after foreclosure sell for less than the loan balance outstanding. For rating purposes, Standard & Poor's assumes larger losses on sale, known as MVD, for higher ratings. So at "BBB," the MVD may be on the order of 22 percent, whereas at "AAA," the MVD is about 34 percent, resulting in a greater loss on sale for the higher rating. Besides the loss in market value, there is unpaid interest on the loan that has accrued since the loan became delinquent, and finally there are costs associated with the foreclosure. These costs include legal fees and costs to maintain the property until sold at auction. The sum of the lost principal and interest, and related costs as a percent of the original loan balance is the LS.

Loss Severity Calculation Example

Property value		$100,000
Loan amount (80% LTV)	$80,000	
MVD 35%		−35,000
Net recovery		65,000
Principal loss (loan amount- net recovery)	15,000	
Lost interest and costs	20,000	
Total loss	35,000	
LS (total loss/loan amount)	44%	

The base LS assumptions for each rating category are affected by factors such as the following:

+ LTV ratios
+ Mortgage insurance
+ Lien status
+ Loan balance
+ Loan maturity
+ Loan type
+ Loan purpose
+ Property type and occupancy
+ Geographic dispersion
+ Mortgage seasoning.

Many of these loan characteristics are also factors affecting the FF and are discussed earlier. Generally, a loan with a higher LTV will experience a higher LS because by definition there is less equity in the property. However, mortgages with LTVs greater than 80 percent may experience lower LSs because these loans may have primary mortgage insurance. Mortgage insurance guarantees a certain percentage of the mortgage loan balance, so the net effect is to reduce the exposure to the lender in the event of a default. In this simplified example, 25 percent of the loan is insured, reducing the lender's exposure. Although the loan has a higher LTV, the insurance results in a lower LS. This is not to encourage the origination of high-LTV loans because the risk of default is much higher than lower LTV loans. The net effect is that there is overall greater risk, and the credit enhancement for these loans is generally higher without offsetting characteristics.

Loss Severity Calculation with 25 percent Mortgage Insurance Example

Property value	$100,000
Loan amount (90% LTV)	$90,000
Uninsured amount	67,500
MVD 35%	−35,000
Net recovery	65,000
Principal loss (loan amount- net recovery)	2,500
Lost interest and costs	20,000
Total loss	22,500
LS	25%

Standard & Poor's LS assumptions are higher for second lien mortgage loans than for first lien mortgage loans because of the inherent risk in a subordinate lien position. The effect of lien status on LS is related to the size of the second mortgage loan relative to the first mortgage loan. The potential LS of a second mortgage loan increases as its LTV decreases relative to that of the first mortgage loan. Other data indicate that mortgage loans with larger loan balances take longer to foreclose and it takes longer to resell the property. The current criteria increase the assumed liquidation time frame for larger balanced loans, resulting in higher carrying costs and larger losses.

The LS, and the required loss coverage, is adjusted for any pool of loans that is more vulnerable to changing economic environments based upon its geographic dispersion. The analysis for this type of risk is based on whether there is any excessive geographic concentration of the underlying properties in any region represented in the pool. In the United States, Standard & Poor's developed the Housing Volatility Index that ranks local housing markets according to their risk of price decline. Loss assumptions are adjusted accordingly for those loans secured by properties in high-risk markets.

Structural Considerations for RMBS

There are different structural forms that RMBS issuers can use. They can be senior/subordinated structures where the lower rated or unrated tranches provide the credit support for the more highly rated tranches, and they can be senior/subordinated/over-collateralized structures where part of the credit support is in the form of over-collateralization usually derived from the value of excess interest, or the spread between the underlying mortgage coupons and the coupon on the rated securities.

The issuer's decision as to which type of credit enhancement structure to use takes into consideration many factors but is primarily investor driven, based upon which structure yields the best economic value. The credit analysis for these structures is the same, regardless of type. Most importantly, it is the use of the shifting interest structure that allows credit support to grow over time, at least until the transaction is through the majority of Standard & Poor's assumed default curve. This occurs through criteria that mandate that the majority of principal cash flow be allocated to the most senior classes, or by requiring that the over-collateralization target be pegged to the initial pool balance during the early stages of a transaction's life.

Only after determining that the mortgage pool is performing well will credit support be allowed to step down. The delinquency and loss levels experienced by the mortgage pool is critical to the determination of how much credit support will be needed over the life of the deal. Adequate credit support or loss coverage will enable all rated classes to receive their promised monthly interest payment and to ultimately receive back their entire principal amount. Accordingly, if the pool is performing well (relative to the initial expectation of delinquency, loss, and the level of credit support), the release or stepping down of credit support is permitted.

Senior/Subordinate Structures

A senior/subordinate structure for RMBS is characterized by the subordination of junior certificates that serve as credit support for the more senior certificates. Generally, in U.S. RMBS, all interest shortfalls and principal losses are allocated to the most junior bond first, resulting in a write-down of its principal balance. In contrast, in the United Kingdom, market bonds are not written down, as losses are experienced on the assets. Instead, principal losses experienced on the mortgage pool are recorded in a principal deficiency ledger (PDL), which tracks the extent to which the liabilities' principal balance exceeds that of the assets' principal balance. At each rating level, Standard & Poor's requires that principal deficiencies do not exceed the existing subordination. For example, in a transaction with £100 million "AAA" senior notes, £9 million "A" subordinate notes, and £1 million unrated notes, the principal deficiency at any point in time should not exceed £10 million in the "AAA" cash flow runs and £1 million in the "A" cash flow runs. If there is insufficient income to fund the principal deficiency, however, Standard & Poor's considers the risk to a transaction to be low if the principal deficiency is remedied within a short period of time using excess spread. In contrast to a structure that uses excess interest, in this structure, the subordinate bonds solely provide credit support. The result is larger subordinate bonds than would have been needed, if excess interest was also used to cover losses.

Allocation of Cash Flow   Most RMBS are structured as pass-through transactions. All principal and interest (including liquidation and insurance proceeds, seller repurchase and substitution proceeds, servicer advances, and other unscheduled collections) generated by the underlying mortgage pool are allocated in a priority order to bondholders. Interest is generally paid to all outstanding bonds, beginning with the most senior, and then in priority order to the remaining junior bonds. After all classes have received in full their promised interest payment, principal will be allocated based upon the terms of the governing documents. According to the rating criteria, since the subordinate bonds provide the only source of credit support in this type of structure, their receipt of principal must be delayed until a majority of borrower defaults have occurred. Amongst the senior classes, principal will be allocated sequentially or pro rata, based upon the average life preferences of investors.

When a loss is realized on a defaulted loan, issuers have two options in allocating cash flow. The most senior bonds can be promised the full, unpaid principal balance of the defaulted loan, or more simply the proceeds generated from the loan's final disposition.

If the full, unpaid principal balance of the defaulted loan is paid to senior classes, all rated classes must receive interest before any payments of principal are made. This is necessary because the payment to senior classes of more cash flow than the defaulted loan generates will result in the temporary shortfall of interest to subordinate bondholders. This violates Standard & Poor's timely receipt of interest criteria.

There is the possibility that the credit composition of a mortgage pool will diminish over time, as the level of defaults increases. This can occur as a result of stronger borrowers refinancing out of the pool, as time goes on. This shift in pool makeup is commonly known as "adverse selection." Accordingly, the rating criteria require that all principal collections be paid first to the most senior class, lowering its percentage interest in the pool and, therefore, increasing the percentage interest represented by the subordinate classes. The resulting "shifting interest" increases the level of credit protection to the most senior bondholders over time.

Typically, the senior bondholders will receive all principal payments for at least three years and until the level of credit support has increased to two times its initial level. After that time, and provided that additional performance-based tests are met, holders of the subordinate bonds may receive a portion of principal collections.

Allocation of Losses In the case of the senior/subordinate structure, the right of the junior class certificate-holders to receive a share of the cash flow are subordinated to the rights of the senior certificate-holders. In addition, losses cause the certificate balance of lower-rated certificates to be written down (in the United States) prior to the more senior bonds. Whenever the mortgage pool suffers a loss that threatens the amount due to the senior certificate-holders, cash flow that would otherwise be due to the subordinated certificate-holders must be diverted to cover the shortfall. Therefore, all interest shortfalls and principal loss will be allocated to the most junior class outstanding. Servicer advances that must ultimately be backed by a highly rated party, usually the trustee, generally cover shortfalls that result from delinquencies.

Stepping Down of Loss Protection As stated earlier, all rated transactions must preserve credit support until the mortgage pool has experienced a majority of its defaults and the remaining borrowers have proven their ability to perform well, as judged by delinquency and loss tests. However, after that point, the decline of credit enhancement over time has traditionally been a feature of Standard & Poor's-rated mortgage-backed securities. This stepping down of credit enhancement is contingent upon collateral performance, measured by loss and delinquency numbers as well as the time elapsed since securitization.

In the senior/subordinate structure, the stepping down of loss protection occurs when principal is allocated to the subordinate bonds. Historical data show that the majority of all defaults occur in the first five years after mortgage loan origination. Accordingly, to protect against severe losses during this stressful time period, a five-year lockout period applies. During this time period, no reduction in credit enhancement is expected. This lockout is also intended to protect certificate holders against deterioration in the collateral pool's credit profile due to adverse selection. Once the determination has been made that principal may be allocated to the subordinate bonds, principal may be allocated to each subordinate bond that has maintained at least two times its original credit support as a percentage of the current outstanding pool balance. Delinquency and loss tests should also continue to be met.

Principal may also be paid to the senior and mezzanine classes pro-rata. To attain pro rata allocation between the senior and the mezzanine classes before the end of the standard lockout period, the mezzanine class must be oversized to compensate for the early receipt of principal.

Excess Interest Valuation and Cash Flow Analysis

The senior/subordinate with over-collateralization structure is a hybrid structure that combines the use of excess interest to cover losses and create over-collateralization. The capital structure for these securities and based on the value of excess interest determined through cash flow analysis. Excess interest is the difference between the net mortgage rates paid by the borrowers in the underlying mortgage pool and the interest rate paid to bondholders. Cash flow analysis is necessary to determine how much excess interest will be available to cover losses over the life of the transaction. The analysis must consider the following variables:

♦ Mortgage interest rates
♦ Weighted average coupon (WAC) deterioration
♦ Fees
♦ Rate and timing of default and prepayment speeds
♦ Length of time for loss realization
♦ Bond pass-through rates
♦ Structural features such as the prioritization of principal cash flow.

An analysis of cash flows is done to determine the amount of over-collateralization and the size of the subordinate bonds necessary at each rating category. Cash flows should demonstrate that each rated class receives timely interest and ultimate repayment of principal. Default and LS projections are made at each rating category, regardless of structure or type of credit support.

For cash flow allocation, interest is generally paid to all senior classes of certificates concurrently based upon their pro rata percentage interest in the mortgage pool. Interest is then allocated sequentially, in priority order, to the subordinate bonds. Excess interest is then used to cover current losses, paid to the most senior bonds to build towards the over-collateralization target, and lastly will be "released" from the deal through payments to a residual certificate holder. The targeted level of over-collateralization is usually set as a percentage of the original pool balance. Principal is then allocated sequentially, pro rata, or in some combination among the senior classes, in order to accommodate investor's varying average-life requirements. Remaining principal is then paid sequentially, in priority order, to the subordinate bonds.

In this hybrid structure, the credit enhancement to each rated class is provided first by the monthly-generated excess interest, second through the decrease in any over-collateralization, and third will be allocated to the subordinate bonds. After all excess interest and over-collateralization has been depleted, subordinate bonds, on a priority basis, are shorted interest or written down for principal loss.

Defaults play a major role in the amount of excess interest available in a given transaction. The frequency of defaults and the timing of those defaults will influence the amount of excess interest that may be on hand to cover potential losses. If the cash flows show that payment of current interest can be maintained and the losses adequately absorbed while ultimately paying the rated class, the transaction will meet the stress test. In addition, the balance of the loan at the time of default is calculated by assuming that only scheduled principal payments have occurred on the loan, and that no prepayments on that loan have taken place.

Typically, a 12-month lag is assumed from the time a loan defaults until the loan is liquidated for U.S. RMBS; the assumption is 18 months for the U.K. market. In other words, 12 (or 18) months after the default occurs, a percentage of the balance (equal to the LS at the rating level being analyzed) will be lost, and the remainder of the balance will be recovered as net proceeds.

The availability of excess interest is also impacted by whether or not advances are being made on delinquent and defaulted loans. Typically, transactions require the servicer to make advances on delinquent and defaulted loans until such time the loan is liquidated. However, the servicer does not have to make an advance on a specific loan if it determines that the amount advanced will not be recoverable from liquidation proceeds. If advances are required, then the excess interest from these loans may be available to offset potential losses. Transactions without an advancing mechanism will not have any interest flowing into the transaction from delinquent or defaulted loans. Therefore, this is assumed in the cash flow analysis. In this case, an added stress is placed on the cash flows. Because no advancing is occurring, analysts will assume in the cash flow modeling that a certain percentage of loans are delinquent at any point in time, in addition to the amount of loans in default at that time. Six months prior to each bullet default, beginning with the default balance in month 12, a like percentage of loans will be delinquent in interest as is in default. Recovery of this delinquent interest occurs six months later; that is, the first delinquent period begins in month 6 with recovery in month 12. This delinquency stress continues for all bullets throughout the default curve.

The prepayment rate significantly impacts the amount of excess interest that is available in a transaction. The greater the amount of loans prepaying, the less excess interest will be available. The prepayment rate that is assumed is based on the historical experience of the industry or the specific issuer. The pricing speed may be used as a proxy for this speed and is typically reported as a constant prepayment rate (CPR). This indicates the "all in" speed at which loans are removed from the pool. That is, the speed at which loans voluntarily prepay combined with the rate at which defaults occur.

However, Standard & Poor's uses this pricing speed to indicate voluntary prepayments only. The rating analysis assumes that poorer credit quality borrowers will not be able to prepay, and that therefore only includes voluntary prepayments. Default assumptions are layered over the prepayment assumptions. In this regard, it is believed that voluntary prepayments are inversely related to the economic scenario as we go up the rating scale to a more stressful economic scenario. However, because defaults increase at a greater pace as the more severe economic downturn occurs, the overall speed at which loans are removed from the pool will increase.

It should be again noted that Standard & Poor's will analyze the speed at which the deal is priced versus the issuer's historical experience, and if it is determined that the pricing speed does not adequately reflect the actual prepayment history for the issuer and the collateral type, the prepayment assumptions will be adjusted accordingly.

Mortgage prepayment history has shown that the WAC of a pool, and therefore the available excess spread, decreases over time in mortgage pools. That is, loans having higher interest rates and greater margins are more likely to prepay if the borrower's credit improves, and more likely to default if it does not. Therefore, the ratings analysis stresses the cash flows in order to reflect this situation.

When a transaction contains mortgage loans with an interest rate index that is different from that of the certificates, basis risk occurs. The changing spread between the two rates may cause shortfalls in the cash flow needed to pay the bonds. To address this issue, Standard & Poor's uses its stressed interest rate scenarios in the cash flow modeling. Several years ago, Standard & Poor's revised its interest modeling approach for U.S. RMBS. The research began with the estimation of a Cox-Ingersoll-Ross (CIR) model for the one-month LIBOR. The estimated CIR model was used in the simulation of hundreds of thousands of interest rate paths. Simulations were repeated for various ranges of starting rates, up to 2.25 percent, 2.25 to 2.75 percent, 2.75 to 3.25 percent, and so on up to 20 percent. For each starting range, the simulation results were selected based on a point-wise quantile, that is, from the month one results the values corresponding to specific quantiles were chosen, from the month two results, from the month three results, and so on. These points were "connected" to create the base curves. Additionally, to reflect the natural movement of rates up and down, a sinusoidal component was added. To ensure consistency, all other indices were modeled against the one-month LIBOR.

Each month the RMBS vectors for about a dozen indices and all rating categories are published. These vectors are used in the U.S. RMBS cash flow model, SPIRE. In the United Kingdom, the interest rate scenarios are more straightforward and perhaps more stressful. LIBOR is assumed to increase at 2 percent per month until a ceiling of 18 percent (12 percent for EURIBOR) is reached. The rate is assumed to remain at the ceiling for the life of the transaction. For falling rate environments, rates are assumed to fall 2 percent per month until a 2 percent floor is reached, where rates remain for life.

Legal Issues in RMBS

Banks or other financial institutions, insurance companies, or nonbanking corporations transfer residential mortgage loans into a securitization structure. Some of the legal issues raised by these transactions differ depending on whether the entity transferring the loans is a nonbanking corporation that is eligible to become a debtor under the U.S. Bankruptcy Code, a bank, other financial institution. Also relevant is whether the entity is an insurance company that is not eligible to become a debtor under the Bankruptcy Code, or an entity subject to the Bankruptcy Code (such as a municipality or public-purpose entity), but which is deemed by Standard & Poor's to be *bankruptcy-remote* in that the bankruptcy or dissolution of such entity for reasons unrelated to the transaction structure is deemed unlikely to occur (a "special-purpose entity transferor"). Unless otherwise indicated, an entity either selling, contributing, depositing, or pledging assets for purposes of securitization, including the originator of the assets and any intermediary entity participating at any level in a structure transaction as a transferor of assets, is referred to as a transferor.

Structured financings are rated based primarily on the creditworthiness of isolated assets or asset pools, whether sold, contributed, or pledged into a securitization structure, without regard to the creditworthiness of the seller, contributor, or borrower. The structured financing seeks to insulate transactions from entities that are either unrated and for whom Standard & Poor's is unable to quantify the likelihood of a potential bankruptcy, or that are rated investment grade but wish a higher rating for the transaction. Standard & Poor's worst-case scenario assumes the bankruptcy of each transaction participant deemed not to be bankruptcy-remote or that is rated lower than the transaction. Standard & Poor's resolves most legal concerns by analyzing the legal documents, and where appropriate, receiving opinions of counsel that address insolvency, as well as security interest and other issues. Understanding the implications of the assumptions and its criteria enables an issuer to anticipate and resolve most legal concerns early in the rating process.

Special-Purpose Entities   Standard & Poor's legal criteria for securitization transactions are designed to ensure that the entity owning the assets required to make payments on the rated securities is bankruptcy remote, that is, is unlikely to be subject to voluntary or involuntary insolvency proceedings. In this regard, both the incentives of this entity, known as an SPE, or its equity holders to resort to voluntary insolvency proceedings and the incentives for other creditors of the SPE to resort to involuntary proceedings are considered. The analysis also examines whether third-party creditors of the SPE's parent would have an incentive to reach the assets of the SPE (e.g., if the SPE is a trust, whether creditors of the beneficial holder would have an incentive to cause the dissolution of the trust to reach the assets of the trust). In this regard, Standard & Poor's has developed "SPE criteria," which an entity should satisfy to be deemed bankruptcy remote.

Trustee, Servicer, and Eligible Accounts The indenture trustee/custodian in a structured transaction is primarily responsible for receiving payments from servicers, guarantors, and other third parties and remitting these receipts to investors in the rated securities in accordance with the terms of the indenture, in addition to its monitoring, custodial, and administrative functions. In a structured transaction, the servicer agrees to service and administer assets in accordance with its customary practices and guidelines and has full power and authority to make payments to and withdrawals from deposit accounts that are governed by the documents.

The servicer's fee should cover its servicing and collection expenses and be in line with industry norms for securities of similar quality. If the fee is considered below industry averages, an increase may be built into the transaction. The increase might be needed to entice a substitute servicer to step in and service the portfolio. If the servicing fee is calculated based on a certain dollar amount per contract, the fee will increase as a percentage of assets due to amortization of the pool. This is an important consideration when assessing available excess spread to cover losses and fund any reserve account.

The filing of a bankruptcy petition would place a stay on all funds held in a servicer's own accounts. As a result, funds held to make payments on the rated securities would be delayed. In addition, funds commingled with those of the servicer would be unavailable to the structured transaction. As a general matter, Standard & Poor's addresses this commingling risk by looking both to the rating of the servicer and the amount of funds likely to be held in a servicer account at any given time.

A structured financing provides for different accounts to be established at closing to serve as collection accounts in which revenues generated by the securitized assets are deposited and to establish reserves funds. Often, the accounts in which the reserves are held contain significant sums held over a substantial period of time. Standard & Poor's has criteria regarding these accounts. The criteria are intended to immunize and isolate a transaction's payments, cash proceeds, and distributions from the insolvency of each entity that is a party to the transaction. An insolvency of the servicer (sub or master), trustee, or other party to the transaction should not cause a delay or loss to the investor's scheduled payments on the rated securities. As a general matter, Standard & Poor's relies on credit, structural, and legal criteria to ensure that a structured transaction's cash flows are protected at every link in the cash flow chain.

Unless collections on assets are concentrated at certain times of the month, for a period of up to two-business days after receipt, any servicer, whether or not rated, may keep collections on the assets in any account of the servicer's choice, commingled with other money of the servicer or of any other entity. Before the end of the two-business day period, the collections on the assets should be deposited into an *eligible deposit account*. As a general matter, all servicers, including unrated servicers, may keep/commingle collections for up to two business days, based on Standard & Poor's credit assumption, made in connection with all structured transactions, that two days' worth of collections on assets will be lost.

If, however, collections on the assets are concentrated at certain times within a month (e.g., the first, 15th, or 30th of a month), a servicer rated below "A-1" should not be able to keep/commingle collections on the assets even for the two-business day period, as described above. Rather, to prevent a potentially significant loss on assets, Standard & Poor's generally requires that, in transactions involving concentrated collections in which the servicer is rated below "A-1," either additional credit support be provided to cover commingling risk or obligors be instructed to make payments to lockbox accounts, which, in turn, are swept daily to an eligible deposit account. The servicer, unless rated the same as the rating sought on the structured transaction, should be prevented from accessing either the lockbox or sweep accounts. If a servicer is rated below "A-1" or is unrated, or if an "A-1" rated servicer's obligation to remit collections is not unconditional, the servicer should deposit all collections into an eligible deposit account within two business days of receipt. All other accounts maintained by the master servicer, special servicer, or trustee in a structured transaction (e.g., reserve accounts) should qualify as eligible deposit accounts.

PART 2: ANALYTICAL TECHNIQUES TO RATE RMBS TRANCHES IN EUROPE

In this part, we review the main modeling features used by Standard & Poor's to come with rated tranches on the European market.

Portfolio Credit Analysis

The credit analysis performed by Standard & Poor's estimates the expected principal loss (EL) that a mortgage portfolio might exhibit under different economic scenarios. At the primary rating level, loan level data is almost invariably available to complete this analysis. The loan level data includes information on the borrower (e.g., income, repeat buyer, and past credit events), loan (e.g., repayment type and interest rate), and property (e.g., valuation, valuation technique, and occupancy status). Two variables are calculated for each loan from this data: the FF and the LS. The FF is the likelihood that the borrower will default on their mortgage payments. Although this is commonly known as FF within the mortgage market, it is simply a default probability estimate (the PD). The LS refers to the amount of loss upon the subsequent sale of the property, once the borrower has defaulted (expressed as a percentage of the outstanding loan balance).

Calculating FF

As described earlier, FF is calculated for each loan in the portfolio. This calculation starts from a base case FF, which is then altered according to the characteristics of the loan. Certain loan or borrower features are assumed to increase (e.g., past credit difficulties) or decrease (e.g., seasoning) the probably of default. There are a few key variables that tend to have the most impact on loan performance. These are widely believed to be the LTV (the loan's balance divided by the value of the property, which can be used to represent the amount of borrower equity within the property), borrower past credit performance, and current indebtedness, although there are many other loan features that will contribute (e.g., potential for payment shock).

e.g., FF Loan(i)=4 percent (base FF)×2 (penalty for high LTV)
× 2 (penalty for poor past credit performance)
=16 percent probability of default.

In order to calculate estimates that represent loan behavior under harsher economic environments (and hence cover higher rating levels), the base FF is adjusted upwards. For example, Standard and Poor's assumes a base of 4 percent at the BBB level, increasing to a maximum of 12 percent at the AAA level.

The FF calculations above result in default estimates for each loan in the portfolio. The FF estimates for each loan are then combined to produce the total mortgage balance of the portfolio assumed to default. A weighted FF is used to achieve this, where the FF for each loan is weighted by the percentage of principal that loan contributes to the portfolio as a whole. The weighted FFs are then summed to produce the weighted average FF (WAFF). A simple and arithmetic average of the FF will not estimate the portfolio default rate accurately. Take the example

TABLE 12.1

Computation of the WAFF

Loan	Balance	FF (%)	Total principal at risk	Pool percent (%)	FF weighted by pool percent (%)
A	100,000	10	10,000	20	2
B	100,000	5	5,000	20	1
C	200,000	5	10,000	40	2
D	75,000	20	15,000	15	3
E	25,000	40	10,000	5	2
Total	500,000		50,000		WAFF = 10

shown in Table 12.1. When the FF calculated for each loan is applied to each loan's balance, this estimates the principal at risk that this loan contributes to the portfolio as a whole (e.g., calculated at 10,000 for Loan A, C, and E, despite markedly different initial principal balances). The total principal at risk is 50,000, or 10 percent of the total outstanding. An arithmetic average of the FFs would give a value of 16 percent, which is clearly well in excess of 10 percent, and as such, inaccurately represents the contributions of each loan. Instead, a weighted average takes into account the initial principal balance a loan contributes to the balance of the portfolio as a whole.

Calculating LS

The LS is the amount of loss that is expected to occur on a loan once it has defaulted (or simply the LGD). Most loans in Europe (with significant exceptions in the Netherlands) are originated with LTVs less than 100 percent. Hence, it appears initially that even if the borrower was to default, the property could be sold to re-coup the full outstanding principal loan balance (excluding any accumulated interest payments). There are two factors, however, that can erode the amount of sale proceeds that is available to repay the loan. First, costs need to be included, as it is assumed that the originator bears the cost of selling the property. Secondly, a downturn in the housing market may mean that the property is sold for less than it was valued at the time of origination. This potential downturn is represented in the LS calculation with the assumption of a MVD. A clear example of a MVD was demonstrated in the UK housing market in the early 1990s, as indicated in Figure 12.1.

FIGURE 12.1

An Example of a MVD, as Demonstrated in the UK Housing Market in the Early 1990s.

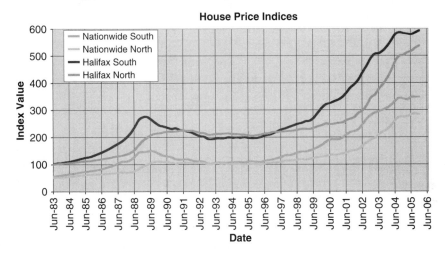

House Price Indices

The LS is the amount of shortfall in sale proceeds to cover the outstanding loan (plus costs), expressed as a percentage of the outstanding loan balance, e.g.,

$$LS = \frac{(\text{loan balance} + \text{costs}) - \text{sale price}}{\text{loan balance}},$$

where costs are calculated as a percentage of the outstanding loan balance, and the sale price is equal to the initial valuation minus the MVD. Take the example in Table 12.2.

In order to calculate estimates that represent LS under harsher economic environments (and hence cover higher rating levels), the MVDs are adjusted upwards. Standard and Poor's also adjust MVDs based on property location. For example, in the United Kingdom, MVDs are assumed to be larger in southern areas where the most aggressive house prices increases have been evidenced.

The LS calculations earlier result in LS estimates for each loan in the portfolio. Note that 1−LS is equal to the recovery on the loan in question. The LS estimates for each loan are then combined to produce the percentage of the defaulted balance of the portfolio assumed to be lost. A weighted LS is used to achieve this, where the LS for each loan is weighted by the

TABLE 12.2

Computing Loss Severity

Loan balance (£)	85,000
Costs (%)	4
Costs (£)	3,400
Loan balance + costs (£)	88,400
Initial valuation (£)	100,000
MVD (%)	35
Sale price (£)	$100,000 \times 35\% = 65,000$
(Loan balance + costs) − sale price (loss in £ amount)	23,400
LS (loss in £ amount expressed as a percentage of outstanding loan balance)	$23,400/85,000 = 27.5\%$

percentage of principal that loan contributes to the portfolio as a whole. The weighted LSs are then summed to produce the weighted average LS (WALS).

As described at the beginning of this section, the credit analysis attempts to estimate the expected loss that a mortgage portfolio might exhibit under different economic scenarios. The WAFF (the defaulted principal balance) multiplied by the WALS (the percentage of the defaulted principal balance assumed to be lost) gives one measure of the EL. A more accurate way of calculating the principal loss on the portfolio as a whole is to take the product of the FF and LS for each individual loan, and then calculate the weighted average overall loss percentage. This approach, however, results in a single variable that measures the loss as a percentage of the initial portfolio. This presents a modeling problem for any transaction that requires a cash flow analysis, as separate estimates of the default and LS measures are required. These estimates are needed in order to test the structure's ability to withstand the appropriate foreclosure period. The foreclosure period is the time between default and the sale of the property, and is therefore the time it takes until the crystallization of losses and recoveries. Hence, separate estimates of both these variables are required.

The WAFF and WALS estimates increase as the required rating level increases, because the higher the rating required on the bond, the higher the level of mortgage default and LS it should be capable of withstanding. Given the variability in mortgage lending and borrower behavior across countries, country-specific criteria are applied in WAFF and WALS assessments. As a consequence, the assumed percentage of defaults and subsequent losses can differ substantially across jurisdictions. It is worth mentioning that WAFF/WALS are measures that work only for large pools, as for smaller pools, idiosyncrasies may not vanish.

Cashflow Analysis

Many RMBS transactions are cash flow based, where the revenue stream generated by the mortgages is used to service rated note obligations. A key feature of the primary rating process for these types of transactions is to assess the adequacy of the cash flow from the mortgage loans to satisfy the terms of the rated debt. Economic stress scenarios are applied to the cash flows, and then the rated note interest payments and principal repayments are assessed for their adequacy in a given rating scenario. Standard and Poor's ensures under any given stress scenario, principal payments will be made in full and interest payments on a timely basis.

A typical RMBS cash flow transaction consists of a number of rated notes that differ in seniority with respect to interest and principal payments from the underlying mortgage portfolio, in so-called senior/subordinated structures. There is usually a first-loss fund provided by the originator of the assets underneath the rated notes, often called the reserve fund. This is used to cover both interest shortfalls and principal losses arising in the transaction. A liquidity facility might also be incorporated, which is used to bridge timing mismatches that can occur between the asset cash flows and the required liability payments. The transaction might also include specific structural features designed to minimize the issuer's exposure to external economic factors (e.g., interest rate hedges).

There are many variants to the generalized case described above. Structures tend to vary depending on the underlying collateral (e.g., prime RMBS transactions tend to differ structurally from nonconforming RMBS transactions), and across different countries (e.g., UK prime RMBS transactions differ structurally from Spanish or Italian prime RMBS transactions). This is generally for practical reasons. For example, UK prime mortgage originators tend to have very large portfolios, and have used "master trust" type structures primarily as a tool to reduce the costs of multiple securitizations over time. In contrast, Spanish and Italian transactions typically swap the entire asset cash flows to receive principal plus a fixed spread, primarily because the underlying mortgage loans tend to have quite variable interest rates, reset dates, and fixed periods.

Standard & Poor's stresses the transaction cash flows to test both the credit and liquidity support provided by the assets, subordinated tranches, cash reserve, and any external sources (such as a liquidity facility). Stresses to the cash flows are implemented at all relevant rating levels.

For example, a transaction that incorporates "AAA," "A," and "BBB" tranches of notes will be subjected to three separate sets of cash flow stresses. In the "AAA" stresses, all "AAA" notes must pay full and timely principal and interest, but this will not necessarily be the case for the "A" or "BBB" tranches, as they are subordinated in the priority of payments. In the "A" case, all "AAA" and "A" notes must receive full and timely principal and interest, but not necessarily so for the "BBB" tranche, as it is subordinated to both "AAA" and "A."

Defaults and Losses

Default, recovery, and loss rates are all estimates calculated in the initial credit analysis of the portfolio. The WAFF at each rating level specifies the total balance of the mortgage loans assumed to default over the life of the transaction. In general, defaults are assumed to occur over a period of time. In Standard and Poor's case, a three-year recession is assumed. Standard & Poor's will assess the impact of the timing of this recession on the ability to repay the liabilities, and chooses the recession start period based on this assessment. Although the recession normally starts in the first month of the transaction, the "AAA" recession is usually delayed by 12 months. The WAFF is applied to the principal balance outstanding at the start of the recession (e.g., in a "AAA" scenario, the WAFF is applied to the balance at the beginning of month 13). Defaults are assumed to occur periodically in amounts calculated as a percentage of the WAFF. The timing of defaults generally follows two paths, referred to here as "fast" and "slow" defaults.

Default Timings for Fast and Slow Default Curves

Recession month	Fast default (percentage of WAFF)	Slow default (percentage of WAFF)
1	30	0
6	30	5
12	20	5
18	10	10
24	5	20
30	5	30
36	0	30

TABLE 12.3
Foreclosure Periods in Different
European Jurisdictions

Country	Foreclosure period (time from default to recovery in months)
Belgium	18
France	36
Germany	24
Greece	72
Ireland	18
Italy	60 (on average, but can be vary depending on location of property)
The Netherlands	18
Portugal	36
Spain	30
Sweden	18
Switzerland	18
United Kingdom	18

Standard & Poor's assumes that the recovery of proceeds from the foreclosure and sale of repossessed properties occurs 18 months after a payment default in UK transactions (i.e., if a default occurs in month one, then recovery proceeds are received in month 19). The value of recoveries will be equal to the defaulted amount less the WALS. The time taken to repossess and sell a property can vary widely across the European countries, primarily because the legal procedures required before a lender can repossess and sell a property differ across jurisdictions (see Table 12.3). Standard & Poor's will therefore adjust the foreclosure period for each country to account for this.

Note that the WALS used in a cash flow model will always be based on principal loss, including costs. Standard & Poor's assumes no recovery of any interest accrued on the mortgage loans during the foreclosure period. In addition, after the WAFF is applied to the balance of the mortgages, the asset balance is likely to be lower than that on the liabilities (a notable exception is when a transaction relies on over-collateralization). The interest reduction created by the defaulted mortgages during the foreclosure period will need to be covered by other structural mechanisms in the transaction (e.g., excess spread).

Delinquencies

The liquidity stress that results from short-term delinquencies, i.e., those mortgages that cease to pay for a period of time but then recover and become current with respect to both interest and principal is also modeled. To simulate the effect of delinquencies, a proportion of interest receipts equal to one-third of the WAFF is assumed to be delayed. This applies for the first 18 months of the recession, and full recovery of delinquent interest is assumed to occur after a period of 18 months. Thus, if in month five of the recession the total collateral interest expected to be received is £1 million and the WAFF is 30 percent, £100,000 of interest (one-third of the WAFF) will be delayed until month 23.

Interest and Prepayment Rates

Three different interest rate scenarios—rising, falling, and stable—are modeled using both high and low prepayment assumptions. Interest rates always start from the rate experienced at the time of modeling. For example, in the rising interest rate scenario, LIBOR (or EURIBOR) rises by 2 percent per month to a ceiling of 18 percent (12 percent), where it remains for the rest of the transaction's life. Where there is a longer-than-average foreclosure period (e.g., Italy or Greece), the effect of high interest rates over the life of the transaction is unduly stressful, and the interest rate is allowed to ramp down after three to four years. For falling interest rates, interest rates fall by 2 percent per month to a floor of 2 percent, where they remain for the rest of the transaction's life. For stable interest rates, the interest rate is held at the current level throughout the life of the transaction. Note that in the "AAA" scenario the interest rate increase will not begin until month 13. Also note that interest rate scenarios will be revised if there is sufficient evidence to warrant it.

Transactions are stressed according to two prepayment assumptions: high and low. These rates of prepayment are differentiated by country of origin, as shown in Table 12.4. Prepayment rates are assumed to be

TABLE 12.4

Prepayment Assumptions for European RMBS

Prepayment level	United Kingdom (%)	European countries other than the United Kingdom (%)
High	30.0	24.0
Low	0.5	0.5

TABLE 1 2 . 5

Stress Scenarios for European RMBS

Scenario	Prepayment rate	Interest rate	Default timing
1	High	Rising	Fast
2	High	Rising	Slow
3	High	Stable	Fast
4	High	Stable	Slow
5	High	Falling	Fast
6	High	Falling	Slow
7	Low	Rising	Fast
8	Low	Rising	Slow
9	Low	Stable	Fast
10	Low	Stable	Slow
11	Low	Falling	Fast
12	Low	Falling	Slow

static throughout the life of the transaction and are applied monthly to the decreasing mortgage balance.

In combination, the default timings, interest rates, and prepayment rates described earlier give rise to 12 different scenarios, as summarized in Table 12.5.

Reinvestment Rates

Unless the transaction has the benefit of a guaranteed investment contract (GIC) with an appropriately rated entity, Standard & Poor's assumes that the transaction will suffer from a lower margin on reinvested redemption proceeds and other cash held in the vehicle than the margin being received on the underlying assets. If proceeds are received and reinvested through-out the quarter, and the long-term rating of the GIC provider is lower than that of the rated notes being subjected to the stress, then the reinvestment rate is assumed to be LIBOR less a rating-dependent margin, with a floor of 2 percent. The rating-dependent margin is a multiple of the contractual margin. The multiple used for this calculation varies from one at the "A" level to five at the "AAA" level.

Originator Insolvency

Mortgage payments from borrowers are typically paid by direct debit into a collection account, transferred to a transaction account in the name of the issuer, and finally credited to the GIC account. The degree to which insolvency of the originator will affect the cash flow from the assets therefore depends on the collection account characteristics. The amount at risk depends on the timing of payments from borrowers and the frequency with which these funds are transferred to the transaction account. If all borrowers pay on the same day of the month, then even with daily sweeping of the collection account, up to one month's cash flow from the assets is potentially at risk.

The collection account is often not in the name of the issuer, as most originators do not want to ask borrowers to change their direct debit instructions as a result of securitization. Under English law, if the issuer has been granted the benefit of a properly executed declaration of trust over the collection account, then insolvency of the originator should not result in a loss of funds, but should only involve a simple delay. This risk will need to be modeled appropriately for each transaction, but normally results in a delay of one month's cash flow for three months over an interest payment date. In other European countries, insolvency of the originator is more likely to result in a loss of funds, the amount of which depends on the frequency of the transfer of money from the collection to the transaction account. This amount is generally modeled as a loss of interest and principal in the first month of the recession.

Expenses

All the issuer's foreseeable expenses should be modeled (e.g., mortgage administration fees, trustee fees, standby servicer fees, cash/bond administration fees, etc.). These expenses should also include any tax liability the issuer may have. These fees are either a fixed amount per annum, or are sized as a percentage of the outstanding mortgage loans (or a combination of both). Standard & Poor's normally requires a schedule of these expenses to be provided. In addition to foreseeable expenses, the model should contain amounts sized for contingent expenses, such as the need for the trustee to register legal title to the mortgages in the event of insolvency of the originator. This amount can vary from £150,000 to £300,000, depending on the size of the transaction, and can be modeled either as a separate contingency reserve or as a haircut to the reserve fund.

Principal Deficiencies

In general, bonds are not written down, as losses are experienced on the assets. Instead, principal losses experienced on the mortgage pool are recorded in a PDL, which tracks the extent to which the principal balance of liabilities exceeds that of the assets. At each rating level, Standard &

Poor's requires that principal deficiencies do not exceed the existing subordination. For example, in a transaction with £100 million "AAA" senior notes, £9 million "A" junior notes, and a £1 million reserve fund, the principal deficiency at any point in time should not exceed £10 million in the "AAA" runs and £1 million in the "A" runs. If there is insufficient income to fund the principal deficiency, however, Standard & Poor's considers the risk to a transaction to be low if the principal deficiency is remedied within a short period of time using excess spread.

Basis Risk

Basis risk occurs when the value of the interest rate index used to determine the interest payments received from the assets differs from that of the liabilities. This can occur when assets and liabilities are linked to different indices (e.g., mortgages are linked to three-month Libor, liabilities to three-month Euribor), or both are linked to the same index, but it is set on a different date (mortgage interest rate set on 1st of the month and liability interest rate on the 20th). Here, there is the risk that the index for the assets falls below that of the liabilities, such that asset interest payments are insufficient to make the required payments to the liabilities. In situations where this risk is not hedged, Standard & Poor's typically assesses the historical performance of the indices in question, and calculates the difference over a certain time horizon (e.g., 20 days in the above example) that has been experienced historically. The average difference between the indices is then calculated, assuming that in periods where the index for the mortgages has been higher than that of the liabilities, the difference between the two is assumed to be zero. This average is then subtracted every month from the asset margin. In addition, two spikes in the liability interest rate index are also modeled. The height of each spike is determined as the maximum difference between the two indices and occurs at the beginning of the first two years of the transaction.

PART 3: A REVIEW OF THE GENERIC QUANTITATIVE TECHNIQUES USED BY MARKET PARTICIPANTS FOR ASSET BACK SECURITIES IN EUROPE

The ABS or structured finance constitutes one of the fastest growing and most innovative sectors of the European bond market. Banks, specialist finance companies, credit card companies, governments, mortgage

FIGURE 12.2

Annual Issuance of European Structured Products.
(Lehman Brothers, European Structured Finance Research)

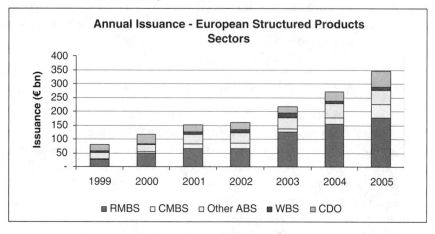

companies and a whole host of other entities use ABS to raise financing and as a tool for risk transfer. The ABS repay interest and principal from the stable and predictable cash flows associated with underlying assets, such as credit card receivables, residential mortgage loans and leases. Figure 12.2 shows the dramatic growth in issuance of European ABS over the past five years. Investors now have access to a regular and diversified supply of asset-backed bonds coming to market from different sectors and jurisdictions. The proportion of asset-backed debt in overall European bond issuance has also increased dramatically over the past few years (see Figure 12.3). While corporate issuance has remained relatively stable over the past years, the proportion of asset-backed issuance has grown significantly in 2005 to 64 percent of corporate issuance.

The U.S. structured finance market is significantly larger than the European market and has a much longer history. The U.S. market dates back to the 1970s when the U.S. government first stimulated the growth of mortgage-backed securities by encouraging government sponsored entities to fund prime mortgages through the capital markets. Annual issuance of U.S. mortgage and asset-backed bonds in 2005 stood at $3,300 billion (*source: Lehman Brothers, Securitized Products Research*).

The ABS can be broken down into two broad types of transaction: cash flow and synthetic securitizations. In the former, the interest and

FIGURE 12.3

Annual Issuance of European Structured Products and Corporates. *(Lehman Brothers, European Structured Finance Research)*

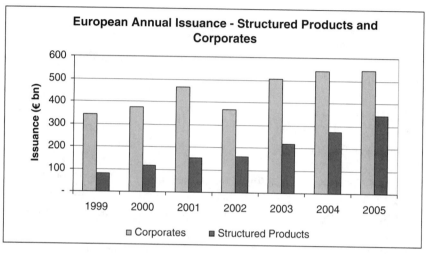

principal associated with the assets as well as their risks are passed on to investors. In the latter, only the risk is transferred.

The RMBSs dominate the structured finance landscape in almost all jurisdictions (see Figure 12.2). In view of the dominating influence of mortgage-type assets on the structured finance market and the growing interest in these sectors, the rest of this chapter will focus on quantitative analysis of mortgage specific deals. Moreover, since there is a lot more commonality across residential mortgage securitisations (RMBS) than commercial mortgage-backed securities (CMBS), which are more bespoke in nature, the focus of this chapter is slanted towards the former asset class, where these methods have wider applicability.

The structure of this part is as follows. In the section "ABS Credit and Prepayment Risks," the broad prepayment and credit risks of underlying assets backing structured finance bonds are described. The section "ABS Credit and Prepayment Modeling" provides a brief overview of statistical models used to project prepayment and default performance. The section "ABS Valuation" then discusses the impact of predicted mortgage cash flows, using the statistical models from previous section, on the liability (bond) side of European structured finance deals. The section "ABS Default Correlation and Tail Risk

Scenarios" presents a methodology for assessing tail credit risk in ABS and the valuation impact this has on ABS bonds. The last section is the "Conclusion."

ABS Credit and Prepayment Risks

The fundamental value of ABS is intimately related to the interest and principal cash-flows due on the bonds and the likelihood and timing of those being made in part or full. There are a number of key risks impacting the likelihood of these payments being made: defaults, delinquencies, losses, and prepayments. The former three of these constitute the credit risk in a collateral pool, whereas the last relates intimately to investment risk. The first three risks interact with each other to reduce the total amount of principal and interest available to bondholders. Note holders are also subject to prepayment risk, as they may receive their proceeds more quickly than originally anticipated, forcing them to re-invest the notional amount at sub-optimal levels. This is a problem when the security they are holding is priced at a premium to par, which has been a fairly common scenario in the European ABS market over the past few years. Conversely, for securities priced at a discount to par, early redemption is beneficial and allows bondholders to find a more efficient vehicle for investing their proceeds.

Figure 12.4 presents a fairly generic overview of the pricing of ABS. Statistical models provide projections of prepayments, and credit risk on the asset side of the transaction. These models often take loan level variables, such as a mortgage's LTV ratio, loan size or term and may combine this with macro-economic information, on, e.g., interest rates. These projections are then used to adjust contractual mortgage cash flows and these are passed through a bespoke cash flow model, which specifies the order and priority of all these payments. By applying a stochastic interest rate model over all months and running many interest rate scenarios, a value for the ABS may be generated as an expectation over the interest rates. Alternatively, a value may be desired that leads to an option-adjusted spread (OAS) to account for the stochastic nature of rates. This approach clearly has the advantage of factoring in the volatility of interest rates.

The current practice in the European ABS market falls some way short of the description above, as historical performance data is quite limited. Since the availability and quantity of such data is intimately linked with the

FIGURE 12.4

Quantitative Modeling of Securitizations.

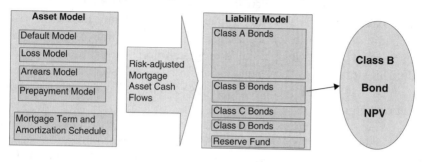

feasibility of creating prepayment and default models, the prevalence of such models in European ABS is quite rare. In practice, many market participants examine historic prepayment curves to infer future prepayment behavior.

The first manifestation of credit risk in any pool of securitized assets is nonpayment of interest and/or principal. In the case of mortgages, this is termed "arrears" or "delinquencies." After a mortgage loan misses a payment in a month from a clean state, it progressively moves through successive delinquency states: 30 days down, 60 days down, and so on. Some originators specify this as the number of days an asset is down in its payments and others as the number of months down. The asset servicer's role is to ensure timely payment from the assets in the pool and to take appropriate action in the event of nonpayment. Thus, many servicers have well-articulated policies for dealing with collections and, ultimately, litigation. Servicing policies typically involve a series of letters and calls encouraging payment and culminate with foreclosure procedures. Up until foreclosure takes place, the originator's main credit risk is delinquency risk associated with nonpayment of interest and principal, as well as the possibility of foreclosure taking place. Foreclosure normally follows a sustained period over which delinquencies are rising and is an absorbing irreversible state. Once the property is in the originator's possession, or REO (real estate owned) the borrower has no recourse to the asset securing the loan.

From the time the property is in possession of the originator, there is a time lag before a suitable sale price can be obtained and the loan balance and costs of foreclosure and delinquencies can be recovered. The foreclosure risk on a loan manifests itself in any losses that are incurred on the loan. Typically, the priority of payments to different claimants is specified according to a schedule. Fees (administrative and legal for foreclosure) are normally senior, followed by arrears interest payments. The most junior payment tends to be the principal balance outstanding on the loan. Depending on the priority of claims, mortgage originators can lose a substantial part of the principal balance outstanding at the time of property sale. This situation is exacerbated if the loan itself is a second or third lien, in which case all cash received is first used to pay off claims on the more senior mortgage loans.

When asset originators generate new loans for securitization, a key risk they bear is that obligors may decide to prepay the obligation earlier to take advantage of more attractive rates or other opportunities in the market. Since assets are priced at a premium to par by originators, in order to maintain the profitability of their business franchise, prepayments tend to limit the interest payments available to them and hence the value of the asset. Effectively, the originator of the asset must re-invest the loan amount lent to the obligor in the event of a prepayment at possibly less attractive rates.

ABS Credit and Prepayment Modeling

Normally, prepayments are expressed as a conditional prepayment rate (conditional on a loan's nonprepayment and nondefault up to a certain point in time) or CPR. This measure is calculated over a specific time horizon and is expressed as an annualized measure. If the asset balance in an asset-backed transaction is expressed at two successive points in time, t, and $t+d$ as $B(t)$ and $B(t+d)$, with scheduled principal payments on the assets of $S(t, t+d)$ over the period and unscheduled principal payments of $U(t, t+d)$, the prepayment rate may then be expressed as:

$$CPR = 1 - \left(1 - \frac{U(t, t+d)}{B(t) - S(t, t+d)}\right)^{(365/d)}$$

where d is the number of days in the time increment.

The default rate can be calculated in a similar way as the proportion of balance going into repossession over a given time period. The constant default rate (CDR) is an annualized default rate. Denoting $DF(t, t+d)$ as the actual total balance of loans in the asset pool going into foreclosure over the time period, we have:

$$\text{CDR} = 1 - \left(1 - \frac{\text{DF}(t, t+d)}{B(t)}\right)^{(365/d)}.$$

Since both the CDR and CPR are conditional rates (on survival up to a certain point in an asset's life), they can be regarded as hazard rates and, thus, be applied to all the contractual cash flows from an asset portfolio.

The third component in determining performance projections and, hence, cash flows in asset pools, is the recovery rate, expressed as a percentage of principal balance outstanding that has gone into default/repossession. Denoting the principal LS as LS(t), one can compute all the expected cash flows, and consequently put them through a typical securitization structure to analyse different bonds' expected performance and valuation.

Figure 12.5 provides a depiction of the three main outcomes that one may observe for a live mortgage loan over the course of a month: a default, prepayment, or mortgage continuation. The likelihood of defaults and prepayments are given by $\lambda_D(t)$ and $\lambda_P(t)$, respectively. The probability of mortgage continuation sums up with these to 100 percent, or all the possible states. These states repeat themselves at each month over the course of the life of live mortgages in a pool. If the beginning loan balance is denoted $B(t)$, there are cash flows from four main sources: principal (scheduled principal payments), interest, recoveries, and prepayments (unscheduled principal payments). The total cash flows for repayment loans based on the beginning month balance at time t is then, TCF(t) with monthly rate, $m(t)$:

FIGURE 12.5

Prepayment and Default Hazards Over a Monthly Time Horizon.

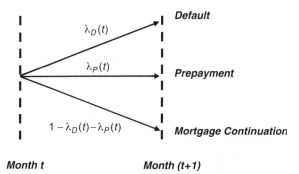

$$TCF(t) = ICF(t) + PCF(t) + RCF(t) + PP(t)$$

where

$$ICF(t) = \left(1 - \lambda_D(t)\right) B(t)\, m(t),$$

$$PCF(t) = \left(1 - \lambda_D(t) - \lambda_P(t)\right) \left(\frac{B(t)m(t)}{1 - \left(\dfrac{1}{1+m(t)}\right)^{T-t}} - B(t)m(t) \right),$$

$$RCF(t) = \lambda_D(t-\Delta)(1-LS(t-\Delta))B(t-\Delta),$$

$$PP(t) = \lambda_P(t)B(t),$$

where Δ is the lag (in number of months) between the time properties are repossessed and sold. $ICF(t)$ is the interest cash flow, $PCF(t)$ is the scheduled principal cash flows, $RCF(t)$ is the recovery cash flow associated with defaulted mortgages, and $PP(t)$ is the unscheduled principal cash flow from full prepayments. The hazard rates are applied to all of the cash flows in the equations above in a multiplicative way. Thus, the expected unscheduled principal payment in month, t, is equal to the beginning monthly mortgage balance, $B(t)$, multiplied by the hazard of prepayments taking place in that month. To determine the cash flows in the next month $(t+1)$, one must determine the next month's *expected* beginning asset balance as the previous month's expected balance minus the expected prepayments in the period, principal cash flow, and default balance:

$$E[B(t+1)] = B(t) - PP(t) - PCF(t) - \lambda_D(t)B(t)$$

In this successive way, future expected cash flows can be generated for all future months. The cash flows arising from the asset pool are then dependent on the deterministic and fixed nature of contractual mortgage loan characteristics (e.g., fixed rate period, interest-only or repayment, and prepayment penalties and rates), as well as the stochastic nature of actual prepayments, defaults and losses, denoted by the hazards $\lambda_D(t)$ and $\lambda_P(t)$ and $LS(t)$. These stochastic rates lend themselves well to econometric modeling.

Given a large enough performance data set, prepayments can be modeled as the conditional hazard of prepayment given survival at a particular month in time following origination. In markets where full prepayments far outweigh partial prepayments (e.g., the UK nonconforming mortgage market), this can be modeled as a binary event.

Suppose that the probability of full prepayment for loan $i \in \{1, \ldots, N\}$, conditional on survival up till month, $t - 1$, is denoted by $\lambda_{Pi}(t)$, in month t after completion, and that this is modeled using the logistic function:

$$\lambda_{Pi}(t) = \frac{1}{1 + \exp\left[-\left(\beta_0 + \sum_{j=1}^{J} \beta_j x_{ji}\right)\right]}$$

The likelihood function for a single loan can be computed as:

$$L_i(\beta) = \begin{cases} \prod_{t=1}^{t=T}(1 - \lambda_{Pi}(t)), \text{ no prepayment.} \\ \lambda_{Pi}(V)\prod_{t=1}^{V-1}\left(1 - \lambda_{Pi}(t)\right), \text{ prepayment in month } V. \end{cases}$$

where T is the last possible monthly observation. It is fairly straightforward to extend this to all loans in a sample to determine the log-likelihood function of the data set. Such a model can easily be estimated using a statistical package such as SAS or S-Plus. The academic literature on such econometric models is vast, largely in the context of U.S. mortgages [see, e.g., Deng et al. (2000) among others as well as references therein]. Less effort has been devoted to econometric modeling of defaults and prepayments of European mortgages. The most statistically significant variables in such models vary by European ABS market.

The covariates themselves fall into a number of broad categories:

♦ *Seasoning variables*:   In most prepayment models, mortgagors are less inclined to prepay in the first few months than later in the life of the mortgage loan. There may be other dependencies over time and these may relate to structural features of the loan.

♦ *Obligor-specific*:   This includes whether the borrower is single/married/widowed as well as the mortgagor's past payment behavior. Bespoke credit scores may also play an important role in predicting prepayments.

♦ *Loan-specific*:   This can include the LTV ratio, which effectively determines the loan's leverage, as well as the term and the presence of any prepayment penalties. These latter features are often found to play a profound role in determining prepayments because of the economic incentives that may exist. The loan purpose may often play a significant role in predicting prepayments, whether the loan is used to finance an investment property or for a mortgagor to be the owner-occupier. The rate on the loan also plays an important role in determining rate incentives for prepaying.

♦ *Macroeconomic variables*:   This includes house prices, unemployment rates, inflation rates, and, crucially, market interest rates. The dependence on these rates varies significantly by jurisdiction. For fixed rate mortgages, the rate incentive is important in predicting prepayment behavior. If rates rally following origination of a fixed rate mortgage loan, borrowers have a higher propensity to prepay, all things equal. Conversely, in a sell-off, mortgagors are less incentivized to re-finance their mortgage.

The first three categories are usually fixed for the life of the mortgage loan, or vary in some deterministic way (e.g., loan term or remaining balance). The last category of variables, however, evolve in a stochastic manner and lend themselves well to this type of modeling. Alternatively, by making specific assumptions on each of these variables, the resultant cash expected flows can be computed under that particular scenario. There is a vast literature on pricing LIBOR market models (see, e.g., Brace et al., 1997) and by running many simulations with such an interest rate model, prepayments on a pool of mortgages can be generated for many possible states of the world.

The covariates themselves may assume quite complex functional forms, such as polynomial functions or nonparametric kernel functions. Another popular approach is the use of cubic splines, which produce a smooth dependence of prepayments on the underlying covariate, while capturing the nuances of this dependence. As in all other univariate modeling, the danger of over-fitting is always a concern and these more complex functional forms must be tempered with an awareness of this potential problem.

As in the case of prepayments, one can create loan level models of defaults, provided there is sufficient performance data, including a sufficient number of defaults. If there are insufficient defaults in a mortgage data set, one may have to resort to using a more conservative default definition and adjust the model for loss severities to account for the higher default rate. One possibility, e.g., is to model the probability of a loan being 90 or 180 days or more down at a particular month after origination. This definition of default fits well with the regulatory framework in most countries, as the Basel II Accord specifies this default definition. The problem with this definition, however, is that 90 or 180 days past due may not technically or historically be a fully absorbing irreversible state. Thus, the modeling of loss severities will need to take this into account by being conditioned on loans being 90 days down. This will introduce a large cohort of cured mortgage loans, which have zero loss. Analysis of mortgage transition matrices is indispensable in informing such modeling decisions. Low transition probabilities from high delinquency states to lower delinquency states suggest that using a more conservative default definition is less likely to be problematic. In other words, credit curing is not very common and so 90 days past due is generally a robust measure of default.

As in the case of prepayment modeling, statistical models of default may depend on macroeconomic variables, such as house prices and rates. By simulating these variables through separate stochastic models, credit risk volatility can be introduced and evaluated in the context of portfolios of mortgage loans.

The above paragraphs have discussed modeling mortgage prepayments and defaults as competing hazards. In other words, there are only two events that can lead to mortgage termination with the former being the decision of the borrower, and the latter the decision of the originator. Another broad modeling approach for mortgage is to model the full transition behavior of mortgages through finer arrears states. This involves modeling the probabilities of transitions one typically sees in a monthly mortgage transition matrix. The disadvantage with this approach, however, is that estimation can be tricky if the performance data is limited and the implementation is more cumbersome. With 300 months for a 25-year mortgage loan one would have to calculate 300 transitions per mortgage loan to generate cash flows, as described earlier. Fortunately, mortgage arrears transition matrices are more sparse than other matrices, such as credit rating transition matrices, as barring prepayments and defaults; the maximum downward migration in any monthly period can only be 30 days of more arrears.

Figure 12.6 shows a typical mortgage transition matrix. In this matrix, each row corresponds to the initial state of a mortgage loan. These states include: {clean, 30 days past due, 60 days past due, 90 days past due, . . . , default, prepayment}. The columns correspond to the final mortgage state

FIGURE 12.6

Mortgage Monthly Arrears Transition Matrix.

$$
\begin{bmatrix}
p_{00} & p_{01} & \cdot\cdot & \cdot\cdot & \cdot\cdot & \cdot\cdot & \cdot\cdot & \cdot\cdot & \lambda_{D0} & \lambda_{P0} \\
p_{10} & p_{11} & p_{12} & \cdot\cdot & \cdot\cdot & \cdot\cdot & \cdot\cdot & \cdot\cdot & \lambda_{D1} & \lambda_{P1} \\
p_{20} & p_{21} & p_{22} & p_{23} & \cdot\cdot & \cdot\cdot & \cdot\cdot & \cdot\cdot & \lambda_{D2} & \lambda_{P2} \\
p_{30} & p_{31} & p_{32} & p_{33} & p_{34} & \cdot\cdot & \cdot\cdot & \cdot\cdot & \lambda_{D3} & \lambda_{P3} \\
p_{40} & p_{41} & p_{42} & p_{43} & p_{44} & p_{45} & \cdot\cdot & \cdot\cdot & \lambda_{D4} & \lambda_{P4} \\
p_{50} & p_{51} & p_{52} & p_{53} & p_{54} & p_{55} & p_{56} & \cdot\cdot & \lambda_{D5} & \lambda_{P5} \\
p_{60} & p_{61} & p_{62} & p_{63} & p_{64} & p_{65} & p_{66} & p_{67} & \lambda_{D6} & \lambda_{P6} \\
p_{70} & p_{71} & p_{72} & p_{73} & p_{74} & p_{75} & p_{76} & p_{77} & \lambda_{D7} & \lambda_{P7} \\
\cdot\cdot & \cdot\cdot & \cdot\cdot & \cdot\cdot & \cdot\cdot & \cdot\cdot & \cdot\cdot & \cdot\cdot & 1 & \cdot\cdot \\
\cdot\cdot & \cdot\cdot & \cdot\cdot & \cdot\cdot & \cdot\cdot & \cdot\cdot & \cdot\cdot & \cdot\cdot & \cdot\cdot & 1
\end{bmatrix}
$$

over the course of a month. The last two columns and rows correspond, respectively, to defaults and prepayments. Since prepayments and defaults are fully absorbing states, the rows corresponding to these have 100 percent probability of remaining in those states.

The leading diagonal, p_{ii}, is the probability of a mortgage loan starting the month off in a state and remaining in that state. The upper diagonal corresponds to the probability of migrating to a worse credit state over the course of a month. Thus, p_{23} corresponds to the probability that a mortgage loan goes from being 60 days down to 90 days down over a monthly period. The final two columns are the monthly hazards of the default and prepayment, respectively, starting the month at each of the initial states.

ABS Valuation

Since every deal is uniquely structured based on the underlying asset pool, there is no commonality across structures. However, certain features are similar across many deals. In view of the bespoke nature of the structures, the next part of this chapter is dedicated to analyzing a particular Dutch residential mortgage-backed transaction. This analysis will highlight some of the most common structural features, as well as their impact on valuation. It should be stressed that the liability side of ABS transactions are for the most part deterministic and pre-determined at the time of structuring. Thus, the main source of uncertainty in terms of the performance of bonds has to do with the asset risks that were discussed earlier.

The BS structures usually have a combination of the following sources of credit enhancement:

+ Senior/subordinate bonds: credit enhancement is provided by more junior tranches in the transaction by structurally forcing them to take earlier losses from the asset pool.
+ Over-collateralization: the notional amount of assets may be larger than the notional of bonds issued. In stressed loss scenarios, there are more assets which can be drawn upon to repay interest and principal.
+ Monoline wraps: large monoline insurers may guarantee the interest and principal payments of senior tranches in transactions, thereby giving extra strength to the deal.
+ Excess spread: this is the remaining interest after all tranches have been paid off and losses incurred and provides the first line of defense in most transactions.
+ Reserve funds: these typically correspond to a percentage of the total deal size of the transaction. They may be funded in full at origination, or be built-up through excess spread over the life of the transaction. In many cases, this fund amortizes over time.

Many European residential mortgage securitizations have a sequential principal structure which reverts to a pro-rata structure. In this arrangement, all principal from the asset side is first used to pay down the principal on the most senior tranche. When a certain pro-rata trigger is met (e.g., the remaining bond balance on the most senior note reaches a fraction of the original amount), the entire deal reverts to a pro-rata pay down of the notes. Principal is paid down on a pro-rata basis across all notes. Interest is first used to pay the AAA class and then the AA class, and so on. If there is a shortfall in any note, the shortfall is registered in that class's PDL. This then becomes senior in the waterfall and is paid off by successive interest payments.

The Bloomberg screen shot (*source: Bloomberg L. P.*) in Figure 12.7 sets out the transaction structure of the Dutch MBS X transaction (deal priced on March 27, 2003), which has quite a few features discussed earlier. The deal included five tranches: a AAA bond (the A class), a longer-life AA bond (the B class), a A bond (the C class), a BBB bond (the D class), and, finally, a BB bond (the E class). The transaction first pays down principal on the A class up to a pro-rata trigger.

FIGURE 12.7

Bloomberg Deal Summary of Dutch X Transaction. *(Bloomberg L. P.)*

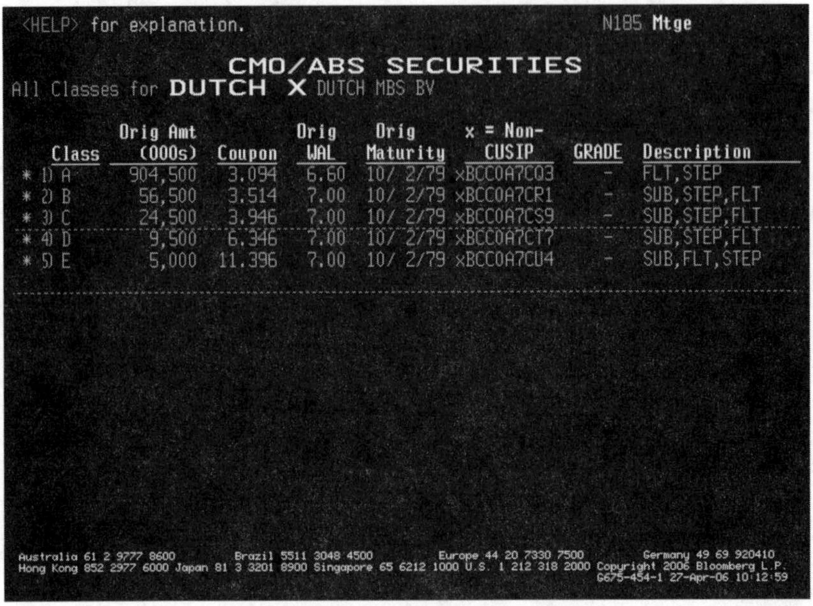
<HELP> for explanation. N185 Mtge

CMO/ABS SECURITIES

All Classes for DUTCH X DUTCH MBS BV

Class	Orig Amt (000s)	Coupon	Orig WAL	Orig Maturity	x = Non-CUSIP	GRADE	Description
* 1) A	904,500	3.094	6.60	10/ 2/79	xBCC0A7C03	-	FLT,STEP
* 2) B	56,500	3.514	7.00	10/ 2/79	xBCC0A7CR1	-	SUB,STEP,FLT
* 3) C	24,500	3.946	7.00	10/ 2/79	xBCC0A7CS9	-	SUB,STEP,FLT
* 4) D	9,500	6.346	7.00	10/ 2/79	xBCC0A7CT7	-	SUB,STEP,FLT
* 5) E	5,000	11.396	7.00	10/ 2/79	xBCC0A7CU4	-	SUB,FLT,STEP

Australia 61 2 9777 8600 Brazil 5511 3048 4500 Europe 44 20 7330 7500 Germany 49 69 920410
Hong Kong 852 2977 6000 Japan 81 3 3201 8900 Singapore 65 6212 1000 U.S. 1 212 318 2000 Copyright 2006 Bloomberg L.P.
G675-454-1 27-Apr-06 10:12:59

An interesting way of analyzing the tranches in this deal is by pricing the bonds at different conditional default rates (CDRs) with prevailing market discount margins. Figure 12.8 shows a table of each bond priced at a CPR of 15 percent, a recovery rate of 85 percent, and a recovery lag of 12 months, with variable default rates. Starting with a CDR of 75 bps, the bonds increase in value going down the capital structure. Since subordinate bonds have larger coupons and the scenario in the first column is quite mild, the most subordinate bonds receive almost all of their principal and interest. As the default scenarios become more adverse, each of the bonds are eventually affected, with the exception of the AAA bond, which is still quite resilient even in the 25 percent CDR scenario. Going down the capital structure, the bonds break at lower CDRs, as one would expect given the decreasing rating levels. Even at very low default levels of 0.75 percent CDR, the E floater bond breaks.

The default rate also has a second-order impact on the weighted average life (WAL) of the bonds. As defaults rise, a larger amount of the mortgage balance amortizes away through the effect of prepayments and

FIGURE 12.8

Dutch X Transaction Bond Pricing at 15 Percent CPR and with Recoveries of 85 Percent and a 12-Month Lag between Default and Property Sale. *(Lehman Brothers, European Structured Finance Research)*

Bonds	Rating (Fitch/Moody's)	Pricing Spread (bps)	CDR 0.75%	CDR 2.5%	CDR 5%	CDR 10%	CDR 25%
A floater (3m€ + 28 bps)	AAA/Aaa	11.5	100.5	100.5	100.5	100.4	97.3
B floater (3m€ + 70 bps)	A/A2	26	101.6	101.6	101.6	59.0	12.7
C floater (3m€ + 130 bps)	BBB/Baa2	52	102.8	102.8	38.0	15.4	8.6
D floater (3m€ + 370 bps)	BB/Ba2	325	101.5	41.6	22.8	14.4	8.4
E floater (3m€ + 875 bps)	B/B1	750	91.6	36.8	26.3	14.7	11.7

defaults. Thus, as default rates increase, the weighted-average life of the bonds decreases.

A shortcoming of this approach to valuation is that each scenario is merely a point projection of performance. In reality, there is scope for substantial volatility in realized default rates, losses, delinquencies, and prepayments.

ABS Default Correlation and Tail Risk Scenarios

An important feature of the rating process is to set rating levels based on highly stressed scenarios. The AAA rating on ABS bonds is an indication of the bond's resilience to the most extreme scenarios. Thus, the AAA rating corresponds implicitly to the ability of the bond to withstand losses up to a certain confidence level among all possible states of the world. There may be some states of the world (with extremely low probability) where even a AAA bond could take a loss. The field of credit portfolio modeling and default correlations allows such extreme tail risks to be quantified. It is only natural that prices of cash ABS bonds should reflect to some degree the tail risk inherent in ABS structures.

A useful starting point for portfolio credit risk in ABS is the popular 1-factor Gaussian copula model by Vasicek (1997). This model provides a good description of portfolio credit risk when the underlying pool of assets is very large with relatively small loan sizes. The Vasicek model corresponds to the limit where the pool of assets becomes infinite in number and the asset size becomes infinitesimally small. The probability density function of the Vasicek formula is as follows:

$$f(x; p, \rho) = \sqrt{\frac{1-\rho}{\rho}}$$
$$\times \exp\left[-\frac{(1-2\rho)N^{-1}(x)^2 + N^{-1}(p)^2 - 2\sqrt{1-\rho}N^{-1}(x)N^{-1}(p)}{2\rho}\right],$$

where x is the actual proportion of losses, p is the unconditional default rate, and ρ is the asset correlation. This distribution is skewed and fat-tailed, as can be seen in Figure 12.9, for a typical parameterization with mean default rate of 2 percent (i.e., $p = 2$ percent) and an asset correlation of 15 percent (i.e., $\rho = 15$ percent). The loss profile of a thin tranche with enhancement levels of 5 percent and 7 percent is also included for reference.

The asset correlation represents the degree to which individual returns are correlated with a single systematic factor. The parameter, p,

FIGURE 12.9

Vasicek Distribution and Loss Profile for a Tranche, with a Default Rate of 2 Percent and an Asset Correlation of 15 Percent.

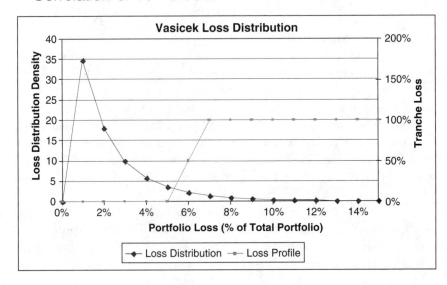

effectively sets the mean for the distribution of defaults, whereas the asset correlation sets the amount of volatility in the distribution.

The density distribution above leads to a closed-form solution for the cumulative distribution function:

$$F(x; p, \rho) = N\left(\frac{\sqrt{1-\rho}N^{-1}(x) - N^{-1}(p)}{\sqrt{\rho}} \right)$$

And, this may be inverted to give actual losses for different quantile levels:

$$x = N\left(\frac{N^{-1}(p) + \sqrt{\rho}N^{-1}(\alpha)}{\sqrt{1-\rho}} \right)$$

where x is the proportion of portfolio losses and α is the quantile level. If, e.g., α is set to 99.9 percent, then the portfolio losses are equal to the amount in this formula, with the twin parameters set to typical levels.

The Vasicek model can be used in the context of European mortgage securitizations to identify the likelihood of certain stressed scenarios. By setting the mean of the distribution of the Vasicek distribution to the expected loss from an econometric model and by making some assumptions about asset correlations, one can obtain stressed default rates based on an objective opinion about the state of the world.

One way of determining such stressed scenarios for defaults and losses is as follows. Suppose one is interested in looking at the 90 percent quantile level of worst possible credit risk scenarios. One can then take the mean projected CDR and LS from an econometric model for these two risks and take their product. This yields a projected curve of annualized expected losses (even though this does not take into account the effect of lags between default and property sale, where the loss is finally booked in the transaction):

$$EL(t) = CDR(t) \times LS(t)$$

One can then compute the upper quantile annualized loss at each point in time using the Vasicek formula above. This then leads to the following formula for the adjusted expected loss:

$$EL_2(t) = N\left(\frac{N^{-1}(EL(t)) + \sqrt{\rho}N^{-1}(\alpha)}{\sqrt{1-\rho}} \right)$$

FIGURE 12.10

Vasicek Distribution Implied CDRs.

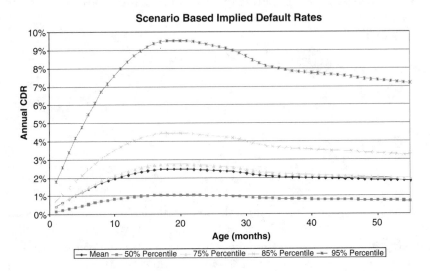

Keeping the LS at the same original level, the adjusted CDR is then:

$$CDR_2(t) = \frac{1}{LS(t)} N\left(\frac{N^{-1}(EL(t)) + \sqrt{\rho}N^{-1}(\alpha)}{\sqrt{1-\rho}} \right)$$

Figure 12.10 illustrates an example of this approach using a typical projected CDR curve for a pool of mortgage loans. Using this methodology, one can determine what the valuation is in the worst 75 percent of states and repeat the valuation of the previous section.

A natural question which arises, however, when using the Vasicek formula is how one can best estimate the asset correlation. Fortunately, the analytical form of the Vasicek distribution function lends itself well to manipulation through maximum likelihood methods. Given a series of realized actual losses, x_i, where $i \in \{1, \ldots, M\}$, one can construct the log-likelihood of these observations being drawn from the Vasicek distribution:

$$L(\theta) = \log\left(\prod_{i=1}^{M} f(x_i, p, \rho) \right)$$

It can be shown that this log-likelihood function leads to the following maximum likelihood estimators for the mean default rate, $\hat{p}$, and asset correlation, $\hat{\rho}$, (see Khadem and Hofstetter, 2006 for details):

$$\hat{\rho} = \frac{(1/M)\sum_{i=1}^{M}N^{-1}(x_i)^2 - \left((1/M)\sum_{i=1}^{M}N^{-1}(x_i)\right)^2}{(1/M)\sum_{i=1}^{M}N^{-1}(x_i)^2 - \left((1/M)\sum_{i=1}^{M}N^{-1}(x_i)\right)^2 + 1},$$

$$\hat{p} = N\left(\frac{\sqrt{1-\hat{\rho}}}{M}\sum_{i=1}^{M}N^{-1}(x_i)\right).$$

An attractive feature of these estimators is the fact that they are available in closed-form and rely only on actual default data. Other approaches of estimating asset correlations based on actual loss data include Gordy and Heitfield (2000). The estimation involves estimating the asset correlation in the Vasicek model before the distribution is taken to the asymptotic limit. This estimation necessitates maximizing the likelihood of a fairly complex function.

The first expression above allows the specification of bespoke asset correlations based on historical performance, and this can easily be manipulated to obtain default correlations:

$$\hat{\rho}_D = \frac{N_2\left(N^{-1}(\hat{p}), N^{-1}(\hat{p}), \hat{\rho}\right) - \hat{p}^2}{\hat{p}(1-\hat{p})},$$

where the estimators are as included in the previous formulae.

Given a sufficient amount of data from individual quarterly asset-backed investor reports or other loan data, one may be able to derive estimates of the asset correlation from the formula above. This, then, gives an indication of the tail risk in that particular asset class.

Conclusion

This brief part has presented a broad approach used for modeling cash ABS transactions. Some attention has been devoted to considering credit volatility and default correlations in ABS. Credit portfolio modeling-techniques are relatively less developed in ABS than in structured credit, and this represents an interesting area of future research in ABS modeling.

REFERENCES

Brace, A., D. Gaterek, and M. Musiela (1997), "The market model of interest rate dynamics," *Mathematical Finance*.

Deng, Y., J. M. Quigley, and R. Van Order (2000), "Mortgage terminations, heterogeneity and the exercise of mortgage options," *Econometrica*.

Dietsch, M., and J. Petey (2002), "The credit risk in SME loans portfolios: modelling issues, pricing and capital requirements," *Journal of Banking and Finance*.

Gordy, M., and E. Heitfield (2000), "Estimating factor loadings when ratings performance data are scarce," working paper, Federal Reserve Board.

Khadem, V., and E. Hofstetter (2006), "A credit risk methodology for retail and SME portfolios," working paper.

Vasicek, O. A. (1997), "Loan loss distribution," working paper, KMV.

Covered Bonds*

Arnaud de Servigny and Aymeric Chauve

INTRODUCTION

The concept of covered bonds has existed for about 200 years. This instrument was initiated by Frederick the Great of Prussia (Germany), with the creation of "Pfandbriefe." The underlying idea was to help project financing. Typically, a bank issuing pfandbriefe bonds would be able to collateralize the bonds with some underlying assets already on its balance sheet.

In simple terms, a covered bond is a financial product whose creditors are benefiting from a pledge. This pledge usually corresponds to mortgage or public sector loans that are on the balance sheet of the issuing bank.

This product has remained a pure German instrument until recently, with mostly German investors purchasing local pfandbriefe issuance. Due to the globalization of the Western European economies as well as to the rising appetite of non-German investors for this kind of very secured product, other countries have enacted laws to replicate the concept, among which the French with "Obligations Foncières" or the Spanish with "Cédulas." New jurisdictions continue to expand the universe of covered bonds, with legal and regulatory frameworks being amended to facilitate this development.

*We would like to thank Karlo Fuchs and Jean-Baptiste Michau for their support and contribution.

Apart from Germany, the fastest growing markets at the moment are the United Kingdom, with its *Structured* covered bonds, the Netherlands and, more recently, Italy. In the Nordic countries, regulation has even widened the scope of the product. Covered Bonds may, for instance, be collateralized by shipping loans.

PRODUCT CONSIDERATIONS

Structural Aspects

Let us clarify first the distinction between *Pfandbriefe-like* Covered Bonds and *Structured* Covered Bonds:

- *Pfandbriefe-like* Covered Bonds are bonds backed by mortgage or public sector assets in a well-defined regulatory environment. Practically, the local Financial Code/Act clearly sets the rules applicable to the product.
- *Structured* Covered Bonds are issued in jurisdictions where there is no specifically adjusted regulatory framework. The robustness underlying this more recent type of product, such as the bonds issued in the United Kingdom, relies on a pure contractual basis and on legal opinions related to the case of insolvency of the issuing bank.

In both cases, the principle is that, upon insolvency of the issuing bank, a trustee (or administrator) would be appointed to service the registered cover pool* and that such a pool would be segregated from the other assets on the balance sheet of the bankrupt bank. One key point to note here is that all covered bonds issued by a bank benefit from the same registered cover pool and are ranked *pari passu*.

Structured Covered Bonds can typically be compared to on-balance sheet replenishing residential mortgage backed securities (RMBS) and reference a portfolio of mortgage assets.

Pfandbriefe-like covered bonds can be split into two main segments: "mortgage-backed" Covered Bonds, which represent about 1/3 of the global market, and "public-sector backed" Covered Bonds, which represent the remaining and historically correspond to a large proportion of the German market (Offentliche Pfandbriefe). However, some jurisdictions

---

*The portfolio of mortgage and/or public loans that are granted as collateral to the covered bonds holders.

like France allow for a mix of these two types of assets, such as in the case of "Compagnie de Financement Foncier."

The structure and the strength of covered bonds depend on the jurisdiction of the product. Its guarantee of robustness is usually translated as the minimum level of overcollateralization required by a given jurisdiction. In order to support their "AAA" rating, rating agencies also require that the Covered Bond issuer commits to a minimal level of overcollateralization and to a reasonable proportion of liquid assets in the cover pool to face stressful market situations.

Basel II Regulatory Treatment

As this asset class is a purely European one, its capital treatment is dealt with at the European level in the capital requirement directive (CRD). Terms employed by the ECB (European Central Bank) 2005 paper (p. 42).

"The covered bonds that meet the CRD requirement are treated as exposures to banks. The risk weighting is based on the credit standing of the issuing bank, while at the same time recognizing the effects of the collateral. The collateral is recognized in the form of reduced risk weights under the standardized approach or in the form of reduced loss given defaults (LGDs) under the IRB approaches.

Under the standardized approach, covered bonds receive reduced risk weights based on the weights of senior exposures to the issuer in the manner described in Table 13.0."

TABLE 13.0

Risk weight of senior exposure to issuer	20	50	100	150
Covered bond risk weight	10	20	50	100

"As regards treatment under the IRB approaches, the EU rules are fully consistent with Basel II, since a bank's internal rating system needs to comprise both a borrower and a facility dimension. Based on the borrower dimension, probability of defaults (PDs) are assigned to exposures, while the facility dimension underlies the assignment of LGDs. The collateral to which the bondholders have a preferential claim affects the facility dimension. While Basel II does not encompass any specific rules for covered bonds, the collateral of the bond would lead to a reduced LGD if the bank was able to get supervisory approval for an estimate of this collateral effect under the advanced IRB. Under the foundation IRB, such

TABLE 13.1

European Covered Bond Issuance in 2005

Country	Type*	Issuance (2005 approx.) (€billion)
Germany	R	138
Spain	R	35
France	R	17
United Kingdom	NR	7
Luxembourg	R	6
Italy	R	4
Switzerland	R	2
Netherlands	R	2
Other (Austria, Belgium, Czech Rep., Hungary, Ireland, Portugal)	R/NR	1
Total		212

*R = Regulated (Pfandbriefe-like), NR = Nonregulated (Structured)
Source: European Securitization Forum, Rating Agencies

covered bonds may receive a reduced supervisory LGD of 12.5 percent. The advanced IRB would require the investing bank to use its own LGD estimates for covered bonds. Under both the foundation and advanced IRB, the risk weights continue to depend also on the PD of the issuer."

Market Considerations

As of today, there are about €2 trillions covered bonds outstanding (including *Structured* covered bonds), with a yearly issuance of about €200 billions (see Table 13.1). This makes it the second largest and homogeneous bond market after sovereigns. These ever-growing volumes demonstrate investors' appetite for this high credit quality product.

The market should continue to grow in the foreseeable future, as more and more mortgage or public sector lenders are looking for cheap financing, in a competitive environment where spreads on the loans they grant tend to shrink and with an increasing number of investors looking for highly secured instruments with low capital charge requirement. The growth of the market is fuelled, in addition, by the use of these assets, paying a coupon of roughly flat Euribor, as a funding collateral in structured finance transactions such as CDOs.

Almost all European countries have now set up a covered bond regulation, with the noticeable exception of the United Kingdom. The latest country to have adopted such a regulatory framework is Italy with state-owned Cassa di Depositi e Prestiti having set up a €20 billion program in March 2005.

Market Momentum

The current market trend is around *Jumbo* issuances, i.e., issuances with a size typically exceeding €1 billion, and where the issuing bank and the arranger commit to market making in order to ensure liquidity. This corresponds to a change as until a recent past most of the issuances where small private deals.

Spanish issuers are the most active in this area of public, high-volume, issues tapping a wide range of investors. According to the European securitization forum, Spain has been overwhelming Germany recently, with about €55 billion new *Jumbo* issuances, compared to a mere €50 billion for Germany.

The size and liquidity of the covered bond market is now such that some investment banks like J.P. Morgan-Chase have started offering Pfandriefe CDSs.

As already mentioned, the CDO market directly benefits from the growth of the covered bond market, with the increasing use of the product as a funding collateral to guaranty the payment of contingent claims arising from defaults in the underlying CDO portfolio.

MODELING RISK IN COVERED BONDS*

In this section, we review the quantitative methodology that underpins the rating process at Standard & Poor's (S&P).

As already mentioned, a covered bond is a debt instrument typically issued by a bank and overcollateralized by sound assets such as residential mortgage loans or loans to the public sector. If the issuing bank is publicly committed to maintaining the overcollateralization levels commensurate with target rating specific stress scenarios, S&P is usually able to assign a rating to the transaction. This rating can be significantly higher than, and delinked from the counterparty issuer credit rating, further enhancing the appeal of the market.[†]

---

*This part is derived from an S&P technical document produced by the authors.
†For more information see "Expanding European covered bond universe Puts Spotlight on key analytics," July 16, 2004, available on S&P website.

S&P has used proprietary models to analyze the quality of pools of assets and the adequacy of cash flow structures for several years. The improved transparency, which the products such as CDO Evaluator and CDS Accelerator have provided to participants in the CDO market, has led S&P to offer the issuer a product Covered Bond Monitor (CBM)—a core analytical tool used in the analysis of covered bonds.

Currently, CBM is used to perform the quantitative analysis of covered bond programs in Germany, Denmark, France, Ireland, and Luxembourg. It will also be used for upcoming Scandinavian covered bonds.

The quantitative piece of the analysis of a covered bond can be broadly split into two parts:

+ A credit quality analysis performed by S&P analysts, which results in the determination of the default and recovery assumptions applicable to the pool of the assets of the covered bond transaction.

+ An analysis of the strength of the structure under these default and recovery assumptions as well as under interest and foreign exchange rate stresses. This analysis leads to the assessment of whether the covered bond is strong enough to withstand these stresses, and may obtain the target rating.

This technical section deals with the latter part of the analysis and provides interested parties with further information on the advanced details of CBM. CBM aims to offer maximum transparency to the market. It consists of three parts. Firstly, an explanation of how the model simulates interest and foreign exchange rates. Secondly, details of how the default risk on the asset side is factored in. Finally, the quantitative rating eligibility test itself.

Interest Rate and Foreign Exchange Rate Simulation

Covered bonds are typically issued by banks whose main activity is mortgage lending or public sector financing. In contrast to securitization transactions like RMBS, covered bonds programs are "on-balance sheet" instruments, collateralized by mortgages and/or public sector assets. Based on its experience, S&P has observed that despite the regulatory and legal frameworks in place, covered bonds can be exposed to significant liquidity, currency, interest rate (fixed–floating) as well as to duration mismatches. It is important to understand how robust structures would be under these stresses. This is the focus of S&P quantitative analysis during the rating process. In this context, interest and foreign exchange rates scenario modeling is an important constituent of the CBM.

Simulation Methodology*

> ### Technical specification
>
> Interest rates and foreign exchange rates are treated jointly, in a similar way. The vector of their logarithms follows a mean-reverting model of the form:
>
> $$d \ln(i_t) = (a - b \cdot \ln(i_t))dt + \sigma dW_t, \tag{1}$$
>
> where $\sigma^T \sigma = \Omega$ is the instantaneous, stable over time (homoscedastic), covariance matrix.
>
> The rates are constantly pulled towards a pivotal value of $e^{a/b}$. The Monte Carlo simulation is based on a simplified version:
>
> $$\tilde{i}_t = \tilde{i}_{t-\Delta t} \exp\left[(\hat{a} - \hat{b}\ln(\tilde{i}_{t-\Delta t}))\Delta t + N_t \sqrt{\Delta t}\right], \tag{2}$$
>
> where N_t is the vector of disturbances.

Figure 13.1 gives an illustration of a possible path generated under the modeling for interest rates.

($i_0 = 2.11$ percent, $b = 0.001$, $a = b \ln(i_0)$, and $\Omega = 0.002213$)

Interest and foreign exchange rates clearly exhibit a lower boundary at zero due to the logarithmic specification in Equation (1). However there is no upper boundary embedded in the model. Consequently, S&P introduces criteria-based upper boundaries corresponding to those used in other areas of structured finance[†] at S&P, shown in Table 13.2.

---

*Because the objective is to model the behavior of rates over a very long horizon, up to the next 50 years, the choice has been made on purpose to prioritise robustness over complexity. In particular we neglected the sigma square term coming from the Ito lemma.
[†]Especially regarding RMBS transactions criteria.

FIGURE 13.1

Simulation of the Euro Interest Rate over 200 Quarters (50 Years).

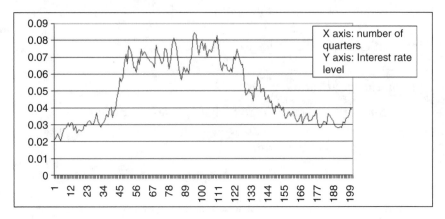

Model Calibration

This mean-reverting model corresponds to a simple parametric set up. Once this model is selected, the second step is the estimation of the parameters.*

In order to find the most robust calibration results, two well-established methods (described in Appendix B) are simultaneously used:—maximum likelihood (ML) and the method of moments.

TABLE 13.2

Country/Region	Upper Interest Rate Boundary (%)
Eurozone	12
United States	18
Japan	8
Switzerland	12
Other countries	18

---

*In order to improve the characteristics of the data with respect to the specification of mean reverting models, a polynomial smoothing of the past time series of interest rates and foreign exchange rates is being performed. This fit increases stability in the rating process over time.

Following extensive econometric work, the following conclusions were reached:

- The results suggest that the pivotal interest rate, $\bar{i}$, should be estimated by the method of moments.
- The simplest way is to use the ML technique to estimate b.
- The instantaneous variance (Ω) is estimated by ML, which provides accurate estimations. It is easy to compute the variance with ML once $\bar{i}$ and b have been estimated.

Definition of the Deterministic Default Rate Patterns

The asset side of any covered bond program is based on securities that are subject to credit risk; typically mortgage loans and/or loans to public entities. In CBM a stress, corresponding to a recession period, is applied to the asset pool in the form of defaults occurring in the first years of the transaction. The level of default is defined as a result of an analytical process performed by S&P analysts.* The timing of default is hard-coded in the CBM in a way that gives maximum consistency with other transactions rated by S&P with similar asset classes.

- If the assets underlying the covered bonds are mortgages, the standard default patterns for RMBS are used. The length of recession is typically three years, and there are two scenarios, as shown in Table 13.3.
- If the underlying assets are public loans, cash CDO-like default patterns are used. The length of recession is five years, and there are four scenarios, as shown in Table 13.4.

TABLE 13.3

Default Patterns for Mortgage Assets

Recession month	1	6	12	18	24	30	36
Fast default (%)	30	30	20	10	5	5	0
Slow default (%)	0	5	5	10	20	30	30

*For any targeted rating, a required asset default rate d is specified; it is determined using Standard & Poor's proprietary models like CDO evaluator or RMBS analyzer.

TABLE 13.4

Default Patterns for Public Loans

Recession year	1	2	3	4	5
Pattern I (%)	15	30	30	15	10
Pattern II (%)	40	20	20	10	10
Pattern III (%)	20	20	20	20	20
Pattern IV (%)	25	25	25	25	0

This structure allows CBM to communicate under which pattern an over-collateralization breach* would be observed. From a user perspective this solution increases the visibility on the cover pool of sensitivities to various default scenarios.

The quantitative rating eligibility test is performed based on a "pass" result on all scenarios and/or patterns.

The Quantitative Rating Component of the Model

(Terms used in this section are explained in a detailed glossary—see Appendix A.)

Description of the Architecture

The Quantitative Rating Eligibility Test S&P approach assumes that the covered bond is independent from the credit strength of the issuer,[†] and that in order to obtain a given level of rating it must, in particular, pass a proper quantitative rating eligibility test. The principle behind the test is that regardless of the environment, the level of assets should be sufficient to cover liabilities. This means that the probability of a loss event should impact bondholders only beyond the confidence level corresponding to the related rating level.

---

*Over-collateralization breach, see Appendix A for a definition.
†Provided that the issuer servicing capabilities are sufficiently robust to avoid operational and moral hazard risk becoming a major rating driver.

In order to determine the rating of a covered bond program, the model focuses on the effects of interest, foreign exchange rates, and default rates on the cash flows generated by the default table assets, net of the cash outflows scheduled for the liabilities. The drivers for cash flow generation are amortization of the principal (both on the asset and liability sides), fixed coupon payments, and floating coupon payments (split between a risk-free and a spread component).

The quantitative rating eligibility test can be summarized as follows: a target rating, e.g., "AAA," is defined by the issuer. Given the average maturity* of the transaction, e.g., five years, a corresponding cumulative default rate is deducted from S&P default tables, in this case is 0.28 percent. A rank ordering of the final net cash balance scenarios generated, conditional on the realization of interest and foreign exchange rates is performed. A specific focus is set on that 0.284 percent worst scenario. If the corresponding final net cash balance is positive, the deal will be likely to receive an "AAA" rating. If the net cash balance is negative, this means that the covered bond transaction does not meet the required target rating eligibility level, from a quantitative view. To remedy this situation, issuers have the option of providing more collateral on the asset side. If the final net cash balance is positive, the rating process can move ahead to the more qualitative aspects.

Impact of the Specification of the Asset Default Rate   At each period,[†] the cash flows generated by the assets are triggered by the default patterns defined in the section "Definition of the Deterministic Default Rate Patterns" and decreased by the cumulative default rate, which increases through time up to the target value (during the length of recession period). Liabilities are not affected by defaults.[‡]

Default leads to two opposite effects:

♦ It reduces the security cushion of the transaction. If, for instance, the default rate at the period under consideration is 10 percent, the cash flows on the asset side will be equal to 90 percent of what they were planned to be.

---

*Taking into account the repayment structure of principal and instalments.
†In the model, a period corresponds to a quarter.
‡See specific presentation on the impact of default on assets.

♦ In contrast, recovery is subsequently inflating asset cash flows with a time lag driven by a "time to recovery." The level of recovery equals a defined proportion of the amount that has defaulted. Different recovery rates are specified for the principal and the coupons. For example, if in a given period t, there is a 10 percent default on a principal amount of €1500 million, a fixed coupon of €400 million, and a floating coupon (based on initial interest rate, i_0, i.e., EURIBOR) of €75 million; then with a "time to recovery" of two years and with a respective recovery rate of 75 percent, 50 percent, and 50 percent, the amount of recovery that will take place two years later is:

$$R_{(t+2)} = 1500 * 10\% * 75\% + 400 * 10\% * 50\%$$

$$+ 75 * \frac{\tilde{i}_t}{i_0} * 10\% * 50\%,$$

where $\tilde{i}_t$ is the simulated interest rate at t.

The Impact of Interest Rates

Unlike default rates, interest rates have an impact on both the assets and the liabilities. They are modeled using the technique described in the section "Interest Rate and Foreign Exchange Rate Simulation."

The input data reported by issuers typically assumes that the floating component of the cash flows corresponds to a constant risk-free interest rate index level over the life of the bond (e.g., EURIBOR = 2 percent).* The model adjusts to each of these quarterly floating contribution to the cash flows, on both the asset and liability sides, by using the Monte Carlo simulated interest rate rather than the initial "frozen" value. For example, if in the cash flow schedule reported by the issuer, the risk-free index component of the floating interest amounted to €100 and the initial interest rate was 2 percent, then with a simulated interest rate of say 3 percent the floating interest that has to be repaid would become €150.

The risk-free interest rate is also a component in the liquidity risk adjustment mechanism. It is used in order to determine the reinvestment

---

*An accounting approach is considered here, which contrasts to a forward approach that would have based the planned repayments on forward interest rates.

rate of the cash balance. In the model, there is a reinvestment margin over the simulated risk-free interest rate if the cash balance is positive and a borrowing margin if it is negative. The margins embedded in the model are −50 bps and 100 bps, respectively.

The Impact of Foreign Exchange Rates   Foreign exchange rates are simulated in a similar way, and in conjunction with interest rates. They are only used to convert the cash balances into the pool's working currency, typically euros. When there are periodic non-euro deposits, then cash balances are transformed into euros at the end of each quarterly period, using the simulated foreign exchange rate for that period.

The Quantitative Rating Eligibility Test   Once all the simulated cash flows generated by assets and liabilities have been computed, the model generates the final net cash balance corresponding to each realization of the foreign exchange/risk-free interest rates. If it is negative, the covered bond is considered to be in default. In order to get to this final net cash balance, the model computes for each simulation the evolution over time of the cumulative cash balance. It then counts the proportion of iterations that end up with a negative final cash balance. If this proportion is smaller than the default rate tolerated for the targeted rating level, then the covered bond passes the quantitative rating eligibility test. In the example given in Figure 13.2, the final cash balance at the required percentile is positive, therefore the covered bond passes the test. Clearly, the percentile is lower for higher ratings and accordingly, the tolerance in the number of failing runs is lower.

Additional Features

Treatment of Recoveries

♦ *Mortgage assets*
As soon as a default occurs, recovery impacts the entire value of the mortgage loan (on the asset side) that was affected by the default.

To illustrate this point, let A_t, P_t, and c_t denote the outstanding asset, the principal repayment and the cumulative

FIGURE 13.2

Total Cash Balance Through Time in Euros.

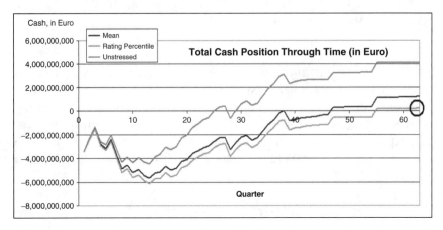

default rate at time t, respectively. Let r be the recovery on principal. S&P assume that the time to recovery and the length of recession are two years and four years, respectively. Table 13.5 summarizes the treatment of default and recovery in the covered bond model.

TABLE 13.5

Treatment of Defaults in the Covered Bond Model for Mortgage Assets

Period	Outstanding Asset	Principal Repayment	Recovery
1	$A_1 (1 - c_1)$	$P_1 (1 - c_1)$	0
2	$A_2 (1 - c_2)$	$P_2 (1 - c_2)$	0
3	$A_3 (1 - c_3)$	$P_3 (1 - c_3)$	$rA_1 c_1$
4	$A_4 (1 - \bar{c})$	$P_4 (1 - \bar{c})$	$rA_2 (c_2 - c_1)$
5	$A_5 (1 - \bar{c})$	$P_5 (1 - \bar{c})$	$rA_3 (c_3 - c_2)$
6	$A_6 (1 - \bar{c})$	$P_6 (1 - \bar{c})$	$rA_4 (\bar{c} - c_3)$
7	$A_7 (1 - \bar{c})$	$P_7 (1 - \bar{c})$	0
8	$A_8 (1 - \bar{c})$	$P_8 (1 - \bar{c})$	0
9	$A_9 (1 - \bar{c})$	$P_9 (1 - \bar{c})$	0
10	0	0	0
11	0	0	0

♦ *Public sector assets*

Public sector issuers often rely on some support from other government levels and ultimately on the tax base in the concerned country. S&P therefore considers that a default would not usually result in an ultimate loss of principal, but that payments, including arrears, would be resumed after a certain period of time. For public sector issuers S&P assumes that recovery rates would be close to 100 percent, although interest rate conditions may be renegotiated after default. An example is shown in Table 13.6, with a two-year time to recovery and a four-year recession.

As a result, S&P focus on the redemption cash flows, rather than on outstanding assets and liabilities for mortgage pools. However, the net effect for both is largely similar. In earlier periods of the remaining life of the pool, cash inflows are lower than planned, owing to payment delays occurring. Later on, most of these amounts are recovered so that in particular for public sector assets simulated cash inflows could even be higher than planned.

TABLE 13.6

Treatment of Defaults in the Covered Bond Model for Public Sector Assets

Period	Outstanding Asset	Principal Repayment	Current Recovery
1	$A_1 (1-c_1)$	$P_1 (1-c_1)$	0
2	$A_2 (1-c_2)$	$P_2 (1-c_2)$	0
3	$A_3 (1-c_3)$	$P_3 (1-c_3)$	$rP_1 c_1$
4	$A_4 (1-\bar{c})$	$P_4 (1-\bar{c})$	$rP_2 c_2$
5	$A_5 (1-\bar{c})$	$P_5 (1-\bar{c})$	$rP_3 c_3$
6	$A_6 (1-\bar{c})$	$P_6 (1-\bar{c})$	$rP_4 \bar{c}$
7	$A_7 (1-\bar{c})$	$P_7 (1-\bar{c})$	$rP_5 \bar{c}$
8	$A_8 (1-\bar{c})$	$P_8 (1-\bar{c})$	$rP_6 \bar{c}$
9	$A_9 (1-\bar{c})$	$P_9 (1-\bar{c})$	$rP_7 \bar{c}$
10	0	0	$rP_8 \bar{c}$
11	0	0	$rP_9 \bar{c}$

Early Repayments on the Asset Side

♦ *Repayments on mortgages*

Borrowers often choose to repay their debts ahead of the schedule specified in their contract. Stressed early repayments are usually specified as a fixed proportion of the nominal outstanding assets. For instance, if this rate is set at 20%, then 20% of the current nominal outstanding assets will be added to the planned repayments each year until the debts on the asset side are fully refunded. More formally, let A_t and P_t be the reported nominal outstanding asset and principal repayment at time t, respectively. Let $\tilde{A}_t$ and $\tilde{P}_t$ be their corresponding values after the stresses have been applied. Finally, r denotes the early repayment rate. Practically:

$$\tilde{P}_t = \tilde{A}_t \; \min\left\{\frac{P_t}{A_t} + r, 1\right\}.$$

With initially $\tilde{A}_1 = A_1$. The minimum function is used to ensure that the amount repaid cannot be larger than the outstanding debt. Consequently, we also have:

$$\tilde{A}_{t+1} = \tilde{A}_t - \tilde{P}_t = \tilde{A}_t \; \max\left\{1 - \left(\frac{P_t}{A_t} + r\right), 0\right\}.$$

As can be seen from Figure 13.3, repayments initially increase because of prepayments; however, as the refunding of the outstanding assets occurs earlier, repayments eventually decrease.

Early repayments tend to reduce the duration of the assets, and could compress yields. As it is dependent on the liability structure, the effect of the inclusion of this extra feature may, or may not, prove more stressful. The quantitative rating analysis is indeed based on a realistic worst-case approach between the scenarios with and without early repayments. Note that S&P has published criteria that define different early repayment rates. They tend to be jurisdiction specific. The objective with the CBM is to keep the approach simple; as

FIGURE 13.3

Principal Repayment of Assets.

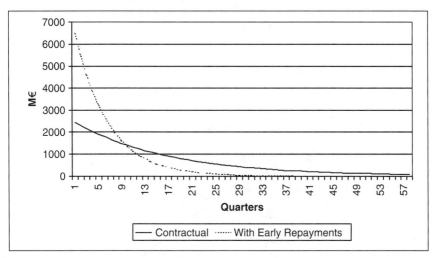

a consequence, the value retained in the model corresponds to a weighted-average of the appropriate prepayment rates.

♦ *Prepayments on public finance*

Public finance assets are typically not exposed to prepayment risk; so early repayment is usually not factored into the analysis.

Servicing Fees   The liquidity stress included in the model implicitly assumes that the parent bank can go out of business and that the rating is performed on an extinguishing cash flow profile. It is therefore reasonable to include servicing fees that represents the management cost of the structure issuing the covered bonds. These fees typically correspond to a fixed proportion of the nominal outstanding assets that should be subtracted each period from the cash balance. If s denotes the servicing fee per year expressed as a percentage, and A_t the outstanding assets at time t, then the servicing fee that has to be paid at quarter t equals $(s/4)^* A_t$.

MacroSwaps   Issuers often buy swaps to hedge interest rate and currency risk, e.g., by converting a flow of fixed interests into floating interests. In the case of macroswaps, i.e., where the notional of the swaps is expected to follow, albeit imperfectly, the dynamics of the asset, two

TABLE 13.7

Example of Pre Swap and Post Swap Reporting on the Asset Side

	Preswap reporting			Postswap reporting			Difference		
	Fixed interest	Floating interest		Fixed interest	Floating interest		Fixed interest	Floating interest	
Quarter		Index	Spread		Index	Spread		Index	Spread
1	225	110	2	110	198	3	−115	88	1
2	200	98	1.9	90	182	2.9	−110	84	1
...	...	...	...	...	...	...	...	...	...

types of risks can arise:

♦ On the positive side, the swaps modify and usually reduce the exposure of the bank to interest rate risk; and

♦ On the negative side, because of defaults on the asset side, the notional of the swap will turn out to only match the underlying exposure approximately and will accordingly put the covered bond transaction at risk.

The input data received by S&P from covered bond issuers does not typically include the detail of the swap contracts in which the issuers are involved with respect to their covered bond programs. Issuers generally provide a pre swap ALM (Asset Liability Management) report (before the effect of swaps is included) and a postswap ALM report (after the effect of swaps is included). Assuming these swaps are in compliance with S&P criteria, the difference between the two reports gives the net series of exposures that has been swapped, including fees. This series is sensitive to interest rate fluctuations, however, it is not sensitive to the occurrence of defaults, as swap contracts are not subject to the realization of events affecting the covered bond asset pool. The easiest way to model the effect of these macroswaps is therefore to add the difference between the postswap and the pre swap reports to the existing liabilities.

Table 13.7 gives an example of pre swap and postswap reports on the asset side. In the first quarter, the bank has swapped €115 of fixed interests into €89 of floating interests [split between €88 risk-free (index) and €1 spread]. As can be seen in the table, the net effect of the swap can easily be identified by observing the difference between the two reports.* Obviously, the value of the risk-free floating component, and therefore the cost of the swap, will be affected by interest rate changes. This explains why each column should be treated separately.

After the realization, $\tilde{i}_{j'}$ of the simulated interest rate has been applied to the risk-free rate component, the impact of the swap can be computed.

For example, in quarter 1, this cost is:

$$-115 + 88\frac{\tilde{i}_1}{i_0} + 1.$$

---

*It should be emphasized that the reported flow corresponding to the risk-free component of the floating interest is based on the initial interest rate i_0.

Similarly in quarter 2, the cost of the swap is:

$$-110 + 84\frac{\tilde{i}_2}{i_0} + 1.$$

This cost should be added to the preswap net cash flow of the corresponding period. Denoting K_t the cash balance and cf_t the net cash flow (preswap) at time t, we have for quarter 1:

$$K_1 = (1 + \tilde{i}_1)K_0 + cf_1 + \left(-115 + 88\frac{\tilde{i}_1}{i_0} + 1 \right).$$

An easy way to take the cost of swaps into account is to add it (see Table 13.7, column 3) to the preswap liabilities. The reason why the cost of macroswaps is included to the preswap liabilities rather than to the assets, is a practical one. It is to ring-fence it from the occurrence of defaults. By including it in liabilities, it will be affected by interest rate changes, but not by the default rate patterns.

Communication of Results

CBM focuses on the value and sign of the final cash balance based on the assets and liabilities after the different stresses have been applied in order to help S&P analysts be able to assign a rating.

In order to improve transparency and communication, Standard and Poor's is careful to articulate results according to the terminology used by covered bond issuers.

Issuers typically target an "AAA" rating for their covered bond programs. They are usually interested to know what collateral margin is needed to secure this rating or to know the quantity of extra assets they need to add or remove as collateral during the life of the transaction in order to maintain the initial rating level (see definition of the break-even portfolio in Appendix A).

Issuers also communicate on their unstressed schedule of assets and liabilities. S&P therefore provides relevant reporting in this respect. Market participants typically focus on two key parameters, one regarding their level of current overcollateralization and another one regarding the duration gap between assets and liabilities.

- Overcollateralization: Issuers are increasingly communicating with the market and the rating agencies in terms of collateral surpluses defined as overcollateralization. Communication can either be provided in terms of a nominal overcollateralization or in terms of a net present value (NPV) overcollateralization (see glossary in Appendix A for the definition of terms).

♦ Duration: Duration is an important communication element as there is increasing focus from customers and regulators on the duration gap.

Identifying the Break-even Portfolio with an Overcollateralization Focus
From a S&P perspective a critical point is to evaluate how far, from a quantitative point of view, the structure is from the break-even portfolio corresponding to the rating level in consideration. Given the initial reporting provided by the bank, there are two simple ways of getting to (and communicating on) the break-even portfolio. One can either initially add or subtract cash, or alternatively, increase or decrease proportionally the amount of assets owned by the bank.

♦ *Initial cash*

There are several ways of communicating the break-even pool. First the model gives the initial amount of cash that could be withdrawn (or that needs to be added) such that the rating is just secured. Let K_t, i_t, and cf_t be the cash balance, the interest rate (risk-free interest rate plus bid/ask margins*) and the net cash flow (flow of assets minus flow of liabilities) at time t, respectively.

We have:

$$K_t = (1 + i_t)K_{t-1} + cf_t$$

As the interest rate i_t comprises borrowing and reinvestment margins that depend on the sign of K_{t-1}, it requires some calculation effort to obtain the initial amount of cash that could be withdrawn from the final cash balance, K_T.

♦ *Proportional increase or decrease of assets*

The other way to communicate on the break-even pool is to give the proportion by which the nominal outstanding assets and the

---

*Under Standard & Poor's criteria, $i_t = \tilde{i}_t + 1\% \cdot I\{K_{t-1} < 0\} - 0.5\% \cdot I\{K_{t-1} \geq 0\}$ where $\tilde{i}_t$ is the simulated risk-free interest rate and I is an indicator. Recall that the indicator is such that

$$I\{A\} = \begin{cases} 1 & \text{if } A \text{ is True} \\ 0 & \text{if } A \text{ is False}. \end{cases}$$

cash flow they generate can be reduced (or increased), so that the final cash balance at the quantile level corresponding to the rating target is zero. However, it is not possible to compute the exact value of this proportion without resorting to an iterative process.

Adjustment of the Portfolio with a Duration Focus

CBM tries to help communication with market participants in a way that enables covered bond issuers to adjust their portfolio within the constraints of their commitments and such that they obtain the desired rating. This section explains how CBM adjusts the portfolio, with a focus on the duration gap, while also maintaining the targeted rating.

Throughout the proposed procedure it is assumed that the duration of assets does not change. In order to change the duration gap, the CBM user can only change the duration of liabilities by adding or repurchasing covered bonds with a given bullet maturity τ. The interest rate, $\hat{i}_t$, paid on these bonds is reported by the user. As illustrated in the calculation below, this allows us to determine the quantity of covered bonds, C_τ, that needs to be issued in order to reach the desired duration for liabilities. Let B_t be the cash flow generated by the newly issued bonds, then:

$$B_t = \begin{cases} \hat{i}_t C_\tau, & t < \tau \\ \hat{i}_\tau C_\tau + C_\tau, & t = \tau. \\ 0, & t > \tau \end{cases}$$

If l_t denote the flow of liabilities and Γ the targeted duration for liabilities, then C_τ must be found such that:

$$\frac{\sum_{t=1}^{T} \left(t \cdot (B_t + l_t) \Big/ \prod_{s=1}^{t}(1+i_s) \right)}{\sum_{t=1}^{T} \left((B_t + l_t) \Big/ \prod_{s=1}^{t}(1+i_s) \right)} = \Gamma.$$

This gives:

$$C_\tau = \frac{\displaystyle\sum_{t=1}^{T}(t-\Gamma)\frac{l_t}{\displaystyle\prod_{s=1}^{t}(1+i_s)}}{\displaystyle\sum_{t=1}^{\tau}(\Gamma-t)\frac{\hat{i}_t}{\displaystyle\prod_{s=1}^{t}(1+i_s)} + \frac{\Gamma-\tau}{\displaystyle\prod_{s=1}^{\tau}(1+i_s)}}.$$

Once these new bullet single maturity covered bonds have been issued, we can apply the described procedure to discover the quantity of assets, or how much initial cash needs to be added in order to obtain a break-even portfolio.

CONCLUSION

This model has been designed to be as simple as possible in order to provide strong visibility to investors and issuers. It is in addition meant to be robust in the sense that it allows for seriously stressed conditions and that its conclusions do not rely on the support of the issuing bank. It is ultimately as consistent as possible with the other rating tools developed by S&P. Note that the quantitative analysis performed with CBM is only part of the rating process for S&P. Potential users shall be aware that S&P reserve the right to assign the suggested rating or not, based, among other things, on qualitative and legal analysis.

APPENDIX A

Glossary of Terms

DEFINITIONS

Break-Even Pool

A pool that just passes the quantitative rating eligibility test, i.e., a pool with final cash balance of zero.

Cash Balance

The cash balance at time t represents the total amount of cash available to the bank at time t. (Note it is a stock rather than a flow.)

Cash Flow

The (net) cash flow at time t is the difference between the cash generated by assets and by liabilities over the tth period.

Duration

The duration of assets and liabilities is the discounted weighted average time at which their respective cash flows occur. Let $\{c_t\}_{t=1}^{T}$ denote a cash flow series, then its duration is defined as:

$$\text{Duration} = \frac{\sum_{t=1}^{T}\left(t \cdot c_t \Big/ \prod_{s=1}^{t}(1+i_s)\right)}{\sum_{t=1}^{T}\left(c_t \Big/ \prod_{s=1}^{t}(1+i_s)\right)}$$

where i_t is the interest used for discounting, typically the forward rate.

Duration Gap

The duration gap between assets and liabilities is one of the key parameters on which banks focus; it gives information on the mismatch in the timing of cash flows. Market practice in the covered bond area is to compute the duration gap as the difference between the duration of the assets and that of the liabilities is,

   Duration gap = duration of assets − duration of liabilities

$$\frac{\sum_{t=1}^{T}\left(t \cdot a_t \Big/ \prod_{s=1}^{t}(1+i_s)\right)}{\sum_{t=1}^{T}\left(a_t \Big/ \prod_{s=1}^{t}(1+i_s)\right)} - \frac{\sum_{t=1}^{T}\left(t \cdot l_t \Big/ \prod_{s=1}^{t}(1+i_s)\right)}{\sum_{t=1}^{T}\left(l_t \Big/ \prod_{s=1}^{t}(1+i_s)\right)},$$

where a_t and l_t denote the asset and liability flows at time t. It is clear from the equation that the duration of assets is computed independently from duration of liabilities. It can also be noted that the duration gap is different from the duration of the net cash flow as usually expressed:

   Duration of assets − duration of liabilities ≠ duration of (assets − liabilities).

Final Cash Balance

The cash balance observed at the last period, after the different stresses (defaults, interest rates, . . .) have been applied. The pool under consideration passes the rating test if and only if the final cash balance is positive.

Net Present Value

The NPV of a cash flow $\{c_t\}_{t=1}^{T}$ is given by:*

$$NPV = \sum_{t=1}^{T} \frac{c_t}{\prod_{s=1}^{t}(1+i_s)}.$$

The interest rate, i_t, used for discounting in the computation of the NPVO/C is given by the prevailing market yield curve, considered as the forward value of three-month interest rates (e.g., Euribor).

Nominal Overcollateralization

Amount by which the outstanding assets initially exceed the outstanding liabilities. If A_1 and L_1 denote the initial nominal outstanding assets and liabilities, then:

$$\text{Nominal O/C} = \frac{A_1 - L_1}{L_1}.$$

NPV Overcollateralization

Amount by which the initial net present value of assets (i.e., the sum of all discounted flows starting from the first period) exceeds that of the liabilities. If NPVA and NPVL denote the initial net present value of those flows, then:

$$\text{NPVO/C} = \frac{\text{NPVA} - \text{NPVL}}{\text{NPVL}}.$$

Overcollateralization

Overcollateralization, amount by which assets exceed liabilities. The two most important measures of overcollateralization are the nominal overcollateralization and the NPV overcollateralization.

---

*The net present value is sometimes computed as:

$$\sum_{t=1}^{T} c_t/(1+i_t)^t.$$

However, the formula reported in the text is more accurate.

Main Relations

Cash Balance and Cash Flows

Let K_t, i_t, and cf_t be respectively the cash balance, the interest rate, and the net cash flow (flow of assets minus flow of liabilities) at time t. We have:

$$K_t = (1 + i_t)K_{t-1} + cf_t. \tag{1}$$

Note: if several currencies are involved, the net cash flows generated in foreign currencies should be converted into euros and added to the domestic cash flows.

Discounted Final Cash Balance and Net Present Value of the Cash Flows

By iterating Equation 1, we obtain:

$$\frac{K_T}{(1+i_1)(1+i_2)\cdots(1+i_T)} = K_0 + \frac{cf_1}{1+i_1} + \frac{cf_2}{(1+i_1)(1+i_2)}$$

$$+ \cdots + \frac{cf_T}{(1+i_1)(1+i_2)\cdots(1+i_T)}.$$

In the special case where i_t is the forward interest rate, then we have:

$$\frac{K_T}{(1+i_1)(1+i_2)\cdots(1+i_T)} = \text{NPVA} - \text{NPVL}$$

There is therefore a link between the final cash balance and the NPVO/C (expressed in euros rather than as a percentage).

NPV Overcollateralization and Nominal Overcollateralization

It turns out that the two measures of O/C are closely related. Let A_t' and A_t'' denote the nominal outstanding fixed and floating assets at time t, respectively; similarly for L_t' and L_t''. Let i_t be the *forward* risk-free interest rate used for discounting and used as index in the computation of the floating interest that has to be paid. Let $\bar{i}_{A,t}$ be the fixed interest rate corresponding to received coupons on fixed assets;* similarly $\bar{i}_{L,t}$ corresponds

---

*The fixed interest rate is time dependent because the aggregate asset is made of different assets having different maturities and paying different fixed interest rates.

to *coupons due on fixed liabilities*. Finally, $S_{A,t}$ and $S_{L,t}$ denote the *spread component* in currency units (e.g., in euros) of the floating interest of assets and liabilities, respectively. We have:

$$\text{Nominal O/C}_1 = \frac{A_1' + A_1'' - L_1' - L_1''}{L_1' + L_1''},$$

and it could be checked that:

$$\text{NPVO/C}_1 = \frac{A_1' + A_1'' - L_1' - L_1'' + \displaystyle\sum_{k=1}^{T} \frac{\left\lfloor (\bar{i}_{A,k} - i_k)A_k' + S_{A,t} \right\rfloor - \left\lfloor (\bar{i}_{L,k} - i_k)L_k' + S_{L,t} \right\rfloor}{\displaystyle\prod_{l=1}^{k}(1+i_l)}}{L_1' + L'' + \displaystyle\sum_{k=1}^{T} \frac{(\bar{i}_{L,k} - i_k)L_k' + S_{L,t}}{\displaystyle\prod_{l=1}^{k}(1+i_l)}}.$$

It can easily be seen that the difference between the nominal O/C and the NPV_O/C is entirely due to the difference between the effective fixed or floating interest rates and the risk-free interest rate.

APPENDIX B

MAXIMUM LIKELIHOOD

The simplified discretized version of the model can also be written as:

$$\ln(i_t) - \ln(i_{t-\Delta t}) = (a - b\ln(i_{i-\Delta t})) \cdot \Delta t + \sigma R_t \sqrt{\Delta t}. \tag{3}$$

The discretized model (3) turns out to be a linear regression model. As ML and Ordinary Least Squares give the same estimates for a and b, we can use this latter technique that is much simple to implement.

METHOD OF MOMENTS

Starting from the discretized version of the model, for a given interest, we have:

$$\ln(i_t) = a + (1-b)\ln(i_{t-1}) + \varepsilon_t$$

where $\varepsilon_t \sim$ normal $(0, \Omega)$. This is a standard AR(1) process, and we can compute the first two terms of its autocorrelation function:

$$\begin{cases} \mathrm{Var}(\ln(i_t)) = (1-b)\,\mathrm{Cov}(\ln(i_t), \ln(i_{t-1})) + \Omega \\ \mathrm{Cov}(\ln(i_t), \ln(i_{t-1})) = b\,\mathrm{Var}(\ln(i_t)). \end{cases}$$

We also have:

$$E(\ln(i_t)) = \frac{a}{b}.$$

This leaves us with three equations in three unknowns, thus:

$$\hat{b} = 1 - \frac{\mathrm{Cov}(\ln(i_t), \ln(i_{t-1}))}{\mathrm{Var}(\ln(i_t))}$$

$$\hat{\Omega} = \frac{[\mathrm{Var}(\ln(i_t))]^2 - [\mathrm{Cov}(\ln(i_t), \ln(i_{t-1}))]^2}{\mathrm{Var}(\ln(i_t))}$$

$$\hat{a} = \hat{b}E(\ln(i_t)).$$

REFERENCES

Standard and Poor's Research:
"Research: Expanding European Covered Bond Universe Puts Spotlight on Key Analytics" (published on July 16, 2004).
"FI Criteria: Approach to Rating European Covered Bonds Refined" (published on March 29, 2004).
"FI Criteria: Rating Pfandbriefe—The Analytical Perspective" (published on April 8, 2004).
"Research: Revised Analytical Approach to Residential Mortgages in Hypotheken-Pfandbrief Collateral Pools" (published on April 19, 2002).
"Research: Criteria for Rating German Residential Mortgage-Backed Securities" (published on Aug. 31, 2001).
"Research: New Mortgage Pfandbriefe Criteria" (published on April 8, 1999).
Frank Dierick, Fatima Pires, Martin Scheicher and Kai Gereon Spitzer "The new basel capital Framework and its implementation in the European Union" ECB Occasional Paper Series NO. 42 / DECEMBER 2005

An Overview of Structured Investment Vehicles and Other Special Purpose Companies

Cristina Polizu

In the recent years, new structures have been developed. Special purpose companies or quasi-operating vehicles are designed to be operating in primarily one type of business: interest rate and FX derivatives or credit derivatives or repo markets or as a traditional asset manager. They are bankruptcy remote entities, nonconsolidated with any other financial institution with which they may interact. They are managed using rigorous tests for capital adequacy, collateral and liquidity adequacy and do not rely on third party capital injection. They own and hold their capital required by the adequacy tests in eligible investments. In this chapter, the most frequent quasi-operating companies will be presented with a more detailed focus on structured investment vehicles (SIVs). The quantitative techniques that build the capital and liquidity adequacy of the company are presented and examples of models are illustrated without trying to be prescriptive in any way.

STRUCTURED INVESTMENT VEHICLES
Definition of What an SIV is

SIVs have been operating in the U.S. and European debt markets for more than a decade. They are designed to be limited-purpose companies that take arbitrage opportunities by purchasing mostly highly rated medium- and long-term assets and funding themselves with cheaper short-term commercial paper and medium term notes (Figure 14.1).

In a nutshell, the SIV issues short-term and long-term liabilities and purchases assets with the proceeds. These assets will pay a coupon that is higher than the interest that the SIV needs to pay on issued liabilities. This price differential is one of the advantages an SIV undertakes to become profitable. If the assets mature and do not default, there would be no other need for resources to cover defaults in the structure. Also, if the commercial paper market were always there, there would never be a risk of having to liquidate assets to repay par on the liabilities, because every time a liability would mature, the vehicle would just roll it. However, the company needs to be equipped with enough resources to repay debt in a scenario where liabilities could not be rolled and assets would need to be liquidated or when assets default.

Similar to a finance company, the SIV's main goal is to generate returns for its shareholders by taking exposure to long-term securities and by funding these assets with shorter-term debt. The SIV manager manages to optimize the mismatch between asset returns and cost of funding while providing stable returns to its capital noteholders.

Perhaps a better way to define what an SIV is, would be to describe what an SIV is not. They are not unrated trading vehicles like hedge funds, neither bank-sponsored ABCP conduits, typically supported by 100 percent liquidity, nor collateral debt obligations (CDOs) which are match funded up front and invest mostly in high-yield assets. SIVs feature a dynamic treasury function that can expand or contract depending on the manager's strategic plans. They are supported by partial liquidity that is sized using a daily dynamic model. All SIVs are rated AAA by Standard and Poor's and are designed to exist and operate in the market

FIGURE 14.1

A SIV Structure.

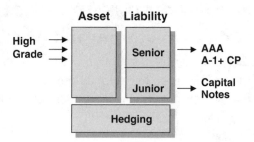

as AAA corporations. They can be funding vehicles, swap counterparties, and repo counterparties in other structured finance transactions.

SIVs and CDOs

The SIVs are not purely credit arbitrage vehicles. This is partially true because their portfolio may exhibit defaults, which constitute a loss to the portfolio in the same way a CDO does. However, having a high-grade portfolio, mainly AA, the default rate is small. Their role is more on managing the mismatch between assets and liabilities and the consequences of a liquidity shortfall. A CDO's main focus is credit risk, as BB portfolio is purchased with AAA debt that is usually longer in tenor than the asset portfolio.

Assets in SIVs and CDOs SIVs purchase usually AAA to A range assets, have limited BBB exposure. There is a subinvestment bucket allowed to pick up the downgrade of an investment-grade security.

Some SIVS have synthetic credit derivative exposure. The assets are diversified per type, geography, tenor, and size and all rated by the rating agencies in a proportion of 95 percent.

In a CDO, the range of assets is wider. It can go from high-grade to high-yield bonds and loans. CDOs can take cash or synthetic exposure. As for SIVs, approved sets of concentration guidelines are applied. For both, concentrated pools or assets are further penalized in the model for quantifying appropriate capital adequacy.

Liabilities in SIVs and CDOs In an SIV, there is no maturity matching. The gap between assets and liabilities is about three to four years. More than 50 percent of the debt is CP (U.S. and EURO). Capital structure is evolving, depending on market conditions. Typically, in an SIV, we see two tranches. Senior liabilities are rated AAA and issued in several classes. Capital notes are the mezz piece and are usually one tranche. In the past couple of years, SIVs have seeked a rating (private or public) on their capital notes. Sometimes, the capital notes are tranched in a rated piece and an unrated first loss position. SIVs roll their debt and issue new debt as they deem appropriate. They could use alternative funding instruments like repurchase agreements and credit-linked notes.

CDOs are more focused on maturity matching than SIVs. Capital structure is multitranched from AAA to BB and usually CDOs have an unrated first loss position. The tenor, rating, and size are determined on day one. The intention is to keep the capital structure fixed during the life of a CDO. Management is allowed on the asset side within certain parameters. The rating on the debt has to remain unaltered during the active management of the portfolio.

It is important to understand that because an SIV carries a corporate rating of AAA, it has to satisfy all its obligation with AAA certainty. In a CDO, given the multiple layers of subordination, some liabilities of the CDO (e.g., swap termination payments) could be subordinated in the waterfall and not addressed in the model.

Liquidity in SIVs and CDOs   Management of liquidity is one of the most challenging elements in the SIVs. Due to a considerable gap between assets and liabilities, the SIV needs to rely on external/internal liquidity in the form of bank lines, breakable deposits, committed repos, put options, and liquid assets. It is monitored through specially designed tests, commonly known as net cumulative outflow (NCO), that monitor the peak liquidity need over the coming year. It is run daily and quantifies what amount of resources has to be in liquid assets. In a CDO, liquidity is managed through internal reserve accounts. Because they do not run a refinancing risk, outside liquidity is not necessary. Cash flow mismatches are mitigated by cash diversion if certain tests do not pass. Some tranches could also have their interest deferrable.

SIVs and CP Conduits

A CP conduit is primarily driven by off-balance sheet regulatory capital relief. An SIV is motivated by profit for its shareholders. The number of CP conduits to date exceeds the number of SIVs.

Assets in SIVs and CP Conduits   Both invest in asset backed and corporates. While an SIV has to have all of its assets rated, a CP conduit can have unrated illiquid assets like trade receivables. CP conduits are not subject to the diversification criteria that an SIV is. For example, there can be CP conduits 100 percent concentrated in one asset class.

Liabilities in SIVs and CP Conduits   CP conduit accesses the commercial paper market primarily. The SIVs have access to both short- and long-term funding. In an SIV, there is a floor on the weighted average life of the liabilities of three-months. This is to mitigate a forced one-day sale, should the commercial paper market be disrupted. In a CP conduit, there is no such limit. The liabilities can be 100 percent one day or very short term. This is mitigated by the credit and liquidity enhancement programs in a CP conduit, which are most onerous than those of an SIV.

Liquidity in SIVs and CP Conduits Due to the range of liabilities, through the NCO test, an SIV does not have to keep 100 percent liquidity as a CP conduit does. The model in the SIV quantifies what the one-year liquidity need is and reserves bank lines for that amount, which is lower than 100 percent (could range from 25 to 40 percent).

SIVs and Hedge Funds

The hedge funds attempt to make profit on their bets on market directionality for interest rates, currency, and stocks. An SIV is designed to not take such bets. For example, when a fixed rate asset is purchased, the manager attaches a swap, which converts the fixed rate asset into a floater. The asset stays in such an asset swap package till its maturity or till the counterparty defaults, case in which it has to be immediately replaced. In an SIV, the profit is made from prudent management of the credit spread of the assets versus liabilities.

It is true that both operate at a leverage to increase profits. But, whereas all the positions of SIVs have to be reported to rating agencies and are subject to stringent compliance tests, a hedge fund does not require full transparency on its positions.

Due to their high-rating and high-management standards, the SIVs can access the commercial paper and medium term notes market for funding purposes, whereas the hedge funds do not.

SIVs are closer to be labeled as buy and hold vehicles with static hedges, whereas hedge funds have active trading and rely on dynamic hedging of their risk.

What Does the Rating of AAA for an SIV Mean?

If a series of trigger events occur that impact the normal operations of the SIV, a wind down event will start and the manager or a third party (i.e., security trustee) will step in and liquidate gradually the portfolio. No debt will be further rolled or issued, and the cash obtained from liquidating the portfolio will be used to repay the senior liabilities. Capital will be used to make up the shortfalls on the asset liquidation. Practically, in a finite time, the SIV will cease to exist. The SIVs wind down when their resources are

FIGURE 14.2

Dynamics of SIV Tests.

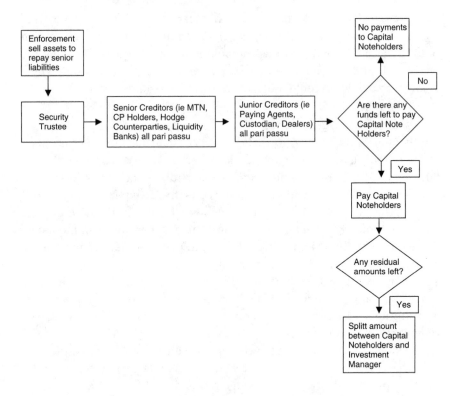

on the verge of being insufficient to repay senior debt. The wind down is called defeasance. The attempt is to repay in full all senior debt or at least with AAA certainty before becoming extinct. Most important is that an SIV does not default on its debt. It is equipped with structural tests to allow an exit strategy prior to downgrade or default. This feature is essential in differentiating an SIV from a regular corporate and understand that an SIV has multiple layers of support, including capital and liquidity tests and various defeasance mechanism that preclude the SIV to default on its debt. The sequence of steps described above can be seen in Figure 14.2.

Portfolio Diversification Guidelines in an SIV

Each SIV has approved diversification guidelines. The main critéria for diversification are asset types, geography, ratings, and tenor. The SIV has to comply with these guidelines. Beside the model that quantifies losses, the diversification requirements are an important feature for the credit enhancement of the SIV. Breach of the guidelines has to be cured either by selling collateral or by capital charging the excess dollar for dollar. For example, in February 2001, when Hollywood Funding was downgraded from AAA to CCC– (default status), Asset Backed Capital Ltd. (ABC) owned approximately $100 million of these notes at the time of downgrade. The asset became ineligible for the SIV and, at that time, ABC had five days to cure. ABC sold massively liquid assets to reduce its leverage and returned into compliance. The rating was reaffirmed by all rating agencies.

Sponsorship, Managers, and Investors

An SIV sponsor is usually a major commercial bank, asset manager, insurance company, or a combination of thereof. It plays an important role, as investors differentiate SIVs by their perception of the sponsor. The sponsor usually is setting up the SIV, may or may not provide liquidity support, may or may not invest its own money in a portion of the capital structure (capital notes).

The asset manager is responsible for daily management of credit and liquidity. Their management style reflects in the asset composition of the portfolio. Some are focused on asset-backed security (ABS) assets, some invest more in bank subdebt, some focus more on certain rating categories.

As for the range of investors, it varies depending on the portion of the capital structure that they are targeting. Commercial paper is attractive to money market funds, banks, and conduits. Banks and corporates are buyers of medium term notes. Banks, insurance companies, as well as private individuals may invest in rated or unrated capital notes.

Table 14.1 presents a snapshot of the market as of December 2005 (as shown by an S&P's update: SIV Outlook Report/Assets Top $200 Million in SIV Market; Continued Growth Expected in 2006—January 2006).

In Figure 14.3, outstanding senior debt is displayed as of December 2005. The asset classes in SIV portfolios cover mostly floating rate USD bullet or soft-bullet ABS and bank debt. However, they are able and some do invest in nonbank corporates and sovereign paper. Assets held by the SIV sector exceeded $200 billion at the end of 2005, and stand at almost $204 billion, a rise of almost 40 percent over the previous year.

TABLE 14.1

SIV Market (as of December 2005)

SIV	Manager/adviser	Date rated	Senior debt (Million $)
Beta Finance Corp.	Citibank International PLC	September 8, 1989	16,455.64
Sigma Finance Corp.	Gordian Knot Ltd.	February 2, 1995	41,089.99
Orion Finance Corp.	Eiger Capital Management	May 31, 1996	2,080.97
Centauri Corp.	Citibank International PLC	September 9, 1996	15,999.33
Dorada Corp.	Citibank International PLC	September 17, 1998	9,677.63
K2 Corp.	Dresdner Kleinwort Wasserstein	February 1, 1999	17,842.94
Links Finance Corp.	Bank of Montreal	June 18, 1999	16,296.81
Five Finance Corp.	Citibank International PLC	November 15, 1999	4,401.66
Abacas Investments Ltd.	III Offshore Advisors	December 8, 1999	972.89
Parkland Finance Corp.	Bank of Montreal	September 7, 2001	1,561.01
Harrier Finance Funding Ltd.	West LB	January 11, 2002	9,301.41
White Pine Corp. Ltd.	Standard Chartered Bank	February 4, 2002	7,858.29
Stanfield Victoria Finance Ltd.	Stanfield Global Strategies LLC	July 10, 2002	8,276.98
Premier Asset Collateralized Entity Ltd.	Société Générale	July 10, 2002	2,780.55
Whistlejacket Capital Ltd.	Standard Chartered Bank	July 24, 2002	6,327.25
Tango Finance Corp.	Rabobank International	November 26, 2002	7,759.37
Sedna Finance Corp.	Citibank International PLC	June 22, 2004	4,111.99
Cullinan Finance Ltd.	HSBC Bank PLC	July 18, 2005	7,292.00
Cheyne Finance PLC	Cheyne Capital Management	August 3, 2005	5,063.46

FIGURE 14.3

Outstanding Senior Debt.

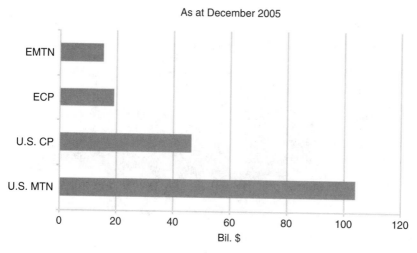

Outstanding Senior Debt

As at December 2005

Figure 14.4 gives an indication on the concentration in different types of assets that current SIVs hold. Figure 14.5 shows a further breakdown of the structured finance bucket. Figure 14.6 shows a composition by rating across SIV sector.

One of the primary features of the SIV is the dynamic nature of capital allocation and leverage. SIVs can increase or decrease leverage, can grow or shrink if they comply with certain capital and liquidity requirements. The capital adequacy focuses on the event that will require the SIV liquidate its assets to repay the outstanding debt. The capital adequacy tests are applied to the market value of the assets.

Generally speaking, the assets may depreciate over time. When the SIV needs to sell them in the market, take the cash and repay the debt, the cash that it has sold the asset for, may be lower than the liability that needs to be repaid. That is why, an SIV needs to be equipped with additional resources in the form of equity to make sure it can cover credit losses and market value depreciation, should it rely only on its current portfolio to repay the debt.

To do that, the SIV issues equity in the form of capital notes. These notes will act as a first-loss position and the return or coupon will be commensurate with the risk. The capital notes are meant to capture the

FIGURE 14.4

Concentration by Industry.

Portfolio Exposure By Industry

Assets held by SIVs at end-2005

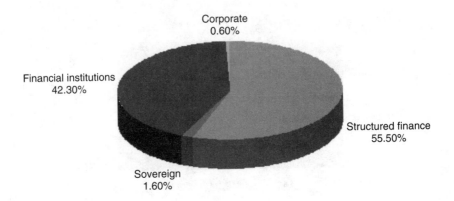

FIGURE 14.5

ABS Holdings.

A Closer Look At ABS Holdings

By sub-sector

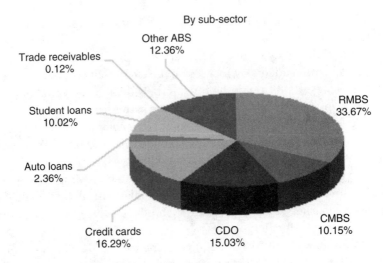

Note: % of ABS assets. ABS assets make up 55.5% of total assets.

FIGURE 14.6

Asset Ratings Breakdown.

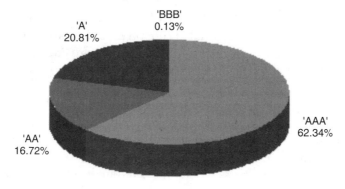

Note: 79% of assets are rated 'AA' or above.

potential depreciation in value of the assets and to make up for the insufficient cash realized when the asset is sold. The capital notes are sized so that, when used in conjunction with the realized market value of the asset, they will be sufficient to repay the debt.

Holding capital in cash is not efficient. Cash would normally accrue at a sub-Libor rate. Any sub-Libor rate is commonly referred to as a negative carry. Cash or cash equivalents have the advantage that they are very liquid resources and hence can be readily used and deployed for payments. However, if the timing of the liabilities is known, cash can be further invested in a positive spread yielding asset. To minimize the negative carry, the capital notes are, themselves, invested in assets.

Cost of Funds

The coupon that the SIV needs to pay on its issued debt is referred to as cost of funding. Usually, CP and MTNs (medium-term note programs) price at Libor rates, perhaps within a range of a few basis points up and/or down.

The SIVs raise funds to acquire their portfolios by accessing the commercial paper market. At a later stage, with the growth of the portfolio, MTNs start playing a bigger role in the portfolio funding. MTNs allow for portfolio match funding, which eliminates partially the risk of liquidation, leaving only the default risk in. However, MTNs are more expensive than short-term debt.

Any disruption in the normal mode of an SIV would be immediately reflected in the cost of funds for its rolled commercial paper. Cost of funds for capital notes includes a stated coupon (25 to 50 above Libor) that is, or not, rated as well as profit or performance coupon. Profit depends on the excess spread of the SIV and ultimately on the excess capital that an SIV has. Capital notes are rated in most cases BBB.

In a CDO, the AAA tranche prices somewhere in the range of Libor +25 and +45. The short tenor of the debt in an SIV (typically senior MTN are 18 to 24 months) is reflected in the spread above Libor which is lower than the CDO AAA spread. Same comparison can be made to European covered bonds where the stated maturity is typically 20 to 30 years.

The BBB CDO tranche prices in the range of Libor +200 to +350 with a five-year average of approximately 250 above Libor. The floating RMBS/CMBS pay a coupon which on average over last five years is Libor +190. Spread raged within 170 to 230. SIVs may pay similar coupon or even higher to their capital noteholders but most of the spread is profit and their stated coupon is much lower.

Leverage

In its simplest definition, *leverage* is the ratio between senior debt and equity. Other equivalent definitions involve net asset value. Irrespective of the capital model outcome, SIVs have to comply with leverage constraints. Typically, SIV leverage is within the range of 12 to 14. At 18 or 19 leverage level, they enter restricted operations, and, at a leverage of 20, they need to wind down.

Quantitative analysis on an SIV focuses mainly on capital adequacy, market neutrality, and adequate liquidity.

Capital Adequacy

Example 1

SIV XYZ issues $100 million one-year note at Libor + 10 bps. It buys a five-year asset of 10 million MTM. The asset pays Libor +30 bps, so the spread differential is 20 bps.

If at the end of one year the SIV cannot roll the liability (e.g., market disruption), it needs to sell the asset (which has four more years to maturity). The SIV will sell it and may get only 9.8 million.

It means that the SIV is 0.2 million short of its debt obligation, so it should have raised 0.2 million in equity. See a simplified example of a SIVs balance sheet:

Sample SIV Balance Sheet

Assets	Liabilities
$10 million	$ 9.8 million
	Capital
	$ 0.2 million
$10 million	$10 million

This example leads naturally to the kind of questions we need to answer in sizing the capital adequacy of such an entity: how much resources should the SIV have so that if the SIV is short on assets due to defaults or market value deterioration, it can still pay in full its debt holders?

In sizing the capital adequacy of an SIV, a series of assumptions are being made: the SIV winds down today with current portfolio, the debt is no longer rolled, and there are no further reinvestments. The analysis is an analysis of a static portfolio that winds down and repays liabilities as they come due.

The winddown timeline is presented subsequently:

Time step 0, day of trigger event or starting day for the simulation

♦ Input in the model the current portfolio of assets with type, ratings, notional, market price, and domicile.

♦ Input debt information with tenor, size, and coupon frequency.

Time step 1

♦ Evolve the ratings of assets, derivative counterparties, and market price of the assets.

♦ Inflows are asset coupons, par on the maturing assets, recovery on defaulted assets, hedging counterparty-related inflows.

♦ Outflows are senior expenses and fees, any derivative-related outflows, coupon or principal which are due in that time step.

♦ Sell assets, if needed, to repay liabilities.

Time step 2 onward

♦ Repeat time step 1 till all liabilities are paid back. If there is a shortfall in assets and they are insufficient to repay the debt, the SIV has inadequate AAA capital.

In evolving the portfolio through its winddown period, key risk factors are:

♦ Credit migration including defaults
♦ Recovery
♦ Asset spreads
♦ Interest rates and
♦ Foreign exchange rates.

The market price of the portfolio changes as a consequence of a change in the rating of the asset but also as a consequence of the fluctuation in the spread.

Some vehicles take the asset-by-asset approach and capital charge each asset for its potential loss in value due to credit and market environment. In these companies, when debt is issued and proceeds are used to buy an asset, depending on its rating and tenor, a capital charge is attached to it. The daily capital adequacy test will check whether current market value of the assets adjusted for the capital charges are enough to cover par on the liabilities. These SIVs are referred to as "matrix" SIVs.

Other vehicles take a portfolio simulation approach where credit and market risk variables are stochastically modeled and integrated with a cash flow model in which the waterfall of payments is input. This means that market paths and credit paths are simulated for each asset in the portfolio. The asset cash flows and their market value are then used to pay the liabilities as they become due. If assets are insufficient to pay liabilities, losses will occur. These SIVs are referred to as modeled SIVs.

Final output is a distribution of losses. The latter can be a distribution of the first dollar of loss on the liabilities. Or, it can be an expected loss metric on each of the vehicle's liabilities. Both are relevant in sizing appropriate resources in the vehicle. Figure 14.7 shows a hypothetical loss distribution.

Figure 14.7 is helpful in sizing the capital requirement in a first dollar of loss framework as well as to quantify other loss metrics.

FIGURE 14.7

SIV Loss Distribution.

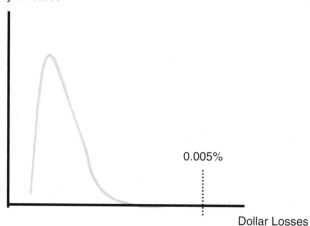

The Two Modeling Approaches: Matrix SIVs versus Modeled SIVs

The purpose of any model proposed by an SIV manager is to measure with AAA certainty the level of capital required to repay all senior liabilities during the enforcement phase. The aim is to ensure that the capital levels calculated and held by the SIV reflect the enforcement operation mode and adequately capture the risks associated with credit loss and market value decline during the winddown. To date, SIV managers have undertaken one of two forms of capital appraisal:

1. Fully modeled simulation of asset and hedge counter-party credit and market value risk for the life of the vehicle's longest liability maturity or

2. Fixed capital charges based upon stressed historical market value declines and credit impaired theoretical worst-case asset portfolios (matrix).

A matrix SIV has an easier daily capital adequacy to test, as each asset has its own capital attached to it. The adequacy test checks whether assets minus liability is always greater than capital.

For a modeled SIV, the adequacy test is the output of a probabilistic model which is run on a portfolio basis without any specific capital allocation to each asset. The model evolves the portfolio through wind-down and checks whether assets are sufficient to repay liabilities. Simulation models, being more accurate, could allow a higher leverage as opposed to matrix SIVs, where the matrix is developed using simple historical spread and transition considerations. However, matrix or modeled, SIVs have to comply with structural leverage constraints that are very close.

Matrix SIVs

- Matrix is easy to calibrate.
- Matrix is easy to measure the attractiveness to different assets using a return on capital.
- Capital charges are fixed using a matrix, but will require regular updates.
- Matrix allows easy and quick identification of the amount of capital than any asset consumes.
- Matrix capital charges are inflexible as not all assets can be accommodated within the one capital charge number concept and there is often a need for several matrices for a SIV's different assets.
- A Matrix calculation does not take into account the actual liability structure that a SIV might have at any particular point in time but determines capital based on a number of set and standard liability structures.
- Substantial work on historical spread volatility is required for a matrix calculation.

Example Matrix* indicating range of capital charges for one asset type.

Tenor Rating	1 year	3 years	5 years	...N years
AAA	2%	3%	5%	...
AA	3%	4%	7%	...
A	6%	9%	12%	...
BBB	10%	15%	18%	...
BB	15%	22%	30%	
...				
N_{Rating}				

* The numbers in this example are for illustrative purposes only.

Without being prescriptive, a methodology of how the matrix is built is presented subsequently. The charge for an asset, let us say AAA five years, is tested to withstand the loss that would occur if it were sold in any month prior to its maturity.

If the charge were, e.g., 5 percent, different liquidation horizons are being tested starting with one month and ending with five year minus one month. The drivers for the decline in value are credit migration which is commensurate with the liquidation horizon, and a spread widening that in the absence of any parametric model could be assumed to be the worst historical widening observed for that asset class and ratings or a multiple of standard deviations (this multiple would cover up to a tail quantile the distribution of absolute changes).

Credit migration is usually described as a homogeneous Markov Chain with a constant transition matrix. An example of such a monthly matrix is given subsequently.

from/ to	AAA	AA	A	BBB	BB	B	CCC	D
AAA	99.184%	0.755%	0.044%	0.001%	0.012%	0.000%	0.000%	0.004%
AA	0.099%	99.216%	0.615%	0.045%	0.004%	0.011%	0.001%	0.009%
A	0.008%	0.215%	99.141%	0.547%	0.049%	0.023%	0.004%	0.012%
BBB	0.005%	0.025%	0.546%	98.711%	0.579%	0.108%	0.013%	0.013%
BB	0.003%	0.010%	0.066%	0.883%	98.086%	0.683%	0.090%	0.179%
B	0.000%	0.006%	0.027%	0.053%	0.484%	98.422%	0.713%	0.295%
CCC	0.016%	0.000%	0.056%	0.125%	0.198%	1.261%	97.331%	1.013%
D	0.000%	0.000%	0.000%	0.000%	0.000%	0.000%	0.000%	100.000%

For example, 99.184 percent is the likelihood that a AAA credit stays AAA over a certain period, in this case a month.

Repricing the asset in a different credit and market environment will result in a decline in price, which should be smaller than the associated capital charge. As most noninvestment data is sparse, one can proxy ratings lower than BB with default (with or without recovery).

As pricing tools one can use either a duration proxy or a more formal pricing tool (discounting the remaining cash flow of the asset in the shocked spread environment).

In the following table, the algorithm given earlier is formalized with a duration proxy for pricing.

Spread move	Loss	Prob from TM	Wghtd loss
$\Delta s_{AAA \to AAA}$	$\Delta s_{AAA \to AAA} \times D_{rem}$	$P_{AAA \to AAA}$	$\Delta s_{AAA \to AAA} \times D_{rem} \times P_{AAA \to AAA}$
$\Delta s_{AAA \to AA}$	$\Delta s_{AAA \to AA} \times D_{rem}$	$P_{AAA \to AA}$	$\Delta s_{AAA \to AA} \times D_{rem} \times P_{AAA \to AA}$
$\Delta s_{AAA \to A}$	$\Delta s_{AAA \to A} \times D_{rem}$	$P_{AAA \to A}$	$\Delta s_{AAA \to A} \times D_{rem} \times P_{AAA \to A}$
$\Delta s_{AAA \to BBB}$	$\Delta s_{AAA \to BBB} \times D_{rem}$	$P_{AAA \to BBB}$	$\Delta s_{AAA \to BBB} \times D_{rem} \times P_{AAA \to BBB}$
$\Delta s_{AAA \to BB}$	$\Delta s_{AAA \to BB} \times D_{rem}$	$P_{AAA \to BB}$	$\Delta s_{AAA \to BB} \times D_{rem} \times P_{AAA \to BB}$
	100%	$P_{AAA \to \leq B}$	$100\% \times P_{AAA \to \leq B}$

Assuming that s_A refers to spread for rating A and s_{AAA} refers to spread for rating AAA:

$$\Delta s_{AAA \to A} = \max(s_A) - \min(s_{AAA})$$

D_{rem} is the remaining duration of the asset and $P_{AAA \to A}$ represents the transition probability from a AAA rating to a A rating commensurate with the liquidation horizon.

Adding the last column gives the loss in value due to transition and spread widening. This loss in value can be further stressed by factors that take into account data imperfections. Most data represent index data. As such data might miss certain bid/offer differentials that can further contribute to the loss in value of the asset. Moreover, if portfolio is not sufficiently diversified to mimic the index data, a correction factor greater than 1 has to be applied to the loss in value. In this way, a decline in price commensurate with the liquidation horizon that is being tested is finally derived.

The above methodology is testing whether the matrix is conservative enough to cover forced sales should the portfolio be 100 percent invested in that asset. This methodology attempts to cover certain stressed scenarios like tail risk, when the portfolio lacks diversity and needs to be liquidated to repay debt.

Further, a cash flow model complements the capital adequacy exercise for matrix SIVs, where different portfolios and liability structures are tested. The goal here is to prove that the derived matrix provides enough resources to repay in full the senior debt.

Simulation SIVs   A stochastic model attempts to model all key risk factors for an SIV. They are credit migration, including default and recovery, asset spreads, interest rate, and FX rates.

Credit migration measures the new credit profile of the portfolio. A downgrade is causing a decline in the market value of the portfolio. Default results in a loss net of recovery for the portfolio.

Asset spreads indicate the evolution in the market price of the portfolio. Both are essential in evaluating the value of the assets that need to be deployed to repay liabilities and hence in measuring any shortfall that might occur. A decline in price can occur because of a downgrade in conjunction with spread widening. Interest rates and FX rates project the mark to market of the derivative contracts. A default of a derivative counterparty could mean a loss for the vehicle and replacement comes at a cost.

Correlation is a key component in the model for each of the above risk factors. There is correlation for pairwise transition. Transition, as well as default correlation, captures joint movements in credit. It helps simulate clusters of default or transition. In projecting spreads, the correlation between intra-and inter-asset classes has to be incorporated. And, finally, there is correlation among interest rates and FX rates. When projecting market rates, correlation between different interest rate curves and foreign exchange curves has to be incorporated.

Calibration of the above-mentioned risk factors is a historical calibration as opposed to risk-neutral. Stability of capital requirement is one of the key components in the risk management of an SIV. Major swings in parameters generated by implied parameters that could cause volatility in the capital requirements are not reflective for the buy and hold business in which an SIV is. Without being prescriptive, examples of such models are being presented subsequently.

A   Correlated transitions
There are a few approaches for modeling correlated transition. Below, three of them are presented:

A1   Historical
The most direct way to estimate joint rating change likelihoods is to examine credit ratings time series across many firms, which are synchronized in time with each other. This method has the advantage that it does not make assumptions as to the underlying process, the joint distribution shape, but has the limitation that it needs extensive data in a pairwise format per region, country, and industry. A factor model can be fit to this data set, hence correlated transition could be modeled using a series of standard normal variates, which will translate via Merton approach into ratings.

A2   Corporate bond prices
A second way to estimate credit correlations using historical data is to examine price histories of corporate bonds. It is intuitive to link bond

prices with changes in credit quality, so a robust history for bond prices may allow estimations of correlated transitions. This approach requires adequate data on bond prices and a model that links bond prices to credit events on a pairwise basis. The main drawback here is historical data. There are a couple of models that attempt to use bond spreads for modeling credit migration.

A3   Asset correlation

There is a third way to model joint transition using as underlying asset correlation.

A3.1.   Asset correlation could be derived from observable firm specific equity returns. This model uses the Merton approach for default simulation, extended to transition. A firm defaults if its asset values go below liabilities. This approach may be extended to derive certain real number thresholds that are linked to a certain rating of the firm. Crossing a threshold is equated to transiting from a rating to another. So a joint migration in the assets' value will be translated in a joint move in credit.

This method has the drawback of overlooking the differences between equity and asset correlations. However, one could make the argument that it is more accurate than using a fixed correlation, is based on more data which is daily available, and is sensitive to countries and industries. Equity variations address market movements as well as credit migration, which is our sole interest in this exercise. In Credit Metrics, Chapter 8, this approach is described in great detail. The reader is referred to Credit Metrics (1997) for a detailed analysis on correlation.

Essentially, a correlation matrix is built that captures joint movements for asset values. Then, each time step (e.g., each month) a multi-normal draw with this correlation matrix is performed and its numeric outcome is used to determine the new credit ratings.

The correlation matrix is derived using the obligor's participation to a country and industry and uses as underlying equity returns.

Looking at equity for a obligor's transition is a well-accepted framework in the Merton/MKMV approach and is one of the few available proxies for defining and simulating performance. What gives comfort is that data for this method is observable, is available daily. Datametrics is a web based product that gives access to such correlation information. The data covers a wide range of countries and industries in those countries. Currently, there is a lot of research done to strip out of the equity returns the credit information and use that to find asset correlation because the aim is to find credit migration and not market movements.

A3.2. The above model can be used with constant historical asset correlations as well. These correlation levels can be derived from the joint transition information. The problem that needs to be solved is the following. Assume for simplicity two states: default and nondefault. Assuming same Merton framework for the asset's value, the question is to find the asset correlation that best matches the theoretical variance of the number of defaults with the observed variance of the number of defaults. The number of unknowns is defined by the number of pairwise correlations one is looking for. Asset correlation can be pairwise constant for an industry and the same for all industries. A second asset correlation can be searched for interindustry. The problem can be further refined to incorporate countries and regions. Extension of the problem to incorporate transition can be easily done, using same Merton assumption for transitions, namely that credit worthiness underlying ratings transition could be modeled with a normal variate.

Finally, a simple example of correlated transition simulation with two obligors is given for illustration purposes only.

First, one needs to use a transition matrix to determine the probability of moving to each rating. These probabilities are further used to set thresholds in a normal distribution. Each threshold is corresponding to a possible rating outcome. Then draw a set of correlated normal deviates equal in number to the number of obligors in the portfolio. Finally, use these numbers, combined with the thresholds, to determine the forward credit rating of each obligor.

A convenient way to think about the thresholds is in terms of Figure 14.8. Underlying ratings transition, there exists a "credit performance" random variable that is normally distributed. Change in letter rating is merely a reflection of the realization of "credit performance." A credit A is migrating with different probabilities to the other ratings and has the highest likelihood to stay A.

A bell-shaped curve representing the asset value as a standard normal density function is sliced in such a way that the areas underneath equate the transition probabilities to other ratings.

Note that the probabilities of moving to AAA, CCC, and D are too small to be seen in the figure. In the bell-shaped figure, the area beneath the curve is divided into smaller areas, each of which is in a one-to-one correspondence with a certain credit worthiness of the asset. The reader can see that the middle area below the curve corresponds to the high probability of the obligor staying in its current state.

To use an example, consider two obligors, A and B, and suppose that obligor A is an A-rated entity, whereas obligor B is an B-rated entity.

FIGURE 14.8

Thresholds for Obligor A in the Example.

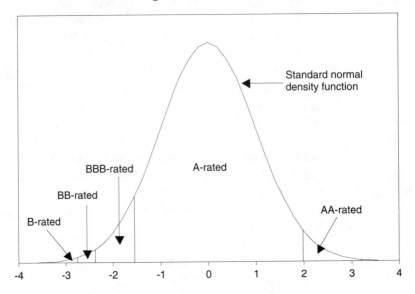

Furthermore, suppose that we have determined that the migration between these two obligors has a correlation of 0.3. Assume that A-rated and B-rated entities have the one-year transition probabilities given subsequently:

Final rating	Obligor A	Obligor B
AAA	0.0007	0.0001
AA	0.0227	0.0010
A	0.9069	0.0028
BBB	0.0611	0.0046
BB	0.0056	0.0895
B	0.0025	0.8080
CCC	0.0004	0.044
D	0.0001	0.05

These probabilities are used to determine the thresholds of a normal distribution.

For example, considering obligor A, we need to determine the threshold such that 0.01 percent of the draws from a normal distribution will be less than this threshold. That is, if we denote by x the asset value, we want to choose y such that

$$P(x \leq y) = 0.0001, \quad \text{where } x \sim N(0, 1)$$

Thus, y will be determined from the inverse normal cumulative distribution function and is given by the value -3.719. Similarly, in order to assure a 0.04 percent probability that obligor A migrates to a CCC rating, we must choose y such that

$$P(-3.719 \leq x \leq y) = 0.0004 \Rightarrow P(x \leq y) = 0.0001 + 0.0004 \quad \text{when } x \sim N(0, 1)$$

This gives a value for y of -3.29. Applying this algorithm iteratively, we may derive the following thresholds (see also Figure 14.8):

Final rating	Obligor A	Obligor B
AAA	na	na
AA	3.195	3.719
A	1.988	3.062
BBB	−1.478	2.661
BB	−2.382	2.387
B	−2.748	1.293
CCC	−3.290	−1.316
D	−3.719	−1.645

There is no threshold for the AAA rating, since everything greater than the AA threshold is by definition AAA. Having determined the thresholds, to conclude our example, we now need to draw two normally distributed random numbers that have a correlation of 0.3. To do this, we draw two normally distributed numbers, say 1.5961 and −2.5299, and multiply by the square root of the correlation matrix (obtained using singular value decomposition or Cholesky decomposition) to obtain the two correlated numbers 1.5961 and −1.9345. The threshold look-up table shows that 1.5961 indicates that obligor A has maintained its A rating, whereas −1.9345 indicates that obligor B has defaulted.

B Recovery analysis

Each time an obligor defaults in the simulation, a recovery cashflow for bond obligations of that obligor will be posted at a later time step. Depending on the time to settlement and settlement mechanism, this recovery time may be further reduced. This cashflow is calculated from the total exposure to that obligor (taking into account investments and derivative exposure and the appropriate netting rules) as follows:

$$\text{Recovery amount} = \text{Obligor exposure} \times \text{Recovery \%}$$

B1 Beta distribution

A Beta distribution is now commonly accepted method for modeling the recovery percentage that has now been adopted for use in a variety of modeling applications.

The constant pdf (the flat line) shows that the standard uniform distribution is a special case of the beta distribution.

This distribution has the following attractive properties for the purpose of modeling recoveries (see Figure 14.9):

1. Bell curve distribution
2. Bounded at 0 percent and 100 percent
3. Ability to derive distribution parameters to fit mean and standard deviation
4. Can be sampled relatively quickly within a simulation

The probability density function for a Beta distribution with parameters a and b is shown as follows:

$$f_{a,b}(x) = \frac{\Gamma(a+b)}{\Gamma(a)\Gamma(b)} x^{a-1}(1-x)^{b-1} \quad \text{for } x \in [0, 1] \text{ else } f_{a,b}(x) = 0,$$

where the gamma function is defined as $\Gamma(a) = \int_{x=0}^{\infty} x^{a-1} e^{-x} \, dx$.

FIGURE 14.9

Range of Shapes Obtainable from a Beta Distribution.

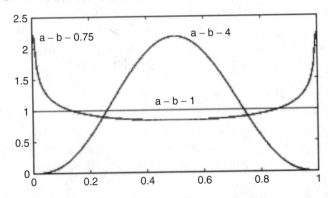

This distribution has analytic mean and standard deviation formulae, allowing easy calibration:

$$\mu = \frac{a}{a+b} \quad \text{and} \quad \sigma^2 = \frac{ab}{(a+b+1)(a+b)^2}.$$

B2 Findings

For corporate bonds, studies show that the seniority of the bond is the key driver in estimating the recovery. The curves in Figure 14.10 have been obtained by matching the mean and variance of the beta distribution with the mean and variance reported in Carty and Lieberman for each seniority.

Structured Finance Issuers The rating agencies have recently published analyses using industry and rating at origination as the primary drivers for recovery.

S&P's study suggests "a fairly significant relationship exists between the original credit rating and the repayment rates and principal loss rates" and have produced Table 14.2:

This study suggests that the principal drivers for recovery for structured finance issuers are asset sector and rating at origination.

FIGURE 14.10

Curves Obtained by Matching the Mean and Variance of Beta Distribution.

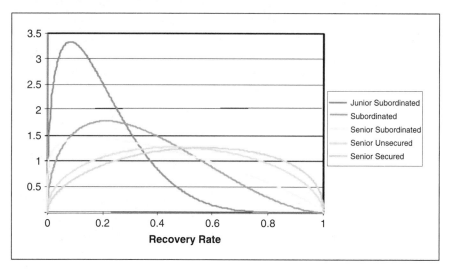

TABLE 14.2

Estimated Ultimate Recovery Rates for U.S. Structured Finance Defaults (%)

Original	ABS	CMBS	RMBS
AAA	78.00	99.00	98.00
AA	52.99	73.00	72.00
A	40.00	62.00	60.00
BBB	33.00	54.00	53.00
BB	25.00	46.00	45.00
B	22.00	43.00	42.00

Source: Standard & Poor's Research—Principal Repayment and Loss Behaviour of Defaulted U.S. Structured Finance Securities, published 10 Jan 2005 by Erkan Erturk and Thomas Gillis.

C Asset spread simulation

In an SIV, fixed rate assets are swapped to floaters using swap derivatives. As such the pure interest rate risk is hedged and the remaining risk for the fluctuation in price comes from the credit spread of the asset. This is the spread over Libor of the floating rate asset swap package. The spread modeling is done for each asset type, rating category and tenor. For missing ratings or tenors, different interpolation methods or other proxies could be considered.

An example of credit spread model is a mixed Brownian and jump diffusion, that would capture fat tails of credit spreads. In the example that follows, obligors in same asset class rating and tenor behave the same. One can refine a model to add a pure idiosyncratic risk.

The process below used for credit spreads guarantees positive spreads while capturing jumps and mean reversion. The jumps are modeled assuming that jump times follow an exponential distribution with jumps equally likely to be up or down.

The spread processes is described by the following equation:

$$dY_t = \alpha(\theta - Y_t)dt + \sigma dW_t + dN_t \quad \text{where } Y_t \text{ is the logarithm of the credit spread,}$$

where W_t is a standard Brownian motion, N_t is a jump of magnitude a with the probability of a jump up and down equal and where the jump times follow an exponential distribution with parameter λ, α is the speed of mean reversion as in the Ornstein–Uhlenbeck specification, θ is the long-term mean of the credit spread, and σ is the volatility parameter.

In summary, the log of the credit spread will mean revert back to the long term mean θ with mean reversion speed α. The process will experience a stochastic movement with volatility σ and it will also experience jumps of size a where the jump times are exponentially distributed.

C1   Estimating the parameters for the jump diffusion process
The credit-spread process is conditionally normal, i.e., given that there is an up-jump, a down-jump or no jump, the distribution is normal with a corresponding mean. We can decompose the likelihood function into a product of normal distributions weighted by the probability of having a jump or no jump at all.*

Let x_i denote the change in log returns over the period $(i-1)\Delta$ to $i\Delta$. We have

$$\mu_i = E_{(i-1)\Delta}[x_i] = (\theta - Y_{(i-1)\Delta})(1 - \exp(-\alpha\Delta))$$

$$\sigma_i^2 = \mathrm{Var}_{(i-1)\Delta}[x_i] = (1 - \exp(-2\alpha\Delta))\frac{(\lambda a^2 + \sigma^2)}{2\alpha}$$

and the log-likelihood function is:

$$L(\mathbf{x}\,|\,\Gamma) = \sum_{i=1}^{n} \ln\Big\{ e^{-\lambda\Delta}\,\phi(x_i, \mu_i, \sigma_i^2)$$

$$+ \sum_{j=1}^{\infty} \frac{1}{2} e^{-\lambda\Delta}\frac{(\lambda\Delta)^j}{j!}\Big[\phi(x_i, \mu_i - ja, \sigma_i^2) + \phi(x_i, \mu_i + ja, \sigma_i^2)\Big]\Big\},$$

where $\phi(h, k, \sigma^2)$ is the normal density at point h with mean k and variance σ^2, $\Gamma = (\alpha, \theta, \sigma, \lambda, a)$ and $\underline{x}$ is the vector of n log credit spread changes.

For practical purposes one should truncate the infinite sum at $j = 15$ or less.

The same model can be used for spread levels as well. Calibration can be done at the univariate level but should be tested at the multivariate level, namely for all ratings and tenors in one asset class. This is important because simulated spreads should not cross each other. This type of constraint should be imposed in any goodness-of-fit exercise.

---

*An Empirical Investigation in Credit Spread Indices, Prigent, Renault & Scaillet, September 2000.

A convenient and robust goodness-of-fit exercise is to check whether the mean of the simulated path statistics match the historical statistics. That means that one needs to compute the average of the statistics (e.g., maxima, tail quantiles, median, minima, standard deviation, kurtosis, etc.) for the simulated paths and compare them with the statistics of the realized historical path. The simulated paths would be simulated for all ratings and tenors in an asset class incorporating correlation of the historical noise and imposing noncrossing constraints. Path analysis is important for simulating portfolio behavior as each Monte Carlo path is a potential realization of a spread evolution. This goodness-of-fit test can be complemented by an analysis of the errors of the fitting exercise as well as by a point in time analysis of the simulated distribution.

Recalibration is done periodically, semiannually, or annually.

D   Interest rate risk

Although not directly exposed to interest rate risk, if a counterparty defaults, there is a cost of replacement. All assets have the interest rate portion of their coupon microhedged with a third party counterparty. Derivative contracts need to be valued and losses covered by capital. A projection of interest rates allows also to capture any basis mismatch between assets and liabilities.

An example of mean reverting interest rate model is the CIR (Cox, Ingersoll, and Ross) (SIV outlook report, 2006) model for interest rate evolution:

$$dr = (\eta - \gamma r)dt + \sqrt{\alpha r}\, dZ_r, \tag{1}$$

where r is the spot interest rate (1/time), η/γ is the steady state mean rate (1/time), $1/\gamma$ is the mean reversion time-scale (time), α is the interest rate volatility parameter (1/time^2), and Z_r is the Wiener process to simulate interest rates it should be scaled to the appropriate time step by multiplying with $dt = 1/0.833$ for a monthly granularity for example.

The three parameters in this model can be chosen to best reproduce the empirical long-term mean, standard deviation, and mean reversion time-scale and/or can also be chosen to impose desired probabilities of exceeding specified thresholds of interest rates. The goal below is to illustrate, as an example, the usage of the CIR model for the short rate by calibrating to historical observations of that rate.

Predicting or reproducing the interest rate term structure by invoking arbitrage-free pricing often involves multifactor models that are more complex that the single factor CIR model used here. Interest rates are assumed uncorrelated to credit spreads. See Appendix A for the calibration of the CIR model.

E   FX rates

FX Evolution may be required by the need of valuing assets in a different currency or cross currency swaps for defaulting counterparties.

Evolution of an exchange rate could be modeled using a lognormal process as in:

$$de(t) = e(t)(r_D(t) - r_F(t))dt + e(t)\sigma(t)dw(t),$$

where $r_D(t)$ is the domestic short rate process, $r_F(t)$ is the foreign short rate process, and $\sigma(t)$ is the volatility parameter determined from historical time series.

SIV Tests

Market Risk

One important feature of the SIVs is that they are market risk neutral. They are not taking position on where interest rates or FX might move. As opposed to most hedge funds, they are not betting on market directionality. The SIV microhedges its positions on an asset-by-asset basis. If the hedge provider defaults, the SIV manager has to find a replacement for the hedging counterparty. When an asset is sold, it is sold as a package with its associated hedge, such that the SIV does not enter into open IR or FX positions.

Each asset is hedged to floating rate USD exposure using interest rate or cross currency swaps. That is why, often, SIVs are referred to as credit arbitrage vehicles.

The hedging counterparties are introducing additional credit risk. As such, they are treated as any other asset and capital is allocated against such counterparties.

An SIV is equipped with IR and FX sensitivity test to provide the verification of its necessary representation of market neutrality. These tests basically measure the change in NAV due to a sudden IR shock of each point of the yield curve or of the entire yield curve. Tolerance limits are set for each structure. These tolerance limits usually allow for a residual basis mismatch. An uncured breach of an IR/FX sensitivity test triggers wind down for the SIV.

In the following figure, the reader can see a simplified example on how a SIV manages its IR/FX exposure by putting on hedges for both assets and liabilities to convert both into floating USD.

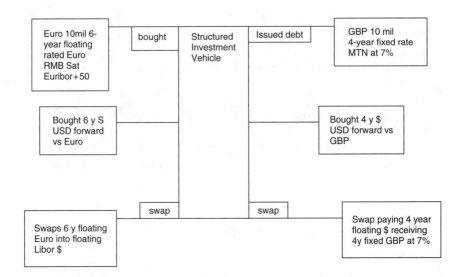

To monitor their exposure to interest rates and FX rates, SIV managers use a simple deterministic test. The test helps identify the absence of a hedge or a significant mismatch between assets and liabilities. They are based on shocking current interest rate curve and revaluing assets and liabilities in the new environment. If there is perfect hedging, there is no sensitivity to the yield curve movement. The change on the asset side is counterbalanced by the change on the liability side. A few such tests are presented subsequently. The tolerance level is positive indicating that there is room for a residual mismatch. Breach of this tolerance level sends the vehicle in a cure period. If the test is not cured within five business days, the vehicle goes into irreversible winddown.

Parallel Yield Curve Shift

All the inflows are discounted with the respective zero coupon LIBOR yield curve for each currency. This test involves a parallel shift in yield curve for each currency by increasing and decreasing every point on the curve by one basis point (see Figure 14.11). The aggregate impact on the present value (PV) of the SIV net asset value of all currencies must not be more than a low tolerance, for example, 0.20 bps.

FIGURE 14.11

Parallel Yield Curve Shift.

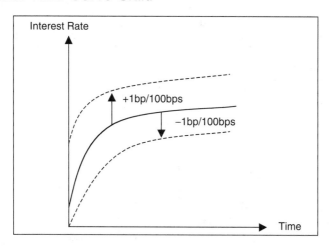

The methodology works as follows:

1. Calculate the PV for each currency portfolio with each respective yield curve using the following minimum monthly points:

1	3	6	9	12	24	36	48	60	84	120

   and such other independent points on the curve as will ensure that this test is applied to the maturity of the longest dated asset or rated liability and also reflects the asset composition of the SIV at the time of the test.

2. Aggregate all PV of all currency portfolios by converting first the non-$ denominated portfolio by the spot rate;

3. Calculate the PV of all senior liabilities, using the same methodology as in steps 1 and 2;

4. Subtract the PV of all currency portfolios from the PV of all senior liabilities. This gives the base NAV or NAV_0;

5. Replicate steps 1 to 4 but move each yield curve up by one basis point and then calculate the new net asset value aggregating the worst case absolute values regardless of positive or negative results (NAV_{Up});

6. Replicate step 5 but move each yield curve down by one basis point and calculate the new net asset value aggregating the worst case absolute values regardless of positive or negative results (NAV_{Down});

7. Compare the results of NAV_0 minus NAV_{Up}, and NAV_0 minus NAV_{Down}. The highest absolute value of these two calculations is called NAV_1.

Example
Assume that an SIV has two bonds, one denominated in US$, and another in Euro and the $/€ spot rate = 0.90. Also assume that outstanding senior liabilities are $180.

The US asset pays: $LIBOR + 50 basis points has a three-year maturity and a PV of $100.

The Euro asset pays: three-month EURIBOR + 30 basis points also matures in year 3 and has a € PV value of 100. PV of asset = $90.

PV of the portfolio is therefore = $190.

Senior liabilities pay three-month LIBOR + 20 basis points and consist of a principal bullet in year 2 with a PV = $180.

Net asset value$_0$ $(NAV_0) = \$190 - \$180 = \$10$.

The parallel shift calculations are followed, resulting in $NAV_1 = \$9.999$.

Thus, the test will be passed if $(NAV_0 - NAV_1)/NAV_0 < 0.2$ bps.

In our example, $(\$10 - \$9.999)/\$10 = 0.01\%$ or 0.1 basis point, therefore the test is passed.

The test is then repeated assuming a 100 bps parallel shift.

Point-by-Point Yield Curve Shift
This test involves an instantaneous one basis point shift (up and down) of the zero coupon LIBOR yield curves for each currency at each specified point along the respective curve. The manager will, therefore, be running NAV tests as described before assuming a yield curve shift of +1 bps at the one-month point only for all yield curves. It will then rerun the tests using a −1 bps shift at the one-month point only. The test will be repeated assessing the same shifts at the three-month point only, etc. The largest NAV change result from all of these runs is compared to NAV_0 in the same way as the parallel shift test (Figure 14.12).

This test assumes that yield curve do not necessary move in a parallel fashion. The test particularly stresses cash flows that might be concentrated in a specific part of the curve.

Spot Foreign Exchange
This test involves individually changing the value of each currency relative to the U.S. dollar by 1 percent (up and down). The aggregate impact for all eligible currencies may not result in more than a preset level of

FIGURE 14.12

Point-by-Point Yield Curve Shift.

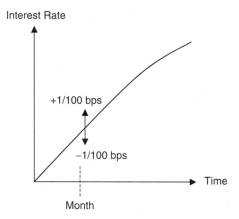

tolerance, for example, 2.0 bps movement (up or down) of the SIV net asset value. Again, the new net asset value is calculated by aggregating the worst-case absolute values regardless of the positive or negative result.

Liquidity Risk

Liquidity risk in an SIV arises in two ways:

1. Rollover of current outstanding debt or
2. Sale of assets to meet senior liabilities.

Because the assets mature in four years on average but the liabilities fall due between one month and 18 months, cash from maturing assets cannot be relied upon to pay liabilities. The SIV relies on refinancing existing debt and repaying outstanding debt with new issued debt. When market conditions are not favorable to roll current debt, the SIV faces a liquidity problem. Not being able to roll debt can cause the winddown of the SIV if it needs to liquidate the portfolio to repay the debt. So liquidity management is a very important task for the manager and that is why in addition to the capital adequacy model, an SIV is equipped with special models to cover for liquidity shortages for limited periods of time.

The liquidity model is a tool to provide information about the vehicle's internal liquidity relative to its liability. This is very important in the context of funding longer term assets with the issuance of commercial paper. The liquidity model usually looks at daily inflow and outflow in rolling five business days intervals to determine the peak cumulative potential cash need over one year. The requirements for liquidity are covered by credit lines, or by assets that are deemed to be "liquid," meaning readily available for sale at a price close to their current market price.

Daily cash inflows and outflows from the vehicle drive the liquidity requirement. Unlike other areas of structured finance, 100 percent liquidity facilities are not required as the SIV is subject to many stringent tests and constraints and benefit can be given to the liquidity of the assets that it holds.

The SIV has to have an appropriate mix of liquidity lines and internal liquidity to be able to repay some level of its short maturing liabilities when they fall due. This risk takes on great importance in an SIV because most vehicles fund the purchase of longer-term assets with the issuance of commercial paper that may be rolling every few days. Medium-term notes can also be issued and as these are not normally maturity-matched to specific assets liquidity risk arises here as well.

Given the dynamic feature of the SIV, it is appropriate to measure the liquidity levels in the SIV on a dynamic basis referred to as the NCO tests. Some SIV managers may actually refer to this test as the MCO (maximum cumulative outflow). This test measures on a deterministic basis the projected one-year net payments for the vehicle. In this way, the manager can reserve liquid resources to cover his short-term need and avoid selling longer-dated assets for these payments which would then make him exposed to market risk unnecessarily.

NCO Tests

NCO tests are normally calculated for each rolling 1, 5, 10, and 15 business day period commencing on the next day of calculation through and including the day which is one year from the day of such calculation (i.e., the vehicle needs to determine on a daily basis its 1, 5, 10, and 15 day peak NCO requirements over the next year). SIV managers may decide to have other NCO tests beside these standards depending on the specifics of the individual vehicle.

The NCO tests are produced by subtracting daily Outflows (i.e., interest and principal on senior and junior debt, all admin and operating expenses, and all net payments on derivatives contracts) from daily Inflows (i.e., all interest and principal received from the SIV's assets) and cumulating the results of these individual calculations over the relevant period. The SIV will need to ensure that the cumulative peak amount from the NCO tests is covered by eligible liquidity. Eligible liquidity is provided through a mixture of bank liquidity lines and liquid assets held by the SIV.

The table that follows shows an example of the NCO5 test for the next six business days. The same "rolling first day" method will be used in calculating the 10-day and 15-day periods.

Such calculation must be done for all NCOs up to one year, i.e., approximately 240 business days.

Time	I	O	I–O	NCO5 T	NCO5 T+1	NCO5 T+2	NCO5 T+3	NCO5 T+4	NCO5 T+5	NCO5 T+6
T										
T+1	5	25	–20	–20						
T+2	4	20	–16	–36	–16					
T+3	2	0	2	–34	–14	2				
T+4	3	4	–1	–35	–15	1	–1			
T+5	4	3	1	–34	–14	–2	0	1		
T+6	2	2	0		–14	2	0	1	0	
T+7	4	3	1		3	1	2	1	1	

For example, for each five-day period, there will be five different cumulative values, except for the last 4, 3, 2, and 1 five business days of the year. The NCO will be the largest of the five different values, calculated as follows:

Day 1 cumulative sum = Daily NCO for day 1

Day 2 cumulative sum = Sum of daily NCOs for days 1 and 2

Day 3 cumulative sum = Sum of daily NCOs for days 1, 2 and 3

Day 4 cumulative sum = Sum of daily NCOs for days 1, 2, 3 and 4

Day 5 cumulative sum = Sum of daily NCOs for days 1, 2, 3, 4 and 5

In the previous example, the largest five business days NCO is –36, which is the two-day cumulative sum of the daily NCO for days $T+1$, and $T+2$. In this example if the NCO5 test was run for the rest of the year (i.e., out to $T+364$) and no higher NCO5 amount was encountered, then the vehicle will need to have eligible liquidity at least equivalent to $36 millions. The vehicle will run the other NCO tests (e.g., NCO1, NCO10, and NCO15) and if any produces a higher NCO requirement than the NCO5 peak discussed, that higher amount will become the eligible liquidity requirement.

Eligible liquidity can be provided through a mixture of external liquidity facilities from A-1+ rated banks and highly liquid assets held by the SIV. The expectation is that the SIV will cover the peak NCO5 Eligible liquidity requirement with external liquidity lines only (on the basis that a five-day liquidity period for even highly liquidity assets is not an appropriate assumption at AAA). So, in the above example, if say the NCO1 test resulted in a peak of $30, the NCO 10 test resulted in a peak of $80 and the NCO15 test resulted in a requirement of $60, the actual liquidity amount held by the vehicle, based on the calculations on that day, would be $80 with $36 provided by bank liquidity lines (i.e., the peak NCO5 requirement) and the remaining $44 coming from liquid assets.

Recent Developments in SIV Land

Most recent SIVs have increased their exposure to non-USD assets and non-USD capital by creating ring fenced subportfolios in non-USD currencies. SIVs have expressed interest in alternative types of funding, via credit linked notes or repurchase agreements. In the past few years, SIVs have attempted to rate their capital notes. This is driven by risk management motivations, in an effort to quantify all exposures for internal purposes or for the benefit of the purchasers of the note. To date more than 11 billion of capital notes has been privately or publicly rated not higher than A. To rate the capital notes A or BBB, one needs to show that the likelihood of losing a first dollar on the capital notes is A or BBB remote. Once the vehicle enters winddown, capital will be used to repay the debt, and hence capital notes will suffer a loss. So, the focus of the analysis is to quantify the likelihood of the vehicle to not enter irreversible winddown. If one makes the assumption that the manager is diligent enough to not force the vehicle into winddown, the only drivers remain to be a massive rating deterioration and a spread widening that would consume all the excess capital and hit the capital adequacy test. So basically, the excess capital will have to cover all the bad credit cycles as well as market spread widening. The excess capital would cover for defaults and any loss in market value of the portfolio. Once it is used, and the minimum level of capital attained, the vehicle is very likely to fall short of the AAA adequacy test and go into winddown, when most likely the capital notes would suffer a positive loss.

Older and newer SIVs have expressed interest in entering other types of markets like credit derivative markets, where they act as protection sellers.

It is also worth mentioning that other types of operating companies have borrowed from SIV technology to a greater or lesser degree (mostly to manage market and liquidity risk), like repurchase agreement vehicles as well as credit derivative companies.

OTHER TYPES OF QUASI-OPERATING COMPANIES

In addition to the SIVs, other operating companies have been designed to serve a special purpose. Derivative product companies are intermediaries between financial institutions (known as their parent or sponsor) and their third party counterparties. Derivative product companies (DPCs) intermediate swaps between the sponsor and third parties under approved ISDA master agreement. Enhanced subsidiaries differ from other derivative-product subsidiaries, as their credit ratings do not rely on their parent's guarantee. A DPC may engage in over-the-counter interest rate, currency and equity swaps, and options as well as certain exchange-traded futures and options depending on its individual structure. A DPC is capitalized at a level appropriate for the scope of its business activities and desired rating. DPCs have been set up in most cases to overcome credit sensitivity in the derivative product markets. There are two types of DPCs: continuation or termination structures. The continuation structures are designed to honor their contracts to full maturity even when a winddown event occurs, whereas the termination structures are designed to honor their contracts to full maturity, or should certain events occur, to terminate and cash settle all their contracts prior to their final maturity. The chart presented subsequently illustrates a DPCs role as an intermediary with offsetting trades.

The DPCs have AAA rating and are often projected as the AAA face of the sponsor. They are market risk neutral by mirroring their trades with third parties with the parent or sponsor. They are exposed to credit risk of third parties. As with the SIVs, the structure is equipped with exit strategies and resources that ensure that even in a winddown scenario, the vehicle meets with AAA certainty its derivative obligations.

The market for derivative product companies started in early 1990. Every bank that wanted to be eligible as an AAA counterparty in derivative contracts, sponsored its own derivative product company. Currently there are 15 active DPCs.

- Bank of America Financial Products, Inc.
- Bear Stearns Financial Products, Inc.
- BT CreditPlus (closed)

- Credit Lyonnais Derivative Program
- GS Financial Products International L.P. (closing)
- Lehman Brothers Derivative Products, Inc.
- Lehman Brothers Financial Products, Inc.
- Merrill Lynch Derivatives Products AG
- Morgan Stanley Derivative Products, Inc.
- Nomura Derivative Products Inc.
- Paribas Derives Guarantis
- Sakura Prime (closed)
- Salomon Swapco, Inc.
- SMBC Derivative Products, Ltd
- JP Morgan Enhanced ISDA Program

Once a trigger event occurs, the DPC freezes its operations and active management. The termination DPCs accelerate all their contracts and exit the market in a short termination window, typically 15 days. Hence, the termination payments that the counterparties owe to the DPC will be passed through to the parent to close out the mirror contracts. If the counterparties default, capital will be used for those payments.

If the DPC owes money to the counterparty, the parent is delivering that termination payment to the DPC from the mirror trade, in which parent owes money to the DPC. That amount is quantified and held as collateral posted by the parent on behalf of the DPC.

Practically, two models are being developed for a DPC: a credit model in which capital is quantified to cover for third party defaults, a VaR type of model in which the amount that the parent owes to the DPC on all its trades is quantified over a 15-day horizon.

Quantitative techniques in sizing capital adequacy for a DPC rely on a market rate generator in which new market environment is projected for the lifetime of the portfolio. This means that interest rates in each currency and foreign exchange rates are projected in a correlated fashion up to the longest tenor of the swap book.

The forward rates require models for the entire yield curve. The financial literature provides a wide range of models from one to multiple factor models.

Principal component analysis (PCA) involves a mathematical procedure that transforms a number of (possibly) correlated variables into a (smaller) number of uncorrelated variables called *principal components*. The first principal component accounts for as much of the variability in the data as possible, and each succeeding component accounts for as much of the remaining variability as possible.

The mathematical technique used in PCA is called eigen analysis: it solves for the eigenvalues and eigenvectors of a square symmetric matrix, the covariance matrix of key points on the yield curve. The eigenvector associated with the largest eigenvalue has the same direction as the first principal component. The eigenvector associated with the second largest eigenvalue determines the direction of the second principal component. The sum of the eigenvalues equals the trace of the square matrix and the maximum number of eigenvectors equals the number of rows (or columns) of this matrix.

In most cases, two or three PCAs are enough to explain more than 90 percent of the variance covariance matrix.

Once the market environment is simulated, valuation modules will be used to project the mark-to-market of each swap contract. By combining market paths with credit paths (in which the credit worthiness of the counterparty is simulated), one can see where capital is being deployed to cover for losses. The potential losses corresponding to each market path can be obtained by combining the results of default simulations and the counterparty exposures. A consideration of losses across all market paths permits the construction of a distribution of potential credit losses. The necessary credit enhancement to protect against losses at a given level of confidence may be obtained. This risk model can also quantify the potential change in the portfolio's value over a period of time.

A DPC with a continuation structure generally receives collateral from the parent to cover its exposure to the parent resulting from the back-to-back trades. This collateral amount, after appropriate discount factors are applied, is equivalent to the net mark-to-market value of the DPC's portfolio of contracts with its parent. Upon the occurrence of certain events, however, the management of the DPC's portfolio will be passed on to a contingent manager.

In the short period prior to the transfer of portfolio management to the contingent manager, the value of the DPC's contracts with its parent could rise. Using the capabilities of the risk model, the potential increase in the DPC's credit exposure to the parent may be quantified.

In a termination structure, the value of the DPC's portfolio can change over the period beginning with the last regular valuation date and ending at the early termination valuation date upon occurrence of a termination trigger event. Again, the potential change in the portfolio's value may be determined at the desired level of confidence by using the same risk model.

The DPC's liquidity needs also require evaluation. The DPC must be able to meet its obligations on a timely basis. These include its payables to its counterparties under its derivative contracts, and to its parent resulting from the back-to-back transactions and, in certain cases, obligation to meet margin calls on the exchange-traded futures contracts used as hedges. The risk model may be used in determining the liquidity needs of the DPC by using simulated market evolution and evaluating the current portfolio of derivative contracts and the likely portfolio of offsetting hedges. Using the model, a distribution of daily portfolio positions can be simulated, thus establishing, at an appropriate level of confidence, the potential liquidity need of the DPC on a daily basis and over a specific time horizon.

CREDIT DERIVATIVE PRODUCT COMPANIES

Since credit default swaps made their debut in 1991, their marketplace has grown exponentially. This has created a new asset type for derivative product companies, called credit derivative product companies (CDPCs).

Generally, a CDPC is a special-purpose entity that sells credit protection under credit default swaps or certain approved forms of insurance policies. Sometimes, they can also buy credit protection. A CDPC is organized to invest in credit risk exposure in certain segments of the markets through the use of credit derivatives or insurance policies.

The following chart illustrates the typical structure of a CDPC that sells credit protection under a credit default swap.

The AAA counterparty rating assigned to a CDPC ensures that all obligations of the company are met with AAA certainty, should a trigger event occur and send the vehicle into winddown.

The CDPCs rated to date are listed:

1- **Primus** AAA ICR—focused on single name primarily
Notional approximately $13 billion
Launch: 2001

2- **Athilon** AAA ICR—focused on tranche business primarily
senior and super senior tranches
Notional approximately $10 billion
Launch: 2005

3- Theta AAA operating program—focused on single name primarily
Notional approximately $2 billion
Launch: 2005

Cdpcs and Cdos

The two structures are indeed in the same type of business: selling protection on a portfolio of reference entities. These reference entities can be single name corporates, single name ABS, baskets of names or structured credit, namely indices or CDO tranches. The tranches can be anywhere in the capital structure of the CDO ranging from the first loss position to super senior.

CDPCs are evergreen vehicles, whereas CDOs have a finite life. In addition, the risk model of a CDPC has to account for all obligations of the CDPC including termination payments on credit default swap contracts. In a CDO, such obligations are subordinated in the waterfall and the risk model does not address the likelihood of such obligations to be paid.

When a credit default swap counterparty defaults, a termination payment may need to be calculated. The termination payment is the potential future mark-to-market of the credit derivative contract. This termination payment on the swap contract is the expected risky discounted value of the remaining cash flows of the swap. The key variables in computing the forward value of the swap are the then-current rating of the entity of which protection is sold or bought and the potential future credit swap premium. For each counterparty, the termination payments on the underlying contracts are computed and aggregated at the counterparty level if netting is applicable. For each out-of-the-money position with each counterparty, capital is reserved. The termination payments on swap contracts of a CDPC are AAA obligations *pari passu* with payments on credit events and other AAA obligations.

The future rating of single names can be explicitly modeled using a multiperiod transition matrix, or a distribution of ratings could be inferred from the timing of defaults of the underlying obligors (in case a time to default model was chosen). Given the current liquidity in the market of certain tenors on the credit default swap curve, it is likely that a model for a full-term structure for the credit default swap premium would be hard to calibrate. As a simple method of implementing proxy, a flat-term structure may be assumed at the most liquid point on the curve (e.g., five years). That point could be projected forward using a model that takes into consideration serial correlation, fat tails, and correlation across different industries and ratings. Further, the simulated premium is used to derive the risky discount factors, which, when applied to the remaining premium payment, would compute the fair market value at the then-current time step. The credit derivative market is expected to become more liquid, and, in the future, term structure models for the entire credit default swap curve are expected to be developed. This would allow further enhancements of the valuation modules currently used by the market.

The fair market value of a credit default swap on a structured credit depends on the behavior of the underlying portfolio of reference entities. As opposed to a single name, where the default is a binary event, a structured credit is approached based on expected loss of the tranche. For example, for a first-loss position, losses due to defaults have a direct impact on the size of the tranche. For a mezzanine tranche, defaults will impact the position in the capital structure of that tranche and, potentially, the size of the tranche. At each time step, the distribution of losses to the tranche can be calculated based on aggregating losses in the underlying portfolio. Then, the incremental expected losses in each period can be derived and discounted to size the net PV of aggregate loss on the tranche. Pricing of the tranche is affected by the defaults in the underlying pool and by the movement of rating/credit spreads of the nondefaulting entities. Correlation among the credits in the portfolio is another key input in the pricing module of a tranche. Reader is referred to recent research papers on correlation term structure and impact on tranche pricing.

CDPCs and SIVs

As with an SIV, the CDPC has a dedicated management team that decides to increase or decrease leverage as they see appropriate. Although the two have different businesses and, perhaps, motivations, in the recent years the two have borrowed from each other important structural features. As such, we have seen SIVs trying to enter the credit derivative market and sell and buy protection. So their risk model had to be adjusted for default of the underlying and swap termination payments.

Also CDPCs, which traditionally held their capital in highly rated investments expressed interest in investing and holding higher yielding assets. If the eligible investments include riskier assets, like corporates and/or ABS, their market value and credit risk needs to be explicitly incorporated by modeling their key risk factors: asset spreads and credit migration. In this way, the model can size appropriately the impact of the investments on the cash flows of the company. It can address, in an accurately and timely fashion, the cash inflows for the coupons and the liquidation risk for the assets that need to be sold to meet the timely "AAA" obligations of the company. The potential future credit rating of the asset that needs to be liquidated, as well as its market value, is modeled.

Hybrid vehicles have attracted the interest of the market and we see this interest growing.

There are currently special purpose companies that combine structural features of a CDPC with SIVs (e.g., Theta) and vice versa.

The CDO technology and tiered capital structures start to attract interest for a more efficient funding strategy. We expect the three types presented earlier to overlap and to lead to the creation of new innovative structures.

REPO COMPANIES

Repo companies are AAA vehicles that engage in repurchase agreements. They provide financing to institutional investors through reverse repurchase transactions and total return swaps. To achieve that, these vehicles finance themselves through repurchase agreements or commercial paper and medium term notes.

A repurchase agreement (or repo) is an agreement between two parties whereby one party sells the other a *security* at a specified price with a commitment to buy the security back at a later date for another specified price. Most repos are overnight transactions, with the sale taking place one day and being reversed the next day. Long-term repos—called term repos—can extend for a month or more. Usually, repos are for a fixed period of time, but open-ended deals are also possible. Reverse repo is a term used to describe the opposite side of a repo transaction. The party who sells and later repurchases a security is said to perform a repo. The other party—who purchases and later resells the security—is said to perform a reverse repo.

Although a repo is legally the sale and subsequent repurchase of a security, its economic effect is that of a *secured loan*. Economically, the party purchasing the security makes funds available to the seller and holds the security as *collateral*. If the repo-ed security pays a dividend, coupon, or partial redemptions during the repo, this is returned to the original owner. The difference between the sale and repurchase prices paid for the security represent interest on the loan. Indeed, repos are quoted as interest rates. Figure 14.13 shows how a typical repo company works with both assets and funding sides.

The assets that are repo-ed range from U.S. Treasuries/agencies, leveraged loans, Investment grade or noninvestment grade Bonds, ABS, CDOs. credit risk, market risk, liquidity risk are the key drivers for capital in the risk model.

Credit Risk occurs when counterparty fails to postmargin or return asset (repo) or $ amount (reverse repo) at maturity. Because most positions are matched, if a counterparty defaults, the risk model has to absorb the open market risk that the vehicles are left with unless they contractually agree to close out the trade.

Market Risk fluctuations in MtM may result in margin calls Loss severity upon termination depends on MtM of collateral. If the asset loses value during the liquidation horizon, this becomes a direct hit to capital.

FIGURE 14.13

Repo Company Works with Both Assets and Funding.

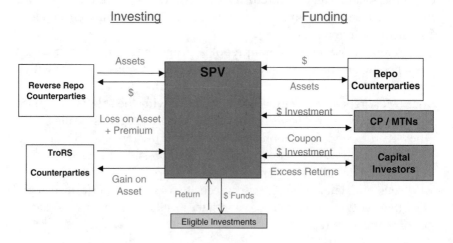

Liquidity Risk

SPV may be required to post additional margin/return excess margin. That is why a spread model is needed to accurately evolve through time the market value of the assets.

In a repo, SPV would post more assets or return cash to counterparty if MtM of original assets falls below maintenance margin.

In a reverse repo, SPV would return assets or send additional cash to counterparty if MtM of asset rises above maintenance margin.

All three risks can be modeled according to the terms of the repo contracts. One could use modules similar with the ones presented as examples given earlier.

LIQUIDITY FACILITIES

Another type of special purpose company is a vehicle that is set up to provide multilateral and bilateral commitment facilities extended to corporate borrowers. It is a limited purpose company that seeks to provide back-up liquidity to its corporate clients.

A structural diagram, like the one presented subsequently, shows the SPV has to raise capital from its capital investors to cover for the potential peak drawdown over the life of the commitments. Funding for such vehicles rely on the fact that not all borrowers draw up to to their limit in the same time.

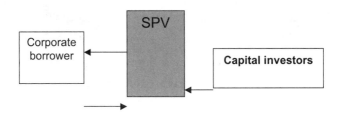

The corporate borrowers usually have a two-year or a five-year commitment line with the SPV. They can borrow any amount up to their commitment size and have the obligation to repay it within the tenor of the facility. A borrower that cannot pay back the amount borrowed is deemed to have defaulted on its obligation. The SPV has to have resources to cover less than the total notional of the commitments, as not all borrowers will draw in the same time. The quantitative exercise here is to size an amount that covers the borrowers who will default and not pay back and, more important, cover the potential maximum drawdown amount over the lifetime of these commitments.

The key risk factors for such an exercise are frequency of drawdown, magnitude of drawdown, and persistence of drawdowns. They are different per rating and certain industries. Credit worthiness is modeled using the technologies presented before, applying a rating transition approach. The other factors are modeled from data collected on them. Each of the factors is a source of randomness and noise in the simulation. By combining credit paths with paths for drawdowns and persistence, a stochastic model is built.

Typically, this Monte Carlo exercise results in a percentage less than 100 percent (the size of the commitments extended), in capital requirement. As mentioned earlier, tranching using CDO technology can provide a more efficient source of funding for the operating company.

A P P E N D I X   A

CIR Model Calibration

The steady state probability and cumulative density functions

$$f_r(r)dr \equiv \text{Prob}\{r < \mathbf{r} \le r + dr\}; \quad F_r(r) \equiv \text{Prob}\{\mathbf{r} \le r\} \qquad (2)$$

of the interest rates following the CIR process is given by

$$f_r(r) = \frac{(2\gamma/\alpha)^\kappa r^{\kappa-1} \exp[-2\gamma r/\alpha]}{\Gamma(\kappa)}, \qquad (3)$$

$$F_r(r) = 1 - \frac{\Gamma(\kappa, r\kappa\gamma/\eta)}{\Gamma(\kappa)}, \qquad (4)$$

$$\kappa = \frac{2\eta}{\alpha}; \quad \Gamma(\kappa) = \int_0^\infty x^{\kappa-1} e^{-x} \, dx; \Gamma(\kappa, z) = \int_z^\infty x^{\kappa-1} e^{-x} \, dx. \qquad (5)$$

A way to infer the three parameters of the CIR model is by calculating statistical moments of quantities involving the interest rates and fitting the parameters to best reproduce the moments. The steady state first statistical moment of the interest rate is given by

$$\bar{r} = \frac{\eta}{\gamma}. \tag{6}$$

The steady state second statistical moment is given by

$$\sigma_r^2 = \frac{\eta\alpha}{2\gamma^2}. \tag{7}$$

It follows directly from Equation (1) that the second statistical moment of the interest rate change Δr over small time intervals Δt is given by

$$\overline{\Delta r^2} = (\eta - \gamma r)^2 \Delta t^2 + \alpha\bar{r}\Delta t. \tag{8}$$

Substituting Equation (6) in (8) gives

$$\overline{\Delta r^2} = \gamma^2 \Delta t^2 \sigma_r^2 + \alpha\bar{r}\Delta t. \tag{9}$$

Equations (6), (7), and (9) along with empirical inferences of $\bar{r}$, σ_r^2, and $\overline{\Delta r^2}$ provide a method for calibrating η, γ, and α. Hence,

$$\gamma = \left(-1 + \sqrt{1 + \frac{\overline{\Delta r^2}}{\sigma_r^2}}\right)\frac{1}{\Delta t}, \tag{10}$$

$$\eta = \bar{r}\left(-1 + \sqrt{1 + \frac{\overline{\Delta r^2}}{\sigma_r^2}}\right)\frac{1}{\Delta t}, \tag{11}$$

and

$$\alpha = \frac{2\sigma_r^2}{\bar{r}}\left(-1 + \sqrt{1 + \frac{\overline{\Delta r^2}}{\sigma_r^2}}\right)\frac{1}{\Delta t}. \tag{12}$$

Using historical time series from 1963–2003, closed form solutions for the three parameters were derived.

The empirical statistics are

$$\bar{r} = 0.071483(1/\text{yr}); \quad \sigma_r = 0.03379823(1/\text{yr}); \quad \overline{\Delta r^2} = 0.000049099(1/\text{yr}^2).$$

The fitted parameters are

$$\eta = 0.018205493(1/\text{yr}^2); \quad \gamma = 0.25468 \ (1/\text{yr});$$
$$\alpha = 0.00813991(1/\text{yr}^2) \quad 1/\gamma = 3.926 \ \text{yr}.$$

In Cox et al. (1985), it is shown that zero-coupon bond prices, with term $(T-t)$ and issued at time t, when the short rate is $r(t)$, have the following general form:

$$P(t, T) = A(t, T) e^{-B(t, T)r(t)},$$

where

$$B(t, T) = \frac{2(e^{k(T-t)} - 1)}{(k+\gamma)(e^{k(T-t)} - 1) + 2k},$$

$$A(t, T) = \left[\frac{2k \, e^{(\gamma+k)(T-t)/2}}{(k+\gamma)(e^{k(T-t)} - 1) + 2k} \right]^{(2\eta/\gamma\alpha)},$$

and

$$k = \sqrt{\gamma^2 + 2\lambda^2}.$$

The continuously compounded rate for a zero-coupon bond is then;

$$R(t, T) = \frac{-\ln(P(t, T))}{T - t}$$

The CIR model allows us to price any bond regardless of maturity, simply by modeling the short rate. For any given term, $L = (T-t)$, both A and B are constants and the earlier equation becomes

$$R(t, L) = \frac{Br(t) - \ln A}{L}.$$

Hence, the long rate is a linear function of the short rate. In this way, a full discounting curve can be built for each currency and used to derive the market value of the assets and the mark-to-market on derivative contracts.

APPENDIX B

Analyzing Capital Notes for a SIV

The rating on the capital notes of an SIV can be assigned either confidentially or publicly—the methodology does not differ—and addresses the SIV's ability to make ultimately payment of the principal amount of the capital notes, plus the minimum interest amount. These interest payments can be addressed in the rating definition as being timely or ultimately. This will depend on whether the capital note (or junior) model is able to produce results that suggest that the minimum coupon can be paid timely, or the transaction documents specify that coupons can be deferred.

We assume that in defeasance, the capital note investors lose at least one dollar of their investment, hence P(first dollar of loss conditional upon defeasance) = 1.

However, capital note investors could suffer losses outside defeasance as well, hence it may be the case that P(first dollar of loss conditional upon no defeasance) > 0.

Therefore, the rating analysis must address three main areas, namely:

- ♦ Analysis of defeasance events
- ♦ Probability of defeasance and
- ♦ Likelihood of first dollar of loss to capital note investors outside defeasance.

For the capital notes, the evaluations that one would make in order to reach comfort to look only at a parametric model are more heavily based on qualitative than quantitative assumptions. They relate to the manager's ability to perform in the future and to avoid noncredit/noncapital related winddown/defeasance events. However, the likelihood or remoteness of triggering defeasance is not an assumption in the rating methodology for the senior debt of a SIV, where defeasance is supposed to occur on day 1, regardless of what caused it.

In practice, the SIV manager requests a desired rating on the capital notes. The majority of managers have requested a rating in the "BBB" range.

It must be noted that the methodology that follows is neither specific to any vehicle S&P currently rates, nor it is prescriptive to any vehicle seeking a rating on the capital notes. Indeed, other issues could

FIGURE 14.14

First Dollar Loss Formula.

| P (first dollar of loss) | = | P (first dollar of loss conditional upon defeasance) * P (defeasance) | + | P (first dollar of loss conditional upon no defeasance) * P (no defeasance) |

Where P is probability.

arise on a case-by-case and the implementation of a rating methodology will be specific to each SIV and will take into account its idiosyncrasies.

The analysis addresses the likelihood of the first dollar of loss in the capital notes. During the lifetime of the vehicle, the most disrupting event is the defeasance event. This event stops the normal operations of the vehicle and, in essence, the portfolio is wound down gradually and the SIV ceases to exist after the last liability is paid.

It then makes sense to divide the rating analysis into two mutually exclusive events, namely defeasance and nondefeasance, and analyze the effect on the first dollar of loss in both events.

Formalizing the rationale above, this translates into an analysis of the conditional first dollar of loss in defeasance and in nondefeasance mode respectively, in the formula shown in Figure 14.14.

USE OF A MONTE CARLO APPROACH IN RATING THE CAPITAL NOTES

The likelihood of first dollar of loss on the interest and/or principal could be estimated using a "Monte Carlo" approach. Although the Monte Carlo exercise is computationally intensive, it provides an excellent tool to accurately model the risk factors. It also provides a framework for accurately inputting into the model the waterfall, including the timely payment of coupon on capital notes and its ranking in the waterfall.

This approach simulates implicitly the steps in the defeasance and nondefeasance scenarios.

As described in the paper, the main risk factors are credit variables (transition/default migration) and market variables (credit spreads, credit swap premiums, interest rates, and exchanges rates).

Following the methodology of our rating analysis, one needs to determine P(first dollar of loss on the capital notes) and benchmark it with the default probability of a corporate bond with a similar rating and tenor. The tenor may depend on certain structural features of the capital notes, typically with expected maturities of seven to 10 years, although this expected maturity can be shorter if puts are exercised by capital note investors.

To do the exercise using a Monte Carlo tool, one needs to evolve the portfolio through time and analyze if timely payment of coupon and principal on the capital notes can be achieved. In each "time step," one would stochastically evolve the credit and market variables and analyze the new profile of the portfolio. This means that in each time step, the creditworthiness and market value of the portfolio are computed and then checked whether the portfolio meets the guidelines and passes the capital adequacy tests (in each time step, the simulated market value of the asset portfolio should be greater than par of all senior debt issued).

Therefore, in each time step, a random process would define the then-current market and credit environment. Assets have a stochastic market value that reflects their new rating, new market spreads, and new tenor. Breaching portfolio guidelines (e.g., rating limits) should be cured to get back into compliance by selling assets or 100 percent capital charging the assets.

In each time step, the waterfall is implemented starting with the "AAA" senior fees and expenses, then the senior debt, and finally incorporating the minimum coupon on capital notes. The remaining funds could be distributed as profit according to the guidelines (with or without a cap). Thereafter, any remaining funds are cash trapped for the subsequent time steps and reinvested at the original ratings and at spread levels simulated stochastically.

In evolving credit spread curves for reinvestment purposes, focus is on stressing the spread tightening as opposed to the same exercise for asset pricing purposes, where focus is on stressing the spread widening. Debt is rolled at a cost of funds that itself is a stochastic variable that needs to be simulated.

In each time step, as long as the adequacy tests (portfolio guidelines, capital, and capital gearing) are met, the model makes assumptions of stochastically reinvesting the cash amount from maturing assets or recoveries, recontracting derivative contracts, and rolling debt (cost of funds may vary as well).

If the capital test is breached during a time step and defeasance is triggered, the vehicle stops issuing debt and sells assets to repay liabilities. It is almost certain that in the defeasance mode, capital would be deployed to repay senior debt. That path should be deemed a failed path for the purpose of rating the capital notes. Let us say there is a total of D paths that trigger defeasance out of the total of N paths simulated. In this way, the Monte Carlo exercise sized the probability of defeasance to be D/N.

The paths in which all the tests are met do not trigger defeasance. Those paths are re-run each time step until the maturity of the capital notes. The challenge is to see whether the minimum coupon and the full notional value of the notes can be paid.

Intuitively, this translates into having enough spread to make up for the defaulted assets, which would be the main consumer of capital.

There may be paths in which, although defeasance is not triggered, there is not enough cash to repay in full the capital notes. These are also considered to be failed paths. Let us say there are E paths in which the notes are not paid in full out of the total of N paths simulated. In this way, the Monte Carlo exercise sized the probability of first dollar of loss if no defeasance occurs to be E/N.

The number of failed paths for the capital notes is therefore $(D+E)/N$, where

- D = Defeasance paths
- E = Non-defeasance paths but notes not paid in full and
- N = Total number of paths.

This has to be commensurate with a default probability of a corporate bond with the desired rating and tenor.

In a Monte Carlo stochastic model, if there is a similar model for the senior notes, parameters are kept the same if they were already calibrated. The level of confidence lower than "AAA" is incorporated in the cut-off point or the tolerance for failed paths.

It is worth reminding readers that this methodology is not prescriptive; in fact, one could use this Monte Carlo tool to simulate defeasance and see how much capital was deployed. There may be paths in which not all the capital is used (e.g., if assets recover in price) and the capital note investors may get a portion of their notes back.

THE NON-MONTE CARLO APPROACH

Given the formula for calculating the probability of the first dollar of loss (see chart 4), one needs to estimate only P(defeasance) and P(first dollar of loss given no defeasance). Besides the Monte Carlo approach, these two probabilities could be quantified with other methods.

For example: P(defeasance) can be quantified by assuming that defeasance occurs due to a drastic downgrade of asset ratings and spread widening over a short horizon, say, one month or three months. Intuitively, this downgrade and spread widening would consume all excess capital and make the "AAA" capital adequacy test trip and hence trigger defeasance.

Performing the earlier exercise amounts to quantifying the probability of a spread widening occurring over a short horizon and compounding it to the tenor of the capital notes (e.g., 10 years).

This requires a probabilistic model to be fitted to the spreads. Furthermore, the analysis has to reflect the composition of the portfolio, hence the asset mix. The spreads usually have "fat" tails and may vary from one asset type to another.

P(loss given no defeasance) can be quantified using a profit and loss approach in which conservatively assessed incomes are counted against stressed defaults, senior fees and other expenses, senior debt, and the minimum coupon on the capital notes.

The methodologies given earlier are only examples of alternative approaches to a Monte Carlo approach. They could be adapted to each SIV's model or technology. For nonstochastic models, parameter stresses may need to be lowered to reflect the increase in tolerance in the exercise of rating the capital notes as opposed to senior debt. For portfolios that are not ramped up, a variety of assumptions on initial asset spreads and cost of funds is tested.

In rating capital notes, to address rating volatility several portfolios should be tested, with low, medium, and high leverage or, respectively, with high, average, and low credit quality. Ultimately, the excess spread (beyond the "AAA" model) is the main contributor to the payment of coupon and principal on the capital notes. Refining the capital structure of the capital notes into a mezzanine and first-loss piece may help absorb the losses and achieve a higher rating.

REFERENCES

Carty, lea V. and Lieberman, D. (1996), "Corporate Bond defaults and Default Rates 1938–1995," Moody's Investors Service, Global Credit Research.

Cox, J.C., J.E. Ingersoll, and S.A. Ross (1985), "A Theory of the Term Structure of Interest rates," *Econometrica*, 53(2), March, 385–408.

CreditMetrics (1997), Technical Document April.

"Global Methodology For Rating Capital Notes In SIV Structures" (published on February 11, 2005).

Jolliffe, I.T. (1986), *Principal Component Analysis*, Springer-Verlag.

Merrill Lynch (2005), Fixed Income Strategy, "SIVs are running strong," January 28.

Merrill Lynch (2005), International Structured product Monthly (jan), "SIV capital Notes vs. CDO Mezzanine Notes and equity," February 1.

Hull, J. (2005), Options, Futures and other Derivative Securities.

Prigent, Renault, and Scaillet (2000), An Empirical Investigation in Credit Spread Indices.

Rating Derivative product Companies S&P Structured Finance Criteria February 2000.

Standard & Poor's Research—Principal Repayment and Loss Behaviour of Defaulted U.S. Structured Finance Securities, published 10 January 2005 by Erkan Erturk and Thomas Gillis.

"Structured Investment Vehicle Criteria: New Developments" (published on September 4, 2003).

"Structured Investment Vehicle Criteria" (published on March 13, 2002).

SIV Outlook Report/Assets Top $200 Million in SIV Market; Continued Growth Expected in 2006—January 2006.

CHAPTER 15

Securitizations in Basel II

William Perraudin*

INTRODUCTION

In this chapter we consider the rules governing regulatory capital for structured products[†] in the new Basel II proposals.[‡] We look at the motives that have influenced regulators in designing the rules, review the different approaches banks will be required to follow, discuss the financial engineering that underpins the main approaches, and consider the likely effects of the new Basel II system on the structured product market. To ensure that the discussion is self contained, we briefly review some relevant features of the market in this introduction.

Growth in structured products began in the 1980s with the emergence of the residential mortgaged-backed security (RMBS) market in the United States. In the 1990s, substantial asset-backed security (ABS) markets emerged in auto loans and credit card receivables. Since the late 1990s, there has been major growth in different types of collateralized debt obligations (CDOs) in which the special purpose vehicle (SPV) pool is made up of illiquid bonds or loans by banks to large corporate borrowers.

---

*The author thanks Patricia Jackson and Ralph Mountford of Ernst of Young for valuable discussions and Robert Lamb for research assistance.
†We use the terms "structured product" and "securitization" interchangeably.
‡See Basel Committee on Banking Supervision (2005).

Recently, the range of collateral types included in structured product pools has widened further, as issuers have created securitizations based on trade receivables of different kinds, equities, commercial property, utility receivables, and even energy derivatives. Issuers have realized that, in principle, any assets that represent claims to future cash flows can be securitized.

As well as classic securitizations in which assets are transferred to an SPV, banks have made extensive use of structures in which off balance sheet conduits issue commercial paper and use the proceeds to purchase revolving pools of assets. Such Asset-Backed Commercial Paper (ABCP) conduits are particularly important in the United States.

Also common are synthetic securitizations. In these, the SPV provides a bank with credit protection on its loans [often, in the form of credit default swaps (CDS)]. At the same time, it issues notes to the market and invests the proceeds in high credit standing bonds such as Treasuries. The premiums the SPV receives from the bank on the CDSs plus the coupons on the Treasuries provide it with income it uses to pay coupons on the notes. Such structures are often cheaper to create than traditional structured products, since the legal complication of transferring ownership of the underlying assets is avoided.

The impact of structured products has been substantial for issuers and investors alike. Structured products have provided investors with a broader and more liquid range of debt instruments in which they can invest, permitted issuers to manage better their balance sheets risks, and opened up new sources of funding for banks. As early as 1998, one estimate suggested that 40 percent of the nonmortgage loan books of the 10 largest U.S. bank holding companies had been securitized.

THE REGULATORS' OBJECTIVES

This section reviews the broad objectives regulators have had in framing the Basel II rules for structured products. The treatment of securitizations is a key part of Basel II. This is not just because of the sheer volume of securitization exposures in bank portfolios, but also because banks have made widespread use of securitization to circumvent regulatory capital requirements through the so-called capital arbitrage. Indeed, the prevalence of such capital arbitrage has been one of the major reasons that regulators have felt obliged to replace the simple rules of the 1988 Basel Accord with the more complex, risk-sensitive regulatory capital requirements of Basel II.

Examples of how securitizations may be used for capital arbitrage are provided by Jones (2000). Consider the following example. Suppose a bank possesses a loan pool worth $100. The chance of losses exceeding $5 might be negligibly small. In this case, the bank could create a securitization and retain a junior tranche with par value of $5. It thereby retains all credit risk in the transaction.

The maximum capital charge that the regulatory authorities can charge is 100 percent. Hence, the bank which would have had to hold capital of $8 under Basel I if the exposures were held on balance sheet now has to hold no more than $5 in capital even though its risk position has not changed.

Under Basel I, even lower regulatory capital charges may be achieved if the pool exposures are actually originated by the SPV. In this case, the bank may provide the SPV with a credit enhancement like a subordinated loan so that it effectively bears the credit risk associated with the pool of assets. Under Basel I, the subordinated loan in this case just attracts an 8 percent capital charge.

In the light of these examples, one may understand how important it has been for bank regulators designing the Basel II system to come up with rules likely to reduce the incentives banks face to engage in capital arbitrage.

To achieve this, regulators have tried, first, to design regulatory capital charges for loans that are aligned with the capital that banks would themselves wish to hold. Second, they have aimed to create a system of capital charges that preserves on and off balance sheet neutrality, i.e., the capital banks must hold should be the same whether they hold a pool of loans on balance sheet or if they securitize it and retain all the tranches. Third, they have sought to ensure that the individual capital charges attracted by the different tranches in a structure are consistent with the relative distribution of risks between the tranches.

The new system of capital charges will inevitably have an impact on the securitization market. One of the major objectives of Basel II after all is to reduce the volume of transactions motivated by capital arbitrage considerations. Nevertheless, an important objective has been not to impede activity unreasonably in particular segments of the market, especially where the transactions are clearly aimed at effecting genuine transfer of risk off the issuer's balance sheet.

As we shall see, in certain key areas, regulators have felt obliged to include additional flexibility to prevent the new regulations having a prejudicial effect upon market segments. In particular, the impact of Basel II on suppliers of liquidity and credit enhancement facilities in the ABCP market has been of great concern to the U.S. regulators because of the importance of this market to U.S. companies.

Given these general objectives, regulators have provided a menu of different approaches that should permit banks to calculate capital for the very diverse range of securitization exposures in their books in a risk-sensitive fashion.

The different approaches permitted in the menu is heavily influenced by the question of how much information one may expect banks to have about the securitization exposure they hold. For example, as arms-length investors, a bank may hold substantial securitization exposures about which they have only hazy information. Typically, they will only have a broad notion of the composition and credit quality of the underlying asset pool. On the other hand, if a bank has originated and continues to manage the securitized assets, it will have very detailed information about the securitization.

An intermediate case occurs when a bank acts as the sponsor of a commercial paper programme. The sponsoring bank may supply credit enhancements and liquidity facilities to the programme that will then represent exposures subject to the Basel II securitization framework. The underlying assets will in most cases have been bought in from other originators, and so the sponsor will only have limited information about them.

The two possible ways in which securitization capital charges might be calculated are either (1) to base charges on the ratings attributed to securitization tranches by external credit rating agencies, or (2) to base charges on a formula supplied by supervisors into which the regulated bank can substitute parameters describing features of the tranche in question.

A ratings-based approach is attractive for its simplicity and the fact that it recognizes the key role that rating agencies play in the securitization market. Agencies are relied on heavily by investors evaluating the credit quality of securitization tranches after issue and strongly influenced by their assessments the form that many deals take at issuance. (In the run-up to an issue, issuers often effectively have to negotiate with the rating agencies on such features as the degree of credit enhancement a tranches must enjoy if it is to obtain a particular target rating, for example.)

Also, the principle of basing capital charges on ratings has been widely applied in the Basel II rules for conventional credit exposures like bonds on ratings. (In some cases, the ratings employed are internal and in others are agency ratings.) One might be concerned, however, that the relationship between capital and ratings is more complex in the case of structured products than in the case of traditional credit exposures such as bonds or loans. In which case, a bottom-up approach to capital calculation based on a stylized model may be an attractive option.

CAPITAL CALCULATION BY BANKS UNDER BASEL II

These objectives and considerations have led regulators to devise a system comprising the following menu of different approaches.

1. The Standardized Approach. This approach consists of a look-up table of capital charges for different rating categories for exposures with long- or short-term ratings. The ratings in question come from designated ratings agencies and are not internally generated by the banks. Banks are required to employ this approach for a particular structured exposure if and only if they use the corresponding "standardized approach" in their Basel II calculations of capital for the predominant assets in the structured exposure pool.

    The standardized approach look-up tables are shown in Tables 15.1 and 15.2. The numbers in the table are expressed in terms of "risk weights." To convert these into percentage capital charges, one must multiply by 0.08, i.e., the standard Basel I capital charge.* For example, the 50 percent risk weight for a BBB-rated exposure translates into a 4 percent capital charge.

TABLE 15.1

Standardized Approach with Long-Term Ratings

	AAA to AA (%)	A+ to A– (%)	BBB+ to BBB– (%)	BB+ to BB– (%)	B+ and below (%)
Risk weight	20	50	100	350	1250

---

*Under Basel, a bank must maintain capital at a level no less than 0.08 times its risk-weighted assets (RWA). The RWA is obtained by summing the bank's notional exposures weighted by risk weights like those in Table 15.1.

TABLE 15.2

Standardized Approach with Short-Term Ratings

	A-1/P-1 (%)	A-2/P-2 (%)	A-3/P-3 (%)	Other (%)
Risk weight	20	50	100	1250

A risk weight of 1,250 percent translates into a 100 percent capital charge, i.e., in effect deduction of the exposure from capital. The risk weights are highly conservative in the standardized approach. A long-term AAA-rated tranche attracts a risk weight of 20 percent and so a capital charge of 1.6 percent. The default probability of such an exposure may be very close to zero, so this is very conservative.

2. The ratings base approach (RBA). The RBA consists of a slightly more elaborate pair of look-up tables for long-term and short-term rated tranches (see Tables 15.3 and 15.4). The risk weights for tranches of a given rating vary according to:

TABLE 15.3

RBA for Long-Term Ratings

External rating	Risk weights for senior positions (%)	Base risk weights (%)	Risk weights for tranches backed by nongranular pools (%)
AAA	7	12	20
AA	8	15	25
A+	10	18	35
BBB+	12	20	35
BBB	20	35	35
BBB+	35	50	50
BBB	60	75	75
BBB–	100	100	100
BB+	250	250	250
BB	425	425	425
BB–	650	650	650
Other rated	1,250	1,250	1,250
Unrated	1,250	1,250	1,250

TABLE 15.4

RBA for Short-Term Ratings

External rating	Risk weights for senior positions (%)	Base risk weights (%)	Risk weights for tranches backed by nongranular pools (%)
A-1/P-1	7	12	20
A-2/P-2	12	20	35
A-3/P-3	60	75	75
Other rated	1,250	1,250	1,250
Unrated	1,250	1,250	1,250

a   Granularity. A pool is said to be highly granular if it contains a large number of exposures none of which contributes a large part of the total risk. A measure of granularity is the statistic

$$N = \frac{\left(\sum_i \text{EAD}_i\right)^2}{\sum_i \text{EAD}_i^2} \qquad (1)$$

where EAD_i denotes the exposure at default of the ith exposure in the pool. In the RBA, tranches rated above BBB+ attract risk weights higher than the base weights if $N < 6$ (see the fourth column of Table 15.3).

b   Seniority.   If a tranche is the most senior in its structure and is rated BBB or above, it attracts a lower risk weight than the base case so long as $N > 6$ (see the second column of Table 15.3). Lastly, as a late amendment to the RBA, a risk weight of 6 percent has recently been introduced for super senior tranches. Such tranches are defined as tranches that have tranches junior to them that would attract a weight of 7 percent, if they were the most senior.

3. The supervisory formula approach (SFA).   This consists of a bottom-up approach to calculating capital in which a set of parameters reflecting the pool credit quality and features of the cash flow waterfall of the structured product are plugged into a formula to yield the capital for a particular tranche. The formula in question depends on five bank-supplied inputs:

a K_{IRB}. The capital charge the bank would have had to hold against the pool exposures if they had been retained on balance sheet and the bank was using the internal-ratings based (IRB) approach, as specified under Basel II.

b L. The attachment point or credit enhancement level of the tranche, i.e., the sum of the par values of more junior tranches.

c T. The tranche thickness.

d N. The effective number of exposures in the pool.

e LGD. The exposure-weighted loss given default of the pool defined as:

$$LGD = \frac{\sum_i LGD_i\, EAD_i}{\sum_i EAD_i} \tag{2}$$

The SFA capital charge for the tranche is:

$$\max\{0.0056\, T, S(L+T) - S(L)\} \tag{3}$$

where the supervisory formula $S(L)$ is defined as:

$$S(L) = \begin{cases} L & \text{when } L \le K_{\text{IRB}} \\[2mm] \begin{aligned} & K_{\text{IRB}} + K(L) - K(K_{\text{IRB}}) \\ & + \frac{d\,K_{\text{IRB}}}{\omega}\left(1 - \exp\left[\omega\,\frac{K_{\text{IRB}} - L}{K_{\text{IRB}}}\right]\right) \end{aligned} & \text{when } L > K_{\text{IRB}} \end{cases} \tag{4}$$

where

$$h = (1 - K_{\text{IRB}}/LGD)^N \tag{5}$$

$$c = K_{\text{IRB}}/(1-h) \tag{6}$$

$$v = \frac{1}{N}((LGD - K_{\text{IRB}})K_{\text{IRB}} + 0.25(1 - LGD)K_{\text{IRB}}) \tag{7}$$

$$f = \left(\frac{v + K_{\text{IRB}}^2}{1-h} - c^2\right) + \frac{(1 - K_{\text{IRB}})K_{\text{IRB}} - v}{(1-h)\tau} \tag{8}$$

$$g = \frac{(1-c)c}{f} - 1 \tag{9}$$

$$a = gc \tag{10}$$

$$b = g(1-c) \tag{11}$$

$$d = 1 - (1-h)(1 - \text{Beta}(K_{\text{IRB}}; a, b)) \tag{12}$$

$$K(L) = (1-h)((1 - \text{Beta}(L; a, b))L + \text{Beta}(L; a+1, b)c). \tag{13}$$

Here, Beta(x; p, q) denotes the cumulative beta distribution evaluated at x and with parameters p and q. The parameters τ and ω are set at $\tau = 1000$ and $\omega = 20$. The underpinnings of this approach are explained at greater length next.

The practical use of these different approaches is best explained by reviewing the flow chart shown in Figure 15.1. This flow chart shows the sequence of questions that a bank must answer in deciding what capital to hold against a given securitization exposure.

1. Is it a securitization? The definition of a securitization in the EU's draft Capital Requirements Directive (Article 4, 36) is: "A transaction or scheme, whereby the credit risk associated with an exposure or pool of exposures is tranched, having the following characteristics: (1) payments in the transaction are dependent upon the performance of the exposure or pool of exposures; (2) the subordination of tranches determines the distribution of losses during the life of the transaction or scheme."*

2. Supposing that the exposure is a securitization, the bank must decide whether it is held as part of the trading or the banking book. In the former case, the capital charge will be based on the usual trading book rules.

3. For the bank to apply the above securitization capital approaches, it must satisfy two sets of conditions: (1) risk transfer requirements if the bank is an originator of the securitized assets, and (2) implicit support requirements if it is either an Originator

---

*This definition encompasses both traditional and synthetic securitizations and is simpler than the definition in Basel Committee on Banking Supervision (2005).

FIGURE 15.1

Flow Chart for Structured Product Capital.

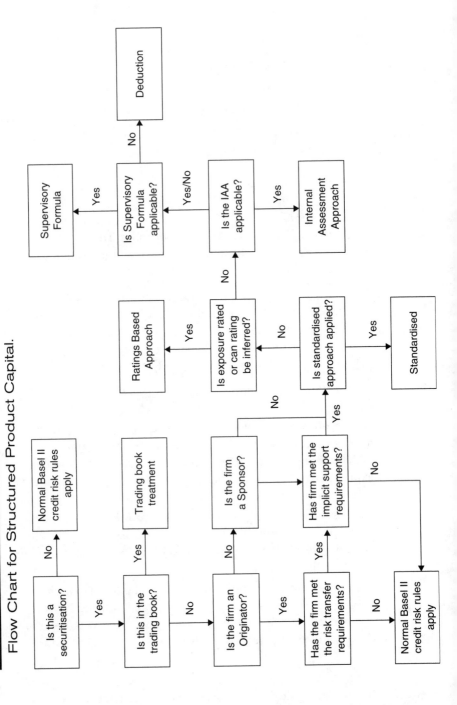

or a Sponsor* of the securitization. If either of these sets of conditions is not satisfied, then the bank must calculate capital for the pool exposures as though they are held on balance sheet.

4. If it satisfies these conditions, the bank must use the standardized approach as described earlier if it uses the standardized approach for on balance sheet assets of the same type as those that predominantly make up the securitization pool.

5. If the bank uses the IRB approach for the assets that predominantly comprise the pool, then it must employ either the RBA or the SFA. If the exposure is rated by an external agency recognized by the bank's national supervisor, the bank must employ the RBA. This is also true if the exposure is unrated, but the bank may infer a rating for the exposure by taking the rating of a more junior tranche with an equal or longer maturity.

6. If an external rating is not directly available and cannot be inferred, then the bank must decide whether the internal assessment approach (IAA) is applicable. This approach applies only to eligible liquidity and credit enhancement exposures to ABCP facilities. In effect, banks are able for this narrow set of exposures to calculate their own internal ratings. In so doing, they must devise a rating process that broadly mimics the approach followed in rating exposures to similar deals by a recognized rating agency.

7. If the IAA is applicable, the bank may choose to employ this approach or it may decide to use the SFA instead. If it implements the IAA, the bank determines its capital charges from the RBA look-up tables based on the the IAA-generated ratings. In general, the bank must adopt a consistent principle in choosing whether to use the SFA or the IAA/RBA.

8. If the IAA is not applicable or if the bank opts not to implement it, it must either use the SFA if that is feasible or otherwise

---

*An Originator is either of the following: An entity which, either itself or through related entities, directly or indirectly, was involved in the original agreement that created the obligations or potential obligations of the debtor or potential debtor giving rise to exposure being securitized; an entity which purchases a third partys exposures onto its balance sheet and then securitizes them. A Sponsor is a firm other than an Originator that establishes and manages an asset-backed commercial paper programme or other securitization scheme that purchases exposures from third parties.

deduct the exposure from its capital, i.e., apply a 1250 percent risk weight.

The sticking point for implementing the SFA in many cases is likely to be the bank's ability to calculate the inputs to the formula. These include most notably K_{IRB}, the capital that the bank would have to hold against the pool of assets backing the securitization if it held the pool on balance sheet. Basel II places rather tight restrictions on the information and data that banks must possess if they are to calculate K_{IRB}. A concession was made in the informational requirements for calculating K_{IRB} for portfolios of purchased receivables at quite a late stage in the Basel II process specifically because it was felt that otherwise many securitization exposures in bank portfolios that embodied relatively little risk would otherwise have to be deducted, disrupting reasonable market activity in several areas.

The IAA requires a substantial investment in procedures and systems by a bank. The idea is that banks will be able to rate tranches themselves in one quite circumscribed area of the securitization market, ABCP, but it must adopt an approach that resembles an approach employed by a recognized rating agency. The bank's procedures have to be audited thoroughly and authorized by the regulators. Banks are allowed to choose which of the SFA or the IAA combined with RBA look-up tables they wish to employ for nonrated ABCP liquidity and credit enhancement facilities. But they must adopt a consistent policy of using one approach or the other and not hop and change between different deals.

The implicit support and risk transfer requirements are an important part of the rules. The former are intended to ensure that originators maintain a clean break with their securitized assets. (Originators are able to support their past securitizations but only if this support is formally implemented, as an exposure against which capital can be levied.) The risk transfer requirements contain potential for some ambiguity.

THE FINANCIAL ENGINEERING OF THE RBA AND SFA

Regulators have been very keen to ensure that the Basel II rules will reduce banks' incentives to engage in capital arbitrage. The only way to achieve this is to maintain a reasonable level of neutrality between the on and off balance sheet treatment of exposures and to make sure that capital charges are similar in absolute level to what a bank would wish to hold as economic capital.

Decisions about the levels of structured product capital charges in Basel II was informed and influenced by financial engineering studies performed by analysts at the Federal Reserve Board and the Bank of England. This section provides a brief summary of these studies. Key contributions are (1) Peretyatkin and Perraudin (2004) on the RBA and (2) Gordy and Jones (2003) and Gordy (2004) on the SFA.

On the RBA, devising a set of capital charges for structured products based on ratings can be viewed as a significant challenge. Indeed, at an early stage in the Basel II process, some regulators disputed whether it could be achieved at all. To understand the issues, one needs some background about the capital treatment of other exposures like bonds and loans in Basel II.

The IRB charges for traditional, on balance sheet credit exposures in Basel II are based on measures of marginal Value at Risk (MVaR) for exposures with given probabilities of default over a one-year horizon. The default probabilities may be mapped into ratings by associating with each rating the historically observed one-year default probability. Hence, the approach may be thought of as one of basing capital charges on ratings. (The standardized approach to on-balance-sheet credit exposures is explicitly framed in terms of ratings rather than default probabilities in any case.)

A justification for linking capital to ratings is that analysis using simple industry standard models suggests that when there is a single common risk factor driving a portfolio of loans, the MVaRs for individual exposures within a large portfolio are a function of the default probability.* Other influences on the MVaR for a given exposure are the expected LGD, the degree of correlation between the claim in question and the single common risk factor and the maturity of the claim. If regulators are prepared to specify reasonable correlation values for each different market segment, suitable capital curves may be deduced.†

Turning to capital charges for structured products, one may be concerned that the mapping from default probability/rating to capital will be more complex, dependent, e.g., on tranche thickness, correlation of the factor risk in the pool and the factor risk in the bank's wider portfolio and the maturities both of the pool and of the structure.

---

*See Gordy (2003).
†This has been the approach followed under Basel II, so there are a set of capital curves or functions for five different credit exposure asset classes (C%I loans, SME loans, revolving retail exposures, and other retail and residential mortgages.) See Basel Committee on Banking Supervision (2005).

TABLE 15.5

Pykhtin–Dev Model Capital Charges

ρ	AAA	AA+	AA	AA−	A+	A	A−	BBB+	BBB	BBB−	BB+	BB	BB−	B+	B	B−	CCC
0.6	0.59	0.98	1.30	1.50	1.70	1.90	3.58	4.96	7.06	7.71	10.07	17.11	23.15	32.88	54.28	60.28	77.05
0.7	0.87	1.47	1.98	2.29	2.61	2.92	5.60	7.76	11.02	12.02	15.61	25.81	34.03	46.34	69.47	75.03	88.29
0.8	1.12	1.99	2.75	3.22	3.70	4.18	8.41	11.84	16.97	18.51	23.97	38.62	49.37	63.72	84.77	88.68	95.95
0.9	1.08	2.12	3.16	3.85	4.54	5.24	12.06	17.85	26.48	29.01	37.80	58.72	71.35	84.49	96.03	97.23	98.72
RBA	0.96	1.20	1.20	1.20	1.60	1.60	1.60	4.00	6.00	8.00	20.00	34.00	52.00	100.00	100.00	100.00	100.00

Note: charges are in percent.

Peretyatkin and Perraudin (2004) examine how MVaRs for tranches in a large set of stylized transactions are related to default probabilities and expected losses. (Moody's base their structured product ratings on target expected losses. Standard and Poor's and Fitch use target default probabilities when they attribute ratings to structured product tranches.) They conduct their analysis by calculating capital (i.e., MVaRs) within the simple analytical models proposed by Pykhtin and Dev (2002a), Pykhtin and Dev (2002b), and surveyed by Pykhtin (2004), and then examining the mapping from tranche default probability and expected loss to this MVaR.

The Pykhtin-Dev model yields MVaRs for tranches within structures that have the same maturity as the holding period of the VaR calculation. Peretyatkin and Perraudin (2004) also devise and employ a Monte Carlo model within which one may calculate portfolio VaRs and MVaRs on tranches in structures when the VaR holding period is less than the maturity of the structure. This is clearly the more realistic case, as CDO maturities are often 10 years or more, while the VaR horizon used by almost all banks is one year.

An example of the calculations performed by Peretyatkin and Perraudin (2004) is shown in Table 15.5. The table shows percentage capital charges based on MVaRs for tranches with different ratings and for different values of ρ, the correlation coefficient between the single common risk factor assumed to drive the credit quality of the bank's wider portfolio and the risk factor driving the exposures in the structured exposure pool. The calculations are performed assuming a highly granular pool of BB-rated underlying exposures. The holding period and confidence level of the VaR are one year and 0.1 percent, and the maturity of the underlying pool exposures is also taken to be one year.

As one may see from Table 15.5, the results depend significantly on the value of the correlation parameter ρ, the correlation between the pool and the wider bank portfolio risk factors. When $\rho = 0.6$, the capital charges are broadly similar to those required under the RBA, as shown in the bottom row of Table 15.5.

The importance of the correlation parameter shows that capital charges for structured product exposures should be distinctly higher if the exposure has underlying pool assets similar to exposures that predominantly make up the bank's wider portfolio. It is perhaps obvious that a bank that invests in a credit card ABS tranche needs to hold more capital against it if much of its on balance sheet risk is associated with downturns in the retail credit market that if it is primarily exposed to large corporate lending. But the differences in the rows shown in Table 15.5 underline the point.

TABLE 15.6

Monte Carlo-Based Capital Charges

	AAA	AA+	AA	AA–	A+	A	A–	BBB+	BBB	BBB–	BB+	BB	BB–	B+	B	B–	CCC
1 year	0.54	0.99	1.36	1.58	1.77	1.96	3.50	4.63	6.25	6.75	8.75	14.78	19.87	28.30	49.53	56.21	76.26
2 years	0.17	0.86	1.72	1.89	2.27	2.70	4.99	6.98	9.30	11.83	14.65	20.50	26.31	35.74	55.72	62.58	78.81
3 years	0.67	1.55	2.68	2.80	3.31	3.93	6.29	8.55	10.91	14.59	18.66	24.57	30.93	40.79	58.84	65.15	77.46
4 years	1.41	2.53	3.86	3.99	4.62	5.45	7.88	10.38	12.86	17.32	20.97	26.49	32.83	42.27	56.79	61.28	67.66
5 years	1.29	2.49	3.82	3.96	4.67	5.62	7.96	10.51	13.03	17.83	23.05	29.14	35.98	45.27	57.17	60.41	64.02

Note: Simulations assume a portfolio of 264 BB-rated exposures, 50 percent LGD, a correlation of 60 percent between single factors driving the pool and wider bank portfolio, and a correlation between individual exposure latent variables of 80 percent.
Capital charges (MVaRs) are in percent.

Peretyatkin and Perraudin conclude that some other aspects of the structured product have only a second-order effect on the appropriate capital charges. For example, the degree to which the underlying pool exposures are correlated with each other or are nongranular leads to relatively small changes in capital. The reason is that when the riskiness of the pool is increased, the rating agencies tend to downgrade the more senior tranches, so capital increases even without a direct rise in the capital charge for tranches with a given rating.

On the other hand, Peretyatkin and Perraudin find that maturity again has a first-order effect on the capital charges for particular rating categories. Using a novel Monte Carlo technique, they are able to calculate MVaRs and hence capital for structured products of different maturities. The results are shown in Table 15.6. The capital more than doubles when one considers relatively senior tranches with the same rating, but a maturity of four years rather than one year.

As described above, the RBA in Basel II provides simple look-up tables for risk weights (and hence implicitly capital charges) by rating category. No distinction is made between tranches (1) backed by different underlying assets (e.g., credit cards versus large corporate loans), (2) of different maturities, or (3) backed by assets similar or dissimilar to exposures predominant in the bank's wider portfolio. While there are reasons for believing that that (1) is not a serious drawback, as factors that affect the riskiness of the securitization pool may have second-order effects on capital, (2) and (3) may be more serious. These might have been dealt with through Pillar II requirements, but Basel II did not take that approach.

Lastly, one may be critical of the RBA on the grounds that agencies assign ratings to securitization exposures taking into account complex sets of factors that they perceive to drive the risk of the transactions. These factors include the probability that the issuer will be able to meet principal and interest payments, the structure of the cash flow waterfall, the type of assets in the pool, other risks, such as market, legal and counter-party risks, and credit and liquidity enhancements of various sorts. The different rating agencies also employ significantly different procedures in assigning ratings. Expecting all of this to be satisfactorily summarized in a stylized calculation of expected losses on tranches as was performed in the parameterization of the RBA is somewhat ambitious.

The counter-argument to the above criticism is that the different rating agencies seem over time to be converging in the approaches they take to rating structured products in that they are increasingly using comparable Monte Carlo methods to simulate pool performance and payoffs to tranches. The RMA parameterization may be viewed as employing a stylized version of these simulations for representative transactions.

The financial engineering background to the SFA is set out in Gordy and Jones (2003) and Gordy (2004). To calculate a bottom-up formula for capital on a structured product tranche, the most obvious approach might be to employ the single asymptotic risk factor model used elsewhere in Basel II as the basis for capital curves linking default probabilities to capital for on balance sheet assets. This model is described in Gordy (2003).

The problem with this approach in the context of securitization tranches is that when the pool is perfectly granular, the implied capital charges turn out to equal 100 percent for junior tranches. For thin tranches, at a certain level of protection,* the capital charge drops abruptly from 100 to 0 percent. This implication of the model makes the model unappealing as a basis for capital calculations, as it implies that a bank might have a portfolio of mezzanine tranches against which it was not required to hold any capital but which would obviously be subject to credit risk.

Therefore, Gordy and Jones devised a model that effectively smooths out the step function for capital charges. In principle, various different approaches could be followed, as the basic aim was just to incorporate some smoothing of capital charges as the level of protection varies. The Gordy–Jones approach consists of assuming that the protection level for a given tranche is uncertain. They argue that in practise, the complexity of typical cash-flow waterfalls means that one cannot be sure of the exact level of protection enjoyed by a given tranche. Assuming a Wishart distribution, they derive a formula.

Figure 15.2 shows the capital for marginally thin tranches implied by the single asymptotic risk factor model plotted against protection as a step function. (Note that the protection level at which the capital jumps to 0 percent equals K_{IRB}, i.e., the capital that the bank would be obliged to hold against the asset pool if it retained it on balance sheet.) The Gordy–Jones smoothing approach yields a reverse S-shaped curve. Their model contains a parameter ω that reflects the degree of uncertainty about the level of protection. The figure shows capital plotted for different levels of ω. The Basel II supervisory formula is based on an ω value of 1000.

The SFA is not based solely on the supervisory formula just described, however, as it includes additional overrides that build in greater conservatism. In particular:

---

*The protection of a tranche here denotes the sum of the par value of more junior tranches tranches. It is also sometimes called the attachment point of the tranche.

FIGURE 15.2

SFA Capital Charges.

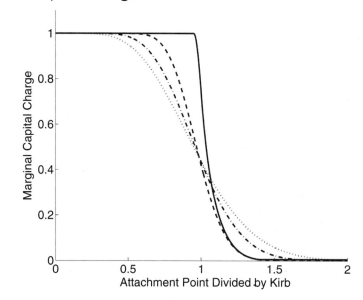

1. Capital charges are constrained to equal 100 percent for any protection level up to K_{IRB}.
2. For protection levels greater than K_{IRB}, the capital curve for thin tranches is then allowed to approach the Supervisory Formula smoothly based on an exponential smoothing.
3. Capital is constrained to be no less than 0.56 percent (corresponding to a risk weighting factor of 7 percent) even for high levels of protection.

These additional overrides yield the SFA formula that appears in Figure 15.2. The overrides may, in some cases, significantly increase the capital charges. Table 15.7 shows capital implied by the SFA for all the tranches

TABLE 15.7

Total Capital Under the SFA

Effective number of exposures in the pool	2	10	100
Total capital	1.42	1.19	1.08

FIGURE 15.3

SFA with Different Granularities.

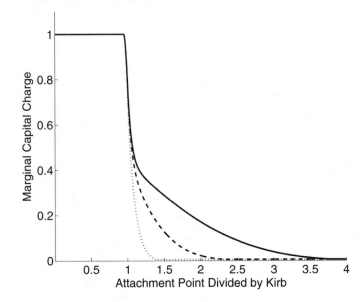

Attachment Point Divided by Kirb

in a structure as a fraction of K_{IRB}. When there are 100 underlying expo-sures, the total capital for all the tranches is just 8 percent higher than K_{IRB}. However, when the effective number of exposures is small such as 10 or 2, total SFA capital is 19 percent or 42 percent higher than the on balance sheet capital, K_{IRB}. To understand what drives this result, one may exam-ine Figure 15.3, which shows the SFA calculated for different effective numbers of exposure, N. As N decreases, the SFA curve becomes flatter; thus, the effect of overriding the basic inverted S-shaped supervisory for-mula by imposing that capital be 100 percent for protection levels less that K_{IRB} has a sizeable impact.

LIKELY CONSEQUENCES OF THE NEW FRAMEWORK

Discussions with banks suggest that the IRB institutions will employ the RBA where possible and, in a limited number of cases, the SFA. Widespread use of the RBA is likely to put originators under greater pressure to obtain agency ratings for more tranches. In some markets, e.g., Japan, one might expect there to be a significant reduction in the currently large number of unrated securitization exposures. In the past, there was considerable concern that large numbers of exposures would not fit into any of the approaches permitted. The less restrictive informational requirements for calculating K_{IRB} with purchased receivables and the introduction of the IAA has calmed these concerns.

Initially, many in the industry were anxious that the securitization market would be impaired by the reduction in capital arbitrage-related deals that the Basel II regulations would bring. However, the scope for securitization is likely to be significantly increased when banks have developed the systematic approaches to measuring and managing portfolio credit risk required by Basel. The nature of the market is likely to shift, therefore, with more transactions being motivated by genuine risk transfer and funding considerations and fewer by regulatory capital arbitrage.

In any case, if regulatory capital on individual securitization exposures is high, capital arbitrage between the banking and trading books may provide a safety valve. The boundary between the trading and banking books has been reconsidered by regulators, following the 2005 review of the trading book completed by the Basel Committee and the International Organization of Securities Commissions (IOSCO). Exposures can be classified as trading book exposures if they "arise out of a financial instrument or commodity" and "are held with trading intent or to hedge elements of the trading book." An increasing number of securitization exposures are sufficiently actively traded to be eligible for such treatment.

The capital charges that securitization exposures attract in a trading book context will depend on the volatility and correlations of market-wide factors driving spread and on specific risk charges. Perraudin and Van Landschoot (2004) show that the volatility of ABS exposures may be low, but that sudden and dramatic increases in risk may occur if shifts occur in the credit quality of particular market segments. To the extent that internal risk models employ relatively short return and spread change data series, the possibility of regime shifts in volatility may not be fully allowed for and capital may be too low.

Under the new rules, securitizations that would attract a 1250 percent risk-weight under the securitization framework or would be deducted will face equivalent charges in the trading book. This will reduce the scope for capital arbitrage between banking and trading books for equity tranches. However, it may remain for mezzanine tranches.

This chapter has focussed on the Pillar 1 part of Basel II, i.e., the rules governing minimum regulatory capital requirements. But other parts of Basel II will affect the securitization market. In particular, Pillar 3 covers rules on disclosure that banks will have to follow. For example, banks will have to reveal to the market qualitative information, such as the aims of their securitizations, the regulatory capital treatment adopted, and which rating agencies they employ to rate their securitizations.

They will also have to supply quantitative information about the bank's total outstanding volume of securitized exposures with a breakdown by type, and by whether the securitizations are traditional or synthetic,* and with information on the volume of impaired assets that have been securitized. They will also have to publish information about their aggregate holdings of securitization exposures. These substantial disclosures will reveal a lot about what directions are being taken in securitizations by individual banks and the market as a whole.

REFERENCES

Basel Committee on Banking Supervision (2005), *Basel II: International Convergence of Capital Measurement and Capital Standards: a Revised Framework* Bank for International Settlement: Basel, November.

Gordy, M. B. (2003), "A risk-factor model foundation for ratings-based bank capital rules," *Journal of Financial Intermediation*, 12, 199–232.

Gordy, M. B. (2004), "Model foundations for the supervisory formula approach," in W. Perraudin (ed.), *Structured Credit Products: Pricing, Rating, Risk Management and Basel II*, Risk Books: London, 307–328.

Gordy, M. B., and D. Jones (2003), "Random tranches," *Risk*, 16(3), March, 78–81.

Jones, D. (2000), "Emerging problems with the accord: Regulatory Capital arbitrage and related issues," *Journal of Banking and Finance*, 24, 35–58.

Peretyatkin, V., and W. Perraudin (2004), "Capital for structured products," in W. Perraudin (ed.), *Structured Credit Products*, Risk Books: London, 329–362.

Perraudin, W., and A. Van Landschoot (2004), "How risky are structured exposures compared with corporate bonds? in W. Perraudin (ed.), *Structured Credit Products*, Risk Books: London, 283–303.

Pykhtin, M. (2004), "Asymptotic model of economic capital for securitization," in W. Perraudin (ed.), *Structured Credit Products*, Risk Books: London, 215–244.

Pykhtin, M., and A. Dev (2002a), "Credit risk in asset securitizations: Analytical model." *Risk*, March, S26–S32.

Pykhtin, M., and A. Dev (2002b), "Credit risk in asset securitizations: The case of CDOs," *Risk*, May, S16–S20.

---

*Where no exposures are retained, this information will have to be disclosed in the first year only.

Securitization in the Context of Basel II: Case Studies*

Arnaud de Servigny

INTRODUCTION

In this chapter, we review the impact of Basel II treatment of securitization on two asset classes: credit cards and residential-mortgage backed securities (RMBS). We focus in particular on the discrepancies between the regulatory approach and S&P approach. One important point to recall is that S&P considers its models as one of the constituents leading to the tranching of a transaction. It is not the only one.

In the first part, we concentrate on credit cards and consider three types of transactions.

In the second part, we analyze four types of RMBS transactions.

PART 1: ANALYSIS OF THE IMPACT OF BASEL II ON THE CREDIT CARD ASSET CLASS†

The main finding in this part is related to the importance of excess spread in the analysis of the credit card asset class. Basel II(*) option to ignore

---

*The author would like to thank Alain Carron, Bernard de Longevialle, Wai To Wong, and Prashant Dwivedi for contribution.
†A definition of terms can be found in Appendix A.

excess spread for assets on balance sheet and to grant credit for it in rated securitized transactions, could generate significant regulatory arbitrage among banks.

The Internal Rating Based (IRB) Approach. Assets are on Balance Sheet and there is No Securitization*

We do not focus on the standardized approach that requires a uniform 75 percent risk weight (RW) for all credit cards transactions.

Regarding the IRB approach for credit cards, there is no distinction in Basel II between the foundation and the advanced approaches. Banks are required to provide an estimation of the probability of default (PD), the loss given default (LGD), and the exposure at default (EAD).

Credit card transactions are categorized in the revolving retail exposures sector:[†]

The Capital Risk Charge Formula[‡]

Within this sector, the pillar I equations are defined as below:

- ◆ Correlation $(R) = 0.04$
- ◆ Capital requirement $(K) =$

$$\text{LGD} \times N\left[(1-R)^{-0.5} \times G(\text{PD}) + \left(\frac{R}{(1-R)}\right)^{0.5} \times G(0.999)\right] - \text{PD} \times \text{LGD} \quad (1)$$

- ◆ Risk-weighted assets $= K \times 12.5 \times \text{EAD}$
- ◆ Risk-weight $= K \times 12.5$

In the Equation (1), $N(x)$ denotes the cumulative distribution function for a standard normal random variable. $G(z)$ denotes the inverse c.d.f. for a standard normal random variable.

Considering Three Transactions

In this section, we present empirical results, based on three credit card transactions:

---

*Basel II—Part 2; Section III.
[†]Basel II—Paragraph 234.
[‡]Basel II—Paragraph 327(ii).

+ Transaction 1 corresponds to a typical transaction in the United Kingdom or in the United States. It is characterized by a high yield, a medium/high level of charge-off.
+ Transaction 2 is typical of a transaction in continental Europe. It corresponds to a low yield, low charge-off pattern.
+ Transaction 3 is a subprime US transaction.

Extracting the Average Probability of Default in Each Pool

In the remainder of this section, we consider two cases. All cardholders are assumed to have a similar average level of risk (PD) that corresponds either to the mean or to a stressed default rate experienced by the bank on this asset class. This dual approach enables us to assess the impact of the conservatism of banks on their capital requirements, with respect to their internal risk monitoring systems.

A time-series of gross losses data typically represents the historical behavior experienced by a bank on its portfolio of credit card transactions. The ratio of the gross loss to the amount outstanding corresponds to the charge-off. This ratio is however different from a Basel II PD, in the sense that a common practice in the credit card industry is not to consider a 90-day past-due trigger for default, but rather a 180-day one. Empirical tests that we have performed show that multiplying the charge-off ratio by 1.35 gives a good proxy for the Basel II PD.

Transaction 1* In transaction 1, we consider Basel II one-year PDs, rolling on a monthly basis from December 1999 to September 2005. We plot the corresponding c.d.f. on which we fit a Gaussian c.d.f. We consider two cases, taking the PD at alternatively the 50 percent and the 95 percent confidence levels. This leads to a PD value of respectively **6.05** percent and **7.77** percent for transaction 1, as shown in Figure 16.1.

The normal distribution for PD of transaction 1 has the following properties: $N(\mu = 6.05$ percent; $\sigma = 1$ percent$)$.

---

*We removed the first year of information related to the time series in order to obtain stabilized PDs and LGDs.

FIGURE 16.1

Historical Distribution of Default Rates in Transaction 1.

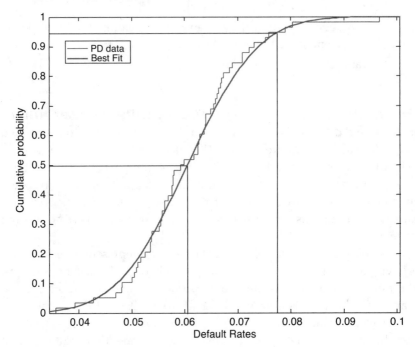

Transaction 2* In transaction 2, we consider Basel II one-year PDs, rolling on a monthly basis from December 2000 to September 2005. We plot the corresponding c.d.f. on which we fit a Gaussian c.d.f. We consider two cases, taking the PD at alternatively the 50 percent and the 95 percent confidence levels. This leads to a PD value of respectively **1.76** percent and **3** percent for transaction 2, as shown in Figure 16.2. In addition, we can observe that the Gaussian fit is less good than in transaction 1, probably given the lower number of cardholders in the pool.

The normal distribution for PD of transaction 2 has the following properties: $N(\mu=1.76$ percent; $\sigma=0.769$ percent$)$.

---

*We removed the first year of information related to the time series in order to obtain stabilized PDs and LGDs.

FIGURE 16.2

Historical Distribution of Default Rates in Transaction 2.

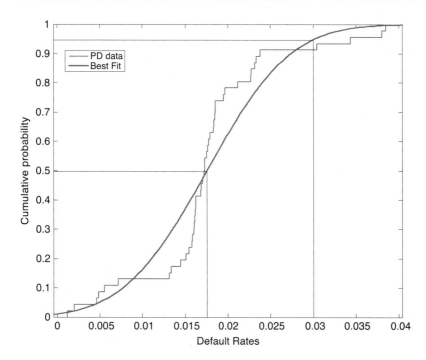

Transaction 3*   In transaction 3, we consider Basel II one-year PDs, rolling on a monthly basis from December 1996 to July 2005. We plot the corresponding c.d.f. on which we fit a Gaussian c.d.f. We consider 2 cases, taking the PD as alternatively the 50 percent and the 95 percent confidence levels. This leads to a PD value of respectively **19.8** percent and **27.7** percent for transaction 3, as shown in Figure 16.3. In addition, we can observe that the assumption of a Gaussian distribution of loss is less accurate than in transaction 1.

    The normal distribution for PD of transaction 3 has the following properties: $N(\mu = 19.8$ percent; $\sigma = 4.8$ percent).

---

*We removed the first year of information related to the time series in order to obtain stabilized PDs and LGD.

FIGURE 16.3

Historical Distribution of Default Rates in Transaction 3.

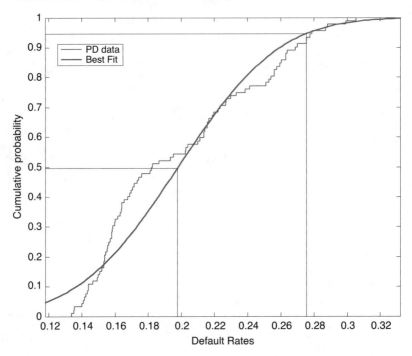

Extracting Loss Given Default

Non-Discounted LGD The Net charge-off = (Gross charge-off) − (Recoveries). The LGD rate can be found by dividing the Net charge-off by the Gross charge-off. As mentioned previously, a common practice in the credit card industry is not to consider a 90-day trigger for default but rather a 180-day one. The 90-day LGD has to be adjusted from the 180-day LGD. It is extracted from the equation below:

$$\text{LGD}_{90} = \left[1 - \left(\left(1 - \frac{1}{1.35}\right) + \frac{1 - (1 - \text{LGD}_{180})}{1.35}\right)\right] \times 100\% \qquad (2)$$

Transaction 1

As earlier, we consider two cases, taking the LGD at alternatively the 50 percent and the 95 percent confidence levels. This leads to an

FIGURE 16.4

LGD Historical Distribution (Transaction 1).

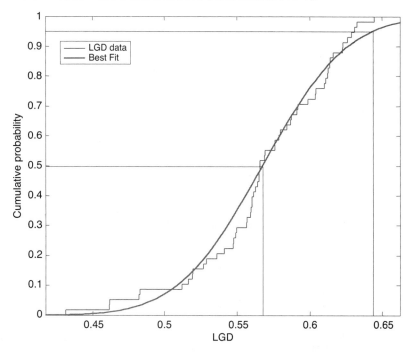

undiscounted LGD value of respectively **56.7** percent and **64.3** percent, as shown in Figure 16.4.

The normal distribution for LGD in transaction 1 has the following properties: ($\mu=56.7$ percent; $\sigma=4.6$ percent).

Transaction 2

As earlier, we consider two cases, taking the LGD at alternatively the 50 percent and the 95 percent confidence levels. This leads to an undiscounted LGD value of respectively **63.3** percent and **75** percent, as shown in Figure 16.5.

The normal distribution for LGD in transaction 2 has the following properties: $N(\mu=63.3$ percent; $\sigma=7.13$ percent).

Transaction 3

As earlier, we consider two cases, taking the LGD at alternatively the 50 percent and the 95 percent confidence levels. This leads to an

FIGURE 16.5

LGD Historical Distribution (Transaction 2).

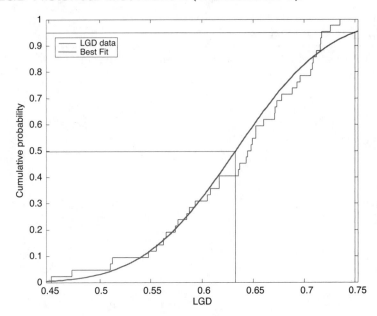

FIGURE 16.6

LGD Historical Distribution (Transaction 3).

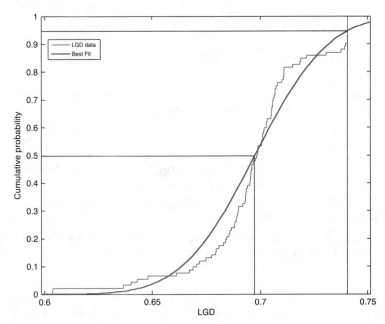

undiscounted LGD value of respectively **69.8** percent and **74.15** percent, as shown in Figure 16.6.

The normal distribution for LGD in transaction 3 has the following properties: $N(\mu = 69.8$ percent; $\sigma = 2.67$ percent).

Obtaining Discounted LGD from the Previous Observations

In this analysis, we consider two rates to discount LGD—the market risk-free rate and the average prepetition rate. Again this will help to gain some understanding of the sensitivity of capital requirements to the degree of conservatism in the measurement of LGD. The discounted LGD is extracted from the formula shown below:

$$\text{Discounted LGD} = 1 - \frac{\text{Recovery}}{(1+R)^T} \qquad (3)$$

Recovery $(\%) = (1 - \text{LGD})$ at the 50 percent and 95 percent confidence levels.

Market interest (R) = Averaged libor interest rate for transaction 1, in UK
= Averaged euribor interest rate for transaction 2, on continental Europe
= Average U.S. libor rate for transaction 3.

Prepetition rate (R) = Average Yield to Maturity (YTM) for transaction 1, 2, and 3.

Time to recovery (T): Since we consider a 90-day trigger for default instead of a 180-day one, we assume a 0.5-year recovery period for transactions that defaulted on a 90-day basis but paid before 180 days. In addition, based on empirical analysis, we consider that it usually takes 1.5 years (t) to recover for transaction 1 and 3, and 2.5 years for transaction 2. We can calculate the recovery time as:

$$T = \left(1 - \frac{1}{1.35}\right) \times 0.5 + \frac{1}{1.35} \times t \qquad (4)$$

= 1.24 years for transaction 1 and 3
= 2 years for transaction 2

Results are listed below:

Discounted LGD in Transaction 1

Transaction 1		
Confidence level (%)	50	95
LGD (%)	56.7	64.3
Average time to recovery (T) (years)	1.24	1.24
Libor interest rate (R) (%)	4.6	4.6
YTM (%)	18.9	18.9
Discounted LGD (using risk-free rate) (%)	59.05	66.24
Discounted LGD (using YTM) (%)	65.06	71.2

Discounted LGD in Transaction 2

Transaction 2		
Confidence level	50	95
LGD	63.3	75
Average time to recovery (T) (years)	2	2
Euribor interest rate (R)	1.86	1.86
YTM (%)	15.9	15.9
Discounted LGD (using risk free rate) (%)	64.63	75.9
Discounted LGD (using YTM) (%)	72.68	81.39

Discounted LGD in Transaction 3

Transaction 3		
Confidence level	50	95
LGD	69.8	74.15
Average time to recovery (T) (years)	1.24	1.24
US libor interest rate (R)	4.85	4.85
YTM	26.85	26.85
Discounted LGD (using risk-free rate)	71.52	75.62
Discounted LGD (using YTM)	77.51	80.75

On Balance Sheet IRB Results We can now compute the RWs obtained when the pool remains on balance sheet, depending on the assumptions on PD and LGD:

Transaction 1

Risk-free discount rate

Transaction 1 (using risk-free rate LGD)		
Confidence level (%)	50	95
PD (%)	6.05	7.77
Discounted LGD (%)	59.05	66.24
Minimum capital requirement (K) (%)	6.5	8.52
RW (%)	**81.27**	**106.51**

YTM discount rate

Transaction 1 (using YTM LGD)		
Confidence level	50	95
PD	6.05	7.77
Discounted LGD (%)	65.06	71.2
Minimum capital requirement (K) (%)	7.16	9.16
RW (%)	**89.54**	**114.48**

Transaction 2

Risk-free rate

Transaction 2 (using risk-free rate LGD)		
Confidence level (%)	50	95
PD (%)	1.76	3
Discounted LGD (%)	64.63	75.9
Minimum capital requirement (K) (%)	3.03	5.22
RW (%)	**37.83**	**65.21**

Yield to maturity

Transaction 2 (using YTM LGD)		
Confidence level (%)	*50*	95
PD (%)	72	3
Discounted LGD (%)	1.76	81.39
Minimum capital requirement (K) (%)	3.4	5.59
RW (%)	**42.54**	**69.93**

Transaction 3

Risk-free rate

Transaction 3 (using risk-free rate LGD)		
Confidence level (%)	*50*	95
PD (%)	19.8	27.7
Discounted LGD (%)	71.52	75.62
Minimum capital requirement (K) (%)	14.94	17.67
RW (%)	**186.77**	**220.9**

Yield to maturity

Transaction 3 (using YTM LGD)		
Confidence Level (%)	*50*	95
PD (%)	19.8	27.7
Discounted LGD (%)	77.51	80.75
Minimum capital requirement (K) (%)	16.19	18.87
RW (%)	**202.41**	**235.89**

Securitization

We consider the same three pools and analyze the capital requirement corresponding to their securitization (assuming that the deals are kept on balance sheet).

The Rating-Based Approach*

Under the rating based approach (RBA) the RW assets are determined by multiplying the exposure by the appropriate RWs provided in the table below:

External rating (Illustrative)	RWs for senior positions and eligible senior IAA exposures (%)	Base RWs (%)	RWs for tranches backed by nongranular pools (%)
AAA	7	12	20
AA	8	15	25
A+	10	18	
A	12	20	35
A–	20	35	
BBB+	35	50	
BBB	60	75	
BBB–		100	
BB+		250	
BB		425	
BB–		650	
Below BB– and unrated		Deduction	

In this case, capital requirements are independent from the confidence level at which PD and LGD are considered. As a result, we obtain only one set of results per transaction. We have added to the calculation the impact of the seller interest (defined in the section "Seller's interest buffer.") with a constant level of 7 percent.

♦ *Transaction 1:*

In transaction 1, the amount outstanding in the pool is £9 billion. It consists of 88 percent "AAA," 6 percent "A," and 6 percent "BBB."

Equivalent RW $= 93\% \times (7\% \times 88\% + 20\% \times 6\% + 75\% \times 6\%)$
$+ (7\% \times 89.54\%) = \textbf{17.3\%}$

Equivalent $K = 17.3\% \times 8\% = \textbf{1.38\%}$

Risk weigh appropriate (RWA) $= 17.3\% \times £9$ billion $= £1.6$ billion

---

*Basel II–Part 2, Section 4D–No. 4(vi).

♦ *Transaction 2:*

In Transaction 2, the amount of outstanding in the pool is
Euros 200 million. It consists of 90 percent "AAA," 4 percent
"A," 5 percent "BBB," and 1 percent "unrated."
Equivalent RW $= 93\% \times (7\% \times 90\% + 20\% \times 4\% + 75\% \times 5\%$
$+ 1250\% \times 1\%) + (7\% \times 42.54\%) = \mathbf{24.7\%}$
Equivalent $K = 24.7\% \times 8\% = \mathbf{1.98\%}$
RWA $= 24.7\% \times$ Euros 200 million $=$ Euros 49 million

♦ *Transaction 3:*

In Transaction 3, the amount outstanding in the pool is $6 bil-
lion. It consists of 50 percent "AAA," 20 percent "A," 15 percent
"BBB," and 15 percent "BB."
Equivalent RW $= 93\% \times (7\% \times 50\% + 20\% \times 20\% + 75\% \times 15\%$
$+ 425\% \times 15\%) + (7\% \times 202.41\%) = \mathbf{90.9\%}$
Equivalent $K = 90.9\% \times 8\% = \mathbf{7.27\%}$
RWA $= 90.9\% \times \$6$ billion $= \$5.5$ billion

The S&P Approach to Rate Credit Card Tranches

The S&P model is summarized in Appendix B.

In a credit card securitization transaction, the four drivers of credit
enhancement analyzed S&P are

1. The payment rate, or the proportion of principal repaid on
   a monthly basis
2. The asset yield
3. The charge-off rate
4. The repurchase rate, or the proportion of new drawings in
   a given month to total outstanding in the previous month.

Two of these variables, i.e., yield and charge-off, are intrinsically com-
menting on the absolute level of risk in the portfolio and the prominence
of the other two is more a consequence of the structural features of these
transactions: Payment rate and repurchase rate are not necessarily per se
major drivers of risk, they have yet a direct impact on how long noteholders are exposed to losses arising from the portfolio once the amortization period has started.

It follows from this that the latter two variables would have much less bearing in a going concern analysis of the type undertaken by S&P analysts when assessing a financial institution's issuer rating. However, it is notable that in both cases the yield, or in other words the excess spread, is a key factor. This is a major difference with Basel II pillar 1, where excess spread or future margin income is given no explicit credit for, and we will see later that there are ensuing consequences.

The Supervisory Formula Approach*

Under the Supervisory formula (SF) approach, the capital charge for a securitized tranche depends on five key inputs: The IRB capital charge had the underlying exposures not been securitized (K_{IRB}); the tranche's credit enhancement level (L); thickness (T); the pool's effective number of exposures (N); and the pool's exposure-weighted average loss-given-default (LGD).

The capital charge is calculated as follows:

Tranche's IRB capital charge = the amount of exposures that have been securitized time the greater of (1) $0.0056 \times T$, or (2) $(S[L+T] - S[L])$, where S[L] is the SF, which is given by the following expression:

$$
S[L] = \begin{cases} L & L \le K_{IRB} \\ K_{IRB} + K[L] - K[K_{IRB}] + \left(\dfrac{d \times K_{IRB}}{\omega}\right)\left(1 - \exp\left(\dfrac{\omega(K_{IRB} - L)}{K_{IRB}}\right)\right) & K_{IRB} \le L \end{cases}
$$

(5)

For more details on the formula, we revert readers to Basel II document on paragraph 624 or to Chapter 15.

Definition of Inputs:

1. K_{IRB}
   ◆ The ratio of (1) the IRB capital requirement including the EL portion for the underlying exposures in the pool to (2) the exposure amount of the pool.
   ◆ The formula is:

$$
K_{IRB} = LGD \times N\left[(1-R)^{-0.5} \times G(PD) + \left(\frac{R}{(1-R)}\right)^{0.5} \times G(0.999)\right]
$$

(6)

---

*Basel II–Part 2, Section 4D–No. 4(vi).

	Transaction 1 (%)		Transaction 2 (%)		Transaction 3 (%)	
Confidence level	50	95	50	95	50	95
K_{IRB} (using Risk-free rate)	10.07	13.67	4.16	7.49	29.1	38.62
K_{IRB} (using YTM)	11.1	14.69	4.68	8.03	31.54	41.24

2. *Credit enhancement level (L)*

   The ratio of (a) the amount of all tranche exposures subordinate to the tranche in question to (b) the size of the pool.

Transaction 1 (%)	
AAA	12
A	6
BBB	0
AAA	10
Transaction 2 (%)	
A	6
BBB	1
Unrated	0
AAA	50
Transaction 3 (%)	
A	30
BBB	15
BB	0

3. *Thickness of exposure (T)*

   The ratio of a) the size of the tranche of interest to b) the size of the pool.

Transaction 1 (%)	
AAA	88
A	6
BBB	6
Transaction 2 (%)	
AAA	90
A	4
BBB	5
Unrated	1
Transaction 3 (%)	
AAA	50
A	20
BBB	15
BB	15

4. *Effective number of exposures (N)*

$$N = \frac{\left(\sum_i EAD_i\right)^2}{\sum_i EAD_i^2}$$

5. *Exposure-weighted average LGD*

$$LGD = \frac{\sum_i LGD_i \cdot EAD_i}{\sum_i EAD_i}$$

The value of LGD is the same as in the IRB approach, as we assume equal weighting for all credit card transactions.

	Transaction 1 (%)		Transaction 2 (%)		Transaction 3 (%)	
Confidence level	*50*	*95*	*50*	*95*	*50*	*95*
LGD (using Risk-free rate)	59.05	66.24	64.63	75.9	71.52	75.62
LGD (using YTM)	65.06	71.2	72.68	81.39	77.51	80.75

Detailed Results
Transaction 1

Transaction 1 (using risk-free rate LGD)		
Confidence level (%)	*50*	*95*
K_{IRB} (%)	10.07	13.67
Discounted LGD (%)	59.05	66.24
Equivalent K (%)		
AAA	0.785	4.95
A	100	100
BBB	100	100
RW (%)		
AAA	9.818	61.82
A	1250	1250
BBB	1250	1250
Overall RW (%)	133.84	180.64
Overall equivalent K value	10.7	14.45

Transaction 1 (using YTM LGD)		
Confidence level (%)	50	95
K_{IRB} (%)	11.1	14.69
Discounted LGD (%)	65.06	71.2
Equivalent K (%)		
AAA	1.98	6.12
A	100	100
BBB	100	100
RW (%)		
AAA	24.72	76.53
A	1250	1250
BBB	1250	1250
Overall RW (%)	147.24	193.88
Overall equivalent K value (%)	11.78	15.51

Transaction 2

Transaction 2 (using Risk-free rate LGD)		
Confidence level (%)	50	95
K_{IRB} (%)	4.16	7.49
Discounted LGD (%)	64.63	75.9
Equivalent K (%)		
AAA	0.56	0.739
A	2.83	100
BBB	93.51	100
Unrated	100	100
RW (%)		
AAA	7	9.23
A	35.35	1250
BBB	1168.84	1250
Unrated	1250	1250
Overall RW (%)	62.98	100.18
Overall equivalent K value (%)	5.04	8.01

Transaction 2 (using YTM LGD)		
Confidence level (%)	*50*	*95*
K_{IRB} (%)	4.68	8.03
Discounted LGD (%)	72.68	81.39
Equivalent K (%)		
AAA	0.56	1.35
A	12.55	100
BBB	99.86	100
Unrated	100	100
RW (%)		
AAA	**7**	**16.85**
A	**156.92**	**1250**
BBB	**1248.29**	**1250**
Unrated	**1250**	**1250**
Overall RW	**69.83**	**107.24**
Overall equivalent K value	5.59	8.58

Transaction 3

Transaction 3 (using Risk-free Rate LGD)		
Confidence level (%)	*50*	*95*
K_{IRB} (%)	29.1	38.62
Discounted LGD (%)	71.52	75.62
Equivalent K (%)		
AAA	0.56	0.56
A	0.56	16.835
BBB	66.12	100
BB	100	100
RW (%)		
AAA	**7**	**7**
A	**7**	**210.44**
BBB	**826.51**	**1250**
BB	**1250**	**1250**
Overall RW	**384.47**	**505.45**
Overall equivalent K value	30.76	40.44

Transaction 3 (using YTM LGD)		
Confidence level (%)	50	95
K_{IRB} (%)	31.54	41.24
Discounted LGD (%)	77.51	80.75
Equivalent K (%)		
AAA	0.56	0.56
A	0.56	29.07
BBB	79.92	100
BB	100	100
RW (%)		
AAA	7	7
A	7	363.36
BBB	999	1250
BB	1250	1250
Overall RW (%)	415.52	539.09
Overall equivalent K value (%)	33.24	43.13

"Seller's Interest" Buffer

In credit card transactions, it is customary to transfer an additional 7 percent of the pool value to the structure. This portion is not rated as it corresponds to a buffer meant to absorb fraud and dilution risks. In this analysis, when we show comparisons, we add to the securitized RWs these 7 percent, considered with the K_{IRB} rate.

The following graph (Figure 16.7) the sensitivity of RW to the percentage of seller's interest when it increases.

FIGURE 16.7

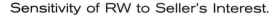

Sensitivity of RW to Seller's Interest.

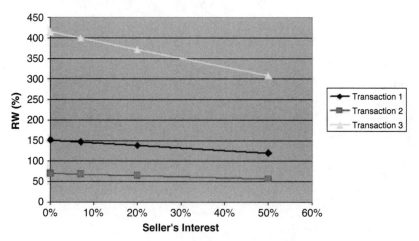

Basel II Drawn and Undrawn Lines and Early Amortization

According to paragraph 595 of Basel II, credit card lines, whether they are drawn or undrawn are considered to be uncommitted.

In a credit card securitization transaction, during the life of the transaction and before the scheduled amortization process starts, all receivables associated with a debtor are relocated in the securitization vehicle, whether they are drawn or undrawn. There is no risk that some of the undrawn exposures get back on the balance sheet of the issuer, unless the issuer keeps some tranches of the transaction on its balance sheet or unless an early amortization process is triggered. There are two categories of early amortization: controlled and noncontrolled ones.

When considering a securitized exposure, paragraph 590 of Basel II refers to "the Investors' interest," i.e., both the drawn and undrawn exposures related to the transaction.

Basel II focuses on early amortization in paragraphs 590 to 605 and 643.

The Issuer Perspective—Early Amortization of the Drawn Portion

Let us define the credit conversion factor (CCF) as a weighting coefficient commensurate with the level of risk that the originator may be facing due to early amortization.

The required extra level of capital is $C = I * CCF * RWA$. Where I stands for the "investor's interest" in this case the drawn balances related to the securitized exposure, and RWA for the risk weight appropriate to the underlying exposures, had they not been securitized.

- ◆ Controlled early amortization (599): for uncommitted but drawn cases, the level of CCF is increasing gradually from 0 to 40 percent while the excess spread is diminishing and becoming negative.
- ◆ Uncontrolled early amortization (602–604): for uncommitted but drawn cases, the level of CCF is increasing gradually from 0 to 100 percent while the excess spread is diminishing and becoming negative.

If we assumed that the controlled case would be applicable, we would note that in all the "prime" cases, the reserve account put in place in the S&P framework (comparable to capital) would look more conservative than the above formula for controlled early amortization. In the "subprime" cases the Basel II formula would look more conservative, but it is the case where a zero or negative excess spread is the most unlikely. Based on a careful reading of paragraph 548, S&P however believes that almost all currently rated credit card transactions should be considered as part of the uncontrolled early amortization situation, as none of them fulfils all required four conditions detailed in that paragraph. In this case, Basel II always looks more conservative than the S&P model.

One additional difference worth mentioning is that in the S&P model triggering some levels above the trapping point opens the reserve account that will be filled gradually, whereas in the Basel II setup additional capital requirement becomes immediate.

The Issuer Perspective—Early Amortization of the Undrawn Portion   Uncommitted and undrawn cases:

+ For transaction 1, the uncommitted undrawn exposure typically represents three times the drawn amount.
+ For transaction 2, the uncommitted undrawn exposure typically represents one time the drawn amount.
+ For transaction 3, the uncommitted undrawn exposure typically represents one-fifth of the drawn amount.

Practically, this means that the required extra level of capital is $C = I * \text{CCF} * \text{RWA}$. Where I stands for the "investor's interest" in this case, the undrawn balances related to the securitized exposure, had they not been securitized. For uncommitted and undrawn cases, the level of CCF is increasing gradually while the excess spread is diminishing and becoming negative. The RWA corresponds to the appropriate risk weight, had the assets not been securitized. The RWA will depend on the assessment of the EAD.

We therefore need to detail the on balance sheet treatment. It can be found in paragraph 83, as well as in paragraphs 334 to 338. We have read that in the case no securitization was taking place, the uncommitted undrawn part would typically receive a 0 percent CCF under the standardized approach and a bespoke low EAD increase under IRB approach, based on the historical track record of the bank.

The S&P methodology does not consider any specific treatment for undrawn exposures in case of early amortization.

Comparisons*

Transaction 1 (Yield to Maturity LGD)

Figure 16.8 shows a comparison of RWs between the standardized, IRB, SF, and RBA approaches in transaction 1 at a 50 percent confidence level.

Figure 16.9 shows a comparison of RWs between the standardized, IRB, SF, and RBA approaches in transaction 1 at a 95 percent confidence level.

Transaction 2 (Yield to Maturity LGD)

Figure 16.10 shows a comparison of RWs between the standardized, IRB, SF, and RBA approaches in transaction 2 at a 50 percent confidence level.

Figure 16.11 shows a comparison of RWs between the standardized, IRB, SF, and RBA approaches in transaction 2 at a 95 percent confidence level.

Transaction 3 (Yield to Maturity LGD)

Figure 16.12 shows a comparison of RWs between the standardized, IRB, SF, and RBA approaches in transaction 3 at a 50 percent confidence level.

FIGURE 16.8

Comparison of RW (Percent) in Transaction 1 (Average Case).

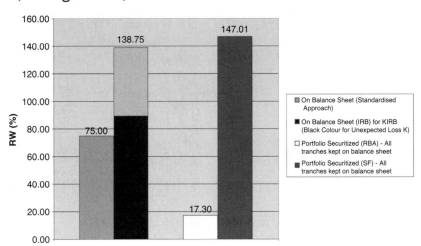

*In this section we include the effect of the "Seller's interest" into the computation.

FIGURE 16.9

Comparison of RW (Percent) in Transaction 1
(Stressed Case).

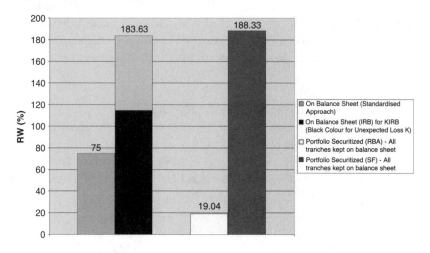

FIGURE 16.10

Comparison of RW (Percent) in Transaction 2
(Average Case).

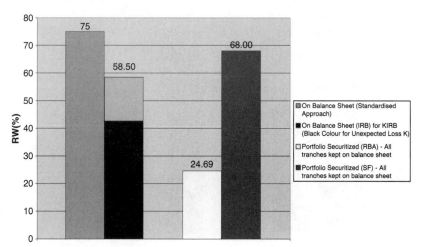

FIGURE 16.11

Comparison of RW (Percent) in Transaction 2
(Stressed Case).

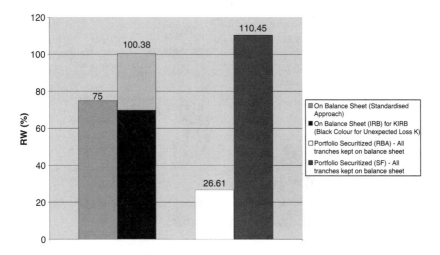

FIGURE 16.12

Comparison of RW (Percent) in Transaction 3
(Average Case).

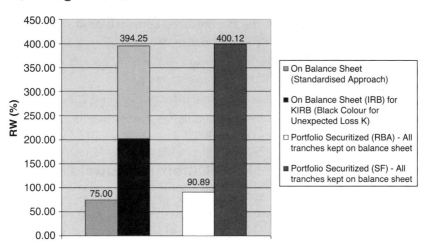

FIGURE 16.13

Comparison of RW (Percent) in Transaction 3
(Stressed Case).

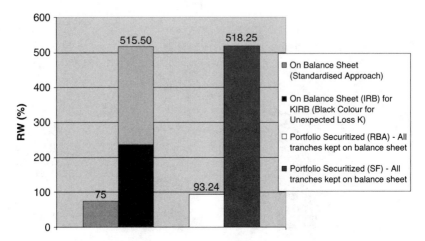

Figure 16.13 shows a comparison of RWs between the standardized,
IRB, SF, and RBA approaches in transaction 3 at a 95 percent confidence level.
The main results of this comparative analysis are:

♦ The IRB approach favors the continental pool with a lower PD
  (pool 2).
♦ Counter intuitively, the standardized approach produces lower
  results than IRB for two of the three pools.
♦ There are strong disincentives to use the SF approach versus the
  RBA approach for all three transactions.
♦ The RBA requirements are similar for pools 1 and 2.
♦ The RBA approach looks generally very attractive as compared
  to owning the assets under IRB.

Sensitivity of the Different Models

Sensitivity to PD*

In this paragraph, we review the sensitivity of the RBA and the SF
approaches to a change in PD level in each of the transactions, everything

---

*We do not integrate the indirect effect of Early amortization when the PD gets sufficiently
high so that the excess spread of the transaction gets close to the trapping point.

else being kept equal. Regarding both the S&P model related to the RBA approach and the SF approach, we change the tranching accordingly to the output of the S&P model (we assume that banks who decide not to get a rating have been able to replicate the S&P model and tranche their transaction accordingly).

50 percent confidence level risk-free rated LGD is used in all calculations. For the SF approach, probabilities of default in each graph are adjusted to correspond to the 90-day past-due Basel II definition (Figures 16.14, 16.15, and 16.16).

Sensitivity to Yield

In this paragraph, we review the sensitivity to a change in yield level in each of the transactions, everything else being kept equal. For both the S&P model and the IRB approach, we change the tranching accordingly to the output of the S&P model.

In this section, we include the impact of the uncontrolled early amortization mechanism on Basel II results.

Fifty percent confidence level risk-free rated LGD and K_{IRB} are used in all calculations (Figures 16.17, 16.18, and 16.19).

FIGURE 16.14

Comparison between K SF and K RBA
Sensitivity to PD (Transaction 1).

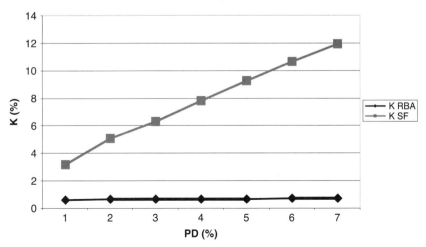

FIGURE 16.15

Comparison between K SF and K RBA
Sensitivity to PD (Transaction 2).

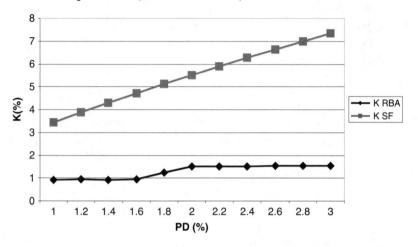

FIGURE 16.16

Comparison between K SF and K RBA
Sensitivity to PD (Transaction 3).

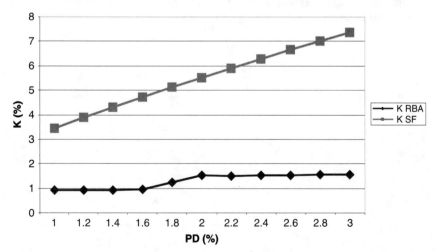

FIGURE 16.17

Comparison between K SF and K RBA
Sensitivity to Yield (Transaction 1).

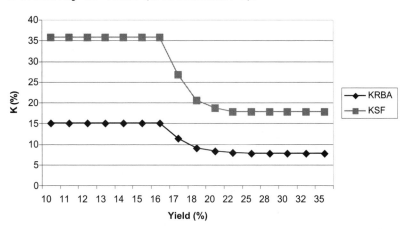

FIGURE 16.18

Comparison between K SF and K RBA
Sensitivity to Yield (Transaction 2).

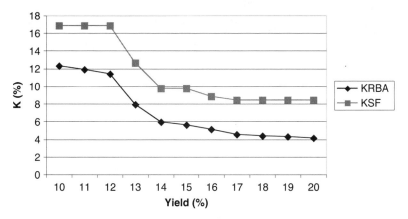

FIGURE 16.19

Comparison between K SF and K RBA
Sensitivity to Yield (Transaction 3).

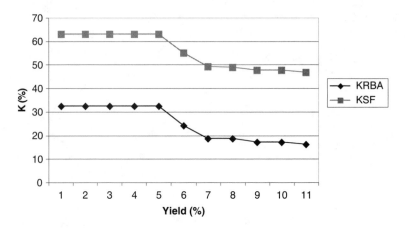

Sensitivity to Payment Rate

In this paragraph, we review the sensitivity to a change in payment rate level in transactions 1, everything else being kept equal. For both the S&P model and the IRB approach, we change the tranching accordingly to the output of the S&P model.

FIGURE 16.20

Comparison between K SF and K RBA
Sensitivity to Payment Rate (Transaction 1).

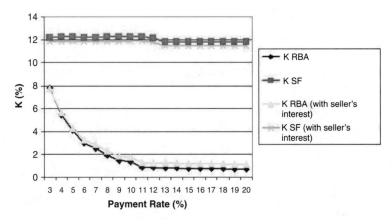

FIGURE 16.21

Comparison between K SF and K RBA
Sensitivity to Payment Rate (Transaction 2).

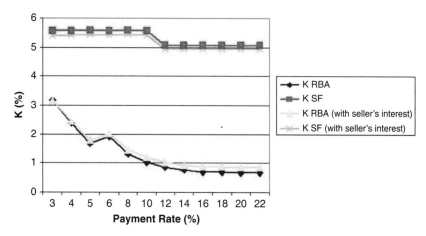

Fifty percent confidence level risk-free rated LGD and K_{IRB} are used in all calculations. Once the payment rate drops below a certain level, we have to introduce an unrated tranche in the S&P model (Figures 16.20, 16.21, and 16.22).

FIGURE 16.22

Comparison between K SF and K RBA Sensitivity
to Payment Rate (Transaction 3).

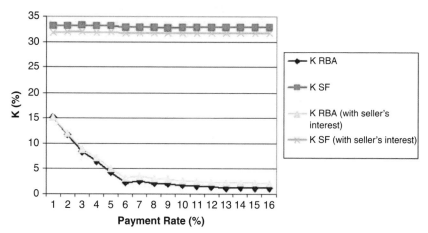

Conclusion of Part 1

Securitization versus Keeping Assets on Balance Sheet: The Impact of Excess Spread

As discussed in the introduction, the level of excess spread in a securitization transaction has a direct effect on the capital structure. This is why in the credit card field, it is not uncommon, even if counterintuitive at first sight, for subprime portfolios to have a AAA tranche as large as or even larger than a prime pool. On the other hand, excess spread or future margin income is not a factor in Basel II's pillar 1. Pillar 1 is meant to measure unexpected loss only.

The credit card sector is probably the one where this discrepancy has the widest consequences, as reinforced by the fact the most junior notes in a capital structure for UK or US assets can often be rated BBB on the basis of the strength of the excess spread alone.

Securitization: Discussion on the Use of the Supervisory Formula

From the three examples we have considered above, it seems clear that the SF has been calibrated to dissuade regulated investors from keeping unrated securitization tranches on their balance sheet. Such capital treatment should represent an incentive for originators to have a systematic recourse to more transparent external rating assessment on their securitization transactions. We can identify two elements that make the SF approach way more conservative than the RBA approach:

- The size of the tranches below BBB seems to be most of the time much smaller than the K_{IRB} level. As a result, some of the mezzanine and even the senior tranches get penalized as if they were junior (with a one for one capital treatment).
- The capital charge related to the most senior tranches in the pool are negatively impacted in the SF framework by the almost exclusive focus on a typically high K_{IRB} level and the absence of credit granted to a high level of excess spread.

PART 2: ANALYSIS OF THE IMPACT OF BASEL II ON THE RMBS ASSET CLASS

The main finding in this part is that apart for subprime deals, regulatory arbitrage will probably not be a key driver for securitization.

The IRB Approach. Assets are on Balance Sheet and there is No Securitization*

We do not focus on the standardized approach that requires a uniform 35 percent RW for all residential mortgage transactions.

Regarding the IRB approach for residential mortgages, there is no distinction in Basel II between the foundation and the advanced approaches. Banks are required to provide an estimation of the PD, the LGD, and the EAD.

RMBS transactions are related to residential mortgage exposures:[†]

The Capital Risk Charge Formula[‡]

Within this sector, the pillar I equations are defined as below:

- Correlation $(R) = 0.15$
- Capital Requirement $(K) =$

$$\mathrm{LGD} \times N\left[(1-R)^{-0.5} \times G(\mathrm{PD}) + \left(\frac{R}{(1-R)}\right)^{0.5} \times G(0.999)\right] - \mathrm{PD} \times \mathrm{LGD} \quad (7)$$

- Risk-weighted assets $= K \times 12.5 \times \mathrm{EAD}$
- Risk-weight $= K \times 12.5$

In the Equation (7) above, $N(x)$ denotes the cumulative distribution function for a standard normal random variable. $G(z)$ denotes the inverse c.d.f. for a standard normal random variable.

Considering Four Transactions

In this section, we present some empirical results, based on four transactions.

- Transaction 1—A prime transaction in the UK.

---

*Basel II—Part 2; Section III.
[†]Basel II—Paragraph 232.
[‡]Basel II—Paragraph 327(ii).

- Transaction 2—A subprime transaction in the UK.
- Transaction 3—A prime transaction in continental Europe–Germany.
- Transaction 4—A prime transaction in continental Europe–Spain.

Extracting the Average Probability of Default in Each Pool In the remainder of this section, we consider two cases. All mortgages are assumed to have a similar average level of risk (PD) that corresponds either to the mean or to a stressed default rate experienced by the bank on this asset class.

A time-series of default rates (90 days) is typically available from which we can extract the average PD.

Transaction 1 In transaction 1, we use rolling one-year PDs on a monthly basis from July 2001 to February 2006. We plot the c.d.f. corresponding to the monthly default rate on which we fit a Gaussian c.d.f. We consider two cases, taking the PD at alternatively the 50 percent and the 95 percent confidence levels. This leads to PD values of respectively **0.53%** and **0.73%** for transaction 1, as shown in Figure 16.23.

The normal distribution for PD in transaction 1 has the following properties: $N(\mu=0.53\%; \sigma=0.12\%)$.

Transaction 2 In transaction 2, we plot the c.d.f. corresponding to the monthly default rate on which we fit a Gaussian c.d.f. We consider two cases, taking the PD at alternatively the 50 percent and the 95 percent confidence levels. This leads to PD values of respectively **15.08%** and **17.37%** for transaction 2, as shown in Figure 16.24.

The normal distribution for PD in transaction 2 has the following properties: $N(\mu=15.08\%; \sigma=1.39\%)$.

Transaction 3 In transaction 3, we consider rolling one-year PDs on a monthly basis from April 2002 to January 2006. We plot the c.d.f. corresponding to the monthly default rate on which we fit a Gaussian c.d.f. We consider two cases, taking the PD at alternatively the 50% and

FIGURE 16.23

Default Rate Distribution in Transaction 1.

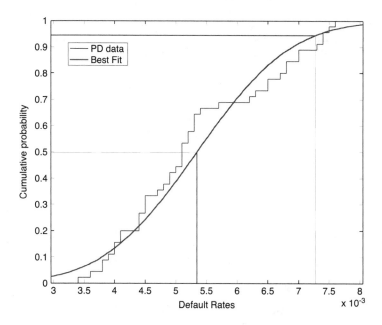

FIGURE 16.24

Default Rate Distribution in Transaction 2.

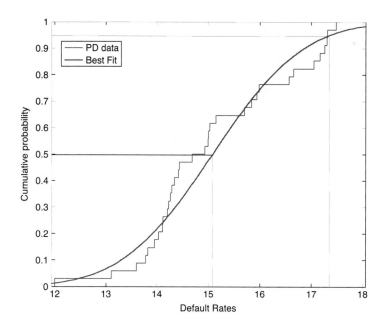

FIGURE 16.25

Default Rate Distribution in Transaction 3.

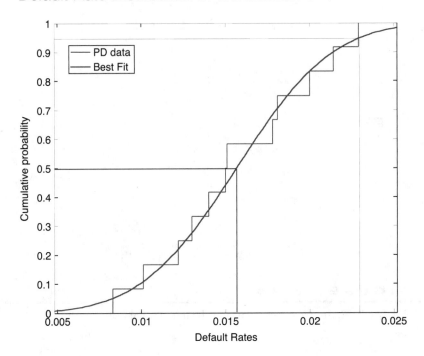

the 95% confidence levels. This leads to PD values of respectively **1.57**% and **2.31** % for transaction 3, as shown in Figure 16.25.

The normal distribution for PD in transaction 3 has the following properties: $N(\mu=2.74\%; \sigma=0.45\%)$.

Transaction 4   In transaction 4, we consider rolling one-year PDs on a monthly basis from April 2002 to October 2005. We plot the c.d.f. corresponding to the monthly default rate on which we fit a Gaussian c.d.f. We consider two cases, taking the PD at alternatively the 50% and the 95% confidence levels. This leads to a PD value of respectively **0.164**% and **0.23**% for transaction 4, as shown in Figure 16.26.

The normal distribution for PD in transaction 4 has the following properties: $N(\mu=2.74\%; \sigma=0.04\%)$.

FIGURE 16.26

Default Rate Distribution in Transaction 4.

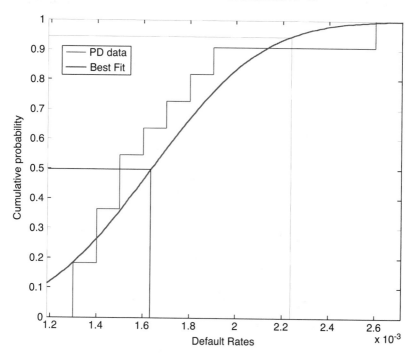

Extracting Lost Given Default

Non Discounted LGD   In RMBS terms, the LGD for each loan is called loss severity (LS), as detailed in the glossary in Appendix 3. LS is defined as:

$$LS = 100\% - \frac{RV}{LTV} + FC$$

Where foreclosure cost (FC) = 4 to 6 percent of the loan
residual value of property (RV) = [100 percent − market value decline (MVD)]
loan-to-value (LTV) = loan/valuation of the property

By considering that the LGD of the pool corresponds to the weighted average of LSs, we can extract the LGD from the data.

As previously, we consider two cases, taking the LGD alternatively as the average LGD and as a stressed LGD. The difference between the average LGD and the stressed LGD is based on the MVD that is used. These values are defined by S&P based on the region and country where the property is located.

Transaction 1

In the average LGD case, the MVD is assumed to be 26 percent for the South of UK and 12 percent for the North of UK.

In the stressed LGD case, the MVD is assumed to be 47 percent for the South of UK and 25 percent for the North of UK.

Results	
Average LGD	5.4%
Stressed LGD	17.2%

Transaction 2

For the average and stressed LGD cases, see transaction 1.

Result	
Average LGD	6.7%
Stressed LGD	21.8%

Transaction 3

In the average LGD case, the MVD is assumed to be 28 percent.
In the stressed LGD case, the MVD is assumed to be 45 percent.

Result	
Average LGD	2%
Stressed LGD	8.1%

Transaction 4

In the average LGD case, the MVD is assumed to be 22 percent.
In the stressed LGD case, the MVD is assumed to be 37 percent.

Result	
Average LGD	7.2%
Stressed LGD	15.6%

Discounted LGD In this analysis, we consider one scenario where the LGD is discounted based on the risk-free rate. The discounted LGD can be derived from the formula shown below:

$$\text{Discounted LGD} = 1 - \frac{\text{Recovery}}{(1+R)^T}$$

$$\text{Recovery (\%)} = (1 - \text{LGD})$$

Market Interest (R) = Averaged libor interest rate for transaction 1 and 2 in UK

= Averaged euribor interest rate for transaction 3 and 4 on continental Europe

Time to recovery (T) = 1.5 years

LGD Results are detailed below:

Transaction 1		
Case	**Average**	**Stressed**
LGD (%)	5.4	17.2
Average time to recovery (T)	1.5 years	1.5 years
Libor interest rate (R) (%)	4.6	4.6
Discounted LGD (using risk-free rate) (%)	11.57	22.6

Transaction 2		
Case	**Average**	**Stressed**
LGD (%)	6.7	21.8
Average time to recovery (T)	1.5 years	1.5 years
Libor interest rate (R) (%)	4.6	4.6
Discounted LGD (%)	12.79	30.59

Transaction 3		
Case	**Average**	**Stressed**
LGD (%)	2	8.1
Average time to recovery (T)	1.5 years	1.5 years
Euribor interest rate (R) (%)	1.86	1.86
Discounted LGD	4.67	10.61

Transaction 4		
Case	**Average**	**Stressed**
LGD (%)	7.2	15.6
Average time to recovery (T)	1.5 years	1.5 years
Euribor interest rate (R) (%)	1.86	1.86
Discounted LGD (%)	9.73	25.33

On Balance sheet IRB Results

We can now compute the RW obtained when the pool remains on balance sheet, depending on the assumptions on PD and LGD:

Case	**Average**	**Stressed**
Transaction 1		
PD (%)	0.53	0.73
Discounted LGD (%)	11.57	22.6
Minimum capital requirement (K) (%)	0.75	1.83
Risk-Weight	**9.4**	**22.9**
Transaction 2		
PD	15.08	17.37
Discounted LGD	12.79	30.59
Minimum Capital Requirement (K)	5.37	13.34
Risk-Weight	**67.1**	**166.78**
Transaction 3		
PD (%)	2.74	3.46
Discounted LGD (%)	4.67	10.61
Minimum capital requirement (K) (%)	0.88	2.29
Risk-Weight (%)	**11**	**33.23**
Transaction 4		
PD (%)	0.164	0.23
Discounted LGD	9.73	25.33
Minimum capital requirement (K)	0.269	0.902
Risk-Weight	**3.37**	**11.27**

Securitization

We consider the same four pools and analyze the capital requirement corresponding to their securitization.

Standardized Approach for Securitization Exposures*

Under the Standardized approach, the RW assets are determined by multiplying the amount of the exposure by the appropriate RWs, provided in the tables as shown:

Long-term rating category[†]

External credit assessment	AAA to AA–	A+ to A–	BBB+ to BBB–	BB+ to BB–	B+ and below or unrated
RW	20%	50%	100%	350%	Deduction

Results:

Transaction 1:

Total risk weight = **47.09 percent**
Equivalent $K = 3.77$ percent

Transaction 2:

Equivalent risk weight = **44.78 percent**
Equivalent $K = 44.78\% \times 8 = 3.58$

Transaction 3:

Equivalent risk weight = **28.79 percent**
Equivalent $K = 28.79\% \times 8\% = 2.3\%$

Transaction 4:

Equivalent risk weight = **40.21 percent**
Equivalent $K = 40.21\% \times 8\% = 3.22\%$

Rating-Based Approach (RBA) for Securitized Exposures[‡]

Under the RBA approach, the risk-weighted assets are determined by multiplying the tranche exposures by the appropriate RWs. Results are provided in the table presented in the section: "The Rating-Based Approach (RBA)."

---

*Basel II—Part 2: Section IV.D.3.
[†]The rating designations used in the following charts are for illustrative purposes only and do not indicate any preference for, or endorsement of, any particular external assessment system.
[‡]Basel II—Part 2, Section 4D—No. 4(iv).

Transaction 1:

Equivalent risk weight = **38.58%**
Equivalent $K = 38.61\% \times 8\% = 3.09\%$

Transaction 2:

Equivalent risk weight = **36.92%**
Equivalent $K = 36.92\% \times 8\% = 2.95\%$

Transaction 3:

Equivalent risk weight = **16.1%**
Equivalent $K = 16.1\% \times 8\% = 1.29\%$

Transaction 4:

Equivalent risk weight = **26.86%**
Equivalent $K = 26.86\% \times 8\% = 2.15\%$

The Supervisory Formula Approach*

See this section in Part 1 regarding the methodology. We present here the results.

Transaction 1

Case	Average (%)	Stressed (%)
K_{IRB}	0.81	2
Discounted LGD	11.57	22.6
Equivalent K		
AAA	0.56	0.56
AA	0.56	0.56
A	0.56	0.56
BBB	0.56	7.75
Unrated	48.16	100
Risk-Weight		
AAA	7	7
AA	7	7
A	7	7
BBB	7	96.87
Unrated	602.03	1250
Overall risk weight	18.69	34.51
Overall equivalent K value	1.49	2.76

*Basel II—Part 2, Section 4D—No. 4(vi).

Transaction 2

Case	Average (%)	Stressed (%)
K_{IRB}	7.3	18.85
Discounted LGD	12.79	30.59
Equivalent K		
AAA	0.56	5.53
AA	0.56	100
A	47.85	100
BBB	100	100
BB	100	100
Unrated	100	100
Risk-Weight		
AAA	7	69.14
AA	7	1250
A	598.07	1250
BBB	1250	1250
BB	1250	1250
Unrated	1250	1250
Overall risk weight	104.08	247.92
Overall equivalent K value	8.33	19.83

Transaction 3

Case	Average (%)	Stressed (%)
K_{IRB}	1.01	2.66
Discounted LGD	4.67	10.61
Equivalent K		
AAA	0.56	0.56
AA	3.33	100
A	69.94	100
Unrated	100	100
Risk weight		
AAA	7	7
AA	41.67	1250
A	874.31	1250
Unrated	1250	1250
Overall risk weight	21.37	36.96
Overall equivalent K value	1.71	2.96

Transaction 4

Case	Average (%)	Stressed (%)
K_{IRB}	0.285	0.96
Discounted LGD	9.73	25.33
Equivalent K		
AAA	0.56	0.56
A	0.56	0.56
BBB	0.56	0.68
Unrated	24.28	74.19
Risk weight		
AAA	7	7
A	7	7
BBB	7	8.52
Unrated	303.51	927.34
Overall risk weight	11.39	20.65
Overall equivalent K value	0.911	1.65

Comparisons

Transaction 1

Figure 16.27 shows a comparison of RW between Standardized, IRB, RBA, and SF approach in the average case.

Figure 16.28 shows a comparison of RW between Standardized, IRB, RBA, and SF approach in the stressed case.

Transaction 2

Figure 16.29 shows a comparison of RW between Standardized, IRB, RBA, and SF approach in the average case.

Figure 16.30 shows a comparison of RW between standardized, IRB, RBA, and SF approach in the stressed case.

Transaction 3

Figure 16.31 shows a comparison of RW between standardized, IRB, RBA, and SF approach in the average case.

Figure 16.32 shows a comparison of RW between standardized, IRB, RBA, and SF approach in the stressed case.

FIGURE 16.27

Comparison of RW (Percent) in Transaction 1 (Average Case).

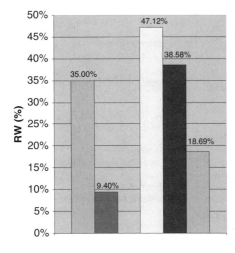

FIGURE 16.28

Comparison of RW (Percent) in Transaction 1 (Stressed Case).

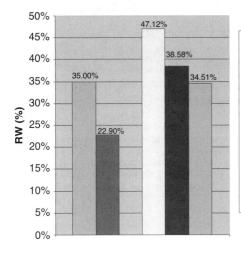

FIGURE 16.29

Comparison of RW (Percent) in Transaction 2
(Average Case).

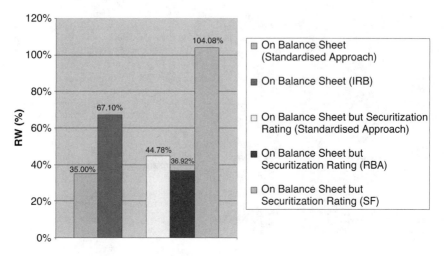

FIGURE 16.30

Comparison of RW (Percent) in Transaction 2
(Stressed Case).

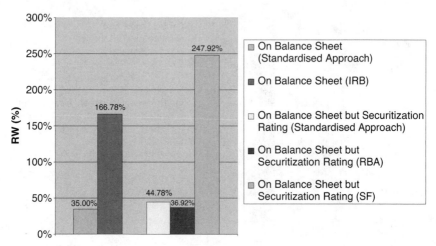

FIGURE 16.31

Comparison of RW (Percent) in Transaction 3 (Average Case).

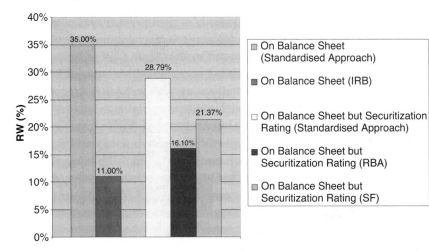

FIGURE 16.32

Comparison of RW (Percent) in Transaction 3 (Stressed Case).

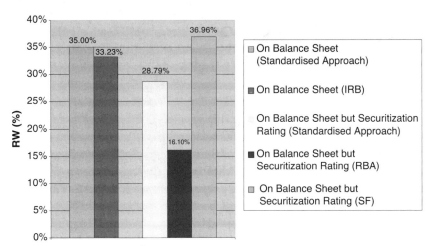

FIGURE 16.33

Comparison of RW (Percent) in Transaction 4 (Average Case).

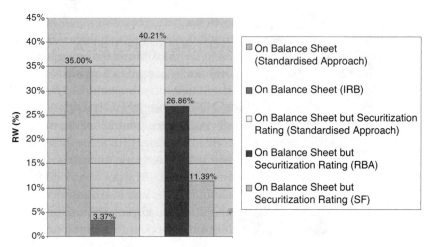

FIGURE 16.34

Comparison of RW (Percent) in Transaction 4 (Stressed Case).

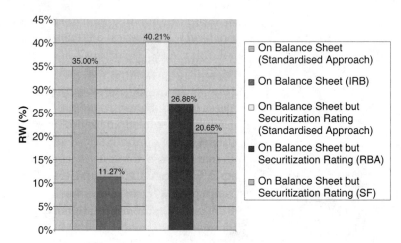

Transaction 4

Figure 16.33 shows a comparison of RW between standardized, IRB, RBA, and SF approach in the average case.

Figure 16.34 shows a comparison of RW between standardized, IRB, RBA, and SF approach in the stressed case.

Conclusion of Part 2

The first conclusion is that the type of arbitrage, we could observe systematically, in the credit card asset class does not occur anymore for the RMBS sector. A point could however mitigate this statement slightly as when no securitization is taking place, the bank needs to provision an amount that should be reasonably close to the expected loss level (see paragraphs 380 to 386).

Another point to mention is that the way banks will measure PDs and LGDs will very much impact the existence of an opportunity of arbitrage linked to securitization transactions.

Lastly, securitization seems to make more sense for subprime pools than for prime ones.

APPENDIX A

Definitions and General Terminology—Credit Cards

Asset side

Payment Rate
The credit card payment rate can be defined as: Principal Repayment this month as a percentage of outstanding receivables in the previous month.

Yield
The yield represents the total revenue collected by the issuer, as a percentage of the outstanding. The numerator of the Yield consists of three items:
- Finance charges, i.e., primarily interest paid
- Fees (late fee and over-limit fee)
- Interchange (It is the fee paid to originators by VISA or MasterCard for absorbing risk and funding receivables during grace periods) [S&P does not take interchange into account in its cash flow model.].

Gross losses (charge off)
Losses on the principal of receivables on the basis of a 180 days past due definition.

Default rate
The default rate corresponds to the 90-day past due Basel II definition.

Gross charge-off (%)
Losses on the principal of receivables due in 180 days divided by outstanding in corresponding month, annualized.

Recovery
Realization on receivables that are charged off. Recovery figures provided by originators are not discounted when received.

Liability side

Tranching (initial class size)
The initial class size is the relative weight of each tranche in a transaction.

Certificate rate (coupon rate)
The Certificate rate is the ratio of certificate interest paid to investors divided by outstanding invested amount annualized.

Beginning coupon (beg. coup)/Max coupon rate (max. coup)
S&P assumes that the certificate rate is a floating rate rather than a fixed rate. The certificate rate is assumed to increase over time from a beginning coupon rate. In floating-rate deals in which interest rate caps are provided, interest rates are increased to the level of the cap (max coupon rate). It is in ratio, since it is the coupon payment to the total notes outstanding.

Beginning loss
The beginning loss corresponds to the initial level of loss assumed in the transaction under stress. It is usually calculated as the maximum of 0 or yield—servicing charge—beg. coup—excess spread.

Step-up
It is the rate of increase of the coupon rate. S&P assumes 1% step up. If the beginning coupon rate is 10% and the max coupon rate is 15%, it will go up from 10%, 11%, 12%, so on, and so far till it reaches 15%.

LGD (%)	LGD is 1 minus the recovery rate. S&P credit card model assumes the LGD to be 100%, i.e., no recovery.
Net losses	Gross losses minus recovery.
Exposure at default	This is the credit exposure in the portfolio at the time of default.
Purchase rate	Purchases keep the amount of principal receivables in the trust from declining. The purchase rate is the ratio of the amount of purchases that cardholders have made this month divided by the total outstanding last month.
Servicing charge (servicing)	Servicing is the service fee, salary, etc. required to manage the transaction. In S&P model, servicing is assumed to be fixed at 2% of the total notes outstanding.
Interest shortfall	Interest shortfall occurs when the SPV does not have sufficient cash to pay the interest due to investors. In S&P model, this information is reported as the ratio of the interest shortfall amount to the total notes outstanding initially.
Servicing shortfall	Servicing shortfall occurs when the SPV does not have enough cash to pay the servicing charge. In S&P model, the information is reported as the ratio of the servicing shortfall to the total notes outstanding initially.
Principal shortfall	Principal shortfall occurs when the SPV does not have enough cash to pay the principal to investors. In S&P model, the information is reported as the ratio of principal payment to the total notes outstanding initially.
CIA	A credit enhancement to the more senior classes, class A and class B, is a subordinated interest known as CIA.
Excess spread	Excess spread can be described as the difference between the returns of both assets and liabilities in the structure. In other words, excess spread is the difference between the yield and the certificate rate, the servicing charge, and the losses. In the stress tests associated with S&P models, all factors mentioned earlier are stressed to the worst case; hence, the excess spread will be negative in most stressed cases. Excess spread = yield − coupon − servicing − losses
Base rate amortization	Base amortization occurs when the yield is not sufficient to cover the coupon interest.

Abbreviations: LGD = loss given default; CIA = collateral invested amount.

Credit Card Model, the S&P Methodology

After assessing the seller and servicer's (SPV) operations and analyzing the performance of the issuer's (Originator) receivables, S&P runs cash flow scenarios that stress five key performance variables:

- Payment rate
- Purchase rate
- Losses
- Portfolio yield
- Certificate rate

If the average three months portfolio yield is insufficient to cover the certificate interest and servicing fees averaged for the same period, a base rate amortization will occur. Different issuers will have different rules for the amortization; In this model, S&P assumes that as an issuer enters in the amortization, it will pay out the principal and the interest to the more senior tranche holder first. For some other transactions, it may be paying back the principal to all investors first and then the payment of interest as per the waterfall.

TRAPPING POINT

All credit card structures incorporate a series of amortization events that, if triggered, cause principal collections allocated to investors to be passed through immediately and before the maturity date. Amortization events include insolvency of the originator of the receivables, breaches of representations or warranties, a servicer default, failure to add receivables as required, and asset performance-related events. Additionally, amortization happens if the three-month average excess spread falls below zero.

In a typical credit card structure, credit enhancement for the Class A and Class B are fully funded at closing. For example, the Class A certificate relies on the credit enhancement provided by the subordination of Class B and Class C notes. In constant, the enhancement for the Class C notes is dynamic. Generally, if excess spread falls below specified levels, excess finance charge collections are trapped in a spread account for the CIA's benefit.

TABLE B.1

Sample Spread Account Trapping Mechanism

Three-month average excess spread (%)	Reserve fund target % of initial series invested amount
4.5	0.0
4.0–4.5	1.5
3.5–4.0	2.0
3.0–3.5	3.0
3.0	4.0

An example of spread account structure and the required trigger levels is shown in Table B.1.

In this example, if the three-month average excess spread is above 4.5 percent, no deposit is required. Should excess spread falls between 4 to 4.5 percent, it will be trapped in the spread account until the spread account balance is equal to 1.5 percent of the initial invested amount. As excess spread falls, the targeted reserve fund balance increases. At less than 3 percent excess spread, the targeted reserve account will be 4 percent. In an adverse scenario, this structural credit enhancement is designed to build the reserve account before the excess spread falls below zero.

VARIABLES

Among the five variables, S&P focuses primarily on three of them—losses (charge-off rate), payment rate, and portfolio yield—for the base case assumption. These three variables are extracted from historical data (S&P averages monthly data from the most recent calendar year for these three variables).

REQUIRED TRANCHES

The initial tranching (class size) suggested by the seller is an input to the model. An example of Transaction 1's class sizes is shown on Table B.2.

TABLE B.2

Initial Class Sizes

Class A (%)	90.00
Class B (%)	5.00
Class C (%)	5.00
Total size (%)	100.00

STRESS FACTORS

After entering the data related to the class sizes and the base case assumptions based on the latest historical data, stress factors have to be chosen for each variable in accordance to a range of stress factors defined globally. Table B.3 shows the range for every factors.

The stressed scenario assumptions are obtained by applying a stress factor within the range listed in Table B.3 to the base case assumptions.

Stressed default rate = base case default rate × default rate stress
factor = "Max loss"
Stressed payment rate = base case payment rate × payment rate
haircut = "Payment rate"
Stressed yield rate = base case yield rate × yield haircut = "Yield"

KEY INPUTS PER RATING CATEGORY

In Table B.4, the values shown in bold correspond to the stressed assumptions; all the other fields are computed from them or are inputs.

An example of an "AAA" stress case for a transaction is shown in Table B.3.

+ The excess spread happens to be –5 percent for "AAA" case, –3 percent for "A" case. The excess spread is negative because in a stress scenario, the loss variable is under a much bigger stress. For example, excess spread = yield – beg. coup – servicing – beg. loss, (where in a stressed case, excess spread = 9.75 percent – 2 percent – 7 percent – 5.75 percent).
+ The excess spread for the "BBB" case is based upon the trapping point. In Transaction 1, it is 4.5 percent.

TABLE B.3

Ranger for Stress Factors

	Default rate (X coefficient)	Payment rate (% of base case)	Yield (% of base case)
AAA	4–5	50–55	65–70
A	2.5–3	60–65	70–75
BBB	1.5–2	70–75	75–80

TABLE B.4

Assumptions (AAA)

Excess spread (%)	–5.00
Yield (%)	**9.75**
Purchase rate (%)	3.00
Payment rate (%)	**10.00**
Servicing (%)	2.00
Beg. coup (%)	7.00
Max coup (%)	15.00
Step-up (%)	1.00
Beg. loss (%)	5.75
Max loss (%)	**30.00**

- The servicing is assumed to be 2 percent for all cases.
- The beginning coupon rate and the max coupon rate are assumed to be, respectively,—7 percent and 15 percent for "AAA" tranche; 7.3 percent and 14 percent for "A" tranche; and 7 percent to 15 percent Fixed coupon rate for "BBB" tranche.
- Step-up rate is always 1 percent for "AAA" tranche and 0.8 percent for "A" tranche.
- The purchase rate is extracted from the historical data.
- The loss rate is increasing gradually from the beginning loss to the max loss.

THE ENGINE

The model will determine four outcomes—the interest shortfall, the principal shortfall, the service shortfall, and the duration of paying back the principal to investors. The underlying calculations are in a waterfall format on a monthly basis.

Step 1: Determine the cash flow (CF = yield rate × beginning month's balance)

Step 2: Determine the interest for the "AAA" tranche (I_{AAA} = coupon rate × tranche amount)

Step 3: Check the remaining amount/shortfall ($CF_2 = CF - I_{AAA}$)

Step 4: Determine the interest for the "A" tranche (I_A = coupon rate × tranche amount)

Step 5: Check the remaining amount/shortfall ($CF_3 = CF_2 - I_A$)

Step 6: Determine the servicing fee (SF = servicing × transaction principal exposure)

Step 7: Check the remaining amount/shortfall ($CF_4 = CF_3 - SF$)

Step 8: Determine the interest for the "BBB" tranche ($I_{BB>B}$ = coupon rate × tranche amount)

Step 9: Check the remaining amount/shortfall ($CF_5 = CF_4 - I_{BBB}$)

Step 10: Determine the loss amount (L = loss rate × transaction principal exposure)

Step 11: Compute the final balance ($CB = CF_5 - L$)

Step 12: The final balance becomes the new beginning month balance

Step 13: Go back to step 1

TABLE B.5

Rating Category Scenarios (AAA)

Month	1	2	3	4	5	6
Beginning Balance	100,000	93,333	86,940	80,824	74,990	69,440
Purchases	3,000	2,800	2,608	2,425	2,250	2,083
Payments	10,000	9,333	8,694	8,082	7,499	6,944
Yield	813	758	706	657	609	564
Losses	479	619	736	833	910	971
Principal Payments	9,188	8,575	7,988	7,426	6,890	6,380
End Balance	93,333	86,940	80,824	74,990	69,440	64,173

Table B.5 shows the results from the model. The table (Table B.5) shows the beginning balance of each month, the purchases rate, the principal payment rate, the yield, the losses, and the end balance of each month.

ADJUSTMENT OF STRESS FACTORS

The interest shortfalls, the principal shortfalls, and the service shortfalls of each scenario are determined in the model as shown in Table B.6. The tranching requirements are accepted if interest shortfall, service shortfall, and the principal shortfall (values in bold) are all below 0.05 percent.

Since all assumptions are determined for each stress case, the principal payment for each stress scenario is obtained as: payment due this month – yield of this month. Hence, the end balance of each month is calculated by: beginning balance + purchase – loss – principal payment. The outcome of this number will be the next month's beginning balance. This process is repeated until principal is paid back to investors, consequently the duration can be found.

TABLE B.6

Credit/Liquidy (AAA)

A sub. size (%)	**9.91**
A Interest shortfall (%)	**0.000**
Servicing shortfall (%)	**0.05**
A write-down (%)	**0.000**
B interest shortfall (%)	3.104
LOC draw (%)	12.50

APPENDIX C

Definitions and General Terminology–Residential-Mortgage Backed Securities

Asset side

Buy-to-let properties	Buy-to-let corresponds to borrowers who purchase properties for rental purposes. Since these borrowers rely on the rental income to pay their mortgage installments, the buy-to-let mortgages are considered to carry greater risk.
CCJs or discharged bankruptcy	CCJs and discharged bankruptcy relate to the credit history of a borrower. If a borrower has CCJs or has been bankrupt in the past, an increased likelihood of a mortgage loan might default in the future.
Default rate	Losses on principal of receivables (expressed as a percentage of the outstanding loan).
Exposure at default	Exposure at default is the credit exposure vis-a-vis an obligor at the time of default.
Foreclosure	A situation in which a homeowner is unable to make principal and/or interest payments on his/her mortgage. The lender, be it a bank or building society, can seize and sell the property as stipulated in the terms of the mortgage contract. So, Foreclosure frequency = default rate.

Liability side

GIC account	GIC account will guarantee a certain level of return on amounts outstanding.
Servicing charge (Servicing)	Servicing charge is the service fee, salary, etc. required to manage the transaction. In the RMBS world, servicing fees vary from jurisdiction to jurisdiction. For UK prime deals, S&P assumes that the servicing fees are in the area of 35 basis points of the total notes outstanding; whereas for the subprime deals, S&P assumes the servicing fees to be around 50 basis points (the lower the credit quality of the underlying borrowers, the greater the effort of the servicer in order to collect the payments). However, in other jurisdictions, e.g., Greece, S&P assumes that the servicing fees are around 70 basis points.
Tranching (initial class size)	In the RMBS world, we see various kinds of capital structure that cover the entire rating spectrum, from AAA moving all the way down the capital structure to BB. It is depending on the jurisdiction and the underlying mortgages (prime versus subprime).

Term	Description	Term	Description
Income multiples	Income multiples is the ratio of the annual income of the borrower to the loan.	Certificate rate (coupon rate)	The coupon interest rate.
Interest rate payable under the mortgages	The interest rate that the underlying borrowers pay on, e.g., monthly basis.	Beginning coupon (beg. coup)/ max coupon rate (ceiling level)/ floor level coupon rate	S&P assumes the certificate rate is a floating rate rather than a fixed rate. Therefore, the certificate rate is assumed to increase/decrease over time from a beginning coupon rate with respect to the Libor interest rate. In floating-rate deals in which interest rate caps and floor level are provided, interest rates are increased/decreased to the level of the cap (max coupon rate)/floor level. It is in ratio since it is the coupon payment to the total notes outstanding.
Jumbo loans	A jumbo loan is defined as a loan exceeding certain amount according to different area we are interested in (e.g., A loan in Germany which exceeds Euros 400,00 is a jumbo loan).	Step-up/ step-down margin	It is the rate of increase/decrease for the coupon rate from the beginning coupon rate according to the trend of the market.
LGD (%)	LGD is 1 minus the recovery rate.	Interest shortfall	Interest shortfall occurs when the SPV does not have sufficient cash to pay the interest due to investors. In S&P model, this information is reported as the ratio of the interest shortfall amount to the total notes outstanding initially.
LS	Loss given default for individual transaction within the pool (a loan to loan LGD). For both prime and subprime pools, SL is defined as: $LS = 100\% - $ residual value of property/LTV $+$ foreclosure costs of the property.	Servicing shortfall	Servicing shortfall occurs when the SPV does not have enough cash to pay the servicing charge. In S&P model, the information is reported as the ratio of the servicing shortfall to the total notes outstanding initially.
Loan repayment type	Methods through which borrowers repay their loan. ♦ IO—the borrower makes monthly interest payments, with the total principal due at final maturity. The interest only loans with maturity between 5 and 10 years are assumed to carry greater risk, as the borrower might have been unable to build up his capital during such a short period. ♦ REP—The principal amortizes over the life of the loan; i.e., the borrower repays principal and pays interest at each mortgage payment date. ♦ PP—Part of the mortgage is based on repayment and the rest is on an IO basis.	Principal shortfall	Principal shortfall occurs when the SPV does not have enough cash to pay the principal to investors. In S&P model, the information is

(continued)

Appendix C (continued)

Asset side		Liability side	
LTV	The LTV is defined as the ratio of aggregate mortgage debt divided by the value of the property.		reported as the ratio of principal payment to the total notes outstanding initially.
MVD	The MVD corresponds to the loss in value of a property backing a mortgage loan.	Excess spread	Excess spread can be described as the difference between the returns of both assets and liabilities in the structure. In other words, excess spread is the difference between the yield and the aggregated amount of the certificate rate, the servicing charge, and the losses. In the stress tests associated with S&P models, all factors mentioned earlier are stressed to the worst case; hence, the excess spread will be an negative percentage in most stressed cases.
SVR	SVR is a standard rate, e.g., floating rate, which is a sum of the current market's rate (e.g., Libor, Euribor, etc.) plus an additional interest rate set by a particular bank (the Margin).		
Non-SVR Loans	The Non-SVR corresponds to loans with interest payments that are not linked to the SVR of the lender (such as fixed, discounted, or capped rate loans).		Excess spread = yield − beg. coup − servicing − beg. loss
Self-certified income	Self-certified income loans are loans made in cases where borrowers cannot supply adequate income documentation, or the underwriting of the loan has not included income documentation requirements (For the self-certified loans, there is no objective measurement of the income of the borrower; consequently, these loans are considered to carry greater risk.).	PDL	The amount by which the principal balance of liabilities exceeds that of the assets (e.g., due to payment).
WAFF	Based on the S&P assumptions, the average default rate in the pool under stressed scenarios.		

Timing of defaults	The WAFF at each rating level specifies the total balance of the mortgage loans assumed to default over the life of the transaction. S&P assumes that these defaults occur over a three-year recession. S&P analyzes the impact of the timing of this recession on the ability to repay the liabilities, and defines the recession starting period specific to each rating level. Although the recession normally starts the first month of the transaction, the "AAA" recession is usually delayed by 12 months. The WAFF is applied to the principal balance outstanding at the start of the recession (e.g., in a "AAA" scenario the WAFF is applied to the balance at the beginning of month 13).
WALS	The loss severity in the entire pool under stressed scenarios. WALS is 1 minus the recovery rate. Calculations are based on S&P assumptions.

Abbreviations: CCIs = county court judgment; LGD = loss given default; LS = loss severity; LTV = Loan-to-value ratio; IO = interest only; REP = repayment; PP = part by part; MVD = market value decline; SVR = standard variable rate; WAFF = weighted-average foreclosure frequency; WALS = weighted-average loss severity; GIC = Guaranteed investment contract; PDL = principal balance of deficiency ledger.

BIOGRAPHIES

Arnaud de Servigny is a Managing Director at Barclays Wealth. He is responsible for Quantitative Analytics. Up until August 2006 he was a Managing Director at Standard & Poor's. He was responsible for Quantitative Analytics in Credit Market Services. One of his dominant areas of focus was Structured Finance Quantitative Analytics. His initial position within Standard & Poor's was as the European head of quantitative analytics and products within S&P Risk Solutions. Prior to joining Standard and Poor's, Arnaud worked in the Group Risk Management Department of BNP-Paribas in France. He is a Visiting Professor of Finance at Imperial College, London. He holds a Ph.D. in Financial Economics from the Sorbonne University, an MSc in Finance from a program associating Dauphine University and HEC Business School, and a Civil Engineering MSc from Ecole Nationale des Ponts & Chaussees.

Publications include many papers and articles as well as three books

- *The Standard & Poor's Guide to Measuring and Managing Credit Risk*, McGraw Hill 2004, with Olivier Renault.
- *Le Risque de Credit*, Dunod Editions 2001—2003—2006, with Ivan Zelenko and Benoit Metayer.
- *Economie Financiere*, Dunod Editions 1999, with Ivan Zelenko.

Norbert Jobst joined DBRS in May 2006 as a SVP, Quantitative Analytics. Prior to that, and at the time of writing this book, he was a Director at

Standard & Poor's Structured Finance Ratings Division and Head of Multivariate Quantitative Research within Standard & Poor's Credit Market Services. He has lead a team of quantitative analysts, focusing on model development for synthetic CDOs, covering also research into portfolio (credit) risk analytics.

He holds a degree in Mathematics from Regensburg (FH), Germany, and a Ph.D. in Mathematical Sciences from Brunel University, U.K. He conducted research into credit risk modeling and optimization under uncertainty, which was funded by Fidelity Investments.

Alexander Batchvarov, Ph.D., CFA, is a Managing Director at Merrill Lynch in London. He has been Head of Merrill Lynch's International Structured Product Research group since 1998 when he relocated from New York to London. He and his team cover a range of structured products originated in Europe and Asia categorized in four main categories: RMBS, consumer ABS, CMBS, and cash and synthetic CDOs.

Prior to Merrill Lynch, he worked at Moody's Investors Service and at Citibank, both in New York City, and has covered the securitization and structured finance markets in the United States, Latin America, Europe, and Asia. He and his team have been consistently ranked in the top three positions in investors' surveys carried out by Institutional Investors, EuroMoney, ISR in Europe, etc.

He has published extensively on numerous topics in structured finance. He co-authored and edited the *Merrill Lynch Guide to International Mortgage Markets and MBS*—the first extensive comparative study of the mortgage markets in 12 European and Asian countries. He is the editor of the first publication on Hybrid Products by Risk Books. He has also contributed chapters to different books; among others, the different editions of the Fabozzi's *The Handbook of Mortgage-Backed Securities* and the *Handbook of European Structured Financial Products*.

He holds a Ph.D. in Economics from the Bulgarian Academy of Sciences and an MBA in Finance from the University of Alberta in Canada.

Sven Sandow has recently moved to a tier 1 international bank. Up until recently he headed the univariate quantitative research group within Standard & Poor's Credit Market services. His responsibilities included developing methods for modeling credit risk, as well as developing specific models for various asset classes. He taught graduate level courses at New York University's Courant Institute of Mathematical Sciences and at Polytechnic University. He is a Fellow in Courant's Mathematics in Finance Program. Prior to joining Standard & Poor's in 2002, he held positions with Lord, Abbett & Co. and with TechHackers/Citibank, where he worked as a quantitative analyst. He worked as a researcher in statistical physics at Virginia Polytechnic University and the Weizmann Institute of Science.

He received a Ph.D. in Physics and a M.Sc. in Physics from Martin-Luther Universität Halle-Wittenberg. He has published articles in physics, finance, statistics, and machine learning journals.

Philippe Henrotte is a Professor of Finance at HEC, a French business school, and Head of Financial Theory, at ITO 33, a software company active in quantitative finance.

He has earned his Ph.D. from Stanford University, and he graduated from Ecole Polytechnique de Paris before that.

Astrid Van Landschoot is an Associate Director in the Structured Finance Quantitative Group at Standard & Poor's. She works in the analytics team, where she focuses primarily on quantitative credit risk modeling for structured finance products, mainly CDOs. Prior to joining Standard & Poor's in 2005, she worked in the Financial Stability Group (Research and Analysis) of the National Bank of Belgium, where she also conducted research on credit risk modeling.

She holds a MSc in Economics and a Ph.D. in Finance from Ghent University, Belgium.

Vivek Kapoor recently joined UBS as an Executive Director. He is responsible for analyzing the risk-reward profile for structured credit trading within UBS's new alternative investment management business, Dillon Read Capital Management. Prior to that, he was the risk-manager for CDO trading at Credit-Suisse, where he was responsible for analyzing and communicating the risk-return profile of individual trades and for the CDO trading in aggregate and for developing a risk-assessment strategy to assess risk-capital on CDO trading. Prior to Credit-Suisse, Vivek worked for S&P, where he developed approaches for rating market and credit risk sensitive structured products.

He holds a Ph.D. from MIT in the area of stochastic modeling of geophysical flows and dispersion.

Andrea Petrelli is a Vice President at Credit Suisse. He initially joined the High Energy Physics Division at Argonne National Laboratory, Argonne, Illinois, U.S.A., mainly working on heavy quarks interaction. In 2002, he moved to Banca Intesa, Milan, Italy, where his work was mainly devoted to credit derivatives modeling. In 2004, he joined Credit Suisse in London, where he is responsible for CDO Trading Risk Management in Europe. His main interest is credit derivatives modeling, valuation and risk, and correlation trading.

He graduated at Pisa University, where he also obtained his Ph.D. in Theoretical Physics, developing his thesis on perturbative QCD at CERN TH Division.

Jun Zhang is the head of CDO Risk Management (U.S.) and Vice President at Credit-Suisse. His main responsibility is to monitor the risks for both synthetic and cash CDO, such as spread, default, and correlation risks. Before joining Credit-Suisse, he was a Credit Risk Quantitative Analyst at Toyko Mitsuibish Financial Group, where his main responsibility was portfolio analysis of credit derivatives products. He has been a speaker at trading and risk management conferences.

He has BS in Engineering from ShangHai Jiao Tong University in China, a MS in Mathematics in Finance from New York University, and a Ph.D. in Engineering from the Johns Hopkins University.

Varqa Khadem is a Director working in the European Structured Finance Research Group at Lehman Brothers, covering ABS, CMBS, RMBS, and other esoteric securitised products. His focus has been on research and modeling of prepayments, and defaults and losses in European residential mortgages and RMBS. Prior to this, he worked at Standard and Poor's Risk Solutions as a Quantitative Analyst working on the credit risk analysis of middle market/SME sectors in the United Kingdom, Germany, France, Italy, and Spain. He started his career in 2001 in the portfolio management and group risk functions at Abbey National Treasury Services (now Abbey Financial Markets, part of Banco Santander) working principally on economic capital and capital allocation across both the wholesale bank and the residential mortgage bank.

He holds a Ph.D. in Finance from Oxford University on the pricing of defaultable corporate and convertible bonds incorporating the effects of strategic game theoretic behaviour. His undergraduate and masters studies were in Physics (Imperial College, University of London).

Francis Parisi is a Managing Director in the Quantitative Analytics group at Standard & Poor's. He joined Standard & Poor's in 1985 as a rating officer in the residential mortgage group. Since then, Frank has held various positions in structured finance, including training director, manager of the surveillance group, member of the research and criteria group, and ana-lytical manager in the residential mortgage group. Prior to joining Standard & Poor's, he worked at Chemical Bank in New York with respon-sibility for mortgage warehouse lending, secondary mortgage marketing, and issuing and servicing mortgage-backed securities.

He earned his BA in Philosophy, his MS in Statistics, and his Ph.D. in Management of Engineering and Technology. His research interests include extreme value theory, time series analysis, applied probability, and Markov decision processes, with applications in finance and climatology.

Olivier Renault recently moved to CDO structuring within Citigroup. He use to be the Head of European Structured Credit Strategy for Citigroup, based in London. He is a regular speaker at professional and academic conferences and is the author of a book and many published articles on credit risk. Prior to joining Citigroup, Olivier was responsible for portfolio modeling projects at Standard & Poor's Risk Solutions and was a lecturer in finance at the London School of Economics, where he taught derivatives and risk. He was also a consultant for several fund management and financial services companies.

He holds a Ph.D. in financial economics from the University of Louvain (Belgium) and MSc from Warwick University (U.K.).

Cristina Polizu is a Director in the Quantitative Analytics group in S&P. Her responsibilities include model, structure, and criteria development for structured finance primarily but also for corporate, financial institutions and insurance departments within S&P. She runs the lead efforts for rating quasi-operating companies and alternative assets in S&P.

She develops models that cover the financial risks of bankruptcy remote companies as well and of structured transactions that include eso-teric assets. Her focus of interest is portfolio credit and market risk mod-eling. Her research is geared to finding new modeling tools and new areas in which S&P can expand business. She joined S&P in 1995.

She holds a Ph.D. in Mathematics from Courant Institute of Mathematical Sciences. Her research focus was probability theory. Prior to that, she was an assistant professor in mathematics in Romania.

Aymeric Chauve is a CDO structurer at SG CIB. Prior to this, he was working with Standard and Poor's as an analyst in structured finance (CDO, RMBS, and Covered bonds). His activity included discussions on structuring with arranging banks, publications, client meetings, etc.

He holds an Engineering degree from Ecole centrale Paris, and a postgraduate degree in finance from Universite Paris Dauphine.

William Perraudin is Head of the Accounting, Finance and Macro-economics Department at Tanaka Business School and Director of the new MSc degrees in Risk Management and Financial Engineering.

His research interests include risk management, structured products, the pricing of defaultable debt, portfolio credit risk modeling, and financial regulation.

For seven years, he worked part-time as Special Advisor to the Bank of England and was deeply involved in the financial engineering behind the current Basel II proposals for bank capital. He has consulted with numerous banks and public bodies.

He was formerly the Head of the Finance Group in Birkbeck College. He is an Associate Editor of Quantitative Finance, the Journal of Banking and Finance and the Journal of Credit Risk.

INDEX